THE CRUSADER STATES

THE
CRUSADER
STATES

MALCOLM BARBER

YALE UNIVERSITY PRESS
NEW HAVEN AND LONDON

For information about this and other Yale University Press publications, please contact:
U.S. Office: sales.press@yale.edu   www.yalebooks.com
Europe Office: sales @yaleup.co.uk   www.yalebooks.co.uk

Set in Minion Pro by IDSUK (DataConnection) Ltd
Printed in Great Britain by TJ International Ltd, Padstow, Cornwall

Library of Congress Cataloging-in-Publication Data

Barber, Malcolm
    The crusader states/Malcolm Barber.
       p. cm.
    Includes bibliographical references.
    ISBN 978-0-300-11312-9 (cl : alk. paper)
1.   Latin Orient—History. 2.   Crusades. 3.   Jerusalem—History—Latin Kingdom, 1099–1244. 4.   Christianity and other religions—Islam. 5.   Civilization, Medieval.   I. Title.
    D182.B37 2012
    956'.014—dc23

                                                                              2012009776

A catalogue record for this book is available from the British Library.

10 9 8 7 6 5 4 3 2 1

To Dominic, Sam, Rhys, Calum and Cieran

Contents

Illustrations

Plates

14 Castle of Kerak in Moab. Reproduced by permisison of Richard Cleave.

15 The Virgin leading an apostle through the perils of Hell. Capital from the shrine-grotto of the church of the Annunciation, Nazareth. Reproduced by permission of Pantheon, Florence.

Maps and Plans

Figures

Preface

THIS is a book about the history of Palestine and Syria in the twelfth century. In 1097, these lands felt the first effects of a series of western invasions that have since become known as the crusades, introducing yet another new element into the complex politics and culture of the region. In one sense my approach has been quite orthodox since I have largely maintained a chronological structure, which necessarily means a relatively continuous narrative. However, less conventionally, within that structure I have tried to incorporate as many aspects of twelfth-century life as possible, rather than dividing the book into a series of separate thematic chapters. Political and military narrative inevitably forces itself upon anybody who reads the sources in any depth, but at the same time the Latins built castles, churches, monasteries, city walls, houses, both urban and rural, mills and harbours, they cultivated the soil and created new settlements, they developed industrial processes for products like sugar, they sculpted, painted, and wrote and copied manuscripts, and they traded with the entire known world. The aim, therefore, is to try to show this society as an integrated whole.

My deepest thanks go to those who have had such a profound influence upon the study of this subject in the last sixty years, whose work I have tried to absorb both through their publications and through personal contact. The bibliography and notes reflect this, especially in their references to Jaroslav Folda, Bernard Hamilton, Rudolf Hiestand, Beni Kedar, Hans Mayer, Joshua Prawer, Jean Richard and Jonathan Riley-Smith. Moreover, I am most grateful for the generous help received in many different ways from Elizabeth Barber, Keith Bate, Peter Edbury, Norman Housley, Nikolas Jaspert, Rachael Lonsdale, Heather McCallum, Sophia Menache, Piers Mitchell, Alan Murray, Helen Nicholson, Denys Pringle and Rita Tyler.

County of Edessa

Baldwin of Boulogne, Count of Edessa, 1098–1100
Baldwin of Bourcq, Count of Edessa, 1100–18
Tancred of Hauteville, Regent of Edessa, 1104
Richard of the Principate, Regent of Edessa, 1104–8
Galeran of Le Puiset, Regent of Edessa, 1118–19
Joscelin I, Count of Edessa, 1119–31
Geoffrey, lord of Marash, Regent of Edessa, 1122–3
Joscelin II, Count of Edessa, 1131–59
Beatrice, wife of Joscelin II, Regent of Edessa, 1150
Joscelin III, titular Count of Edessa, 1159–1200

The Ecclesiastical Rulers

Latin Patriarchs of Jerusalem

Arnulf of Chocques (not consecrated), 1099
Daibert of Pisa, 1099–1101
Evremar of Chocques, 1102–8
Gibelin of Arles, 1108–12
Arnulf of Chocques, 1112–18
Warmund of Picquigny, 1118–28
Stephen of Chartres, 1128–30
William I, 1130–45
Fulcher, 1145–57
Amalric of Nesle, 1157–80
Eraclius 1180–91

Latin Patriarchs of Antioch

Bernard of Valence, 1100–35
Ralph of Domfront, 1135–40
Aimery of Limoges, 1140–93

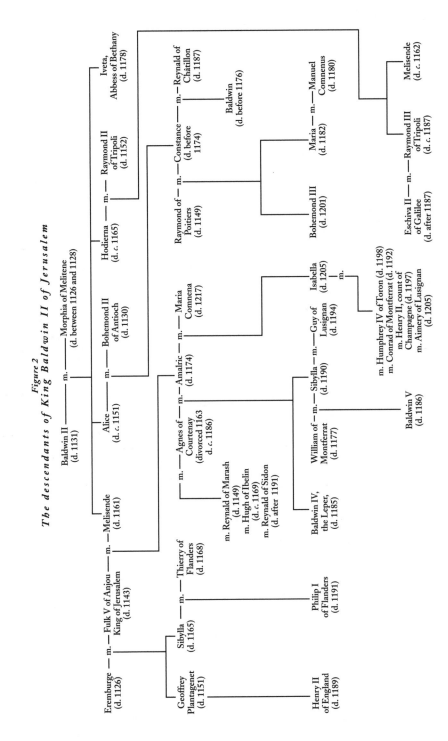

Figure 2

The descendants of King Baldwin II of Jerusalem

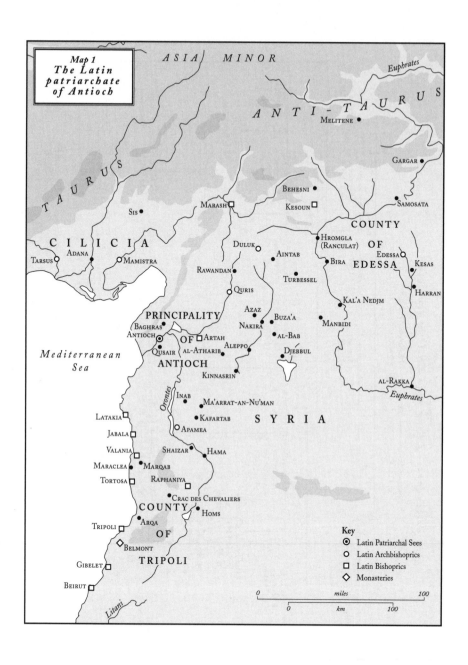

Map 1
The Latin
patriarchate
of Antioch

ASIA MINOR

ANTI-TAURUS

Euphrates

MELITENE

GARGAR

TAURUS

SIS

MARASH

BEHESNI

KESOUN

SAMOSATA

COUNTY

CILICIA

ADANA

DULUK

AINTAB

HROMGLA
(RANCULAT)

OF

EDESSA

KESAS

TARSUS

MAMISTRA

BIRA

EDESSA

RAWANDAN

TURBESSEL

HARRAN

QURIS

KAL'A NEDJM

PRINCIPALITY

AZAZ

NAKIRA

BUZA'A

MANBIDI

BAGHRAS

ANTIOCH

OF

ARTAH

AL-BAB

QUSAIR

AL-ATHARIB

ALEPPO

DJEBBUL

Mediterranean
Sea

ANTIOCH

KINNASRIN

al-RAKKA

Euphrates

INAB

MA'ARRAT-AN-NU'MAN

SYRIA

LATAKIA

KAFARTAB

JABALA

APAMEA

VALANIA

SHAIZAR

HAMA

MARACLEA

MARQAB

TORTOSA

RAPHANIYA

CRAC DES CHEVALIERS

COUNTY

HOMS

TRIPOLI

ARQA

OF

BELMONT

GIBELET

TRIPOLI

BEIRUT

Litani

Orontes

Key

◉ Latin Patriarchal Sees
○ Latin Archbishoprics
□ Latin Bishoprics
◇ Monasteries

0   miles   100

0   km   100

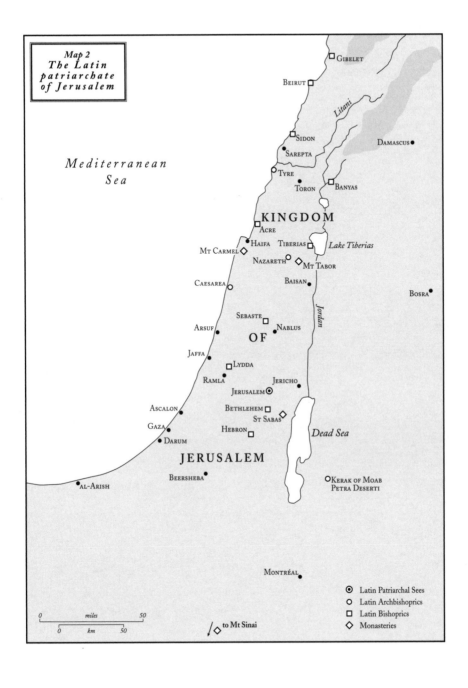

Map 2
The Latin
patriarchate
of Jerusalem

Mediterranean
Sea

GIBELET

BEIRUT

Litani

SIDON
SAREPTA
DAMASCUS

TYRE
TORON
BANYAS

KINGDOM

ACRE
HAIFA TIBERIAS *Lake Tiberias*
MT CARMEL
NAZARETH MT TABOR

CAESAREA BAISAN

BOSRA

SEBASTE
ARSUF NABLUS

OF

JAFFA

Jordan

LYDDA
RAMLA JERICHO
JERUSALEM
ASCALON BETHLEHEM ST SABAS
GAZA HEBRON *Dead Sea*
DARUM

JERUSALEM

AL-ARISH BEERSHEBA

KERAK OF MOAB
PETRA DESERTI

MONTRÉAL

◉ Latin Patriarchal Sees
○ Latin Archbishoprics
□ Latin Bishoprics
◇ Monasteries

0   miles   50
0   km   50

to Mt Sinai

Introduction

O N 18 October 1191, in the course of extended negotiations with Saladin, King Richard I of England instructed his envoy as follows:

> You will greet him and say, 'The Muslims and the Franks are done for. The land is ruined, ruined utterly at the hands of both sides. Property and lives on both sides are destroyed. This matter has received its due. All we have to talk about is Jerusalem, the Holy Cross and these lands. Now Jerusalem is the centre of our worship which we shall never renounce, even if there were only one of us left. As for these lands, let there be restored to us what is this side of the Jordan. The Holy Cross, that is a piece of wood that has no value for you, but is important for us. Let the sultan bestow it upon us. Then we can make peace and have rest from this constant hardship.'

After the sultan had read this message, he summoned the leading men of his council and consulted them about what to reply. What the sultan decided to say in reply was:

> Jerusalem is ours as much as it is yours. Indeed, for us it is greater than it is for you, for it is where our Prophet came on his Night Journey and the gathering place of the angels. Let not the king imagine that we shall give it up, for we are unable to breathe a word of that amongst the Muslims. As for the land, it is also ours originally. Your conquest of it was an unexpected accident due to the weakness of the Muslims there at that time. While the war continues God has not enabled you to build up one stone there. From the lands in our hands we, thanks be to God, feed on the produce and draw our benefit. The destruction of the Holy Cross would in our eyes be a great offering to God, but the only reason we are not permitted to go that far is that some more useful benefit might accrue to Islam.[1]

This exchange was recorded by Baha al-Din Ibn Shaddad, who was qadi (judge) of the army under Salah al-Din Yusuf, or Saladin, between 1188 and 1193. Saladin was the most successful proponent of the *jihad* in the twelfth century, for it was for the cause of Islam that he had made himself ruler of Egypt, Damascus, Aleppo and Mosul, and Ibn Shaddad makes no attempt to hide his admiration for him. Nevertheless, Ibn Shaddad was no credulous hagiographer, for he remained close to the centre of power throughout, and his account of those years offers an invaluable insight into Saladin's thinking. An abiding theme of the later part of the narrative is the negotiations between King Richard I and Saladin, negotiations impelled both by mutual exhaustion and by the inability of either side to deal a decisive blow. When Richard finally sailed away from Acre in October 1192, he left an agreement for a three-year truce and a division of territories between what Ibn Shaddad calls the Uplands and the Coast, in which the Muslims retained Jerusalem, but the Christians were granted visitation rights to the holy places.

As Ibn Shaddad shows, this was not a satisfactory outcome for either side. The armies of the First Crusade had wrested Jerusalem from the control of the Fatimids of Egypt in July 1099, and had established a hegemony over the holy places in Palestine that had lasted for nearly a century. Four viable states had been created, centred on Antioch, Edessa, Tripoli and Jerusalem, and a constant stream of crusaders, legates, pilgrims, mercenaries and merchants had flowed into the land. Although Edessa had been lost to Zengi, atabeg of Mosul, in 1144, and the Second Crusade had failed in its attempt to capture Damascus, the Latins of the East did not lose confidence, for, during the 1160s, determined efforts were made to conquer Egypt. Ultimately these attempts were unsuccessful, mainly because they had been opposed by Shirkuh and his nephew, Saladin, two members of a Kurdish family in the employ of Nur al-Din, son of Zengi and ruler of Mosul, Aleppo and Damascus. They had prevented Amalric, king of Jerusalem, from extending his power into the Nile Delta, and, after the deaths of Nur al-Din and Amalric in 1174, Saladin had set about creating an empire that united the Muslim lands of Egypt and Syria. In July 1187, he won a great victory over the Christians on the hillside of Hattin within sight of the Sea of Galilee, and in the following months cut a swathe through the crusader states so that, by the end of the year, the only major cities left in Christian hands were Tyre, Tripoli and Antioch. The greatest prize was the city of Jerusalem, captured on 2 October, enabling him to purge the city of 'Christian pollution' and the Muslims once more to attend Friday prayers in the al-Aqsa mosque. Saladin now seemed to be on the verge of fulfilling his plans, but the events of 1190 and 1191 prevented their realisation. Waves of crusaders came from the West and their efforts culminated in the recapture of Acre in June 1191, soon followed by Richard I's victory in the battle of Arsuf in September. The truce of 1192 therefore represented a major diminution of Saladin's ambitions, and his death only a few months later, in March 1193, meant that he was unable to take advantage of Richard's departure.

The crusader states were unique in their own time, for they were carved out of a part of the world that had been fought over more times than any other region, a characteristic it still retains. Past civilisations, previous political structures and many different phases of settlement had all left their mark, so that the crusader inheritance was both rich and complicated. Thus, although it was a relatively small area, it had a significance far beyond its physical extent. Moreover, although the Latins settled there governed the lands independently, at the same time they were part of a wider Christian community, for Jerusalem and the holy places were seen as belonging to all Christians, a belief expressed in papal rhetoric, and demonstrated by crusaders, pilgrims and the constant contacts between East and West through trade, letters, embassies and prayer networks. Nor was that community drawn entirely from the Latin world, for the most recent Christian rulers had not been westerners, but the Byzantines, who regarded themselves as the only true successors of the Roman empire and saw the region at the very least as belonging to their sphere of influence even if they found it difficult to bring it back directly under their lordship. This is the story of how the new conquerors from the West adapted to these circumstances and produced a distinct cultural entity of their own.

CHAPTER 1

The Expedition to Jerusalem

B ETWEEN 18 and 28 November 1095, Pope Urban II held a church council at Clermont in the Auvergne. Its climax was a great speech in which he called upon the Christians of the Latin West to take up arms in order to free their eastern brethren from Muslim oppression. Soon after, as his publicity campaign gathered momentum, he wrote to the faithful of Flanders, explaining the theme of his speech.

We believe that you, brethren, learned long ago from many reports, the deplorable news that the barbarians in their frenzy have invaded and ravaged the churches of God in the eastern regions. Worse still, they have seized the Holy City of Christ, embellished by his passion and resurrection, and – it is blasphemy to say it – they have sold her and her churches into abominable slavery. Thinking devoutly about this disaster and grieved by it, we visited Gaul and urged most fervently the lords and subjects of that land to liberate the eastern churches. At a council held in Auvergne, as is widely known, we imposed on them the obligation to undertake such a military enterprise for the remission of all their sins and we appointed in our place as leader of this journey and labour our dearest son Adhémar, bishop of Le Puy.[1]

The audience at Clermont was largely clerical and therefore, as Urban says in his Flanders letter, he set out to spread the message more widely, partly through a personal tour of southern and western France, and partly by involving local bishops and their hierarchies. He may, too, have commissioned individuals like Robert of Arbrissel, a famous popular preacher and leader of a group of ascetics living in the Loire valley; certainly other charismatics took up the cause, whether officially sanctioned or not, the most famous of whom was an ex-monk from Amiens known as Peter the Hermit.

This set in motion a series of events that, within the next twelve months, led to the assembly of nine major armies from a very wide geographical area, which encompassed northern France, Flanders, Lorraine, Toulouse and Apulia, as well as fleets from Genoa, Venice, Pisa, Greece and England. Even this is in some senses an oversimplification, in that the larger elements were made up of a coalescence of many smaller groups.[2] The priest Fulcher of Chartres, one of the chroniclers of the expedition and a participant and settler, says that they came from all the countries of the West and that, over a period, they formed into a group of armies. The numbers involved were uniquely large for the time, a fact reflected in Fulcher's acceptance of a figure of 600,000 fighting men, noncombatants excluded, derived, he says, from those who knew what they were talking about. If everybody who set out had actually reached Asia Minor, he thought there would have been 6 million warriors.[3] Modern estimates inevitably reduce these numbers, but, even so, the total may have been as high as 80,000 – that is, about 20,000 followers of Peter the Hermit and Walter Sans Avoir, who were the first to engage the Turks, and perhaps 50,000–60,000 in the major armies that came after them.[4] They did not form a single force, says Fulcher, until they besieged Nicaea in June 1097.[5] To these can be added at least 10,000 sailors and troops who, between the summer of 1197 and that of 1100, arrived on the ships of the Italian cities of Genoa, Pisa and Venice, as well as other maritime contingents from the western Mediterranean and northern Europe.[6] The Muslims, too, realised that this was exceptional. Ibn al-Qalanisi, a contemporary from an important Damascene family, heard that the Franks were assembling at Constantinople in the course of the year 490 – that is, 1097 – 'with forces not to be reckoned for multitude'. As the news spread, 'the people grew anxious and disturbed in mind'.[7]

The very first crusaders were the least prepared. Inspired by popular preachers, some set out as early as December 1095, so there can have been little planning. The bulk of these people were not 'arms-bearers', although there may have been a few hundred knights involved.[8] Shipped across the Bosphorus by the Byzantines in an effort to remove them from the vicinity of Constantinople, the great majority were killed or enslaved after engaging with the Seljuk Turks in September and October 1096, although Peter the Hermit was not present and survived to join the better-equipped armies, which began to arrive that autumn. Three largely German armies drawn from similar social groups followed, but after attacking Jewish communities in the Rhineland in May and June 1096, they were themselves massacred by Hungarian troops sent by King Koloman, who was unwilling to tolerate their depredations.

The members of the major armies described by Fulcher of Chartres had required time to raise money and to equip themselves, as well as to arrange

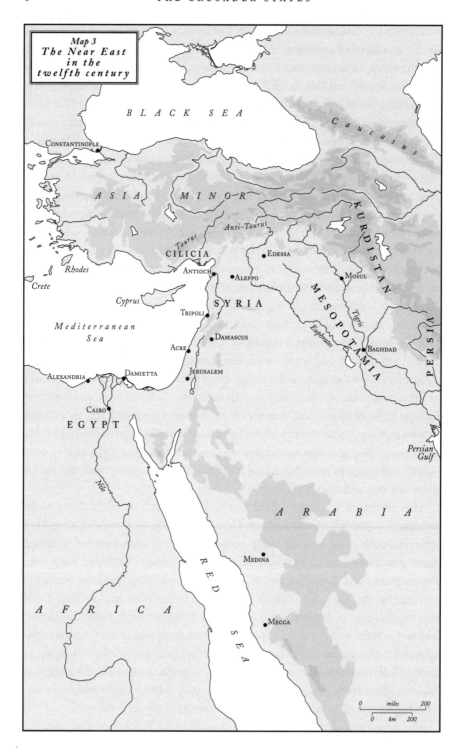

Map 3
The Near East
in the
twelfth century

BLACK SEA

Caucasus

CONSTANTINOPLE

ASIA   MINOR

KURDISTAN

Taurus   Anti-Taurus

CILICIA

Rhodes

Crete

EDESSA

ANTIOCH   ALEPPO   MOSUL

Cyprus

SYRIA

MESOPOTAMIA

Tigris

TRIPOLI

Mediterranean
Sea

DAMASCUS

ACRE

Euphrates

BAGHDAD

PERSIA

ALEXANDRIA   DAMIETTA   JERUSALEM

CAIRO

Persian
Gulf

EGYPT

Nile

ARABIA

AFRICA

MEDINA

RED
SEA

MECCA

0   miles   200

0   km   200

their affairs for what many rightly anticipated could be a lengthy absence. They had assembled considerable information from past pilgrimages, Italian merchants and the Byzantines, so they must have had a good appreciation of the tasks ahead.[9] Urban's appeal attracted some of the great territorial rulers of the time, some of whom, like Robert II, count of Flanders, and Raymond IV, count of Toulouse, were among the wealthiest in the West; others, such as Stephen, count of Blois, Robert, duke of Normandy, and Hugh of Vermandois, the brother of King Philip of France, were equal in rank if not quite so well resourced. As well as the men from Francia and Languedoc, Eustace, count of Boulogne, Godfrey of Bouillon, duke of Lower Lorraine, and Baldwin of Boulogne, three brothers from the imperial borderlands, committed them-selves to the expedition, despite the pope's continuing quarrel with the emperor, while the Normans established in southern Italy during the eleventh century, led by Bohemond of Taranto and his nephew, Tancred, son of Emma, his half-sister, left their internecine conflicts to join the army of God.[10]

These leaders needed to establish a relationship with the Byzantine emperor, Alexius Comnenus, since they could not reach the Holy Sepulchre unless they travelled through his lands, nor were they likely to defeat the Seljuk Turks, their mutual enemy in Asia Minor, without some degree of co-operation. For Stephen of Blois, deeply impressed by imperial largesse, this presented no problems. 'It seems to me,' he wrote to his wife, Adela, in June 1097, 'that in our times no other prince has had a character distinguished by such complete integrity.'[11] However, Alexius did not intend to rely on presents alone. Before the journey into Asia Minor began the emperor attempted to protect his own interests by extracting an oath, the essence of which was that the Latins were to return to the Byzantines all reconquered lands that had belonged to the empire before the Turkish invasions, and that they should accept Alexius as overlord for any other lands that they might take beyond these. The reaction to this was inconsistent, although in principle there was no reason for refusal, since aristocratic society in the Latin West could not have functioned without acceptance of the idea of multiple homage.[12] According to Albert, who was probably a canon of the cathedral church of St Mary at Aachen: 'Bohemond became the emperor's man, and with an oath and a pledge of trust he made an agreement with him that he would not keep for himself any part of the emperor's realm, except by his favour and consent.'[13] Nevertheless, Tancred tried unsuccessfully to evade the oath, while Godfrey of Bouillon resisted for some time before he was eventually reconciled. Once he had agreed, he, too, in Albert's words, 'not only gave himself to him as a son, as is the custom of that land, but even as a vassal with hands joined, along with all the nobles who were there then, and those who followed afterwards'.[14] In the end, all the leaders accepted the imperial conditions, although Raymond of Toulouse would only agree in general terms to respect the emperor's life and possessions. According to the Provençal chronicler Raymond of Aguilers, who was the count's chaplain, he told Alexius that 'he had not taken the cross to pay allegiance to another lord'.[15] Part of the problem was that Raymond of Toulouse wanted the emperor to accompany the crusaders to Jerusalem, but this would have been too risky an enterprise for a ruler in his position. Instead he provided a small escort led by Tatikios, one of his experienced generals, as well as considerable logistical support, especially from the sea in northern Syria.

Anna Comnena, the emperor's daughter, looking back on these events from the 1140s, claimed that, 'while in appearance making the journey to Jerusalem, in reality their object was to dethrone the emperor and to capture the capital', an enterprise they had adopted through the persuasion of Bohemond.[16] However, Anna was writing to record the achievements of her father, whose deeds seemed to her to have been appropriated by his successors, John and Manuel, to emphasise the glory of their own reigns. This was especially galling to Anna, who believed that she and her husband, Nicephorus Bryennius, had been robbed of the succession by her brother, John. In her version of events, therefore, her father had diverted the crusaders from Constantinople by his skilful handling of men she saw as western barbarians.[17] Although Anna's story is tendentious and heavily coloured by the contemporary scene at the time of writing, it is important because it reflects the Byzantine view of the superiority of the empire and the belief of its rulers that the crusader states were established on imperial territory.

In fact, during the next three years, the crusaders sustained huge losses and experienced almost unimaginable horrors until, on 15 July 1099, they succeeded in storming the walls of Jerusalem and regaining control of the holy places. Once they had broken in they slaughtered large numbers of the defenders and inhabitants as they finally requited their longing for the cherished city.[18] Those who had set out from northern France had covered approximately 2,700 miles.[19] It had taken three great sieges, at Nicaea in May and June 1097, when they had combined with the Byzantines, at Antioch between October 1097 and June 1098, and at Jerusalem in June and July 1099, and two decisive battles, at Dorylaeum on 1 July 1097, and outside Antioch on 28 June 1098. At Dorylaeum they had defeated the Seljuks under Kilij Arslan and at Antioch a Turkish coalition under Kerbogha, atabeg of Mosul, while at Jerusalem they overcame the Egyptians, who had recaptured the city from the Turks the previous year and held the lands as far as the Dog River, north of Beirut. Separate engagements against Duqaq of Damascus and Ridwan of Aleppo, the sons of Tutush, the late Seljuk ruler of Syria, on 31 December 1097 and 9 February 1098 respectively, were each major confrontations, their insignificance only relative in comparison with Dorylaeum and Antioch. At the same time squadrons of ships had struck out for the Levant, much of the time sailing along hostile coasts and with little knowledge of either the fate or the position of the land forces.[20]

Contemporaries immediately recognised that this was an exceptional – indeed, unique – event; for them, it was *inauditus*, 'unheard of'.[21] Yet it cannot be explained simply by a papal speech at a church council in one of the minor towns of south-central France, however eloquent the individual concerned. If, therefore, Urban tapped a potential that was already present it is important to identify those involved, for ultimately the new settlements in the East emerged from the interplay of their interests and actions. The conventionally accepted view is that Alexius I, the Byzantine emperor (1081–1118), sent ambassadors to a previous council, held by the pope at Piacenza in March of the same year, at which he appealed for military help for a campaign planned against the Seljuk Turks, who had invaded Asia Minor and occupied all but three small areas, one of which was opposite Constantinople and two of which were on the Black Sea coast.[22] This was in keeping with problems experienced by the Byzantines ever since the heavy defeat of a previous emperor, Romanus IV, at the battle of Manzikert in 1071, a defeat that had opened up Asia Minor to the Turkish tribes, many of which had been moving west over the course of the eleventh century. Westerners routinely served in the Byzantine army – indeed, the emperors had actively recruited them – so the concept was not unfamiliar, even if the scale was larger than in the past.[23] It may be that the appeal was pitched in terms of helping eastern Christians owing to a need to tailor the message to the sensibilities of the church council at which Alexius's messengers had been received. Urban took this up both because he felt genuine anguish at the news of Christian suffering and because he saw an opportunity to heal the schism that had opened up between the Roman and Greek Churches following a quarrel between the papal legate and the patriarch of Constantinople in 1054. However, in Urban's hands the imperial appeal for military help was moulded into something quite different, leaving Alexius to adapt his plans as best he could to the huge response which the pope elicited.

More recently, the actions of the principals have been interpreted rather differently. As there is no evidence to suggest that Alexius was planning a campaign at this time, nor that he ever appealed for westerners to serve in his army, it may be that the initiative came from the pope in that he actually invited the imperial representatives to Piacenza.[24] In one sense, the latter event had a Byzantine origin as well in that the idea may have been stimulated by Symeon II, the Greek patriarch of Jerusalem, through a message brought to the pope by Peter the Hermit, who had visited Jerusalem on pilgrimage, where he had seen for himself the wretched state of the Christian inhabitants.[25] This is a partial revival of a view, long rejected, that Peter had been the instigator of the crusade, but which is to be found in the chronicle of Albert of Aachen, the only contemporary writer to attempt to explain the origins of the crusade.[26] Albert was an important member of the cathedral church at Aachen and, although he did not take part in the expedition, he had many informants who did. He had written the first six books of his work by 1102.

Some confirmation of the general circumstances in Palestine can be found in the chronicle of world history of Michael I Rabo, known as Michael the Syrian, Jacobite patriarch of Antioch between 1166 and 1199. As might be expected, although he provides more detail on the later twelfth century, Michael is nevertheless a valuable independent source for the whole period. According to him:

> When the Turks ruled in the countries of Syria and Palestine, they inflicted evils on the Christians who were going to pray at Jerusalem, beating and pillaging them, and levying a poll tax at the gate of the city and also at Golgotha and at the Sepulchre; as well as this, every time they saw a caravan of Christians, especially those (who came) from Rome and the country of Italy, they contrived to cause them to perish in various ways. And when countless people had perished in this manner, the kings and counts were seized by zeal and set out from Rome; forces from every country joined them, and they went by sea to Constantinople.[27]

All interpretations place the papacy at the centre of affairs, as did the leading crusaders who, in September 1098, described the pope as 'our spiritual father, who began this expedition'.[28] Whether Alexius or Peter and Symeon were the catalysts for action, Urban was already receptive. In the early 1090s, he had encouraged resistance to Muslims elsewhere in the Mediterranean, both in Tarragona and in Sicily, and he was heir to half a century of increasing papal assertiveness, arising from his predecessors' attempts to free the Church from what they had come to see as the corrupting effects of lay control. Indeed, as early as 1059, Pope Nicholas II had promoted the conquest of Islamic Sicily when he received Robert Guiscard, the most prominent member of the Hauteville family in Apulia, as his vassal, granting him titles which included that of duke of Sicily. The Normans, who had been settling in southern Italy since the later years of the tenth century, were thus able to present their attack on the island as a means of restoring the Church in lands wrongfully seized by Islam in the past, thus offering an obvious precedent for Urban's justification for the invasion of Palestine.[29]

Among Urban's predecessors, Gregory VII (1073–85) stands out, for not only had he been the most uncompromising of the moral reformers in Rome, but he had imagined that the papacy could place itself at the head of a community of devoted seculars, who would become 'soldiers of Christ', fighting the very visible forces of evil in the material world around them.[30] In 1074, he planned to make this a reality by leading an expedition to the aid of the eastern Christians. In a letter to his ally Matilda, countess of Tuscany, he wrote: 'How serious my intention and how great my desire to go overseas and with Christ's help to carry succour to the Christians being slaughtered like sheep by pagans, I hesitate to say to some persons lest I seem to be moved by too great a fickleness of purpose. But to you, my most dearly beloved daughter, I have no hesitation in declaring any of these matters; for I have more confidence in your good judgement than you yourself could possibly express.'[31] At the same time such initiatives were underpinned by a powerful intellectual structure which, despite some dissenting voices, maintained that force could be used in certain circumstances, the centrepiece of which was a threat to the faith. Drawing on biblical and patristic texts, it was possible to compare the situation with the slaughter of the Israelites found worshipping a golden calf by Moses (Exodus 32: 26–8), while St Augustine's formulation of precise conditions of legitimate authority, just cause and right intention fitted comfortably with the self-image of the contemporary papacy.[32]

However, Gregory, heavily embroiled in an all-consuming struggle for supremacy with the German emperor, Henry IV, never did lead an expedition to the East and, indeed, such an operation would probably not have been practical even in more favourable circumstances. Urban II, more realistic, appointed Adhémar of Le Puy as his legate, not only to maintain his influence over the crusade, but also to take steps to heal the division between the two Churches.[33] Whether or not he played a part in stimulating the crusade in the first place, the patriarch, Symeon, certainly worked to support the expedition once it was in being. In 1097 and 1098, he sent supplies to the crusaders at Antioch from his place of exile in Cyprus and again to the siege of Jerusalem in 1099, while in the winter of 1097–8 he associated himself with two letters urging potential crusaders in the West to join their brethren as soon as possible.[34]

At the same time Urban set about exploiting the conditions in the West that would turn rhetoric into actual armies. The most important of these was the long pilgrimage tradition of the Christian faith, evident since the fourth century. In Urban's time this had been strongly promoted by the Cluniac

Order, from which the pope himself came. The mother house of Cluny was situated in the Mâconnais in southern Burgundy, a region that can be seen as the epicentre of monasticism in the eleventh and twelfth centuries. Local Cluniac abbots urged laymen associated with their house to undertake penitential journeys to expiate their sins, an approach that had the effect of increasing secular awareness of the need for individual moral reform which was integral to the wider papal programme. Such monastic houses probably held sway in an area extending to a radius of about 20 to 25 miles; within this territory local lords, themselves usually related through extensive marriage links, naturally supported the house with gifts and even armed protection if the monastery was under threat. In return it took their children as oblates and their elderly relatives as pensioners, as well as offering a place within the cloister for those who wished to leave secular life. In the longer term it provided an appropriate place of burial and intercession for the souls of the dead in its prayers.[35] Aristocratic and monastic society in the West was founded upon these ties, a fact that Urban II, a former Cluniac prior, comprehended perfectly.

The need for expiation of sin heavily reinforced this structure. Even the well-intentioned could hardly avoid violence if they were to protect their lands, while the pursuit of chastity was not an option for those with dynastic responsibilities.[36] Yet the prospect of permanent residence in Hell, tormented by the Devil and his demons, was terrifying. Strikingly illustrated by the vivid imagery on the tympana of local abbeys and churches, it was a powerful reason for taking the papal call seriously. Again, Urban was attuned to contemporary lay sensibilities, since the offer of full remission of sin for taking part in this most daunting of tasks undoubtedly proved a major attraction. Even Tancred of Hauteville, whose actions during and after the crusade show him to be one of the most materially minded of the participants, was apparently anxious because, in the words of Ralph of Caen, who wrote an account of his deeds, 'his military life contradicted the Lord's command'. Urban's appeal energised him, 'as if the vitality of the previously sleeping man was revived'.[37] It is probable that the pope's offer was meant to apply to penances imposed by the Church in this life, but it was sufficiently ambiguous to encourage lay participants in the crusade to believe that death in Christ's service would make them instant martyrs, opening up a direct route to Heaven.[38] When Adhémar of Le Puy and Symeon of Jerusalem wrote their joint letter to the pope in mid-October 1097, they recounted the story of the patriarch's vision in which the Lord appeared 'and promised that all who strove in this expedition would stand crowned before Him on the fearful day of the Last Judgement'.[39]

This interrelationship between monastic houses and the local aristocracy can be seen most strikingly in Burgundy (see plate 1). Thus, in 1090, a knight, Peter Charbonnel, expressing 'the desire to go to Jerusalem', assigned to the abbey of Saint-Marcel (near Châlon-sur-Sâone) his possessions at Servigny in such a way that 'if he came to die or to remain in these countries' the property would be retained by the priory. This grant was extended to include other property that he had left in the hands of Boniface, his brother, so that if he died during the journey the monks would celebrate services for the dead for his sake and for that of his brother. In fact, Boniface was unco-operative and it took three years for the matter to be fully resolved, but it nevertheless shows the mindset of those upon whom Urban II needed to rely to fulfil his plans. Six years later, in April 1096, as preparations were being made for the crusade, Achard, lord of Montmerle, pledged his estate to the abbey of Cluny in a transaction that is recognisably of the same genre as that of Peter Charbonnel, but which had been adapted to the needs of an armed expedition. In return for his pledge, Cluny provided Achard with 2,000 *sous lyonnais* and four mules to enable him to leave 'well-armed' with 'all that immense mass levée and expedition of the Christian people desiring to go to Jerusalem to combat against the pagans and Saracens for God'. Achard was well aware of both the hazards and the possibilities: 'in case I die during this pilgrimage to Jerusalem, or if I should decide to remain in this land in some way, the abbey of Cluny will no longer hold the title to the mortgage which it holds at the moment, but will be in legitimate possession and for always.'[40]

The 'expedition of the Christian people desiring to go to Jerusalem' was fundamentally a religious movement; an appeal for colonists could not have produced such an amazing response within such a narrow timescale.[41] Few of the aristocratic participants could have seen it as a source of potential profit: it cost four to five times the annual income of a knight to equip one.[42] Achard certainly needed the funds and mules provided by Cluny: in contemporary Burgundy horses cost between 20 and 50 *sous*, while a hauberk cost 100 *sous*.[43] Achard's experience was repeated many times over, which is why there are so many extant charters detailing the arrangements made to finance the expedition.[44] Moreover, when they had fulfilled their vows, many returned home, an action entirely consistent with their image of themselves as pilgrims. Among these were three of the most important leaders, Robert, count of Flanders, Eustace, count of Boulogne, and Robert, duke of Normandy, who, together with many of their followers, departed soon after the defeat of an Egyptian army on 12 August 1099, their status as pilgrims emphasised by a visit to bathe in the Jordan and the collection of palms in the Garden of Abraham near Jericho.[45] Both Albert of Aachen, who derived much of his information from returnees, and Fulcher of Chartres, who stayed in the East, described the exodus; indeed, Fulcher claimed that, as a result, the land of Jerusalem remained 'empty of people'.[46]

Even so, the impact of the pilgrimage tradition was not entirely one-sided. Although crude material theories that the First Crusade was driven by over-population in the West, or by changing inheritance customs that excluded younger sons and co-lateral lines, have largely been discarded, Urban was not above suggesting that a good reason for going was that life would be better in the East. The chronicler known as Robert the Monk, from the Benedictine abbey of St Rémi at Reims, heard Urban's speech at Clermont, and presents him as telling potential participants not to hold back because of ties at home. 'For this land you inhabit, hemmed in on all sides by the sea and surrounded by mountain peaks, cannot support your sheer numbers: it is not overflowing with abundant riches and indeed provides scarcely enough food even for those who grow it.'[47] But even an entirely religious explanation of the crusade does not exclude the possibility that at least some participants would choose to stay in the East. For many, pilgrimage to the holy place was the culmination of their earthly existence and the desire to end their lives in this unique land was as powerful as the drive that had led them to join the expedition in the first place, especially after the suffering they had endured in order to reach their goal. Moreover, survivors must have realised that the remission of sins that they had been granted would be eroded by actions which they took once the crusade had ended and that therefore their continued service in the cause would be the best means of mitigating the new sins that they would inevitably commit.[48]

Indeed, for many the success of the crusade and the liberation of the holy places must have been crucial, since failure would have obliged all the survivors to return home, whatever their possible aspirations in the East. When Achard of Montmerle allowed for the possibility that he might 'decide to remain in this land in some way', he may simply have been making the arrangements of a prudent man, but it is equally likely that he had not, at that time, made up his mind. In his case, the opportunity never arose, for he was killed in fighting near Jaffa in June 1099, shortly before the fall of Jerusalem.[49] Even Raymond of Toulouse, the only secular lord to have been informed in advance of the appeal at Clermont, does not seem to have made a definitive decision before he left home, or, if he did, he did not tell anybody, since, as late as April 1099, Raymond of Aguilers refers to the actions the count should undertake when he returned to Provence, including the founding of a church near Arles to house the Holy Lance, which a member of his army claimed to have found in the cathedral at Antioch, and the stabilisation of the coinage in his lands.[50] Three months later, after the election of Godfrey of Bouillon as ruler, he was forced to give up the Tower of David in Jerusalem, a circumstance that made him so angry that, after gathering palms in Jericho and receiving baptism in the Jordan, 'he made plans to return with a great part of the Provençals'. He was certainly under some pressure from his followers: according to Raymond of Aguilers, when the princes asked him to accept the rulership of Jerusalem, the Provençals spread 'malicious lies to block his elevation as king'.[51]

In the event, Raymond did leave, but for Constantinople not Saint-Gilles, and in 1101 he returned to lay the foundations of what became the county of Tripoli. Despite the many frustrations he suffered during the course of the crusade, he may ultimately have been influenced by a near-death experience for, in early August 1097, during the journey across Asia Minor from Dorylaeum to Iconium, he had recovered from an illness so serious that the bishop of Orange had administered the last rites.[52] Thus, in retrospect, Raymond became one of the heroes of the crusade, praised for his steadfastness by William, archbishop of Tyre, looking back from the perspective of the 1170s.[53] He may eventually have come to see himself as among those who had intended to leave but changed their minds because they saw the capture of Jerusalem as 'quasi-miraculous', a situation that convinced them that they had been 'called'.[54]

Godfrey of Bouillon seems to have seen himself in this way. As duke of Lower Lorraine, he had gained the maternal inheritance from his father Eustace II's marriage to Ida, daughter of Godfrey the Bearded, duke of Upper and Lower Lorraine. Although the duchy had been difficult to govern and Godfrey had not found it easy to raise the money needed for the expedition, his arrangements before departure show that he had made no final decision about whether to return. Nor was there anything irregular about his participation, despite the continuing quarrel between Henry IV and the pope, for the emperor had granted permission and did not reassign the duchy until 1101, after Godfrey's death.[55] However, his election as ruler of Jerusalem in late July 1099 seems to have persuaded him that he was especially chosen, as well as convincing many of his household staff, together with a good proportion of his vassals, to remain with him. Albert of Aachen presents the situation in the form of a dream by a canon of St Mary's church in Aachen. In the dream the pilgrims, envisioned as birds of Heaven surrounding the duke, are given permission to fly away, and indeed many do, but by no means all. 'But very many birds remained fixed and motionless, as many were attached to him by dutiful love, and having delighted in his intimate and comforting speech they vowed to stay longer with him.'[56] As his election was not foreseeable, it is most likely that both Godfrey and his men decided at this time about their plans rather than when they had set out on the crusade. Indeed, for most vassals and members of his immediate circle, a final decision could not have been made until they knew their leaders' minds.

Nor was Godfrey alone. His younger brother, Baldwin, had struck out towards Edessa, and the two Normans, Bohemond of Taranto and Tancred, his nephew, showed a powerful determination to establish themselves in Antioch and Galilee respectively, while, in 1101, Raymond of Toulouse, Stephen of Blois and Hugh of Vermandois all returned to the fray as members of a second group of armies launched into Asia Minor in the spring of 1101. Here again there is no set pattern. As the third son of an important family, Baldwin had been steered into the Church, where he accumulated prebends at Reims, Cambrai and Liège.[57] This practice, however, although common, was contrary to canon law, and it is likely that his clerical career was cut short as a consequence of pressure from church reformers, leaving him to find support by other means. Marriage to Godehilde, daughter of the wealthy Ralph II of Tosny, brought the prospect of a share in the lands of a leading Norman family. He had not at first intended to join the expedition, as in his own pre-crusade arrangements Godfrey had ensured that Baldwin would receive the county of Verdun, so that when he did decide to set out he had probably taken Godehilde as an insurance against losing the Norman inheritance. If this was so, then Godehilde's death in mid-October 1097 may have been the decisive event that persuaded him to seek out a lordship in the East.[58]

Tancred lacked a decent patrimony and could see that his prospects in the East were much more favourable than in Apulia, but Bohemond, although initially disinherited by his father, Robert Guiscard, had been successful in creating a lordship for himself in the territories between Melfi and the Gulf of Taranto at the expense of his half-brother, Roger Borsa.[59] Bohemond had had a glimpse of greater possibilities, however, for, in the late 1070s, he and his father had attempted to carve out lands for themselves in those parts of the Byzantine empire across the southern Adriatic, and in 1081 they had taken Corfu and Durazzo. While the story of the chronicler Richard of Poitiers that Guiscard had intended that Bohemond should be made emperor and that he himself should become 'king of Persia' sounds far-fetched, it may reflect a caste of mind prevalent among the Normans of the Hauteville family; indeed, it was credible enough for a version of it to appear in Anna Comnena's *Alexiad*.[60] Another member of the clan, Richard of the Principate, nephew of Robert Guiscard and cousin of Bohemond, was the third son of William of Hauteville and unlikely to gain any substantial lordship in the family lands in the principality of Salerno. He had apparently tried his hand in the campaigns led by his uncle, Roger, in Sicily in the 1080s and 1090s, during which his brother had acquired Syracuse in 1091, but was attracted by Bohemond's expedition to the East in 1096. His subsequent career shows that he too was interested in acquisitions in Syria.[61]

With little written evidence, it is difficult to identify the motivations of the non-noble crusaders. Ekkehard of Aura, a monk from Bamberg, and a participant in the expedition of 1101, describes how many of the Frankish peasantry had left because of wretched conditions at home, including local warfare, famine and the disease of ergotism, caused by eating bread made from grain that had been badly stored and had grown a poisonous fungus.[62] Although many were inspired by religious enthusiasts such as Peter the Hermit, it is evident that, if they survived the crusade, they were the least able to return to the West at its conclusion and therefore the most likely to settle in the East, where they must have displaced at least some of the indigenous peasantry.[63] Moreover, the guarantee of their freedom, which appears to have been given during the course of the expedition, would certainly have been a further incentive to stay.[64] This was reinforced by the manner in which Jerusalem was taken, as those involved were rewarded with possession of whatever they were able to seize, a situation that, according to Fulcher of Chartres, led many of the destitute to become rich.[65] Even though a disproportionate number of those who died would have been those who had the least means of defending and feeding themselves, nevertheless, the majority of the 14,000 or so who survived to besiege Jerusalem would still have been non-noble.[66] There is no way of knowing how many of the earliest settlers had set out on the original expedition, but it must be significant that there were sufficient freemen of western origin to populate the twenty-one villages (*casalia*) granted by Godfrey of Bouillon to the canons of the Holy Sepulchre in the region of al-Bira, about 10 miles north of Jerusalem, during the year after his election in July 1099.[67]

Those who did stay faced immense practical problems, all of which grew out of the circumstances that had first created and then sustained the crusade. Bohemond had engineered the fall of Antioch on 3 June 1098, and Baldwin of Boulogne had pushed east from Marash to be welcomed by Armenians resentful of Turkish rule. Ravendel and Turbessel (Tell Bashir) submitted to him before he reached Edessa in February 1098. In March, an internal conspiracy (in which Baldwin was probably involved) overthrew Thoros, its Armenian ruler, and he was able to take control.[68] However, the other crusader leaders had been forced to leave Antioch because of popular pressure and, although most local rulers were keener to pay them off than to fight them, the drive to Jerusalem precluded a systematic conquest. Long sieges were not practical. When Raymond of Toulouse had tried to take Arqa, north-east of Tripoli, in 1099, he found himself sucked into a fruitless siege lasting three months between February and May, and in the end was forced to abandon it.[69]

Apart from the capture of Antioch and Edessa, the crusaders had been buttressed on the coast by the Byzantine possession of the ports of Saint Simeon and Latakia (apparently taken before the crusaders had reached northern Syria), and in the course of the expedition they had captured Tortosa (February 1099) and Jaffa (June 1099), the second of which was the nearest port to Jerusalem. Inland they took the towns of Rugia and Albara (September 1098) and Ma'arrat-an-Nu'man (December 1098) in the north, and Ramla (May 1099) in the south, while Tancred had seized Bethlehem, just to the south of Jerusalem, shortly before the city fell. Their main centres of power were far apart: the distance between Antioch and Jerusalem was over 360 miles and that between Antioch and Edessa 160 miles. On this slender basis the crusaders had to attempt to construct viable states so that the holy places could be protected from what they saw as Muslim tyranny and thus become properly accessible to pilgrims from the West. Whatever their ultimate physical condition, it could be said that those who did eventually settle in 1099 and immediately after were the best fitted psychologically for the hugely demanding task that lay before them.

The first requirement was a military leader, a matter so pressing that, on 22 July, within eight days of the capture of Jerusalem, they had elected Godfrey of Bouillon. This was very much the decision of the secular leaders on the expedition; the crusade may have been initiated by the papacy, but the Roman see was too far away to be consulted, while the pope's chief representative, Adhémar of Le Puy, was dead. Indeed, Raymond of Aguilers reports that they had discussed the question in early July, even before the capture of Jerusalem, apparently provoked by Tancred's seizure of the church of the Nativity at Bethlehem the previous month. Clerical attempts to argue that they should not elect a king as he could become a David and 'degenerate in faith and goodness', thus inducing the Lord to overthrow him, and that they should appoint an advocate instead, simply increased the conflicts within an already tense army. 'Nothing good came from this quarrel,' said Raymond.[70] As the most senior and wealthiest of the leaders, Raymond of Toulouse was the obvious choice, but at around sixty he was also the most elderly as well as being the least popular, having been identified as the chief reason for the excessive delay at Antioch after the defeat of Kerbogha in June 1098, which he had been reluctant to leave in Bohemond's hands. Raymond was undoubtedly asked but, according to Raymond of Aguilers, he baulked at taking the title of king in the city of Christ.[71] The English chroniclers William of Malmesbury and Henry of Huntingdon later claimed that Robert of Normandy had been offered the kingdom, but had turned it down 'through fear of its insoluble difficulties', as William put it, but there is no contemporary evidence for this.[72] Godfrey, however, did not attempt to become king, and is usually described in the sources as *princeps* or *advocatus*, titles which may have reflected the current political thinking that kings could only be created by popes or emperors.[73] As prince, he evidently believed that he exercised full authority under God, while the title of advocate implied a special responsibility for the defence of the Church, a role that was obviously fundamental in such a unique place. It is true that in Germany an advocate would have meant a lay protector of an ecclesiastical institution, but in this case it did not signify any kind of subordination to the patriarch. Advocates were often dominant figures, but in any case there was no cleric available for the patriarchate who had anything like the status necessary for such a role.[74]

The need for military leadership was quickly proved, for within three weeks of Godfrey's election the crusaders were forced to fight a major battle with the Egyptians under their vizier, al-Afdal. Initial contacts with the Egyptians had not been unfriendly. As adherents of the Shi'ite cause, the Fatimids of Cairo had been regarded with extreme hostility by the Seljuks, who saw themselves as the chief representatives of the Sunnite caliphs in Baghdad. The arrival of the crusaders at Antioch encouraged the Egyptians to send envoys in the hope of achieving co-operation against a mutual enemy.[75] However, the Christian victory over Kerbogha in June 1098, followed soon after by the restoration of Egyptian control over Palestine as far north as the Dog River (including Jerusalem), discernibly weakened the Turks and changed al-Afdal's perspective, so that he was less inclined to be accommodating. Perhaps misunderstanding the ideological drive that lay behind the crusade, he was prepared to allow parties of pilgrims into Jerusalem on a restricted basis, but he had no intention of giving up control either of the city itself or of the surrounding holy places.[76] Only when the crusaders captured Jerusalem did he fully grasp that their aims were incompatible with Egyptian policy, and realise that he would have to fight them. According to Fulcher of Chartres, he was particularly angry when he heard that Jerusalem had been captured 'with such savagery', and set about equipping an army based at Ascalon with the intention of either provoking a battle or of besieging Jerusalem.[77] For what was the last time, despite the evident tensions within the crusader ranks, they gathered together their combined forces and, taking the Egyptians by surprise, fell upon their encampment near Ascalon in the early morning of 12 August 1099. Robert of Normandy was particularly prominent, charging into the centre of the Egyptian camp, an action later commemorated in the stained glass at the abbey of Saint-Denis.[78] Such a bold tactic was fully rewarded and the much larger Egyptian army was completely overcome and put to flight, many in such a panic that they suffocated as they tried to force their way back into the safety of the city.[79] The author of the *Gesta Francorum*, who has a penchant for putting imaginary speeches into the mouths of his Muslim opponents, has al-Afdal wailing that he had been defeated by 'a wretched little force of Christians', and swearing that he would never raise another army against the Franks, a pronouncement that turned out to be a piece of wishful thinking on the part of the anonymous author.[80]

After Dorylaeum and Antioch, this was the third decisive battle of the campaign. On each occasion the crusaders had defeated different forces from the Muslim world, but the nearest Islam had come to putting together a coalition was under Kerbogha, and even then it was both partial and fragile. Informed contemporaries were well aware of this. According to Ibn al-Qalanisi, viewing events from Damascus: 'the peoples of Khurāsān, 'Irāq and Syria were in a state of constant bickering and hatred, wars and disorder, and fear of one another, because their rulers neglected them and were distracted from the task of governing them by their dissensions and mutual warfare.'[81] Even so, on any one of these occasions the whole project could have foundered;[82] it had not done so because of a combination of religious conviction and military boldness. Such characteristics continued to be displayed by those who stayed in the East, for the only alternative to returning home was to make a life in Palestine and Syria. Bohemond and Baldwin had already taken the first steps at Antioch and Edessa, and Tancred, vigorous from the very beginning in protecting his own interests and unimpressed by Godfrey's authority, whatever his title, now attempted to create a viable lordship centred on Galilee. He had taken Bethlehem before the fall of Jerusalem, but lands farther north seemed to represent a more realistic opportunity for establishing his own lordship, and he seized Samaria and Galilee, including the important towns of Nablus and Baisan. Then, in a foray across the Jordan into Damascene territory he forced its ruler to divide the revenues of the area. When, in August 1100, he gained a port at Haifa, the outline of a potential state began to emerge.[83]

Tancred, however, was not entirely free from external restraint; ultimately he knew he could not survive without some degree of co-operation with Godfrey of Bouillon and the other leaders, including the clergy. The crusade had been created by the pope and it was evidently closely woven into the reform agenda that had dominated papal thinking for a generation. Yet the project depended upon the willingness of the 'arms-bearers' to put ecclesiastical plans into some form of practical action, a situation that was certain to produce strain among the crusaders, especially since the papal legate, Adhémar of Le Puy, had died in August 1098. Again, the men on the spot had been obliged to take matters into their own hands and it is not surprising that they had given priority to military survival.

Nevertheless, they were attentive to the claims of the Church, for the election of a patriarch took place on 1 August, only ten days after Godfrey had been chosen as ruler, and before the great battle with the Egyptians on the 12th.[84] The man selected was Arnulf of Chocques, the chaplain of Robert of Normandy, who came from the diocese of Thérouanne in the Pas-de-Calais and who had originally set out in the retinue of Odo, bishop of Bayeux, half-brother of William the Conqueror.[85] He appears to have been the only surviving cleric with legatine powers and this may have influenced the choice, as may his association with Robert of Normandy, a leader who, shortly before, perhaps came into consideration as the first ruler.[86] According to Ralph of Caen, a former pupil of Arnulf at the cathedral school at Caen, as he lay dying, Adhémar had entrusted the spiritual care of the army to Arnulf.[87] Further support came from the bishop of Martirano, who was a close associate and, having established himself in Bethlehem, was seeking patriarchal recognition.[88] In any case there was only a narrow range of candidates, for nearly all the bishops on the crusade returned to the West,[89] while the only other Latin bishopric in the patriarchate at this time was that of Lydda-Ramla, to which Robert of Rouen had been hastily appointed the previous June before the siege of Jerusalem.[90]

As the alleged son of a priest and, according to the very hostile account of Raymond of Aguilers, a known fornicator, Arnulf of Chocques was not exactly an exemplar of the kind of prelate to which the reform papacy aspired.[91] Nevertheless, he had become well known in the course of the crusade as an effective preacher and, says Guibert, abbot of Nogent, who appointed himself to rewrite the *Gesta Francorum* for more sophisticated readers, 'since a man's voice is of more concern than the life he has led, he was called to the patriarchy of Jerusalem'.[92] Moreover, he was a learned man, who had had a successful teaching career, something that could not be said for the bishop of Martirano, of whom Ralph of Caen alleges that he was 'not much better educated than the common folk and hardly well read'.[93] Ironically, if the arguments about his supposed role in the genesis of the crusade have any validity, Symeon II, the Greek patriarch of Jerusalem, still living in Cyprus, was ignored.[94]

Such personal failings did nothing to dent Arnulf's confidence or undermine his assertiveness, although Raymond of Aguilers thought he should

have been frightened by the capture and disappearance of the bishop of
Martirano soon after his election, which Raymond ascribed to divine punishment.[95] Almost immediately he came into conflict with Tancred, whose
acquisitiveness during the taking of Jerusalem had extended to stripping away
gold, silver and gems from the Temple (that is, the Dome of the Rock), apparently on the pretext that they represented Muslim idolatry and that he was
acting for the common good. Arnulf later described in detail the clash that
followed to Ralph of Caen, who had come out to Antioch in about 1111. He
had assembled the leaders and made a speech about his role. There seems to
have been little pretence that the election had been free of secular influence.
'You,' he said, meaning the crusade leaders, 'have vested me as the vicar of the
pope.' His major theme, though, was the misconduct of Tancred, who had
despoiled the churches and persecuted the new patriarch, a denunciation that,
in the time-honoured fashion of polemical abuse, included an attack on
Tancred's ancestry, in particular Robert Guiscard, father of Bohemond and
the most powerful of the south Italian Normans until his death in 1085. Given
Guiscard's character, it was, he said, necessary to make 'allowances' for the
behaviour of his descendants. Tancred replied in kind, claiming that Guiscard
was 'second only to Alexander' and that there was no one in Arnulf's family
who could compare with him. Moreover, he had been assured by Arnulf
before the capture of Jerusalem that whoever occupied a property could keep
it, but now it appeared that Arnulf had changed his mind. In the end the
leaders decided that Tancred should pay back 700 marks to the Temple.
Struggling to reconcile his friendship for Arnulf with his admiration for the
deeds of Tancred, Ralph concluded by blaming the others. 'Both were
renowned, both had become powerful from meager beginnings, and both
were the subject of jealousy by everyone else, although neither one was jealous
of the other except by chance.'[96]

When Robert of Normandy and Robert of Flanders sailed from Latakia in
September 1099, they left behind a Frankish presence that was precarious in
the extreme. Huge losses during the journey, as well as the return home of
many pilgrims, left only a thin military establishment spread over a very wide
area. Nor were the settlers helped by the expeditions of autumn 1100 and
spring 1101, which, even though led by powerful lords and backed by large
numbers of soldiers, did not form a united army and were defeated piecemeal
by Kilij Arslan and his allies in Asia Minor. As a result, relatively few of them
actually reached Syria and Palestine, and even fewer settled permanently.[97]
Although Islam had failed to offer united opposition to the initial invasion,
it is evident from Fulcher of Chartres's chronicle that the Latins left in the
East were highly nervous. Fulcher says that there were insufficient people to

defend Jerusalem from the Saracens 'if only the latter dared attack us'. He could not understand why they did not. 'Why did they not gather from Egypt, from Persia, from Mesopotamia, and from Syria at least a hundred times a hundred thousand fighters to advance courageously against us, their enemies? Why did not they, as innumerable locusts in a little field, so completely devour and destroy us that no further mention could be made of us in a land that had been ours from time immemorial?' His only explanation was that the Christians enjoyed the protection of God, but he knew that 'His mercy aids in their tribulations those who trust in Him alone'; in other words, it depended upon their conduct.[98]

Such conduct was always at risk given the evident divisions caused by the ambitions of the competing leaders and their followers, and by the unresolved relationship between ecclesiastical and secular power, itself entangled with those ambitions. Nor could they rely on help from the Byzantines, since, although Greeks and Latins shared a common goal in their wish to undermine Islam, there were fundamental differences both in their strategic objectives and in their perceptions of the world. Like the crusaders, the Greeks saw the defence of the holy places as the responsibility of all Christendom, but their priority was to regain control of Asia Minor and northern Syria, for they knew that they could not hold Jerusalem without them. Whatever the imagined limitations covered by the oath sworn to Alexius by the crusade leaders, they certainly believed that Bohemond's seizure of Antioch was a blatant violation of it.[99] Moreover, although Byzantine military traditions had deep roots in the Roman era, roots reinforced since then by the adoption of Christianity and the cult of warrior saints like St Demetrius and St George, the Greeks did not see the waging of the just war in Augustinian terms, nor did they believe that warfare, whatever the cause, was a means of expiating sin.[100]

This divergence of outlook found a focus at Antioch. By the latter part of 1098, the crusaders had become convinced that they had been betrayed by Alexius, who had failed to bring them help at the time of their direst need. In the late spring of 1098, threatened by Kerbogha's army approaching from the east and apparently unable to break the resistance of the defenders of Antioch, they were in greater danger than at any other time during the expedition. At this point Stephen of Blois abandoned the crusade and, in the course of his return across Asia Minor, met Alexius at Philomelium in central Anatolia around 20 June. When the count gave him news of what appeared to be a hopeless situation, the emperor decided to retreat.[101] The meeting at Philomelium was crucial, creating a depth of anti-Greek feeling among the crusaders not previously present.[102] Indeed, after the crusaders had taken Antioch and defeated Kerbogha, but apparently before they were aware of

Alexius's retreat, they had sent Hugh of Vermandois and Baldwin of Hainault to arrange for the handover of the city to imperial power.[103]

However, Bohemond had begun to act as if he were the legitimate ruler of Antioch almost at once, for he had no intention of conceding the city to the Byzantines, and in September, in a letter heavily influenced by him, the crusaders referred to the Greeks as heretics, along with the other eastern Christian Churches: the Armenians, Syrians and Jacobites. Urging the pope to come out to head them, the leaders asked that they be separated 'from the unjust emperor who has never fulfilled the many promises he has made us. In fact, he has hindered and harmed us in every way at his disposal.'[104] Nine months before, Adhémar had ensured close liaison with the patriarch, Symeon, but Adhémar's death on 1 August had removed the one leader with the weight and prestige to moderate these resentments. The powerful anti-Byzantine propaganda contained in the *Gesta Francorum* stemmed from these circumstances and thereafter was taken up in the West by the many chroniclers influenced by the *Gesta*.[105] Although Adhémar's death did not completely extinguish feelings of fraternal solidarity with the Greeks, nevertheless Urban II's wish to rescue the eastern Christians from infidel oppression had never inspired the crusaders in the way that his call for an armed pilgrimage to liberate Jerusalem had done.[106]

Anna Comnena, too, was aware of the long-term importance of the failure to relieve Antioch and felt the need to justify it. Alexius, she says, was very anxious to go to the aid of the Franks, but was deterred both by Stephen of Blois and the news of Kerbogha's relief army. 'For he calculated what would probably happen in the future, namely, that it was an impossibility to save a city which had only just been taken by the Franks and while still in a state of disorder was immediately besieged from outside by the Hagarenes; and the Franks, in despair of all help, were planning to leave only empty walls to the enemy and to save their own lives by flight.' He therefore decided not to proceed, 'lest by hastening to the assistance of Antioch he might cause the destruction of Constantinople.'[107]

Finally, the polities founded by the Latins in the East were quite unique in that whatever the nature of the states that emerged from the First Crusade, they could never act solely in terms of their own concerns, for all western Christians had a stake in the holy places. Every day the settlers were reminded of this, as pilgrims and other visitors streamed into their lands and as they themselves were obliged time after time to appeal for the outside help that would ensure their survival. In a letter to his suffragan, Lambert, bishop of Arras, written in November or December 1099, Manasses, archbishop of Reims, expressed the essence of this caste of mind. 'Jerusalem,' he declared, 'the city of our redemption and glory, delights with inconceivable joy, because through the effort and incomparable might of the sons of God it has been liberated from the most cruel pagan servitude.' He therefore commanded 'that you have every one of your parish churches, without fail, pray with fasts and almsgiving that the King of Kings and the Lord of Lords crown the King of the Christians with victory against the enemy, and the Patriarch with religion and wisdom against the sects and deceptions of heretics'.[108] To the modern eye, the crusader states may appear no more than narrow strips of territory clinging to the coast on the farthest fringe of Christendom, but to contemporaries they were the guardians of the holiest shrines and therefore at the very heart of the Christian world.

CHAPTER 2

Syria and Palestine

'So at last our knights came into the valley where stands the royal city of Antioch, capital of Syria, which was granted to blessed Peter, prince of the Apostles, to restore to the holy faith, by Our Lord Jesus who liveth and reigneth with God the Father in the unity of the Holy Ghost, One God, world without end.'[1] With these words the author of the *Gesta Francorum* describes the emergence of the crusader army from the Amanus mountains into the Orontes valley in mid-October 1097. There is a palpable sense of relief in the text at this point since, for the past month, the crusaders had been struggling over the Anti-Taurus range through Coxon and Marash, sometimes along mountain paths so narrow that they had been obliged to adopt single file. Even then, horses had fallen over precipices and baggage animals, roped together, had pulled one another over the edge. Many knights were so 'frightened and miserable', the author says, that they had thrown away their armour rather than carry it.

They secured the so-called Iron Bridge over the Orontes on 19 October and, within two days, they were arrayed before Antioch. The debate that followed – whether to make an immediate assault or settle down for a long siege – must have reflected their mixed feelings at what they saw around them. Antioch was attractively situated. According to the *Gesta*, there were 'plenty of provisions, fruitful vineyards and pits full of stored corn, apple-trees laden with fruit and all sorts of other good things to eat'. Ralph of Caen, who did not take part in the First Crusade, but had direct experience of Antioch during the later years of Tancred's rule until the latter's death at the end of 1112, describes how nearby Daphne supported Bohemond. Daphne, he says, means delightful and had been so named by the Greeks. It held 'a position of glory among the other valleys, having an abundance of fruits, vines, trees and water'.[2] Half a century before, Ibn Butlan, a Christian Arab physician from

Baghdad, had travelled from Aleppo to Antioch through a populous and productive countryside in which 'the villages ran continuous, their gardens full of flowers, and the waters flowing on every hand'.[3]

Yet to an attacker, the city was daunting. Although the population was much diminished from its height under the later Roman empire, Ibn Butlan thought Antioch immense. Set out in a semicircle on the left bank of the Orontes, protected by a double line of walls and, he claims, 360 towers, it backed onto Mount Silpius, near the summit of which was the citadel, and the Iron Gate, approachable only by means of a narrow defile. The mountain overshadowed the city so that the sun only began to shine about the second hour of the day.[4] Ralph of Caen explained that the plain on which Antioch lay was, in fact, constrained between two mountains to the north and the south-south-west, and that the mountains grew broader farther east.[5] Raymond of Aguilers was so in awe of its situation that he claimed that neither the impact of machines nor the assault of men would have any effect, 'even if all mankind gathered to besiege it'.[6]

Moreover, although the crusaders had arrived in the autumn when grain and fruit were abundant, they were only days away from the rainy winter season, which began in November and lasted until March or April.[7] Indeed, the crusaders were fortunate not to experience the exceptional conditions recorded by Michael the Syrian in the autumn of 1172. In September, the rain and the snow arrived much earlier and more suddenly than usual, ruining the harvest. 'It destroyed the vines, the olive trees, the cotton and the sesame, which looked like black charcoal, as if they had been burned by fire. This calamity made itself felt not only in Assyria, in Mesopotamia and Syria, but also in the countries of Persia and Armenia, and even in Palestine and Egypt. The whole land resembled a heap of wood shavings which the fire had devoured and which had become burnt and powdered.'[8] Ralph of Caen knew what a Syrian winter could be like. During the siege of Antioch, 'there were floods of water, sometimes in sudden downpours, and sometimes in continuous streams. There was great movement of both the heaven and earth so that it appeared that the two elements had been joined together with the one rising up and the other coming down. But what about the storms, what shall I say about the raging of the winds? While they were blowing, neither tent nor hut could stand. Indeed, it was hardly possible for the palace and the tower to survive.' The weather was no respecter of persons; in Ralph's view, the nobility felt it more than the peasants because the former were 'accustomed to luxury'.[9]

Stephen of Blois certainly thought so. In his letter to Adela on 29 March 1098, he told her that 'all winter long . . . we suffered extremely cold temperatures and an endless downpour of rain for Christ the Lord. When some people say that the heat of the sun throughout Syria is unbearable, this is wrong, since their winters are similar to our western winters.'[10] However, Stephen did not stay to experience a Syrian summer. In August, Godfrey of Bouillon left for the mountains, where he stayed in Ravendel and Turbessel. Albert of Aachen says that, having seen Bishop Adhémar succumb to disease on 1 August, he feared 'that this was the same illness which he had remembered had afflicted Rome long ago with a very similar disaster when he was on an expedition with King Henry IV'. At that time it had killed 500 in the army and had led the Germans to abandon Rome.[11] If it was the same disease, it was almost certainly malaria, endemic in the swamps around Rome, but the crusaders were afflicted by dysentery as well, common in the East whenever sanitary conditions were poor. Ralph of Caen calls it a 'vile illness', and Ibn al-Qalanisi says it was 'a disease to be feared and one from which its victim scarcely ever recovers'.[12]

The experiences of the crusaders at Antioch in 1097–8 were in many ways a reflection of the broader physical environment. In c.985, Muhammed al-Muqaddasi, a theologian and merchant born in Jerusalem, wrote a description of Syria in which he divided the country into four belts. The first bordered the Mediterranean, which he calls 'the plain-country, the sandy tracts following one another, and alternating with the cultivated land'. The second was 'the mountain-country, well wooded, and possessing many springs, with frequent villages, and cultivated fields'. The third belt 'is that of the valleys of Ghaur, wherein are found many villages and streams, also palm trees, well cultivated fields, and indigo plantations'. Finally, there were the lands along the edge of the desert. 'The mountains here are high and bleak, and the climate resembles that of the Waste; but it has many villages, with springs of water, and forest trees.'[13]

The coastal plain varied considerably in width and fertility, depending on the proximity of the mountains to the sea. Thus, in what became the county of Tripoli, the main cultivable area was the wedge of the 'Akkar plain, formed by the Kebir River and its tributaries and the volcanic soils of al-Buqai'ah farther east towards the mountains. However, to the north and south around Maraclea and Gibelet respectively, the littoral is much narrower.[14] Even so, relatively small areas could be productive. William of Tyre was especially proud of the hinterland of his own city. 'It was famous for its unique beauty of location and the fertility of its soil. Although lying in the sea itself, entirely surrounded by waves like an island, yet it had before its gates extensive arable fields, excellent in every respect, while a level plain of rich and productive soil stretched out from the city itself and furnished the people of Tyre with abundant supplies.' This terrain was only about 10 miles long and between 2 and 3

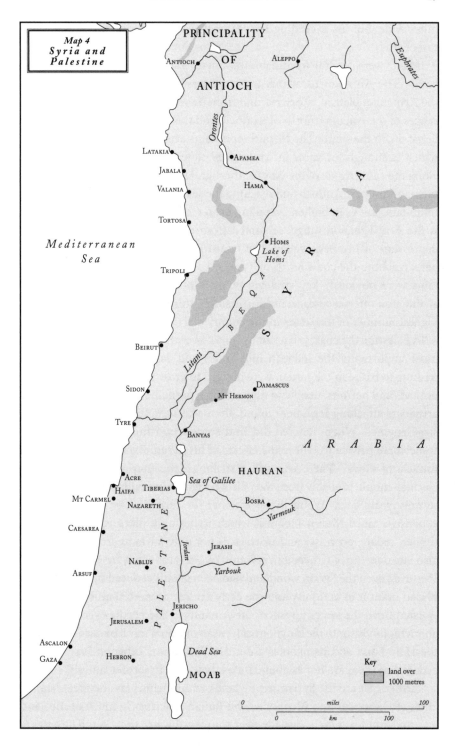

Map 4
Syria and
Palestine

PRINCIPALITY
OF
ANTIOCH

ANTIOCH

ALEPPO

Euphrates

Orontes

LATAKIA
APAMEA

JABALA

VALANIA
HAMA

TORTOSA

HOMS
Lake of
Homs

Mediterranean
Sea

TRIPOLI

B E Q A A

S Y R I A

BEIRUT

Litani

SIDON
DAMASCUS

MT HERMON

TYRE

BANYAS
A R A B I A

ACRE
HAIFA   TIBERIAS   Sea of Galilee   HAURAN

MT CARMEL
NAZARETH
BOSRA

CAESAREA
Yarmouk

Jordan
JERASH

NABLUS
Yarbouk

ARSUF

P A L E S T I N E

JERICHO

JERUSALEM

ASCALON
Dead Sea

GAZA
HEBRON

MOAB

Key

land over
1000 metres

miles

0   100

0   km   100

miles wide, but 'its exceeding fertility makes it equal to acres of boundless extent'.[15]

Inland were several formidable mountain ranges, mostly limestone and basalt. The Anti-Taurus, which the crusaders endured, projects south from the Armenian plateau into Syria, and from there are the shorter and narrower ranges of the Amanus, north of Antioch, and the Nosairi (Ansariyah) and the Lebanon, to the south. The Nosairi mountains average 1,000 metres in height, which is enough for snow in winter (see plate 2). The Orontes flows north along the eastern side of the Nosairi through Homs, Hama and Shaizar before turning west past Antioch and reaching the sea at Saint Simeon. The Lebanese mountains are even higher, averaging nearer 2,000 metres. Further south still is the Anti-Lebanon range, separated from the Lebanese mountains by the depression of the Beqa valley. The Litani River flows south and west from here, reaching the coast north of Tyre. Accessible routes across these mountains were obviously key strategic points. South of the Nosairi mountains al-Buqai'ah offers a passage; not surprisingly, this region always contained the highest number of fortresses in the county of Tripoli.[16]

In Palestine the coast is backed by hills rather than mountains on this scale, most importantly the Judaean hills south and east of Jerusalem. Pilgrims wishing to bathe in the Jordan were obliged to cross this arid region, a land of nomads and hermits, unable to support large permanent communities. As the crusaders attacking Jerusalem found, there was little timber for constructing siege engines. When Tancred did find some wood in a cave while seeking somewhere private to relieve the effects of his dysentery, it was regarded as a miracle of God.[17] There was still a striking deficiency when Theoderic, a German monk, probably from the well-wooded Rhine valley, visited Jerusalem seventy years later. 'Wood there, whether for carpentry or for firewood, is expensive, since Mount Libanus, which is the only place which has much timber, cedars, cypresses and fir trees, is not only far away from the city, but also no one can go there on account of the ambushes by the Gentiles.'[18] However, even the Syrian woodland had been greatly reduced by the demands placed upon it in antiquity and the early middle ages, so that it had become isolated from the larger forests of the Amanus to the north. According to an anonymous visitor to the kingdom of Jerusalem who wrote a treatise describing the Holy Land and its peoples around 1170, Mount Lebanon 'has very tall cedars, but these are not as abundant as they were in former times'.[19]

Farther east are the Syrian steppe lands within which lay the great Islamic cities of Damascus and Aleppo. As Ibn Butlan describes it, much of this land was under cultivation, especially near sources of water such as the Orontes.[20] The only Latin state established beyond these regions was that created by

Baldwin of Boulogne at Edessa (Urfa), about 160 miles to the north-east of Antioch in Upper Mesopotamia. This was really an extension of the steppe lands, rising in a series of ridges towards the Euphrates. Edessa itself is farther still, situated about 45 miles east of the river. Nevertheless, despite the distance, it had its attractions. 'This city,' says Fulcher of Chartres, who accompanied Baldwin, 'is very famous and is in a most fertile area.'[21] However, according to the Armenian chronicler Matthew of Edessa, it did not always realise its potential, for it was sometimes subject to sudden changes in its weather patterns. In 1099–1100, there was an acute drought, causing the land to become dessicated and thus leading to a severe famine. Fortunately, the rain returned the following year, so there was an abundance of the main products of the region, which included wheat, barley, fruit and grapes.[22]

To the south is the great rift valley, which encompassed the Jordan. This flowed into the Sea of Galilee (Tiberias) and then on to the Dead Sea. Between the Sea of Galilee and Mount Carmel, overlooking Haifa on the coast, is the Galilean plain which, like parts of the Syrian steppe, offered good agricultural land. Just to the south-west of the lake stood the extraordinary Mount Tabor, much visited by pilgrims, who believed it was the site of the Transfiguration (see plate 3). Abbot Daniel of Kiev, who visited the kingdom of Jerusalem between 1106 and 1108, says that it took six hours of steady climbing to reach the top. 'Mount Tabor is a marvel and wonder and is beyond description, made beautiful by God. ... It is situated in a beautiful plain far from other mountains like a round haycock and a river flows through the plain at its foot. And Mount Tabor is covered all over with trees of every kind, figs and carobs and olives in great abundance.'[23]

In November and December 1100, Baldwin of Boulogne, the new ruler of Jerusalem, set out to explore the south and south-east. As his chaplain, Fulcher was again with him. Fulcher was fascinated by the wonders of the natural world. 'There is there a great lake which is called the Dead Sea because no living thing is born in it. It extends five hundred and eighty stades in length and one hundred and fifty in width. It is so salty that no beast or bird of any kind whatsoever can drink from it. This, I, Fulcher, learned by experience when I dismounted from my mule into the water and took a drink with my hand, testing it by the taste and finding it to be more bitter than hellebore.'[24] A few years later, Abbot Daniel was similarly amazed.

And there are high rocky mountains here with many caves in those mountains, and holy fathers lived in these mountains in this fearful waterless wilderness. Here are the lairs of the panther and there are many wild asses. The Sea of Sodom is dead and has no living thing in it, neither fish nor crayfish, nor shellfish, and if the

swift current of the Jordan should carry a fish into this sea, it cannot live even an
hour but quickly dies. And from the depths of this sea red pitch rises to the surface
and this pitch lies on the shore in great quantity and a stench comes up from this
sea as if from burning sulphur.[25]

Penetrating farther south, Baldwin, Fulcher and his party reached Wadi
Musa (west of Petra), which impressed them because of the fertility of the
valley and because they identified it as the place where Moses had struck the
rock to bring forth a spring. Above was the mountain where Moses and Aaron
spoke with God (Numbers 20). They rested here for three days before
returning to Jerusalem on the day of the winter solstice (21 December).[26]
Fulcher seems never to have travelled beyond this but, in 1116, Baldwin took
a force of 200 knights down to the Red Sea 'that he might see what he had not
yet seen and along the way fortuitously find something good which he
wanted', a journey of about seven days via his new castle of Montréal
(Shaubak). This meant crossing the desert lands of the Negev and Sinai, or the
Waste, as al-Muqaddasi called it, before reaching Ailah (al-'Aqabah).[27]
    As the armies at Antioch soon came to realise, this terrain encompassed
wide variations in precipitation and temperature. Around Antioch itself the
average annual precipitation is about 46 inches (1,181 mm), most of which
falls during the winter, leaving long, hot, dry summers, with little in the way
of spring or autumn. Although the average annual temperature is between 15
and 20°C, this conceals much greater extremes. In the mountains the midwinter
temperature can fall below freezing, while in the plain summer levels can rise
above 30°C.[28] Once the crusaders left Antioch and, urged on by popular
pressure, began to push south towards Jerusalem, they found that precipitation decreased as the temperature climbed: in what became the kingdom of
Jerusalem, average temperatures of around 20–22°C could be transformed
by the desert winds of early summer into highs of 40°C or more. In 1185, John
Phocas, a Greek pilgrim from Crete, visited the Holy Land, where he had a
particular interest in Orthodox monasteries and their sites. Among these
was the monastery of Choziba, near the Jericho road. 'Indeed the recesses of
the caves are the monks' cells. And the Church itself and the cemetery are set
in the chasm of the rock, and everything is so blasted by the burning sun
that one can see the rock emitting tongues of flame like pyramids. In fact the
water which the monks drink is of the kind which comes from a pool, when
the midsummer sun hangs above the pools and heats it to boiling-point with
its fiery rays.'[29]
    Rainfall in Palestine, again almost exclusively in the winter, is less than half
that in Antioch, diminishing to almost nothing in the hills and deserts of the

east and south. In al-Muqaddasi's time, in the late tenth century, water was plentiful in Jerusalem, but it was entirely because of the city's conservation measures, which included the provision of three great tanks, twenty underground cisterns in the Haram area and two pools in the Muristan.[30] The natural condition of the region was one of aridity. It was 'entirely lacking in water', says William of Tyre, with no springs or rivers, and therefore depended upon the winter rains to replenish the cisterns.[31] Even so, there are still microclimates: Tiberias and the borders of the lake experience very mild winters of around 14°C. Indeed, al-Muqaddasi places this area within his third belt, characterised by palms, cultivated fields and indigo plantations.[32]

The pressures experienced by the crusaders in northern Syria could all too easily be repeated elsewhere. Raymond of Aguilers is one of several writers to describe how starvation gripped the crusaders' camp during the winter of 1097–8, a situation exacerbated on the kalends of January (1 January 1098), when there was a frightening earth tremor.[33] The twelfth century was a particularly active period for earthquakes in this region, culminating in May 1202, when, according to Philip of Plessis, master of the Temple, 'we suffered the sort of earthquakes not seen since the creation of the world'.[34] In the twenty years between 1097 and 1117, Fulcher of Chartres recorded six separate earthquakes, including the most serious in 1114, which, although the epicentre appears to have been at Marash, which was destroyed, was strong enough to damage buildings in Antioch, 60 miles to the south.[35] Equal in severity to that of 1202 was the Syrian earthquake of 29 June 1170, which brought down the cathedral of St Peter in Antioch, as well as the walls of the city, and ruined many of the great castles of the military orders in the county of Tripoli. Muslim cities were similarly struck, especially Aleppo, Hama, Homs and Baalbek. Tremors were felt as far south as Jerusalem and as far north and east as the Jacobite monastery of Mar Hanania, near Mardin, over 100 miles east of Edessa. Aftershocks continued for three to four months.[36]

The earthquakes of August and November 1114 had been preceded in the spring by locusts, which, says Walter, the chancellor of Antioch between c.1114 and c.1122, 'stole nearly all the things necessary to feed the farmers of Syria. Then they were dispersed partly by crawling along the ground, partly through the air, and they afflicted almost the whole region of the eastern Christians to the same devastating effect'.[37] It was not only crops that were vulnerable. Ambroise, the Norman poet who took part in the Third Crusade, describes the afflictions of King Richard's army in August 1191. Encamped south of Haifa, they were disturbed during the night by an 'attack from stinging worms and tarantulas which harassed them greatly, stinging the pilgrims who would at once swell up'.[38]

While earthquakes were prevalent in the north, crossing the desert lands south of the kingdom of Jerusalem presented its own hazards. In 1167, Shirkuh, one of the most important generals of Nur al-Din, ruler of Aleppo and Damascus, was caught in a terrible sandstorm while trying to lead an army into Egypt. William of Tyre witnessed such phenomena for himself.

> Particles of sand raised aloft swirled through the air like clouds or dense fog. The men dared not open their mouths to speak to one another, nor could they keep their eyes open. Dismounting from their horses, they lay prostrate clinging to the ground, their hands pressed into the sand as far as possible, lest they be swept aloft by the violence of the whirlwind and again dashed to the ground. For in that desert waves of sand like those of the sea are wont to rise and fall as in a tempest, a fact that renders the crossing of these perilous reaches not less dangerous than sailing over the sea.[39]

The crusaders were well aware that they could do nothing to change the basic facts of topography and climate, and usually attributed natural disasters to God's will, a scourging inflicted as punishment for riotous living and plundering, as Raymond of Aguilers put it.[40] However, human geography presented both different problems and new opportunities, for this was a populous and diverse land, dominated by ancient cities and ports, inhabited by many races, and deeply marked by the impact of three great religions and their offshoots. A web of communications followed the coast, crossed the mountain passes and the inland valleys, and spread out across the plains and the desert.[41]

The remains of the past confronted them at every turn.[42] Latakia was an important port, but it had seen better days. Ralph of Caen, describing Tancred's siege of 1101–2, was very impressed.

> It could be seen from the ruins that this city had once been noble, having churches, a large population, riches, towers, palaces, theatres and all of the other things which make a place great. Aside from Antioch, no other city had within its circuit such great signs of ancient nobility. The multiple series of columns, aqueducts which ran over rough terrain, towers built toward the heavens, statues lying around in fitting places, all of which were well constructed from precious materials. All of these noteworthy works, still present after so much time and so many ravages, provide evidence of its past from its present, its former state from its destroyed remains, and its large population from its current state of abandonment.[43]

In 1121, pursuing the Muslims across the Jordan, King Baldwin II destroyed a fortress built the previous year by Tughtigin, atabeg of Damascus, within the ruins of the second-century Roman city of Jerash (see plate 4). Fulcher of Chartres describes it as 'marvellously and gloriously founded upon a strong site in ancient times'.[44] Similar sights could be found at Sidon and Gibelet or Jubail (the Greek Byblos), and even in the thirteenth century the past continued to impinge. When the Templars began to dig the foundations of their great new castle at 'Atlit, on a promontory south of Haifa, in 1217 and 1218, they uncovered ancient walls and found coinage of a type quite unknown to contemporaries.[45] There were equally impressive remains in the south. When, in 1149–50, Baldwin III sought to rebuild Gaza, on the coast below Ascalon, he encountered a site too large for him to fortify in its entirety. It had been, says William of Tyre, one of the five cities of the Philistines. 'It was celebrated for its buildings, and many handsome churches and spacious houses of marble and huge stones, though now in ruins, still gave splendid evidence of its ancient glory. Many reservoirs and wells of living water also still remained.'[46]

At Tyre, Archbishop William set down this historical context. At the beginning of book 13 of his chronicle, he describes what he considers to be the most important characteristics of the place he designates 'the metropolis of all Phoenicia'. According to Justinian's great law code, the *Digest*, published in 533, Tyre held a special legal position within the Roman empire, having been granted 'Italian rights' as a reward for its loyalty. Its origins, however, were much earlier. Drawing on his knowledge of Solinus and Ovid, William claims that it had belonged to King Agenor and his children, Europa, Cadmus and Phoenix, from the last of whom, 'as the Phoenicians claim, that the whole region derives its name'. Initially it had had two names: Sor, which was Hebrew; and Tyre, Greek in origin, from its foundation by Tyrus, the seventh son of Japhet, the son of Noah. It was already famous 'in early times', as can be seen from Old Testament references in Ezekiel and Isaiah, the stories told of the relations between Hiram, king of Tyre, and Solomon in the *Antiquities* of Josephus, the first-century AD Jewish historian, and the account of the great faith of the Canaanite woman from the city given in chapter 15 of Matthew and prophesied in Psalm 45. As presented by the archbishop, therefore, Tyre can be seen as a model of the renowned cities of the region: founded in legend, integrated into biblical history, and an established political and economic entity in the Hebrew, Greek and Roman worlds.[47]

William calls this region 'Syria'. It is, he says, a name used 'sometimes in a broad sense as applying to the whole province, and again in a more limited way to designate only a part of the same'. Greater Syria extended from the Tigris to Egypt and from Cilicia to the Red Sea. It was divided into twelve provinces: Mesopotamia, lying between the Tigris and the Euphrates; Coelesyria, which includes Antioch; the two Cilicias; Phoenicia, now divided between Phoenicia Maritima, the metropolis of which is Tyre, and Phoenicia Libania, the capital of which is Damascus; the two Arabias, centred on Bostrum and Petra respectively; the three Palestines, Jerusalem, capital of Judea, maritime Caesarea and Scythopolis, also called Bethsan (Baisan); and, finally, the last province, Idumea, extending towards Egypt.

While there was nobody on the First Crusade with William's education and access to books, nevertheless the participants had answered Urban's call because at one level or another they understood the meaning of what the pope had described as 'our lands', that is, they adhered to the distinctly Latin Christian interpretation of the region's history. They knew, too, however, that they were not entering a land of neat administrative divisions, but one soaked in the blood of past conflicts to an extent unparalleled in the known world. The geopolitics of the Middle East had determined that Syria was a frontier region across which powers whose epicentres were far to the west or the east fought out their many wars. In the late tenth century, al-Muqaddasi praised Syria as a place of glorious renown, but nevertheless presented its inhabitants as victims of outsiders, corrupted by the circumstances that trapped them. 'But the people live ever in terror of the Byzantines, almost as though they were in a land of exile, for their frontiers are continuously ravaged, and their fortresses again and again destroyed. Nor are the Syrians the equals of the Persians in either science, religion or intelligence; some have become apostates, while others pay tribute to the infidels, thus setting obedience to created man before obedience to the Lord of Heaven. The populace, too, is ignorant and seditious, and the Syrian people show neither zeal for the Holy War, nor honour to those who fight against the infidel.'[48]

These conflicts had deep roots. Persian expansion into Asia Minor in the fifth century BC led to clashes with the Greeks; the ultimate response was the invasion of Alexander of Macedon who, in 337 BC, eliminated the Archaemenid rulers of Persia. After Alexander's death in 323 BC, his empire was carved up by his generals. One of them, Seleucus, established Seleucia Pieria in Cilicia and founded, among other cities, Antioch, Apamea and Latakia. Antioch became a key centre both because of its strategic and commercial position and because it was consciously created as a Hellenistic centre within an oriental setting. With Roman expansion into the region in the first century BC, it developed into a prosperous city, particularly favoured by Augustus (27 BC–AD 14).[49] Persia, however, remained a threat, and Armenia, Syria and Palestine were integrated into a Roman defensive system that lasted in various forms until the Muslim conquests of the seventh century.

Muhammad's revelations transformed this world. Until the early seventh century, the framework of the ancient order had survived. The Byzantines, secure in their great capital of Constantinople on the Bosphorus, maintained that they were the true heirs of the Romans, despite the collapse of the empire in the West in the fourth and fifth centuries. They continued to see other mighty powers as their main rivals, most obviously the Persians, based at Ctesiphon on the Tigris. When these two giants clashed they took little account of the other peoples of the Middle East. But Muhammad had appeared at an opportune moment. Worn down by the coruscating wars of the first three decades of the seventh century, neither the Byzantines nor the Persians were ready to face a new and unforeseen challenge. During the 620s, Muhammad overcame political and military opponents in the Arabian peninsula and convinced a large proportion of the population that he was, as he had claimed, the prophet chosen by God as the vehicle for the final revelation. After his death in 632, his successors, driven by what had become a dynamic new religion, committed themselves to an unprecedented territorial expansion. Antioch, which Emperor Heraclius had won back from the Persians in 628 and thereafter used as his eastern base, succumbed soon after the main Byzantine army was defeated at Yarmuk in 636. Heraclius retreated to Constantinople, never to return.

Within a century, the Muslims had encompassed Syria, Palestine and Egypt, the entire southern shore of the Mediterranean, and most of the Iberian peninsula. Significantly, these new conquests included the city of Jerusalem, taken in 637, and seen as the third great religious centre of the Islamic world after Mecca and Medina. The Byzantine empire was deeply wounded and later twice had to fight off determined attempts to take Constantinople itself, but at least it survived; for the old Persian empire, the rise of Islam was fatal. Westward expansion was matched by eastern conquests, initiated by the defeat of the Persians at al-Qadisiyah in 637. When the last shah was killed by his own men in 651, the way was open to central Asia. Historians have long been divided about the nature of the impact of Islam upon the medieval West, sometimes arriving at diametrically opposite conclusions about the economic and political effects of the division of the great inland sea the Romans had seen as their own. It is, though, indisputable that the creation and expansion of this new religious force were both a threat and a challenge to a world that, since the late fourth century, had been dominated by Christianity, and the long-term effects were as profound as the replacement of Greece by Rome and Rome by the Germans.

The crusaders, therefore, represented yet another outside invader of a region long fought over by Greeks, Persians, Romans, Byzantines and Arabs, all of whom had left their cultural imprint. They were not there, however, to admire the remnants of Antioch's agora or its great colonnaded street; they had come, in the pope's mind at least, to rescue their co-believers from Turkish oppression and to liberate the holy places from the control of the infidel. For them, the most important feature of Antioch's history was its formative role in the establishment of Christianity as a distinct religion after the martyrdom of Stephen in Jerusalem in AD 34 or 36. As the author of the *Gesta* saw it, Antioch was the city of 'the blessed Peter, prince of the Apostles'.[50] For the crusaders, Peter's presence there in the middle of the first century meant that he was the first bishop of the Church, a view reinforced by contemporary papal thinking which, basing itself on the Gospel of Matthew (16: 18), believed to have been written there, stressed the importance of the see of St Peter as the rock upon which the Church was founded.[51] William of Tyre saw it as fundamental to the adoption of Christianity. 'In this city the first gathering of the faithful was held and here also the name of Christians was adopted. Before this time, those who followed the teachings of Christ were called Nazarenes. Afterwards, by authority of that synod, all the faithful were known as Christians, a name derived from that of Christ. This city voluntarily and eagerly received the preaching of the apostle and was converted as one body to the Christian faith. She was the first to embrace and to teach the Name which, like a precious anointment, diffuses its fragrance far and wide.'[52]

While both religious feeling and strategic necessity made it inconceivable that the crusaders would ignore Antioch, their ultimate goal was Jerusalem, 'the Holy City beloved of God', as William of Tyre described it. In William's history, the most salient points were its foundation by David (which took place in c.1000 BC), its prophesied destruction by the Romans (in AD 70), and its rebuilding on top of the hill by Hadrian (in AD 135 as Aelia Capitolina), when its new walls encompassed the sites of the Passion and the Resurrection.[53] As William's emphasis shows, it was its association with the events of the Crucifixion and as the place from which the Apostles began their mission that mattered most to the crusaders.[54] Like the other cities of the region, it had been subject to a whole succession of invaders, including the Babylonians in the sixth century BC and the Greeks and the successors of Alexander. Although the Maccabean revolt of 168 BC inspired a Jewish revival, in 63 BC Jerusalem was conquered by Pompey and thereafter ruled by Rome, albeit sometimes through client kings such as Herod the Great (37–34 BC). It only became important in the Christian Church as a whole after the penetration of Christianity into imperial circles under Constantine, particularly after Helena, Constantine's mother, visited the city in AD 326. Even then it did not become one of the great patriarchates of the Church until 451.[55] It is not surprising

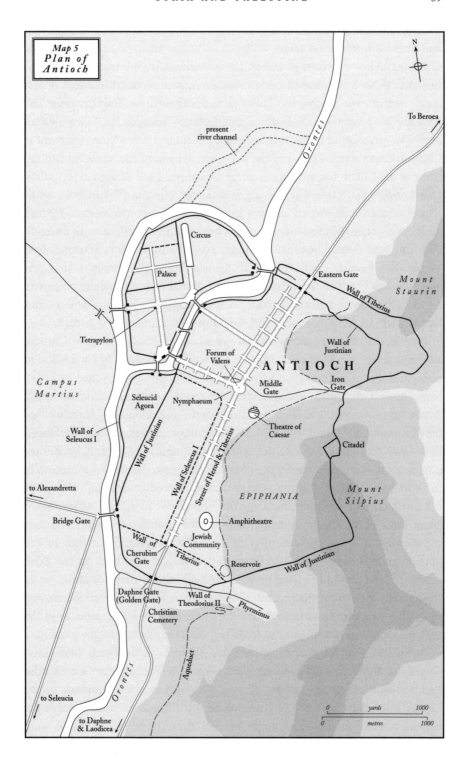

Map 5
Plan of
Antioch

that, during the twelfth century, the ecclesiastical rivalry between Antioch and Jerusalem remained acute.

All the major accounts of Urban II's speech at Clermont stress the pope's call to help their persecuted eastern brethren, accompanied by more or less lurid descriptions of what the Turks were doing to them. Baldric, prior and then abbot of Saint-Pierre-de-Bourgueil (west of Tours in the Loire region), before his promotion to the archbishopric of Dol in 1107, who was present at Clermont, wrote in c.1108 that the pope had spoken of the 'dreadful tribulations' of the Christians, who are 'scourged, oppressed and injured in Jerusalem and Antioch and other cities along the eastern coastline'.[56] However, while these brethren may indeed all have been 'our brothers, members of Christ's body', in practice they were made up of a heterogeneous collection of different Churches and races. The great earthquake of 1114 in Antioch, acknowledged Walter the Chancellor, affected 'Latins, Greeks, Syrians, Armenians, strangers and pilgrims',[57] while the pilgrim John of Würzburg, visiting Jerusalem in c.1165, felt unable to give an account of the 'people of every race and tongue' he found there, ranging as they did, he claimed, from Greeks to Indians.[58]

By 'Greeks' the crusaders meant members of the Orthodox Church, adhering to the tenets of the faith as set down at the council of Chalcedon in 451. After the fall of Jerusalem to the Arabs in 638, these were called Melkites; some spoke Greek and used it as their liturgical language, but others spoke Arabic and used Syriac as their liturgical language, a distinction largely based on education and class.[59] Under Muslim rule these communities had followed their own liturgies and retained their traditional legal forms, and they continued to do this even after the crusader conquest, despite a diminution in the numbers of patriarchal clergy in Jerusalem. Moreover, although after 1099 a Latin hierarchy replaced them, so that the Greek patriarchs of Jerusalem spent most of their time in exile, the powerful monastic tradition that they represented still commanded respect, providing a continuous link to the anchorites and early monastic communities, which went back to the third century.[60] The Orthodox were present throughout the crusader lands, in all the coastal cities, in the major centres like Antioch, Edessa and Jerusalem, and in smaller communities in places like the south-eastern Transjordan or in the scattered monasteries sought out by John Phocas in the 1180s (see plate 5).

In his list, John of Würzburg includes Armenians, Jacobites, Maronites, Copts and Nestorians, all of whom were seen as heretical by the Greeks, who had persecuted them in the past. At best, they were seen as schismatic by the Latins, since they were not in communion with Rome. It is not clear if the crusaders thought they had come to save these from the Turks as well, although Michael the Syrian says that, during the expedition, the Franks had

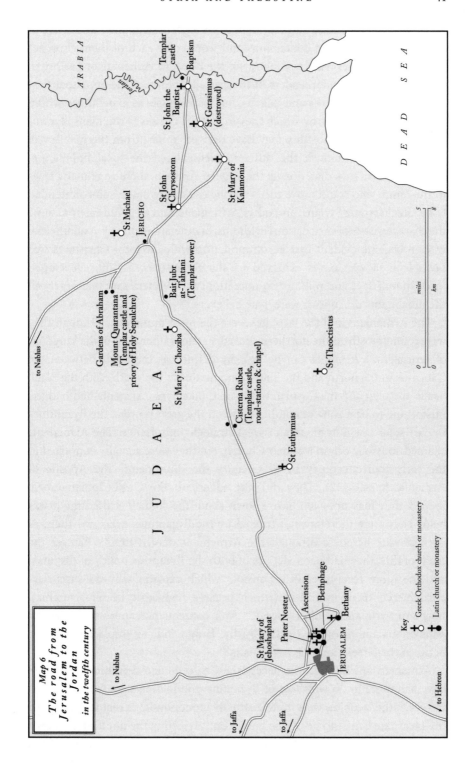

Map 6
The road from
Jerusalem to the
Jordan
in the twelfth century

ARABIA

Jordan

DEAD SEA

Templar castle
Baptism
St John the Baptist
St Gerasimus (destroyed)

St John Chrysostom
St Mary of Kalamonia

St Michael
JERICHO

Gardens of Abraham
Mount Quarantana
(Templar castle and
priory of Holy Sepulchre)

Bait Jubr at-Tahtani
(Templar tower)

J U D A E A

St Mary in Choziba

St Theoctistus

Cisterna Rubea
(Templar castle,
road-station & chapel)

St Euthymius

to Nablus

to Nablus

to Jaffa

to Jaffa

St Mary of Jehoshaphat
Pater Noster
Ascension
Bethphage
Bethany
JERUSALEM

to Hebron

Key
Greek Orthodox church or monastery
Latin church or monastery

miles
km
5
8
0
0

promised God that, if he allowed them to enter Jerusalem, they would live in peace with all Christian confessions and would give each of them churches and convents.[61] Nevertheless, following the death of Adhémar of Le Puy in August 1098, the secular leaders of the crusade informed the pope that they had driven out the Turks and pagans, but were unable to expel those whom they called the heretics, by which they meant the Greeks, Armenians, Syrians and Jacobites.[62] This hostility may have derived in part from the inability of the Latins to distinguish the different elements in the local population. William of Tyre says that, during the siege of Antioch, there were many spies in the camp, who could move easily among the troops since 'some pretended to be Greeks, some Syrians, and other Armenians, and all could easily assume the characteristics of such nations in idioms, manners, and dress'.[63] Nonetheless, it soon became evident that accommodation with the local Christians was possible in a way never achieved by the Byzantines, as links developed through marriage and military co-operation, and William says that nearly all the inhabitants of Antioch were 'true believers'.[64]

The Armenians and the Jacobites were the most numerous, although they were found mostly in the northern crusader states rather than in the kingdom of Jerusalem.[65] Armenia can be broadly defined as the lands between the Caucasus to the north and the Taurus mountains to the south, with the Black Sea to the west and the Caspian to the east. Like Syria, Armenia had had the misfortune to be a zone of conflict between the great powers; the Byzantines in particular saw it as an area of great strategic importance. The Armenians claimed apostolic origin for their Church, but they were actually converted in the early fourth century by St Gregory the Illuminator, 'the Apostle of Armenia' (c.240–332). They did not adhere to the Chalcedonian creed; indeed, they may not even have known about the council at the time it was held. They were therefore not trusted by the Byzantines, who saw them as monophysite heretics, although the Armenians denied this. Whatever the truth of this, they had been victims of both the Byzantine policy of dispersal and the more recent Seljuk expansion, which explains why the crusaders encountered them in Cilicia (which became known as Lesser Armenia), northern Syria and around Edessa.[66] As a consequence, there was, says the anonymous author of the treatise on the Holy Land, 'an implacable hatred' between the Greeks and the Armenians.[67]

Armenian unwillingness to accept the Chalcedonian definitions may well have had more to do with fear of Byzantine domination than with doctrine. However, the Jacobites were quite distinctly monophysite in that they believed the Incarnate Christ to be of one nature only, rejecting the doctrine set down at Chalcedon of two natures, divine and human, mystically united, while the

Maronites were monotheletes, accepting that Christ had two natures, but only one (Divine) will.[68] The Jacobites were named after Jacob Baradaeus, who became metropolitan of Edessa in c.542, during a career of consistent opposition to the Byzantines. As the Syrian Orthodox Church, they had communities in all the crusader states, but were particularly strong in northern Syria, under the leadership of their own patriarch of Antioch.[69] Although there were fewer of them in the south, nevertheless they had a continuous line of metropolitans in Jerusalem in the twelfth century, among whom was Ignatius Hesnun (who died in 1124 or 1125), who rebuilt the church of St Mary Magdalene and Simon the Pharisee, situated in the north-east corner of the city, which had been virtually deserted at the end of the eleventh century.[70]

The Maronites had originally been based at Antioch, but when the crusaders arrived they were mainly to be found in the northern Lebanese mountains, where they had taken refuge from Byzantine persecution. They were less dispersed than the Armenians and the Jacobites; William of Tyre estimated that there were about 40,000 of them living in the region of Gibelet. Their heresy was, he says, 'that in our Lord Jesus Christ there exists, and did exist from the beginning, one will and one energy only'.[71] This seems to be a reference to the doctrine of monotheletism, which Heraclius had tried to introduce in an unsuccessful attempt to reconcile dissident Churches in the midst of the Persian crisis of the 620s. They took their name from St Maro (350–433), who founded a monastery on the Orontes not far from Apamea in the late fourth century, although their monophysite beliefs were most likely to have been derived from another Maro, Maro of Edessa, who lived in the late sixth century.[72]

The Copts and the Nestorians were less important to the crusaders, although, as John of Würzburg shows, they clearly had a presence in the kingdom of Jerusalem. The Copts, in fact, might have become of much greater interest to the Latins had King Amalric succeeded in gaining control of northern Egypt during the 1160s, since their main centre was Alexandria. Coptic tradition claimed unbroken succession from St Mark, martyred in Alexandria in AD 68. Their opposition to Chalcedon was therefore less a doctrinal matter – they did not deny the two natures of Christ – than one of authority.[73] The Nestorians were different from the other four eastern Christian Churches in that they believed in two separate natures in Christ Incarnate, although it is not clear that Nestorius, the patriarch of Constantinople after whom they were named, actually taught this himself. Nestorius had certainly been a controversial figure, having been made patriarch in 428, only to be deposed in 431 and exiled to Upper Egypt five years later. Whatever the truth of this dispute the Nestorians had been very successful in the early middle ages, spreading east through Persia, so that by c.1000 they had at least twenty metropolitan dioceses.[74]

One other group of Christians included in John of Würzburg's list was the Georgians, whose monastery and church of the Holy Cross stood about a mile to the south-west of Jerusalem. It was a special place, as it was believed to encompass the stump of the tree from which the wood of the Cross was made.[75] The Georgians had been converted by the mid-fourth century and accepted the Chalcedonian tenets; as monks, hermits and pilgrims, they had had a presence in and around Jerusalem since at least the fifth century. Although it had been damaged in the eleventh century, Abbot Daniel mentions that the monastery was functioning at the time of his visit, and there was also a convent of Georgian nuns, one of whom, the former wife of King David (1089–1125), had probably founded the house at about this time.[76] The Georgians had considerable military strength: in 1120, Ansell, cantor of the Holy Sepulchre, described the kingdom as 'a rampart for us against the Medes and Persians', and, after the Latin defeat in 1187, they were strong enough to insist that Saladin restore their losses in Jerusalem as a consequence of the war.[77] However, the core of their power between the Black Sea and the Caspian Sea was too far north to have much direct effect upon the crusader states. Even so, after 1187, Queen Tamar (1184–1213) took the opportunity to assume the role of protector of the Christians in the East on the basis that both the Latins and the Greeks had failed in this task.[78]

The crusaders, of course, believed that Syria and Palestine were 'the lands of the Christians'. This was not the way the Jews saw it. For them, ever since the Diaspora, as early as the eighth century BC, the land of Israel had been in the hands of invaders. The famous thirteenth-century Jewish scholar from Gerona known as Nahmanides (Moses ben Nahman) (d. c.1270) wrote a commentary on Leviticus 26:32, 'I will destroy your land and the enemies who occupy it will be appalled.' Conceived in the light of events in the East in the twelfth and early thirteenth centuries, it took this form: 'And these are good tidings proclaiming in all the lands of the Diaspora that our land does not accept our foes. And this is a decisive proof and a great promise, because you will hardly find in all the inhabited world a country which is so fair and spacious, settled from time immemorial, and which is as much ruined as this one. For ever since we departed from it, it has not accepted a single other nation or language. They all try to settle it, but it is beyond their power.'[79]

The capture of Jerusalem by the crusaders in July 1099 was yet another of these enemy blows. Jews who had remained in the city suffered badly in the massacre, but not all of them were killed, since Tancred would not otherwise have been able to ransom some of them after the crusader frenzy had died down.[80] Jewish leaders in Cairo were aware of the situation and sent representatives to Ascalon with funds to pay ransoms, a practice that continued until 1102.[81] After this, Jews were not allowed to remain in Jerusalem, but they continued to live in some of the crusader cities such as Tiberias and in the larger Galilean villages, where they were within walking distance of the synagogues.[82] In fact, by c.1170, limited settlement had again been permitted in Jerusalem, for the Jewish traveller Benjamin of Tudela, who meticulously recorded the Jewish communities scattered around the Mediterranean and the Middle East, said that a small group of about 200 lived 'under the Tower of David in one corner of the city', where they specialised in dyeing, over which they had been given a monopoly by the king in return for a small rent.[83]

However, even before Jerusalem fell, Tancred and Eustace of Boulogne had made a raid on Nablus, 32 miles to the north. There, they found not only local Christians, but also a substantial community of Samaritans, perhaps as many as 1,000 people. There were probably another 500 living in Acre, Caesarea, Ascalon and Gaza.[84] The Samaritans were a separate Jewish group, who based their religious rites upon a version of the Pentateuch and centred their worship on their temple on Mount Gerizim. They had been excluded from the main body of the Jews since the time of the Babylonian exile in the sixth century BC, in which they had no part, and since the time of the Muslim invasions had been Arabic-speaking, although continuing to pray in Hebrew.

The Arabs had swept into this complicated world of different peoples and beliefs in the 630s. Muhammad believed that he was the unworthy instrument of God's final revelation and thus the ultimate successor of the Jewish prophets, including Christ. Islam imposed a strict monotheism and moral code, which entailed a series of obligations, most importantly, as Ibn Shaddad, Saladin's qadi of the army, expressed it, 'testimony that there is no god but God, performance of the prayers, the giving of alms, fasting in Ramadān, and the Pilgrimage to the Sacred House of God'.[85] This had been set down in the 114 *suras* (chapters) of the Koran, later supplemented by the *Hadith*, or sayings of the Prophet. After Mecca, the place of pilgrimage, and Medina, which had sheltered Muhammad during his exile from Mecca, Jerusalem was the third of the great holy cities. Here the Archangel Gabriel had taken Muhammad to the rock from which the Prophet ascended through the seven heavens to receive Divine revelation. When Saladin besieged Jerusalem in early October 1187, there followed, claimed Ibn al-Athir, 'the fiercest fight that anyone had ever seen, as each side of the two sides believed that it was a religious task and a binding duty'.[86]

However, when Muhammad had died in 632, Islam was a faith that was still evolving, with only a fraction of the adherents and territory it was to gain over the next two centuries. Inevitably, as it expanded, it was modified by circumstances: the Islamic world of the crusader era was not one dominated by the desert tribes of Arabia, but by military and intellectual leaders whose bases were urban mosques and madrasas, and who followed a literature that had not been consolidated until the ninth century.[87] Not surprisingly, under the pressure of such development, Islam had splintered. If they had not been fully cognisant of it before, the crusaders at Antioch were soon aware that the Muslims were far from unified in their faith, for, in February 1098 envoys representing the Fatimid caliph at Cairo presented themselves at the crusader camp. According to Albert of Aachen, they not only offered them the city of Jerusalem, which they had recently retaken from the Turks, but also urged them to continue their attack on Antioch. 'There had been,' he says, 'very severe discord and hatred between [the caliph] and the Turks long before this expedition of the Christians.'[88]

This hatred was based on more than cultural and racial antagonisms, for the Fatimid caliphate had been established in 969 as the chief Shi'ite power within Islam, thus consolidating a long-standing schism that found its origins in the generation that followed Muhammad's death. William of Tyre, who wrote a history of the Muslim world, describes how Muhammad's successors, beginning with Abu-Bakr (who had been one of his earliest associates), had ruled as caliphs, 'because they succeeded their famous master and were his heirs'. They were, however, challenged by Ali, a cousin of Muhammad, who 'considered it unfitting that he should be called the successor of his cousin and not rather a great prophet himself'. Not everybody accepted this, but there were some who believed him, 'so a schism developed among that people which has lasted even to the present. Some maintain that Muhammad is the greater and, in fact, the greatest of all prophets, and these are called in their own tongue, Sunnites; others declare that Ali alone is the prophet of God, and they are called Shiites.'[89] William's presentation of the schism as a rivalry between two prophets was not entirely accurate in that Ali claimed to be the first true successor of Muhammad rather than his rival; nevertheless, it is clear that the Latins soon grasped that this represented a fundamental fissure within Islam, which, although political in origin, had over time developed religious dimensions as well.[90]

From 750, the Sunni had been represented by the Abbasids, the second of whom built a new city at Baghdad, near the former Persian capital of Ctesiphon. The Abbasid dynasty achieved great longevity, lasting until 1258, when they were exterminated by the Mongols. However, from the mid-tenth century, they were largely in the hands of a new element in Islam, the Seljuk Turks; in 1055, the reigning caliph had installed Tughril Beg as sultan or temporal ruler, and from this time the Turks represented the cutting edge of the Sunnite cause. The first crusaders were much impressed by the Seljuks, even when describing their atrocities. Survivors of the crusade of 1101 told Albert of Aachen that they were 'wicked and dreadful men, whose heads were shaved in front and behind, on right and left sides in the manner of a neck, and whose sparse hairs hanging down from these four necks bristled as an uncut crest, with also untrimmed and flowing beards, and who are reported to resemble in their appearance nothing so much as ugly and filthy spirits.'[91] In a powerful passage, the author of the *Gesta*, the battle of Dorylaeum fresh in his mind, wrote: 'What man, however experienced and learned, would dare to write of the skill and prowess and courage of the Turks, who thought that they would strike terror into the Franks, as they had done into the Arabs and Saracens, Armenians, Syrians and Greeks, by the menace of their arrows?' He claimed they had a saying that they were of common stock with the Franks and, he says regretfully, if only they adhered to the true faith 'you could not find stronger or braver or more skilful soldiers.'[92]

However, by the later twelfth century the Franks had become aware of another Muslim enemy, the Kurds, seen as equally formidable. Their home-lands were in southern and eastern Anatolia and north-eastern Iraq but, not surprisingly, since Saladin was a Kurd, they played a prominent part in his armies. According to an anonymous Christian survey of the forces gathered by Saladin during the battles for the control of Acre between 1189 and 1191, the Kurds were the best knights and were characterised by the greatest nobility. 'They serve all the Saracen princes as soldiers, just like the English and Danes in Constantinople.'[93]

The Shi'ites, for their part, asserted that they represented the only legiti-mate line of imams, by which they meant those who were divinely guided in their exposition of the true faith, and from these there would appear the Mahdi or Guided One. There was much disagreement over who this would be and when this event would occur, but for the crusaders the most significant element was the Fatimids at Cairo, who adhered to an imam called Ismail, who died sometime before 765. His successor had appeared in 909 and his descendants established themselves at Cairo sixty years later. There was evidently a powerful messianic element among the Shi'ites, which itself was always likely to provoke further splits. In 1090, one such group of dissidents set themselves up at Alamut in Persia and adopted political murder as their preferred method of operation. These became known as the Assassins, and their western branch, established in the 1130s in enclaves in the Nosairi mountains, became very well known to the Latins, although they were to be found farther east around the Jabal as-Summaq at the time of the First Crusade.[94] According to William of Tyre, in the 1170s they numbered around 60,000 and possessed ten fortresses together with adjacent villages.[95]

The majority of indigenous Muslims living in the lands conquered by the crusaders were to be found in the south. The main Muslim villages were in Samaria and eastern Galilee, while the Franks settled in the area north of Jerusalem as far as Sanjil (Saint-Gilles), that is, in the places already inhabited by eastern Christians. There was, therefore, a distinct Muslim region, determined by cultural rather than ecological frontiers, and already established centuries before the arrival of the crusaders.[96] These must have been the people described by the German pilgrim Theoderic in the early 1170s around Nablus. 'When we were going along this road we saw a crowd of Saracens, who were all beginning to plough with their oxen and asses a very well-kept field. And they uttered a horrid cry, which is not unusual for them when they start any work, but they filled us with great terror! There are a great number of pagans there, who stay everywhere in cities and villages and farms of this province.'[97]

Many Muslims were nomadic or engaged in some form of transhumance. In his description of the origins of the Turkish race, William of Tyre explains that, initially, all the Turks were nomadic, 'constantly roaming around here and there in search of the best pasture for their flocks', but that thirty to forty years before the arrival of the crusaders they had established much more stable political entities in Persia. Even so, there continued to exist those whom he calls Turcomans, who 'still retained their rude and primitive mode of life'.[98] Michael the Syrian describes how in the winter the Turcomans were accustomed to migrate from the north into southern Syria, where there was no snow or frost and where they could find pasture, returning in the spring. In 1185, they were attacked en route by a band of Kurds intent on stealing their animals, an incident that escalated into a large-scale conflict that left many dead.[99] The Bedouin Arabs were similarly nomadic, living mostly along the outer edges of the crusader lands in the Transjordan and the Sinai and Negev deserts. Raids upon the Jewish and Muslim settlements in eastern Galilee were not uncommon, but often quite unconnected to the wider war between the Muslims and the Franks.[100] Nor were the nomads always the predators. In February 1157, King Baldwin III attacked Arabs and Turcomans grazing their flocks and herds in the woodlands near Banyas. These people, says William of Tyre, 'live in tents and are accustomed to support life from the products of animals'.[101]

When they crossed the Iron Bridge over the Orontes in October 1097, the crusaders were entering an ancient land, just one more invading army over

the centuries. As Fulcher of Chartres was soon to discover, it was an environment that would change them far more than they could ever have imagined.
In the course of spending thirty years in the East, Fulcher became imbued
with a strong sense of the need for co-existence, reflected not only in his
empathy with the Greeks, Syrians and Armenians, but even with the
Muslims.[102] A generation after the crusade, in the mid-1120s, he reflected on
this. 'Indeed it is written,' he said, quoting Isaiah, "The lion and the ox shall
eat straw together".[103]

CHAPTER 3

The First Settlers

IF one of the objections to Raymond of Toulouse as ruler of Jerusalem was his age, then it is ironic that he outlived Godfrey of Bouillon, who died only a year after his election, on 18 July 1100. Returning from a campaign in the lands of Duqaq of Damascus, Godfrey had begun to make his way south along the coast, where he was met by the emir of Caesarea, who offered him dinner. The duke, however, says Albert of Aachen, 'refused food with every polite expression of thanks, tasting only some oranges'. Soon after, he began to feel ill, and was secretly taken to a guesthouse at Jaffa, where four of his companions supported his head and feet. But news soon spread and both Vitale Michiel, doge of Venice, who had just arrived with his fleet at Jaffa, and Tancred hurried to visit him. Godfrey was aware that his condition was deteriorating, and had himself moved to Jerusalem, closely followed by the Venetians. In Jerusalem the Venetians visited the Holy Sepulchre and the other holy sites, having been reassured by the duke that he was improving, before returning to Jaffa. Two weeks later, a combined force led by Tancred and Daibert of Pisa, who had replaced Arnulf of Chocques as patriarch of Jerusalem the previous Christmas, set out to besiege Acre, although they were obliged to leave behind Godfrey's deputy, Warner, count of Grez, who had himself become so ill that he had had to be carried to Jerusalem on a stretcher. Four days later, Godfrey's illness became critical. 'He made confession of his sins in true remorse of heart and with tears, took communion of the Lord's body and blood and, thus secured and protected by a spiritual shield, he was taken from this light.' He was buried at the entrance to the Holy Sepulchre. His illness had lasted five weeks. Six days later, on 22 July, Warner of Grez also died, and was buried in the entrance to the church of the Tomb of the Virgin in the valley of Jehoshaphat.[1]

The causes of Godfrey's lingering death are not known. William of Tyre speaks of 'a violent and incurable disease', perhaps basing himself on Ekkehard of Aura, who says that, during the summer, many (including Godfrey) died of a *pestilentia*, that is, an infectious or contagious disease. As Ekkehard visited the kingdom personally the following year, he was probably well informed.[2] At the same time, the physical stress of the crusade, together with the severe injuries he had received when attacked by a bear in August 1097, must have made him vulnerable.[3] Although by no means the most distinguished or influential of the leaders during the expedition itself, he was uniquely associated with the achievements of the First Crusade in the minds of contemporaries, and remained an inspirational figure for later generations. Within twenty years of his death, Albert of Aachen was able to present his career as foreseen in a dream by a knight called Hercelo of Kinzveiler. In the vision, Hercelo had seen Godfrey on Mount Sinai, receiving the blessing of two men in white. As interpreted by Albert, this meant that 'in the spirit and gentleness of Moses there may arise a spiritual leader of Israel, preordained by God and prince of the people'. This leader was Godfrey, who succeeded where all others had failed and was 'made ruler of the city and commander of the people'.[4]

The reality was more mundane. The victory over the Egyptians near Ascalon on 12 August 1099 had temporarily removed the threat that the Fatimids would immediately retake Jerusalem, a very real danger since, only the year before, in July 1098, they had driven out the Artukid emirs, Soqman and Il-Ghazi. The Franks were aware of this and sought to follow up with an assault on Ascalon itself. Apparently, a few days after the battle, the citizens secretly offered to hand over the city to Raymond of Toulouse, as the only Christian leader they could trust. However, Godfrey and Raymond, already rivals after Godfrey's election and the dispute over the possession of the Tower of David, quarrelled over the command of the army, and therefore failed to present a credible threat.[5] In Albert of Aachen's version, this was the result of Raymond's envy of Godfrey's 'glory', a state of mind that led him to advise the citizens to hold out as the bulk of the army was about to return home.[6] Albert clearly reflects the Lotharingian viewpoint, but Ralph of Caen, too, blames Raymond's 'arrogant and vain acts' for this failure, a judgement influenced by what he discerned as the great damage the city had subsequently caused to the Christians, while William of Malmesbury, writing about twenty years later, presents Raymond as filled with resentment and says that, as a consequence, he 'handed over the keys of the city to the enemies of God'.[7] Although Godfrey did attack Ascalon, he was abandoned by Raymond and, left with an inadequate force of 700 mounted men, decided that the siege was no longer tenable.[8]

The Franks could not afford such internecine conflict. William of Tyre, perhaps anxious to emphasise the importance of divine protection, may have exaggerated the insecurities of the time, but it is nevertheless clear that the crusaders' grip on the few enclaves they held in Palestine was too shaky to ensure safe travel or to support a settled agriculture. Indeed, the situation was exacerbated by a strike of Muslim peasants 'in order that our people might suffer from hunger'.[9] Fulcher of Chartres, the only chronicler to have visited Jerusalem at this time, when he took part in the pilgrimage of Bohemond and Baldwin at Christmas 1099, describes the privations of the journey from Edessa, including hunger, cold and heavy rain. Nobody would sell them supplies and many stragglers were picked off despite the size of the army. When they reached Jerusalem, the rotting bodies of its defenders still lay in the streets and outside the walls, creating a miasma that intruded upon the joy of worshipping at the holy places.[10]

Godfrey's failed attack on Arsuf in the autumn of 1099 did nothing to alleviate the situation. Although this was a serious assault lasting two months, from 15 October to 15 December, it was undermined by lack of sea power and the destruction of two of his siege engines, finally ending when the weather became too bad.[11] As a result, in the winter of 1099–1100 he was left with no option but to conduct *chevauchées* and foraging expeditions in order to survive. One of these, in February 1100, on the hinterland of Arsuf, took advantage of the need for local Muslims to begin preparations for the new agricultural year by attacking the populace while they were in the fields, and was sufficiently ferocious to persuade the emirs of Ascalon, Caesarea and Acre to pay tribute in money and kind, as well as gaining the release of Gerard of Avesnes, a knight from Hainault who had been held as hostage and was thought to have been killed.[12]

Combined operations with Tancred in May 1100 against the emir of Sawad, whose lands lay immediately to the east of the Jordan, had a similar effect. He was, says Albert of Aachen with some relish, called the Fat Peasant, 'on account of his very great and gross corpulence and his worthless character, in which he seemed to be entirely a peasant'. The Franks spent a week in his lands 'inflicting fire and slaughter' before returning to Jerusalem with 'immeasurable booty'. Tancred now set his sights on Damascus, sending six men to demand the surrender of the city and Duqaq's submission to the Christian faith. It was a risky mission and the ruler's response was to decapitate five of the envoys, sparing only the one who agreed to accept 'the Turkish religion'. Tancred retaliated by devastating his lands for two weeks before a settlement was made.[13]

Brutal and sometimes desperate fighting was an integral part of these encounters. Albert of Aachen recorded how, during the siege of Arsuf, Gerard of Avesnes had been tied to a mast in the form of a crucifix, with the result

that, during Godfrey's assault, he had been pierced by ten arrows, while over
fifty men manning one of the siege engines were killed when it was set on fire
by the defenders. 'Some had broken backs and necks, others legs half cut off,
hips or arms, certain had burst intestines from the unbearable weight of the
timbers; having no strength to free themselves, they were reduced to ember
and ash along with the timbers.' Albert's account of Godfrey of Bouillon's men
setting upon the peasants and townsmen while they were cultivating their
vineyards and fields outside the walls is equally gruesome: 'they attacked with
a sudden cavalry charge some thousand Saracens who came out of the city,
and, destroying them with savage wounds, they left over five hundred half-
dead on the battlefield, their noses cut off, or hands and feet, while the victors
returned to Jerusalem with citizens' wives and sons as prisoners.' Albert's
description of this as a battle can hardly be justified, but it does encapsulate
the balance of weakness in southern Palestine at this time.[14]

In the end, slash-and-burn could not achieve long-term results; only the
capture of the sea ports in combination with the establishment of fortified
strong points in the hands of capable lords could offer the Franks a measure
of security. Although he had failed at Ascalon and Arsuf, Godfrey rebuilt the
walls of Jaffa and improved the port facilities, an action, Albert of Aachen
says, that led to the subjugation of the other Muslim cities and to a great
increase of Christians arriving by sea. He strengthened Tiberias with 'a
rampart and invincible defences on the steep slope of the mountain'.[15]
Moreover, the exodus that followed the ending of the expedition was not as
dramatic as has sometimes been suggested. Although some of the major
leaders returned home, many of those who remained or arrived soon after
derived from important families in the West, so that, from the beginning,
despite (or perhaps because of) the evident fragility of some dynastic lines
and the heavy losses in the unavoidable battles, there developed a degree of
aristocratic cohesion which strengthened in the course of the twelfth century.[16]
Equally importantly, Godfrey had also retained a small group around him
which Albert of Aachen describes as the *domus Godefridi*, an immediate circle
of men who had decided to stay in Palestine, which included at least twenty-
one seculars, about half of whom were Lotharingian, and three clerics.[17]

At the same time Godfrey began a process of enfeoffment: Tancred was
granted Tiberias and Gerard of Avesnes compensated for his near-martyrdom
with fiefs worth 100 marks and possession of the castle of Hebron
(St Abraham). This 'castle' was, in fact, a large enclosure dating from Herodian
times, now known as the Haram al-Khalil.[18] Robert of Apulia, who had taken
part in the massacre of the populace around Arsuf, was given the tribute from
the town in return for a cash payment.[19] While he lay sick in Jerusalem in

early July 1100, Godfrey made an anticipatory grant of Haifa to a crusader from Dargoire in the Upper Loire region, Geldemar Carpenel, 'if they managed to capture it'.[20] He evidently made several smaller grants as well, for, only days after his arrival to claim the kingship following Godfrey's death, Baldwin assembled all the holders of equipment, money and *beneficia*, that is, fiefs, so that they could account for their holdings and then swear fealty to him, 'returning the fiefs individually to each person'.[21] In addition, Godfrey issued an edict declaring that each year a written record (*prescriptio*) should be made of those who had stayed in their tenure for a year and a day, a measure aimed at preventing those who had left from returning to claim property after a year.[22]

He began, too, the endowment of religious institutions, granting the canons of the Holy Sepulchre twenty-one villages in a key area to the north of Jerusalem.[23] These were settled by westerners who, initially at least, must have been survivors of the crusade. Whatever their previous status, these were now freemen, occupying allocated plots of land and paying tithes and a proportion of their harvests. Many must have established themselves as family units, marrying local Christians, widows of dead crusaders or former prostitutes who had come on the crusade as penitents. The presence of western women in the crusading host is well attested, in particular in the denunciations of clerics intent on explaining military failures in terms of immorality, although self-preservation rather than sexual laxity must have been the main determinant of female behaviour given the circumstances they were obliged to face during the expedition.[24] The rapid establishment of such communities was essential since Jerusalem was dependent upon its rural hinterland to supply its markets with fresh fruit, vegetables and meat, as well as processed food and drink. The canons particularly needed regular production of oil and wine.[25] As well as their obvious economic value, these villages had a strategic role, for they were developed along the main routes to the north towards Nablus, and the west towards Lydda, Ramla and Jaffa.[26] In 1124, Fulcher of Chartres mentions a tower at al-Bira, one of the larger villages, constructed, he says, 'in our time', strong enough to provide refuge during a raid from Ascalon.[27] Given the insecurity of the rural areas and the roads at the beginning of the century, it is likely that some fortification of settlements had been erected almost immediately.

Godfrey himself held a corridor of land from Jaffa to Jerusalem, encompassing Lydda and Ramla, and extending a short distance south to Bethlehem. Such a limited territory could only sustain a relatively small force. According to Albert of Aachen, the raids into the lands of the emir of Sawad had been conducted by 200 knights and 1,000 infantry under Godfrey, to which

Tancred had contributed a further 100 knights.[28] Ralph of Caen, who presumably obtained his information from Arnulf of Chocques and Tancred, says that, after the departure of the leaders in late August, 'barely 200 men, who were equipped with breastplates, remained to defend Jerusalem', about eighty of whom belonged to Tancred's household.[29] To put this in perspective, at the battle of Ascalon on 12 August, the Franks had mustered 5,000 knights and 15,000 foot soldiers, an army that, the crusaders claimed, had even then been outnumbered by twenty to one.[30] His one port was Jaffa, which was in such poor condition that its inhabitants had abandoned it as indefensible shortly before the crusaders arrived,[31] while the road from there up to Jerusalem was described by the English pilgrim Saewulf, in the summer of 1102, as very hard and dangerous because of Saracen ambushes and the lack of water.[32] In contrast, as Daibert, archbishop of Pisa, Godfrey and Raymond of Toulouse explained to the pope in a letter of September 1099, any one of the many coastal cities in Muslim hands had more men than the entire crusading army.[33]

Godfrey was evidently worried that if the situation became widely known in the West it would deter new crusaders. Guibert of Nogent, writing a decade later, recalled that he had been told by Baldwin of Bourcq, a kinsman of Godfrey, who had travelled with him on the First Crusade, that he was with Godfrey when they had fought off an ambush of 120 Turks with only twenty knights, 'made the more audacious by the aid we had continually experienced from God'. On this occasion, in order to inspire those who had remained in France, Godfrey had asserted that he had a vast fortune, derived from ten castles and an abbey, which paid him a sum of 1,500 marks annually. 'And if God favours my taking Aleppo, I shall soon have 100 castles under my command. Do not believe those who have retreated, claiming that we grow weary with hunger, but rather trust in my words.'[34]

However, at this time ports were more important than Aleppo and they could not be taken without the help of the Italian fleets. Most were held by emirs, largely independent of higher authority since the tenth century, when the bureaucratic government of the Abbasids at Baghdad had begun to fall apart. As a result, none of these rulers possessed forces comparable in size to Mesopotamian atabegs like Kerbogha, nor could they assemble viable coalitions, but even so their 'askar, or mounted guards, reinforced by local troops and mercenaries, often seemed to be sufficient to see off the Frankish threat.[35] Moreover, at various times they received help from Egyptian ships, which had by no means conceded the sea to the Christians.[36] The arrival of a large Pisan fleet at Jaffa in late December 1099 therefore offered Godfrey an unprecedented opportunity. The Pisans were led by their archbishop, Daibert, who had landed at Latakia two months before with what they claimed were 120 ships, a fleet too large to be challenged by the Egyptians at Ascalon, where poor harbour facilities precluded the retention of shipping on this scale.[37] The archbishop himself reached Jerusalem on 21 December, accompanied by Bohemond and Baldwin, now established in Antioch and Edessa respectively.[38] Daibert's exact status remains unclear, although it is generally held that he possessed legatine powers received from Urban II. He had certainly been strongly associated with the late pope, as he had taken the Cross at Clermont and, in 1098, had acted as his legate in Castile. His record in Pisa suggests a strong commitment to the papal reform programme, so it is reasonable to see him as an emissary of Urban II and therefore carrying all the prestige and weight that this implied, even though any legatine powers he may have possessed would have lapsed with the pope's death.[39]

Urban II had originally intended the Pisan ships to be used to help the crusaders at Antioch, but in these new circumstances they provided an ambitious prelate like Daibert with the leverage he needed to establish his own position within a state in which the institutional structure had by no means been properly formed. He proceeded to translate this into his own election as patriarch, when he was crowned on Christmas Day.[40] It was not difficult to find reasons for the removal of Arnulf of Chocques, whose clash with Tancred even Ralph of Caen had been unable to present as a high-minded issue of principle, although in this case Ralph describes Arnulf as acceding with grace, because 'he hoped that the other would be more successful in spreading Christianity than he might be'.[41] Indeed, there is good reason to think that Daibert did not believe that Arnulf was patriarch in the first place, since his election had not been confirmed, which may explain why Fulcher of Chartres, Albert of Aachen and William of Tyre all present Daibert as the first Latin patriarch. In 1102, with Daibert out of office, Arnulf reappears as archdeacon of Jerusalem, a not insignificant role despite his demotion.[42]

According to William of Tyre's later account, Daibert now established his authority over the secular leaders when 'both Duke Godfrey and Prince Bohemond humbly received from his hand, the former the investiture of the kingdom, and the latter that of the principality, thus showing honour to him whose viceregent on earth they believed the patriarch to be'.[43] This was evidently the work of Bohemond, whose Christmas pilgrimage to Jerusalem cannot have been a coincidence, whatever the degree of personal piety involved, since it gave him sanction for his seizure of Antioch, made in clear contravention of his oath to Alexius.[44] Daibert had originally landed at Latakia, still in Greek hands, and was in the process of helping Bohemond attack the city when they had both been stopped by Raymond of Toulouse,

Robert of Normandy and Robert of Flanders returning north after the battle of Ascalon.[45] Daibert's common front with Bohemond must have been formed at this time, leading to the archbishop's Christmas election and Bohemond's investiture. Daibert followed this up by appointing three Latin archbishops and one bishop within the patriarchate of Antioch, ignoring the authority of the Greek patriarch, John IV. This had evidently been planned in advance, as Ralph of Caen says that the four, 'namely Roger of Tarsus, Bartholomew of Mamistra, Bernard of Artah and Benedict of Edessa, had come with Bohemond and Baldwin after being elevated to the priestly office'.[46] As subsequent events demonstrate, Godfrey was a good deal less enthusiastic, since he had no need of such confirmation, but without Daibert's co-operation he would not have had access to the Pisan fleet and his recent failure to take Arsuf, directly attributable to his naval weakness, must have been fresh in his mind.

Neither Bohemond nor Baldwin could afford to linger long in the south. On the eve of Epiphany (5 January), they met Godfrey and Daibert at the Jordan, 'in which', says Albert of Aachen, 'they bathed and enjoyed them-selves'. After this, 'Baldwin and Bohemond rejoiced with the duke in all happi-ness and in shared friendship, and there in the region of Jordan they kissed with tears and took their leave of each other'.[47] Daibert was now in a dominant position. At the time of his election he had received the 'patriarch's quarter' in Jerusalem, together with new revenues, but he was evidently not satisfied. In William of Tyre's words: 'The patriarch demanded that the duke give over to him the Holy City of God with its citadel and likewise the city of Jaffa with its appurtenances'. Although presented in an emollient form by William, this clearly provoked a furious dispute, but by stages Godfrey made the required concessions, granting the fourth part of Jaffa on 2 February 1100, followed by the city of Jerusalem and its citadel on Easter Day (1 April). Jerusalem, however, would not actually be handed over until Godfrey had gained control of what William describes vaguely as 'one or two other cities', but which Daibert himself calls 'Babylon and other cities'. If he died without a legitimate heir, all these possessions would pass under the control of the patriarch.[48]

When these events took place, neither Fulcher of Chartres nor Albert of Aachen was present, while William of Tyre was writing more than seventy years later. Even so, this was no passing reference by William, who had researched the subject with some intensity, perhaps at least partly because he had ambitions to be patriarch himself. He could find no evidence that Godfrey had been appointed by the leaders of the crusade on these conditions, but instead traces the origin of 'the patriarch's quarter' to the period of Egyptian rule under Caliph al-Mustansir in 1063. The Christian inhabitants had been assigned a fourth part of Jerusalem to rebuild but lacked the resources to do so. They therefore appealed to the Byzantine emperor, Constantine X (1059–67), for help, which he granted on condition that the quarter concerned be assigned exclusively to the Christians, a condition to which the caliph agreed. 'From that day, then, and in the manner just described, this quarter of the city had had no other judge or lord than the patriarch, and the church therefore laid claim to that section as its own in perpetuity.'[49]

However, although William goes on to describe the exact extent of the patriarch's quarter – which he was able to do from direct personal experience – he offers no explanation for the additional, very sweeping concessions in Jerusalem and Jaffa. William clearly derived his information from a letter written by Daibert himself to Bohemond after the death of Godfrey on 18 July. Probably William has not reproduced the text verbatim, but he was at least recording the main elements of a letter that had really existed, for reference is made to it by Albert of Aachen.[50] Since it must be assumed that, ultimately, Godfrey's main concern was not 'fear of the rebuke of the Lord', as William asserts, but the deployment of the Pisan fleet against the Muslim ports, then the most convincing explanation is that the concession of the quarter in Jaffa was aimed at satisfying the Pisans in a manner that was to become familiar in future agreements with the Italian maritime cities.[51] Moreover, the city of Jerusalem and its citadel, the latter the subject of such bitter dispute with Raymond of Toulouse, would not be handed over until Godfrey had captured other cities, a condition that surely obliged the Pisans to act if they wanted the terms of the agreement carried out. William, however, is not helpful in identifying these cities. His version of Daibert's letter refers to Babylon, which, if it means Cairo, is so unlikely as to negate the concession entirely, given that Godfrey had not even been able to take Arsuf.[52] Much closer to the time than William is a compilation of an anonymous scholar known as the *Work on Geography*, which can be dated to between the years 1128 and 1137. Godfrey, it says, vowed 'that if the Divine Piety allowed him to capture Ascalon, he would give the whole revenue of Jerusalem into the hands of the Soldiers of God in the Holy Sepulchre and to the authority of the Patriarch.'[53]

In this light the settlement between Godfrey and Daibert looks much less one-sided than it first appears. Daibert's acquisition of Jerusalem would have had to be balanced by the acquisition of other, more strategically important cities, which, if on the coast, would have been more lucrative as well. Nor does the agreement demand that Godfrey marry and produce male heirs, which was an unlikely circumstance, but only that he should be succeeded by a legitimate male heir, which would have meant either of his brothers, Eustace or Baldwin.[54] Presumably Baldwin was well aware of this when he helped make Daibert patriarch at Christmas 1099.

In fact, nobody knows what instructions Urban II gave Daibert but, in any case, like the crusaders, to some extent he was obliged to react to the situation as he found it.[55] On the face of it, he was apparently exploiting the shortages of men and money to further his own personal ambition. Yet such a view distorts contemporary perceptions, for he had been sent by a reforming pope, whose central tenets were that fornicating priests be removed and that secular appointment to ecclesiastical office was a sin punishable by excommunication. Daibert would have been very conscious of the importance of the unresolved conflict over investitures. Moreover, the apparent attempt to build a patriarchal patrimony was little different from the papacy's own efforts to create a territorial base in central Italy, a policy vigorously pursued from the mid-eleventh century and continued into the thirteenth century.[56] Indeed, it was not in his interest to weaken the new state and, after Easter 1100, he sent an appeal to the clergy and people of the Teutonic regions, to whom 'God has given riches beyond all other peoples'. Jerusalem, he said, was under attack from all sides, but after its capture many had returned home. Others followed after celebrating Easter on 1 April, taking advantage of the presence of Pisan and English ships. It was costly to keep those who remained, and without German help they could not continue to pay the promised wages.[57] Whatever may have been Urban's specific instructions, he surely must have told Daibert to strengthen the Latin Church in the East as far as he was able.

However, if reform ideas lay behind his actions in dealing with others, there is little to indicate that Daibert thought they applied to himself. His election to the patriarchate was blatantly the result of secular influence. Fulcher of Chartres, who was there at the time, says that the pilgrimage of the leaders to the Jordan was 'after the Duke and the other chief men had chosen the above-mentioned Lord Daimbert to be Patriarch in the Church the Holy Sepulcher', while Daibert himself, as quoted by William of Tyre, reminded Bohemond that he had brought about his election, and that Baldwin had supported him 'in choosing me as a patriarch and rector of the church at Jerusalem'.[58] Put in place by three seculars, two of whom had been hostile to church reform, accepting an office that made him 'a pluralist on a grand scale',[59] and completely disregarding Greek rights and claims in both Latakia and Antioch hardly made Daibert a shining example of the new prelacy that the reformers had sought to create. In the end it is difficult to see these events as an attempt to found a theocratic state or indeed as an example of the application of Gregorian principles; instead, they look much more like a power struggle between Godfrey and Daibert in which each attempted to exploit whatever advantages came to hand. Such factional conflicts became common-place in the crusader states during the twelfth century. Not surprisingly, therefore, Albert of Aachen presents Daibert as ingratiating, treacherous and venal, while William of Tyre saw him as a 'man of God', who was the Lord's earthly representative.[60] Ironically, all this political manoeuvring eventually proved fruitless, as the Pisan fleet does not seem to have been used in any systematic attack on the coastal emirates, although the sailors did help in the rebuilding of Jaffa in the middle of January. Then, immediately after Easter, in early April, the Pisans sailed for home, soon to be replaced by an even larger fleet of 200 Venetian ships under the doge, Vitale Michiel, and Enrico Contarini, bishop of Castello (Venice), which, having overwintered at Rhodes, arrived on about 10 June.

Warner of Grez and Tancred now negotiated a treaty with the Venetians, the terms of which set the pattern of future agreements with the maritime cities and, in that sense, began the process of establishing the Italian communes in the East, whose inhabitants became a characteristic element in the social structure of the Frankish littoral in the course of the twelfth century. In any cities which the Franks captured then or in the future, whether on the coast or inland, the Venetians should have a church and a square suitable for a market. Booty would be divided one-third to the Venetians and two-thirds to the Franks, except in the case of Tripoli, when the division should be in equal parts. The city of Tripoli itself, if captured, would be granted to the Venetians in its entirety, except for an annual payment to Jerusalem as a mark of reverence to the holy places. The Venetians evidently regarded the allowance of two-thirds of the booty to the Franks elsewhere as a concession 'because they [the Franks] were not wealthy'. Beyond this, they were to have security against claims of right of wreck for all their merchandise. Godfrey, though still incapacitated, was nevertheless able to confirm these terms.[61]

As the departure of the Pisans shows, the use of fleets was constrained by sailing conditions, so the agreement covered the period between 24 June and 15 August, evidently based on the hope that success could be achieved during a summer campaign before the arrival of the autumn made it imperative to leave.[62] Around 2 July, they chose Acre as the target and, two weeks later, the army left Jaffa. At some point, however, they decided to besiege Haifa first, perhaps influenced by news of the deaths of Godfrey and Warner of Grez, which effectively gave Tancred and Daibert a free hand.[63] Albert of Aachen says that initially Tancred was unenthusiastic 'on account of envy', but was encouraged by Daibert, who effectively promised him possession of the city if he could take it. In the face of what now became a ferocious attack, the city, isolated by the Venetian blockade, fell on around 20 August, and the Franks massacred the population and seized large quantities of plunder. Tancred, supported by Daibert, then forced out Geldemar Carpenel, to whom Godfrey had granted the city if it should be taken, thus adding a vital component to the territories he already held by gaining an outlet to the sea.[64]

On the face of it, the fall of Haifa presaged the triumph of the faction led by Daibert and Tancred, but in the twelfth century thrones could be won by speed of thought and action, as well as by the chance of proximity to the seat of power. Their preoccupation with the siege of Haifa meant that, when Godfrey died, Jerusalem itself was open to seizure by Godfrey's vassals, led by Warner of Grez, and the Lotharingians and other members of Godfrey's *domus* at once occupied the Tower of David which, as Godfrey, Raymond and Daibert had all demonstrated in the previous months, was the key to control of the city. Although Warner survived Godfrey by less than a week, a delegation led by Robert of Rouen, bishop of Lydda-Ramla, and sent by Geldemar Carpenel and Arnulf of Chocques, at once set out for Edessa, inviting Baldwin to 'take over the kingdom in your brother's place and sit on his throne'.[65] Daibert and Tancred were slower to react. Daibert's appeal to Bohemond, as presented in William of Tyre's version of his letter, was sent after the news had reached them of the seizure of the Tower of David and the departure of the delegation to Baldwin, and therefore was probably not dispatched before the beginning of August. Daibert belatedly realised the danger and his letter to Bohemond is couched in apocalyptic terms. The coming of Baldwin, he said, would 'bring about the downfall of the church and the destruction of Christianity itself', and he asked Bohemond to prevent Baldwin from attempting to take the throne, by force if necessary.[66]

Looking back on these events, William of Tyre clearly believed that Daibert had right on his side, calling Warner of Grez the leader of 'a troublesome faction' and pointing out that he had died within five days of his seizure of the citadel. 'This was regarded as a miracle, and it was ascribed to the merits of the patriarch that the enemy and persecutor of the church had met a sudden death.'[67] However, even Daibert's letter says only that Jerusalem and Jaffa should be restored to the Church if Godfrey died 'without a male heir'.[68] In contrast to William, Albert of Aachen described Daibert's letter as 'sent in deceit and against the oath which that same patriarch had made with Tancred to the duke, that if he happened to die they would not confer the throne on anyone except his brothers or one of his blood'.[69] Moreover, Warner of Grez was the most senior of Godfrey's men, a kinsman who acted as his deputy, who must have known what Godfrey expected. Indeed, when Godfrey had been preparing to depart on crusade, before Baldwin had decided to take part, he had quite explicitly made him his heir in a series of charters that Warner himself had witnessed.[70]

In the event, legal arguments proved irrelevant, for circumstances favoured Baldwin. Around 12 August, Morellus, the patriarch's secretary, who was carrying the letter to Bohemond, was intercepted by men of Raymond of Toulouse and the message never reached its destination, while in about mid-August Bohemond himself was captured by the Danishmend Turks during a campaign in the region of Melitene.[71] After a fruitless attempt to find and rescue Bohemond, Baldwin returned to Edessa at about the same time as the messengers arrived from Jerusalem.[72] As presented by Fulcher of Chartres, Baldwin himself had no doubts: 'When it was announced to the Lord Baldwin that all of the people of Jerusalem expected him to succeed as hereditary prince in the kingdom, he grieved somewhat over the death of his brother but rejoiced more over his inheritance.'[73] He then conferred Edessa on Baldwin of Bourcq, a kinsman who was the son of Hugh of Rethel in the Ile-de-France, whom he summoned from Antioch, and, on 2 October, set out for Jerusalem with a force of nearly 200 knights and 700 foot soldiers.[74] Such an expedition needed money and, before his departure, Baldwin subjected the population of Edessa to 'all sorts of extortions', including seizing 'a goodly amount of gold and silver', according to the contemporary Armenian chronicler Matthew of Edessa.[75]

The journey took about five weeks, which was about the same length of time as his return to Edessa the previous January after bathing in the Jordan, although on that occasion he had followed a route via the Jordan valley, Tiberias, Banyas and Baalbek.[76] This time he went first to Antioch, which he reached very quickly, covering the 160 miles in six days. All his actions there-after suggest that he had complete confidence in his succession. At this point he sent his wife and her household, together with the heavy baggage, to Jaffa by sea, evidently expecting some opposition on the forthcoming march, but apparently not fearing that they would encounter any problems when they arrived in the south.[77] He stayed four days at Antioch, where, according to Albert of Aachen, he declined an offer of the rulership, before moving to Latakia, where he stopped for another two days.[78] Here he met Maurice, cardinal-bishop of Porto, who had been appointed legate by Paschal II and had arrived at the port the previous month with a Genoese fleet. This reinforced his already strong position, for he received the backing of both the legate and the Genoese.[79]

However, news of a threatened attack by Duqaq of Damascus provoked a number of desertions and excuses, so he left with a considerably diminished force. This was the critical part of the journey, for, although he received supplies from the emir of Tripoli, on 25 October he was obliged to force a passage along the coast north of Beirut in a serious battle at the Dog River. Fulcher admits, during the sleepless night before, he had been so frightened he would rather have been anywhere other than where he was.[80] Five days later they passed Haifa, whose citizens sold them bread and wine, but they did not attempt to enter the city because, although Tancred was not there, he was ill-disposed towards Baldwin.[81] In fact, in late October, Baldwin's supporters had prevented Tancred from entering both Jerusalem and Jaffa, which shows that they had retained the upper hand in the interval since Godfrey's death.[82] Baldwin himself stopped two days at Jaffa and then, on 9 November, he came within sight of Jerusalem where, Fulcher says, he was greeted with joy by the citizens who, already receiving him as their king, conducted him to the Holy Sepulchre. Daibert was not present, because 'he was under accusation by certain men around Baldwin' and he had therefore retired to Mount Sion.[83]

Baldwin, as William of Tyre describes him, 'was a man who loved work and disdained idleness',[84] and, indeed, within six days of his arrival he gave a graphic demonstration of how he intended to rule. Having received oaths of fidelity from his new vassals, he at once set out towards Ascalon, engaging its defenders in a brief but evidently fierce encounter. Then he smoked out and killed some local robbers who had been hiding in caves, apparently near Bait Jibrin, before turning east towards Hebron and the Dead Sea. From there he travelled south into what Fulcher of Chartres calls the mountains of Arabia, as far as Wadi Musa, about 50 miles south of the Dead Sea, before returning to Jerusalem on 21 December.[85] According to Albert of Aix, he took only 150 knights and fifty foot with him,[86] which suggests a mobile reconnaissance force intended both to demonstrate his presence and to allow him to familiarise himself with the region south of Jerusalem, which he had never before visited. It is a measure of his confidence that, despite the presence of Daibert and Tancred in the immediate vicinity, he was able to leave Jerusalem for over a month, between 15 November and 21 December.

On 25 December, Baldwin was crowned king in the church of the Nativity in Bethlehem by Daibert. This was an entirely appropriate setting, for it had not been damaged in the conflict and was only 8 miles to the south of Jerusalem.[87] Built over the place of the nativity of Christ which was beneath the main altar, it took the form of a great cross, the interior of which was decorated with Greek mosaics.[88] Even Fulcher of Chartres, so terse in his account of relations between the secular and ecclesiastical authorities, could hardly pass over such a significant event without comment. 'This,' he says, 'had not been done for his brother and predecessor because Godfrey had not wished it, and there were others who did not approve of it. Still, upon wiser consideration they decided that it should be done.'

As Fulcher presented it, kingship was an honourable calling, approved by God for the fundamental purpose of rendering justice.[89] Anselm of Bec, archbishop of Canterbury, and a personal friend of Countess Ida of Boulogne, Godfrey's mother, seems to have regarded both brothers as kings. In his letter of congratulation to Baldwin, probably written in the spring or summer of 1101, his main concern is that Baldwin should ensure the liberty of the Church, a role that he evidently did not regard as incompatible with a Jerusalem monarchy. Indeed, in a second letter he calls on Baldwin to reign in such a manner as to become an exemplar for all the kings of the earth.[90] Even so, at this point in his narrative, Fulcher devotes considerably more space to a lengthy description of the Dead Sea, while William of Tyre simply records the coronation without further elaboration, although agreeing with Fulcher that a reconciliation had taken place between Baldwin and Daibert.[91] In fact, Bethlehem was probably chosen as a location for the ceremony to avoid an overt confrontation over Daibert's claims to Jerusalem, since there was no physical impediment to a coronation in the church of the Holy Sepulchre. For Albert of Aachen, however, Baldwin had similar scruples to Godfrey in not wishing to be crowned in Jerusalem, 'where Lord Jesus, King of kings and Lord of lords, was brought low and subject even to death for the redemption of the world'.[92]

CHAPTER 4

———— ✴ ————

The Origins of the Latin States

BALDWIN's situation was actually very unpromising. When Geldemar Carpenel complained that he had been unjustly deprived of Haifa by Tancred, the king, in his role as dispenser of justice, summoned Tancred to Jerusalem. Albert of Aachen, the only chronicler to describe this, says that Tancred answered that 'he was not going to reply concerning these things in Baldwin's presence, because he would not recognise him as king of the city and judge of the kingdom of Jerusalem'. Given the history of enmity between the two men, particularly arising from their conflict in Cilicia in the autumn of 1097, as well as the extent of the landed base built up by Tancred, this defiance had the potential to undermine Baldwin's authority and prestige even before he was fully established as king. Two further summonses eventually led to a meeting, not in Jerusalem, to which Tancred claimed he was afraid to come, but at a place on the river that ran between Jaffa and Arsuf, a location that implied a kind of frontier between their lands. They failed to reach agreement, so a new date was set for Haifa in early March 1101, but by that time events beyond the control of either man had changed the political landscape, for a delegation of Antiochene nobles had asked Tancred to take over the government in Bohemond's absence. This enabled Baldwin to restore Haifa to Geldemar Carpenel and to grant Tiberias to Hugh of Fauquembergues, although Tancred protected his own interests by ensuring that he would receive 'these lands and cities as a fief held from the king' if he returned within a year and three months.[1] Ralph of Caen, writing at a time when Baldwin had long been established, says quite bluntly that Baldwin's accession 'raised up the flames of great dissension and war', which were avoided by Tancred's summons to Antioch, but neither Fulcher of Chartres nor William of Tyre discusses the implications of this crisis.[2] William of Tyre, usually so scrupulous in his regard for lawful authority, unconvincingly presents Tancred's opposition as that of a man unable 'to be bound by the oath of fidelity to a lord whom he could not love with a pure affection'.[3]

The Latin states were indeed highly volatile. Less than eighteen months after the capture of Jerusalem all four of the main territorial blocs established by the crusaders had changed hands, a pattern that can be seen among the major fief-holders as well. When Tancred left for the north, one of these four potential states disappeared, leaving the Latins with three isolated entities in Palestine, Syria and Mesopotamia, the last of which had no access to the coast. The number of fighting men available to improve the situation appears quite inadequate, not only to modern historians but to contemporaries as well. Fulcher of Chartres, so reticent about the key stages of Baldwin's rise to power in Edessa and Jerusalem, is eloquent about manpower deficiencies, asking rhetorically why the many thousands of Muslims in Egypt, Persia, Mesopotamia and Syria did not come in force and wipe out the Latins completely, as they could easily have done. He found his answer in the skill and courage of Baldwin and in the consequent divine protection of the righteous.[4]

More specifically, in early 1101, Fulcher says that in the kingdom of Jerusalem they could muster no more than 300 knights and the same number of foot soldiers. In these circumstances Baldwin certainly expected the patriarch and the canons of the Holy Sepulchre to make a contribution, for he did not consider the donations they received from the faithful to be exclusively for their own use. When the patriarch or his representative carried the True Cross into battle, he was indeed surrounded by his own corps of knights, as well as by some members of the chapter itself. Moreover, he also provided a contingent of sergeants drawn from the clients and dependants of the chapter, mostly burgesses from Jerusalem and peasants from the villages endowed by Godfrey of Bouillon.[5] There seems to have been a core of 250–300 knights, which only reached as many as 500 in the battle with the Egyptians at Ramla in August 1105, a figure probably inflated by temporary residents.[6] During the summer months there was a regular flow of maritime traffic, much increased from the pre-crusade days. Albert of Aachen claims that 200 ships arrived in the summer of 1102 and that pilgrims from them fought the Egyptians near Jaffa; certainly, demand for passage was so high that the English pilgrim Saewulf had difficulty finding a ship to take him to Jaffa from Apulia during that sailing season.[7] However, at the time of Baldwin's accession, Fulcher records no help from anybody travelling by land (indeed, there was no direct link with Antioch), while those coming by sea appear to have been unable to transport horses.

The varied backgrounds of these men reflect the heterogeneous nature of the crusade. This heterogeneity had swelled the numbers of recruits who had responded to Clermont, but made it more difficult to mould those who did stay into a coherent body whose first loyalty was to their new country. Flemings and Picards were the single largest group, despite the Lotharingian origins of the first two rulers. This link persisted throughout the twelfth century: at least four of the six counts of Flanders in the period upto 1193 participated in the crusades, two of whom were offered the rulership of Jerusalem, while one died at the siege of Acre in 1191. Thierry of Alsace, who was count for forty years between 1128 and 1168, visited the Holy Land four times, his wife, Sibylla, became a nun at the monastery of Bethany, and their son, Philip, made three expeditions.[8] In Baldwin's time the Lotharingians were not as numerous, although they did include some of the king's most important advisers, while smaller numbers came from the Ile-de-France, Normandy, Languedoc, northern and southern Italy and England.

The king had an acute need for the help of his vassals, but at the same time they knew that their survival depended upon mutual co-operation, essential both to achieve military success and to ensure God's approval and support. These lords were nearly autonomous as long as they supplied the forces needed by the king, for the absence of any institutional infrastructure meant that there were no public courts outside the royal demesne through which the king could enforce any form of closer control.[9] Nor was the king well supplied with ready cash, much needed to augment the forces owed by the major fief-holders. Indeed, initially, the rulers of the crusader states even lacked their own currencies, as can be seen by the circulation of both billon *denarii* from Lucca and *deniers* from Valence in Jerusalem and Antioch during these early years.[10]

In these circumstances, as William of Tyre puts it, the king devoted 'his entire attention to extending in every possible way the narrow limits of the kingdom'.[11] During the first five years of the reign he captured three major coastal cities, Arsuf (29 April 1101), Caesarea (17 May 1101) and Acre (26 May 1104), and survived three serious Egyptian invasions, in September 1101, May 1102 and August 1105, engagements more dangerous than the urban sieges, for failure in such circumstances usually meant there would be no second chance.

The arrival of a Genoese fleet in Jaffa at Easter 1101 was the key to the fall of both Arsuf and Caesarea. The Genoese had already mounted two expeditions, in April 1098, when they had helped the crusaders at the siege of Antioch, and in May 1099, when their appearance at Jaffa had provided the crusaders with much needed timber during the siege of Jerusalem. Their third sailing, however, was in much greater numbers: according to Caffaro, the Genoese chronicler, who was a participant in this expedition, it consisted of twenty-six galleys and four other ships.[12] Arsuf capitulated in three days, but Caesarea proved tougher, holding out for fifteen days. Control of the coast from Jaffa to Haifa having been secured, the next objective was Acre, since, according to William of Tyre, Caesarea, while having well-watered gardens, lacked a proper port.[13] Acre, however, had the best harbour on the Palestinian coast, as well as serving as an effective base for Egyptian attacks. Baldwin failed to take it in April 1103, but the next year, the arrival of a new fleet of perhaps seventy ships, both Genoese and Pisan, enabled him to overcome it on 26 May. 'This city,' says Fulcher of Chartres, 'was very necessary to us since it contained a port so commodious that a great many ships could be safely berthed within its secure walls.'[14]

These successes owed more to Genoese help than to any other Christian power. The crusade had been preached in Genoa by Hugh of Châteauneuf, bishop of Grenoble, and William, bishop of Orange, in 1097, and the powerful noble class that dominated both the city and its hinterland had responded by fitting out fleets most years thereafter. By Italian standards it was not a huge city, having a population of about 10,000 at the beginning of the twelfth century, and little is known about the development of its sea power before this time.[15] However, the needs of the crusader states presented Genoa with obvious commercial opportunities, especially since Venice and Pisa were already drawing large profits from the spice trade, which was channelled through Egypt.[16] Baldwin's charter of 1104, issued after the fall of Acre, sets out the privileges the Genoese received for their help. The basis was a grant of a third of the cities conquered, both those already gained and those that might be obtained in the future. In the latter case they were to receive an income of 300 besants per annum as well, provided the help given consisted of fifty or more Genoese. Territorial concessions were buttressed by commercial and legal rights, by which they were exempted from the regular tax on trade known as the *commercium* and were free of royal jurisdiction in cases involving capital punishment, maiming or imprisonment, as well as in all testamentary arrangements.[17] Sometime between spring 1106 and early July 1109, the Genoese were permitted to record their privileges in a golden inscription placed in the Rotunda of the church of the Holy Sepulchre.[18] The Genoese crusaders were not concerned exclusively with economic advantage, however, for they were equally impelled by the desire for pilgrimage to the Holy Sepulchre. Their disappointment at the failure of the Holy Fire at Easter 1101, as described by Caffaro, is palpable, as is their exaltation when it did finally appear.[19]

Such alliances did nevertheless present problems. When Acre fell, the Genoese and the Pisans attacked and plundered Muslims leaving the town under a royal safe-conduct, an action that incited the Frankish soldiers as well.[20] Yet it was evident to the king and his advisers that gratuitous destruction of cities and their populations was unsustainable for a regime with such meagre resources. Arsuf, which capitulated with little resistance, seems to have escaped unscathed; Albert of Aachen says that Baldwin spared the inhabitants, allowing them to leave with any possessions they could carry. The attack on Caesarea was more destructive, since it involved the clearing of the immediate vicinity to prevent ambushes. Albert's informant had been very impressed by the 'extraordinary orchards all round the walls, as closely planted as woodland, of great beauty and providing an invaluable abundance of fruit.'[21] Moreover, stiffer resistance tended to provoke greater retribution and, when the city fell, most of the male populace were killed. Even then it was not an unrestrained sack, since the emir and the qadi were ransomed, while most of the women were spared to be sold as slaves or used to turn hand-mills.[22] As this suggests, Baldwin had also learned the value of taking ransoms rather than killing prisoners, a practice well established in the Levant, but which had not initially been considered by the crusaders, who had seen their actions as representing God's will.[23] Moreover, a depopulated city was of little use to the conquerors if they wished to retain it as a functioning entity: sixteen years after the massacre of 1099, Baldwin was still trying to fill the gaps in Jerusalem by offering privileges aimed at persuading Syrian Christians from the Transjordan to settle in the city.[24] By the spring of 1108, when Baldwin made an unsuccessful attack on Sidon, this cooler assessment of monetary advantage had become policy. During the bombardment of the city's towers, Arnulf of Chocques, at this time archdeacon of Jerusalem, persuaded the king to desist. 'For Arnulf said that so outstanding a piece of work would cost at least two thousand bezants to rebuild, and if it was not ruined and subjected to a bombardment of stones it could be taken by storm and handed over into the king's hands after a few days.'[25]

The emirs of the coast were often supported by Egyptian shipping, but the real danger from Egypt arose on the occasions when al-Afdal managed to put together a large army, which could be landed at Ascalon and used to attack the kingdom from the south. In August 1099, the main crusader armies had not yet dispersed, so the victory of the Frankish forces, hardened by over two years of desperate fighting, is not surprising. A new invasion in the spring of 1101 was much more threatening, for the Christians were clearly outnumbered, even though contemporary Frankish estimates of the size of the Egyptian army cannot be relied upon. The Franks were wary of advancing from Jaffa, fearing that they would be trapped under the walls of Ascalon, so, although fully aware of the Egyptian presence from at least late May, they did not move until 6 September, when the enemy advanced onto the plain near Ramla. Baldwin therefore had time to assemble his forces, drawn from Jerusalem, Tiberias, Caesarea and Haifa. Fulcher says these amounted to 260 knights and 900 foot soldiers, a figure that must represent the maximum available, as it includes squires who were hastily knighted. The battle was fought on 7 September and within an hour the ground was covered with bodies and equipment, while riderless horses picked their way through the debris. Fulcher of Chartres, who was present, says that there was such slaughter on both sides that it turned his stomach. The Egyptians finally fled back to Ascalon, leaving eighty Frankish knights and many more foot soldiers dead. Nobody could have been confident of the outcome. In Jaffa a report that the Christians had been defeated was accepted as fully credible and led to panic; an appeal for help to Tancred had to be rescinded when it was found to be false.[26]

Having lost nearly a third of his knights the previous autumn, with the survivors too exhausted to pursue the enemy, Baldwin had to face a new invasion the following May. As Fulcher put it, they had been sent to destroy the Christians completely. This time the king, apparently overconfident after the victory the previous year, rushed into battle with only 200 knights and little infantry support. In Fulcher's view, this was an act of great recklessness, since the Egyptian army was much larger than he realised. Arpin of Bourges, chastened by recent experiences in Asia Minor, had tried to persuade Baldwin to wait for reinforcements, but the king scornfully told him that if he were frightened, he should flee back to Bourges. The resulting carnage claimed the lives of 'the greater part' of his knights, as well as those of Stephen of Blois and Stephen, count of Burgundy, also survivors of the crusade of 1101, who had been waiting at Jaffa for a favourable wind to return home. Arpin was taken prisoner and held in Cairo until his release was obtained by Alexius Comnenus, the Byzantine emperor.[27]

Baldwin himself escaped first to Ramla and then, after spending an anxious night hiding in the mountains, reached Arsuf. This brief disappearance was sufficient to fuel a rumour that the king had been killed, which was quite likely in the circumstances and, like the panic in Jaffa the previous year, indicative of the state of nerves prevailing among the early settlers. Once safe, Baldwin sailed to Jaffa, where he gathered what forces he could find, perhaps amounting to 170 knights plus foot soldiers, and counterattacked to such effect that the Egyptians were once more put to flight. In Fulcher's account the role of the foot soldiers, not present at the initial encounter, was crucial. Even so, it is evident that Fulcher thought that this near-disaster, spread over ten days between 17 and 27 May, was largely of the king's own making, a criticism to be taken seriously in view of Fulcher's admiration for Baldwin.[28]

Unsurprisingly, the Egyptians were not able to muster an immediate response, but the danger of a crushing defeat, which, as Fulcher of Chartres shows, could change everything in a single day, remained for the next three years. In August 1105, al-Afdal sent a combined force of Arab cavalry and Ethiopian foot soldiers, intended to act in combination with 1,000 Turkish archers from Damascus, supplied by its ruler, Tughtigin. This was the first time that the Franks had been faced by an alliance between Sunni and Shi'ite, and it resulted in the biggest battle since the victory of the first crusaders in August 1099. Baldwin's army was larger than on any previous occasion since he had become king. There were about 500 knights and 2,000 foot soldiers, as well as an unspecified number of mounted warriors 'who were not counted as knights', which suggests that, perhaps for the first time, the Franks were enlarging their armies with contingents of local Christians and baptised Turks – the turcopoles, as they were later called.[29] The battle was fought on 27 August and, after another fierce encounter, the Muslims retreated to Ascalon, losing Jamal al-Mulk, one of their leading emirs, in the process.[30]

Contemporaries were well aware that the four victories over the Egyptians were extraordinary achievements and, thus, like the capture of Jerusalem, should be attributed to divine intervention. The latter was manifested in the form of wood from the True Cross, which, according to Raymond of Aguilers, had been found thanks to the efforts of Arnulf of Chocques during his brief period as patriarch-elect.[31] Albert of Aachen presents Godfrey as explaining to 'the prefect of Ramla' that it was 'a spiritual shield against all the enemy's missiles'. This was why the Christians had such belief in their battles with the Egyptians, for 'we have been redeemed by this wood of the Holy Cross from the hand of death and hell, and by angelic power from harm, and we have been cleansed in the blood of Lord Jesus, son of the living God, from all the filth of former error, and we have confidence in eternal life'.[32] Fulcher of Chartres stresses that the True Cross was carried before the army by leading clerics in all the battles with the Egyptians, the only exception being Baldwin's reckless attack of May 1102, when he had neither waited for reinforcements, nor sent for the True Cross, which of course proved Fulcher's point: 'If indeed this benevolent Cross had been carried with the king in the previous battle, it cannot be doubted that the Lord would have favored His people'.[33] Baldwin fully absorbed the lessons, both military and spiritual. Before the battle with the Egyptians in August 1105, he did not engage until he was ready, making sure that the patriarch, Evremar, had brought the True Cross to the army and apparently engineering the confrontation for a Sunday when, in the eyes of the soldiers, the relic may have been thought most efficacious.[34]

Map 7
The kingdom
of Jerusalem
in the twelfth century

*Mediterranean
Sea*

BEIRUT
BAALBEK
Litani
SIDON
DAMASCUS
MARJ AYUN
MT HERMON DARAYYA
BEAUFORT
TYRE
BANYAS
TORON
SCANDELION
CHASTEL NEUF
MONTFORT
GALILEE
ACRE SAFAD JACOB'S FORD HAURAN
HAIFA *Sea of Galilee*
MT CARMEL HATTIN
DESTROIT NAZARETH TIBERIAS HABIS JALDAK
MT TABOR DER'A BOSRA
CAESAREA LA FÈVE BELVOIR
BAISAN *Yarmouk*

SAMARIA
SEBASTE JERASH
ARSUF NABLUS *Yarbouk*
JAFFA MIRABEL *Jordan*
LYDDA
IBELIN RAMLA
MONT GISARD JERICHO AHAMAT (AMMAN)
JERUSALEM
BLANCHEGARDE JUDAEA
ASCALON BETHLEHEM
GAZA BAIT JIBRIN
DARUM HEBRON
MOAB
Dead Sea
KERAK

N E G E V

T R A N S J O R D A N

MONTRÉAL

LI VAUX MOISE
PETRA

S I N A I

0   *miles*   50
0   *km*   50

AILAH

Key
— — Boundary of the kingdom

Baldwin's military achievements effectively marginalised Daibert; indeed, apart from the brief mention of the appointment of an archbishop to the see of Caesarea in May 1101, Fulcher of Chartres makes no reference to ecclesiastical affairs until the autumn of 1104, when Daibert, 'who had been Patriarch of Jerusalem', decided to depart for Rome to present his case to the pope and make known the injury done to him by the king. Although he must have known much more, Fulcher offers only the laconic statement that in Rome Daibert 'gained what he sought, but he did not come back for he died on the way'.[35] William of Tyre, dependent on his sources for his facts if not for his opinions, offers little more, claiming that, in 1103, Daibert was driven out of the kingdom by the intrigues of Arnulf of Chocques, who had revived the conflict with the king as well as stirring up the clergy against him. Daibert left for Antioch where he was well received by Bohemond, his old ally, who endowed him with the church of St George, which had considerable estates and revenues. Arnulf then used his influence with the king to promote to the patriarchate 'a simple-minded priest of deeply religious character, named Ebremar', who came from his home village and had been a companion on the crusade.[36] Having successfully appealed to the pope, Daibert then set out for the East, armed with an apostolic letter, but died on 15 June 1105 while waiting for a ship at Messina.[37]

Albert of Aachen offers a much fuller account in which the nub of the conflict seems to be money, although his hostility to the patriarch might suggest that he overplays Daibert's role as villain. Baldwin needed paid soldiers to defend the kingdom and therefore had no intention of leaving control of the resources of the Church in the hands of an ambitious prelate whom he did not trust. In early March 1101, the new legate, Maurice of Porto, arrived in Jerusalem, having overwintered in Latakia.[38] The king seems to have taken this as an opportunity once again to voice his allegations against Daibert and, at a council convened in Jerusalem, the patriarch was suspended, pending his answer. Pushed into a corner, Daibert secretly handed over 300 besants to the king, who then interceded with Maurice to restore him.[39] However, the money did not last long. Faced with the Egyptian invasion of September 1101, and under pressure from soldiers who had not been paid, Baldwin demanded more money from Daibert in a confrontation so furious that Maurice of Porto could do no more than stand on the sidelines, vainly trying to calm the protagonists. According to Albert, Baldwin was so angry that he said he would 'devour not only the offerings of the faithful and distribute them to our soldiers', but that he would 'even rip out the gold from the Lord's Sepulchre and altar in order to sustain the soldiers'. Daibert finally gave in when an envoy from Roger Borsa, Bohemond's half-brother, revealed that he had brought 1,000 besants to the patriarchate for distribution in three parts, to the canons of the Holy Sepulchre, the hospitaller brothers, and the king for maintaining soldiers, but that all this had disappeared into the patriarch's coffers. Albert says that, because of 'this enormous fraud and treachery', Daibert was deposed and forced to withdraw to Jaffa. The following spring he sailed for Antioch.[40]

Daibert made one more effort to regain his position, returning to Jaffa in May 1102 with the forces of Tancred and Baldwin of Bourcq, who had come south in response to Baldwin's appeal for help against the Egyptian invasion of that year. The king, still angry, was reluctant to accept him, but did agree to a council at Jerusalem, presided over by the new legate, Cardinal Robert of St Eusebio, the replacement for Maurice of Porto, who had died the previous winter. As Albert saw it, the patriarch's perfidy was clearly proved and he was again deposed, leaving him with no option but to return to Antioch with Tancred, to be replaced by Evremar, 'a man and cleric of good character, an excellent and cheerful distributor of alms'.[41]

Fulcher's reticence about these matters is hardly surprising. He knew very well that Baldwin's determination to dominate the Church was not compatible with papal attempts to shake ecclesiastical life free from the tentacles of secular power, but he had seen enough fighting to realise that the survival of the kingdom of Jerusalem depended upon its soldiers, led by a king who expected unquestioning spiritual and material support from the patriarch. Evremar was a more pliant instrument than Daibert, but it soon became evident that Baldwin had a low opinion of his abilities; according to Albert of Aachen, accusations were made against him by Baldwin and Arnulf and, in 1107, he too travelled to Rome to absolve himself.[42] Fulcher of Chartres presents this as an attempt to 'inquire from the Apostolic See whether he would remain patriarch' in view of Daibert's death.[43]

The pope's version, set out in a letter to Baldwin of 4 December 1107, was that Evremar arrived in Rome seeking confirmation as patriarch, having heard news of Daibert's death, but that he was closely followed by Arnulf bringing letters from the king and the canons of the Holy Sepulchre asking that Evremar be removed from office on the grounds that he was 'completely useless'.[44] Paschal's answer was to send a new legate, Gibelin, archbishop of Arles, to sort out the problems and, in a council held in Jerusalem in 1108, Gibelin decided that Evremar could not be lawful patriarch as he had assumed office when the incumbent was both still alive and in communion with the Church.[45] Evremar was then translated to the see of Caesarea, while Gibelin himself reluctantly accepted the patriarchate, which he held concurrently with the post of legate. William of Tyre, whose hostility to Arnulf of Chocques is unshakeable, thinks he discerns the real reason for this: 'It is claimed that this choice also was brought about by the subtle plotting of Arnulf, who thought that Gibelin, being old and decrepit, would not survive long in the patriarchal office.'[46] Albert of Aachen does not blame Arnulf so overtly, but makes no secret of his view that the whole business was quite contrary to the principles of papal reform: 'Although it was wrong that this dispute should take place, unless one of them had been condemned by decree and sentence of canon law, yet because the Jerusalem Church was still unformed and fragile the pope allowed it to happen, and so by the king's gift and the assent of all the faithful, each of them was elevated to office.'[47]

When Baldwin left Edessa for Jerusalem on 2 October 1100, almost three years had passed since he had abandoned the main body of the crusade on the road to Antioch and headed east.[48] Fulcher of Chartres, who was the only chronicler who went with him, says that they were only three days north of Antioch at this point, but he offers no explanation for the diversion, nor does he record the opinions of the other leaders. The foray into Cilicia the previous month, undertaken apparently in conjunction with Tancred, may have been part of a wider plan intended to make contact with the Armenians and to open up a supply route for the coming siege of Antioch. If so, Baldwin may have convinced the leaders that the establishment of a redoubt east of Antioch would similarly bring strategic advantage.[49] Albert of Aachen says that Baldwin sent gold, silver, horses and arms to the leaders during the siege of Antioch and, as the situation outside the city grew more dire, ceded the revenues of Turbessel to Godfrey in the form of corn, barley, wine and oil, together with an annual income of 50,000 besants.[50] There is some evidence of forward planning. The Franks had not only informed Constantine, the Roupenid prince of Cilician Armenia, about their arrival, as might be expected, but also Thoros, the Armenian governor of Edessa appointed by the Greeks, but now largely cut off by Turkish expansion.[51] Moreover, as early as the spring of 1097, when the crusaders were still in Nicaea, Baldwin had made contact with an Armenian soldier called Pakrad (or Bagrat), the brother of another local Armenian lord, Kogh Vasil, who held castles east of Marash.[52]

However, if strategy and provisioning were the sole reasons for the expedition, then it was an extremely risky enterprise, since Fulcher of Chartres says that when Baldwin crossed the Euphrates in February 1098, he had only eighty knights.[53] The more likely driving force was Baldwin himself, evident both from his subsequent actions and what is known of his character. The death of Godehilde, his wife, in mid-October, which weakened any claim he had on part of the Tosny inheritance in Normandy, may have convinced him that he needed to concentrate on gaining land in the East.[54] Even before this, he had done little to hide his ambitions in Cilicia, where his quarrels with Tancred over the possession of Tarsus and Mamistra had culminated in a violent fight between their followers, resulting in several deaths. Even Albert of Aachen, whose pro-Lotharingian sympathies are never far from the surface, could find no credit in this: the next day, 'they recalled that both sides had done wrong in the Lord's sight, and their devotion to the most sacred way of Jerusalem had been violated'.[55] As their bad relations at the time of Baldwin's accession to the kingship of Jerusalem show, this reconciliation was mere form, for the rivalry remained.

Fulcher of Chartres should be the major witness for the establishment of what became the county of Edessa, but his sparse and minimal narrative conceals as much as it tells. As Baldwin moved east, the local Armenians submitted to him, most importantly the town of Turbessel. He then received an offer of an alliance from Thoros, which included the inheritance of Edessa should Thoros die without direct heirs. As Thoros was childless, this drew Baldwin across the Euphrates, a highly dangerous move, since Edessa was about 160 miles from Antioch and there was little chance of any aid from the main Latin armies. Indeed, Baldwin's force was obliged to beat off an attack by Turks based in Samosata on the Euphrates to the north. Around 20 February 1098, they reached Edessa, where they were received 'with rejoicing' and the promises made by Thoros were fulfilled. However, within a fortnight Thoros had been overthrown and killed, and replaced by Baldwin. Fulcher says that this was an entirely internal affair, arising from local hatred of Thoros. 'Baldwin and his men were much grieved because they were not able to obtain mercy for him.'[56]

In Albert of Aachen's more detailed version, which appears to be soundly based on both oral and written sources, Baldwin also took Ravendel, which he entrusted to Pakrad, before crossing the Euphrates at the second attempt, having first been deterred by Turkish forces.[57] At Edessa he was adopted as a son by Thoros in a ceremony that involved 'binding him to his naked chest', but he was then unable to prevent the overthrow of his new 'father', who was killed in the uprising. Albert makes clear that Baldwin knew what was happening, although, in contrast to Matthew of Edessa, he does not accuse him of collusion. Once in control, Baldwin set about extending his power, buying the support of Balduk, emir of Samosata, when he found he did not have the necessary forces to take the town, probably with resources obtained from the treasury of the late Thoros, and forcing out Balak ibn Bahram, the Artuqid ruler of Saruj, south-west of Edessa, a capture that opened up the route between Antioch and Edessa.[58]

By the spring of 1098, while the main body of crusaders was still struggling to bring down Antioch, Baldwin and his small force had created the basis of a viable lordship, stretching from Ravendel in the west to Edessa in the east, and dominating the previously Turkish-controlled towns of Samosata and Saruj to the north-west and south-west of Edessa respectively. It was defined in the north by the Anti-Taurus mountains and in the west by the Jaihan (Pyramus) and Afrin Rivers, although its southern limits are more difficult to identify. Edessa itself was an ancient and well-fortified site, claiming apostolic conversion to Christianity and containing a great cathedral, richly decorated with mosaics. In 1032, the Byzantines had retaken it from the Turks, but it had been lost again after the battle of Manzikert in 1071, vicissitudes that emphasise its position on the frontier between the powers of the region, making it difficult for its rulers to use it as the nucleus of a state.[59]

Ravendel had been granted to Pakrad, but he was soon tortured into giving up control because of what Albert of Aachen calls treachery, although there is no way of knowing whether Baldwin had always intended to be rid of him once his value had evaporated.[60] Nor did Balduk long survive his association with Baldwin who, in the summer of 1098, had him beheaded on the pretext that he had not provided the hostages he had promised to guarantee his good behaviour.[61] Moreover, once news of Baldwin's success began to reach the main army, the numbers of Franks started to increase; Albert of Aachen mentions frequent journeys in the summer of 1098 after the victory over Kerbogha. Some took service in Edessa, while the others became temporary residents in their efforts to escape the spread of disease around Antioch, including Godfrey of Bouillon, who lived for a period in Turbessel and Ravendel.[62]

Of course, Baldwin had left the main army shortly after the march from Marash had begun, which meant he had been unable to take any further direct role in the crusade. This must have provoked criticism, for when Bohemond and Baldwin eventually completed their pilgrimage to Jerusalem at Christmas 1099, Fulcher felt the need to stress the importance of the protection provided by guarding cities that acted as a barrier against the Turks, 'now driven back as far as Persia', something that had been achieved through the many battles fought by Baldwin in Mesopotamia.[63] Most dramatically, when Kerbogha brought his huge army of perhaps 35,000 men west from Mosul, he spent three fruitless weeks besieging Edessa, between 4 and 25 May, before giving up and continuing to Antioch. William of Tyre, always keen to find evidence of God's favour, thought that the delay had saved the crusaders, who only broke into Antioch on 3 June.[64]

Edessa itself had a developed administrative and financial structure, with a council of twelve, variously called governors, senators or *curopalates*.

Ecclesiastical life was led by an archbishop who, indeed, had been among the representatives sent by Thoros to encourage Baldwin to become co-ruler.[65] Baldwin himself quickly adapted his appearance and style to this new milieu. Guibert of Nogent, who seems to have gained his information from Baldwin of Bourcq, says that 'whenever he went out he had a gold shield carried before him, which bore the image of an eagle, in the Greek manner. Like the pagans, he went about in a toga, let his beard grow, accepted bows from worshippers, and ate on rugs laid on the ground.'[66] The population was mainly Armenian Christian, potentially supportive because resentful of both Greek and Turkish control, and Baldwin's marriage to a daughter of another Thoros, the brother of Constantine of Cilicia, in the course of 1098 was evidently an attempt to identify with the local Christians.[67] According to William of Tyre, unlike that of the surrounding region, the population of the city was entirely Christian and had been so since apostolic times.[68] However, relations between Latins and Armenians began to sour quite quickly, as the latter found themselves displaced from positions of authority.[69] Later in the summer of 1098, Baldwin had to suppress an internal rebellion, apparently generated by resentment of the increasing influence of the Franks now arriving in the city. 'From that day,' says Albert of Aachen, 'Duke Baldwin became a man to be feared in the city of Edessa, and his name was spread among the people to the limits of the land.'[70]

For such a man, the offer of the rulership of Antioch made in early October 1100 would, in most circumstances, have been impossible to turn down, but the coincidence of Godfrey's death less than a month before Bohemond's capture meant that Baldwin had his sights set on Jerusalem. It was therefore Tancred who accepted the regency of Antioch in March 1101. Bohemond, together with Richard of the Principate, had been taken prisoner in mid-August 1100 while responding to an appeal from Gabriel, Armenian ruler of Melitene, under siege by the forces of Malik-Ghazi, the Danishmend Turk who dominated the eastern Anatolian plateau. While it was politic to maintain good relations with at least some of the Armenian princes, this was a very long-range expedition indeed. Ralph of Caen says it was at least ten days' journey to Melitene, which is about 190 miles north-east of Antioch over mountainous terrain. Malik-Ghazi took advantage of what Ralph calls Bohemond's 'stupid audacity' in refusing to rest in the city itself after the journey, and he fell upon a force that Matthew of Edessa describes as quite unprepared.[71]

In contrast, Tancred concentrated upon more immediate problems, for Byzantine pressure in Cilicia and along the north Syrian coast had prevented Bohemond from expanding much beyond the immediate territory of Antioch

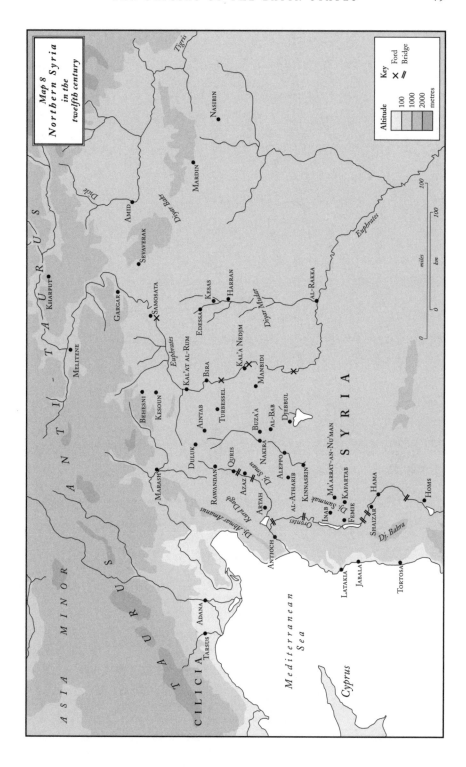

Map 8
Northern Syria
in the
twelfth century

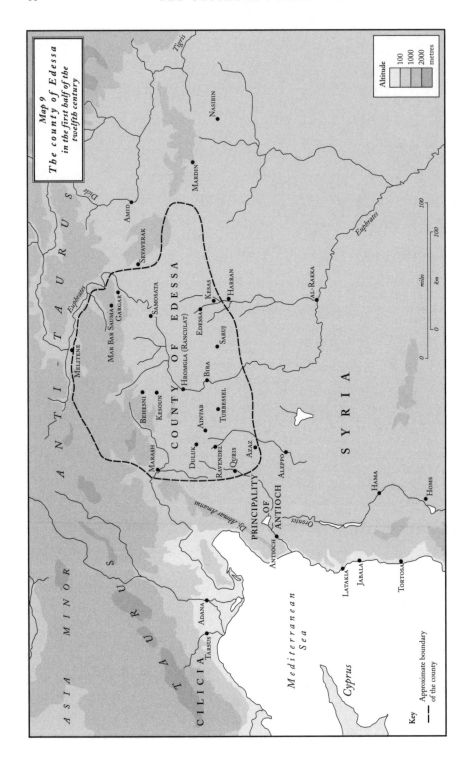

Map 9
The county of Edessa
in the first half of the
twelfth century

itself. His attempt to take Latakia was blocked in September 1099 by the returning crusade leaders, still concerned to preserve Byzantine co-operation. Yet, within eighteen months, Tancred had regained Mamistra, Adana and Tarsus, and, most importantly, after a long siege, had succeeded in driving the Byzantines out of Latakia.[72] He took care to ensure that he had the necessary sea power, reinforcing Bohemond's alliance with the Genoese, consolidated a little more than two weeks after the defeat of Kerbogha in June 1098. In November 1097, a fleet of twelve galleys and a supply ship had arrived at Saint Simeon, providing military and technical support for the siege of Antioch over the winter and into the spring of 1098. After the fall of the city they were established in Antioch by Bohemond, even though he was still contesting its control with Raymond of Toulouse. In a charter of 14 July 1098, he granted them the church of Saint John, with a warehouse (*fondico*), well and thirty houses around the square on which the church stood. It was a pact of mutual convenience: on the same day seven named *boni homines* (leading citizens) of Genoa agreed to defend the city 'against all men' except for the count of Toulouse.[73] Tancred built on this. In 1101, he conceded the Genoese a third of the port revenues of Saint Simeon and a half of those of Latakia, as well as a quarter (*ruga*) with a church and a well in Latakia. He also promised them an anchorage (*fundus*) in the port of Gibelet when it was captured.[74]

The only attempt to rescue Bohemond had been made by Baldwin of Edessa, who set off in pursuit of Malik-Ghazi a few days after the capture but, understandably reluctant to penetrate too deeply into Anatolia, he was obliged to fall back on Melitene, where he left a garrison of fifty soldiers.[75] Within weeks he had departed from the north to claim the rulership of Jerusalem. Thereafter, Ralph of Caen says that both Bernard of Valence, patriarch of Antioch, and Baldwin of Bourcq kept pressing to obtain Bohemond's release, but he was not freed until May 1103, after a ransom payment of 100,000 gold coins, probably negotiated by the Armenian Kogh Vasil.[76] Tancred had done nothing, and even Ralph of Caen strained to present his conduct in a good light: 'Nor did Tancred stand in the way of these efforts, although it seemed that Bohemond's return would be a hindrance to his continued prosperity.' Bohemond, says Ralph, then obliged Tancred to hand over everything he held, including the places 'he had gained by his own effort'. In the end, 'he had to beg for two small towns'. Ralph is perhaps trying too hard; Fulcher of Chartres says Bohemond made Tancred 'proper compensation from his lands and joyfully pacified him'.[77]

Bohemond, however, had barely a year to enjoy his freedom before he was drawn into a battle that Fulcher of Chartres describes as 'far more dreadful than all previous battles'.[78] Even from the much longer perspective of the

1180s, William of Tyre does nothing to moderate this judgement; indeed, he presents it in apocalyptic terms. 'Never during the rule of the Latins in the East, whether before or after this event, do we read of a battle so disastrous as this one, which resulted in so terrible a massacre of brave men and so disgraceful a flight of the people of our race.'[79] This was the battle of Harran, which took place on 7–8 May 1104. No Latin chronicler was present, but both Ralph of Caen and Albert of Aachen were well placed to collect information from those who had been. This was especially true of Ralph, who accompanied Bohemond on his Balkan campaigns in 1106–7 and lived in Antioch during the last year of Tancred's life in 1111–12.

Bohemond and Tancred were responding to a call for aid from Baldwin of Bourcq, besieged in Edessa by a formidable combined Turkish force led by the emirs Soqman ibn Ortuq and Jikirmish, lord of Mosul. The Antiochene leaders were accompanied by Joscelin, lord of Turbessel and Ravendel, Baldwin's cousin, who had come to the East in 1102 with the remains of the army of Stephen of Blois. Having no patrimony and probably poorly resourced after the losses of 1101, he had been endowed by Baldwin with the Edessan lands west of the Euphrates, creating an important link between the two main parts of the county.[80] According to Ibn al-Qalanisi, the Turkish leaders had 'made a solemn agreement with one another to prosecute the Holy War against the Franks, the enemies of God', although William of Tyre suggests that Baldwin's attempts to subjugate Harran, which lay about 22 miles to the south-east of Edessa in an area made productive by irrigation from the Balikh River, were the immediate cause of the attack.[81] This seems likely, as possession of Harran would not only have increased Baldwin's resources, but also have made Edessa itself safer from attack from Mesopotamia.

The Christian forces seem to have lacked cohesion from the outset. Fulcher of Chartres thinks that quarrelling brought the army close to disintegration, while William of Tyre says that Bohemond and Baldwin were wrangling over who was entitled to hold Harran itself. The Muslim leaders drew the Christians across the river in a feigned retreat, and then fell upon them, capturing Baldwin, Joscelin and Benedict, archbishop of Edessa, although the archbishop was quickly rescued. Despite the disappearance of Baldwin, Bohemond and Tancred were prepared to fight again the next day, only to find that most of the troops had fled back across the river to Edessa.[82] Matthew of Edessa says that the Franks went two days' march beyond Harran, to a place called Oshut, in order to engage the Turks. Here, 'in this strange and alien Muslim land', they fought a 'frightful and violent battle'. He claims that there were 30,000 Christian dead, 'so the region was depopulated', enabling the Muslims of Harran to bring 'more destruction upon the Christian faithful than the Turks had ever done'.[83] Ibn al-Qalanisi was triumphant, although his judgement that it was 'the turning of fortune against them' proved to be premature. 'This was,' he says, 'a great and unexampled victory for the Muslims; it discouraged the Franks, diminished their numbers and broke their power of offence, while the hearts of the Muslims were strengthened, and their zeal for the victory of the Faith and the war against the heretics was whetted and sharpened.'[84]

Tancred was now chosen as regent of Edessa, although for a period the survival of the city hung in the balance, as the Turks tried to follow up their victory.[85] Bohemond once more lost ground to his immediate enemies, for the Byzantines retook the Cilician cities and refortified Latakia, while Ridwan of Aleppo, although largely estranged from Sunnite Islam, nevertheless took the chance to seize Artah, only 20 miles to the north-east of Antioch itself. Ibn al-Qalanisi says that it was surrendered to him by the Armenians 'because of the injustice and grievous tyranny they had suffered from the Franks'.[86] At the same time the Turks devastated the entire region as far as the Orontes River. As Ralph of Caen saw it, the defeat had the direct consequence of persuading Bohemond that he should raise new forces in the West. In the autumn of 1104, with Daibert of Pisa in train, he set sail, leaving Tancred once more as regent. Even allowing for Ralph's prejudice in favour of Tancred, his claim that Antioch was left 'without protection, wages and mercenaries' rings true.[87] In the West, however, Bohemond retained his status as a heroic figure, an image upon which he capitalised over the next two years, finally convincing Paschal II to support a crusade against Byzantium. It was not successful: Bohemond's expedition to Dalmatia, which began in October 1107, was finally ground down by Alexius's forces in September the following year, and, by the treaty of Devol, Bohemond was obliged to agree to govern Antioch as a vassal of the emperor, as well as to give up his lands in Cilicia.[88]

This failure must have diverted potential soldiers from Antioch itself, as well as deterring new crusaders, but, on the other hand, it did leave Tancred free to develop the principality in his own way, for he had no intention of submitting to the Byzantines. In one sense, Tancred was paying back both Alexius and Bohemond since, according to Ralph of Caen, he considered the oath he had sworn to the emperor in 1097 as having been made under pressure from Bohemond; he therefore saw it as 'a small matter' to violate it.[89] Tancred put Richard of the Principate in charge of Edessa, but in the circumstances it is not surprising that it took nearly four years to regain what had been lost in the aftermath of the battle. Richard's acquisitive and sometimes violent rule was deeply resented by the local population, while his absence in the West between late 1105 and 1108 meant that he was often unable to supervise the government of the county in person.[90] Ridwan's aggression was the most easily reversed; by the spring of 1105, Tancred once more controlled Artah, Sarmin and Tell Aghdi, and in April he defeated Ridwan in battle, effectively neutralising the threat from Aleppo for the next five years. The Byzantines were tougher, but over the winter of 1107–8 he retook Mamistra and, in the spring, Latakia.[91] In the latter case he needed sea power and the Pisans were given quarters in both Latakia and Antioch in return for their help.[92] A measure of Tancred's confidence can be seen in the striking of his own copper coinage at around this time, one type of which shows, on the obverse, a full-face bust of a bearded Tancred holding a large sword on his shoulder. Such coinage cannot have been confined to the years 1111–12 – that is, after Bohemond's death – and must be seen as a clear indication that Tancred regarded himself as sovereign ruler of the principality rather than as some kind of regent for Bohemond.[93]

Tancred, of course, had no more interest in obtaining the release of Baldwin and Joscelin than he had had in obtaining that of Bohemond. An early attempt by King Baldwin to persuade Bohemond and Tancred to use a high-status female captive as a bargaining counter was met by 'smooth and flattering replies', according to Albert of Aachen, but they had no real intention of giving up Edessa, which Albert claims provided an income of 40,000 besants per annum, plus additional revenues from dependencies.[94] In fact, Joscelin managed to negotiate his own release in 1107 and that of Baldwin the following year, but when Baldwin tried to gain access to Edessa 'he could not go in', says Fulcher of Chartres, 'because Tancred and his men forbade entrance'.[95] Not the least of the effects of the Harran defeat was the disintegration of any attempt at a unified front among the powers of the north, just at a time when the Turks were beginning to pose a serious threat and the Armenians were becoming increasingly disaffected. This enmity culminated in a battle between Tancred and Joscelin near Turbessel in September 1108, in which both sides deployed Turkish allies. Initially nearly overcome, Tancred recovered and defeated Joscelin, a victory approved by Fulcher of Chartres, who ascribes it to the help of God, although, in an apparent non sequitur, he goes on to say that 'when the chief men of the land saw the damage being done, they took mutual counsel and brought the contestants to agreement'.[96]

Tancred's ambitions, however, were not confined to the county of Edessa. An idea of the perception he had of the territories of Antioch can be gained from the oath he extracted from Raymond of Toulouse when he fell into his hands in the winter of 1101–2. At a time when King Baldwin's reach extended no farther than Haifa, Raymond was obliged to promise that he 'would not seize any land whatsoever on this side of the town of Acre', a demand in keeping with Tancred's concession of an anchorage in Gibelet, around 25 miles to the south of Tripoli, to the Genoese in 1101, if they should help in its capture.[97] In September 1106, Tancred took advantage of internal dissensions to gain Apamea, which lay to the south-east beyond the Orontes.[98] This was potentially very important, for further expansion along the Upper Orontes would have brought Tancred within reach of Shaizar and Hama, control of which would have laid the foundations of one of the most powerful states in northern Syria. Raymond of Toulouse had understood the possibilities when, in September 1098, he had set up a priest from his army, Peter of Narbonne, as bishop of Albara, about 20 miles to the north of Apamea. Although Peter had continued on to Jerusalem, when he later returned, in 1102, he was made archbishop by Bernard of Valence, patriarch of Antioch, and then, in keeping with the previous Orthodox structure, archbishop of Apamea, after its capture.[99] Peter's defection to the Normans greatly strengthened Tancred's hold on the region, since Albara lies within the plateau known as the Jabal as-Summaq, which was very important to the south-eastern defences of Antioch, and which Bohemond and Raymond had contested between September 1098 and January 1099.[100]

In fact, Raymond took no notice of his promise to Tancred for, if he wished to stay in the East, it was evidently impractical for him to try to carve out a domain south of Acre, where King Baldwin was already dominant. In contrast, the coast and hinterland between Baldwin and Tancred offered tempting opportunities, while at the same time the Byzantines were apparently willing to send supplies to the Provençals from Cyprus in return for an oath of allegiance, a matter Raymond probably discussed with Alexius while he was in Constantinople in 1101.[101] Moreover, Raymond was already familiar with the area from his military operations there in 1098 and 1099, notably spending three frustrating months trying to take Arqa, as well as leaving small garrisons in a number of towns and castles.[102] Although there was by this time little left of the acquisitions he had made during the crusade, he was aware that he could exploit divisions among local Muslim powers to his profit.[103] When he had left Kafartab in January 1099, nearby rulers had scrambled to send envoys and gifts, together with what Raymond of Aguilers describes as 'promises of future submission', while Fakhr al-Mulk Ibn Ammar, emir of Tripoli, had given the crusaders large sums of money, horses, mules, clothing and food to divert them from Tripoli, Arqa and Gibelet.[104]

Once Tancred had released Raymond, the leaders and their followers who had survived the traumas of the Anatolian campaigns of August and September 1101 set out for Jerusalem. Apart from Raymond himself, these included Stephen of Blois, Welf of Bavaria and William of Aquitaine. These forces consisted of only a small proportion of the original strength of the crusade of 1101 but, in concert with the Genoese, they were sufficient to bring about the fall of Tortosa in mid-February 1102. The city was, says Albert of Aachen, handed over to Raymond by 'common agreement', although Fulcher of Chartres emphasises there was considerable resentment when Raymond then refused to continue to Jerusalem.[105] To have left, however, would have been to lose yet another opportunity to establish himself in the East, a course to which he now seems to have been committed. Both Tortosa and the hill fortress of Hisn al-Akrad (later Crac des Chevaliers) had been captured by the Provençals in January and February 1099, only for them to be retaken by Fakhr al-Mulk of Tripoli once the crusaders had turned their backs, while it is unlikely that Tancred would have held back if Raymond had contented himself with leaving a garrison there.[106]

With Tortosa under his control, Raymond now assembled his meagre forces for an attack on Tripoli itself, a city described by Ibn al-Athir as one of the greatest of Islam and 'one of the most handsome and rich'.[107] Fakhr al-Mulk was not willing to give it up easily, especially as Raymond appears to have had only about 300 knights available to him. The emir therefore called in help from Duqaq of Damascus and Janah al-Daula of Homs, creating an army that may have been as much as twenty times the size of Raymond's force. As was so often the case in the early days of the Latin settlement, there was no alternative but to fight despite the unfavourable odds, and a battle took place near Tortosa on 14 April 1102. However, the contingent from Homs panicked and fled, enabling the Provençals to concentrate their attack on the Tripolitans.[108] There was no Latin chronicler to report these events and the Muslim sources inevitably do not provide much detail about an engagement that Ibn al-Qalanisi saw as a shattering defeat.[109] Nevertheless, this victory was the equivalent of Baldwin's successes against the Egyptians, for Homs and Damascus were the main threat to any power attempting to establish itself on this section of the Syrian coast.

Free from external attack, Raymond could now once again turn his attention to Tripoli, but while small forces can sometimes succeed against great odds in the very risky and short-term circumstances of a battle, they are much less likely to bring a prolonged siege to a successful conclusion. Raymond therefore established himself on a ridge about 2 miles east of Tripoli along the main route from the north and the east, which became known as Mount Pilgrim. This was more than a temporary camp, for here he built a permanent castle with a rectangular keep and walled bailey, which became known as Qal 'at Sanjil (Saint-Gilles).[110] This castle was used both as a residence and as a long-term threat to Tripoli, a technique later adopted in the kingdom of

Jerusalem against both Tyre and Ascalon. By these means Raymond extracted an annual tribute from Tripoli, but he could not take it before his death on 28 February 1105.[111] In one sense, however, Fakhr al-Mulk had the last word, since, on 12 September 1104, he launched a surprise attack upon Mount Pilgrim, killing many members of the garrison, setting fire to parts of the settlement and taking much plunder. According to a late twelfth-century source, Ibn al-Athir, this was the direct cause of Raymond's death, since he died from injuries received when a burning roof collapsed underneath him.[112]

Even so, by this time he had extended his conquests sufficiently for the outlines of a new state to emerge, most importantly capturing Gibelet, south of Tripoli, with the help of the Genoese, probably in spring, 1104.[113] In 1103, he started to call himself the count of Tripoli, while at about the same time he named one of his followers, Albert, abbot of St Evrard, as bishop of Tripoli.[114] In 1102, he had begun to make pious grants, both actual and anticipatory, which show that he intended to make the city of Tripoli his capital. He particularly favoured religious institutions established in the East that aided pilgrims or took care of the holy shrines, interests closely related to his own original motivation for taking the Cross.[115]

Both the Holy Sepulchre and the Benedictine monastery of St Mary Latin were beneficiaries. In c.1103, the canons of the Holy Sepulchre were granted a former mosque on Mount Pilgrim, on the site of which they built a church, as well as the church of St George, located somewhere in the Lebanese mountains. Raymond also promised them that, after the conquest of Tripoli, they would receive the second most important church in the city, together with the funds to support thirteen clerics to serve it.[116] The Benedictine monastery of St Mary Latin was already maintaining a pilgrim hospice in Jerusalem before 1071, and since then had added two further refuges for men and women. Early in 1102, Raymond had offered to found a church for this monastery, a promise he and his wife, Elvira, fulfilled the following year, when they granted a site for a church next to the new castle of Mount Pilgrim, together with a mill, a terrain and a *casal* (village) with its dependants: 'I do this for my soul and that of my wife Elvira and all my relatives and in order that the good beginning achieved with the new castle should terminate with a better end.'[117] Part of the 'better end' involved the colonisation of what was already a prosperous agricultural area with Christian settlers owing allegiance to Latin ecclesiastical institutions, in a manner already demonstrated by Godfrey of Bouillon in his grant of 1100 to the canons of the Holy Sepulchre to the north of Jerusalem.

At the same time Raymond appreciated the value of consolidating links with his homeland, where the two great congregations of Augustinian canons,

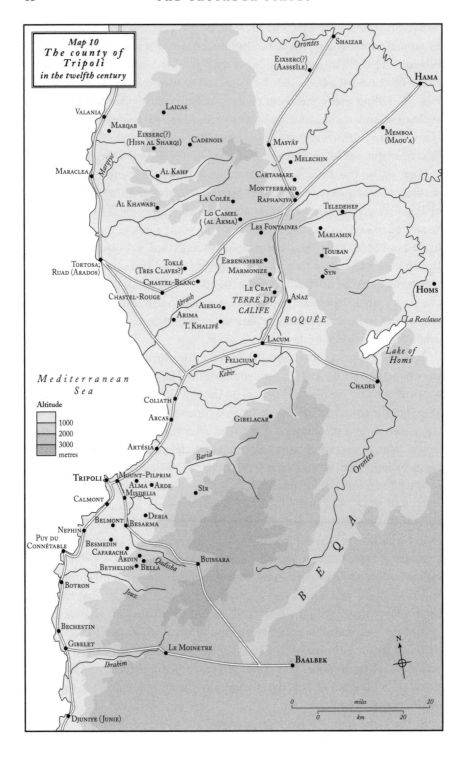

Map 10
The county of
Tripoli
in the twelfth century

Orontes   Shaizar
Eixserc(?)
(Aasseïle)   Hama

Valania   Laicas
Marqab
Eixserc(?)
(Hisn al Sharqi)   Cadenois   Masyâf   Memboa
(Maou'a)
Melechin
Maraclea   Al Kahf   Cartamare
Montferrand
La Colée   Raphaniya   Teledehep
Al Khawabi
Lo Camel
(al Akma)   Les Fontaines
Mariamin
Touban
Tortosa;   Toklé
Ruad (Arados)   (Tres Claves?)   Erbenambre   Syn
Chastel-Blanc   Marmonize
Chastel-Rouge   *Abrash*   Aieslo   Le Crat   Añaz
Arima   TERRE DU
T. Khalifé   CALIFE   BOQUÉE   *La Resclause*
Lacum   Lake of
Felicium   Homs
Mediterranean   *Kebir*
Sea   Chades
Altitude   Coliath
Arcas
1000   Gibelacar
2000
3000   Artésia
metres   *Barid*
Orontes
Tripoli   Mount-Pilprim
Alma Arde
Calmont   Misdelia   Sîr
Deria
Belmont Besarma
Nephin   B
Puy du   Besmedin   E
Connétable   Cafaracha   *Qadisha*   Q
Abdin   Buissara   A
Bethelion Bella
Botron   *Jouz*
Bechestin   N
Gibelet
Le Moinetre   Baalbek
Ibrahim
miles   20
Djuniye (Junie)   km   20

St Victor of Marseille and Saint-Ruf of Avignon, had already spread their influence into northern France, Spain and Italy. It is noticeable that the first witness to the 1103 charter to St Mary Latin is Richard of Marseille, abbot of St Victor, who, on 16 January, was promised half the city of Gibelet for his monastery, while during the next two years Raymond built a new church for Saint-Ruf, 'in the region of Tripoli', at his own expense.[118] These links were strengthened by Pons, count from 1112, who established the church of St James in Tripoli for Saint-Ruf sometime between 1114 and 1122. By 1123, Saint-Ruf held at least four churches, as well as three mills in the county.[119]

Raymond of Toulouse was not popular in his own time. His bitter enmity with the Normans and his unwillingness to co-operate with the Lotharingians, together with his alliance with Alexius Comnenus, had made him an isolated figure, unable to gain control of either Antioch or Jerusalem as he appears to have wanted. The pro-Norman Ralph of Caen claimed that it was hatred that had brought Raymond and Alexius together.[120] As count of Toulouse, he was by far the most prestigious and wealthy of the crusade leaders, yet he died while attempting to conquer the only strip of the Syrian coast left after men of lower status and power had seized the bigger prizes. The failure of the crusade of 1101, in which he was deeply involved, meant that he had very little leverage when he did return to Syria, giving him no opportunity to change the balance of power in what at that time was still a fluid situation. Even so, he had not settled for a minor role. Not only had he been intent on gaining Tripoli and the coast, but he had evidently planned to expand inland, since Albert of Aachen describes William-Jordan, count of Cerdagne, as succeeding by hereditary right 'to the land and towns of Camolla', which was the name used by the crusaders for Homs and its hinterland.[121]

Such actions and attitudes are consistent with what is known of Raymond's character. As the second son of Pons, count of Toulouse, he had not originally been among the great lords of Languedoc, yet by the mid-1090s he had built up a large agglomeration of fiefs, adding the titles of duke of Narbonne and marquis of Provence to that of count of Toulouse. At the same time he had been a supporter of the papal programme since the 1070s, when, with William I, count of Burgundy, he was named among those magnates willing to bring armed force to support Gregory VII against the Normans of southern Italy. After that, said Gregory, they would be able to cross over to Constantinople 'to bring aid to Christians who are grievously afflicted by the most frequent ravagings of the Saracens'.[122] His commitment was reaffirmed by his meeting with Adhémar of Le Puy in 1087,[123] and it is not surprising that Urban chose to contact him in advance of his Clermont speech. Later generations therefore saw Raymond's exploits in a quite different light, which made him an appropriate choice for William of Tyre when he wished to inspire what the archbishop saw as the lesser men of his own generation. 'We believe,' says William,

> that the notable perseverance and courage of the venerable Raymond should be admired and lauded not only by the present generation but by those of the future as well. For when he had once undertaken the pilgrimage for Christ, he patiently and resolutely continued on that way to the very end of his life. In his native land he was a distinguished man of very great power, possessed of extensive ancestral holdings, and he might have had in abundance everything he desired. Yet he chose to leave land and kindred in humble obedience to the Lord rather than flourish in the tabernacles of sinners among his own people. After the Holy City had been restored to freedom, the other leaders who had undertaken the same pilgrimage felt that they had obtained fulfillment of their desires and returned to their own lands. But he, having once assumed the cross, feared to lay it aside. Even when his own friends and members of his household eagerly suggested that, since his vow had been accomplished, he should return to the country which so longed for his presence, he preferred to offer himself as a holocaust to the Lord, rather than to return to the attractions of the world.[124]

A state based on Tripoli and Homs would have made its ruler a major player in Syrian politics, but in the end Raymond captured neither, and the county he founded was mainly confined to the coastal region between the sea and the Lebanese mountains. In this situation the defence of the passes became vital, especially in the north of the county, where the mountains were lower and the coastal plain around the Kebir River more accessible through al-Buqai'ah. Equally, however, conflict with the inland cities of the valleys of the Litani and the Upper Orontes was muted by the commercial needs of both Christians and Muslims, for Tortosa and Tripoli were the natural outlets for Hama, Homs and Baalbek.[125]

Not surprisingly, therefore, Raymond's designated successor, William-Jordan, his cousin and a companion on the crusade between 1096 and 1099, continued to press Tripoli, aided at times by Byzantine ships, and its ruler, Fahkr al-Mulk, became increasingly desperate. In 1108, the latter paid a personal visit to the caliph and sultan in Baghdad, where he was lavishly treated but ultimately gained no more than promises of support. When he returned, he found the Tripolitan nobles had called in the Egyptians, and he was obliged to take refuge in Jabala.[126] Tripoli, situated at the limit of the range of the Egyptian fleets, now became a key strategic goal for the Latins but, partly because of this, it also served as a focal point for Frankish rivalries.

These rivalries were complicated by Raymond's legacy, for as well as leaving an adult son, Bertrand, from his first marriage, by his second wife, Elvira, he had also fathered another son, Alfonso-Jordan, who was aged only three at the count's death. Moreover, he seems to have maintained links with the county of Toulouse, which served to unsettle even further the succession in Tripoli.[127] Thus, although Bertrand had been accepted as ruler of Toulouse, when the barons invited Elvira to bring Alfonso-Jordan to the West in 1108, he naturally looked towards Raymond's Syrian lands. Bertrand's arrival in the East in March 1109, with a large force of 4,000 soldiers and forty galleys, as well as about sixty Genoese ships, was, in one sense, a welcome addition to the exiguous forces trying to conquer Syria, but at the same time it constituted a direct threat to William-Jordan, who had exerted enough pressure on the Tripolitans to force a change of ruler, and had added Arqa to Raymond's conquests in 1108.

The events that followed culminated in the defining moment for the settlers of the first generation. Bertrand first tried to gain Tancred's support, but when this failed he brought his forces to the siege of Tripoli, while at the same time pressing William-Jordan at his base on Mount Pilgrim. Both sides looked for outside help, William-Jordan to Tancred and Bertrand to King Baldwin. According to Albert of Aachen, Bertrand sent envoys to the king, complaining that William-Jordan and Tancred were using force to prevent him entering his father's cities and 'on this account he badly needed his help to deal with these injustices, asserting that he himself would remain in his allegiance'. This appeal to Baldwin's overlordship opened an opportunity that the king immediately grasped, for he sent Pagan of Haifa and Eustace Grenier, two of the kingdom's leading nobles, to summon the parties concerned, as well as Baldwin of Bourcq and Joscelin of Courtenay to what Albert calls 'an assembly and council'. Eustace Grenier may well have played a key role in preparing the ground, for he appears to have been one of Baldwin's long-term companions, probably a rear-vassal of Eustace of Boulogne, the king's brother, who had accompanied him on crusade.[128]

At the assembly, which took place near Tripoli in June 1109, when 'all the injuries on both sides had been recited in the presence of the king and his loyal men', Baldwin handed down his judgments. Baldwin of Bourcq and Tancred were reconciled and Tancred returned Baldwin's lands. The king regranted to Tancred his original conquests in what had since become the kingdom of Jerusalem, which were listed as Haifa, the Temple of the Lord in Jerusalem, Tiberias and Nazareth, 'when he had received loyalty from him'. Bertrand, who had already sworn allegiance to the king, was granted his father's inheritance, except for Tortosa and Arqa, which were to be held by

William-Jordan.[129] In fact, William-Jordan did not benefit, as he was murdered soon after, either in a night ambush or in a dispute with Bertrand's squires over his crops. Fulcher of Chartres says that 'all asked who had done it, but they were not able to find out'.[130] Whoever was responsible, the effect was to further the king's influence for, by 1111, William, an illegitimate son of Robert of Normandy, had become lord of Tortosa. William had come to the kingdom of Jerusalem in 1106 after the defeat of his father at Tinchebrai and had since become one of Baldwin's trusted military leaders, so his acquisition of Tortosa was evidently an expression of the royal will.[131]

The assembly was a landmark in the early history of the crusader states, for which it had no precedent. However, it can readily be compared to contemporary judicial practices in north-western Europe, which are closely associated with the development of royal power. There are striking similarities with the great trials ordered by William the Conqueror in England, which were instituted by royal writ and presided over by the king's representatives. At Pinnenden Heath, near Maidstone, for example, in 1072 or 1075–6, a long-running dispute between Odo of Bayeux and Lanfranc, archbishop of Canterbury, was settled through the judgment of Geoffrey, bishop of Coutances, acting in the king's name.[132] The difference lies in the context. By holding sessions in the shire courts, William was able to make use of existing Anglo-Saxon legal customs, but such traditions were not available to the embryonic Latin states in the East, so that the parties concerned were obliged to look back to their places of origin for models of dispute settlement. Baldwin was aware of the potential difficulties, according to Albert of Aachen, carefully using the phrase 'it pleases the whole church of Jerusalem' when summoning Tancred and William-Jordan, neither of whom was his vassal as such.

The immediate military consequence was the collapse of the long-standing resistance of the Tripolitans, faced now by both the combined forces of the major leaders and a maritime blockade. On about 26 June, they therefore surrendered to the king on the basis of a safe-conduct out of the city, evidently fearing a repeat of the massacre that had occurred at Acre. Even so, according to Fulcher of Chartres, the king was unable to control the lower classes (*minores*) among the Genoese, who scaled the walls and killed any inhabitants they came across.[133] Ibn al-Qalanisi's account of plunder and enslavement is therefore plausible, painting a picture of a prosperous and cultured city badly damaged by the Franks: 'the quantities of material that fell into their hands from its merchandise and storehouses, and the books in its college and in the libraries of private owners, exceed all computation.'[134] Whatever the full extent of the seizures, the Genoese were granted a third of the city for their help, while their existing third share of Gibelet was now converted into full possession.[135]

The significance of the fall of Tripoli can be measured by the behaviour of the Egyptian fleet, which was sent to help the city resist but arrived eight days late. Ibn al-Qalanisi describes it as 'such a fleet as had never before been dispatched by the Egyptians in regard to the number of men and vessels and quantity of equipment and provisions.' Despite this, its commanders could not help; the populations of Tyre, Sidon and Beirut 'made representations of their lamentable condition, and their incapacity to fight the Franks, but the fleet could not stay and returned to Egypt.'[136] The fleet could not stay because, lacking watering facilities, its range and time at sea were subject to rigid constraints, and its failure to arrive in time inevitably forced it to return to Egypt or risk destruction.[137] Shipping lost could not easily be replaced, for Egypt had very little timber and, from now on, access to supplies would be limited mainly to contraband.[138] The wood that was available was now exported through Syrian ports such as Latakia and Tortosa, which the Latins controlled.[139] The capture of Tripoli therefore not only gained the Franks a valuable city, it also severely limited the operational viability of Egypt's navy, conceding domination of the north-eastern Mediterranean to Christian shipping until the 1180s, when Saladin once more tried to challenge Christian naval supremacy.

With the fall of Tripoli, as William of Tyre perceived, 'there still remained on our shore four rebellious cities: namely Beirut, Sidon, Tyre, and Ascalon, a circumstance which greatly hindered our plans for enlarging our young kingdom.'[140] While Tripoli held out, these managed to survive by paying tribute but, as their plea to the fleet shows, they were now very aware of their vulnerability. Two of them – Beirut and Sidon – fell in the course of 1110, on 13 May and 5 December respectively. Both capitulated because of the combined use of land and sea power, by the Genoese at Beirut, and by the Norwegians and Venetians at Sidon. The Norwegians were led by Sigurd Jorsalfar, joint king of Norway, and had arrived with a fleet of about sixty ships. Such a presence was certainly intimidating, and the Egyptian ships in Tyre did not dare leave harbour to challenge it. Neither siege was easy: Beirut resisted for seventy-five days and Sidon for forty-seven. On both occasions the Egyptians tried to send help, and Ibn al-Qalanisi described the battle for Sidon as more hard-fought than any the Franks had encountered before or since.[141] The king granted Sidon to Eustace Grenier, who had played such an important role in arranging the assembly of the previous year.[142]

By the end of 1110, the shape of the crusader states in Syria and Palestine can be discerned. Baldwin was the head of a feudal hierarchy in the kingdom of Jerusalem, including the lands held by Tancred, and overlord of the rulers of Tripoli and Edessa.[143] His kingdom extended as far north as Beirut, while his expedition beyond the Dead Sea in 1100 and his persistent attempts to overcome Ascalon suggest plans for southern expansion once circumstances allowed. In this year, too, is found the first mention of the existence of burgesses (*burgenses*), whose activities came under the control of a royal official, the viscount. Burgesses were key subjects of the king, covering a great range of non-noble occupations, including administrators, professions, traders and farmers, and were clearly numerous enough by this date to form a definable group. They are listed as the third of the Crown's lay orders, after the magnates (*optimates*) and knights (*milites*). By the 1140s, they were encompassed within a more formal legal structure in the shape of a Court of Burgesses, found not only in Jerusalem but also in other royal cities, most notably Acre and Tyre, although it is likely that a court of justice for burgesses was established in Jerusalem much earlier than this, probably in the first decade of settlement.[144] Burgesses held tenancies which came to be known as *burgesia* or *borgesies*, for which they paid a *cens* or fixed rent proportional to the size and value of the property.[145]

The patriarch of Jerusalem was the ruler of the Church, perceived as key both as spiritual leader and as a source of supply for defence, as well as presiding over an embryonic diocesan structure that included the archbishop of Caesarea and the bishops of Lydda-Ramla, Bethlehem and Nazareth, and a developing network of monastic houses, endowed by seculars prompted both by piety and economic necessity. In turn, the monks and canons were the driving forces behind the creation of agricultural settlements, essential underpinning for the military establishment upon which survival depended. However, quite contrary to the vision of a previous generation of ecclesiastical reformers the Church remained subordinate to the king, for whom military needs overrode all other considerations.

This in itself may have reinforced the determination of the Latin hierarchy to emphasise its own superiority over the Greeks. The defeat of the Fatimids in 1105 had enabled Baldwin to place greater pressure on the coastal cities still in Egyptian hands and this, in turn, had increased the fear of the Muslim authorities that resident Christians might be tempted to collaborate. In these circumstances, John, the Orthodox bishop of Tyre, seems to have fled to Jerusalem in c.1106, where he was appointed by the local Orthodox community to the patriarchate, vacant since the death of Symeon II. While this appears to have been acceptable to the king, whose pragmatic attitude to government meant that he wanted to maintain good relations with Byzantium, it was not welcome to the Latin clergy, especially as John proved to be quite a militant opponent of Latin supremacy as well as a polemicist of some fervour on the issue of the Latin use of unleavened bread in the Eucharist. Not surprisingly, at some point soon after, John left for Constantinople and never returned to Jerusalem.[146]

The Italian maritime cities of Genoa, Venice and Pisa had been instrumental in capturing the ports and had been rewarded with grants of specific areas of varying size and significance within which they held a privileged jurisdictional and fiscal status. This created a substantial settlement of Italians in Palestine and Syria, although not all of them were permanent residents. However, for those who were prepared to stay and take responsibility, new possibilities offered themselves in the same way that they did for the noble fief-holders, burgesses and peasant freemen. The government of Genoa, for example, was still evolving; the grants in Acre in 1104 and in Tripoli in 1109 are described as having been made 'to the Genoese of the church of St Lawrence', reflecting the continuing power of the bishop and chapter in the city. In fact, direct government of these enclaves was no more feasible than centralised control by the monarchy: both were obliged to delegate. In the case of Genoa, the chief beneficiary was the family of the Embriachi, which had taken a prominent role in the expeditions of 1099, 1101 and 1109. The head of the family, William, was a leading member of the commune, where he was a consul between 1102 and 1106. In c.1125, the brothers William and Nicholas Embriaco leased from the commune all the Genoese property in Antioch and Tripoli, including the whole town of Gibelet, a position from which the commune was unable to dislodge them thereafter.[147] It was probably during this time that the family built a small seigneurial castle at the south-eastern corner of the town, the centrepiece of which was a two-storey keep, set above a large cistern. Around the keep, enabling the castle to be defended independently, was a curtain wall with towers on each corner and a gate on the northern side protected by an extra tower.[148]

The creation of the county of Tripoli provided a vital link between north and south, making the Christians masters of the coast and isolating the two remaining Muslim enclaves of Tyre and Ascalon, thus greatly reducing the threat from Egypt. This meant control of the ports and little danger to western shipping, essential for military aid, pilgrim access and maritime trade. Moreover, the county of Tripoli, despite the fact that it was the newest and smallest of the crusader states, was more than a mere corridor, for it impeded the activities of the rulers of the great cities of Hama, Homs and Baalbek and, to some extent, even Damascus, strung out along the Latins' flank. Subsequently the defence of the passes through to the coast became one of the highest priorities for the rulers of Tripoli, affecting not only their own position but that of the crusader states as a whole. Edessa remained vulnerable, but it continued to serve as a shock absorber against the formidable armies emanating from Iraq, where Mosul often acted as a focal point for dangerous Turkish coalitions. Antioch, as Bohemond had imagined, had begun to develop as a major state, encompassing Cilicia and the associated mountain passes, the Syrian plain and the former Greek ports to the south, the most important of which was Latakia. In practice, the beneficiary had been Tancred, whose energy and ambition had proved far more influential than the efforts of his uncle, brought to a premature end in 1104. Antioch, nevertheless, had the additional threat of attack from both east and west, for persistent Byzantine claims added to the pressure of the Turkish *jihad*. Neither Bohemond nor Tancred was prepared to accommodate the Byzantines; indeed, the virtual expulsion of the Greek patriarch in 1100 emphasised the Norman determination to Latinise the principality.

Fundamental to the formation of these new political entities was a need for 'self-definition', especially important in a region already moulded by the great civilisations of the past, giving it a cultural and religious depth unmatched in the experience of any of the new settlers. The labels 'Franks' and 'Latins' that they applied to themselves evidently encompassed a wide variety of ethnic groups and to some extent there were concentrations of such groups in the different states. Antioch was predominantly Norman (from both northern and southern Europe), Tripoli was Provençal, and Jerusalem northern French, Picard and Lotharingian.[149] Such differences may sometimes have intensified their rivalries, but by 1110 there is already evidence that integration was beginning to take place. One sign was the creation of their own 'origin myth', emanating from shared experiences, both triumphs and disasters, and the success they had achieved despite all the hardships they had endured. This confirmed their view of themselves as chosen by God and therefore protected by Him. As they had newly arrived, they could hardly have claimed ancient descent, so useful in cementing the loyalties of, for example, the French around the Capetian dynasty, but they could apply the equally potent imagery of the Bible, comparing themselves to the Israelites and seeing their victories against the odds as Maccabean.[150]

Moreover, although he did not as yet have a formal chancellery, Baldwin naturally could not function without issuing charters, and these provided an ideal opportunity to emphasise his majesty. In the charters of 1109–10, drawing on both Capetian and imperial traditions, he was presented as the successor of his brother Godfrey, 'the most serene prince of the whole Orient', while he himself was 'the most exalted and most Christian king'.[151] Baldwin's assembly at Tripoli in 1109 was not only crucial in implementing the necessary political arrangements of a practical man, but also in crystallising the self-image of both the monarchy and the Franks in the East. 'We shall,' the king is quoted as saying by Albert of Aachen, 'hold an assembly and council among us and return to harmony. Otherwise we shall never be able to keep the land which we have recently entered against these Turkish and Saracen enemies all around.'[152]

CHAPTER 5

The Military, Institutional and Ecclesiastical Framework

FAKHR al-Mulk, emir of Tripoli, set out for Baghdad in March 1108 in order to seek help from Sultan Muhammad, the son of Malik-Shah, but he knew that he was taking a great risk in doing so. Raymond of Toulouse had tried to capture Tripoli six years before and the siege had continued after his death in 1105. Meanwhile, the other Muslim coastal enclaves had crumbled around him: Tortosa and Maraclea in 1102, Botron and Gibelet in 1104. As Ibn al-Qalanisi describes it, by spring 1108, the situation had become critical because of 'the continued procrastination in sending assistance'. Fakhr al-Mulk took precautions, paying his troops six months in advance and binding them by oaths of allegiance, yet almost immediately there was a revolt in favour of the Egyptians led by his cousin, which he managed to have suppressed without abandoning his journey. On arrival in Baghdad, he was, says Ibn al-Qalanisi, 'received by the Sultan with such marks of honour and esteem as even exceeded his hopes', and the sultan commanded a number of great emirs to help him to drive away the Franks, as well supplying an accompanying 'askar. Yet he was still in Baghdad in August and, becoming impatient, he set out for Damascus. But he had delayed too long; once more the Tripolitans had turned to Egypt and al-Afdal had sent them a governor and much needed supplies. All the partisans of Fakhr al-Mulk had been arrested and taken to Egypt; he himself had no alternative but to take refuge in Jabala.[1]

In these circumstances it is not surprising that the coastal cities continued to fall into Frankish hands. The ability to build and transport effective siege machinery enhanced the chances of success, for superior logistics could hardly be countered by such a fragmented Muslim response.[2] Apart from the great prize of Tripoli, Tancred took Jabala and Valania in May and July of 1109, while Baldwin and Bertrand had gained Beirut and Sidon in the course of 1110. Beirut was especially important since the Franks could

set watchmen on the mountains above, enabling them to monitor (and sometimes intercept) naval traffic passing along the coast.[3] Each capture made the
task of the Egyptian fleet more difficult, while the schism in the Muslim world
made co-operation between al-Afdal and the Sunni regime in Baghdad
impossible. Local rulers often took their own paths, which in Ridwan of
Aleppo's case meant a predilection for the Assassins, or Batini, as Ibn
al-Qalanisi calls them, whose 'detestable doctrine' alienated the rest of the
Muslim world, whether Sunni or Shi'ite. Not until after Ridwan's death in
1113 were decisive moves made to undermine the power of the Assassins
in Aleppo.[4]

However, while Baldwin was besieging Beirut in May 1110, the king
received a message from Baldwin of Bourcq, who told the king that Edessa
was in imminent danger because 'Turkish chiefs, namely Ahmadil and
Il-Ghazi and Soqman, had come from the kingdom of Khurasan in a great
host' and had devastated the region. The king, however, kept the news secret
as he did not want to lose the opportunity to take Beirut, and indeed thought
that he had time to return to Jerusalem to celebrate Pentecost before setting
off north again with a relief army. In fact, nobody in the Christian world
seems to have understood what was actually happening. Albert of Aachen
thinks that the Turks had been called in by Tancred, still pursuing his vendetta
against Baldwin, while Matthew of Edessa claims that Baldwin and Joscelin
had asked for Turkish aid against Tancred in a misconceived plan that had
rebounded on them.[5] Fulcher of Chartres does not even name the Turkish
leaders, nor make any attempt to explain these events.[6]

Ibn al-Qalanisi, however, tells a different story. The sultan, he says, had
commanded Soqman al-Qutbi, lord of Armenia and Mayyafariqin, and Sharaf
al-Din Mawdud, lord of Mosul, 'to set out with their troops to the Holy War
against the Franks and the defence of the territories of Mosul'. Together with
Najm al-Din Il-Ghazi, they assembled 'in such force as all the Franks would
not suffice to withstand', and determined to begin the holy war by capturing
Edessa. When Tughtigin heard about this, he too set out from Damascus with
his 'askar. News of the Frankish reaction persuaded the Turks that there was
an opportunity for a decisive confrontation and they retreated to Harran in
order to lure the Franks across the Euphrates, where they hoped to catch them
on open ground.[7]

As presented by Ibn al-Qalanisi, this was a serious attempt to bring together
major Turkish leaders in a commitment to a *jihad* against a Frankish presence
that had become all too pervasive.[8] The apparent failure of the Franks to
understand this brought them close to disaster. Baldwin assembled a combined
force, which included a reluctant Tancred, still disinclined to help Baldwin of

Bourcq, as well as Bertrand of Tripoli, Joscelin of Turbessel and a large contingent of Armenians. Although the Latin sources present the Turkish resort to Harran as a cowardly retreat, the Franks were mindful of what had happened in 1104 and, having resupplied Edessa, rapidly headed back towards the Euphrates. Part of the army managed to cross, but most of the baggage train, together with many of the Armenians, was caught on the wrong side, and the Frankish leaders were obliged to watch impotently as the Turks plundered and slaughtered them.[9] Mawdud, says Matthew of Edessa, 'filled the land from the gates of Edessa to the Euphrates river with blood'.[10]

The Muslim invasion did not in itself fundamentally undermine the Latin conquests, even though the destruction inflicted upon the Edessan hinterland and the massacre of the Armenians contributed to a long-term process of decline in the Frankish lands beyond the Euphrates. Indeed, on the surface it looked as if the Frankish expansion would continue: by the end of the year Baldwin had taken Sidon and Tancred had seized al-Atharib from Ridwan of Aleppo, successes that may explain the apparent lack of awareness of the changes in the Islamic world. But viewed from Damascus, there was a new recognition among the Sunni Turks of the need to revivify the concept of *jihad* if the Franks were not to become a permanent presence in Syria and Palestine.

An immediate consequence was an increase in pressure on Baghdad by the Syrians. 'On the first Friday of Sha'bān (17th February, 1111),' says Ibn al-Qalanisi, 'a certain Hāshimite sharīf from Aleppo and a company of Sūfīs, merchants and theologians presented themselves at the Sultan's mosque, and appealed for assistance. They drove the preacher from the pulpit and broke it in pieces, clamouring and weeping for the misfortunes that had befallen Islām at the hands of the Franks, the slaughter of men, and the enslavement of women and children. They prevented the people from carrying out the service, while the attendants and leaders, to quieten them, promised them on behalf of the Sultan to dispatch armies and to vindicate Islām against the Franks and the infidels.' The next Friday they repeated this performance at the caliph's mosque, disrupting the lavish arrival of the wife of the caliph, the sultan's daughter, from Isfahan, to such an extent that Caliph al-Mustazhir wanted to mete out 'condign punishment' to the instigators. 'The Sultan prevented him from doing so, and excused the action of those people, and directed the amīrs and commanders to return to their governments and make preparations for setting out to the Holy War against the infidels, the enemies of God.'[11]

Byzantine agents were undoubtedly aware of the situation, for in late December 1110 or early January 1111 envoys arrived from Emperor Alexius, bringing gifts and letters urging the Turks to exterminate the Franks 'before they were too firmly established in their menacing position and their malice became uncontrollable'. Alexius claimed that he had tried to prevent them crossing his lands, but 'their ambitious designs upon the land of Islām led to a constant succession of their armies', a circumstance that impelled him to come to terms with them. The envoys concluded 'with exhortations and incitements in the strongest of terms to take concerted action to fight them and root them out of these lands'.[12] Ibn al-Athir, writing from a perspective moulded by Saladin's *jihad* in the 1180s, represents the Aleppan delegation as rebuking the sultan because 'the Byzantine emperor shows greater zeal for Islam than you'.[13] In fact, Alexius tried to influence Frankish affairs as well, although at this time without success. Bohemond died in Apulia in 1111, probably in March, but Tancred refused to give up Antioch as set down in the treaty of Devol, made three years before. Alexius therefore attempted to reinvigorate the tie with the house of Toulouse by persuading Bertrand to attack Tancred, but this was prevented by King Baldwin, thus breaking a link established since Bohemond's occupation of Antioch during the crusade.[14]

Mawdud now began annual attacks on the Franks, often in association with Tughtigin of Damascus, a friendship that Ibn al-Qalanisi says 'took firm root'.[15] In 1111, he invaded the weakened and depopulated Edessa; in July, he went as far as besieging Turbessel, thus taking the fight west of the Euphrates. Later in the year Tughtigin brought his forces to the relief of Tyre, which Baldwin had put under extreme pressure now that he had control of the adjacent coast. The siege lasted for four and a half months, but by April 1112 the Franks had had enough and retreated because, in Ibn al-Athir's view, they feared that Tughtigin would destroy their crops.[16] The Tyrians, initially in a panic, now reneged on their promise to hand over the city to Tughtigin but, according to Ibn al-Qalanisi, he simply said: 'What I have done I have done only for the sake of God and the Muslims, not out of desire for wealth or kingdom.'[17] It is impossible to know his real feelings, but it is significant that such sentiments had become the convention among Muslims fighting the Franks. Indeed, the next year, Tughtigin even went as far as making contact with al-Afdal, telling him that he had put in a Turkish garrison but that as soon as he sent an Egyptian governor he would withdraw.[18] Al-Afdal agreed, sending a fleet with supplies in August 1113, with the result that Tyre's 'situation was firmly re-established and the desire of the Franks to possess it was quenched'. Baldwin now made a truce and 'the highways became safe for travellers, merchants and dealers coming from all parts'.[19]

Mawdud returned once the winter had passed, attacking Edessa between April and June 1112, and the next year, more dangerously, allying with

Tughtigin to confront Baldwin in Galilee, much farther south than he had come before. William of Tyre describes this as a new idea, since previous Persian attacks had concentrated on Antioch.[20] They defeated the king at as-Sennabra, the crossing point on the Jordan just to the south of the Sea of Galilee, and Baldwin was only saved by the arrival of Pons of Tripoli and the new ruler of Antioch, Roger of Salerno.[21] It was therefore a huge stroke of good fortune for the Christians when, on 2 October 1113, as he was leaving the mosque in Damascus together with Tughtigin, Mawdud was suddenly stabbed by a single attacker and died of his wounds a few hours later. Ibn al-Qalanisi offers a very complimentary obituary, admitting that he had at first been a tyrannous ruler in Mosul, but claiming that his conduct had been transformed 'when he heard of the Sultan's change of attitude towards him'. Thereafter he became a fair and just ruler and, says Ibn al-Qalanisi in a sentence that may be the key to this favourable verdict, he became 'assiduous in religious exercises and almsgiving, and in practising and enforcing the precepts of the Faith'. He died 'the death of a blessed martyr'.[22]

Responsibility for the murder is unclear although, inevitably, Tughtigin was seen as the most likely suspect. Ibn al-Athir, writing three generations later, recounted what he had heard, probably from his father. 'It has been said that the Bātinis [Assassins] in Syria killed him because they feared him, or that Tughtakīn feared him and so arranged for someone to assassinate him.'[23] The Christians had no doubts. 'Maledoctus [Mawdud],' says Fulcher of Chartres, 'was very rich and powerful and very renowned among the Turks. He was extremely astute in his actions but could not resist the will of God. The lord permitted him to scourge us for a while but afterwards willed that he should die a vile death and by the hand of an insignificant man.' Fulcher claimed that Tughtakīn was 'odious' to the Turks because he had been involved in Mawdud's murder.[24] Unsurprisingly, Matthew of Edessa's view is totally uncompromising, for the bulk of the damage inflicted by Mawdud had been in the Edessan lands east of the Euphrates. Mawdud, he says, was 'a wicked and evil beast', who had brought about his own death by plotting to kill Tughtigin.[25]

Ibn al-Athir says that his father told him that Baldwin had written to Tughtigin when he heard of Mawdud's death, telling him: 'A people that has killed its main prop on its holy day in its house of worship truly deserves that God should destroy it.' Whether or not such a letter was ever written, Mawdud's removal certainly undermined the sultan's jihadist drive. He appointed Emir Aqsunqur al-Bursuqi as governor of Mosul and sent his son, Mas'ud, 'at the head of a vast army, and ordered him to fight the Franks. All the emirs were instructed by letter that they should obey him.' The result was another large-scale attack on Edessa in April and May 1115, causing further damage to the surrounding environment. However, al-Bursuqi was a much weaker vessel than Mawdud. Soon after the Edessan campaign he confronted one of his rivals in Mesopotamia, Il-Ghazi ibn-Artuq of Mardin, over his failure to take part, and was defeated in battle. The sultan was much angered and his threats to Il-Ghazi so alarmed him that he took refuge with Tughtigin in Damascus. Tughtigin was himself out of favour, says Ibn al-Athir, 'because the sultan attributed the murder of Mawdūd to him'.[26]

The efforts of Sultan Muhammad to raise up the *jihad* against the Franks belie the view that there was a fundamental indifference in Baghdad to the plight of the Syrian Muslims. Indeed, more often it was internecine conflict among the Syrian emirs that prevented a united front against the infidel. Aleppo never represented a sustained threat, for Ridwan feared Turkish domination more than he did the Franks, a situation that did not change after his death in December 1113. In Damascus, Tughtigin's conviction that he would be overwhelmed by the Islamic champions chosen by the sultan considerably blunted his effectiveness, while idiosyncratic personalities like Il-Ghazi could not be relied upon to act in any way that did not serve their own immediate interests.

In contrast, the Franks had begun to pull together under Baldwin's leadership. With the collapse of the Byzantine alliance, Bertrand and Tancred had recognised their common interests and, when Bertrand died in February 1112, Tancred had accepted the succession of his young son, Pons, apparently granting him the fiefs of Tortosa, Safita, Hisn al-Akrad and Maraclea.[27] Tancred died in December, and in 1115 Pons married his widow, Cecilia of France. The heir to Antioch was in fact Bohemond's young son, also called Bohemond, but as he was both absent and a minor, Tancred had given the regency to Roger of Salerno, son of Richard of the Principate, now lord of Marash, the most northerly of the Antiochene lands.[28] Roger was married to another Cecilia, the sister of Baldwin of Bourcq, establishing a web of relationships that seems to have been aimed at stabilising the northern crusader states in the face of increasing Turkish pressure.[29] The only real conflict was Baldwin of Bourcq's sudden and unexplained quarrel with Joscelin of Courtenay, whom he deprived of his fief and imprisoned in 1113, before allowing him to leave Edessa for the kingdom of Jerusalem, where Baldwin granted him the valuable Galilean lands centred on Tiberias. It has been speculated that Baldwin of Bourcq was attempting to rebuild his position, deeply undermined by the regular Turkish assaults on Edessa and its hinterland between 1110 and 1112, leaving it in a poor economic state barely fifteen years after its foundation, a situation exacerbated by a recent severe famine.[30]

In February 1115, the sultan put Emir Bursuq ibn Bursuq, lord of Hamadhan, in charge of a large force that included troops from Mosul and the Jazira. 'The sultan ordered them first of all to engage Īlghāzī and Tughtakīn and, when they had dealt with them, to march into Frankish territory, wage war on them and harass their lands.' According to Ibn al-Athir, Il-Ghazi and Tughtigin were so alarmed they sought the protection of Roger of Antioch or, as Walter the Chancellor puts it, they made 'a pretended peace.'[31] Challenged by Roger and Baldwin, Bursuq apparently retreated, a move that persuaded Baldwin to turn back to Jerusalem in the expectation that the Muslim forces were about to disperse. However, with the departure of the king, Bursuq reappeared, taking Kafartab and besieging Zardana, and obliging Roger to reassemble his forces. Bernard of Valence, patriarch of Antioch, called on the soldiers to confess their sins: 'those who would die in the war which was at hand would acquire salvation by his own absolution and also by the propitiation of the Lord.'[32] On 14 September, Roger caught the bulk of Bursuq's army near Sarmin in the valley of Danith, about equidistant from Antioch and Aleppo, and although Bursuq himself was able to take refuge on a hill, he could not prevent the slaughter and flight of his forces. Huge booty was acquired and many prisoners taken. When Roger returned to Antioch he was met by a procession headed by the patriarch bearing holy relics: 'they resounded with angelic voices, "Fear God and keep His commandments", and they received him, praised him highly and revered him.'[33]

The assassination of Mawdud in October 1113, followed less than two years later by Roger of Antioch's victory at Sarmin, severely weakened the Turkish *jihad* and, for a brief period, until the disastrous Christian defeat at Balat in 1119, left the northern states reasonably secure, enabling the king to pay greater attention to the defence of the south of his kingdom. Baldwin had been interested in the region to the south-east even before he was crowned. In the autumn of 1115, he set out to consolidate his control over an area he had first visited in November 1100 by building a castle on a prominent ridge at Shaubak, which, according to Fulcher of Chartres, was about four days' journey from Jerusalem and three from the Red Sea. 'He decided to name this castle Montréal in honor of himself because he built it in a short time with a few men and with great boldness.'[34] It was situated in a strong defensive position upon a conical hill separate from the adjacent plateau of Edom, but there is no contemporary description of its construction. William of Tyre later ascribed a curtain wall, towers, barbicans (*antemurali*) and a fosse to it, although it had evidently been much developed by his time.[35] Within the enceinte there were two churches, the larger of which, on the eastern side, was apparently used as the parish church. A smaller chapel in the outer ward seems to have served the local Orthodox population. In both cases the churches created a focus for Christian settlement in the region, establishing a pattern that was repeated elsewhere.[36] William of Tyre says that the castle had a productive hinterland which supplied grain, wine and oil. The choice may also have been influenced by the presence of springs within the rock which were used to feed internal cisterns.

Montréal appears to have been the first completely new castle built by Baldwin (as opposed to strengthening and extending existing fortifications), and was evidently part of a wider plan, for the next year Baldwin mounted another expedition, accompanied by 200 knights, as far as the Red Sea, which resulted in the construction of two more fortresses, Li Vaux Moise at Wadi Musa, near the ancient city of Petra, and Ailah, at the head of the gulf of Aqaba.[37] His aim was both to dominate the caravans passing between Egypt and Damascus and to have advance warning of any attacks from this direction.[38]

In the early twelfth century, however, founding a new state was not solely a question of the conquest of territory and the capture of cities. Baldwin knew he needed to develop the Crown's own institutions for those functions central to his rule. Crucial to this was the creation of a chancellery, first seen in the crusader states in 1115 with the appointment as chancellor of Pagan, probably a lay notary from southern Italy.[39] Baldwin I's first genuine extant charter dates from 1106, but there is no doubt that both Godfrey and Baldwin issued charters from the very beginning. Lotharingian, Norman and Pisan influences can all be detected in these early efforts, which initially were probably the work of a cleric who had accompanied Godfrey on the crusade and who may be the same person as the Lotharingian called Robert who drafted Baldwin's charters until the advent of Pagan. His chief employment was very likely at the Holy Sepulchre, where he almost certainly held a canonical benefice and wrote charters for the patriarchs as well as for the king. Pagan's appearance may well have been connected to a reorganisation of government in which the king replaced a single viscounty with several, a decentralisation of power that needed an institutional framework.

It is hardly surprising that the establishment of a proper chancellery such as this took time; many of the chancelleries of the West were themselves quite primitive in the late eleventh century. It does appear, however, that Godfrey the Bearded, grandfather of Godfrey and Baldwin, drawing on his experience as margrave of Tuscany, had begun to see the value of producing his own charters rather than leaving them to be drawn up by the recipients of grants; he may not have had an organised chancellery, but he had clerics who could at least edit the charters provided by the recipients into a standardised form.

Moreover, he was using a ducal seal from 1069, and he was followed in this by Godfrey of Bouillon, so that it is easy to see that charter seals would be used in the diplomas of Jerusalem, although the heat necessitated the use of lead rather than wax.[40]

Closely associated with the chancellery were the court clerics, whose formation into a royal chapel suggests a further strengthening of the Crown's institutional structure. All the important leaders of the First Crusade had had their own chaplains, men whose education had enabled them to write their lords' letters and, in some cases, even act as their historiographers. Fulcher of Chartres was the chaplain of Baldwin of Boulogne and continued in that role after the latter had become king, probably sustained by a canonical benefice either in the Temple of the Lord or the Holy Sepulchre, while Arnulf of Chocques, after his removal as patriarch, is recorded as the *scriniarius* of the king, guardian of the relics and treasures of the royal chapel.[41] In the course of Baldwin's reign the royal chapel came to serve the Crown in many ways. Most obviously it provided the means by which the king could worship regularly, even when he was on campaign, as well as offering prayers for the kingdom on a daily basis. To these spiritual duties were added practical responsibilities: the guarding of the royal relics and altar vessels, the keeping of the royal archives, the drafting of royal correspondence with both the West and Byzantium, and even the issuing of charters in times of necessity.[42]

Medieval governments did not of course seek to establish total control, a role that monarchs found neither practical nor desirable, and most were willing to cede 'social service work' to the Church, not the least because of its cost.[43] The development of facilities for pilgrims is a good example of this process. When Jerusalem fell in 1099 the only specifically Latin establishments in the city were: the Benedictine monastery of St Mary Latin, situated just to the south-east of the church of the Holy Sepulchre, and built sometime before 1071 with funds provided by merchants from Amalfi; a nunnery dedicated to St Mary Magdalene, dating from before 1081–2, where the sisters took care of female pilgrims; and a special hospital for men, dedicated to St John the Baptist, established soon after, perhaps to cope with the increasing numbers arriving as a consequence of the growing popularity of pilgrimage in the second half of the eleventh century.[44]

The hospital had been administered for many years before 1099 on behalf of the abbot and convent by a man named by William of Tyre only as Gerard, who apparently came from Provence or southern Italy.[45] Either just before or very soon after the conquest it was separated from St Mary Latin and, like other contemporary religious institutions, was the recipient of donations by the rulers of Jerusalem. Within months of the fall of Jerusalem, Godfrey had ceded a village and two ovens and, in September 1101, euphoric after the victory over the Egyptians at the battle of Ramla, Baldwin had granted them a tenth of the spoils and plunder, a striking concession given the king's constant monetary needs.[46] In 1110 and 1112, the king, the patriarch and the archbishop of Ceasarea all made donations, giving the hospital property not only in Jerusalem, but also in the other major centres of Nablus, Jaffa and Acre. As well as this Arnulf exempted the hospital from the payment of tithes in the patriarchate.[47] There is no doubt these resources were needed, for many pilgrims arrived exhausted and penniless after long and difficult journeys, where the conditions were sometimes exacerbated by the insecure state of the routes from Jaffa to Jerusalem and other desirable places on the Jordan and in Galilee.

After the separation from St Mary Latin, a link seems to have been established with the Augustinian canons of the Holy Sepulchre, who would have provided for their religious needs, notably church services and confession, and many donors continued to associate them with the Holy Sepulchre until the middle of the century.[48] However, they obtained practical autonomy in 1113 when they received a privilege from Pope Paschal II known as *Pie postulatio voluntatis*, which established them as a company of *fratres* directly under papal protection, exempt from tithes on their own properties, effectively creating a new monastic order, that of the Hospitallers. In keeping with the principles of reform, the pope gave them the right to elect their own leader.[49]

To some extent they were little different from other embryonic ecclesiastical institutions in the East, but the publicity generated by increasing pilgrimage traffic attracted donations from the West. The continued flow of funds from Amalfi may have drawn the attention of Roger of Sicily. At any rate a third part of a grant of 1,000 gold besants that Albert of Aachen alleges had been embezzled by Patriarch Daibert in 1101 had been sent for 'the support of the hospital for the feeble and other sick'.[50] Thereafter they received a steady supply of endowments in the West; by 1121, the year after the death of Gerard, they had sufficient property in Languedoc, southern Italy and Catalonia to justify an administrative centre at Saint-Gilles, adding one more strand to the web of interconnections between the crusader states and the Latin West.[51]

These facilities were crucial because a fervent desire to visit the holy places drew pilgrims in greater numbers than to anywhere else in Christendom. Between 1106 and 1108, a Russian abbot, Daniel, possibly from Chernigov, just to the north of Kiev, made an extensive tour, perhaps even leading a diplomatic mission since he brought an entourage with him. Whatever his official status, the visit was an intensely personal experience for him and his account of his feelings articulates what many others must have felt. 'And by the grace of God I came to the holy city of Jerusalem and saw the holy places and travelled round the whole of the Galilean land and the holy places about the holy city of Jerusalem, where Christ our God walked with his own feet and where he performed great miracles. And all this I saw with my own sinful eyes, and merciful God let me see what I had long desired in my thoughts.'[52]

The focal point was the church of the Holy Sepulchre. After the crusaders had broken into Jerusalem in July 1099, slaughtering many of the inhabitants in a bloodbath recalled by Saladin when he besieged Jerusalem in October 1187, the author of the *Gesta Francorum* records how 'they all came rejoicing and weeping from excess of gladness to worship at the Sepulchre of Our Saviour Jesus, and there they fulfilled their vows to him'. Later, in a brief appendix, he describes Golgotha, the place of the Crucifixion, and continues: 'From thence, a stone's throw to the west, is the place where Joseph of Arimathea buried the holy Body of the Lord Jesus, and on this site there is a church, beautifully built by Constantine the king. From Mount Calvary the navel of the world lies thirteen feet to the west.'[53]

The building which the author of the *Gesta* believed to have been the work of Emperor Constantine was in fact a reconstruction paid for by a much more recent emperor, Constantine Monomachus, in the 1040s, made necessary by the destruction wrought by Caliph al-Hakim in 1009. Constantine the Great had indeed ordered the excavation of the cave identified as the tomb of Christ, as well as the construction of a large basilica to the east known as the Martyrium. Between the two sites was a paved and enclosed court, the *triporticus*, so that pilgrims visiting the tomb would first have entered the Martyrium from the street to the east and then passed through the *triporticus*. However, al-Hakim's orders had been quite thoroughly carried out, so that the Martyrium had been razed, leaving the remains of the rotunda which had been built over the tomb in the seventh century. The repairs of the mid-eleventh century produced a larger rotunda resting on eighteen pillars, in the centre of which was the edicule around the tomb itself. Abbot Daniel described the paving as marble and walls as decorated with mosaics of Christ and the Prophets.[54] The Byzantines had built additional chapels attached to the rotunda, one on the north side and three on the south, as well as a large semicircular apse to the east.[55]

As soon as he was able, Godfrey of Bouillon had established a chapter of twenty canons at the Holy Sepulchre, for the church needed their services to assist the patriarch in the liturgy, to conduct masses and to manage the pilgrims and their offerings. Albert of Aachen says that bells were cast so that 'when the brothers heard the signal and sound of these they would hurry to the church to celebrate the praises of the psalms and the prayers of masses, and the faithful people would as one make haste to hear these things'. Until then, he said, there had been no signals of this kind in Jerusalem.[56] The canons were supported by prebends, the allocation of which was set down by Patriarch Evremar in late 1102 or early 1103.[57] As this implies, however, the canons did not live at the Holy Sepulchre and, in April 1112, as he lay dying, Gibelin of Arles, the patriarch, asked the king to establish them as a community living according to the customs of the churches of Lyon and Reims. Two years later, Patriarch Arnulf, who, as archdeacon, seems to have steered Gibelin towards this idea, imposed the Augustinian Rule on the canons, endowing them with a range of incomes, including offerings, tithes and churches. Their role as custodians of the True Cross was emphasised by the grant of all the offerings made, except on Good Friday and when it was carried by the patriarch 'for any necessity'.[58]

Although William of Tyre comments sourly that Arnulf had only done this to distract attention from his own shameful life, this reform was evidently in accordance with contemporary developments, since the Gregorians believed that the communal table was the best way of maintaining standards and avoiding the distractions of the secular world, while in the county of Tripoli, Raymond of Toulouse had already built a church for the Augustinians of Saint-Ruf.[59] Even so, the patriarch inevitably met resistance, since the reform impinged on a number of vested interests, as well as obliging the canons to live under much closer patriarchal supervision than had previously been the case. As late as 1121, the cantor and the succentor were censured by Pope Calixtus II for continuing to live in their own houses and were threatened with expulsion if they did not conform.[60]

In these circumstances it was important that appropriate accommodation be provided as soon as possible and, over the next five years, a cloister, chapter house, dormitory, refectory and kitchen were constructed on the ruins of the Martyrium to the east of the rotunda, as well as an infirmary to the north. The cloister was built over the top of the chapel of St Helena, the dome of which stood out at its centre.[61] It is unlikely that this was part of an overall plan to rebuild the church of the Holy Sepulchre itself, as the axis of the cloister is aligned with the old Constantinian church and not with the rotunda. Both the axis and the unusual situation to the east (rather than to the south, as was more often the case in northern Europe) were determined by the nature of the site and the space available.[62] Although he does not comment on it, the extension of the patriarch's already spacious residence at the same time would undoubtedly have confirmed William of Tyre's view of Arnulf's self-interestedness.[63]

The shrine of the Holy Sepulchre was the most important holy place in the Christian world. However, the first rulers of the crusader states were well aware that, as soon as it became possible, they needed to endow communities at other leading holy sites, all of which had been in the hands of the Greek Orthodox until this time. According to Fulcher of Chartres and William of Tyre, Godfrey had therefore similarly established canons in what the Christians called the Temple of the Lord in the middle of the Temple platform.[64] In 691–2, Caliph 'Abd al-Malik had built a great dome over the rock here, a place sacred to all three great religions. This was substantially rebuilt in 1022–3 after a previous collapse and its rich mosaic decoration restored. For Christians, there was disagreement about its Old Testament associations, but it was universally recognised in the Latin world for its central importance in key episodes in the life of Christ, including the place of circumcision, the scene of the Presentation and the meeting with the teachers. Here, too, was the one recorded act of violence, when Christ drove out the money-changers.[65] Initially, it was served by secular canons, but they probably became an Augustinian community soon after 1114, in the same period in which the canons of the Holy Sepulchre were undergoing reform. They had a prior called Achard by 1112 and he presided until his death in c.1137. In his time a marble floor was installed over the rock and by the 1120s they had erected an altar and a choir on top of this.[66]

Both Saewulf and Daniel report that Christian sites outside Jerusalem were in a poor state, but there are signs that here too under the first generation of settlers considerable effort went into restoration. Apart from the Temple of the Lord, there were canons at the church of St Mary on Mount Sion to the south of the city, a church that incorporated the room of the Last Supper. This had been damaged a century before the arrival of the crusaders, but both Saewulf and Daniel saw a church there, so the Latins must have begun repairs from an early date.[67] At the place of the Resurrection on the Mount of Olives to the east, Daniel describes a small round chapel without a roof or floor situated in a paved court surrounded by a wall.[68] All three churches had priors by 1112, and it has been assumed that they had adopted the Augustinian Rule by this time.[69]

Godfrey also established a monastery at the church of the Tomb of the Virgin in the valley of Jehoshaphat on the western slope of the Mount of Olives.[70] If William of Tyre is correct, the core of the initial community was drawn from monks who had accompanied the duke's army, who had specifically requested to be settled there.[71] Briefly they seem to have been under the jurisdiction of Baldwin, a cleric who had been part of the Lotharingian contingent, but by the time Saewulf saw a community of monks there in 1102, he had become archbishop of Caesarea and had been replaced by Hugh, the first abbot.[72]

In Galilee there were two other famous sites at which the Latins began building almost immediately. William of Tyre says that Tancred, at this time expecting to carve out a principality in the region, 'devoted much attention to establishing churches in that diocese, namely, at Nazareth, Tiberias and on Mt. Tabor', which he generously endowed.[73] Saewulf describes Nazareth as 'wholly ruined and all pulled down by the Saracens', but says that 'a very fine church marks the place of the Lord's Annunciation'. Four years later Daniel saw a tall church with three altars, within which there was a cave with two doors and steps leading down to 'a cell with little doors and in this little cell lived the Holy Mother of God with Christ'; the 'place where Gabriel stood is the third column from the door of the cave'. Daniel was impressed, for he was travelling with the royal party, which was welcomed by the 'very rich Latin bishop there', enabling them to spend a comfortable night in the town.[74]

About 10 miles to the south-east of Nazareth was Mount Tabor, where the Transfiguration took place. Here there were two monasteries, one of which, situated on the south-east corner, had been changed from a Greek Orthodox to a Benedictine house centred on the church of the Transfiguration.[75] In 1100, the Latins had appointed an abbot, Gerard, and for a period, until there was a bishop in Nazareth, he took on the role of metropolitan.[76] However, as both Saewulf and Daniel emphasise, there were few men available to protect either travellers or institutions situated outside the major cities and castles and, even though the whole area was surrounded by a wall, Tughtigin's forces occupied the mountain in June 1113, and it seems unlikely that any of the monks survived. It took two years to re-establish the community.[77]

Nevertheless, however dynamic his military interventions and bold his solutions to the problems posed by the defence of the kingdom, and despite the progress made in establishing a governmental administration and creating an appropriate ecclesiastical structure, Baldwin knew that the ultimate constraint on his activities was money and, throughout the reign, his actions were conditioned by the need to pay his soldiers. He had made considerable progress in establishing a royal demesne, especially in Judaea and Samaria, and had control of important ports, including Acre and Beirut. The demesne varied in size, partly as a consequence of changing political circumstances, but in the twelfth century it remained a substantial source of income, providing returns from proportional taxes and seigneurial monopolies, as well as capitation taxes and forced labour from non-Christian dependants. Incomes from ports were a key resource; despite the privileges granted to the Italian cities, the Crown could still draw on a wide range of taxes. The Italians were essential if ports were to be conquered, but their very presence greatly increased both the volume of trade and the numbers of pilgrims; and although they were exempt from taxes on the sale of goods, their purchases both from locals and long-distance Asian traders had to be made in the royal markets, which attracted a range of relevant taxes. Incomes from non-Italians, including taxes on entry to the ports, anchorage and gate tolls, added further to royal revenues.[78] Moreover, the activity generated by the presence of the Italians further stimulated the economies (and therefore the revenues) of the ports; some of the profits were invested in building, consumption of goods and services, and social climbing.[79] It must be assumed that Baldwin had established some kind of exchequer, which would have been controlled by the seneschal, although, not surprisingly given the embryonic state of many royal and seigneurial exchequers in the West, it has not left clear traces at this early date.[80]

The building of the southern fortresses was, at least in part, a result of the king's desire to exploit the caravan routes, the profits from which he had already experienced when, in 1113, he had gained over 50,000 dinars from plundering a caravan in the pass of 'Azib, about two days from Jerusalem. 'There was not a town [in Syria],' says Ibn al-Qalanisi, 'but had some merchants among the victims of this caravan.'[81] The proceeds must in part have compensated for the failure to take Tyre in April 1112, a siege that had begun so promisingly at the end of the previous year when Baldwin had intercepted a train of camels and wagons loaded with the Tyrians' goods which they were sending to Damascus for safe-keeping. A great part of the proceeds 'the king bestowed with a generous hand on his soldiers, who until now had been weighed down by long want'.[82] Even so, although Baldwin captured 'wonderful and incredible treasures', they were still not sufficient to finance the campaign against Tyre, which was abandoned 'on the advice of his magnates who were tired of the long-drawn-out siege and completely out of possessions and food supplies'.[83]

The withdrawal from Tyre underlined the kingdom's shortage of resources: plundering could only fill gaps temporarily, while the lack of a fleet meant dependence on others to enable a concerted attack on a coastal town to be undertaken. These were the circumstances in which Baldwin and his advisers conceived a plan to draw in the aid of the Norman rulers of Sicily, whose main city of Palermo was the most populous and wealthy on the northern shore of the Mediterranean, except for Constantinople itself. Chief among those advisers was Arnulf of Chocques, in the late winter of 1112 chosen as successor to the patriarch, Gibelin of Arles, who had just died, in an election evidently determined by the king.[84] It appeared to be a propitious moment, for in 1112, Adelaide del Vasto, widow of Count Roger I, who had died in 1101, had relinquished the regency which she had held for her young son, Roger II. Envoys were dispatched to Palermo, proposing that Adelaide come to Jerusalem and marry Baldwin. As ever, Fulcher of Chartres is discreet about this matter, but William of Tyre makes quite explicit the financial needs that prompted the initiative. The king, he says, 'instructed the envoys when they left that they should agree to any conditions and should endeavor by every possible means to bring the countess back with them. For he had heard, as was true, that the countess was rich and possessed everything in great abundance, since she was in good favor with her son. Baldwin, on the contrary, was poor and needy, so that his means scarcely sufficed for his daily needs and the payment of his knights. Hence, he longed to supplement his scanty resources from her superabundance.'[85]

The Norman Sicilians were fully cognisant of Baldwin's position, for the marriage was agreed on condition that any offspring would succeed to the kingdom of Jerusalem, but that if there were no issue then Roger himself would become king on Baldwin's death. Any claim to the throne by Eustace of Boulogne, Baldwin's elder brother, was apparently ignored at this time.[86] This was a deal entered into cynically by both parties, for Adelaide was at least forty years old and had last given birth seventeen years before, while Baldwin had already been married twice and fathered no children by either wife. His probable homosexuality, about which he was discreet but which even so appears to have been known both to contemporary chroniclers and to William of Tyre, makes it even more unlikely that the king would have had any direct heirs.[87] As neither party can seriously have expected children from this third union, in effect the Normans were buying the throne of Jerusalem for Roger II, at this time a youth of sixteen or seventeen, at least twenty-five years younger than Baldwin. The acquisition of a royal title for the son of a Norman adventurer was an obvious inducement.[88] If the conditions described by William of Tyre had been met, Norman domination of the eastern Mediterranean would have been possible. At the very least Sicilian fleets would have had important trading bases in both the principality of Antioch and the kingdom of Jerusalem, and the Normans would very likely have become the main ethnic group in the crusader states.

Adelaide's arrival at Acre in August 1113 was appropriately splendid. According to Albert of Aachen, she had two trireme dromons, each with 500 men, and seven other ships laden with gold, silver and precious objects, as well as a whole range of weaponry, together with a specialist squad of Saracen archers. This was a powerful armada, quite strong enough to beat off an attack by Egyptian ships despite being blown off course into the bay of

Ascalon.[89] William of Tyre's description is not quite so colourful, but it does emphasise that she came with mounted men and foot soldiers, supplies of grain, wine, oil and salt meat, and 'an immense sum of money'.[90] It is likely that Pagan, the future chancellor, and his relative Brando, who became a notary in the chancellery, formed part of her entourage, and it may be that the Sicilian connection brought trained administrative personnel as well, enabling the Crown to establish a proper chancellery in 1115.[91] Baldwin was not the only beneficiary. Roger of Antioch attended the wedding feast and was rewarded with 1,000 marks of silver, 500 besants and high-quality goods, horses and mules, gifts that confirm the Sicilian interest in cultivating the Norman connection throughout the crusader states.[92]

There was a complication, however, for the king was still married to the Armenian wife he had taken in 1098 as part of his policy of establishing himself in Edessa. They had long been estranged, for Baldwin had repudiated her several years before, possibly in 1103 or 1104, and had obliged her to enter the convent of St Anne in Jerusalem, then a small house of three or four women only, although he had added extra endowments at the time of her entrance.[93] William of Tyre, who, of course, knew of the later marriage to Adelaide, says that some thought the repudiation was to enable Baldwin to marry 'a richer woman of higher rank', others that the king had put her away because of sexual misconduct. William himself, who later accuses her of promiscuous behaviour while living in Constantinople, nevertheless claims that, at this time, she had not been convicted of any crime and that Baldwin had acted 'regardless of the rights of matrimony and without the procedure of law'.[94] At any rate, her life as a nun was short-lived, for she gained permission from the king to visit relatives in Constantinople on the pretext of acquiring more endowments for the house, a fiction that was convenient for both parties, as it was evident that she did not intend to return.[95]

Adelaide, claims William, knew nothing of this; indeed, the archbishop presents her as the innocent and naïve victim of the machinations of Arnulf of Chocques, whom he sees as the mastermind behind the plan. This cannot have been the case. Adelaide had had eleven years' experience as regent in the tough world of Norman Sicily, protecting the inheritance of her son Simon, who died in 1105, and then that of his younger brother, Roger. Moreover, Baldwin's repudiation of his wife was known to western chroniclers, one of whom, Guibert of Nogent, always interested in prurient stories, alleges that she had been captured and raped by pirates while sailing from Saint Simeon to Jerusalem and that, consequently, the king had 'banished her from his bed'.[96] It is inconceivable that the Sicilians were unaware of Baldwin's marital state and it therefore follows that, in 1112–13, both parties ignored this inconvenience in view of the advantages they stood to gain from the new marriage.

However, in 1117, a combination of circumstances revived the issue in such a way as to have serious long-term consequences for the kingdom of Jerusalem. Towards the end of the previous year, Baldwin seems to have had a crisis of conscience, brought on by a serious illness. Believing that he was about to die, he ordered the distribution of money and goods to the poor and instructed that all his debts should be paid.[97] 'For this reason,' says Fulcher of Chartres, 'he dismissed his wife, Adelaide, the Countess of Sicily mentioned above, whom he had unlawfully wed, since she whom he had lawfully married in the city of Edessa was still alive.'[98] He was advised, says William of Tyre, by 'certain religious and God-fearing men' to restore his Armenian wife to her former status, an action that necessarily meant sending Adelaide back to Sicily.[99]

Remorse was not the only reason for this course of action, however, for he was further persuaded to it by Patriarch Arnulf who, ever since 1112, had been fending off criticism of the circumstances of his election, his personal conduct and, most importantly, his role in the marriage of Baldwin and Adelaide. In 1115, Arnulf had actually been deposed by Berengar, bishop of Orange, the papal legate, and had been obliged to travel to Rome in an effort to obtain reinstatement. He had succeeded only on condition that he ensure that Baldwin's bigamous marriage be brought to an end.[100] Arnulf therefore convened a council in the church of the Holy Cross at Acre, at which Baldwin and Adelaide were formally separated, with, says Albert of Aachen, 'all the clergy and people giving judgement', their resolve stiffened by the knowledge that an influx of Normans would have a serious impact on their own control of church appointments and lay fiefs.[101] Accordingly, Adelaide was dispatched to Sicily on the spring sailing, leaving Acre on 25 April in the company of seven ships.[102] Later, in the summer, on 19 July 1117, Arnulf himself was restored to the patriarchate in a bull of Paschal II in which the three main arguments against him were put aside, that is, election through royal influence, illicit relations with women and illegitimacy.[103] Sixty years later William of Tyre assessed the damage caused by the collapse of the agreement with the Sicilians. Not only was Adelaide herself highly indignant and insulted, but Roger II was so angry that 'he conceived a mortal hatred against the kingdom'. William of Tyre says that the Norman Sicilians offered no help to the kingdom during his lifetime, although they were best placed among all the powers of the West to do so.[104]

Despite his fears, Baldwin recovered from his illness of the winter of 1116–17 and, characteristically, turned again to the problems posed by Tyre and Ascalon. Both had proved very difficult to take and both had been used as bases for Fatimid attacks. In 1117, the king decided to try to keep the inhabitants of Tyre pinned within the walls, in much the same way as Raymond of Toulouse had used Mount Pilgrim, by building a new castle about 5 miles away, which he called Scandelion.[105] Ascalon had been particularly dangerous because, although no great armies had been landed since the early years of the reign, it still enabled the Egyptians to inflict regular damage on the southern part of the kingdom. At the beginning of 1111, Shams al-Khilafa, the governor of Ascalon, apparently impressed by Baldwin's recent capture of Sidon, allowed a garrison of Christian troops (probably Armenian) into the city, only for the governor and the troops to be killed while the king was away in the north helping Baldwin of Bourcq fend off a threat to Turbessel.[106] Opportunistic attacks from Ascalon therefore remained a problem. One such foray, in 1113, made while the king was preoccupied with Mawdud at as-Sennabra, had caused serious damage to the fragile agricultural infrastructure around Jerusalem, while in August 1115 an attempt had been made to take advantage of Baldwin's absence in the north to besiege Jaffa, initially in concert with an Egyptian fleet.[107]

Baldwin therefore determined to take the war into Egypt itself, an idea he seems to have had in mind since the early years of the reign.[108] Albert of Aachen says that he 'decided to conquer the realm of Egypt itself' which would prevent the city from being supplied, thus making it less 'proud and rebellious', a plan also alleged by a later Muslim observer, Ibn al-Athir.[109] This seems unlikely, since the force of 216 cavalry and 400 infantry that Albert says accompanied him appears inadequate for such an undertaking; indeed, Albert himself calls it 'a tiny army'.[110] Nevertheless, it was a serious invasion, for an eleven-day march brought them to the eastern Nile Delta, where, on 22 March, the inhabitants of Farama (Pelusium) took flight, leaving Baldwin in possession of the town.

Baldwin's vassals now urged him to strike at Cairo before the Egyptians had time to organise themselves, since they claimed it was only three days' journey. However, while the king and his men were in the process of dismantling the defences of Farama, Baldwin once more became seriously ill, news that almost immediately drained the men of confidence. Baldwin was now fully convinced that his end was near and urged them to take him back to Jerusalem so that he could be buried next to his brother, Godfrey, and not be left in the land of the Saracens, where his grave would be 'an object of mockery and derision'. Given the heat and the distance, it would be necessary for his body to be eviscerated and his internal organs discarded so that the rest could be preserved with salt, a task entrusted to Addo, his cook, who had sworn an oath to carry out his wishes.[111] Fulcher of Chartres says that Baldwin's problem was 'the renewal of pain from an old wound'.[112] This probably refers to injuries sustained in July 1103, when, while hunting near Caesarea, he was struck in the back by a spear in a skirmish with forces from Ascalon.[113]

The king survived until the forces reached al-Arish, where he died on 2 April; his remains were carried back to Jerusalem five days later, on Palm Sunday. He was buried in the Calvary Chapel, in the porch of the Holy Sepulchre next to Godfrey, as soon as the Palm Sunday service was completed, for his body was decomposing rapidly and it was considered unseemly to keep it any longer. The interment was notably dignified and splendid, perhaps reflecting the ceremonial that marked imperial burials both in Byzantium and the West.[114] The mausoleum was, says Albert of Aachen, one fitting for kings, 'of great and wonderful workmanship, and white polished marble, grander than the rest of the tombs'.[115]

By coincidence Baldwin's body reached Jerusalem just as the Palm Sunday procession was descending from the Mount of Olives into the valley of Jehoshaphat, and therefore they were able to carry it through the Golden Gate on the eastern side of the city through which they believed Christ had entered in triumph a week before the Resurrection, and which was only opened on that day and on the Feast of the Exaltation of the Holy Cross.[116] This provided an impressive setting, for it was an integral part of the liturgy of the Latin Church of Jerusalem. The patriarch had processed from Bethany accompanied by the guardian of the True Cross as well as the canons and monks of the monasteries of Mount Sion, the Mount of Olives and the valley of Jehoshaphat. When the procession arrived at the Temple, it was met by an assembly of clergy and people carrying palms blessed by the prior of the Holy Sepulchre.[117]

In the twelfth century burials of this kind are closely linked to the development of dynastic cults, based on the assumption of hereditary succession. Albert of Aachen's description therefore lends credence to his account of Baldwin's arrangements for the succession, made in the presence of his vassals on 26 March while they were still in Egypt. 'Baldwin resolved the kingdom should go to his brother Eustace, if by chance he would come. If indeed he was unable because of his age, Baldwin of Bourcq should be chosen . . .'[118] In fact, Baldwin of Bourcq had the immense advantage of arriving in Jerusalem at almost the same time as the bier carrying the king's body, a circumstance that William of Tyre ascribes to coincidence but that must have owed something to an earlier arrangement, since Fulcher of Chartres says he had come to consult with the king.[119] Albert of Aachen's version, that he had come to Jerusalem for Easter worship and knew nothing about the king's death, is not inconsistent with Fulcher's account, although William of Tyre's story that he speeded up his march when a messenger brought news of Baldwin's death sounds more realistic.[120] Eustace, on the other hand, would take time to reach the East, nor would the prelates and nobles of Jerusalem have known whether he was willing to come, even after he had been informed of his brother's death. They were aware, of course, that he had been the only one of the brothers who had returned to the West after the crusade, which might suggest no particular enthusiasm for settling in Palestine.[121]

A council was held and, according to both Fulcher of Chartres and Albert of Aachen, Baldwin of Bourcq was the general choice, and he was accordingly consecrated on Easter Day (14 April).[122] Then, according to Albert, 'on an appointed day', all the leading nobles assembled at the royal palace in what the Latins believed had been the Temple of Solomon, and Baldwin 'granted each his fief, receiving fealty and an oath of allegiance from them, and sending each back home with honour'. He then took a series of key places under his direct control, including Nablus, Samaria, Jaffa, Haifa, Hebron, Acre, Sidon and Tiberias, using some of the revenues to reward 'his nobles'.

The apparent smoothness of the succession is, however, deceptive, for there had been a vigorous debate, vaguely referred to by Albert of Aachen, but described in detail by William of Tyre, who says that some wanted to wait for Eustace and 'not interfere with the ancient law of hereditary succession', while others argued that, given the circumstances in which they lived, a leader was urgently needed. The decisive voices were Patriarch Arnulf and Joscelin of Courtenay, lord of Tiberias, the latter seeing an opportunity to fill the vacancy in the county of Edessa, although William claims that this ambition was not evident at the time. Certainly, Joscelin's voice gained added force from the fact that it was well known that Baldwin had previously deprived him of his fief at Turbessel, and it might therefore be thought that he would consequently have opposed him. Moreover, since his enforced transfer to the south in 1114, he had become 'a man of very great influence in the kingdom'.[123]

William describes the new king as 'a just man, pious and God-fearing', adding, with considerable exaggeration, that he was successful in all he undertook. Nevertheless, William had misgivings, for he felt that the legitimate heir had been fraudulently excluded, a view influenced both by his legal training and by his strong belief in hereditary succession. Indeed, he says that some 'great nobles' had been sent to offer the throne to Eustace, who had reluctantly agreed, only to turn back in Apulia when he heard of Baldwin's election. This supports William's view that there were two parties, although he admits he does not know whether the envoys had been acting on the wishes of Baldwin I, or whether they had been sent by 'the princes of the realm'. William's doubts can be easily understood. Baldwin's relationship to his predecessor is by no means clear; there is no evidence that he was his cousin, as is sometimes said. Indeed, the families of his parents, Rethel and Montlhéry, were much more closely connected to the Ile-de-France than to Lotharingia, where they had spent much of their time in rebellion against the Capetians.[124] In these circumstances the attitude of some sections of the Jerusalem nobility is understandable, for the whiff of opportunism was all too strong.

However, this is a puzzling story in that William says that the envoys set off 'on the death of the king', which would imply a departure so rapid that they had left before Baldwin of Bourcq's election.[125] Hans Mayer sees a debate that developed in two stages. In the first it was decided to send envoys to ask Eustace, but once they had departed a second meeting took place at which Arnulf and Joscelin convinced the others that they should elect Baldwin. This would have been easier than before as the main supporters of Eustace were no longer in the kingdom.[126] That would explain Eustace's journey to Apulia, where news of the choice of Baldwin would have come as a surprise. This scenario is just about possible, but it presupposes an extremely tight timescale, for Baldwin was consecrated only a week after his predecessor's death. Moreover, it assumes that the supporters of Eustace were so incautious as to leave no powerful representatives to prevent what was, in effect, a coup d'état.[127] It may be, of course, that the envoys had set off despite Baldwin's election, to which they were not prepared to accede, since William presents them as urging Eustace to continue on his journey even after he had learnt of Baldwin's election, which they describe as 'contrary to law both human and divine'. Such strength of feeling had some basis. Eustace and his family were proud of his crusading feats, especially during the siege of Jerusalem, and both Guibert of Nogent, who was a contemporary, and William of Tyre rated his reputation as equal to that of his brothers. In these circumstances he must have seemed the logical choice to many of the nobles of the kingdom, although, of course, they were taking no account of Eustace's own concerns in the West.[128] If the legitimists 'were prepared to risk civil war' at this point, then this may have been their attitude from the beginning.[129]

William's account, put together many years later, unsurprisingly leaves loose ends, while those better placed to know, especially Fulcher of Chartres and Albert of Aachen, choose not to draw attention to the evident divisions among the kingdom's elite. Although Baldwin had been consecrated within a week of his predecessor's death, there was a delay of twenty months before his coronation, which took place in Bethlehem at Christmas 1119.[130] Matthew of Edessa says that he had first refused the regency, but that he had agreed to wait a year for Eustace to appear, after which the throne would be his.[131] This does not seem to be very plausible, as consecration, rather than crowning, was the determinant in making a king. Nevertheless, it is difficult to explain the delay entirely in terms of contingent events, such as the time taken to replace Arnulf, who died two weeks after the consecration and was not succeeded by Warmund of Picquigny until August or September, or, more importantly, the need to rush to the defence of Antioch after the defeat and death of Roger of Antioch near al-Atharib on 28 June 1119.[132] Most likely, Baldwin wanted a joint coronation with his wife, Morphia, who was not in the kingdom at the time of his accession.[133] Whatever the exact circumstances, however, Baldwin II was in a weaker position than his predecessor, and this helps to explain the discernible undercurrent of dissent that persisted throughout his reign and that had continued repercussions under his successor, Fulk of Anjou.

CHAPTER 6

Antioch and Jerusalem

NAJM al-Din Il-Ghazi was the son of Artuq, the leader of the Turcoman tribe of the Oghuz that, in the course of the eleventh century, had joined the Seljuk migration from the region to the north-east of the Caspian Sea into Persia. In 1086, Artuq was made governor of Jerusalem by Tutush, brother of the sultan, Malik-Shah, and when he died, in 1091, the city was left under the control of his sons, Soqman and Il-Ghazi. In July 1098, a year before the arrival of the crusaders, they were besieged by al-Afdal, vizier of Fatimid Egypt, and forced to surrender, although al-Afdal allowed them to go free to Damascus.[1] This gave them the opportunity to establish themselves elsewhere: by 1102, Soqman held Hisn Kayfa on the Tigris, north of Mosul, and in 1108 Il-Ghazi took Mardin, about 40 miles to the south-west. These fortresses were well away from the original Artuqid centre in Palestine, but they were much more likely to bring them into contact and conflict with the Franks in Edessa and Antioch. Soqman fought the Franks in the army of Kerbogha outside Antioch in 1098 and again at Harran in 1104, but he died in 1105, and it was Il-Ghazi who made the real impact in the second decade of the twelfth century.[2]

Il-Ghazi was not amenable to outside control. Indeed, most of his career was spent in manoeuvring for power among other minor Seljuk rulers in Diyar Bakr in the Upper Tigris region to the north-west of Baghdad. This was an unstable world of raiding and looting, for Il-Ghazi could not function without satisfying the needs of the Turcomans who comprised his forces, and their chief interests were pasture and booty.[3] Although he contributed to the coalition of Muslim forces led by Mawdud in 1110, he was not responsive to calls from the sultan to take part in the *jihad* and consequently was not present at the defeat of Bursuq by Roger of Antioch in 1115. Indeed, according to Matthew of Edessa, until 1119, Roger and Il-Ghazi were 'very intimate friends', but in that year they became enemies, a situation brought about by Roger's capture of the fortress of 'Azaz, about 26 miles to the north-west of Aleppo.[4] Roger was ambitious to extend his power, most importantly to the key city of Aleppo, which was situated about 66 miles to the east of Antioch and was desired by the Franks for obvious economic and strategic reasons. 'Azaz was seen as Aleppo's 'gate of entry and exit'.[5]

By the early summer of 1119, Roger had placed such suffocating pressure on the city that it could no longer survive without outside help, for the Franks now controlled a semicircle of fortresses to the west of Aleppo which included 'Azaz, Sarmada, al-Atharib and Zardana.[6] The city itself was in a poor state, suffering from decades of misrule, compounded by the pervasive presence of the Isma'ilis, and economically undermined by the ravages of the Turcomans in its hinterland. Although he clearly preferred Mardin, in 1117–18 Il-Ghazi responded to a call for help from Aleppo, a move that brought him into direct confrontation with the principality of Antioch.[7] According to the thirteenth-century Arab historian of Aleppo Kamal al-Din, 'Messages were sent to all the kings of the oriental provinces and to the Turcomans asking for help', for the Franks from al-Atharib were making incessant attacks upon Aleppo and the town was in despair.[8] This atmosphere of crisis is confirmed by the contemporary witness of Ibn al-Qalanisi, who says that throughout the year 512 (April 1118 to April 1119) there had been many rumours that the Franks desired 'to possess themselves of fortresses and cities' and that this was 'owing to the neglect of Islam to make raids upon them and to prosecute the Holy War'.[9]

In reaction to this, Tughtigin of Damascus and Il-Ghazi began to assemble forces and, by the spring of 1119, had gathered them at Aleppo 'in vast numbers and manifest strength, as lions seeking their prey and gerfalcons hovering over their victims'.[10] Kamal al-Din claims that Il-Ghazi had brought more than 40,000 men from beyond the Euphrates.[11] When the news reached Antioch, Roger put together his own army, including a considerable number of Armenian troops whom he had used successfully in the past, and set out for Artah. Here he was counselled by Bernard of Valence, patriarch of Antioch, to remain, since, according to Walter the Chancellor, it was a place well supplied with food and drink, and difficult to approach from the east because of the hills of the Jabal Talat and the dense vegetation in the valleys and along the crags.[12] Bernard must have known that Roger had sent for help from King Baldwin of Jerusalem, at that time campaigning against the Damascenes in the Jordan valley.[13] However, Walter the Chancellor says that Roger 'was advised by certain barons, whose possessions the enemy was accustomed to lay waste every single year', not to wait any longer.[14] As it happened, Il-Ghazi had himself been delayed, for he was awaiting promised reinforcements from Tughtigin but, as Kamal al-Din puts it, 'his emirs, tired of the immobility he had imposed on them, joined together and asked to march on the enemy at once'.[15] On this occasion, the well-known military convention that direct confrontation should be avoided unless the outcome was certain was ignored by both leaders, each of whom was taking an immense risk.

In the event, Il-Ghazi proved the better tactician. While Roger settled his army into its new camp at Balat, near Sarmada, on 27 June, Il-Ghazi began to besiege al-Atharib, a move that Walter the Chancellor saw as a diversionary tactic, but that may, in fact, have been a genuine attempt to capture the fortress.[16] Both sides were now very close and well aware of each other's presence; indeed, cavalry skirmishes led Roger to decide to relieve al-Atharib the next day, and before daybreak the soldiers assembled for public confession and mass.[17] In that sense the Antiochene army was not unprepared, but it was not until warned by his scouts that Roger realised that the Turks had already begun an encircling movement, having apparently reached their positions along routes the Christians thought to be impassable.[18] An immensely fierce battle followed, but from Walter the Chancellor's description it is evident that the Antiochene army had not had time to organise itself properly and sections of it began to run away before others had even engaged the enemy. The turcopoles were apparently the first to take flight, but became entangled in Roger's own battle line as it moved forward. The confusion was increased by what Walter calls a 'whirlwind', which brought up huge clouds of dust. With his men being cut down all around him, Roger was killed by a sword thrust from below that ran though his nose and penetrated his brain, 'and settling his debt to death in the name of the Lord, in the presence of the symbol of the Holy Cross he gave up his body to the earth and his soul to heaven'.[19] Many had already fled by this time, anxious to escape over the Jabal Talat before it was too late. After Roger's death, says Walter, 'the battlefield was so hemmed in and access and paths to the mountains and valleys so observed, that not a single person trying to escape was able to get through unscathed'.[20]

The human cost of the battle was immense. Both Walter the Chancellor and Matthew of Edessa assert that almost all the Frankish military force of Antioch was lost, killed or captured.[21] If Walter's assessment of the size of the army is correct, this would mean 700 knights and 3,000 foot soldiers. Such an assessment may not be incompatible with Fulcher of Chartres's statement that there were 7,000 dead from Antioch, given that Roger appears to have gathered as many men as he could find when he heard news of Il-Ghazi's advance.[22] Matthew of Edessa says his army consisted of 600 horsemen, 500 mounted Armenians, 400 infantry and what he calls 'a rabble' of about 10,000 men. In the twenty-four hours after the battle alone, Il-Ghazi slaughtered over 500 prisoners who were captured when they took refuge on a hill near the battlefield.[23] Apart from Roger himself, the principality was shorn of its major leaders: Robert of St Lô and Guy Fraisnel disappear from the records and were probably killed, and Rainald Mazoir, later constable of Antioch, was taken prisoner.[24] Robert fitz-Fulk, lord of Zardana, was captured when his fortress fell to the Turks in early August, and beheaded.[25]

Roger's death was a huge shock to the Christians; no other Latin ruler in the East had, until then, fallen in battle.[26] Walter the Chancellor is concerned to draw the moral that the defeat was the consequence of pride, which he expresses in general terms, but he does say that Roger himself had lived 'steeped in worldliness'.[27] Fulcher of Chartres, perhaps reflecting resentment in Jerusalem at the need to bail out Antioch, is much blunter, describing the Antiochenes as sunk in materialism and accusing Roger himself of many adulteries.[28] Not surprisingly, both chroniclers believed that God had withdrawn his favour.

Antioch was now very vulnerable. There were few Frankish defenders, and the city was dependent on the leadership of the senior clergy under Patriarch Bernard. At the same time the indigenous population, which Walter the Chancellor openly admits had been unjustly treated by the Franks, 'wanted to return evil for evil', raising the possibility of internal treachery, as had occurred during the crusaders' own siege in 1098.[29] This undercurrent of discontent may well be the reason why Matthew of Edessa describes Roger as 'an arrogant and prideful man'.[30] Il-Ghazi's army certainly terrorised the principality: Matthew says that the Turks ravaged the whole country from the Euphrates to the Mediterranean, 'bringing bloodshed and enslavement', while Walter the Chancellor describes how 'he often sent thousands of soldiers throughout regions far and near who returned to him day after day refreshed and laden with spoils both of men and of other things'.[31] The monastic communities established on the Black Mountain were especially easy targets and many of the monks were massacred.[32] Il-Ghazi, however, did not attack Antioch, as its inhabitants clearly feared, but instead used the time before the appearance of King Baldwin – probably about a month – to take the Frankish fortresses of Artah and 'Imm in the region to the west of Aleppo, and then, while the king was assembling his forces, al-Atharib and Zardana.[33]

Baldwin, together with Pons, count of Tripoli, probably arrived in late July, having already encountered groups of Turcomans raiding the principality, some as far west as the coast. The one detailed account of what followed is by Walter the Chancellor, who must have put this together from witnesses and perhaps from his own archival research, since at this time he was almost certainly in captivity in Aleppo.[34] Baldwin's first action was to establish his authority in the principality. He was accepted as prince until the rightful heir, Bohemond II, came of age, when he would marry Alice, the king's second daughter. However, all existing landholdings were to be protected, a provision apparently aimed at preventing any major redistribution of fiefs by Bohemond.[35] This was a long-term commitment, since Bohemond was only about nine years old at this time and was living in Apulia. Uncharacteristically, Fulcher of Chartres rather grandiloquently says that 'God conceded him [Baldwin] the length and breadth of the land from Egypt to Mesopotamia', a power much greater than that of his predecessors, although it proved a heavy responsibility that was to cause the king much trouble throughout the 1120s.[36]

There was no way that Il-Ghazi could now avoid another great battle if he were to keep the gains made after what the Franks called the 'Field of Blood'. Baldwin assembled all the forces he could call on, including Edessene troops (apparently not present at Balat) and Alan, lord of al-Atharib, whose departure may well have enabled Il-Ghazi to take the fortress there. After a great show of penitence the combined army set out from Antioch, protected by the True Cross, which had been brought from Jerusalem. Baldwin encamped near Tell Danith, south-west of Zardana, apparently at the same place as Roger before his victory in 1115. By this time Tughtigin had finally joined Il-Ghazi, and further reinforcements had arrived under the local Bedouin leader, Dubais ibn Sadaqa.[37] On 14 August, the Turks attempted to encircle the Christians, as they had done in June, but Baldwin was wary enough to prevent this from succeeding. Nevertheless, both sides suffered heavy casualties in what became a very confused battle. Evremar of Chocques, archbishop of Ceasarea, holding the True Cross, was hit by an arrow, and Baldwin's horse was wounded. In the end, Walter the Chancellor claims it as a Christian victory, although Matthew of Edessa is probably more accurate when he says that 'neither side was defeated or was victorious'.[38] Fulcher of Chartres says that Baldwin remained at Tell Danith for another forty-eight hours, waiting to see whether the Turks would return, and only departed when he was sure that the fighting had finished, which indicates that he believed that a substantial part of the Turkish army was still intact.[39] Walter's view is nevertheless understandable, for the king had fought off the immediate threat to Antioch and was given 'a victor's welcome' by the patriarch and people when he returned to the city.[40]

Although the leadership was decimated, the territorial losses of the principality were small in comparison with the aftermath of the battle of Harran in 1104.[41] This accords with the views of Fulcher of Chartres and William of Tyre, both of whom emphasise the seriousness of the defeat at Harran in

Map 11
Losses of territory in the principality of Antioch after the battles of Harran (1104)
and the Field of Blood (1119)

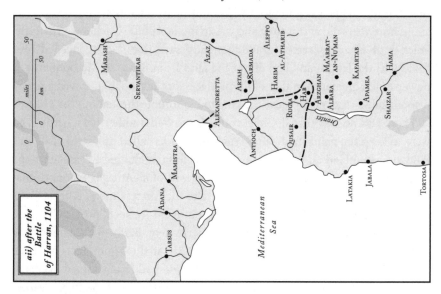

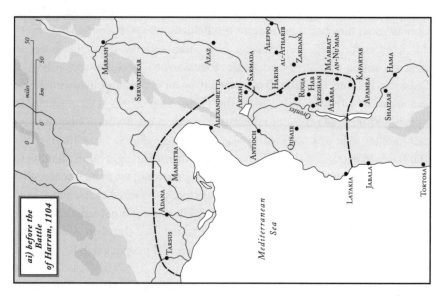

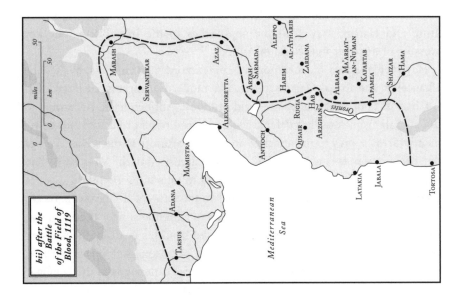

bii) after the Battle of the Field of Blood, 1119

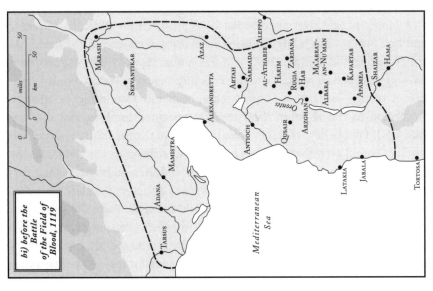

bi) before the Battle of the Field of Blood, 1119

comparison with other battles.[42] The main impact was along Antioch's eastern frontier, where Roger's aggressive attempts to threaten Aleppo had been negated, and the important fortresses of Sarmada, al-Atharib and Zardana, which formed an outer circle facing Aleppo, had fallen to the Turks. Il-Ghazi now also controlled most of the lands beyond the Orontes, including Artah, 'Imm and Harim, as well as the approaches to the Iron Bridge, the key crossing of the river to the east of Antioch.[43]

However, the two most important contemporary chroniclers, Walter the Chancellor and Ibn al-Qalanisi, were, like modern historians, surprised that Il-Ghazi did not attack, after the Field of Blood, Antioch itself. According to Ibn al-Qalanisi, it was 'left defenceless and bereft of its protectors and trusty men-at-arms, a prey to the attacker, and an opportunity to the seeker'. Part of the explanation is suggested by Ibn al-Qalanisi himself, who says that, although Antioch lay open, no one thought to take it, as Tughtigin was not there.[44] This suggests that the answer lies in the flaws of Il-Ghazi's character, which were well known to both Muslims and Christians: he was easily incapacitated by wine, while he could be diverted from his goals by the pleasure he took in plunder and the sadistic treatment of prisoners.[45] Muslim writers, who had their own agendas, liked to frame these campaigns in the language of jihad, but Il-Ghazi himself had never shown much interest in the wider aims of the Islamic world.[46]

A longer perspective suggests that he appreciated the difficulty of taking and holding Antioch while Baldwin's relief army remained in the field.[47] As the crusaders had found in 1097–8, it was not an easy city to overcome; even Saladin was baulked in 1188 after his crushing victory at Hattin. For Il-Ghazi, reliant on his Turcomans, it may have been too formidable to attempt. According to Ibn al-Athir, they never campaigned for long and Il-Ghazi himself did not believe that they were the equal of the Frankish cavalry. 'Each of them would arrive with a bag of wheat and a sheep and would count the hours until he could take some quick booty and then go home. If their stay was extended, they would disperse.'[48] Moreover, although Il-Ghazi was better able to control them than most other Turkish chiefs, there are signs that, towards the end of his career, his influence over them was waning, and that he himself was well aware of this.[49] When Baldwin returned after the battle of Tell Danith, the citizens 'wept from piety and sang for joy', but perhaps they had not been in as much danger as they had imagined.[50]

The affairs of Antioch were to play a major part in Baldwin's reign, but in 1119 he was not able to stay in the north indefinitely. It is likely that, during this period, he settled Edessa on Joscelin of Courtenay, as well as making the best arrangements he could for the maintenance of the Antiochene fiefs.[51]

According to Fulcher of Chartres, this meant ensuring that the lands of deceased nobles were received by the rightful heirs and finding husbands for the many widows.[52] William of Tyre adds that the new husbands were of appropriate rank, although it is not clear how this could have been achieved after what had happened.[53]

In Edessa, Joscelin inherited from his cousin a feudal structure similar to that in north-west France. As well as Turbessel, by 1104, there were Frankish lords of Marash, Saruj, Aintab, Duluk and Raban. Galeran of Le Puiset is known to have been lord of Bira by 1116. Two further lordships appear in the 1120s: Quris in the south-west of the county, and Gargar, on the Euphrates north of Edessa, recaptured from the Turks by Michael, son of Constantine, its Armenian lord, in 1123–4.[54] Although the evidence is scanty, it seems that the counts ruled through their own court and officers, which included a chancellor, a constable and a seneschal, and adapted the Byzantine financial and monetary system to their own use.[55] Under Joscelin, the ecclesiastical institutions implanted in the kingdom of Jerusalem began to establish them-selves in the county; both the abbey of St Mary of Jehoshaphat and the Hospital received grants in the 1120s.[56] Matthew of Edessa calls Joscelin 'a brave and mighty warrior', which appears to reflect the count's determined effort to conciliate the indigenous population. 'Joscelin, abandoning his former cruel nature, now adopted a very humane and compassionate attitude towards the inhabitants of Edessa.'[57] Some limited evidence of the existence of Armenian lordships and of administrators in Frankish employ suggests that Joscelin had indeed recognised the value of co-operation.[58]

King Baldwin returned to Jerusalem later in the year, having sent the True Cross ahead of him (he was well aware that its removal from Jerusalem was always a matter of unease in the kingdom). At Christmas 1119, he, like Baldwin I, was crowned king at Bethlehem, together with his Armenian wife, Morphia,[59] and then, once the Christmas period was over, he and the patri-arch convened a general council in the city of Nablus.

The council of Nablus was held on 16 January 1120. It is recorded by William of Tyre, writing over sixty years later, but not by Fulcher of Chartres, the contemporary chronicler most likely to have known about it.[60] William places it in the context of what he calls a kingdom 'tormented by many hard-ships', the most damaging of which were constant enemy attacks and, for four successive years, the ruin of the crops by locusts and mice. These troubles he attributes to 'our sins', and he describes how the new patriarch, Warmund of Picquigny (a town about 10 miles north-west of Amiens), who had succeeded Arnulf of Chocques in the late summer of 1118, had opened proceedings with a sermon calling on people to assuage God's wrath by turning to a better life

and by undertaking pious works. This took practical form in the promulga-
tion of twenty-five articles, 'ordained by communal judgement as having the
force of law', and intended to improve moral standards and discipline.
William, however, does not incorporate the text of the articles, stating that
they were easily available as copies were kept in the archives of many churches.
This is confirmed by the surviving text from Sidon, which lists the same
major participants as those set down in the archbishop's chronicle.[61]

The list shows that this was not an ecclesiastical synod, but a general
assembly involving all the leading clergy and secular lords of the kingdom,
gathered together under the aegis of both the patriarch and the king. The
council was attended by the former patriarch, Evremar, archbishop of
Ceasarea, who had carried the True Cross in the recent Antioch campaign
and was the second most important cleric in the kingdom, and the bishops of
Nazareth, Bethlehem and Ramla. As this made up the entire episcopate of
the kingdom at this time,[62] it seems certain that the others listed also represent
the elite. Thus there were two abbots from the monasteries of St Mary in the
valley of Jehoshaphat and Mount Tabor, and three priors from the communities of the canons of the Temple, Mount Sion and the Holy Sepulchre. Apart
from Pagan, the chancellor (1115–29), who at this time may or may not have
been a cleric, there were four leading seculars, Eustace Grenier, lord of
Ceasarea and Sidon (1110–23), William of Bures, prince of Galilee (1120–42),
Barisan, constable of Jaffa, later lord of Ibelin (1141–50), and Baldwin, later
lord of Ramla (died 1138), but who was probably the administrator or
castellan of the fief at this time.[63]

The first three clauses record a 'concordat', the central element of which was
the confirmation of the Church's right to the tithes.[64] Baldwin I, in constant
need of money to pay his soldiers, had had little patience with patriarchs who
did not deliver what he wanted. Arnulf of Chocques had survived because he
understood this, but he had been shaken by the furore over the repudiation of
Queen Adelaide and had been under pressure from the papacy for most of his
period in office. It is therefore possible that he had attempted to ingratiate
himself with the ecclesiastical authorities in Rome by extracting a promise
about the restoration of tithes from Baldwin of Bourcq in return for his
support in the struggle for the Crown.[65] Evidently Baldwin I and other seculars, such as Tancred, had used the tithes for their own needs, although this
was supposedly 'an emergency measure' rather than the norm. Tithes were, in
theory, paid to bishops and chapters on all sources of income, and at Nablus
it was established that they should be spent within the diocese in which they
had been collected, preferably on parish churches where these had been instituted.[66] In practice, the system was far from uniform. The papacy itself was

responsible for granting exemptions, especially to monastic institutions on their demesne lands, and both the Hospitallers and the abbey of St Mary of Jehoshaphat used these privileges to help fund their much needed charitable activities in and around Jerusalem.[67]

The largest group of canons lays down the punishments for sexual and marital misdemeanours: adultery (4–6), procuring (7), sodomy (8–11), sexual relations between Franks and Saracens (12–15) and bigamy (17–19). Canon 5, for example, decrees castration and expulsion from the kingdom for male adulterers and rhinotomy (cutting of the nose) for females. The last punishment was waived if the husband forgave her, but in that case both spouses were to be expelled. Sodomy was even more serious: canon 8 says that all adult offenders should be burned, although canon 9 imposes only a penance on a child or an adult who had lodged a legal complaint. As the prologue to the council shows, there is a clear appeal to God's mercy here: Sodom had been brought down by the sexual sins of its inhabitants, and the Latins wanted to make their penitence as overt as possible. One consequence of past laxity had been the defeat of Roger of Antioch, directly referred to in the prologue, and it may be no coincidence that Fulcher of Chartres ascribed this disaster to Roger's promiscuity. At the same time canons 12–15 display an anxiety to avoid miscegenation, whether for their own self-protection as a distinct Latin elite, or because they believed God disapproved, or both.[68]

The final six canons refer to matters of more general importance, although one of them has a very specific relevance to the states in Outremer. Canons 20 and 21 deal with clerics who bear arms or abandon their ecclesiastical status, while canon 22 warns against false accusation and canon 23 sets out a scale of punishments for theft. Most startling is canon 20, the first part of which overtly contradicts normal practice in the rest of Latin Christendom: 'If a cleric bears arms in the cause of defence, he is not to be held culpable.'[69] Of course, clerics over the centuries had often disobeyed the prohibition on the carrying of arms, or tried to evade it on a technicality, but they were nevertheless in contravention of canon law. Here, however, where military crises were so common, there was no such reservation. When the need for action arose nobody was exempt from participation, for survival depended upon the ability of the Franks to beat off an enemy superior in both numbers and resources.[70]

Nobody knows who drew up this list of canons, but the drafter(s) were willing both to absorb Byzantine legislation and, where the problems demanded it, to innovate. Between nine and eleven canons show Byzantine influence and four others are related to these, but other canons are adapted to specific circumstances and do not follow any model. Early examples of miniature painting in the kingdom of Jerusalem have similar links to Byzantine prototypes,[71] underlining the problem of creating a distinctive cultural identity in the midst of a world so heavily moulded by its rich and complex past history.

Evidently the participants in the council believed they were facing a major crisis. In the same year, in an effort to alleviate the food shortages caused by the destruction of the harvests, the king removed the tax on those bringing grain, barley or vegetables into Jerusalem, whether they were Christian or Muslim. Tolls on pilgrims were also abolished, evidently in the hope that their presence would provide an economic stimulus.[72] Although it is not dated, it must have also been in 1120 that the patriarch and Gerard, prior of the Holy Sepulchre between c.1119 and c.1125, who had attended the council, wrote a joint letter to Diego Gelmírez, archbishop of Santiago de Compostela, which has evident links with both the council of Nablus and the crop failures.

> We beseech you to protect us with your prayers and temporal arms and to extinguish our hunger with your alms and those of the rest of the faithful, and your holy encouragement. This we write in no little sadness, for as a result of our sins, God has allowed us to be afflicted by more frequent plagues than usual. This is now the fourth year running that the sky has not produced rain and our land has not brought forth its usual crops. The little the earth does produce is consumed stalk and ear alike by the locust and innumerable grasshoppers. Why harp on the enemy invasions? We are surrounded by the Saracens on all sides.[73]

If Diego could not come himself, they appealed to him to 'send those forces you can'. In return, 'we have decided to pray constantly for you and your church, while requesting you to do likewise'. Remission of sins was offered to those willing to undertake penance.[74]

The patriarch and the prior do not explain why they wrote to the archbishop: he was no crusader and seems to have had little interest in the wars against the Moors, which were taking place well away from his Galician territories. Moreover, there was little chance that he would make a personal visit to Jerusalem, for he needed to remain in Galicia to protect his own position (epitomised by his often fractious relationship with Queen Urraca), as well as to pursue his ambitious building projects which continued throughout his episcopate. He was, however, a great man, whose reputation had been developing since he was elected to the bishopric of Santiago de Compostela in 1100. He presided over one of the most important pilgrimage centres in the Latin West and, after several attempts, in 1120, had convinced the papacy that his see should be elevated to metropolitan status, as were all others that held an apostolic body. His successes were in no small part the result of his influence in royal and papal circles, and it may be that news of this change of status was widely disseminated, perhaps prompting the letter from Jerusalem later in the same year as the council of Nablus.[75] Nor were the patriarch and prior relying simply on reputation, for they were building directly on past contacts. The letter shows that the archbishop had been generous before, while very recently, in the summer of 1119, two of the canons of Compostela, Pedro Anáyez and Pedro Díaz, had made a pilgrimage to the Holy Sepulchre.[76]

The letter had the required effect. At some point between 1123 and 1125, Diego held a council at Compostela, at which he promised support for the pilgrims going to Jerusalem and called for a new route to the Holy Sepulchre to be opened up through the Iberian peninsula.[77] Warmund's successor as patriarch, Stephen of Chartres, in a letter of c.1129 thanked Diego for his support and generosity, and sent a representative, Aimery, a canon of the Holy Sepulchre, both to solicit donations and to accept properties already given. Aimery was also to organise the administration of the churches already made over to the Holy Sepulchre in Galicia.[78] As Compostela was visited by pilgrims from all over the West, it was a likely place to obtain donations for the Holy Land.[79]

These contacts created a mutually beneficial relationship, based not only upon respect for two of the great shrines of Christendom, but also upon self-interest. The chapters were united through their confraternities which established a fellowship of prayer, while at the same time both gained distinct advantages for their own churches. The Holy Sepulchre received grants and support from the West, while the status of Compostela was elevated by its acceptance as a sister church of one of the five great patriarchates. Moreover, the strengthening of the links between Jerusalem and Compostela was paralleled by those between Antioch and Toledo, their respective rivals.[80] Warmund's letter served not only as a plea for help, but also to reinforce links with a key figure and a famous see that might offer further potential, and indeed presages the policy of seeking to build up networks in the West that came to characterise the leaders in Outremer in the twelfth century.

Part of the crisis set out in the letter to Diego was caused by the internal state of the kingdom: 'nobody dares venture a mile or even less from the walls of Jerusalem or the other places without an armed escort of knights and foot-soldiers.' Both the accounts of individual pilgrims and descriptions in the chronicles of Fulcher of Chartres and Albert of Aachen stress the dangers of such travel, while the preamble to the canons at Nablus refers to the deaths of many pilgrims and citizens as a result of Saracen ambushes.[81] These were the circumstances in which two French knights, themselves closely involved with the Holy Sepulchre, Hugh of Payns (in Champagne) and Godfrey of St Omer (in Picardy), together with a group of companions, either volunteered or were asked to provide some protection for pilgrims travelling up to Jerusalem from the port of Jaffa.

Hugh and his companions were probably already living in the Muristan on Hospitaller property to the south of the church of the Holy Sepulchre; there they were following a structured life as some kind of lay associates of the canons of the Holy Sepulchre.[82] However, they lacked a focus for their piety and the plan to protect pilgrims provided them with one. William of Tyre dates this to 1118, although in this instance his chronology is not reliable, and the next year seems more likely. Perhaps the initiative was discussed at Nablus; in any case William of Tyre says that it was welcomed by both king and patriarch who, together with other nobles and prelates, endowed the group with benefices to provide food and clothing. The king gave them a temporary home in his residence on the Temple platform in the al-Aqsa mosque, believed by the Latins to have been the Temple of Solomon, and the canons of the Temple of the Lord (the Dome of the Rock) gave them a square near the al-Aqsa to celebrate their offices. The canons of the Holy Sepulchre granted them 150 besants annually for their sustenance and for defence.[83] The knights followed a quasi-monastic regime, living in chastity, obedience and poverty 'in the manner of regular canons', evidently a reference to the reform of the canons of the Holy Sepulchre introduced by Patriarch Arnulf in 1114. The duty to protect pilgrims was enjoined on them by the patriarch and other bishops 'for the remission of their sins'.[84] At some point during the 1120s, when Baldwin II moved the royal residence next to the Tower of David on the west side of the city, they were able to take over the Temple of Solomon entirely, although it is unlikely that its condition had greatly improved since the early years of the century when Baldwin I, desperate for money, had sold the lead from the al-Aqsa roof.[85]

Surprisingly, Fulcher of Chartres makes no mention of either the council of Nablus or the beginnings of the Templars. It is plausible that, if he was indeed a canon of the Holy Sepulchre, he saw no reason to distinguish the early Templars from his own community: in short, to him they were a *militia* of the Holy Sepulchre, little different from the knights who protected the patriarch when he carried the True Cross into battle.[86] In any case it is unlikely he would have foreseen their later importance, for he died in 1127 or very soon after, about two years before they received papal recognition as an order of the Church at the council of Troyes. It is more difficult to explain the omission of the council of Nablus. Neither the view that he did not want to record a royal defeat on the issue of tithes, nor the idea that his chronicle was designed to attract more settlers who would have been deterred by the image of depravity implied by some of the canons is really convincing.[87] It is questionable whether the restoration of tithes should be seen as more than a regularisation of an existing situation, while the picture of life in the East that Fulcher conveys in some other parts of his work is far from idyllic.

William of Tyre is more forthcoming in that he records the holding of the council and lists the major participants, but he does not incorporate the canons themselves. He may not have wished to undermine the image of a generation that he liked to use as a model to inspire what he regarded as his own inferior contemporaries: by contrast, he did include the text of the decree authorising the special tax of 1183, even though it was readily available elsewhere. However, the 1183 decree was far more relevant to his own time than a set of canons relating to sins committed over sixty years before. More likely, William disliked the content of the canons on legal grounds, especially the extraordinary canon 20, which allowed clerics to bear arms.[88] Nevertheless, if the canons do have any grounding in reality, they present an unsavoury picture of life in Outremer, and it does appear that, for their own reasons, neither chronicler was anxious to be specific about the sins for which the Christians were being punished.

Not long after the grant to the Templars, Baldwin invited the Cistercians to establish themselves at Nabi Samwil, a hill situated 5 miles to the north-west of Jerusalem, which was known to the Latins as Mountjoy. Jews, Christians and Muslims all honoured the Prophet Samuel and, since the sixth century, it had been believed that his tomb was here. Pilgrims coming from Jaffa expected to have their first sight of Jerusalem from this spot, and it is probable that this was one of the routes patrolled by the first Templars, a circumstance that may have encouraged Baldwin to make the offer to the Cistercians in the first place.

There was a Greek monastery situated there before the era of the crusaders, and it still existed in the time of Abbot Daniel's visit between 1106 and 1108.[89] However, Baldwin II, evidently aware of the impact of the Cistercian reform in the West, clearly wanted to encourage them to establish a monastery in the kingdom, for there still existed many holy sites without Latin communities.[90] In fact, Bernard of Clairvaux was not enthusiastic, apparently believing that military insecurity and the climate made it undesirable. He later wrote that he had given the site, together with Baldwin's grant of 1,000 gold pieces, to the Premonstratensians.[91] St Bernard remained consistent, for there were no Cistercian houses in the crusader states until after his death in 1153. Even then, in contrast to their phenomenal expansion in the West, they had a very small presence, most notably in 1157 at Belmont to the south-east of Tripoli on land taken from the count's demesne, and in 1169 in a daughter house known as St John in the Woods, at 'Ain Karim, 5 miles south-west of Jerusalem.[92]

The Premonstratensians, however, readily took up the offer, building a church and an abbey there on land given by the king, and expanding their holdings around Jerusalem, Nablus and the ports of Jaffa and Ascalon.[93] They never achieved the influence of the Augustinians in the crusader states but, like them, they were the product of a wider canonical reform and, in 1121, had similarly adopted the Rule of St Augustine. Their founder, Norbert of Xanten, had a strong belief in a communal way of life based on ascetic principles, combined with a desire to convert this into practical action through missionary work.[94] Although this missionary calling became very evident in the Slav lands of eastern Europe, there is no sign of any attempt to convert Muslims, even though this may have been an intention of Pope Innocent II.[95]

As the case of Nabi Samwil shows, prestigious sites in Jerusalem attracted funds and pilgrims, but it was more difficult for the guardians of other shrines that, in a different environment, would nevertheless have been very famous. Samuel's tomb was at least in relatively close proximity to the holy city, but Hebron was 20 miles to the south in the hills of Judaea, and, therefore, despite the antiquity of the site, which contained the mausolea of Abraham, Isaac and Jacob, and their wives, found itself low in the hierarchy compared to the chapters at the Holy Sepulchre and the Temple of the Lord. However, Hebron was of evident strategic and economic importance and the rulers of Jerusalem maintained direct control over it through the appointment of a series of castellans, while in early 1100, Godfrey of Bouillon had established a community of canons there under a prior called Rainier, the members of which were probably drawn from the ranks of the crusaders. Like the other canons, they probably adopted the Augustinian Rule in 1114.[96]

One hot June afternoon in 1119 or 1120, the canons' discovery of a chamber beneath the Haram al-Khalil, which contained the bones of about thirty people, therefore held out the promise that they had found the actual remains of the patriarchs. Almost at once they were identified as such and, on 6 October, were raised and presented in the church above. The canons believed in the discovery based on their reading of Genesis, and their uncritical acceptance of the find reflected their conviction that this was part of a divine plan, which had prevented the bones being carried away to Constantinople by the emissaries of Emperor Theodosius II in the early fifth century.

The story was written up in two treatises – one soon after 1130, the other at sometime between 1168 and 1187 – but it was not received with enthusiasm either by the patriarch or the castellan. Warmund did not want the presence of the relics to be used to promote the claim of Hebron to become a bishopric, while Baldwin, the castellan, had, it was said, hoped to find treasure rather than bones. The patriarch had a point, since Hebron had not been an Orthodox diocese in the way that, with the exception of Bethlehem, all the other sees in the kingdom had been.[97] Nevertheless, the discovery had its effects, for there was a considerable increase in pilgrimage traffic, including Jews and Muslims (which in itself provided an extra source of income, since they could usually only obtain access by bribery) as well as Christians. As a result the canons were able to convert the mosque, itself based on a Byzantine building, into a three-aisled basilica, which, in turn, had an impact on the wider recognition of the church at Hebron, with the founding of a prayer fellowship and the acquisition of many more properties.[98] Ultimately, in 1168, Hebron was raised to a bishopric, partly because of its increased ecclesiastical and strategic importance, and partly because of, as William of Tyre says, 'her connection with those servants of God, whose memory is ever blessed, Abraham, Isaac, and Jacob.'[99]

King Baldwin, however, had scant time to attend to the ecclesiastical affairs of the kingdom. Il-Ghazi, dependent on his Turcoman troops, could not afford to remain immobile for long and, in June 1120, messengers arrived in Jerusalem to inform the king that he had once again crossed the Euphrates and was threatening Antiochene territory.[100] As regent, Baldwin was obliged to muster forces to help and, indeed, it was strategically unwise to allow Antioch to become too weak, given the Turkish threat from Aleppo, Damascus and Mosul.[101] This, nevertheless, created what Fulcher of Chartres calls two parties (*bipertita*), a situation that manifested itself in the form of opposition to the removal of the True Cross from the kingdom. For some, this was a cover to avoid campaigning in the north, while for others, like Fulcher of Chartres, it was a genuinely emotive issue.[102] Royal vassals were obliged to serve for a year at the maximum but, in the end, Il-Ghazi agreed to a truce, which enabled the Jerusalem forces to return by October.[103]

Even so, it was an indication of the cracks beneath the surface of Baldwin's rule, for there appears to have been a growing resentment among the Jerusalem nobility at the need to protect the increasingly vulnerable principality of Antioch. Between June 1119 and December 1126, Baldwin spent less than 40 per cent of his time in the kingdom of Jerusalem, either because he was preoccupied with Antiochene affairs, or because he was imprisoned. In the last months of 1122, between August and December, he even took his chancellor, Pagan, with him to Antioch, depriving the kingdom of it chancellery and obliging those needing a diploma from the king to travel to the north.[104] The removal of both the True Cross and the royal seal must have strengthened opposition to the king's frequent absences and may be the reason why Baldwin did not repeat the experiment of taking the chancellor away from the kingdom.

Fulcher of Chartres was among the sceptics: when Tyre fell in 1124, he commented sourly that the people of Antioch had failed them, 'for they offered no help to us nor wished to be present for this work'.[105] Viewed from William of Tyre's longer perspective, Baldwin's solicitude for Antioch was a matter for praise, as he might have been expected to favour the kingdom which, unlike the principality, he could hand on to his successors. For William, indeed, it seemed that he actually showed greater care for the affairs of Antioch, but this was hardly likely to go down well with the baronage of Jerusalem.[106]

Baldwin's recalcitrant vassals had some justification for their attitude. Fighting in the north was indeed a dangerous activity. On 13 September 1122, Joscelin of Courtenay, count of Edessa, and his kinsman Galeran of Le Puiset, lord of Bira, were ambushed and captured by Nur al-Daulak Balak, Il-Ghazi's nephew, near Saruj to the south-west of Edessa. More than 100 of their men were killed.[107] Matthew of Edessa criticises the Franks as 'mindless and fool-hardy' to attempt an attack across marshy ground.[108] The next spring Balak achieved an even greater coup when, on 18 April, he surprised Baldwin at Shenchrig, west of Gargar, and took him prisoner as well. Joscelin refused to surrender the city of Edessa in exchange for his freedom, and all three leaders were incarcerated in Balak's castle at Kharput. As it was about 110 miles north of Edessa, it was very remote from any of the Frankish centres of power and rescue was therefore extraordinarily difficult.[109] To some extent this was cause and effect, for Baldwin had been campaigning in the region of Gargar in the Artuqid stronghold of Diyr Bakr in an effort to gain the release of Joscelin and Galeran.

Joscelin escaped on 8 August 1123 with the help of some local Armenians, but Baldwin was unable to negotiate his own release until over a year later, on 24 August 1124, when agreement was reached with Timurtash, Il-Ghazi's son, the ruler of Aleppo. The terms were not easy, for he had to promise to ally with Timurtash against his enemies, hand over the fortress of 'Azaz, pay a large ransom and provide high-status hostages, the most important of whom were Iveta, Baldwin's youngest daughter, and a son of Count Joscelin.[110] This did provide some respite, for by this time both Il-Ghazi and Balak were dead. Il-Ghazi had been taken ill and died on 8 November 1122.[111] Walter the Chancellor, who had suffered so much at Il-Ghazi's hands, claimed that 'his filthy soul issued forth from his anus along with a flux of dung from his belly and it was dragged away by the claws of infernal scorpions to tumble into the halls of deepest hell'.[112] The Franks were equally glad to see the end of Balak, who was killed by an arrow on 6 May 1124 while besieging the city of Manbij (called Hierapolis by the Franks). His head was brought to Joscelin as confirmation of his death, and then circulated around the cities of Antioch, Tyre and Jerusalem.[113]

The news of Balak's death was brought to the Christian camp outside Tyre, for the bulk of Jerusalem's forces were engaged in a siege of the city, a circumstance that emphasises how different the priorities of the kingdom's nobility were from those of the north. Baldwin I had been well aware of the need to capture the two remaining coastal cities of Tyre and Ascalon, but he had failed in his attack on Tyre in the winter of 1111–12, while his foray to Farama in the eastern Nile Delta in 1118 had done nothing to dislodge the Egyptians from Ascalon.[114] Both campaigns suffered from insufficient resources, notably lack of naval support. Baldwin II and Patriarch Warmund had therefore appealed to Calixtus II (who had become pope in February 1119) and to the Venetians, probably in the course of 1120 after the council of Nablus, although the chronology is not entirely clear.[115] Thereafter the pope had issued a decree at the Lateran council in March 1123 offering remission of sins to those who went to help the Holy Land and threatening excommunication to those who had so far failed to fulfil previous vows unless they did so in the year following Easter (15 April).[116]

The Venetians had not taken a prominent role in the crusader states since the fall of Sidon in December 1110; most of the other coastal cities had fallen with the help of the Genoese.[117] The doge and leading men of Venice, says William of Tyre, 'had heard of the needs of the kingdom of the East' and had now put together a large fleet.[118] As in 1100, once the Venetians decided to commit themselves, they did so in force. Fulcher of Chartres, evidently informed by participants, describes a mixed fleet of 120 ships, loaded with timber for siege engines and carrying 15,000 men and 300 horses. Setting out on 8 August 1122, the fleet wintered in Corfu, where it failed to overcome the Byzantine garrison, and then sailed by slow stages to the East, constrained as ever by the need to make regular stops to take on fresh water.[119] Fulcher includes 'pilgrims' in his overall figure, which may mean that other, probably German, crusaders had sailed with them.[120] The Egyptians evidently knew of the approach of this formidable force and, in May 1123, seized the opportunity to launch a series of pre-emptive attacks on Jaffa from their base in Ascalon, which were only beaten off with great difficulty. When the Venetians arrived, however, they pursued and destroyed the Egyptian fleet and captured large quantities of booty.[121]

The Venetians were led by the doge, Domenico Michiel, the son of Vitale Michiel, who had taken part in the siege of Haifa in 1100. William of Tyre says that he had wanted to visit the holy places for many years.[122] Christmas was celebrated in Bethlehem and Jerusalem, and it was agreed with the leaders in the kingdom that after Epiphany (6 January) they would launch a joint attack 'upon Tyre or Ascalon'.[123] The Venetians appear to have primed the pump with a loan of 100,000 gold pieces to help pay the costs of the soldiers, always a chronic problem in the East when mounting a large campaign.[124] In lieu of the king, William of Bures, lord of Tiberias and the royal constable, had been appointed as 'guardian', having succeeded Eustace Grenier, who had died on 15 June 1123.[125] Together with Patriarch Warmund, Eustace and William were the most prominent participants at the council of Nablus; indeed, Eustace Grenier had helped negotiate the agreements over which Baldwin I had presided outside Tripoli as long ago as 1109.[126] At some time in the second half of 1123, after Eustace's death, a ruling triumvirate of Warmund, William of Bures and Pagan, the chancellor, had formalised the promises previously made by Baldwin II in a treaty which William of Tyre records in full in his chronicle.[127]

A pattern had been set in the first decade of the settlements, but the Venetian treaty was the most comprehensive. The Venetians would receive a church, street, square and oven in every royal and baronial city in the kingdom, 'free from all exactions as are the king's own properties', together with a square in Jerusalem equivalent to that of the king. The treaty confirmed their street in Acre, granted 'on the acquisition of Sidon'.[128] If they desired to set up their own facilities there, they could use them freely, including their own measures, except when purchasing goods from other parties, when the royal measure would apply. In addition, the king agreed to pay the Venetians an annual sum of 300 besants, drawn on the revenues of Tyre. Lawsuits between Venetians and against Venetians by outside parties were to be settled in Venetian courts, although if a Venetian had a complaint against another party, that would come under the royal jurisdiction. Property left by Venetians who died (including shipwreck) would be under Venetian control. Finally, the Venetians would have a third part of the cities of Tyre and Ascalon and the lands subject to them, although this excluded territories already in the hands of the Christians. The same privileges were to apply to the principality of Antioch, since the leaders knew that the king had previously granted these, presumably in his capacity as regent. Despite the king's captivity, the kingdom continued under the same leadership: all the signatories had been present at the council of Nablus.[129]

However, the treaty left open the question of which city to attack, apparently because the Jerusalem nobility could not agree among themselves.

According to William of Tyre, who says he found this out from certain
elderly men who had been present, there was a heated debate in which
the viewpoints were determined by the geographical proximity of the
various fief-holders to the two cities.[130] William says that the matter was
eventually settled by lot, and the choice fell on Tyre. The advocates of
Ascalon had argued that it would be cheaper and easier to take, whereas
those who wanted Tyre saw it as a city that could, if it remained in Muslim
hands, be used as a base for bringing down the whole realm. It is, though,
difficult to believe that the matter was left entirely to chance. Tyre was
hemmed in by estates held by some of the most powerful nobles of the
kingdom, including Humphrey of Toron, William of Bures and Joscelin of
Edessa, as well as by the castle of Scandelion, built by Baldwin I for that
purpose in 1117,[131] while Warmund had already appointed a cleric called
Odo as the first archbishop, probably in 1122.[132] The presence of the
Venetian fleet offered an ideal opportunity, for Tyre itself was almost entirely
surrounded by water, having only one main gate on the landward side.[133]
Indeed, the Venetians would hardly have been interested in Ascalon with
its limited harbour facilities when they had the opportunity to establish themselves in a great city like Tyre.[134] At the same time, Ibn al-Qalanisi says that
the affairs of the city were in disorder, a situation created by the division of
responsibilities between the Egyptians and Tughtigin of Damascus, and not
helped by the assassination of the vizier, al-Afdal, in December 1121, after
which the government in Cairo 'fell into disrepute'. When the Egyptians
decided to cede the city to Tughtigin, 'he deputed as its governors, a body of
men who had neither ability, capacity, nor bravery'. The Christians, he
says, were well aware of this vulnerability, and 'their desire for it was stirred
up and they persuaded themselves that the opportunity for capturing it was
now come'.[135]

The siege began on 16 February 1124, and lasted until 7 or 8 July, when
Tughtigin agreed terms of surrender.[136] Despite harassment from Ascalon, the
Christians were not to be diverted from what was a unique opportunity. At
Tyre, the besiegers gradually wore down resistance, helped by the arrival of
Pons of Tripoli, whose additional forces undermined the morale of defenders
already suffering an acute shortage of food.[137] Siege towers and mangonels
had been constructed, and an Armenian called Havedic was called in from
Antioch to direct operations. His ability to hit predetermined targets with a
high degree of accuracy was evidently a rare skill since he was paid a handsome salary, 'so that he could support himself in his usual sumptuousness', a
sign of the increasing professionalisation of warfare in the twelfth century, as
well as of its rising costs.[138]

Tughtigin did bring up forces to within a few miles of the camp, but retreated when challenged by Pons of Tripoli and William of Bures.[139] He was, says Ibn al-Qalanisi, now 'aware of the true state of affairs and the impossibility of remedying the critical situation of the town', and he agreed to terms that allowed the citizens to leave with whatever possessions they could carry, an outcome bitterly resented by the Christian rank-and-file, who had hoped for the opportunity to pillage one of the richest cities on the coast.[140] The news was immediately relayed to Jerusalem by the patriarch, where Fulcher describes how prayers and fasts gave way to great celebrations marked by the ringing of bells and an elaborate procession to the Temple of the Lord.[141] It was a highly significant victory. The next year an Egyptian fleet sailed up the coast, but was forced to land near Beirut in order to obtain water, since there was no harbour open to it. Attacked by the inhabitants, the Egyptians had no alternative but to retreat.[142]

However, although he had obtained his release at the end of August 1124, the king did not reappear in Jerusalem. Once again Baldwin was occupied with northern affairs, reneging on his agreement with Timurtash by turning to attack Aleppo in alliance with Joscelin of Edessa and Dubais ibn Sadaqa, the most powerful of the local Bedouin leaders. Fulcher of Chartres, far away in Jerusalem, says that he was either trying to force Timurtash to give up the hostages or he actually intended to take the city, known to be suffering from famine at this time. In the end a siege lasting nearly four months between October 1124 and January 1125 achieved neither objective, and Baldwin retired to Antioch, before eventually returning to Jerusalem in early April 1125, two years after he had been captured.[143]

He did not stay much longer than a month, but some of the time must have been spent renegotiating the treaty with the Venetians since, on 2 May, the *Privilegium Balduini* superseded the *Pactum Warmundi*. The king was particularly concerned to prevent the erosion of royal authority and, with an eye to the future, struck out the clause in the *Pactum* that committed his successors to the agreement, as well as insisting that the Venetians provide military service in return for their property in Tyre.[144] Within days of completing the negotiations, he must have heard news of the fall of Kafartab on 9 May to al-Bursuqi, atabeg of Mosul since the murder of Mawdud in 1113.[145] The fortress was situated about 53 miles to the south-west of Aleppo, and the attack suggests that al-Bursuqi was attempting to fill the vacuum left by the deaths of Il-Ghazi and Balak. According to Ibn al-Qalanisi, he had already gained 'great merit and renown' for his role in the relief of Aleppo and now, as Fulcher of Chartres puts it, he was 'trampling over Lower Syria', having allied with Tughtigin of Damascus.[146] The king had no alternative but to react, but by the time he had put together a small army al-Bursuqi was already besieging Zardana, another 44 miles to the north, midway between Antioch and Aleppo. When he heard of Baldwin's approach he retreated north to attack 'Azaz, strategically important to the Franks because of its position between Antioch and Edessa. Pursued by the king, Pons of Tripoli and Joscelin of Edessa, on 11 June, he was defeated with heavy losses. Not surprisingly, Fulcher of Chartres offers no real details of the fighting, but Matthew of Edessa claims that the Franks adopted the Turkish tactic of feigning retreat.[147] This victory not only relieved the pressure on Antioch, but also enabled Baldwin to retrieve the hostages, including his five-year-old daughter, Iveta.[148] It cost, says William of Tyre, a large sum of money, but was at least partly paid for by spoils collected after the battle.

Baldwin must have been intimately familiar with the territories and fortresses that lay between Antioch and Aleppo east of the Orontes, for he had spent most of his time when not in prison campaigning in the region. The Antiochenes saw the maintenance of their eastern frontier, extending from 'Azaz to al-Atharib and Zardana, as an essential shield and, as ruler, Baldwin had been obliged to try to rebuild the defences shattered by the defeat at the Field of Blood. One method was to bring pressure on Aleppo itself. Frequent changes of regime in the city gave hope that it could be taken, but ultimately the Franks were never able to land what surely would have been the decisive blow. Nevertheless, when Bohemond II arrived in Antioch in the autumn of 1126, he took over a principality little different in territorial extent from that held by Roger of Salerno before 1119.[149] William of Tyre is full of praise. For ten years, he says, Baldwin had given almost all his attention and resources to the principality, and for this cause he had endured nearly two years in prison. God's reward had been the protection of his kingdom of Jerusalem despite his absence.[150]

The strategy of defending the Antiochene frontier made sense for all the crusader states, but it cannot be expected that the nobility of Jerusalem would see their king's almost total preoccupation with the north in the same light. When Baldwin left to tackle al-Bursuqi in the summer of 1125, having spent only a few weeks back in the kingdom, Fulcher remarks that 'he had only a few men from Jerusalem, since in the present and preceding years they had been much fatigued'.[151] This created opposition to Baldwin among at least a section of the Jerusalem nobility and it appears that in 1123, while Baldwin was still in captivity, one group actually offered the crown to Charles the Good, count of Flanders.[152] According to the Flemish notary and administrator Galbert of Bruges, writing in 1127, these men hated Baldwin 'because he was grasping and penurious and had not governed the people of God well'.[153] Charles was the overlord of Eustace of Boulogne, whose failure to claim the throne in 1118 had so disappointed a substantial party in the East. Some of them may have seen the count as a promising choice in lieu of Eustace, now advanced in age and by this time probably a monk at Cluny. Charles, indeed, was in the prime of life and was known to many of them because of an extended pilgrimage he had made to Jerusalem about fifteen years before.[154] In fact, Charles refused the offer and Galbert, whose aim was to present the count as a martyr after his assassination in 1127, used this to reinforce his portrayal of Charles's outstanding qualities. The count, he says, did not wish to desert Flanders, which he had governed so well, but Charles would have been naïve indeed if he had not foreseen the possible dire consequences of any attempt to seize the throne from Baldwin.

Galbert was well informed about Flemish affairs, so it is unlikely that this story is a complete fantasy, and even in Fulcher of Chartres's account there are signs that there was discontent in the kingdom of Jerusalem. It may be that the expedition against Tughtigin of Damascus in late January 1126, apparently heavily supported by the Jerusalem nobility, was aimed at demonstrating Baldwin's commitment to the kingdom, for it resulted in a major battle on the plain of Marj as-Suffar, about 16 miles south of Damascus, eventually won by the Christians after a seven-hour struggle, but nevertheless representing a considerable risk.[155] Fulcher of Chartres and William of Tyre offer no explanation for this undertaking, but Ibn al-Qalanisi says that the intention was 'to invade the region of Hawrān in the government of Damascus, in order to ravage and devastate it', which suggests an attempt to provide opportunities for plunder after the expense of the northern campaigns.[156] Nevertheless, it is possible to overplay Baldwin's unpopularity: neither Fulcher of Chartres nor William of Tyre mentions the approach to Flanders, nor is it possible to identify any barons who may have been involved in the plot.[157] Moreover, there is no sign that Baldwin was worried about a coup, or he would have hurried back to Jerusalem as soon as he had been released from prison in 1124, whatever the circumstances in the north. At any rate the problem was solved for Baldwin by the arrival of Bohemond II in the late autumn of 1126. He was quickly married to Alice, the king's second daughter, and was then invested as prince, after which he received oaths of fealty from the Antiochene nobles.[158]

After the death of Fulcher of Chartres in 1127, there is no contemporary Latin chronicler resident in the East. The chief narrative source for the period is William of Tyre, but William was not born until 1130 and by the time he was writing there were few direct witnesses left for him to consult. Unsurprisingly, William sometimes omits events believed to be important by

Muslim contemporaries like Ibn al-Qalanisi, while on other occasions he has to admit that he does not really know why something had happened. As a consequence, the latter part of Baldwin's reign and those of his successors, Fulk and Melisende and their contemporaries in Tripoli, Antioch and Edessa, are among the least known in the history of these states, and they have been the subject of much speculative argument among historians.

It is clear, however, that Baldwin had decided to continue the 'western policy' implemented after the council of Nablus, which had resulted in the successful conquest of Tyre. Tyre had held out for a quarter of a century, despite its isolation, but a combined attack in conjunction with the Venetians and the other crusaders they had brought with them had ended its resistance. Baldwin now conceived of a similar strike against the great inland city of Damascus, which would have had immense significance for the long-term future of the kingdom and would have complemented the acquisition of Tyre. There was a further compelling reason for seeking outside help: Baldwin had four daughters but no male heirs, and it was imperative that he find a husband for his eldest daughter, Melisende. The death of his wife, Morphia, served to underline the problem, for there was no immediate prospect of further legitimate children.[159]

The embassy that set off from the kingdom in the autumn of 1127 therefore had a double aim: to find a suitable husband for Melisende and 'to invite powerful men (*potentes*) to come to besiege the city of Damascus'.[160] The leaders were William of Bures, prince of Galilee, the constable, who had taken over the governance of the kingdom in 1123 when Eustace Grenier had died, and Guy Brisbarre, a member of a family that had apparently only recently settled in the East but that had quickly risen to prominence, for his brother, Walter, was lord of Beirut.[161] They were accompanied by Hugh of Payns, described as 'master of the Temple' in the confirmation of Venetian privileges of May 1125, who took with him five companions.[162]

After taking the advice of his barons, the king had decided to offer the marriage to Fulk V, count of Anjou. Fulk's western connections were both extensive and significant, especially with England and Flanders, and their importance to the crusader states is reflected in the inclusion of a detailed genealogy in William of Tyre's chronicle.[163] Fulk himself was well known in the kingdom, having visited on pilgrimage in 1120, when he had paid for the maintenance of 100 knights for a year.[164] While he was in the East, Fulk had been attracted by the work of Hugh of Payns and his companions and had become the first western ruler to be associated with them. When he returned to Anjou he gave them an annual grant of 30 *livres angevines*, an example followed by other lords. These links would have been maintained during the

1120s, and Fulk must have known in advance that when the embassy arrived a formal offer would be made.[165]

Indeed, it seems to have been part of a comprehensive settlement, closely tied to the political situation in western Francia. Once again Charles the Good, count of Flanders, had an important role, although this time in death rather than life. Charles had no heirs, and when he was assassinated in March 1127, there was inevitably a struggle for power in one of the richest fiefs in Francia. For Henry I of England, it was essential that he prevent William Clito, son of his older brother, Robert Curthose, from gaining power in the county and forming an alliance not only with Louis VI of France, but also with the count of Anjou; it was to counter this that he proposed to Fulk that his daughter, Matilda, widow of Emperor Henry V and the king's only legitimate heir, should marry Geoffrey, Fulk's young son. Henry had already persuaded his barons to accept the succession of Matilda in January of that year, so this plan opened up the prospect that, if Henry died without a legitimate male heir, Geoffrey would become ruler of Anjou, Normandy and England.[166] Since Fulk's wife, Eremburge, did not die until late 1126, the offer from Jerusalem could not have preceded these events, but it certainly complemented the agreement between Henry and Fulk, which may itself have provided a model for female succession in a world with few such precedents.[167] William of Bures and Hugh of Payns were certainly at Le Mans on Ascension Day (31 May) 1128, when Fulk took the Cross, and would also have been present during the celebrations surrounding the marriage of Geoffrey and Matilda just over two weeks later, on 17 June.[168] The interlocking nature of these agreements is underscored by the presence of a papal legate, Gerald, bishop of Angoulême, and by the papal commendation of Fulk to Baldwin in a letter of 29 May.[169]

Baldwin and the barons of Jerusalem knew, of course, that Fulk needed guarantees, so William of Bures had been instructed to promise that the count would be married to Melisende within fifty days of his arrival in the kingdom and that, in the words of William of Tyre, this would be 'with the expectation of the kingdom after the king's death'.[170] When Fulk arrived in the spring of 1129, the marriage took place before Whitsun (2 June) and Fulk and Melisende were endowed with Tyre and Acre, the two most valuable ports in the kingdom.[171] Meanwhile, Hugh of Payns and his companions had spent 1128 recruiting men for the Damascus campaign and gaining publicity, grants and men for the Templars, culminating in their recognition as a religious order of the Church at the council of Troyes in January 1129. At the council, presided over by Matthew of Albano, the papal legate, and heavily influenced by Bernard, abbot of Clairvaux, they received a Latin Rule of seventy-one clauses. For such a small organisation, this was a huge step, showing the value of creating and sustaining networks of support for the crusader states in the West in the manner developed after the council of Nablus in 1120. Between them, the Templars persuaded 'many bands of noblemen' to take the Cross, not only from the areas that had provided major support for the First Crusade, such as Normandy, Flanders and Provence, but also from Champagne and the British Isles.[172]

The Christians were therefore able to assemble a formidable army for the assault on Damascus. All the other major princes in the crusader states were present, including Bohemond of Antioch, Pons of Tripoli and Joscelin of Edessa. Fulk himself had brought a large contingent of knights and foot soldiers, and was accompanied by important Angevin lords such as Hugh of Amboise, a veteran of the First Crusade.[173] The expedition was given additional impetus in early November, when the Assassins handed over the city of Banyas to the Franks. Banyas was on the main route to Damascus and was an excellent acquisition, as it had a good water supply and had been refortified by Bahram, the Isma'ili leader in Syria, after it had been ceded to him in 1126 by Tughtigin, who was concerned to conciliate a force that he feared might gain as much power in Damascus as it had in Aleppo. But when Tughtigin died in February 1128, Böri, Taj al-Muluk, his son and successor, attacked the Assassins, killing Bahram, and in September 1129 induced a popular uprising against members of the sect in Damascus, during which many of them were massacred. According to Ibn al-Qalanisi, who hated 'the Batinis' as he called them, their new leader, Isma'il al-'Ajami, realised he was in great danger and 'slunk away from Bānyās into the Frankish territories in the utmost abasement and wretchedness'.[174]

Ibn al-Qalanisi says that this news 'stirred up in them [the Franks] a covetous desire for Damascus and its provinces', but it is evident that it simply strengthened a project already long planned. Initially, the Franks established a base at Banyas, before moving to a position near Darayya, about 6 miles to the south-west of Damascus. For his part, Taj al-Muluk drew in Turcoman reinforcements who, according to Ibn al-Qalanisi, were inspired by the obligation of holy war against the infidel, although at the same time he took care to promise them 'such an amount of money and grain as moved them to hasten to answer his summons'.[175] William of Bures was sent out to the south to the region of Hauran to forage for the army, but it appears that he lost control of his forces, which broke up into small groups, each intent on gaining plunder for itself. Taj al-Muluk quickly took advantage, killing and dispersing both the foragers and the knights detailed to guard them. The main forces, now fired up by a desire for revenge, immediately ran into a heavy storm and fog, which made the roads impassable, and, although they tried to struggle on, they soon realised that it was a hopeless task. An enterprise that, says William of Tyre, had so frightened the enemy now disintegrated, to the extent that the Franks regarded a safe return as 'an immense victory'.[176] Even so, the campaign may not have been entirely fruitless, for Michael the Syrian says that, in return for peace and the Frankish retreat, Taj al-Muluk agreed to pay a lump sum of 20,000 dinars and an annual tribute.[177]

William dates the retreat to 6 December, although the army must have set out in mid-November. In any case it was very late in the year to begin such a major operation, especially one expected to take some time, since nobody could have imagined that Damascus would fall easily. Given the fragmented nature of the reinforcements from the West, the late start was probably to enable as many groups as possible to arrive. Ibn al-Qalanisi makes no mention of the storm, but this is perhaps because a victory gained by the bravery of the Muslim forces was more glorious than a retreat induced by the weather.[178] As a resident of Damascus, he certainly saw it as a very significant victory: 'So the hearts of the Muslims were relieved from terror, and restored to security after fear, and all men felt assured that after this disaster it was scarcely possible for the infidels to assemble in full force, so many of their knights had perished, such numbers of their men were destroyed, and so much of their baggage lost.'[179]

CHAPTER 7

———— ⁘ ————

The Second Generation

THERE was no contemporary chronicler present to record the death of Baldwin II in Jerusalem on 21 August 1131. However, according to William of Tyre, he had fallen ill after returning yet again from Antioch, where the death of Bohemond II in Cilicia early in 1130 had obliged him to intervene to prevent a coup by Alice, the king's second daughter and widow of Bohemond. Realising that his illness was probably fatal, he had himself carried to the patriarch's palace, to which he summoned Fulk, Melisende and their new son, Baldwin, who must have been less than eighteen months old at this time. William says that, in the presence of the patriarch and the prelates and some of the nobles, he commended the kingdom to them. He then took monastic vows in case he should live. He did not and was buried at Golgotha with his two predecessors, 'with the magnificence worthy of a king'.[1] On 14 September, the Feast of the Exaltation of the Holy Cross, Fulk and Melisende were crowned in the church of the Holy Sepulchre, the first monarchs for whom this had been done.[2]

Baldwin's death was appropriately pious for the secular guardian of the most important shrines in Christendom. William was only an infant at the time and could not possibly have remembered him, but he must have talked to his own elderly contemporaries in the late 1160s, since he reported that Baldwin was said to have been tall and striking in appearance, with a ruddy complexion, a long beard and thin, fair hair streaked with white, a description that must reflect his looks in the years immediately before his death. William was almost certainly telling the truth when he declared that 'up to the present day' Baldwin was venerated as a man of 'surpassing faith and distinguished service', a verdict in keeping with the archbishop's insistence on the greatness of the first generation of settlers. Even before he became king, he had developed a hard layer of skin on his hands and knees from constant kneeling in prayer and from religious devotions, while his selfless conduct in defending Antioch, even though it was not his own patrimony, was testimony to his integrity.[3] Matthew of Edessa, who, unlike William, was a contemporary, described him as 'a valiant man and a warrior, exemplary in conduct, an enemy of sin, and by nature humble and modest'.[4]

His actions substantiate their opinions. His concern for the moral well-being of the kingdom is strikingly illustrated by his promotion of the council of Nablus in concert with the patriarch, while his strategic sense can be seen in his frequent attempts to bring pressure on Aleppo and Damascus, the two great Muslim cities most capable of inflicting decisive damage on the crusader states. In 1129, had he not been thwarted by the weather, he stood a real chance of actually taking Damascus in a campaign as significant as the more famous failure of the siege of 1148. In the coastal lands, the capture of Tyre, although it took place while he was in captivity, had been an integral part of his plans. At the same time he had recognised the potential of the Templars both as defenders of the crusader states and as providers of links with the West that he was so keen to promote. His initiative in inviting the Cistercians to the kingdom and his endowment of the Premonstratensians are further evidence of his recognition of the need to strengthen the network of western support. In his last years, with the marriage of Melisende to Fulk in 1129, he fulfilled the most basic duty of all medieval kings by providing for the succession of a vigorous adult leader.

Nevertheless, there is always another way of looking at events. Bernard of Blois, famous as an ascetic and founder of what is described as a priory at Jubin on the Black Mountain in the Amanus range, north of Antioch, and fearless in his denunciation of sin, whether committed by Muslims or Christians, railed at Baldwin for what he described as 'certain enormities in his way of life', a criticism for which Bernard's biographer, Gerard of Nazareth, says 'many praised him'.[5] Writers as different as Matthew of Edessa and Galbert of Bruges saw Baldwin as avaricious and grasping; for the former, often the mouthpiece for Armenian grievances against Frankish oppression, despite his qualities, he had 'an intolerable love for money'.[6] As ever more discreet, Fulcher of Chartres appears to imply that Baldwin's captivity was a punishment for sin when he embarks on a series of reflections on the difference between the perfection of the heavenly ruler and the inadequacies of earthly kings. Fulcher comments that 'perhaps he was no king whom we had lost by accident, but He who recently won the victory is not only King in Jerusalem but over all the Earth'. How, he goes on, can one be a king when one is assailed by vices? He had, he says, reached his sixty-fifth year, but had never seen a king imprisoned in this way, although only God knew if it signified anything.[7]

Moreover, his reign was not without internal tensions. His preoccupation with Antioch's affairs seems to have caused resentment among the Jerusalem nobility and there may have been a faction (perhaps derived from the supporters of Eustace of Boulogne in 1118) who would like to have seen him replaced.[8] The manner of his accession had left open the possibility of a later challenge, and it is noticeable that his chancery took care to draft his charters in ways that justified his rule. Three charters issued in 1119 and 1120 in the early years of the reign emphasise both the dynastic and institutional continuity of his rule and his military prowess as shown in his victory in Antioch in 1119.[9]

For a brief period he was also in direct conflict with the patriarch of Jerusalem, for when Warmund died in July 1128, he was replaced by Stephen of La Ferté, former abbot of Saint-Jean-en-Vallée in Chartres, who had renounced his position and emigrated to Jerusalem a short time before. Stephen was a well-educated man of wide experience in both secular and ecclesiastical affairs, as well as being a member of the extended Montlhéry family, related to the king through a common maternal grandmother. He had seemed an appropriate choice. He appears to have been responsible for the creation of the see of Sebaste, an important suffragan of Caesarea, as it was the burial place of John the Baptist and therefore a key site.[10] However, perhaps because of these qualities, he was not content with the status quo and revived a controversy that had seemingly been put to rest with the death of Daibert in 1105, when he claimed that both Jaffa and, once Ascalon had been captured, Jerusalem itself belonged to the patriarchate.[11] The consequence was 'deep hostility' between the king and the patriarch, only ended by Stephen's premature death in June 1130, accompanied as was usual in such circumstances by rumours of poisoning.[12]

Whatever the king's alleged defects, the Muslims had seen him as a formidable enemy and ultimately this was what really mattered in Syria and Palestine. Ibn al-Qalanisi, the Arab chronicler who knew him best, saw him as a much superior ruler to his successor. 'After him there was none left amongst them possessed of sound judgment and capacity to govern. His place was taken after him by the new Count-King, the Comte d'Anjou, who came to them by sea from their country, but he was not sound in his judgment nor was he successful in his administration, so that by the loss of Baldwin they were thrown into confusion and discordance.'[13] There was, indeed, confusion and discordance, for Fulk was faced by two serious challenges in quick succession, firstly in 1132 in Antioch where Princess Alice took the opportunity to try again to seize power, and then in 1134 in the kingdom of Jerusalem itself in the form of an armed revolt by the leading barons of the kingdom, Hugh of

Le Puiset, count of Jaffa, and Romanus of Le Puy, former lord of Transjordan. In both cases the alliance of the disaffected parties with Muslim powers gave the opposition a more dangerous dimension beyond that of internal quarrels.

During the last months of his life, Baldwin had once again been troubled by events in the principality of Antioch. He had evidently hoped that the arrival of Bohemond II and his marriage to his second daughter, Alice, in 1126 would stabilise the government and provide the principality with the military leadership it had lacked since the death of Roger of Salerno in 1119. In William of Tyre's view, Bohemond had made a promising start: in 1127, he had begun a campaign to regain control of the Jabal as-Summaq to the south, and had retaken Kafartab, lost two years before to al-Bursuqi.[14] William had some justification for his optimism: the death of Tughtigin in February 1128 had been preceded by the murder of al-Bursuqi by the Assassins in Mosul at the end of 1126.[15] According to Ibn al-Athir, 'Syria lay open to them [the Franks] on all sides, lacking a man to undertake to fight for his people.'[16] Bohemond was less successful along the Aleppan frontier, partly because of rivalry with Joscelin of Edessa in 1127, and partly because, the next year, the sultan granted Aleppo to 'Imad al-Din Zengi, atabeg of Mosul, whose military skills and ambitions far exceeded those of his predecessors in the city.[17] Nevertheless, Bohemond did appear to have excellent prospects until, in February 1130, he was killed while fighting in Cilicia, provoking a fresh crisis in the north.[18]

In William of Tyre's presentation, the key figure in this crisis was Princess Alice, whose character and motives he consistently shows in an unfavourable light. Her attempts to gain power between 1130 and 1135 were the result of her 'malice' and were steadfastly opposed first by Baldwin and then by Fulk. In 1130, she closed the gates of the city to her father and even sent for help from Zengi, but eventually submitted and was obliged to retire to her dower lands of Latakia and Jabala. Joscelin of Edessa was left in temporary control until a marriage could be arranged for Constance, Alice's infant daughter.[19] However, the deaths of Baldwin and Joscelin within weeks of each other in 1131 seemed to offer her another opportunity and Alice again took over Antioch, this time in concert with Pons of Tripoli and Joscelin II, 'the Younger', of Edessa, together with William, lord of the important castles of Saone and Zardana. William of Tyre says that this provoked an appeal to Fulk from what he describes as 'the barons of that region'.[20]

This was a serious challenge to the authority of the new king. Baldwin I had received the rulers of Tripoli and Edessa as his vassals in 1109, but, in 1121–2 under Baldwin II, Pons had tried unsuccessfully to escape this bond.[21] This was clearly another and more dangerous bid for independence, backed by

Pons's refusal to allow passage to Fulk's forces, obliging them to sail to Saint Simeon. Using his bases in the fortresses of Arzghan and Rugia, Pons then directly confronted the king, resulting in a prolonged and bitter battle. William of Tyre does not mention casualties, but in 1132–3 Ibn al-Qalanisi heard reports that fighting had taken place among the Franks 'in which a number of them had been killed'. Such a dispute, he says, was 'not usual among them'.[22] Fulk eventually prevailed and this enabled him to impose a new government in Antioch under the control of the experienced Rainald Mazoir, lord of Marqab and constable of Antioch.[23]

It soon became clear, however, that, as in the early 1120s, without authoritative leadership, the affairs of Antioch would not remain stable for long. Fulk's intervention was again required in 1133, when he was obliged to take another army north, first to relieve Pons of Tripoli, besieged in his castle of Montferrand (Barin) by Turcoman forces, and then to beat off the emir Sevar, Zengi's governor in Aleppo, at Qinnasrin, about 23 miles south-west of Aleppo.[24] A new prince in Antioch was evidently needed and, not surprisingly, Fulk looked to France for help. In concert with the Antiochene nobility, it was agreed to ask Raymond of Poitiers, younger son of William IX, duke of Aquitaine, who had been one of the leaders of the expeditions of 1101. Fulk himself was familiar with the family, having spent part of his youth as William's cupbearer before succeeding to the county of Anjou.[25] Raymond had recently been knighted at the court of Henry I of England and, as a cadet member of a distinguished family, seemed an appropriate choice as a husband for Constance, Alice's young daughter. In contrast to the very public deputation sent to bring back Fulk himself in 1127–8, this plan was kept secret to prevent pre-emptive action either by Alice or by Roger II of Sicily, who was believed to be interested in picking up the Norman inheritance in Antioch. Consequently, a low-profile emissary in the form of a Hospitaller brother called Gerald Jeberrus was chosen.[26]

Even so, during this time Alice appears to have maintained her independence, styling herself 'princess of Antioch' and issuing her own charters from Latakia, suggesting that she had more support than William of Tyre admits and that her attempts to gain power cannot simply be dismissed as the wilful behaviour of a selfish woman.[27] The importance of this enclave should not be underestimated, for Latakia was the main port of Antioch and thus strategically and economically significant; indeed, it might well have been difficult for Rainald Mazoir to govern the principality without Alice's co-operation. Moreover, Hugh of Le Puiset, the leader of the revolt against Fulk in the latter part of 1134, is known to have been there in July of that year and it is quite possible that 'she acted as a focal point of resistance to Fulk of Anjou's rule'.[28]

William of Tyre relates that, shortly after the king had returned from dealing with the affairs of Antioch, Hugh of Le Puiset, count of Jaffa, and Romanus of Le Puy, lord of Transjordan, 'are said to have conspired' against the king. Hugh was the son of Hugh II of Le Puiset, in the diocese of Orléans in the royal demesne south of Paris, who had come to the East on pilgrimage in 1106, where he was later given the lordship of Jaffa by Baldwin II. The younger Hugh had been born in Apulia in the course of his parents' journey to the East, where he had been left in the care of Bohemond, to whom he was related. But when Hugh II died, he came to the kingdom of Jerusalem, where he received his inheritance, presumably soon after 1120, when he would have been fourteen years old. He must have been favoured by Baldwin II, because after the death of Eustace Grenier in 1123 he was allowed to marry his widow, Emma, the niece of Patriarch Arnulf.[29] William of Tyre is mistaken in identifying Romanus of Le Puy as lord of Transjordan in 1134, but he had held this key frontier fief until sometime before 1126 when, for an unspecified reason, he and his son, Ralph, had been deprived of it by Baldwin II, leaving Romanus with much less substantial possessions in Samaria.[30] He might have been involved in the opposition to the king, an action that Baldwin could not have punished until he returned to the kingdom in 1125.[31] Whatever the reason, William is certainly justified in describing these two men as among the leading nobles of the kingdom.

Matters were brought to a head by Walter of Caesarea, one of the twin sons of Eustace Grenier and Emma, who, in the *curia regis* or 'high court', publicly accused Hugh of planning to assassinate the king. Hugh denied this and agreed to settle the matter by single combat, which William says was the custom of the Franks, but he failed to appear on the designated day and, as a consequence, was declared guilty of the accusations in the *curia regis*. Hugh then called in help from the Egyptians at Ascalon, who responded by raiding the kingdom as far as Arsuf, north of Jaffa. As with Pons of Tripoli, Fulk was now obliged to use armed force, besieging the count in Jaffa, thus forcing his vassals to make a choice. Unsurprisingly in the circumstances, led by Barisan, constable of Jaffa, who had been one of the most prominent men of the kingdom since at least 1120, they abandoned Hugh, but the intervention of the patriarch, William of Messines, seems to have effected a compromise by which the count would be banished for three years, after which time he would be able to return without further recrimination.[32] This was not quite the end of the affair, however, since before his departure, Hugh, absorbed in a game of dice in Jerusalem, was stabbed several times by a Breton knight, an act many attributed to Fulk's instigation. The knight was tried and sentenced to mutilation, but at no point did he admit that he had acted with the king's knowledge, saying only that, by his deed, he had hoped to gain royal favour. The wounds, though, may have had a long-term effect, for Hugh never returned, dying soon after in Apulia, where he had been given the lordship of Gargan by Roger II of Sicily.[33]

William of Tyre devotes three chapters of book 14 to the revolt, so he clearly thought that it was important, but at the same time, dependent upon the fallible memories of elderly men, he really did not know why it had happened. Some, he says, claimed that Fulk believed that Hugh and Melisende were too intimate, so that the king developed 'an inexorable hatred' of Hugh.[34] Others, however, dismissed these rumours, instead alleging that the count's arrogance had led him to disobey the king and to refuse allegiance to him. While the two explanations are not mutually exclusive, their implications are different, since the first suggests that it was the king who took the initial action, while the second suggests a revolt to which the king had to respond. It may or may not be true that the queen and Hugh were having an affair but, taking the three chapters together, the whole tenor of William's story is that there had been a revolt involving a good deal more than personal animosity based on marital infidelity.

It looks as if two parties had developed within the kingdom apparently because Fulk had tried to marginalise Melisende, despite the intention of Baldwin II in 1130–1 that Fulk, Melisende and the infant Baldwin should be associated in power.[35] Like most new rulers, the king also brought in his own men, replacing the older established families with what Orderic Vitalis calls 'Angevin strangers', an action that was particularly relevant to Hugh as the first cousin of Baldwin II and an obvious beneficiary of the previous regime.[36] This would not only have deprived him of patronage, but possibly even of Ascalon, which in 1126 appears to have been promised to Hugh by Baldwin II in anticipation of its capture. Others, such as Romanus of Le Puy, were nursing their own grievances; in 1126, for unknown reasons, he had been deprived of his fief of Transjordan.[37]

The Angevin 'invasion' encompassed more than Fulk's military followers and political staff, for there are signs of a cultural colonisation of the kingdom as well, reflected in the development of sculptural motifs and styles character-istic of west-central France. Capitals and friezes decorated with acanthus leaves, vines and symbolic animals became increasingly common from the late 1120s, suggesting that Fulk's entourage included not only his vassals and administrators, but sculptors and probably other craftsmen as well.[38] It is not fanciful to suggest that at several social levels the early settlers and their fami-lies would have felt disparaged by the new regime.

A substantial body of opposition had thus built up against Fulk, who may have used Walter of Caesarea's challenge to bring it into the open, for Walter and his brother must have been materially affected by their mother's remarriage to Hugh.[39] In the end Hugh was undone by his attempt to use Egyptian forces, not because alliances with Muslim powers were unique, but because of the real danger posed by Ascalon and the damage its garrison had done to the southern part of the kingdom, for the Egyptians had not given up their goal of regaining Palestine, despite their defeats at the hands of Baldwin I.[40] Nevertheless, the outcome cannot be seen as a total defeat for Hugh – any more than Fulk's intervention in Antioch was completely successful in undermining Alice – for the count received only a three-year exile for an offence that could have ended with his execution. The attempt by the Breton knight to take matters into his own hands serves to emphasise this: there were evidently some who thought the treatment of Hugh had been too lenient.

Melisende's role remains unclear, but she must have been involved. Her later history shows that she was no passive consort, but a powerful personality fully conscious of her lineage as the hereditary link with the founding rulers. William of Tyre's contrasting treatment of the two sisters, Melisende and Alice, should not obscure the similarities between them.[41] In these circumstances, it is possible that Fulk may have been about to repudiate the queen and was using rumours of adultery as a means of achieving this, although there is no solid evidence for such a risky course of action.[42] Whatever his original intentions, after the revolt the king seems to have taken extreme care to involve Melisende even in relatively unimportant matters.[43] For at least a year afterwards the queen kept up the pressure, persecuting Fulk's supporters and making life as unpleasant as possible for the king.[44]

However, once she had been restored to what she regarded as her rightful position and influence, it was not in the queen's interests to maintain hostilities at this level. Fulk, perhaps wisely, spent at least part of 1135 in Antioch, where he was fulfilling his administrative responsibilities. On 2 August, he restored to the canons of the Holy Sepulchre the properties the church had held in the Byzantine era in a charter in which he is described as 'governor and guardian' of Antioch.[45] He returned to Jerusalem soon after, since in late 1135 or early 1136 Fulk and Melisende's second son, Amalric, was conceived.[46] There are two evident reasons for Melisende's changed attitude: firstly, with only one son, the succession of her family rested on fragile foundations; and, secondly, she wished to influence Fulk's policies in Antioch, for at about the same time Alice once more seized power in the city. 'Her sister,' says William of Tyre, 'interceded with the king not to interfere with her actions', adding significantly that 'she [Alice] had the support of certain nobles'.[47]

Melisende was equally concerned to use her position to make provision for her two younger sisters, Hodierna and Iveta, both of whom had still been children when their father died in 1131. Hodierna's marriage to Raymond, son of Pons of Tripoli, which took place sometime before 1138, must have been the result of Melisende's influence, ensuring that the lines of the rulers in Jerusalem, Antioch and Tripoli would all continue through the daughters of Baldwin II.[48] Melisende remained a presence in her sister's life, for when Hodierna quarrelled with Raymond shortly before his assassination in 1152, it was the queen who tried to reconcile them and, having failed, who accompanied the countess on her departure from Tripoli.[49]

Iveta, the youngest, had been given as hostage to Timurtash, Il-Ghazi's son, in August 1124, and ransomed nine months later. This must have been a traumatic experience for a child of four or five.[50] Her mother, Morphia, had died between 1126 and 1128, and at that time Iveta may have been entrusted to the care of the sisters at the convent of St Anne, situated north of the Temple platform near the gate of Jehoshaphat on the eastern side of the city. When she reached an appropriate age, perhaps about 1134, she took vows as a nun there. The convent had been established very soon after the capture of Jerusalem and Baldwin I's second wife had entered the house in c.1103, when the king repudiated her.[51] The pilgrim Saewulf visited Jerusalem at about the same time and mentions a church there that, repeating a tradition that stretched back to the seventh century, he associates with Joachim and Anna, the Virgin's parents, and identifies as the birthplace of Mary.[52] Baldwin had provided extra endowments at the time of the repudiation and it is probable that these were considerably increased when Iveta was professed there, which perhaps enabled the church to be enlarged.[53]

However, Melisende had more ambitious plans, made possible after 1134 by the king's accommodating attitude, for she decided that her sister needed a position in the monastic world more in keeping with her status. As in her relations with Alice and Hodierna, it is difficult to know how far she was motivated by genuine affection. Any political threat that Iveta may have represented as the only sister born while Baldwin was king had been negated when she became a nun. Even so, there is no way of knowing whether she had really wished to become a nun, or whether Melisende had played a role in inducing her to take vows.[54]

Melisende chose to establish a new house at Bethany, about a mile and a half east of Jerusalem, famous as the site of the resurrection of Lazarus and the home of his sisters, Martha and Mary. On Palm Sunday, Jesus had begun his journey from Bethany, culminating in his triumphal entry into Jerusalem through the Golden Gate.[55] For the queen, its proximity to Jerusalem meant that it would be easy to maintain contact. In a charter of 5 February 1138, Fulk and Melisende therefore persuaded the patriarch and the canons of the Holy Sepulchre to abandon their rights on the church at Bethany and its dependent villages, so that they could establish a convent of monks and nuns on the site. The small community of a prior and canons that appears to have already been established there was compensated with the grant of the *casal* of Thecua (al-Tuqu) in Judaea, together with lands stretching as far as the Dead Sea, where they were conceded valuable rights over the extraction of bitumen and salt.[56]

The new structures took shape over the next six years. The original church, by this time over six centuries old, was remodelled and, in the longer term, a second church to the west was built above the actual tomb of St Lazarus, which was therefore now contained in a crypt chapel below. The place was popular with pilgrims both because of the New Testament associations and because it was on the road to the Jordan, so it seems that access to the desired sites was provided from a courtyard on the north side from which visitors could visit the church of SS. Mary and Martha to the east and the tomb of St Lazarus in the rock-cut crypt to the west. This was especially desirable since it was widely believed that Mary was Mary Magdalene.[57] The new abbey church of the sisters was above the crypt and quite separate from the pilgrims.[58] To the south of the church were a cloister, chapter house, dormitory and other conventual buildings. The whole site was heavily fortified with a wall and towers as, although it was close to Jerusalem, it stood on the eastern slopes of the Mount of Olives and could not be seen from the city.[59]

This may have been a double monastery of men as well as women, modelled upon the pattern of the great house of Fontevrault, founded in 1100 by Robert of Arbrissel about 8 miles to the south-east of Saumur in the county of Maine. This, like Bethany, was under the rule of an abbess. Indeed, it is possible that one of the functions of what later charters describe as 'brothers' of the house was to cope with pilgrim visitors, a role that would have been incompatible with the secluded lifestyle of the nuns. If, indeed, Bethany was created as a double monastery, it suggests that the king's interest in it was greater than William of Tyre admits, for Fulk was familiar with Fontevrault and may have conceived Bethany in those terms.[60]

William of Tyre says that Melisende endowed the house with estates that made it richer than any other monastery or church in the kingdom. These included Jericho, to which Bethany was connected by road, ironically confiscated by Fulk when Hugh of Le Puiset was exiled, even though it had originally belonged to the patriarchate.[61] At the same time she made sure that Bethany was lavishly equipped with sacred vessels made of gold and silver and

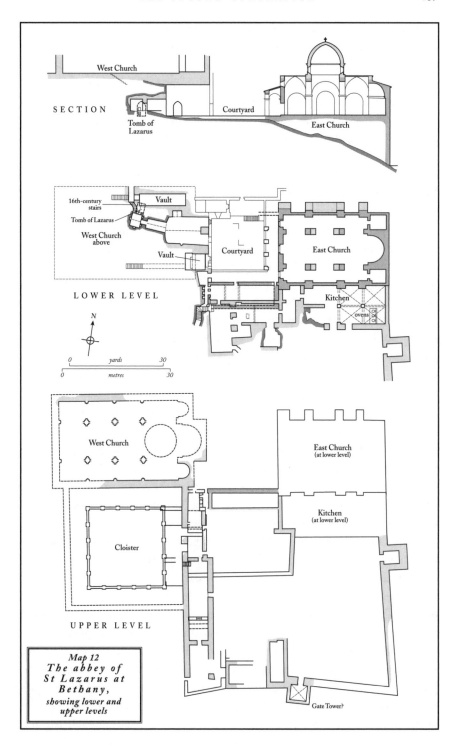

SECTION

West Church

Courtyard

Tomb of
Lazarus

East Church

LOWER LEVEL

16th-century
stairs

Tomb of Lazarus

West Church
above

Vault

Vault

Courtyard

East Church

Kitchen

ovens

N

0   yards   30
0   metres   30

West Church

East Church
(at lower level)

Kitchen
(at lower level)

Cloister

UPPER LEVEL

Gate Tower?

Map 12
*The abbey of
St Lazarus at
Bethany,
showing lower and
upper levels*

decorated with precious stones, silks and ecclesiastical vestments. Initially she placed it under the control of 'a venerable woman full of years and of ripe religious experience', named in a confirmation of 1144 as Matilda, but when she died the queen 'put her original intention into effect' and Iveta became abbess, which was the occasion of further gifts of chalices, books and ornaments.[62] The sisters over whom she presided were exclusively aristocratic, again in keeping with Melisende's perception of Iveta's status, although there would have been insufficient such women among the native Franks and their numbers were supplemented by pilgrims who decided to end their days in the East. These included, most famously, Sibylla, wife of Thierry, count of Flanders, Fulk's daughter by his marriage to Eremburge, who, against the wishes of her husband, entered the convent after their pilgrimage of 1157–8.[63]

The new house at Bethany was not the only tangible result of Fulk's reconciliation with Melisende. Around 1135, he commissioned for her a luxurious psalter, bound in ivory covers joined by a spine of embroidered silk.[64] This was possible because, by the 1120s, following the completion of the cloister, the canons of the Holy Sepulchre had established both a scriptorium and a school. William of Tyre, born in 1130, went to the cathedral school there as a child and adolescent, where he was taught by John the Pisan, later archdeacon of Tyre, and eventually cardinal under Eugenius III.[65] The scriptorium may have been founded by an Englishman, William, prior of the Holy Sepulchre, who became archbishop of Tyre in 1127, and, indeed, the liturgical calendar in the book does contain a high proportion of English saints.[66] The scriptorium must have been producing liturgical books on a regular basis, but the earliest surviving decorated codex can be dated to between 1128 and 1130. This was a sacramentary, used by the celebrant of the Mass for the recited and chanted text. It originally contained full-page miniature paintings, but now only the ornamental initials remain (see plate 6).[67]

The sacramentary shows southern French, Italian and English influences and, inevitably, a strong sense of the Byzantine context. Just as the crusader states occupied a unique position within Christendom, so their artistic products reflect the combination of Latin, Greek and Armenian cultures that defined them. Both the Melisende Psalter and a near-contemporary missal made for an Augustinian house in Jerusalem show the importance of the Armenian world, in the former case in the use of colour, and in the latter through the scribe, who seems to have been Armenian.[68] At the same time the powerful presence of the Byzantine artistic tradition was unavoidable, despite the ambivalent relationship of the Latin states with Constantinople. The use of Byzantine models, the employment of Greek or Greek-trained artists and craftsmen, and even the accessibility of the Greek patriarchal library in

Jerusalem all served to reinforce this pervasive presence.[69] The psalter made for the queen therefore was one of many books produced by the scriptorium down to its demise when Jerusalem fell in October 1187.[70] Illustrated gospel books of St John and St Mark, from the 1140s and c.1167 respectively, demonstrate the quality achieved during these years (see plate 9).[71]

The Melisende Psalter is a small book intended for private devotion by a lady of high social status, but the covers are a very overt assertion of the royal patronage that lay behind it. Both contain six paired medallions within a frame. On the front are scenes from the life of King David, warrior and unifier of the Israelites, and believed to be the author of the Psalms (see plate 7). In the interstices are the individual combats of the Virtues and the Vices, taken, as was common in the West at this time, from the *Psychomachia* by the late fourth-century Spanish poet Prudentius. On the back, a Christian king, wearing different types of Byzantine imperial costume, performs the six works of mercy as set out in verses 35 and 36 of the Gospel of Matthew, chapter 25. The themes are entirely appropriate for a king in Christ's holy city, a title Godfrey of Bouillon had been so reluctant to adopt: a leader fortified by the Virtues who combats the Vices of the infidel, while at the same time extending his hand to protect the vulnerable and the sick, acts intended to ensure that the king will be among the righteous who will be saved. The use of the Old Testament on the front and the New Testament on the back reasserts the continuity of the two in which the one prefigures the other. The miniatures within are the work of four different artists: twenty-four full-page New Testament scenes on one of which the artist identifies himself as Basil (who may have been Greek or a Greek-trained Latin); a calendar with twelve signs of the zodiac contained within medallions by a north European artist; eight full-page gold initials marking the liturgical divisions of the psalms by a Mediterranean artist (Italian or Levantine); and nine portraits of saints at the head of the final prayers by a western artist who is thought to have been employed to help Basil, perhaps a relative newcomer to the Latin East (see plate 8).[72]

However, despite the revolts in Antioch, Tripoli and Jerusalem in the early 1130s, Fulk was not the incompetent successor of a previously effective ruler that Ibn al-Qalanisi portrays him as being. As the arrangements he had left for the succession of his son Geoffrey show, he was the head of a leading French dynasty, whose members had, over two centuries, built up a great power base around the middle Loire. Since his accession to Anjou in 1109, he had further developed its territories and, by his marriage to Eremburge, daughter of Hélie, count of Maine, had added another county to this complex of lands. Such an experienced ruler could not be content merely to react to circumstances –

indeed, it appears to have been his very vigorous approach to government that contributed to the alienation of some of the baronage in 1134 – and there are signs of an increasingly systematic approach to the military and economic needs of the kingdom.

Ascalon was clearly a priority. In 1123, when the decision had been taken to concentrate on Tyre, a strong body of opinion had favoured an attack on Ascalon instead. Egyptian forces based there remained troublesome, despite the isolation of the city from other Muslim powers. William of Tyre says that the government in Cairo took the matter very seriously, rotating the garrison every three months and keeping the city well supplied with arms and provisions.[73] The forces there had the capability to strike at the lands around Jerusalem itself, and it was to counter this that, in 1132–3, the patriarch and the citizens built Castle Arnold, about 12 miles from Jerusalem, near the more northerly of the two roads from Jaffa. It was sited at the point where the plain met the hills leading up to Jerusalem since there was a narrow defile in which, despite the Templar initiative, pilgrims were still being ambushed.[74] The consequence was not only a safer passage for pilgrims, but also easier transit for goods, leading to a drop in the price of food in Jerusalem.[75]

The king, however, decided to confront Ascalon more directly. William of Tyre claims that 'the Ascalonites were becoming increasingly bold and insolent and overrunning the entire region without restraint'.[76] In about 1134, Fulk therefore began the construction of a castle at Bait Jibrin (Bethgibelin) about 20 miles east of Ascalon. William of Tyre says that it was strongly fortified with walls, towers, ramparts and a moat.[77] In 1136, it was given to the Hospitallers, a grant that suggests that the order had by this time acquired military capabilities.[78] It developed these defences in the following decades, although the chronology is unclear. Remains show that an additional, outer wall was built, forming a concentric castle.[79] In 1141 and 1142, two further castles were built at Ibelin (near Ramla), about 20 miles to the north, and at-Tall as-Safiyah, about 17 miles to the east. The second of these was called Blanchegarde and was nearest to Ascalon, which could be seen from the top of the new towers. Both castles were situated on small hills, again with square enceintes and corner towers. Blanchegarde was initially very small, with an enclosure of only 16 × 16 metres, which suggests that it was primarily intended to provide early warning of any military activity in Ascalon itself rather than having any offensive capability of its own, and that any counterattack would come from the garrison at Bait Jibrin.[80] Ibelin was granted to Barisan, the former constable of Jaffa, perhaps partly as a reward for his loyalty during Hugh of Le Puiset's revolt, and his family thereafter took its name from this place.[81]

These castles were not exclusively military in function, although they had been built to hem in Ascalon in the some way that pressure had been put on Tripoli and Tyre in the past. Forays by the Egyptians from Ascalon had made even the settlements around Jerusalem unsafe, so much potentially useful land in the south was wasted because of the danger of attack. However, the establishment of Blanchegarde led to extensive agricultural development in the vicinity, supplying food for the region, while charters to burgesses and craftsmen confirming grants of Raymond du Puy, the Hospitaller master, set down the rights and obligations of colonists living around Bait Jibrin.[82] Indeed, the choice of the site of Bait Jibrin had been as much an economic as a military decision, for it was situated in a valley with a spring at a place where roads from Gaza, Ascalon, Jerusalem and Hebron converged, the importance of which had already been shown by the presence there of a ruined Byzantine city.

At the same time there are signs that a concept of an eastern frontier was emerging, not in the modern sense of a specific line, but rather as a series of territories, often related to a specific fortification. The existence of these castles along the borders, although unevenly distributed, contributed greatly to the security of the crusader states, since they could often delay enemy penetration, giving time for defensive forces to be gathered.[83] When Thierry, count of Flanders, Fulk's son-in-law, came to Jerusalem on pilgrimage in the summer of 1139, the king took advantage of his presence to seize a cave fortress near Ajlun, in Gilead beyond the Jordan, from which raids had been made into the kingdom, although the force he took was so great he left insufficient defenders behind and some damage was done to the crusader lands on the western side of the Jordan while he was away.[84]

Baldwin I had been interested in the Transjordan since the beginning of his reign, and in 1115 and 1116 he had built the castles of Montréal, Li Vaux Moise and Ailah, extending his reach to Aquaba.[85] In 1142, Pagan the Butler, lord of Transjordan, built another castle, at Kerak about 44 miles north of Montréal and about 12 miles east of the Dead Sea, which thereafter became the main seat of the lordship. Kerak was situated on a ridge, with the town at the northern end, separated from the castle by a deep rock-cut ditch.[86] Pagan's successors, his nephew Maurice and Philip of Milly, added huge square towers and a reservoir in the ditch to the south.[87]

Three more castles along the eastern flank were built or reconstructed in 1139–40: Belvoir, set high above the Jordan valley about 9 miles south of the Sea of Galilee; Safad, held by the crusaders since 1101–2, about 25 miles east of Acre; and Beaufort, above the Litani River in the Leontes valley, about 17 miles east of Tyre. All three commanded the heights and were extensively developed in later years, especially Belvoir and Safad, after they were acquired by the Hospitallers and Templars respectively in 1168. These were important long-term projects, serving both as defences and as bases for raids into Muslim territory: Safad, for example, situated at an altitude of over 2,600 feet, commanded views of Mount Carmel to the west and the Golan Heights to the east, and overlooked the main routes between Damascus and Acre.[88]

Fulk may have been influenced by the loss of Banyas, fortuitously acquired from the Assassins in 1129 and used as a base for the attack on Damascus soon after. In December 1132, while the king was in the north, Shams al-Muluk, Böri's son and successor as atabeg of Damascus, had regained the castle and the town, slaughtering many of the defenders and inhabitants, and taking the rest back to Damascus, where they had been paraded through the city. Rainier of Brus, its lord, was absent at the time, presumably with the royal army at Antioch, but his wife was among the prisoners.[89] Ibn al-Qalanisi says this loss had come as a severe shock to the Franks, who 'were greatly astonished that Banyas should have been taken with such ease and in so short a time in spite of the strength of its fortifications and the number of its defenders'.[90]

Banyas was both a key strategic point and an important emotional focus for the Franks, who believed it had been the northern limit of the land of the children of Israel.[91] Situated on the road from Tyre to Damascus, it was roughly midway between Safad and Beaufort but in a more advanced position, and was both a threat to Damascus and a defence for the important Frankish settlements in Galilee. However, in the past it had been of considerable economic importance to Damascus. In the late tenth century, al-Muqaddasi called it 'the granary of Damascus' and described how its river, which ran through the city and was one of the sources of the Jordan, was used to irrigate cotton and rice fields.[92] The establishment of the crusaders cut an artificial line across the Damascene hinterland and possession of the city continued to be fiercely contested until it was finally taken by Nur al-Din, Zengi's son, in 1164.[93]

Not surprisingly, when the opportunity presented itself, Fulk made a huge effort to regain it. Shams al-Muluk had been assassinated in 1135 and, although he had been replaced by his brothers, first by Mahmud and then, in 1139, by Muhammad, the real power in Damascus was the atabeg, Mu'in al-Din Unur. Unur was deeply concerned at the increasing power of Zengi, whose determination to take Damascus was all too obvious. In 1137, Zengi gained the adherence of the governor of Banyas and in these circumstances Unur was prepared to offer the city to the Franks if they would provide him with military support. William of Tyre says that the decisive factor in accepting the alliance was the offer of Banyas, and the rulers of both Antioch and Tripoli were called in to help with the siege. Such overwhelming force brought the surrender of the city on 12 June 1140, after nearly a month of effort. With Banyas back in Christian hands, Rainier of Brus was restored and Adam, archdeacon of Acre, was chosen as its first bishop, established as a suffragan of the archbishop of Tyre.[94]

Zengi presented an even more direct threat to the county of Tripoli, where the counts had considerable difficulty defending themselves. Fulk was obliged to intervene twice – in 1133 and 1137 – to counter the atabeg's attacks on Montferrand, and on the second occasion the consequences were near fatal. Pons of Tripoli was killed in battle with the Damascenes on 25 March 1137, and Zengi sought to take advantage of the lack of defenders that resulted. Montferrand was within the count's demesne but it was situated on the heights above Raphaniya, more than 50 miles to the north-east of the city of Tripoli itself. Pons and Baldwin II had taken Raphaniya in a joint attack in March 1126, but now, facing the Muslim cities of Shaizar, Hama and Homs on the Upper Orontes, this had become a vulnerable frontier region, the defence of which, Fulk decided, took priority over Antioch, which was simultaneously faced by the appearance of a huge Byzantine army led by the emperor, John Comnenus.[95]

Fulk's campaign, however, was a disaster. Misled by guides, according to William of Tyre, his army was caught in the narrow defiles of the mountains, most of the foot soldiers were killed and the supplies he had brought for the relief of the fortress entirely lost. Raymond of Tripoli was captured and Fulk himself, together with the leading nobles of the kingdom, was forced to take refuge in Montferrand, now heaving with people and close to starvation. Urgent calls for help were sent to all possible sources, including Raymond of Poitiers, Joscelin of Edessa and William of Messines, patriarch of Jerusalem.

Zengi now concentrated his forces against the castle, hurling huge rocks from his siege engines and keeping up unremitting pressure by using his men in shifts. Food shortages forced the besieged to eat their horses. They must have been surprised when, in the third week of August, Zengi offered terms. In return for the surrender of Montferrand and a payment of 50,000 dinars, Fulk and his men were allowed free passage and the prisoners, including Raymond of Tripoli, were released. Zengi's uncharacteristic show of mercy was, in fact, brought about by his knowledge that the relieving forces were now close by and, perhaps most of all, because he feared the approach of the Byzantine emperor.[96] Even so, this victory left Zengi in a dominant position in the region; he already held Hama and, in June 1138, he took over Homs as well, obliging its governor to take Montferrand in its place.[97]

In these circumstances Raymond II appears to have decided that the eastern defences of the county needed to be fundamentally reorganised. In a charter of 1142, he ceded to the Hospitallers all his rights over Montferrand, Raphaniya and Mardabech, as well as fishing rights on the western side of the lake of Homs. Most importantly he granted them the four castles of Le Crat, La Boquée, Felis and Lac. Montferrand and Raphaniya were, of course, no longer under his control but, in an evident attempt to induce the Hospitallers to try to retake them, Raymond conceded them the rights he had held there five years before.[98]

The key element in the grant, however, was the cession of the castles, which were situated in al-Buqai'ah between the Jabal Ansariyah to the north and Mount Lebanon to the south. This was a fertile and well-watered region through which ran the main routes from the Upper Orontes to the coast. In the centre of this was Hisn al-Akrad, or the Castle of the Kurds, originally built by the emir of Homs in 1031. Raymond of Toulouse had held the castle briefly in 1099 and had tried unsuccessfully to take it again three years later. In 1109, it had fallen to Tancred and, in 1112, he had granted it to Pons of Tripoli.[99] By 1142, it was known as Le Crat and its lord, William, who also held La Boquée, was compensated with a new lordship based on a castle known as 'the cave (*cavea*) of David the Syrian'. This came with what is described as the *rasagium* of the mountain (probably a collection of villages associated with it governed by the local *rais* or headman), and the fief of Pons Guilhem, consisting of two knights' fees. In addition he received a payment of 600 besants and all the knights' fees on the mountain worth seven besants each for the next ten years. Gilbert of Puylaurens had held Felis, Lac and Gibelacar, the last of which he retained, and received 1,000 besants in compensation for the other two castles.[100]

These dispositions were seen both at the time and since as highly significant. They were made in Raymond's court and the barons and the bishop of Tripoli each contributed 200 besants to the compensation received by William of Le Crat. The charter itself was witnessed by the prelates, barons and burgesses of Tripoli. Among the other witnesses were Rainier, the constable, and Fulcrand, the marshal, while the charter was written by Peter, the chancellor, clear indications that under Raymond II the county had an established administrative structure.[101] In 1145, confirmation was made by King Baldwin and Queen Melisende, as suzerains of Felis and Lac, and Raymond of Antioch and Princess Constance, as suzerains of Le Crat.[102]

The Hospitallers themselves had been a presence in the county since before 1112, when they were granted a church, and between 1125 and 1127 they had received further lands and income.[103] However, these were all intended to support their charitable functions, whereas in 1142 they were established as a quasi-autonomous lordship, owing no feudal obligations to the count, and were quite unambiguously the designated military guardians of the area. No truces could be made without their consent and all booty acquired belonged to them unless the count were personally present, when it was divided equally. The extent of the order's militarisation in 1136, when it had taken over Bait Jibrin, may remain in doubt, but this grant clearly shows an institution regarded as possessing a developed military capacity.[104]

At the same time the Hospitaller presence was intended to keep the local population in check. In 1137, Raymond had blamed the death of his father on the treachery of Syrians living on Mount Lebanon and had exacted savage retribution on them and their families.[105] Mountainous regions on the borders of the Christian and Muslim lands were not easy to control and local chiefs often managed to gain a considerable degree of independence.[106] Indeed, the cave-fortress of David the Syrian may well have been the stronghold where those who had betrayed Pons had been based.[107]

Fulk had been deterred from intervening in Antioch, the affairs of which had taken up so much of the first five years of his reign, first by Melisende when Alice had once more seized power in late 1135 or early in 1136, and then by the arrival of Raymond of Poitiers, designated husband of Constance, Alice's daughter, very soon after in the spring of 1136.[108] With the defeat at Montferrand, his practical ability to act there was in any case seriously undermined and this helps to explain his apparent break with the policies of his predecessor, who had devoted so much of his time to the defence of the principality.

The situation in Antioch was complicated by the death of Bernard of Valence, the first Latin patriarch and the last direct link with the veterans of the First Crusade, in the autumn of 1135. In the absence of a resident lay ruler it appeared that the clergy of Antioch could make their own choice of a successor unimpeded, but while they were deliberating, Ralph, archbishop of Mamistra, was, according to William of Tyre, swept to power by popular acclaim, 'without the knowledge of his brethren and fellow bishops'.[109] However, Ralph came from a military background in Domfront in southern Normandy and he was probably supported by some of his fellow Normans among the Antiochene nobility. Evidence that his elevation was not entirely spontaneous can be seen from the fact that he was the only one of the leading prelates not present at the council called to consider the matter and that he moved swiftly to secure his position, imprisoning ecclesiastical opponents and, in contrast to his predecessor, assuming the *pallium* without reference to Rome. As the Church was locked in the schism between Innocent II and

Anacletus II, there was little the papacy could do about this. His elevation may have been the work of Rainald Mazoir, who was attempting to counter the faction that supported Princess Alice.[110]

As William of Tyre says, Raymond of Poitiers was 'of noble blood and ancient lineage' but, unlike Fulk, he had not been able to bring any military help with him, having been obliged to travel through Italy disguised as a pilgrim in order to avoid Roger II of Sicily. As William presents it, this situation was manipulated by 'the crafty patriarch of Antioch, a man well versed in wiles', who persuaded Alice that Raymond had come to marry her, while inducing Raymond himself to swear an oath of fealty to him in return for organising his marriage to Constance, at this time a child of eight. In addition, if Henry, Raymond's brother, came to Antioch, the patriarch would arrange for him to marry Alice, who would bring with her dower lands of Latakia and Jabala. When Alice realised she had been tricked, she retreated to these lands, but ever after 'pursued the prince with relentless hatred'.[111]

William of Tyre does not tell this as a continuous story, and his childhood memories (which included actually meeting Ralph of Domfront) were of limited value when describing such a complex political scene. Most of his information seems to have come from those who could cast their minds back forty years or so and, understandably, historians have found these events difficult to interpret.[112] Alice must have known that Raymond had come to marry Constance, but it may be that the speed with which it was done caught her off-guard.[113] She must, too, have realised that she could not prevail over Raymond and the patriarch together, and have accepted the possibility that she might still command some influence through marriage to Henry. Once Raymond had appeared in Antioch, she knew she had little hope of retaining control of the government.

Ralph had therefore manoeuvred his way to power in Antioch, but his position was distinctly precarious. According to John Kinnamos, who, as secretary to the Byzantine emperor, Manuel Comnenus, grandson of Alexius I, wrote an account of these years based on his own observations and those of other witnesses, after Bohemond II's death in 1130, 'the principal personages' in Antioch wrote to Emperor John Comnenus asking for a marriage between Constance and Manuel, John's youngest son, promising that 'immediately after the marriage between Constance and Manuel the Antiochenes' realm would be in his power'. This might have been attractive to John since the Byzantines had never accepted the legitimacy of Latin rule in Antioch, nor the removal of the Greek patriarch, and such a marriage would have restored Byzantine power at relatively little cost. However, Kinnamos says that the offer was almost immediately withdrawn when the Antiochenes decided instead to ally with Leon, the Roupenid prince of Cilicia, whose desire to re-establish Armenian rule in Cilicia inevitably made him an enemy of the Byzantines.[114]

John Comnenus had succeeded his father in August 1118, despite the efforts of his sister, Anna, to prevent him, but he did not intervene directly in Antioch until the summer of 1137. The early years of the reign were dominated by conflicts in the Balkans where, in 1122, he had defeated both the Patzinaks and the Serbs, and by uneasy relations with Hungary, which led to war between 1128 and 1130. He knew, too, that Antioch offered no direct threat, whereas the Normans in Sicily had a long record of attacks on Byzantine lands and needed particularly careful attention, especially after Roger II's coronation as king of Sicily in 1130. John's alliance with the German rulers, first Lothar III and then, on his death in 1137, Conrad III, was designed to counteract potential Sicilian ambitions.

The manifold problems of the Byzantine empire had given the Latin principality of Antioch a long respite, but in the summer of 1137 the emperor appeared in Cilicia with what William of Tyre describes as 'a countless number of cavalry and a vast array of chariots and four-wheeled carts'. William evidently reflects the fear of contemporaries that John intended direct conquest; he had already defeated the Danishmend Turks in 1135 and only Leon of Armenia stood between him and Antioch. He quickly took Tarsus, Adana, Mamistra and Anarzarba, and in mid-August laid siege to Antioch itself, obliging Raymond to hurry back from Montferrand, where he had helped to rescue Fulk from Zengi.[115] John, says William of Tyre, was intending to force the Latins to fulfil the terms of their oaths to Alexius, which obliged them to hand over the fortresses which they had captured when the emperor appeared with his army. William agrees that this had been the case, but alleges that since Alexius 'had dealt fraudulently with them and had been the first to break his own pledges', they were no longer bound by their agreement. John's invasion of Cilicia, held by the Latins for forty years, was therefore 'contrary to all justice and right'.[116] Even so, the emperor effectively removed Cilicia from the control of the princes of Antioch and it was never regained.

The Byzantines could not be expected to see the situation in the same light; even William of Tyre acknowledges John's anger when he learned that Constance had been married to Raymond of Poitiers without reference to him. In fact, in the face of overwhelming force there was little that Raymond could do but submit, although William of Tyre presents this as an agreement worked out by arbitration. Raymond was obliged to swear 'allegiance and fealty' to the emperor and to allow him free access to the city of Antioch and its citadel. If John were able to take the cities of Aleppo, Shaizar, Hama and Homs, these would be granted to Raymond as hereditary possessions. Once this had been agreed, the imperial standard was raised above the citadel of Antioch and John himself retired to spend the winter on the coast at Tarsus.[117]

In the spring the emperor made a serious assault on Shaizar. William describes his energetic attempts to capture it and his success in gaining the lower town. However, he received little help from Raymond of Poitiers and Joscelin of Edessa, who are condemned by William for wasting time playing dice. As he could not take the citadel John therefore decided to abandon the siege and to accept the citizens' offer of a large sum of money, together with a very fine cross made of reddish marble, lost at the battle of Manzikert sixty-seven years before.[118] Prince Raymond now apparently regretted his conduct, but the emperor could not be persuaded to change his mind, and he returned to Antioch. Here he demanded control of the citadel on the grounds that he could not prepare for the campaign against Aleppo, as promised in his agreement with Raymond, in any of the lesser cities of Cilicia.[119] Despite his personal admiration for John, William's view is that this would have been a disaster, for ceding Antioch to 'the effeminate Greeks' would be tantamount to throwing away the principality that had cost the Latins so much blood and toil.[120]

William sees Joscelin of Edessa as the arch-intriguer in these circumstances, anxious to undermine Raymond (whom he resented) in the eyes of the emperor, while at the same time stirring up the population into a series of violent attacks upon the Greeks in the city. In the end the emperor decided to leave, perhaps believing that at this time it was not feasible to hold either Antioch or Shaizar. Nevertheless, he promised to return with a strong army in order to carry out the terms of the agreement with Raymond.[121] John Kinnamos does not offer the same degree of detail in his account, admitting that he was not an eyewitness, but he does present the campaign as a triumph: 'Yet with fortune looking on favourably, so much had I think been achieved in two years.'[122]

Kinnamos seems to be suggesting that this was a first step and, indeed, in 1142, the emperor again set out with a formidable army. All four of his sons accompanied him, but the two eldest died during the expedition, while the third, Isaac, who was himself unwell, was sent back to Constantinople to accompany the bodies. Only the fourth, Manuel, continued with him, and Kinnamos says the emperor 'intended that Cilicia and Antioch along with Attaleia and Cyprus should be granted to Manuel for his portion.'[123] If this really was the emperor's plan, then it seems that he wanted more than just acknowledgement of his overlordship, for this would mean that Antioch would be under direct Byzantine control, including the reinstatement of the Greek patriarch. Although William of Tyre asserts that Raymond and the people kept asking for Byzantine help against Zengi, Kinnamos sees the new expedition as action against a ruler whom he believed had rebelled. The emperor's sudden and quite unexpected appearance at Turbessel in September 1142, which caught Joscelin completely off-guard and obliged him to hand over one of his daughters as a hostage, seems to confirm the interpretation offered by Kinnamos.[124]

Having neutralised Joscelin, the emperor moved his army to the castle of Baghras (Gaston) on the southern approaches to the Syrian Gates (Belen Pass) in the Amanus mountains north of Antioch, and demanded that Prince Raymond cede the citadel and the city. William of Tyre accepts that this was quite justified in the light of previous agreements, but repeats his view that if they had surrendered Antioch to 'the indolence of the Greeks', it would have fallen into the hands of the Muslims again. A delegation of leading nobles was sent to the Byzantines 'on behalf of the blessed Peter and the patriarch and all the citizens', to inform the emperor that Raymond had no legal right to hand over his wife's dowry. This obvious piece of dissembling predictably provoked John to anger, but it served to delay him long enough for him to seek winter quarters on the Cilician coast as he had done in 1137–8.[125]

At the same time he turned his attention to the kingdom of Jerusalem, announcing to King Fulk that he wished to come to the city 'for prayer and devotion' and that he would bring military aid. The ambivalence of the relationship between the Greeks and Latins appears very obvious in this request; at the time of John's attack on Antioch in 1137, William of Tyre commented that, even though 'both sides professed the same faith, they fought with one another as with enemies'.[126] Fulk had no wish to see such a huge army enter his territories, yet it was difficult to refuse a fellow Christian ruler access to the holy places. A high-level delegation was dispatched to explain that the kingdom could not sustain such numbers without risking famine, but that the emperor was welcome to come with a smaller entourage of 10,000 men. As Fulk must have hoped, the Byzantines appear to have regarded this as inadequate for a ruler of John's standing and the plan was abandoned.

Even so, William must be reflecting the worries of contemporaries in saying that John 'in his heart' planned 'great deeds' in Syria the following summer. Latin suspicions about the nature of these ambitions are to an extent confirmed by Niketas Choniates, who rose to high office under the emperors of the late twelfth and early thirteenth centuries. He presents the emperor as having 'a burning desire to unite Antioch to Constantinople and then to visit the holy lands trodden by God and adorn the life-giving tomb of the Lord with precious gifts, and, in addition, to clear away the barbarians round about'.[127] However, whatever his long-term goals, the emperor was unable to fulfil them, for, in April 1143, he was accidentally poisoned by the tip of an arrow while hunting and, although he survived a few days, his doctors were unable to prevent his death. He chose his youngest son, Manuel, as his successor.[128]

Raymond of Poitiers had survived seven years as prince of Antioch, but it had been a traumatic time. While the Byzantine presence had deterred Zengi from throwing his full weight against him, nevertheless John Comnenus had evidently meant both to displace him and to reinstall the Greek patriarch. Raymond's problems were therefore exacerbated throughout by the behaviour of Ralph of Domfront, the patriarch, who had his own ambitions.[129] Ralph had not been canonically elected, nor had he sought papal confirmation, acting instead as the ruler of an autonomous patriarchate which, like Rome, had the authority of Petrine foundation. Raymond, for his part, had resented the need to swear fealty in return for a marriage he had been freely offered. Inevitably this meant a struggle for power not dissimilar to that between Daibert and Baldwin I in Jerusalem, but perhaps postponed for a generation by the longevity of Bernard of Valence. The mutual hostility of the prince and the patriarch was obvious even to Ibn al-Qalanisi, who knew that, in the winter of 1137–8, Raymond had actually imprisoned the patriarch, apparently to stop him upsetting the agreement he had reached with John Comnenus.[130]

In the autumn of 1137, the threat of an imperial takeover induced Ralph to appeal to Pope Innocent II. The ending of the papal schism with the death of Anacletus II in January 1138 enabled Innocent to take a more active role and, in the course of the year, both Ralph and his clerical opponents in Antioch travelled to Rome to make their cases.[131] The pope, at first reluctant to give Ralph an audience, knew he needed a strong supporter in the Antiochene Church if a Greek patriarch were to be avoided and this must have persuaded him to recognise Ralph. Innocent then sent a legate to the East to investigate matters on the ground.

A synod was convened in December 1140 under a new papal legate, Alberic, cardinal-bishop of Ostia, attended by the prelates of Outremer, including William, patriarch of Jerusalem.[132] William of Tyre's description of this can be supplemented by that of an eyewitness at the council, whose account shows that the implications of the proceedings went beyond the personal conduct of Ralph of Domfront. Ralph himself appeared on the first day, bringing with him his suffragans and chapter and, in a direct challenge to the authority of the legate, made a show of displaying his patriarchal cross. This witness – evidently antipathetic to Ralph – presents a series of exchanges between the legate and the patriarch in which Ralph chose to represent the legate as insulting the bestowal of his insignia. Proclaiming that he would appeal to Rome, he then walked out, installing himself in his palace, surrounded by his household and knights.[133]

Ralph made no further appearance at the synod and on the third day was deposed and degraded from the clerical order. The tensions at the council were therefore exacerbated by the patriarch's attempt to widen the issue under debate beyond that of his personal conduct into one of principle, that is, the unresolved status of the patriarchate within the Church as a whole. It is impossible to tell how seriously Ralph took this: the potential for conflict had existed ever since a Latin patriarch had been installed in Antioch and Antiochene claims had been strongly defended by Ralph's predecessor, Bernard of Valence. If, however, Ralph had been using this simply as a diversionary tactic, it failed, since Count Raymond could now imprison him without violating clerical immunity, and he was not free to travel to the West until around 1144. William of Tyre says that another appeal to the pope was successful but, again like Daibert, Ralph died before he was able to return to Syria.[134]

King Fulk, like John Comnenus, died in a hunting accident, on 10 November 1143, although in his case it was the result of a blow to the head from his saddle after he had pitched off his horse.[135] Throughout the period of imperial intervention there is no sign of the presence of Fulk, who, in the second half of his reign, appears to have concentrated on the affairs of his kingdom. This was partly a matter of circumstance, but it seems too to have been a conscious decision that contrasts with the policies of Baldwin II and, indeed, with his own approach in the first five years of the reign. Baldwin II's preoccupation with Antioch had provoked serious opposition, while Fulk himself had been the first ruler to face an outright revolt, so this attitude is understandable; nevertheless, it had serious implications for the future.[136] As William of Tyre says, quoting Horace, 'When your neighbor's house is burning, your own property is in danger too.'[137]

CHAPTER 8

The Zengid Threat

BALDWIN III and Melisende were crowned by the patriarch, William of Messines, in the church of the Holy Sepulchre at Christmas 1143 in the presence of the nobles and prelates. As Baldwin II had intended, they were co-rulers, but necessarily the dominant presence in government was the queen, since as a thirteen-year-old Baldwin had not reached his majority, while his mother was a seasoned politician who, even as a young woman, had obliged her much older and more experienced husband to recognise her importance. When she died, in September 1161, she had, as William of Tyre recorded, ruled the kingdom for thirty years during the reigns of both her husband and her son. To William, she had been 'wise and judicious beyond what is normal for a woman'.[1] This was the final verdict in the archbishop's highly favourable account of her life and career, given extra potency because he was not usually appreciative of female intervention in public affairs.[2]

William must therefore be seen as 'a partisan of Melisende', an attitude he adopted partly because she was an important benefactor of the Church, and partly because William's own patron was her younger son, Amalric, who took her side in the conflict that eventually arose between her and Baldwin III in 1151–2.[3] William may too have remembered her when he himself was at an impressionable age, since he was a direct contemporary of Baldwin, but left the kingdom two or three years later to begin his studies in France and Italy, not returning until mid-1165, when she had been dead nearly four years. William also favoured her because of her 'symbolic importance', as the link in the succession from Baldwin II down to the 1180s, a succession that ultimately derived from the heroic age of the first crusaders whom he so admired.[4]

Not everybody has seen Melisende in the same way as William of Tyre. Two of the greatest disasters suffered by the Latins in the East took place during

the period of her direct rule – the fall of Edessa to Zengi in 1144 and the
failure of the Second Crusade to take Damascus in 1148 – although the extent
of her personal culpability for either of these events is arguable. In contrast, in
1153, the year after Baldwin III had forced her to relinquish much of her
power, the Latins took Ascalon which, for more than half a century, had
presented a direct threat to the south of the kingdom and had held out for
nineteen years since the fall of Tyre in 1124.

Some sense of contemporary unease can be seen in the letters of Bernard
of Clairvaux, by this time the outstanding monastic figure in the Latin world
and head of the Cistercians, the most dynamic of the reformed orders of the
first half of the twelfth century. His information came from Andrew of
Montbard, seneschal of the Temple, and the abbot's uncle, who had sent a
favourable view of the queen to Clairvaux. In 1144–5, Bernard responded in
a similar way to that of Anselm when he heard of the accession of Baldwin I,
giving advice on just rule. 'The king, your husband, being dead, and the young
king still unfit to discharge the affairs of a kingdom and fulfil the duties of a
king, the eyes of all will be upon you, and on you alone the whole burden of
the kingdom will rest. You must set your hand to great things and, although a
woman, you must act as a man by doing all you have to "in a spirit prudent
and strong".'[5] However, in a later letter, he adopts a more ambivalent tone,
perhaps partly because he has not heard from her for some time.

> I have heard certain evil reports of you, and although I do not completely believe
> them I am nevertheless sorry that your good name should be tarnished either by
> truth or falsehood. But my dear uncle Andrew has intervened with a letter signi-
> fying better things of you, and I cannot disbelieve anything he says. He tells me
> that you are behaving peacefully and kindly; that you are ruling yourself and the
> kingdom wisely with the advice of wise men; that you love the Brothers of the
> Temple and are on friendly terms with them; and that, according to the wisdom
> given you by God, you are providently and wisely meeting the dangers which
> threaten the Holy Land with sound counsels and help.[6]

Bernard may have picked up the 'evil reports' through the monastic grapevine. One very hostile source was an anonymous Premonstratensian continu-
ator of the *Chronica* of Sigebert of Gembloux (who died in c.1112), probably
written in the diocese of Laon or Reims and covering the period 1114 to 1155.
He may have derived his information from returning pilgrims or even from
someone in the Premonstratensian abbey established at Mountjoy, the site of
the tomb of the Prophet Samuel, in c.1130. According to him, in 1148
Melisende was responsible for the poisoning of Alfonso-Jordan, count of

Toulouse and son of Raymond IV, who had been born in the East in 1102, as well as for engineering the capture of his son and daughter by Saracens.[7] Her motive, he claimed, was to remove a possible rival for the possession of Tripoli, held by Raymond II and Hodierna, the queen's sister. As ever, unexpected deaths were attributed to poisoning; William of Tyre says that such a rumour was in circulation, but that the perpetrator had never been discovered.[8] In fact, Melisende was on good terms with the Premonstratensians, to whom she made donations and in whose Obituary both she and Baldwin III are later recorded.[9] The source of this particular author's hostility is therefore difficult to locate, but inevitably the endemic misogyny of the monastic world found its way into the works of some chroniclers.[10]

The first action of any new ruler in the twelfth century was to appoint supporters to positions of power, just as Fulk of Anjou had done in the early 1130s. As a woman, Melisende particularly needed a military commander, and for this role she chose her cousin, Manasses of Hierges, as royal constable. He was the son of Hodierna of Rethel, Baldwin II's sister. It is not known whether he was a direct replacement for the long-serving William of Bures, who had been constable since 1123 under both Baldwin II and Fulk and a leading noble in the kingdom for a decade before that, but there is no evidence of anybody else holding the post between these two.[11] Manasses had come to the East very recently, since he could not have left earlier than the spring sailing of 1142 and had therefore been in the kingdom for less than two years before he was promoted to the most powerful position in the realm beneath the queen.[12] In these circumstances his appointment was bound to cause resentment, but he did not make his acceptance any easier by, in the archbishop's judgement, adopting 'an insolent attitude of superiority toward the elders of the realm', causing intense hatred of him among some of the nobles, from which he was protected only by the queen's favour.[13] This may explain why the queen was unable to procure an advantageous marriage for him until 1150, even though he was a bachelor throughout the 1140s. The queen's choice provoked further animosity, for he was married to Helvis of Ramla, widow of Barisan of Ibelin, who died that year. Although Barisan had been one of the queen's supporters, his three sons, Hugh, Baldwin and Barisan, were alienated because by this marriage they lost the family's lands in Ramla.[14]

Manasses was the most prominent member of an inner group by which the queen maintained her power, a group that included Philip of Nablus, Elinand of Tiberias, prince of Galilee, and Rohard the Elder, viscount of Jerusalem. When he was old enough, this circle also included her younger son, Amalric, whom she made count of Jaffa in 1151. Philip of Nablus was the son of Guy of Milly, a Norman who had been a prominent landholder in the kingdom since at least 1108, and had been a close confidant of Baldwin I. Philip inherited Guy's lands in Samaria and from 1144 is described as *Philippus Neapolitanus*.[15] His family may well have been adversely affected by Fulk's anti-Norman policy a decade before, which could explain his adherence to Melisende. Elinand of Tiberias was the second son of William of Bures and, in 1144, judging by the knight service owed, the holder of the most important lordship in the kingdom. Rohard the Elder was viscount of Jerusalem between 1135 and 1147 and had previously been an enemy of the queen – indeed, she had apparently victimised him because of his support for King Fulk in 1134 – but he was a key figure in the city of Jerusalem itself and it seems that neither party saw much advantage in allowing the feud to fester. The support of these three individuals meant the queen was able to retain a dominant position through control of Jerusalem, Samaria and Galilee, in all of which there were important areas of royal demesne.[16]

As well as a military commander the queen needed a new chancellor to head her administration and, in 1145, she filled this post with another newcomer, Ralph, whom William of Tyre describes as English by birth, although he may have originated in the county of Boulogne. His predecessor, Elias, is not recorded in office after 1142, and by 1144 he was bishop of Tiberias, clearing the way for the queen to appoint a replacement.[17] Ralph is almost certainly the same man who, between 1137 and 1141, served as chancellor to Queen Matilda of England, wife of King Stephen, a role in which he had become highly skilled. Since Matilda was related to the first three rulers of Jerusalem through both the Boulogne and Rethel families, he must have seemed an appropriate choice to Melisende, who had learned a great deal from her experiences in the 1130s about the importance of appointing one's own men if the principal levers of government were to be successfully manipulated.[18]

Melisende had an equally tight grip on the Church. Indeed, her influence here had deeper roots since her increased role in government after 1134 expressed itself most strongly in ecclesiastical affairs in which she was intensely interested. The foundation of Bethany represents her most spectacular monastic achievement, but it is clear that from the late 1130s she oversaw the expansion of other religious institutions in the kingdom. Among these was the Temple of the Lord, which she endowed with large estates in Samaria, and she was perhaps influential in the promotion of the new prior, Geoffrey, to abbot within months of his appointment in 1137.[19] Geoffrey completed the conversion of the Dome of the Rock into a church and in 1141 had the satisfaction of seeing its consecration by Alberic of Ostia, the papal legate. This was one of the focal points of the city, around which had been created a monastic precinct, encompassing not only the canons' buildings but also houses and baths. Thereafter, Geoffrey was regarded as one of the leading ecclesiastics of the kingdom, appearing regularly on royal and patriarchal charters, and twice participating in important diplomatic missions to the Byzantine emperors, John II (in 1142–3) and Manuel I (in 1158–9), having been chosen at least partly because he was one of the few Greek-speakers among the Latins of the East.[20]

At the same time, Melisende's support for the Jacobite Church in Jerusalem was consistent between 1138 and 1148, when she ensured that the Jacobites regained villages they had lost since the Frankish conquest. Given her own religious background, it is evident the Jacobites expected a sympathetic hearing. According to a contemporary Syrian monk called Mar Simon, in 1148, when Ignatius III, the head of the convent of St Mary Magdalene and the metropolitan for Palestine, wanted to obtain a village called Dayr Dakakiya, once held by the convent but now in Latin hands, she and Baldwin intervened on his behalf and he was able to repurchase it. 'Because they were moved by God and because they had great respect for and trust in Ignatius, they gave him much assistance.'[21]

However, her ability to extract Elias of Narbonne from his position as abbot of Palmaria, near Tiberias, in the late 1130s, is perhaps more typical of her more routine interventions. Elias was a former precentor of grammar in the region of Narbonne, who had a penchant for self-sacrifice and the deprivations of the eremitical life, tastes not shared by his monks, who, among other customs, objected to the imposition of heavy cowls of the Cistercian type in the heat of the Palestinian summer. Although the archbishop of Nazareth later persuaded him to return, it is significant that Elias appealed to Melisende for help in the face of the community's opposition.[22]

More controversially, her insistence that Ralph, the chancellor, should be appointed to the archbishopric of Tyre after Fulcher, the incumbent, had become patriarch in January 1146 may have been one of the sources of the 'evil reports' that had come to the ears of Bernard of Clairvaux. Although Fulcher could not have become patriarch without Melisende's support, he nevertheless led the opposition to Ralph, who, as William of Tyre saw it, 'obtained the church and its goods by violence'. William's view may well have been influenced by John the Pisan, archdeacon of Tyre, who was the most vocal opponent of Ralph's election, for William was a former pupil of his at the cathedral school of the Holy Sepulchre in the 1130s. There is a parallel here with the case of Manasses of Hierges, for Ralph had held no previous ecclesiastical position in the kingdom, and his insertion into the most important see in the kingdom after the patriarchate seems to have engendered similar resentment. The queen was well aware of this and ensured that Ralph was elected in February 1146, as quickly as possible after the choice of the patriarch the previous month. However, the move did not succeed, for the dispute dragged on until 1151, when Peter, former prior of the Holy Sepulchre, is recorded as archbishop.[23]

The first major crisis faced by Melisende and Manasses occurred barely a year after Fulk's death. In the course of November 1144, Zengi, atabeg of Mosul, seized the opportunity to launch a full-scale attack upon the city of Edessa. The sources agree that he was taking advantage of the absence of Joscelin II who, according to William of Tyre, was living in Turbessel, west of the Euphrates: 'He was far from the disturbance caused by his enemies, he had time for luxurious pleasures of every kind, and he felt no responsibility, as he should have done, for the noble city.' William clearly despised Joscelin, contrasting his behaviour with that of his predecessors, Baldwin of Bourcq and Joscelin I, who lived in the city and did not rely on mercenaries for its defence.[24]

Zengi gathered a formidable army of Turcomans, mainly from the Jazira between the Upper Euphrates and the Upper Tigris, a region that, Ibn al-Athir claims, had been badly affected by Frankish raids in the past.[25] Although Edessa had strong defences with a large perimeter wall and as many as forty-five towers, as well as a citadel defended by an internal wall, it had no proper defenders nor organised leadership. After battering the walls with siege engines and using miners to tunnel beneath, Zengi opened up a large breach through which his forces poured into the city. Mass panic ensued and, according to Gregory the Priest, as many as 2,000 died from suffocation as the inhabitants fought to gain access to the citadel.[26] Among the dead was Hugh, archbishop of Edessa, a man whom William of Tyre implies deserved his fate because he had failed to use his riches to pay for soldiers to defend the city. He had apparently forbidden the defenders of the citadel to allow anyone entry until they saw him in person, but when he arrived the way was blocked by the mass of bodies outside. As he tried to get through he fell into the middle of the corpses, where he was struck down and killed by a Turk.[27]

Zengi's troops, says Ibn al-Qalanisi, 'set to pillaging, slaying, capturing, ravishing and looting, and their hands were filled with such quantities of money, furnishings, animals, booty and captives as rejoiced their spirits and gladdened their hearts.' In his graphic account of the scenes within the city, Michael the Syrian describes how aged priests, still holding relics of the martyrs, continued praying in the midst of all this until 'the sword rendered them silent'. Finally, Zengi, seeing such carnage, ordered the massacre to stop and a herald was sent out to announce that all those who had escaped death could return to their homes. Two days later Zengi promised the defenders of the citadel that their lives would be spared and they handed it over to him. The city fell on 23 December 1144, after a siege of twenty-eight days.[28]

In the course of this, Zengi encountered an elderly man, naked, his beard shaven, who was being dragged along on a rope. He turned out to be Basil bar Soumana, the Jacobite bishop of Edessa, and Zengi had him dressed and brought to his tent. He was impressed not only by his courage, but also by his ability to speak Arabic, and together they discussed the reconstruction of the city. 'As long as Zengi ruled in Edessa,' says Michael the Syrian, 'that is to say until his assassination, this venerable bishop was very influential,' and he was given responsibility for repopulating the city. It was not, however, intended that this should include the Franks. 'The Turks preserved the lives of all our people, the Armenians and the Greeks who had survived, but they killed the Franks wherever they could.'[29]

News of the siege soon spread to Antioch and Jerusalem. Joscelin at last realised the danger and asked for help from Raymond of Antioch, but William of Tyre says that he deliberately delayed because of his hatred of Joscelin. Indeed, the Armenian bishop Nerses Snorhali complained bitterly that Antioch had allowed Edessa to be delivered into the hands of the infidel 'out of envy'.[30] In Jerusalem, Melisende called a council and it was decided to send a relief army led by Manasses of Hierges, Philip of Nablus and Elinand of Tiberias. This did not include King Baldwin, even though, earlier in the year, he had led a successful expedition to put down a revolt at Wadi Musa in the Transjordan.[31] However, Baldwin was only fourteen in 1144 and the crisis in Edessa was so grave it might be expected that Melisende would want an army led by experienced adults rather than by Baldwin, whose presence would nonetheless have acted as a focal point for the troops, even if the constable had actually been in command. In fact, the army did not have time to reach Edessa before its fall since, even if it had marched directly to the city, it is unlikely to have completed the journey in less than the five weeks it took Baldwin of Boulogne to travel there from just north of the Dead Sea in January 1100.[32] Given that Zengi's forces occupied Baalbek, it was, in any case, unlikely that this route was practical. The Jerusalem army therefore probably met Raymond at Antioch, and must then have been part of the force driven back by Zengi in February or March 1145.[33]

Viewed in a longer perspective, Zengi's capture of Edessa was of great strategic importance, enabling him to seize the rest of the Frankish lands east of the Euphrates, except for al-Bira, which was only just beyond the river.[34] It made Antioch, with which Edessa had been closely linked since 1098, much more vulnerable and this, in turn, meant that when the kings of Jerusalem wished to invade Egypt, a policy pursued by both Baldwin III and (much more vigorously) by Amalric, his successor, they could never be sure that the northern crusader states were secure. Ibn al-Athir, writing in the light of subsequent victories by Nur al-Din, Zengi's son, and by Saladin, and relying on information from his father, describes how a pious man, after Zengi's death, had seen 'the Martyr' in a dream and had been told that God had forgiven him his sins 'because of the conquest of Edessa'.[35] Perhaps predictably, modern historiography sees Zengi as the first of three great Islamic leaders of the twelfth century, whose jihadist actions ultimately led to Saladin's capture of Jerusalem in 1187.

In practice, however, Zengi's attack on Edessa was more opportunistic than such a teleological presentation suggests. Joscelin was not in residence and in the winter of 1144–5 Raymond was preoccupied by a conflict with Byzantine forces in Cilicia, a campaign in which he was chased back to the city of Antioch itself, leaving him with no alternative but to travel to Constantinople and submit himself as the emperor's vassal.[36] The two outside powers most likely to help – Byzantium and Jerusalem – both had new rulers, hardly established after the deaths of John Comnenus and Fulk the previous year. In the county itself it was unlikely that an embittered and demoralised Armenian population would have offered Zengi any effective opposition, while the attritional effects of previous Muslim attacks over more than four decades must have undermined the infrastructure upon which the city depended.[37]

'The amīr 'Imād al-Dīn Atābek,' says Ibn al-Qalanisi, 'had long been desirous of it, ambitious to possess himself of it, and on the watch to seize any opportunity against it.'[38] This is in keeping with Zengi's record, which was not that of a leader of the jihad, but one of a man always ambitious to extend his power whenever he perceived weakness within the fragmented structure of contemporary Iraq and Syria. As the son of Aq Sunqur, governor of Aleppo, who had been killed by Tutush in 1092, he had been brought up in the violent and unstable world of Seljuk politics. His base was always Mosul, where he had been adopted by its governor, Jikirmish, after his father's death, and where eventually, in 1127, he himself became atabeg under the sultan, having previously ruled Basra and Wasit in southern Iraq (1122–3). His interest in Syria was initially in Aleppo, which he had known as a child, and he took over there in June 1128. Damascus was an obvious goal after this, but, although he gained control of Homs, Hama and Baalbek in the late 1130s, he was never able to take the city, whose ruler and inhabitants were deeply fearful of the consequences of his rule. He was, indeed, seen as a grave threat in Syria by both Muslims and Christians, not only because of his military talents, but also because of his exceptionally cruel and treacherous behaviour.[39] The pact between the Franks and Unur of Damascus in 1140 was made, says Ibn al-Qalanisi, in order to drive him away and 'prevent him from attaining his ambition at Damascus, before he should become too firmly settled to be dislodged and his might should become invincible, and he should be victorious over the Frankish bands and attack their cities'.[40] When Zengi was assassinated in September 1146, it is not surprising that suspicion fell on Damascus, to which the murderer fled after he had stabbed Zengi to death while he was asleep.[41]

Zengi's death emboldened the Franks, for there was an inevitable hiatus before a new ruler established himself. His two sons, Saif al-Din Ghazi and Nur al-Din Mahmud, immediately took steps to secure their own positions, Saif al-Din (the elder) in his father's base in Mosul and Nur al-Din in Aleppo.[42] Relatively few Turks were left in Edessa and messages were secretly sent to Count Joscelin. Late in 1146, in November or December, together with Baldwin, lord of Marash, he moved swiftly to take advantage of the situation and was let into the city at night. Baldwin's presence is significant, since his lordship lay on the edge of eastern Cilicia and was quite isolated from Antioch, over 100 miles to the south. After the fall of Edessa, it was very vulnerable, for it included not only Marash itself, but also the fortresses of Behesni, Raban and Kesoun to the north-east.[43]

However, crucially, they could not take the citadel, having apparently left in such haste that they failed to bring siege equipment, and when Nur al-Din suddenly appeared with his 'askar, they found themselves trapped in the city. Desperate to save themselves, the Franks tried to break out, followed by many of the citizens, who feared retribution if they stayed. William of Tyre calls the scenes around the gates 'a pitiable sight', for not only armed knights, but the elderly, women, children and the sick were all struggling to escape, pressed from the rear by the garrison of the citadel and attacked from the front by Nur al-Din's forces. Most were hacked or trampled to death or suffocated in the crowd, and only a few of those on horseback managed to get away. Even so, many were killed by the pursuing Turks, including Baldwin of Marash, although Joscelin did reach the Euphrates and gain the safety of Samosata, to the north-west of Edessa.[44]

Cruel as these deaths were, says Michael the Syrian, the victims did not suffer like those who were still alive. When they fell into the hands of the Turks, 'they stripped them of their clothes and shoes. Beating them with sticks, they forced them, men and women, naked and with their hands tied behind their backs, to run with the horses. These perverted men pierced the guts of any who weakened or who fell to the ground, and left them to die on the road.' The air, he says, was polluted with the stench of cadavers. In

Michael's estimate, the two capitulations of Edessa had cost 30,000 lives, while another 16,000 had been taken into slavery. Only about 1,000 men had escaped and no women or children. The city itself was deserted, except for looters, leaving the bodies as food for vultures and jackals.[45]

The reaction in Jerusalem was equally vigorous, but no less disastrous. Incited by a disaffected Armenian governor, who claimed he would surrender Bosra and Sarkhad to the Franks if suitably recompensed, in the spring of 1147 King Baldwin gathered together an army to invade the Hauran, south of Damascus. The Hauran consisted of a great plateau extending south to the Yarmuk River and east as far as the desert lands. It was around 47 miles from west to east, and its relative isolation from the crusader lands would have made it difficult to incorporate, which suggests that Baldwin may have intended to establish some kind of protectorate rather than direct rule. It was certainly a desirable area, since its fertile volcanic soils supported a flourishing production of wheat and barley and even in its drier parts there was a strong pastoral economy. Its main limitation was an uncertain water supply in those areas not fed by the waters of Mount Hermon and Gabal al-Arab to the south-west and south-east respectively. It was vital to Damascus, which relied on the region for much of its food. Bosra itself, situated on the traditional caravan routes, was an important commercial centre and for that reason had good fortifications, the centrepiece of which was the citadel, adapted from the Roman theatre, and reinforced by the Fatimids and the Seljuks in the eleventh century. An extensive system of reservoirs, in which were collected the winter rains, enabled the town to survive the summer droughts. Moreover, the combined effects of a legend that Muhammad had visited when he was a boy and the fact that, in 634, it had been the first Byzantine town to be captured by the Arabs meant that it had considerable emotive significance in the Muslim world.[46] No ruler of Damascus would relinquish the Hauran without a tremendous struggle.

As far as Unur was concerned, the Christian invasion was a violation of the agreement between them, although Baldwin attempted to stay within the parameters of convention by informing Unur in advance of his intentions. The chronology of events is by no means clear, but the delivery of this warning seems to have led to a considerable delay and it may have been during this time that Unur negotiated the marriage of one of his daughters to Nur al-Din, evidently as insurance, since it is unlikely that he would have trusted a son of Zengi any more than he did the Christians.[47] There were, indeed, serious divisions about the wisdom of this expedition among the Christian leaders, although William of Tyre blamed 'the rash populace' for the decision to go ahead.[48] In fact, the army had already assembled near Tiberias and the True

Cross had been brought from Jerusalem and, as with a modern mobilisation, it was difficult to check the momentum.

In any circumstances it was a risky enterprise, for Bosra was farther east than any of the other possessions of the kingdom of Jerusalem, and some may have questioned whether it could have been held even if they had managed to take it. Having crossed the mountains and entered what William calls 'the plain of Medan', west of Der'a on the Yarmuk River, they were almost at once hemmed in by Turkish forces in much greater numbers than they had expected. As their march forward became slower and slower, their ranks packed tighter together and they became short of water. The large numbers of Turks were probably the result of the arrival of Nur al-Din on 27 May, called in by Unur following the warning sent by Baldwin.[49]

After several days Baldwin's forces actually came within sight of Bosra, only to learn that it had already been surrendered to the Turks, forcing the Franks to retreat in the same painful manner as they had advanced, but this time exacerbated by the firing of the crops and brushwood by the enemy. Offered a chance to escape using the horse (reputed to be the fastest in the army) of one of his vassals, John Gotman, Baldwin chose to stay, presumably because his reputation would never have recovered had he fled at this point.[50] In William of Tyre's narrative, the army is only saved by miracles: first, when Robert, archbishop of Nazareth, raises the True Cross towards the flames, causing the wind to change direction; and, second, in a scene perhaps deliberately reminiscent of the accounts of the First Crusade, when an unknown knight riding a white horse and carrying a red standard leads the army back to Christian territory.[51] More germane was Unur's decision 'to restrain the Muslims and prevent them from attacking and pursuing the Franks on their retreat'.[52] Ibn al-Qalanisi says that Unur feared a counterattack if they were provoked too much, but he also knew that he might still need the Frankish alliance if Nur al-Din became too powerful.

The Christians in the East therefore failed to capitalise on the situation following Zengi's death. However, western opinion had been greatly shocked by the fall of Edessa, the seriousness of which had been reinforced by Hugh, bishop of Jabala, whom Otto, bishop of Freising, had seen at the papal curia in Viterbo making 'pitiful lament concerning the peril of the Church beyond the sea since the capture of Edessa'. Present at the same time were envoys from Gregory III, the Armenian Catholicus (Patriarch), who must have brought news of their own even more immediate dangers.[53] Both parties had their own separate reasons for being there, but the combined effect must have been to reinforce papal determination, and on 1 December 1145, Eugenius III issued the bull *Quantum praedecessores*, addressed to Louis VII of France and his nobles, calling on them to 'gird themselves to oppose the multitude of the infidels who are now rejoicing in the victory they have gained over us'. Those who died during the expedition 'will receive the fruit of everlasting recompense from the rewarder of all good people'.[54] William of Tyre, who was studying in the West at this time, probably in Paris, says that the pope sent out preachers to many regions and that above all Bernard of Clairvaux stirred the hearts of people 'with a longing to avenge such wrongs'. The effect, he says, was that Conrad, whom he describes as emperor of the Romans (although he was never crowned), and Louis, king of the Franks, together with many princes from both kingdoms, 'embraced the word with an equal desire for the same end'.[55]

In fact, the response was not as structured as William presents it, since Louis had already been desirous of making a pilgrimage to the East, while Conrad III had apparently not intended to go until persuaded by Bernard of Clairvaux at Christmas 1146.[56] The pope reissued the bull on 1 March 1146, but the real impetus came when Bernard, supported by Louis VII, preached at a great gathering at Vézelay in Burgundy at the end of the month.[57] Moreover, not all potential crusaders intended to succour the Holy Land, for they had their own ideas about how best their resources could be used. Indeed, although the expeditions that have become known as the Second Crusade represented the largest western response to the needs of the crusader states since their foundation, it is ironic that the increase of crusading interest that accompanied them also stimulated campaigns against the Wends east of the River Elbe and against the Moors in Iberia, leading to a diversification of crusading effort that did not prove to be in the long-term interests of the Latin settlers in the East. Although the Wendish Crusade between June and September 1147 produced little in the way of concrete results, it did inaugurate an era of military expansion in the Baltic, which eventually led to the conquest of the Slavs, while the Iberian expeditions captured Lisbon in October 1147, in conjunction with Anglo-Flemish fleets, and Almeria and Tortosa in October 1147 and December 1148 with the help of the Genoese.[58]

Understandably William concentrates on the two great armies of Conrad and Louis, for there had been nothing on a comparable scale since 1101, and the kings of Germany and France had never before taken the Cross. The sheer size of the enterprise created serious problems. Whereas Fulk of Anjou and Thierry of Flanders had been able to travel by sea, in the mid-twelfth century it was not possible to transport armies on this scale by such means, so both kings decided to take their forces overland through Asia Minor. However, in 1097 and 1098, the first crusaders had twice been on the brink of disaster, while the majority of the crusaders of 1101 were either killed or captured.

Relations with the Byzantine empire remained ambivalent and recent events in Antioch had done nothing to encourage a belief in Greek co-operation. In the late 1140s, neither the military and logistical obstacles nor the political problems had diminished.

Therefore, when the two kings attended a great assembly at Palmarea, just outside Acre, on 24 June 1148, they did so as leaders of forces much undermined by journeys that had been traumatic for all concerned. Conrad's army had been defeated by the Turks near Dorylaeum around 25 October 1147, and had been forced to flee back to Nicaea. Many of the survivors returned home, but Conrad, sick and exhausted, made his way to the coast at Ephesus. Although the king presented this as a strategic retreat, intended to keep the army intact for the future, in reality he had lost so badly that the chronicler Otto of Freising, Conrad's half-brother, who was a participant, could not bear to write about what he describes as a tragedy.[59] Conrad himself returned to Constantinople, before sailing to Acre, arriving in early April 1148. He then travelled to Jerusalem, where he was met by the patriarch and ceremonially led into the city.[60] Conrad's relations with Emperor Manuel were initially uneasy, partly because of the behaviour of his army, but when he returned to Constantinople after the defeat at Dorylaeum, he was well treated by the emperor and was able to consolidate the link that had already been established when Manuel had married his wife's sister, Bertha of Sulzbach, in January 1146.

Contacts between the French and the Greeks were more fraught – indeed, an element in Louis's army had even been willing to attack Constantinople – but eventually, in November 1147, the French too began their march across Asia Minor. Louis had visited Conrad to commiserate with him, but could not afford to wait until he had recovered from his illness and reassembled his army. Initially the French were more successful in that in late December they defeated the Turks at the ford on the Meander River, but ultimately they too found the logistics of the march beyond their capabilities. In early January 1148, as they made their way towards Attalia, their long and disjointed column was broken up by the Turks as it attempted to struggle across Mount Cadmus. Although the bulk of the army reached Attalia on 20 January, the chances of a successful march to Tarsus and from there to Antioch did not seem good. After some argument Louis and his wife, Eleanor, sailed to Saint Simeon, but there was insufficient shipping for all the army, and those obliged to travel through Cilicia suffered heavy losses.[61]

Ibn al-Qalanisi was well informed about these disasters. Reports from Constantinople warned that huge armies were 'making for the land of Islām'. The rulers of neighbouring lands, however, had time to make preparations and, when the armies appeared, waited to attack them in the high passes of the mountains.

> Death and slaughter commingled with the Franks until a vast number of them perished, and their sufferings from lack of foodstuffs, forage and supplies, or the costliness of them if they were to be had at all, destroyed multitudes of them by hunger and disease. Fresh reports of their losses and of the destruction of their numbers were constantly arriving until the end of the year 542 [i.e. to May 1148], with the result that men were restored to some degree of tranquillity of mind and began to gain some confidence in the failure of their enterprise, and their former distress and fear were alleviated in spite of the repeated reports of the activities of the Franks.[62]

Even so, Ibn al-Qalanisi acknowledges that large numbers of Franks did succeed in reaching Syria and Palestine, but that then 'there was a divergence of views amongst them as to which of the lands of Islām and Syrian cites they should proceed to attack, but at length they came to an agreed decision to attack the city of Damascus'.[63] Conrad III had set out with the intention of recovering Edessa; indeed, despite his defeat at Dorylaeum, in a letter to Wibald, abbot of Corvey, written from Constantinople at the end of February 1148, he was still talking of collecting a new army in Jerusalem at Easter and then pushing on to Edessa.[64] An oath to Manuel that he would return via Constantinople presupposes a successful recapture of Edessa, for the Byzantines wanted to confirm their overlordship of the region before he returned to Germany.[65]

Louis seems to have had a similar plan, but he had always intended to make a pilgrimage to Jerusalem and his determination to fulfil this vow must have been reinforced when he heard that Edessa was so wrecked as to be indefensible even if retaken.[66] Not surprisingly, he could not be persuaded by Raymond of Antioch to attack Aleppo and Shaizar. According to William of Tyre, Raymond had hoped and believed that such conquests would be possible with the help of the French army, and had been planning as much before Louis left France. His elaborate welcome of the king reinforced the gifts sent beforehand, while his cultivation of Eleanor, who was the eldest daughter of William, count of Poitou, his brother, seems to have been motivated by the same end. The acquisition of Shaizar at least was quite feasible and would have strengthened his hand in the conflict with Byzantium.[67]

But the situation quickly turned sour. 'The king, however, ardently desired to go to Jerusalem to fulfil his vows, and his determination was irrevocable.' Raymond's welcome turned to hatred and, as William presents it, he determined to injure the king as much as possible, most notably by committing adultery with Eleanor, whom William calls 'a foolish woman'.[68] William was, of course, basing his information on French sources and writing at least twenty years after the king and queen had been divorced, so it is not possible to know if this was true, but John of Salisbury, who was closer to the events in time if not in place, reports strong rumours of the queen's infidelity, which resulted in the king forcing Eleanor to leave, creating what John calls 'mutual anger'.[69] Clearly, after this, any military target in the northern crusader states was out of the question.

William of Tyre explains that all the leaders of the crusader states had their personal goals, and that each wished to take the opportunity to strike at enemies most threatening to them. Initially, the rulers of Jerusalem had feared that Louis would be diverted by Raymond of Antioch, and were therefore pleased by his estrangement from the king. A lavish welcome, led by Patriarch Fulcher, was arranged, and before the meeting at Palmarea, Louis and his entourage were conducted on a tour of the holy places. William devotes an entire chapter to a record of the great dignitaries present and, even though his list is by no means complete, it was certainly the most impressive gathering ever held in the Latin East. Among the Germans were Otto of Freising, Conrad's half-brother, Henry Jasomirgott, duke of Austria, his brother, and Frederick, duke of Swabia, his nephew. Louis's followers included Robert, count of Perche and Dreux, the king's brother, Henry, count of Troyes, and Thierry of Flanders, now on his second expedition to the East. Both the Germans and the French were accompanied by papal legates. The Jerusalem contingent included King Baldwin, Queen Melisende, the patriarch, seven archbishops and bishops, and the masters of the Temple and the Hospital, as well as all the leading nobles of the kingdom.

This was such a large gathering that it is unlikely that there could have been a meaningful debate about strategic objectives: William of Tyre lists thirty-nine of the most notable individuals, while acknowledging that many others were also present.[70] This lends credibility to Otto of Freising's claim that the decision to attack Damascus was in fact made in April at a much smaller meeting between Conrad, Baldwin, the patriarch, and the Templars, before the arrival of the king of France.[71] The Templars may have been instrumental here for Conrad had been staying in the Temple of Solomon, while the order already had the confidence of Louis both for its role in defending the column after the defeat at Cadmus Mountain in January 1148, and for the provision of essential loans needed to keep the king's crusade in being.[72] Conrad then travelled to Acre, where he spent the money he had received from the Byzantines for the campaign in Edessa on recruiting more soldiers from the many Latins visiting the Holy Land over the Easter period. At the same time his behaviour strongly suggests that he now saw himself as the head of the hierarchy of Christian princes, emperor in all but name.[73]

In the circumstances Damascus was the obvious target. Louis had no intention of helping Raymond of Antioch, while Raymond himself had shown little interest in either saving or regaining Edessa which, in any case, was several weeks' march away. Raymond II of Tripoli was not present, further weakening the case for a more northerly objective. His absence is unexplained, but it may have been connected to the unexpected death of Alfonso-Jordan, count of Toulouse, who had taken the Cross at Vézelay, but had died at Caesarea on his way to Jerusalem, and in the overheated atmosphere of crusader aristocratic society was rumoured to have been poisoned.[74] William of Tyre did not know who the culprit was, but as the son of Raymond of Toulouse, the founder of the county of Tripoli, Alfonso-Jordan might have been seen as a rival of the incumbent, Raymond II. In contrast to the rulers of Antioch and Tripoli, the capture of Damascus could be seen as in the direct interest of the kingdom of Jerusalem and would have compensated Baldwin and the leading nobles involved in the failed campaign into the Hauran the previous year, especially as they now regarded the agreement with Unur as being at an end.[75]

The host mustered at Tiberias in mid-July and proceeded as a body to Banyas, crossed Mount Lebanon and then descended into the plain at Darayya, from where they could see Damascus. As William of Tyre describes it, Damascus was set in arid land but it was irrigated by canals from the Barada River, which flowed to the north of the city in a south-easterly direction. This enabled the citizens to cultivate large orchards along the river banks and to the west and north of the city. The orchards were divided by narrow access routes, defended by mud walls, and the Damascenes used these confined spaces to harass the crusaders. Eventually, however, the Latins forced their way in and the defenders fled into the city. They then took control of the river when the troops sent to defend it were overcome by the Germans, whose cavalry dismounted and fought on foot in a manner William thought was characteristically Teutonic. William's informants told him that the city was now almost within their grasp; inside the walls citizens put barriers across the streets so that the invaders would be sufficiently delayed for them to escape from the other side.

At this point William says that the army was betrayed by certain persons who had been bribed to give false advice. They persuaded the kings to move round the city to the southern and eastern sides where, it was claimed, the defences were poor, with weak walls and no moat. This would obviate the need for siege engines, as well as avoiding the dangers involved in a direct assault. In fact, when they established themselves in the new position they soon discovered they had inadequate supplies and no water. Any chance of moving back to the western side was now blocked by the defenders, whose barricades were heavily manned by archers. Convinced now that they could not take the city and 'covered in confusion and fear', the crusaders were obliged to retreat.[76]

Ibn al-Qalanisi has a different version of events. He says that the crusaders first approached a site known as Manāzil al-ʿAsākir, which lies to the south of the city, but, finding no water, on 24 July moved to the village of al-Mizza on the south-east, where water was available, fought their way into the orchards and took control of the river. He admits that this caused horror and discouragement within the city. The Latins then constructed a series of barricades and enclosures from the trees, but were so fiercely opposed that they were obliged to retreat inside their defences. All the time new Muslim forces were arriving, having responded to the city's call for help, and in three days of fighting the Christians found it difficult to emerge from their stockades. 'Meanwhile reports reached the Franks from several quarters of the rapid advance of the Islamic armies to engage in the Holy War against them and of their eagerness to exterminate them, and they became convinced of their own destruction and of the imminence of disaster.' Their main interest thereafter was not to take the city but, like Baldwin's abortive campaign to Bosra, to extricate themselves, and they fled back to Christian territory under fire from clouds of arrows. Thereafter the bodies of men and horses were to be found all along the route and 'there were stenches from their corpses that almost overcame the birds in the air'.[77]

For the Christians this was an appalling and humiliating defeat. Both William of Tyre and Ibn al-Qalanisi say that the attackers had been confident that the city would be taken, which, given the combined strength of the armies, must surely have been likely. Even allowing for the losses in Asia Minor, at no other time in the history of the crusader states in the twelfth century did the Latins have three formidable armies at their disposal, in whose ranks there must have been a high proportion of fighting men, given that, as always, the losses en route must have been disproportionately high among the lower ranks and noncombatants.[78]

However, there are considerable discrepancies between the stories told in the two main narratives. William was remote from the action, but depended on eyewitnesses who, judging by Conrad's bitter letter to Wibald of Corvey written in autumn 1148, firmly believed the version he recorded. Conrad says that, although it was a unanimous decision to attack Damascus, the crusaders had been betrayed, for when they were encamped before the gate, where 'it was almost certain that the city would be taken', they were purposely led to another side 'where there was no water for the army and no obvious access'.[79] Ibn al-Qalanisi, who was probably in the city at the time, says nothing about changing position, a move that would not have fitted his overall narrative, since he has the crusader army coming from the south. This would be the expected direction of approach of a force coming from Banyas, which, as William of Tyre says, then reached Darayya, to the south-west of the city, and indeed was the route used by Baldwin II and Fulk of Anjou in the autumn of 1129.[80] If this were so, then they would have seen the defences and terrain on the southern side before deciding to hack their way through the orchards on the western side. Even if they had not, it seems scarcely credible that the leaders, with their combined experience, would have shifted so many men and horses and such quantities of baggage without first checking for themselves if the site were suitable.

One other source, further removed from the events than the others, is Ibn al-Athir. He did not have Ibn al-Qalanisi's knowledge of Damascus, but his association with the Zengids enabled him to offer a different perspective. He says that Unur sent for help from Saif al-Din and Nur al-Din, who assembled their forces at Homs. From here Saif al-Din threatened the besiegers, enabling Unur to use his presence as a bargaining counter. In these circumstances, the eastern Franks convinced Conrad that they would not be strong enough to resist an attack from Saif al-Din, who at the same time would take Damascus for himself.[81] This seems quite convincing, even though no direct confrontation with Zengi's sons actually took place.[82] Given the scale of the defeat, it may be that the story of treachery was convenient for both the participants and the promoters of the crusade, especially as it appeared to shift the blame onto the local Franks.

Once the idea of treachery had been established, speculation as to the guilty party was inevitable.[83] William of Tyre reports that some believed that Thierry of Flanders was at fault, not because he had betrayed the army himself, but because his ambition to be granted Damascus had angered those who had spent their entire lives in the struggle to defend the Holy Land.[84] Others blamed Raymond of Antioch who, in his hatred of Louis VII, had incited some of the nobles to sabotage the siege. A third idea was that some had been bribed, although they were appropriately recompensed when the money turned out to be worthless.[85] Michael the Syrian named Baldwin III as the culprit, claiming that the Damascenes had secretly warned him that if the city fell Conrad would take over Jerusalem as well, and that he would be better advised to accept their offer of 200,000 dinars to retreat. However, when they were examined the coins turned out to be no more than copper with a covering of gold.[86] None of these theories is very convincing and William is unwilling to draw any conclusions, but the belief in betrayal persisted and accusations continued to be made in the West. The Würzburg annalist, for example, apparently unaware of the role of the order in the original plan to attack Damascus, believed that 'the abominable deceit of the Templars' was responsible.[87]

Whatever the losses, when the armies returned to the kingdom there were still sufficient men to contemplate further action, which might have helped salvage reputations. Ascalon had remained uncaptured for nearly a quarter of a century after the fall of Tyre, but William says that this, along with other suggestions, was rejected. Conrad, however, claimed that he thought a plan to attack it had been decided upon, only to find that he was the only one to take it seriously. 'When we reached the agreed spot we found virtually no-one. For eight days we waited there in vain for them all to arrive then went back to our own camp when we realised we had been tricked a second time.'[88] Conrad saw no further point in staying in the East and, on 8 September, set sail from Acre. Louis, whose original goal had been pilgrimage, stayed until the following Easter, and it may have been during this time that links were forged that led to the later belief among the eastern Franks that Louis would be prepared to come to their aid again in the future.[89]

This preoccupation with the fate of the great armies and their leaders is perhaps natural in the circumstances but the loss of Edessa and the failure before Damascus had an impact upon the local population as well. According to a contemporary Syrian, Mar Simon, in 1148, 'Jerusalem was filled with no end of poor people and there was want of food and other necessaries', since the city was teeming with refugees, many of whom had fled from Edessa and the surrounding region. Mar Simon describes how the religious houses were virtually besieged by the indigent and, for a period, struggled to cope. He wrote to praise the efforts of Archbishop Ignatius, who 'had compassion on all the poor whether of our own community or that of the Franks'.[90] The result was a settlement of refugees around the church of Dayr Dakariya, which probably refers to Zakariya, 8 miles north-east of Bait Jibrin.[91] The Syrians would not have been the only providers. Every year there was a large-scale distribution of alms at the church of the Holy Sepulchre on the third day after the anniversary of the taking of Jerusalem on 15 July, and in 1148 this must have been particularly important.[92]

William of Tyre, like Otto of Freising, drew moral lessons from these events. To him, it was evident that divine favour had been withdrawn because of the unworthiness of the participants, although he admits he could not understand the judgment of the Lord.[93] In fact, he treats the equally decisive defeat of Baldwin's expedition to Bosra the year before quite differently, trying to show that, even in adversity, God did not desert his people, saving the army by a series of miracles appropriate for those who were descended from the warriors of the First Crusade.[94] 'No one now living,' he says, 'can remember any equally perilous expedition during the period of the Latins in the Orient which did not result in a decisive victory for the enemy.'[95]

William felt that he needed to show that God still approved of the Christian establishment in the East despite the obvious blows of 1144 and 1147–8, for he was aware that perceptions of Outremer had been fundamentally changed.[96] Whether the charges of treachery were true or not, they all related to the eastern Franks in some way, and many crusaders evidently returned to the West bearing a grudge. 'Even when permitted to return to their own lands, the memory of the wrongs which they had suffered still rankled, and they regarded with abhorrence the wicked conduct of those nobles. Not only was this true in regard to themselves, but their influence caused others who had not been present there to slacken in love toward the kingdom. As a result, fewer people, and those less fervent in spirit, undertook this pilgrimage thereafter. Moreover, even to the present day, those who do come fear lest they be caught in the same toils and hence make as short a stay as possible.'[97] At the same time he thought that the military prestige of the Latins had been seriously undermined. Writing about the defeat of Louis's army at Cadmus Mountain, he says: 'That day the glorious reputation of the Franks was lost through a misfortune most fatal and disastrous for the Christians; their valor, up to this time formidable to the nations, was crushed to earth. Henceforward it was as a mockery in the eyes of those unclean races to whom formerly it had been a terror.'[98]

From this time, William says, the situation of the Latins in the East became 'manifestly worse'. His gloom was deepened by events in Antioch in the summer of 1149, when Nur al-Din seized the opportunity to invade the southern part of the principality. He was at once challenged by Prince Raymond who, according to William of Tyre, left Antioch in such a hurry he did not wait for the assembly of the main body of his knights. Nur al-Din retreated but, once he realised the relative weakness of the Christian forces, returned to the offensive, reinforced by a contingent of troops from Damascus. Ibn al-Qalanisi says that this gave him an army of 6,000 men. They found the Antiochenes in a camp surrounded by marshes near Inab, which lay on the plain east of the Orontes about 60 miles south-west of Aleppo, and during the night of 28 June encircled them. Both William of Tyre and Ibn al-Qalanisi say that Raymond's army was outnumbered; even so, Ibn al-Qalanisi gives a figure of 5,000 men, curiously made up of 4,000 horsemen and 1,000 foot soldiers, contradicting William's statement that Raymond had left Antioch without his cavalry. In either case the result was the same. The Franks were slaughtered and when the dust had settled the Muslims found Raymond's body on the battlefield. They hacked off his head and right arm and presented them to Nur al-Din; when the prince's body was later recovered and taken back to Antioch for burial, his men were only able to identify him because of certain known scars. Nur al-Din sent the head and the arm to the caliph and they were passed around the other Turkish leaders of the region.[99]

This was a great triumph for Nur al-Din, underlined in the Muslim sources by their emphasis on the formidable character of the man they had overcome. 'This accursed one,' says Ibn al-Qalanisi, 'was amongst the Frankish knights who were famed for their gallantry, valour, power of cunning, and great stature, and had acquired special repute by the dread which he inspired, his great severity, and excessive ferocity.' For Ibn al-Athir, he was 'one of the most intransigent of the Franks and one of their great leaders'.[100] His death plunged the principality into crisis. Raymond's heir, Bohemond III, was only a small child, and many of Antioch's defenders had lost their lives in the battle. Nur al-Din took immediate advantage, bringing his forces up to the gates of Antioch itself and demanding its surrender, although he was temporarily appeased by gifts and perhaps diverted by the opportunity to take Harim and Apamea. The key figure was the patriarch, Aimery of Limoges, of whom William of Tyre generally has a low opinion, but whom on this occasion he describes as the defender of the region, using his wealth to hire troops.

Ibn al-Qalanisi does not properly explain Nur al-Din's subsequent willingness to grant an armistice based on a broad division of the lands between Antioch and Aleppo, although it is likely that a relief force under Baldwin III, which probably set out in the late summer, deterred him from undertaking the siege that would have been needed to take the city. Included in Baldwin's army was a strong contingent of Templars under Andrew of Montbard, the order's seneschal and acting head while the master, Everard des Barres, was away in France. In a letter to Everard, pleading with him to return as soon as he could with arms, knights, sergeants and money, the seneschal said that he had raised a force of 120 knights and up to 1,000 squires and sergeants for this army, a huge effort that needed a loan of 7,000 besants of Acre and 1,000 besants of Jerusalem to pay for it. According to Andrew, who was present, they had been trapped in the city of Antioch for a time by a twin attack from Mas'ud, the Seljuk sultan of Iconium, and Nur al-Din.[101] This was unlikely to have been a serious attempt to take the city, for William of Tyre says that Baldwin was able to make a foray against Harim, but that he failed to retake it. Even so, Nur al-Din fully exploited the propaganda value of his victory;

before returning to Aleppo, he had reached the coast, where he saw the sea for the first time, symbolically bathing in it in the presence of his troops.[102]

The remains of the county of Edessa were similarly assailed, for when Ma'sud heard of Raymond's death he invaded and besieged Turbessel, pinning Count Joscelin and his family inside. The siege was raised when Baldwin sent his constable, Humphrey of Toron, with sixty knights to protect the fortress of 'Azaz, giving Joscelin the opportunity to negotiate. Ma'sud accepted the release of all Joscelin's Turkish prisoners, together with twelve suits of armour, in exchange for peace.[103] However, in May 1150, while travelling to Antioch to meet the patriarch, Joscelin was fortuitously captured by some of Nur al-Din's troops, apparently after he had stepped aside from his escort to urinate. Taken to Aleppo, he was imprisoned and tortured, eventually dying there in 1159. William of Tyre has little sympathy. Throughout his narrative he stresses how inferior he was in comparison with his father, characterising him as lazy and dissolute, and castigating him for his intense hatred of Raymond of Poitiers, which prevented the two men from co-operating against their common enemy.[104] He was no better regarded by the local population. Michael the Syrian was particularly angry about his pillaging of the Jacobite monastery of Mar Bar Sauma, south of Melitene, in 1149, and about his imprisonment of Basil, the Jacobite bishop of Edessa, who had been forced to flee to Samosata after the second fall of the city. Joscelin had accused both the monks and the bishop of collaboration with the Turks, leading Michael to call him a tyrant who had abandoned God and 'devoted himself to the cult of demons'.[105]

Beatrice, Joscelin's wife, was left with a young son and two daughters, and almost at once her predatory neighbours fell upon the remnants of the county. Ma'sud of Iconium reappeared, forcing the Latins to retreat to Turbessel, abandoning their remaining fortresses, while Nur al-Din ravaged the southern parts of the county, grinding the people between two millstones, as William of Tyre puts it.[106] Although Ma'sud subsequently withdrew, at the end of June Nur al-Din was able to take 'Azaz.[107] As he had the previous summer, Baldwin responded, although he was unable to derive any support from the nobility 'in the part in which the queen ruled', which suggests that relations with his mother had severely deteriorated, and he had to rely on Raymond of Tripoli. However, when Baldwin arrived he decided that the situation was hopeless. He knew he could not remain in Antioch, and even had he been able to, he did not have the resources to govern both provinces. He therefore accepted an offer from envoys of Manuel Comnenus to take over what remained of the county of Edessa in return for providing the countess and her family with a fixed annual revenue. William of Tyre claims that the king had little confidence in this arrangement, although of course when William wrote he knew that the land had been lost within months by 'the soft and effeminate Greeks'.

Meanwhile in August, the king and Count Raymond set about the evacuation of all those Latins and Armenians who wished to leave, an operation made all the more difficult by the constant attacks of Nur al-Din upon the slow-moving column. The Muslims harassed the refugees for two days, obliging them to take cover in the fortress of Aintab after the first day, but finally gave up when they ran out of supplies. William of Tyre, who must have interviewed many of those who had experienced this traumatic march when they later settled in the kingdom of Jerusalem, presents a dramatic picture of people distressed at leaving 'the land of their birth', a region of productive woods and fields capable of supporting 500 knights. As well as the blow to their military capacity, the Latins had also lost three archbishoprics in Edessa, Hierapolis (Manbij) and Corice (Quris).[108]

In contrast, in the kingdom of Jerusalem, in July 1149, the rebuilt church of the Holy Sepulchre was consecrated by the patriarch, once more providing an appropriate setting for the most important shrines in Christendom. Even here, however, beneath the surface unity of the dedication ceremony, fissures were appearing, most critically in the growing animosity between Baldwin III and his mother, Queen Melisende. William of Tyre emphasises that she ruled by hereditary right and that it was appropriate for Baldwin to co-operate with her.[109] Nevertheless, by 1151, Baldwin was twenty-one, six years older than the age required in the kingdom for independent rule, and he appears to have lost patience with his exclusion from power and patronage. Thus, when Elinand of Tiberias died in c.1149, there appears to have been a struggle over who should succeed him in the key lordship of Galilee, while in the summer of 1150 Baldwin was unable to muster the southern lords, despite a series of personal summonses.[110] Moreover, in 1150 and 1151, there are signs that the queen was consolidating her position, both in the marriage of Manasses of Hierges to Helvis of Ibelin and in the promotion of her younger son, Amalric, to the county of Jaffa.

William of Tyre is reluctant to blame Melisende for the ensuing conflict, so he falls back on the cliché of the evil counsellor. The real trouble was caused by Manasses of Hierges, he says, who provoked intense hatred among the baronage by his treatment of them. On 31 March 1152, the day after Easter Sunday, Baldwin appeared in procession in Jerusalem 'crowned with the laurel'.[111] This was quickly followed by a demand in the High Court that the kingdom be divided between him and Melisende, and it was determined that the queen should hold the south, centred on Jerusalem, Nablus and Samaria, while Baldwin should rule in the north, including the key cities of Acre and Tyre. Apparently the king was given the choice, although William does not say what options had been presented. Chief among the king's supporters was Humphrey of Toron, who held extensive lands around Tyre and was one of the kingdom's outstanding soldiers. Baldwin appointed him constable in direct opposition to Manasses of Hierges; indeed, it is possible that he had already been using the title even before this open breach between the two sides.[112] Soon after, in April, Ralph, the former chancellor, reappears as the royal chancellor, having evidently decided that Baldwin was the more likely to win.[113]

Although William rather piously states that 'the people' hoped that the settlement would be maintained, there was in reality no chance that it would, for it would have been impossible to combat the Egyptians in the south and the Turks in the north in a divided kingdom. It seems unlikely therefore that Baldwin intended this to be any more than a temporary arrangement. Baldwin now moved against Manasses in his castle at Mirabel, where he forced a surrender, and then, undeterred by the peacemaking efforts of Patriarch Fulcher, continued on to Jerusalem, where he was joined by southern nobles who had deserted the queen. Although the gates of the city were opened to him it took several days of fierce fighting before Melisende would concede the citadel in which she had taken refuge. The queen was now obliged to retire to Nablus and its territory, leaving Jerusalem to her son.[114] In the circumstances, Manasses clearly could not survive and was banished from the kingdom, but men like Philip of Nablus and Andrew of Montbard, seneschal of the Temple, were too powerful to ignore, and were incorporated into the new regime. Amalric's restoration may have been slower: he lost the county of Jaffa after Baldwin's victory and did not regain it until 1154.[115]

Throughout this period William of Tyre has nothing to say about the affairs of the county of Tripoli. Raymond II had not been present at the siege of Damascus, perhaps feeling that it was wise to keep a low profile after the death of Alfonso-Jordan earlier in the year. However, even with Alfonso-Jordan dead, his natural son, Bertrand, remained a potential rival. Bertrand had taken part in the Damascus campaign, and was living with his mother in the fortress of al-'Arimah, situated midway between Tripoli and Tortosa. Ibn al-Qalanisi describes how, in September 1148, the castle was suddenly attacked by Nur al-Din and Unur of Damascus, falling to them after a fierce struggle. Bertrand and his mother were captured and Bertrand was not seen again until he was released in 1159 after negotiations by the Byzantine emperor, Manuel Comnenus.[116] Despite al-'Arimah's proximity to the main cities of the county, there is no mention of any help from Raymond, which lends credibility to Ibn al-Athir's later claim that it was Raymond himself who had encouraged the Muslim attack. For Alfonso's son, says Ibn al-Athir, the following saying is appropriate: 'The ostrich went out, seeking two horns and returned home minus both ears.'[117]

As the possessor of the only adult male ruler in the three northern states, Tripoli appears to have been better equipped to survive than Antioch or Edessa. Raymond's creation of a Hospitaller enclave east of the Homs gap provided a screen against Nur al-Din, and in the summer of 1150 the count was in a position to reinforce Baldwin III's depleted army on its way north after the capture of Joscelin of Edessa. However, with Antioch and Edessa in tatters, Tripoli became vulnerable. Nur al-Din had already demonstrated his capacity to reach the coast and, in April 1152, he repeated the feat, penetrating the county's defences to take Tortosa, where he left a garrison. The arrival of Baldwin III in Tripoli soon after must, in part, have been a response to such a worrying development and appears to have persuaded the Muslims to abandon the town, which was left largely ruined.

William, bishop of Tortosa, who was overlord of the town, moved quickly to fill the vacuum. A charter of 1157 shows that, a very short time after the Muslims left, he granted the Templars land on which to build a castle. Raynouard of Maraclea, who is recorded as lord in 1151, must have been compensated elsewhere. During the 1150s, the Templars built a strong fortress in the north-west corner of the town with access to the sea. They received a series of ecclesiastical privileges from the bishop, including control of parish churches on Templar lands and exemption from tithes on their own demesne and on booty taken in military expeditions. It is probable that Raymond granted additional land and feudal exemptions equivalent to those of the Hospitallers, although the charter recording this is now lost. The choice of the Templars was a logical step, for the Hospitallers already had heavy responsibilities to the east, and the 1157 charter shows that the Templars had previously been granted Chastel-Blanc (Safita), which was only about 10 miles to the south-east.[118] By this time the Templars also probably held al-'Arimah, just to the south beyond the Abrash River, perhaps acquiring it after the capture of Bertrand, together with Chastel-Blanc. From this time the military orders dominated the northern part of the county of Tripoli.[119] These grants reflect the changing nature of the county, which, after the mid-century, increasingly lost its ties with Toulouse, whose feudal lords had, until then, been drawn largely from southern French families. From this time more outsiders began to appear, not only from northern France, but also from other Syrian lands, such as Armenia, Antioch and Edessa, the last of which must have included refugees from the disasters of recent years.[120]

However, it appears that Baldwin's primary purpose was the holding of a session of the High Court in Tripoli, the first since he had removed his mother from power. In contrast to 1150, he was able to command the full attendance of his vassals from both Jerusalem and Tripoli and, in an assembly reminiscent of that held by Baldwin I near the city in 1109, also the presence of Patriarch Aimery of Antioch and his suffragans and Princess Constance and her leading nobles. At the same time Queen Melisende travelled to Tripoli, although her primary purpose was an attempt to persuade her niece, Constance, to take a husband, rather than to participate in any of the public acts of the High Court.[121] Constance, however, was not amenable. William of Tyre blames her intransigence on Patriarch Aimery, who he believes preferred the greater freedom of manoeuvre available to him when there was no prince ruling in Antioch, but subsequent events show that Constance had her own ideas about marriage.

Melisende was also involved in the marital affairs of her sister, Hodierna, whose relations with Raymond II were breaking down, a consequence, says William of Tyre, of jealousy (*simultas*). She failed to reconcile them and the sisters set out for Jerusalem, accompanied for a short distance by Count Raymond. But, as he returned to Tripoli, Raymond was suddenly attacked and killed just outside the city by Assassins, together with Ralph of Merle and one of his knights, an event that led to a riot in the city with indiscriminate killing of anyone who did not look or dress like a Latin.[122] The reason for the murder is unknown, for it was unusual for the Assassins to target a Christian ruler. Presumably conflict had arisen with the Syrian Assassins, whose bases in the Jabal Nahra, north of al-Buqai‘ah, were close to Raymond's territories.

Therefore, between 1149 and 1152, all three of the northern crusader states had been deprived of their adult male rulers, and Edessa had effectively been liquidated, while simultaneously in Nur al-Din they were faced with the most formidable opponent seen by the Franks in Syria since they had first settled in the region. Il-Ghazi had been a terrible enemy, but the evident flaws in his character, his apparent indifference to the aims of the *jihad* and his sometimes uncertain control over the Turcomans upon whom he relied undermined his credibility in the Muslim world. Nur al-Din, on the other hand, was genuinely committed to the holy war, and from this time worked assiduously to create an image of selfless devotion to the cause of defeating the infidel Franks. Although his military campaigns made it obvious that he believed the chief object of the *jihad* to be the elimination of the Franks, as a Turk he realised the need to convince the local population. An extensive building programme of madrasas and convents for Sufis, together with the repair and restoration of many mosques, enabled him to inspire a renewed interest in Sunnite doctrinal studies, which he saw as the basis for a unified Islamic Syria.[123]

CHAPTER 9

The Frankish Imprint

BEFORE he left the Holy Land in May 1241, Richard, earl of Cornwall, had made the rebuilding of the fortifications of Ascalon his greatest priority. Having agreed a truce with as-Salih, the Egyptian sultan, he was anxious to ensure that the town was now as secure as possible. In a letter of July 1241, he describes how at the time of writing 'it is totally protected by a double wall with high towers and ramparts made of cut stone', and that it lacked only a fosse for completion. Richard was proud of his efforts because he understood the central importance of Ascalon to the kingdom of Jerusalem. The reason for this reconstruction, he explained, was that 'if the truce was broken we would have a secure stronghold in the march on the edge of their territory, previously held by them, to which we could retreat if necessary'. The castle 'is also useful in times of peace, since it is the key and protector of the kingdom of Jerusalem by land and sea, while it threatens danger to Babylon and the southern regions'.[1]

Richard of Cornwall's concern for Ascalon had deep roots in the kingdom of Jerusalem. His uncle, Richard I of England, had rebuilt its defences at great expense in the spring of 1191, and even when he had abandoned his hopes of a march on Jerusalem he could not bring himself to accede to Saladin's demand that he dismantle its walls and towers. According to Ibn Shaddad, Saladin's *qadi* of the army, in July 1192, the king is supposed to have told the sultan's emissary, 'It is impossible for us to demolish one stone of Ascalon. Such a thing shall not be spoken of in the land. The boundaries of these lands are well known and there is no dispute about them.'[2] In the end Richard was obliged to give in and, in the truce of 2 September 1192, it was at last agreed that Ascalon's defences be destroyed for three years.

All the twelfth-century rulers of Jerusalem had been preoccupied with Ascalon. Attacks launched from there had been the most persistent danger to

Jerusalem, and both Godfrey and Baldwin I had fought crucial battles for survival against Egyptian forces emanating from the town. At the end of his life Baldwin was exploring the possibility of an invasion of Egypt, and in 1123–4 there had been a vigorous debate about whether to use the Venetian fleet to besiege Tyre or Ascalon. Under Fulk, practical steps had been taken to control the threat by the building of Bait Jibrin, Ibelin and Blanchegarde.

Baldwin III returned to the matter as soon as he was able and, in the winter of 1149–50, began the task of fortifying the ancient city of Gaza so that, as William of Tyre says, Ascalon would be hemmed in from the south as well as the north and the east. Although the hill on which the city had stood was too large to be completely encircled, part of it was fortified with walls and towers before handing it over to the Templars, who were left with responsibility for completing the interior. An immediate attack by the Egyptians proved fruitless and William says that from then onwards they could only supply Ascalon by sea. At the same time Frankish settlements in the south were far more secure, since Gaza served 'as the fortified boundary of the kingdom'.[3] The Egyptians, though, were by no mean cowed. In April 1152, when Baldwin was distracted by Nur al-Din's seizure of Tortosa, Ibn al-Qalanisi reports a 'victory of the men of Ascalon over the Franks in their neighbourhood at Gaza, when a great number of them perished and the remainder fled'.[4]

Further pressure was evidently needed and at the end of the year the Franks decided to destroy the orchards around Ascalon in the hope of undermining the city's economic base. These orchards were valuable to the town since the sandy soil in the immediate vicinity was unsuitable for agriculture, although the Egyptian government regarded Ascalon as sufficiently important to send troops and subsidies on a regular basis. Given the difficulties such an action entailed, both in the danger of attack from Christian ships and in the problems of making safe anchorage along a windswept coast, this shows the high priority given to the town in Cairo and suggests that it was unlikely that the Franks could bring it down through an economic blockade. William of Tyre's belief that, if Ascalon fell, Egypt would be open to invasion was apparently shared in Cairo.

If William of Tyre is correct, the destruction of the orchards was not initially intended to be a full-scale attack, but the terror of the inhabitants persuaded the Christian leaders that the town could be taken and, on 25 January 1153, they encamped around the walls. The seriousness of the operation can be seen by the presence of the True Cross and by the level of participation. The leading prelates and secular nobles and the heads of the military orders were present, as well as newcomers from the West such as Reynald of Châtillon, a younger son of Hervé II, lord of Donzy, about 25 miles north of Nevers in central France, who served for pay. A fleet of fifteen warships, commanded by Gerard of Sidon, was deployed to blockade the town, while scouts were posted around Gaza in case the Egyptians sent a relief force by land.

Preparations on this scale were fully justified, despite the isolation of the town. The walls and towers were kept in good order and the Greater Gate, facing east, was protected by a series of bent entrances which precluded direct assault. Outworks in the form of embankments prevented direct access to the walls. Although Ascalon had no natural springs, it was well supplied with water by wells and cisterns. As William of Tyre points out, it had resisted all attempts to take it for fifty years. Not surprisingly, after two months' hard fighting the besiegers had made no progress, so the additional forces provided by the arrival of ships from the West in the annual spring crossing were very welcome. Ships were purchased so that their timbers could be used to construct a siege engine and mangonels, and the extra forces enabled them to clear the ground so that the engine could be brought close to the walls. This occurred around Easter, which fell on 19 April, and more or less coincided with the murder of Ibn al-Salar, the Egyptian vizier, in Cairo. Apparently resentment at his autocratic rule had arisen among the emirs and one of them, his stepson, al-Abbas, had assassinated him in his bed.[5] As there had not been an adult caliph since 1149, the occurrence of a struggle for control of the vizirate at the same time that Ascalon was under siege can only have helped the Christian cause.[6]

In fact, the instability of the Egyptian government did not prevent the sailing of the fleet that Ibn al-Salar had been organising to relieve the town. In early June, seventy galleys accompanied by transports loaded with supplies arrived at Ascalon, and soon drove off Gerard of Sidon's squadron.[7] This revived the spirits of the defenders, who determined to destroy the siege engine, piling up debris in the gap between the engine and the wall and setting it alight. However, a strong easterly wind blew up and the fire was driven against the wall, causing a whole section to crumble during the night and leaving a breach through which the Christians could enter. The Templars under their new master, Bernard of Tremelay, were manning that sector and immediately rushed into the town. William of Tyre alleges that they then prevented others from entering so that they could claim all the spoils, but more probable are some western accounts, apparently based on eyewitnesses, which say that the rest of the army was slow to follow, leaving the Templars isolated.[8] When the defenders realised they were faced with only about forty knights, they slaughtered them, while at the same time shoring up the breach with large beams derived from the fleet. The disaster was compounded by the abandonment of the siege engine, which had been damaged by falling masonry when the wall collapsed. Triumphant at their success, the Muslims hung the bodies of the dead Templars from the walls, taunting the besiegers with their failure.[9]

This was a huge setback after five months of toil, expense and many deaths. When the Christian leaders held a conference, it became clear that opinion was divided between those who were ready to abandon the siege, which included most of the nobility and even the king himself, and those who wanted to persevere, led by Patriarch Fulcher and Raymond du Puy, master of the Hospital. In the end they decided to carry on and the assault that followed was so furious that the defenders felt obliged to call for a truce during which the bodies of the dead of both sides could be exchanged. This was the beginning of the end for the inhabitants, overcome by the extent of their losses at a time when there was little prospect of any further outside help. Negotiations followed and the populace was allowed to leave. Baldwin provided an escort as far as al-Arish, but after this they were suddenly attacked by a Turk called Nocquinus, who had actually been involved in the defence of the city but who now seized his opportunity to rob the refugees of all their possessions, leaving them, William says, 'wandering in destitution'.[10]

The taking of Ascalon had involved a massive effort extended over seven months, which had included a reverse so serious that the siege had almost been abandoned. The Christians entered the town on 22 August, where, following the True Cross, they processed to the principal mosque, later consecrated as the church of St Paul.[11] Patriarch Fulcher ordained Absalom, a canon of the Holy Sepulchre, as bishop, and established prebends to support a chapter of canons, although the protests of Gerald, bishop of Bethlehem, and of his successor, Ralph, eventually led Pope Hadrian IV to overturn the appointment of the bishop on the grounds that the town appertained to the see of Bethlehem.[12] Baldwin assigned a series of fiefs, some of which he sold, and the following year appointed his brother Amalric as count of Ascalon as well as Jaffa. William of Tyre says that these actions were taken 'with the advice of his mother', a phrase that suggests that, despite the events of the previous year, Melisende retained at least some influence in royal government.[13]

For the Egyptians, the fall of Ascalon was compounded by the struggle for the control of the government in Cairo. After al-Abbas had seized power, his son, Nasir al-Din, murdered the caliph, replacing him with his five-year-old son, al-Fa'iz, but news of the caliph's death leaked out before they had time to consolidate their position, and they found themselves facing an uprising. They decided to flee from Cairo and seek help from Nur al-Din, enabling

Tala'i 'ibn Russuk, governor of Middle Egypt, to take over the vizirate. In early June 1154, as they hurried across the desert towards Damascus, they were ambushed by the Franks, who killed al-Abbas and captured Nasir al-Din.[14] William of Tyre says that Nasir was held by the Templars, now the established power south of Ascalon, where they were able to operate from their base at Gaza. Nasir allegedly expressed an interest in converting to Christianity, but when the opportunity arose the Templars sold him to the Egyptians for 60,000 gold pieces. Taken back to Cairo in an iron cage, he was torn to pieces by the populace.[15]

This incident emphasised the value of the capture of Ascalon, for it enabled the Franks to patrol the desert south of the kingdom and often provided tangible returns in the form of plunder from caravans. For Baldwin, however, it meant much more, for it opened the possibility of conquering Egypt itself. For the king, this was a very serious project. In a lost diploma, which can be dated between 1157 and 1159, the king granted Joscelin Pisellus an antici-patory fief of 100 knights in Egypt after its conquest. Joscelin must have been one of Baldwin's supporters in the civil war of 1152, since he first appears as a member of the king's inner circle, the *homines regis*, in April 1152. The trust placed in him can be seen in his role as one of the royal envoys sent to nego-tiate with the Byzantine emperor, Manuel, in 1157 and 1159.[16]

A fief worth 100 knights would have been a huge step up for Joscelin, who held only a money fief of 1,200 Saracen *hypereroi* drawn on the *cathena* (port dues) at Acre, for which he owed a mere two knights. In contrast, in the 1260s, the jurist John of Ibelin reckoned a noble holding lands owing service of 100 knights was one of the four great barons of the kingdom.[17] Nothing like that was available in the kingdom in the 1150s, although the king had also promised Joscelin the next vacant fief worth twenty knights. In fact, even a fief of this size was highly unlikely to materialise, for new opportunities were increasingly rare after the mid-century. The conquest of Egypt therefore held a strong attraction for a kingdom that needed more manpower but had insuf-ficient resources to sustain it. In this context, Baldwin's agreement with Pisa in 1156 to embargo all arms and ship-building materials to Egypt gains added significance, and lends credibility to the view that Baldwin III was hoping to convince Manuel to ally with the crusader states in order to overcome Nur al-Din and to conquer Egypt.[18]

The main source for the siege and fall of Ascalon is the vivid account of William of Tyre, who, as later in his narrative, demonstrates his great skill at retelling the stories of the participants as if he himself had actually witnessed the events.[19] Nevertheless, he attributes the fall to divine mercy in a manner that he by no means applies consistently throughout his work, and he seems to be trying to balance the failure at Damascus with the success at Ascalon, both of which he links to the will of God in an attempt to counter the view commonly held in the West that the Franks in Palestine had betrayed the Christian cause for their own selfish and material ends.[20] Indeed, William had already set out to show that God intended these Christians should hold Jerusalem, even though from time to time he withdrew his favour. In November 1152, just before the decision to attack Ascalon, in an extraordinary incident, the city of Jerusalem was suddenly assailed from the east by a large army of Turks led by men whom William describes as claiming the city by hereditary right. The leader appears to have been Timurtash of Mardin, whose father, Il-Ghazi, and uncle, Soqman, had been driven out of Jerusalem by the Fatimids in 1098.[21] Although the Damascenes tried to dissuade him, he nevertheless pushed on with the plan, urged on by his mother. He arrived at Jerusalem when the bulk of the Christian army was at Nablus, but even so the inhabitants of the city were still able to beat him off, falling upon the Turks in the narrow defile of the road to the Jordan. 'The hand of the Lord,' says William, 'was indeed heavy upon our enemies that day.'[22]

Ascalon had received no help from Nur al-Din, but he had taken advantage of Baldwin's concentration on the siege to bring renewed pressure on Damascus, which remained his primary goal. Unur's ambivalent relationship with his overbearing neighbour meant that he hesitated to commit himself to the *jihad* against the Franks, despite continued raids from Tyre and Acre into Damascene territory.[23] He contributed forces to Nur al-Din's armies, but was not willing to cede control of Damascus itself, even though Nur al-Din's increasingly powerful self-presentation as the champion of Islam had attracted widespread support, including from some in Damascus itself. In the years after the Second Crusade, Nur al-Din frequently brought his army into the vicinity of Damascus, sometimes posing as the protector of the peasantry of the Hauran, whom he claimed had suffered at the hands of the Franks. However, he restrained himself from actually besieging Damascus on the grounds that it would involve the shedding of Muslim blood, although he must have been well aware that it was not an easy target, especially after what had happened to the crusaders.[24] Unur's death in August 1150 certainly strengthened his hand, but it was not until April 1154 that he finally managed to enter the city, where he met little resistance. He was, says Ibn al-Qalanisi, received with joy by the people 'because of their sufferings from famine, the high cost of food, and fear of being besieged by the Frankish infidels.'[25]

The implications of this triumph went beyond the city's strategic importance. In 1156, the Banu Qudama, a family that followed the strict precepts laid down by the jurist Ahmad ibn Hanbul in the ninth century, emigrated from the villages around Nablus, complaining of their maltreatment at the hands of the overlord, Baldwin of Ibelin. They were led by Ahmad ibn Qudama, who had been accused of diverting the peasants from their work through his Friday preaching and who now claimed he was in fear of his life. There were, however, evident positive reasons for the move to Damascus, for there the family could hope for a status appropriate to those who believed in Nur al-Din's commitment to the *jihad*.[26] Only eight months after the conquest of the last Muslim enclave on the Palestinian and Syrian coast, the crusader states were faced with a regime more threatening than ever before. As William of Tyre saw it, nothing worse could have happened to the Christians.[27]

Moreover, although in 1153–4 Damascus took priority in Nur al-Din's plans, he was alert to the possibilities that the fall of Ascalon opened up for the Franks, and in 1158 he started negotiations with the Egyptians despite their Shi'ite allegiance. An embassy led by his chamberlain, Mahmud al-Mustarshidi, arrived back in Damascus on 7 October, bringing one of the leading Egyptian emirs, as well as gifts of money and horses. It was a timely initiative. Since 1153, the Franks had become accustomed to intervening in the lands south of Gaza, and Mahmud's party had itself been attacked. Soon after, in a typical skirmish, Ibn al-Qalanisi says that the Egyptians had defeated a force of 400 Frankish horsemen at al-Arish, another striking indication of the scale of the Frankish presence in the region.[28]

Reynald of Châtillon had not stayed to see the victory at Ascalon. At some point in the course of 1153, he had travelled to Antioch where he appears to have convinced Princess Constance that he would make a suitable husband. This was kept secret until they could obtain the king's consent, but the moment was well chosen as Baldwin was entirely focused on the siege and must have been pleased to see Antioch in the hands of an adult male ruler, given Constance's previous rejection of proffered husbands. William of Tyre, influenced by Reynald's subsequent behaviour, thought this a very poor match, calling him 'a knight of the common sort', although in fact he came from a distinguished family, even though he himself had no personal wealth.[29] Most probably Reynald had come to the East in an attempt to rebuild his position, having, as he later put it in a letter to Louis VII of France, had a part of his patrimony 'violently and unjustly confiscated'.[30]

Almost immediately Reynald came into conflict with the patriarch, Aimery of Limoges. Antioch had been without a resident prince for four years and, according to Michael the Syrian, Baldwin had left Aimery as regent.[31] The patriarch, says William of Tyre, was a very rich and powerful man who held the highest authority.[32] He had established himself as a leader in the crisis that followed the death of Raymond of Poitiers in June 1149, when he had used a

1 The Ascension of Christ. The tympanum of the church of Montceaux-L'Etoile (Saône-et-Loire). The theme is derived from Acts 1: 9–11, when the appearances of Christ after the Resurrection are finally concluded with the ascent into Heaven. On the lintel the Virgin Mary and the Apostles stare upwards and two angels point to the mandorla in which Christ is encompassed. Sculpture on local churches such as those of the Brionnais would have been familiar to those contemplating pilgrimage and crusade.

2 Castle of Saone, seen from the west. The castle is built on a spur formed by two water-courses in the Nosairi Mountains about fifteen miles north-east of Latakia. It is divided into two enceintes, of which the upper, north-eastern end is the more heavily fortified. Here the Franks greatly strengthened the defences of what was primarily a Byzantine castle, built after its capture by Emperor John Tzimisces in 975.

3 Mount Tabor rises 500 metres above the plain of Jezreel, making it the most striking physical feature of the area. From the mid-fourth century, it was identified as the high mountain described as the place of the Transfiguration in Matthew 17: 1–8. A Byzantine church and associated buildings were situated there when the crusaders first arrived and Tancred established a Benedictine community soon after the fall of Jerusalem in July 1099. Although this was destroyed in 1113 it was restored soon after and survived until raided by Saladin's forces in June 1187.

4 Roman Jerash was an impressive example of the achievements of past civilisations. Although it was not occupied permanently by the Franks, it was certainly known to them, for King Baldwin II reached it in 1121.

5 St George's Monastery, Choziba, stands on the north side of the road to Jericho and the place of Christ's baptism in the River Jordan, an event recorded in the first three gospels. This was an important pilgrimage route, most of which was through rocky desert. By the second half of the twelfth century it was protected by Templar forts.

6 Ornamental initial P from a sacramentary produced by the scriptorium of the church of the Holy Sepulchre, 1128–30. The scriptorium was established by the 1120s and capable of producing required liturgical books from that time. This page is from the earliest surviving example.

7 Melisende's Psalter, c.1135. It has ivory covers, the front of which shows the life of King David together with the traditional battles between the Virtues and the Vices.

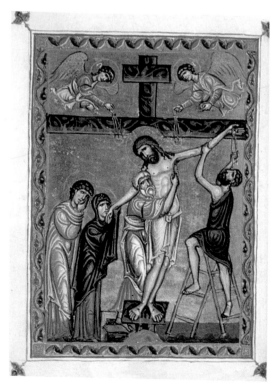

8 Melisende's Psalter contains 24 New Testament scenes. This example shows the Descent from the Cross.

9 Full page miniature of St John, from the Gospel of St John, produced by the scriptorium of the Holy Sepulchre in the 1140s.

10 Aqua Bella, eastern side. This was part of a series of associated Hospitaller buildings in the vicinity of the road between Jerusalem and Ramla. The Hospitaller estates in the area were protected by the castle of Belmont. The function of Aqua Bella is not known for certain, but it was probably an infirmary of some kind.

Obverse: BALDVINUS REX

Reverse: + DE IERUSALEM (Tower of David)

Obverse: AMALRICUS REX

Reverse: + DE IERUSALEM (interior of the Holy Sepulchre)

11 Billon *deniers* issued by King Baldwin III (top), c.1152, and by King Amalric (bottom), c.1163–4. Amalric recoined his *deniers* and *oboles*, reissuing them with a new design.

12 The site of Chastellet at Jacob's Ford on the Upper Jordan situated between Lake Huleh and the Sea of Galilee. The unfinished castle was destroyed by Saladin in August 1179.

13 Castle of Belvoir, Galilee. The castle is set high above the Jordan valley, eight miles south of the Sea of Galilee. It was bought by the Hospitallers in 1168 and during the 1170s they rebuilt it in concentric form. Its defences were strong enough to defy Saladin's besiegers until January 1189, eighteen months after the defeat at Hattin.

14 The castle of Kerak in Moab lies ten miles to the east of the southern end of the Dead Sea. It was refortified by Pagan the Butler and his successors from 1142 onwards. Despite his best efforts, Saladin was unable to overcome it and it did not fall until October or November 1188, when, isolated by the sultan's other conquests, its defenders were starved out.

15 Capital from the church of the Annunciation at Nazareth. This is one of five capitals intended for the shrine-grotto inside the church, which was believed to have been the childhood home of Christ. It would probably have been attached to the arcading of the lower storey. Here, the Virgin leads an apostle through the perils of Hell, all the while assailed by demons brandishing weapons.

part of what William describes as his great wealth to hire soldiers, although he adds that such expenditure was 'against his custom'.[33] Even so, William presents him as a mediocrity, elected to replace Ralph of Domfront in 1140 by bribery, although he had neither the education nor moral qualities to justify such a position. He had benefited from the patronage of both Prince Raymond and Ralph of Domfront, becoming archdeacon and then dean. He had shown no loyalty to Ralph, for he was among those who had plotted the patriarch's deposition, supported by his kinsman Peter Armoin, castellan of Antioch and one of the count's immediate entourage.[34] William's opinion, however, needs to be treated with caution, as he was undoubtedly influenced by the continuing dispute over jurisdiction between Antioch and Jerusalem. Aimery controlled the dioceses of the county of Tripoli, as had his predecessors, a situation to which William was never reconciled as he saw these bishops as his suffragans.[35]

In fact, Aimery was much more accomplished than William presents him. Before his decision to settle in Antioch, Aimery had been a member of 'the school of Toledo', presided over by Raymond, archbishop of Toledo between 1124/5 and 1152. Toledo had been an important seat of learning well before the Christian reconquest in 1085, but had since flourished as a centre of translation, especially of Arab works obtained through Hebrew and vernacular intermediaries. Aimery could not have held his own in such a high-powered intellectual environment without sophisticated linguistic skills, probably including Hebrew and Greek, and a solid grounding in biblical studies. He was the author of a description of the Holy Land called *La Fazienda de ultra mar*, written in Castilian and produced sometime before 1145, which incorporated not only Classical geographical knowledge but also sought to record the story of the people of Israel through the historical and prophetic works of the Old Testament, making use of the Hebrew text.[36] Moreover, Aimery was also what Gerard of Nazareth, bishop of Latakia, calls 'a sedulous promoter of the monastic life'. As patriarch, he showed particular concern for the numerous individuals living on the Black Mountain in the Amanus range to the north of Antioch, many of whom were not well prepared for the life they had chosen. He forbade them to live as solitaries unless they had a supervisor, evidently preferring that they remain within the institutionalised Church, perhaps in Jubin, Machanath or Carraria, houses of ascetics already established on the mountain.[37]

When he emigrated to Antioch, Aimery may well have had his eye on preferment within the Church, but he also knew he was not entering an intellectual wasteland. Western scholars were aware that the larger cities of the Middle East contained important libraries and collections of manuscripts, including glossed Arabic translations of Greek works and original materials from Persia and India. When Tripoli fell in 1109, both the college and the libraries of private individuals were looted, which shows not only that the city had contained large numbers of books, but also suggests that some of them may have been sold in the aftermath, a proportion of which was likely to have ended up in Antioch.[38] The boldest scholars sought out this learning. From about 1110, Adelard of Bath, one of the most radical scientific thinkers and mathematicians of the early twelfth century, embarked upon a series of journeys to Sicily, Greece and Syria, apparently financed by the English king, Henry I. He was particularly interested in acquiring knowledge of Arab and Greek learning and in about 1114 visited Antioch in order to study its manuscripts.[39]

Aimery's own correspondence with Pope Eugenius III in c.1150, and with the famous theologian Hugh Eteriano, resident in Constantinople, in the mid-1170s, confirms that contemporary scholars knew that Antioch and its neighbouring monasteries held important texts, some of which were not available to them in the West. In 1177, Aimery even tried to tempt Hugh to come and live in Antioch by the offer of a prebend worth 1,000 besants, which he clearly did not believe was an outlandish suggestion for a man of such eminence.[40] Aimery was not therefore an isolated figure among the warriors and traders of the East: among previous works produced in Antioch were Walter the Chancellor's chronicle and, in 1127, Stephen of Pisa's translation of the Arabic medical work *Kitab al-malaki* (or *Royal Book*) of 'Ali ibn al-'Abbas. Aimery himself was replaced as archdeacon of Antioch by Rorgo Fretellus, a former chancellor to the prince of Galilee and chaplain of the church of Nazareth. Rorgo was the author of a popular *Descriptio* of the Holy Land, widely copied in the West and datable to c.1137–8.[41]

Such a man was never likely to welcome Reynald of Châtillon, who would inevitably expect to displace the patriarch as the dominant figure in the principality. This would have been all the more galling to Aimery since his ecclesiastical authority had already been reduced by the loss of the three Edessan archdioceses and that of Apamea, as well as the Cilician archbishoprics, held by the Greeks since the expedition of John Comnenus in 1138.[42] William of Tyre's suggestion that Aimery may have been behind Constance's refusal to take any of the husbands offered to her at Tripoli in 1152 probably has some substance, while it cannot be imagined that Aimery would have been any more enthusiastic about the Caesar John Roger sent by the Byzantine emperor, Manuel, as a possible husband in the same year.[43] But it was not simply a question of authority. Antioch was under continuing pressure from Nur al-Din, and Reynald, with no resources of his own, was in dire need of money, which the patriarch was unwilling to supply. In a letter to Louis VII in 1155 or 1156,

Reynald appealed to the king to come to the East again, telling him that it was impossible to describe 'what deprivation and anxiety we have to endure', and asking him to arrange marriages for Maria and Philippa, the two daughters of Raymond of Poitiers, deprived of husbands locally because of 'the harshness of their country and the problems of consanguinity'.[44]

Aimery's refusal to co-operate enraged Reynald of Châtillon, whose volatile nature would be demonstrated throughout his career. William of Tyre, usually more given to moral outrage than dry comment, calls him 'a most impetuous man, both in transgressing and in making satisfaction'.[45] In revenge for his intransigence, Aimery was stripped, thrashed and forced to sit naked in the sun, his wounds smeared with honey, while he was plagued by the insects of a Syrian summer. Naturally enough, he agreed to hand over his wealth. Reynald, having achieved his end, then dressed the patriarch in his ecclesiastical vestments and led him through the streets on horseback, while he himself held the cord of the saddle. Baldwin, shocked by this behaviour, sent Frederick, bishop of Acre, and Ralph, his chancellor, to sort out the quarrel, and Reynald restored the goods he had taken. However, in one sense, Reynald had his own way, for the patriarch left the city, probably in the company of the envoys, and did not return until 1159.[46]

Like his predecessor, Reynald was caught between the demands of the Byzantines to the west and the Zengid attacks from the east. In 1155, he was asked by Emperor Manuel Comnenus to put a stop to raids into Byzantine Cilicia by the Roupenid ruler, Thoros II, based at Tarsus. He seems to have done this effectively enough, but Manuel delayed the payment promised, provoking Reynald's temper in the same way as had Aimery of Limoges two years before. Indeed, the cause was basically the same: Reynald's acute shortage of resources. Manuel's motives are not clear, but the delay may have been connected to Reynald's grant of some of the land regained from Thoros to the Templars, apparently including the castles of Baghras, Darbsak and La Roche Guillaume. Manuel's caution was justified, for the Templars substantially rebuilt the castles, forming a screen along the northern approaches to the principality.[47] Reynald's retaliation was extravagant, taking the form of an attack on Byzantine Cyprus, which his troops ravaged for several days, raping and looting, before returning to the mainland 'laden with a vast amount of riches and spoils of every kind'. William of Tyre calls this 'a shameful deed', provoked by 'evil men' who were a great influence on Reynald. Cyprus, he says, was an island 'which had always been useful and friendly to our realm and which had a large population of Christians'.[48]

Although the gratuitous violence of the raid on Cyprus was extreme, none of the rulers of the Latin East was immune from the pressures that had driven

Reynald. Baldwin III was 'burdened by debt and held fast by many obligations which he had no means of satisfying', and therefore easily tempted by any plan that might alleviate his problems.[49] The kind of warfare involved in the siege of Ascalon was extremely costly. The wood used for building the siege engine had been made from ships that had sailed over in the spring crossing of 1153 and was therefore very expensive. Moreover, Reynald of Châtillon was only one of many who had served for pay; all those who arrived on the spring crossing had been added to the wage bill.[50] In February 1157, therefore, Baldwin fell upon nomadic Arabs (presumably Bedouins) and Turcomans grazing their flocks in the area known as the forest of Banyas, despite the fact that they were covered by a treaty and had the king's permission to be there. Totally unprepared, they were massacred or enslaved and huge booty was taken. Ibn al-Qalanisi says that the Franks had been encouraged to do this because they wished to take advantage of the arrival of reinforcements from the West, although it seems unlikely they had crossed during the winter. Whatever the reason, it proved counterproductive, for Nur al-Din considered it had broken the one-year truce made with the Franks in the previous September under which he had agreed payment of tribute from Damascus of 8,000 dinars of Tyre.[51] In accordance with the usual chroniclers' formula, William of Tyre blames evil counsellors, but his indignation is unambiguous. Such action brought down the vengeance of the Lord.[52]

Vengeance took the form of Nur al-Din. Banyas was an important target for any ruler of Damascus, as it could be used as a base or assembly point for Christian armies intending to invade the Hauran (and thus threaten food supplies) or even to attack Damascus itself. As it was so vulnerable, it was expensive to maintain and its lord, Humphrey of Toron, the royal constable, decided to share control with the Hospitallers. However, on 26 April 1157, Nusrat al-Din, Nur al-Din's brother, attacked a Hospitaller supply train, killing most of the escort and seizing materials intended for the defence of Banyas. As a consequence the Hospitallers withdrew from their agreement with the constable, while Nur al-Din was encouraged to launch an attack on Banyas itself. After a siege lasting a month in May and June 1157, his forces broke into the town, although they could not take the citadel. Only a large relief army under the king caused them to withdraw, although not before they had wrecked parts of the town and its defences.

Baldwin then refortified the town before setting off to return to Jerusalem, apparently unaware that Nur al-Din was still in the area. His army was therefore prematurely disbanded (perhaps for reasons of cost), and important contingents such as those led by Philip of Nablus were allowed to leave the host. Nur al-Din's ambush at Jacob's Ford on the Upper Jordan between Lake

Huleh and the Sea of Galilee on 19 June therefore caught them totally off-guard. Although the king escaped to Safad, Nur al-Din captured several important leaders, including Hugh of Ibelin, Odo of Saint-Amand, the marshal, and Bertrand of Blancfort, master of the Templars.[53] It was reported to Pope Hadrian that eighty-seven Templars were captured and another 300 knights captured or killed, while huge quantities of horses, arms and other equipment were lost.[54] In many ways the taking of high-status prisoners was of greater value to Nur al-Din than their deaths, since their subsequent parade through Damascus served to confirm the legitimacy of Nur al-Din's leadership of the *jihad* and therefore his right to control the city. Huge crowds turned out to see the heads of the dead tied to the Frankish standards, while the prisoners were carried along on horses roped together in groups. Ibn al-Qalanisi calls it a 'brilliant victory' and says that the Damascenes 'multiplied their praises and glorification to God, and their fervent prayers for al-Malik al-'Ādil Nūr al-Dīn, their defender and protector'.[55]

This turned out to be the high point for Nur al-Din in 1157. A second attack on Banyas was aborted when he realised that, at Chastel Neuf, Baldwin had assembled forces from Tripoli under Count Raymond III and from Antioch under Reynald of Châtillon, as well as what he had left from the kingdom of Jerusalem.[56] Then, from the middle of July, a renewed series of earthquakes hit the region, exacerbating the damage of the previous autumn and having a particularly devastating impact on Aleppo, Hama and Homs.[57] Finally, Nur al-Din himself fell so seriously ill that he appeared to be on the verge of death, provoking the pillage of his possessions by those who believed his end had come. As Nur al-Din was carried on a litter to Aleppo, Ibn al-Qalanisi says that 'the armies of the Muslims dispersed, the provinces were thrown into confusion, and the Franks were emboldened'.[58]

At about the same time, probably in early September, Thierry of Alsace, count of Flanders, and his wife, Sibylla, Baldwin's half-sister, landed at Beirut. This was Thierry's third expedition and it offered an opportunity to mount a new campaign. The Christians, including Raymond of Tripoli, gathered their forces at La Boquée, but failed in their attack on Chastel Rouge (Rugia). However, Reynald of Châtillon was anxious to use this army for his own advantage and they moved on to Antioch. There they were joined by Thoros II and the combined force returned south along the Orontes towards Shaizar, probably arriving in November. The army soon broke into the lower city, driving the inhabitants into the citadel, which was protected by the river on one side and the residential area on the other. William of Tyre says that it was primarily a commercial centre rather than a military camp, and that the people had been unaware of Nur al-Din's illness and therefore had not expected to be attacked. Confident of success, Baldwin assigned the city to Thierry of Flanders on the basis that he had the resources to defend it, but Reynald claimed that it was part of the principality of Antioch and that its lord owed him homage. Not surprisingly, as a tenant-in-chief of the king of France and count of one of the richest fiefs in north-west Europe, Thierry was willing only to do homage to King Baldwin III. The issue could not be resolved and, despite the progress made, the attack was abandoned.[59] The failure to take Shaizar was partly compensated by the recapture of Harim in January 1158, only possible, thought William of Tyre, because of Nur al-Din's incapacity.[60]

Baldwin III was now twenty-seven years old. In the summer of 1157, he had barely escaped capture; indeed, there were strong rumours that he had been killed and Nur al-Din's men made a careful search of the battlefield at Jacob's Ford in an effort to find his body. 'If our lord had fallen that day,' says William of Tyre, 'the whole realm would, without question, have been plunged into the deepest peril. Which may God avert! For in the case of a knight, however great, the fortune of one man only is concerned; but the peril of the king involves danger to the entire nation. Thus, loyal David, when full of anxiety about his king, implored, "Lord, preserve the king."'[61] There was an urgent need for a male heir and at a meeting of the High Court it was decided to seek a wife for the king in Constantinople. In the autumn, envoys led by Lethard, archbishop of Nazareth, and Humphrey of Toron, the constable, supported by Joscelin Pisellus and William of Barra, were sent to negotiate with Emperor Manuel. William of Tyre says that they considered various options before reaching the conclusion that only the Byzantines had the necessary resources to relieve the financial problems of the crusader states.[62] Moreover, the king was well aware that Manuel was no more willing to grant Antioch autonomy than his father had been, while in the wake of the Second Crusade the enthusiasm for crusading displayed by Thierry of Flanders was unlikely to be replicated by other powerful men.

Although Archbishop Lethard died during the mission, the embassy was successful in obtaining a bride for Baldwin and, in September 1158, Theodora, the twelve-year-old niece of the emperor, landed at Tyre. Manuel had granted her a dowry of 100,000 *hypereroi* of standard weight (which seems to have meant Byzantine gold *solidi*, still valuable, although less stable than in the past), plus another 14,000 for the wedding. According to Gregory the Priest, he promised that he would personally come to the assistance of Jerusalem.[63] For his part, Baldwin gave her the city of Acre as her marriage portion. Theodora was consecrated and crowned and, within a few days, married to Baldwin.[64] The ceremonies were carried out by Aimery of Limoges, patriarch of Antioch, still living in Jerusalem, since Fulcher, patriarch of Jerusalem, had died in November 1157 and Amalric of Nesle, his successor, had not yet been consecrated.[65]

Manuel was now determined to deal with both Thoros II and Reynald of Châtillon. Thoros was caught almost completely by surprise, escaping only because he had been warned by a Latin pilgrim who had encountered the Byzantine army in the course of his journey. During December 1158, Manuel took Tarsus and began to march through Cilicia, throwing Reynald into a panic. Reynald, accompanied by Gerard, bishop of Latakia, hurried to meet the emperor at Mamistra where, in an elaborate display of penitence, he appeared wearing a woollen tunic, barefooted and with a rope around his neck. He then presented the hilt of a sword to the emperor, while he held the point. Finally, he lay prostrate on the ground beneath the raised dais on which the emperor was seated. According to John Kinnamos, this exhibition astonished the envoys present, who had come from all over the Middle East and Asia; William of Tyre described it as shameful to the Latins. At length Manuel relented, but on condition 'that he would act according to the emperor's will, especially that according to old custom a bishop would be sent to Antioch from Byzantion'. In short, Manuel had achieved his major aims for Antioch: the vassalage of its ruler and the restoration of the Greek patriarch. Aimery of Limoges, who, according to Kinnamos, had several times offered 'to betray' Reynald to the emperor, once more found he had been marginalised.[66]

The Byzantines now moved into the principality itself and encamped near Antioch. Baldwin III hurried north, where he was warmly received, although his inferior status was emphasised by his being given a throne slightly lower than that of the emperor. It was worth it: during the ten days he was with Manuel, he seems to have established a good relationship with him, and he was granted a subsidy of 22,000 *hypereroi* and 3,000 marks of silver, as well as receiving a range of lavish gifts. Baldwin, too, was able to intercede for Thoros, who now re-emerged from the Taurus mountains into which he had fled and took an oath of fealty to the emperor. At the same time he surrendered an unnamed fortress, perhaps as a symbol of submission. Gregory the Priest says that he promised to 'remain obedient and subject to the emperor's commands, a promise he scrupulously carried out'.[67] The imperial triumph was completed on 12 April 1159 by a ceremonial entry into the city with Reynald of Châtillon holding the bridle of his horse and King Baldwin riding some distance behind. Reaching the cathedral of St Peter, he was met by the patriarch and clergy bearing the Holy Scriptures, and welcomed with great ceremony. Even so, Manuel did not entirely trust the Antiochenes. Although ostensibly unarmed, he wore a breastplate under a costly outer garment, decorated with precious stones, and was escorted by a company of the Varangian Guard carrying axes.

This certainly had its effect in Aleppo, where Nur al-Din released a large number of prisoners, including Bertrand of Toulouse and the Templar master, Bertrand of Blancfort. Some of these he had held since the time of the Second Crusade. According to Ibn al-Qalanisi, the emperor 'recompensed this generous act with gifts rivalling those of the greatest and most powerful sovereigns: magnificent brocade robes of various kinds and in large numbers, precious jewels, a brocade tent of great value, and a gratifying number of local horses'.[68] In addition, says John Kinnamos, Nur al-Din agreed to ally with Manuel 'in his wars in Asia', presumably meaning the Byzantine campaigns against the Turks in Asia Minor. This alliance nearly broke down when Manuel's party was attacked by some Turks while out hunting, for which he seems to have blamed Nur al-Din. Nothing came of this, says Kinnamos, because rumours from the west 'reported that matters were in uproar there'.[69]

It was an impressive performance. The entry into Antioch had been a great piece of Byzantine stagecraft, intended to play to the wider audience of representatives of other powers, and exactly suited to the Byzantine perception of the role of the empire.[70] Manuel had even demonstrated his medical skills by attending to Baldwin's broken arm, sustained in an accident dangerously similar to the one that had killed his father when he fell from his horse while hunting. Using little actual force, Manuel had established his supremacy in the crusader states, had brought Armenian Cilicia back under imperial control and had obliged Nur al-Din to tread cautiously in his dealings with Christians. It had led to a major reorientation of policy in the region and had opened the way for further intervention in the future. Moreover, it facilitated Baldwin's southern policy, for Nur al-Din no longer emphasised the liberation of Jerusalem in his propaganda, leaving the Fatimids largely isolated.[71]

Manuel's alliance with Nur al-Din committed the latter to campaign in the lands of the sultan of Iconium, Kilij Arslan II. William of Tyre believed that the sultan was actually stronger than Nur al-Din, but that he was too far away to prevent him from taking Marash and other strongholds. Baldwin, for his part, took advantage of Nur al-Din's absence to ravage and plunder the Hauran and consequently was able to extort 4,000 pieces of gold, together with the release of six knights from Najm al-Din, the governor of Damascus. Late in November 1161, Reynald of Châtillon sought to do the same, moving into the lands between Marash and Duluk to plunder the herds of the local population. However, this region was far to the north-east, nearly 100 miles from Antioch, making it difficult to drive back large numbers of animals on the hoof. William of Tyre was highly critical, as most of the inhabitants were

Syrian and Armenian Christians; the only Turks were in the urban garrisons. As William saw it, Reynald paid an appropriate price for an action the archbishop considered ill-omened; on the way back he was captured by Majd al-Din, the governor of Aleppo. Once more the king of Jerusalem was obliged to go north to arrange the affairs of Antioch, and Aimery of Limoges was left in control until such time as Baldwin could return.[72]

Manuel's return to Constantinople did not, however, signal a retreat from the affairs of the crusader states. The emperor had no male heirs and the death of his wife, Irene, necessitated a new marriage. Links had already been established through Theodora, and it was now proposed that Manuel marry Melisende, sister of Raymond III of Tripoli. William of Tyre was still in the West at the time and could not have been fully conversant with the details, but it appears that, although the marriage was agreed, what the Latins saw as a series of obscure delays followed. An embassy to Constantinople returned with the reply that the emperor had changed his mind, and his envoys in Tripoli left in some haste, aware that the insult to both the king and the count might provoke retaliation. John Kinnamos says that Melisende had become very ill, blighting her appearance, and that there were rumours that she was illegitimate, which, if true, would not have made her an ideal wife for a man wanting an heir.[73]

The capture of Reynald of Châtillon had changed the political landscape, offering new opportunities to consolidate the imperial grip on the principality, and soon after the king found Byzantine envoys in Antioch negotiating a marriage with Maria, the younger daughter of Constance. William of Tyre says that Baldwin was deeply offended, but concealed his anger out of consideration for Maria. In fact, there was little to be gained from opposing Manuel, whom William calls 'the most powerful prince in the world' and whose help in any future attack on Egypt might prove essential.[74] Raymond of Tripoli, however, was unable to exercise Baldwin's restraint, sending 'pirates and nefarious and vicious men' to ravage any imperial lands within reach along the coast and on the islands. This reaction was little different from Reynald of Châtillon's attack on Cyprus, but William of Tyre, whose later narrative shows that he much approved of Raymond, offers no similar moral condemnation.[75]

This situation did not encourage stable government in Antioch, for it left an unresolved tension between Constance and Patriarch Aimery. Moreover, the evident heir was Bohemond, the eldest of Constance's four children by Raymond of Poitiers, who was sixteen years old in 1161 and could not be expected to remain passive for long. A year or so later, in 1163, a coup by Antiochene nobles and Thoros, the anti-Byzantine ruler of Cilicia, removed his mother and Bohemond III took power.[76]

Baldwin had made effective use of his position since overcoming his mother in 1152, but there are signs that she had not been completely excluded, despite her residence in her dower lands at Nablus. The losses of the rulers of Tripoli and Antioch meant that her sisters retained influence in the north and it is noticeable that Melisende appeared in Tripoli at the time of Baldwin's important meeting of the High Court there in the summer of 1152.[77] In Baldwin's absence she seems to have acted on her own initiative: the recovery of the fortified cave of al-Habis beyond the Jordan late in 1157 is attributed by William of Tyre to her 'zeal and diligence', even though Baldwin of Lille had actually been left in charge of the kingdom.[78] She certainly maintained her interest in ecclesiastical affairs and must have continued to exercise patronage in the way she had done in the past.[79] When Patriarch Fulcher died on 20 November 1157, William of Tyre says that, despite an assembly of prelates gathered to chose a new patriarch, his successor, Amalric of Nesle, was chosen 'against the rules of law' through the intervention of Melisende, her sister Hodierna, and Sibylla of Flanders, the wife of Count Thierry.[80]

There were limits to this independence. The rulers of the crusader states had adopted a position of neutrality in the papal schism that followed the death of Hadrian IV in September 1159, but the arrival in Gibelet of a legate sent by Alexander III forced them to confront the issue. This was far more than an internal matter, for Alexander's opponent, Cardinal Octavian, who took the name of Victor IV, was the candidate of Frederick Barbarossa, the German emperor, and any decision was certain to have repercussions for the kingdom of Jerusalem in the Latin West. The matter was discussed in a major assembly held sometime in 1160 at Nazareth, including both prelates and barons. The king, once more with an eye to the potential costs since a legate would inevitably burden the Church with what he described as expenses and extortions, wished to maintain neutrality by allowing the legate to visit only as a pilgrim. However, the legate was finally accepted, an action that committed the crusader states to the side of Alexander III.[81] Later in the year, Amalric of Nesle wrote to Pope Alexander III, accepting the regularity of his election and condemning 'the rash perversity and perverse rashness of Octavian'. 'We have,' says the patriarch, 'unanimously and wholeheartedly chosen you and willingly received you as our temporal lord and spiritual father.'[82]

Melisende's last public act was to join with Baldwin in assenting to a grant of her other son, Amalric, count of Jaffa and Ascalon, to the canons of the Holy Sepulchre, dated 30 November 1160.[83] At some point in the course of the following year she was taken ill, perhaps with a stroke, and confined to bed. Her sisters, Hodierna and Iveta, took care of her, allowing few people to see her. She died on 11 September 1161, probably in her early fifties.[84]

During the last months of her illness she was unaware of the outside world and it was in this period that Baldwin took the opportunity to make an important change to the feudal map of the kingdom. The greatest of the lords who had supported Melisende in 1152 was Philip of Nablus and, on 31 July 1161, Baldwin exchanged his fief of Nablus for that of Transjordan, apparently in anticipation of his mother's death, since at that time Nablus and Samaria would revert to the royal demesne.[85] The fief of Transjordan was over 170 miles long, extending from Amman in the north to the Red Sea in the south, and included the important castles of Montréal, Kerak, Amman and Ain Mousa. It straddled the routes between Egypt and Damascus which Baldwin had striven to control since the rebuilding of Gaza and the capture of Ascalon. In that sense it seems to have been an impressive acquisition for Philip of Nablus and, indeed, some historians have taken this view.[86]

On the other hand, it does not seem to have generated the same income as Nablus, which, according to John of Ibelin's list of the 1260s, owed eighty-five knights, whereas Kerak and Montréal owed forty knights, and one of its potential sources of profit – that of tolls from Bedouins and caravans – was reserved for the Crown.[87] Moreover, the responsibilities associated with Transjordan were daunting; Nablus, situated in the centre of the kingdom, might seem to be the easier option. This may have been the final reckoning with Melisende's supporters, achieved while she was incapable of opposing it.[88] However, over the previous nine years Philip of Nablus had given no reason to believe that he was disloyal, and it is unlikely that Baldwin would have granted a fief like Transjordan to an untrustworthy man. Perhaps Baldwin's chief interest was in absorbing Nablus into the royal demesne, which, like so many of his actions, was driven by his financial needs.

Baldwin himself barely outlived his mother, dying on 10 February 1163, less than eighteen months after Melisende. He was probably thirty-two years old; a premature death by any standards. William of Tyre believed that he had been poisoned by his eastern physicians, whom the archbishop, deeply imbued with the mores of the contemporary Latin intellectual world, instinctively mistrusted. However, William himself says that he was struck by dysentery while on a visit to Antioch in the autumn of 1162.[89] As he realised his illness was becoming worse, he left Antioch for Tripoli and, finally, was carried from there to Beirut. Here he died and, over the next eight days, his body was carried in procession to Jerusalem, where he was buried in the church of the Holy Sepulchre with his predecessors.

Baldwin III had been slow to assert himself and, even when he finally did, he reigned for a much shorter period than might have been expected. Nevertheless, in the last decade of his life he had had a distinct impact upon the crusader states, most obviously in his southern policy, first, against Ascalon, and then, at least in embryo, against Egypt itself, initiatives that both shaped the policies of his successor, Amalric, and had repercussions in Tripoli and Antioch, where the double threat of Byzantine claims and Nur al-Din's growing military strength closely circumscribed the policies of their rulers. Moreover, in a very overt demonstration of his authority, Baldwin made the first real attempt to take control of the currency, hitherto dominated by coins from Lucca and Valence. At some point in his reign, probably in the 1150s, the king called in all these coins and used the bullion for a large-scale recoining of deniers and oboles, estimated to be in the region of 11 to 12 million billon coins.[90] It is probable that an *établissement* (law) forbidding vassals to mint their own coins is Baldwin III's, as it would be natural to assert the Crown monopoly at the same time.[91]

By the time of his death the Franks had occupied the Levantine littoral for more than sixty years and in the city of Jerusalem especially the signs of that presence were now very evident. Ever since 1115, when Baldwin I had endeavoured to attract Syrian Christians to Jerusalem, the Franks had made a conscious attempt to repopulate, restore and rebuild the Holy City and the shrines in its immediate vicinity in a manner appropriate to the most important place in the Christian world.[92] In fact, Jerusalem was a relatively modest size in comparison with many of the other great cities of the Middle East, but even so its repopulation had been an extended process, especially since Muslims and Jews were, at least theoretically, forbidden to live there.[93] On the basis of a notional population density of 125 persons per hectare (just under 2.5 acres), the population of Antioch would have been about 40,500 and that of Edessa about 24,000, both of which, at 325 and 192 hectares respectively, were much larger than the Holy City. Jerusalem, which had no sprawling suburb like Montmusard at Acre in the thirteenth century, was only 82 hectares and on that basis would have had a population of no more than about 10,000 by the 1160s.[94]

However, the nature of the city meant that large parts of it were not available as living space for permanent residents. It had never been significant as a trading emporium like Tyre or Acre, but it was hugely important as the emotional heart of the crusader states and as a powerful attraction to pilgrims from across the Christian world. The pilgrims themselves restricted the size of the local population, for in spring and summer the city was flooded with visitors, all of whom needed accommodation. This must have provided valuable income for burgesses with sufficient property to rent space to pilgrims, not only in Jerusalem, but in the port cities as well.[95] Their arrival may easily have doubled the population, but most did not stay beyond the strict limits

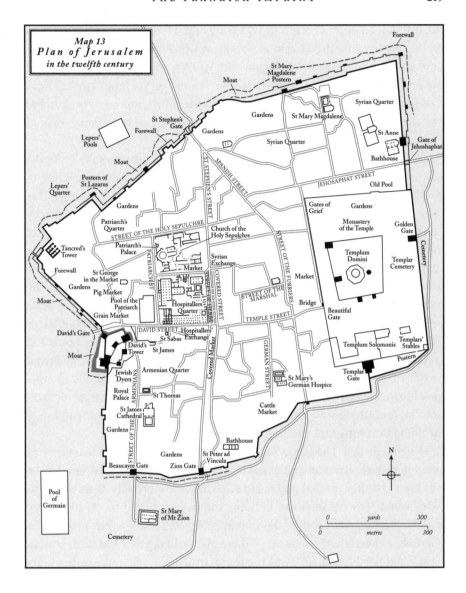

Map 13
Plan of Jerusalem
in the twelfth century

imposed by the autumn sailing season, a situation that must have left many unoccupied rooms during the winter months. The consequence of its role as a focus for government and pilgrimage was that, in the time of Baldwin III, Jerusalem contained a whole series of monumental buildings and complexes that housed far fewer people than would usually be accommodated in equivalent urban areas. Most importantly, it contained on the western side the Tower of David, the royal palace, and the Armenian cathedral of St James, in the centre the church of the Holy Sepulchre and the conventual buildings of the

Augustinian canons, adjacent to which was the Hospitaller compound, and on the eastern side the Haram al-Sharif on which stood the Temple of the Lord (the Dome of the Rock), again with its own conventual buildings, and the headquarters of the Templars in the Temple of Solomon (the al-Aqsa mosque). As well as these, Denys Pringle has identified around sixty churches and chapels, the great majority of which would have existed in some form in the twelfth century.[96]

The centrepiece was the church of the Holy Sepulchre. Around 1170, the visiting German pilgrim Theoderic copied part of an inscription painted in gold letters on a commemorative wall plate in the chapel of Golgotha. This recorded that the chapels above and around had been consecrated at dawn by Fulcher, patriarch of Jerusalem, on 15 July 1149, 'the fiftieth anniversary of the taking of the city'.[97] William of Tyre was in Chartres at this time and the crusaders in the great armies of the previous year had returned home, so there is no chronicle account of an event that must have been as impressive as the consecration of the rebuilt choir of the abbey church of Saint-Denis five years before. The events of 11 June 1144 are known in detail because Abbot Suger wanted them to be and he carefully recorded the presence of King Louis and Queen Eleanor, as well as that of seventeen archbishops and bishops, and what he described as countless numbers of seculars ranging from counts to ordinary knights.[98] Fulcher was no Suger, but it must be assumed that the dedication in Jerusalem was attended by an equally distinguished gathering, including the monarchs, the episcopacy and the great barons.

The church that Theoderic saw was the culmination of half a century of effort to restore, remodel and extend the buildings on the spot where Christ had been crucified, buried and resurrected. Most importantly, there seems to have been a series of intensive building campaigns during the 1140s – very much in keeping with similar developments in the West – which produced a pilgrimage church in the manner of those great edifices that had been built in France and northern Spain along the routes to Compostela in the earlier years of the century. The aim was, as William of Tyre later said, to enlarge the original church in such a way as to include within it all the holy places on that site.[99] This was a hugely ambitious undertaking and planning may have begun as early as the patriarchate of Arnulf of Chocques, although most of the work was probably conceived under the patriarchs William of Messines (who died in 1145) and Fulcher (who died in 1157).

This must therefore have been a very busy and complex site during the 1140s when several ateliers were working there simultaneously, requiring skills of all sorts and employing Latins, Greeks, Armenians and Arabs. The great Byzantine Rotunda was retained but its eastern wall was removed and

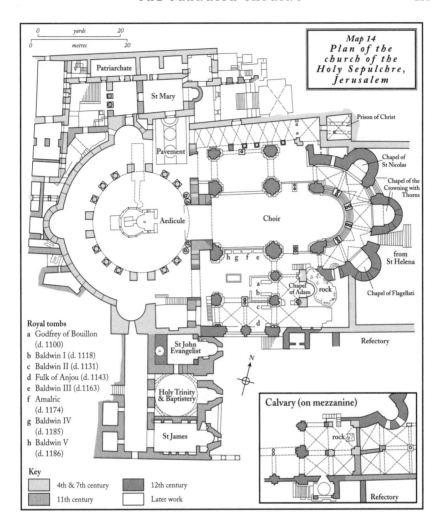

Map 14
Plan of the
church of the
Holy Sepulchre,
Jerusalem

Patriarchate

St Mary

Prison of Christ

Pavement

Chapel of
St Nicolas

Chapel of the
Crowning with
Thorns

Aedicule

Choir

from
St Helena

h g f e

a
b
c
d

Chapel
of Adam

rock

Chapel of Flagellati

Royal tombs

a Godfrey of Bouillon
    (d. 1100)
b Baldwin I (d. 1118)
c Baldwin II (d. 1131)
d Fulk of Anjou (d. 1143)
e Baldwin III (d.1163)
f Amalric
    (d. 1174)
g Baldwin IV
    (d. 1185)
h Baldwin V
    (d. 1186)

St John
Evangelist

N

Holy Trinity
& Baptistery

St James

Refectory

Calvary (on mezzanine)

rock

Key

| 4th & 7th century | 12th century |
| 11th century | Later work |

Refectory

the church extended by two bays to make a choir with an ambulatory and three radiating chapels, incorporating the holy sites previously situated in the *triporticus*, which now disappeared. Galleries linked up with those of the Rotunda. The western bay formed a crossing and was covered by a dome over the place that the pilgrims believed to be the centre of the world. South of the crossing was a transept that on the eastern side contained the tombs of the kings and the chapel of Golgotha, above which was the Calvary chapel. On the south façade was a double portal intended to facilitate the movement of pilgrims into and out of the church.[100]

The whole building was embellished with mosaics, frescoes and sculpture, all of which contributed to a series of detailed programmes that were appropriate to the holy sites now enclosed under the new roof. Most strikingly, the

Latins moved the Byzantine Anastasis mosaic from the now dismantled apse of the Rotunda and reassembled it on the ceiling of the central apse of the new choir. This depicted Christ's Harrowing of Hell, a key scene in the cycle of the Passion. 'In his [Christ's] left hand,' says Theoderic, 'he carries the Cross and in his right hand Adam. He looks regally into heaven, and he is entering heaven with an enormous stride, his left foot raised and his right foot still on the ground. Surrounding him are these people: his Mother, Blessed John the Baptist, and all the Apostles.'[101]

During the 1150s, a large bell tower was erected to the west of the south façade, while the façade itself was decorated with carved lintels, mosaics in the tympana over the portals, and a series of gadroons around the archivolts. This was an important space, for it would be the pilgrim's first sight of the church and it was where the patriarch, speaking from the Calvary chapel, customarily preached to the people.[102] The contrasting lintels above the double portal showed, on the eastern (right-hand) door, a carving of a vine scroll within which could be seen humans and birds, which represented the Tree of Life, and, on the western (left-hand) door, a series of six narrative scenes, the first five of which followed the path of the Palm Sunday procession, beginning in Bethany and proceeding from there through the Golden Gate into Jerusalem. These sites, together with the sixth scene which illustrates the Last Supper, completed a sequence of events that preceded the Passion and Resurrection, and represented the route frequently followed by visiting pilgrims.[103] Above the lintels the tympana were decorated with mosaics showing the Virgin and Child, probably above the western door, and, above the other door, Noli me tangere, the scene where Christ meets Mary Magdalene in the garden after the Resurrection.[104]

At the same time, both the king and the orders of the Hospital and the Temple were actively extending and developing their buildings. Just to the south of David's Gate by the western entrance to the city was the Tower of David and to the south of that the royal palace. Originally a Herodian struc-ture, the tower seems to have housed the royal chapel as well as the main royal administration and it was from here that the viscount and the castellan could monitor entries to and exits from the city, as well as collecting tolls and other taxes. This too seems the most probable site for the mint since it is unlikely that the silversmiths in the centre of the city could have coped with recoining on the scale ordered by Baldwin III. The royal palace was fortified with a crenellated wall with, on its eastern side, a large square tower at its northern end and a round tower on the south, together with further defences in the form of ditches and barbicans. Theoderic says the palace had been 'newly built', although it is difficult to tell how much of this had already been completed under Baldwin III.[105]

Further along David Street, the visitor came to the Hospitaller Quarter. The German pilgrims John of Würzburg and Theoderic, both of whom visited in the 1160s, were in awe of the 'great palace of the sick' built by the Hospitallers in the Muristan to the south of the church of the Holy Sepulchre. According to an anonymous cleric who described the Jerusalem hospital in the 1180s, this was divided into eleven wards, in addition to which there was a separate *palacium* for women.[106] John of Würzburg was told by the servitors that it held 2,000 sick persons, while Theoderic said he could not judge the numbers of people but that he had seen 1,000 beds.[107] However, it is very difficult to determine the exact function of many of the buildings on what was already a complicated site.[108] It seems that the hospital wards were located to the south and east, adjacent to David Street, and that, contrary to the generally accepted view, the large vaulted hall in the north-west corner was part of the conventual buildings of the brothers themselves, over the three most northerly bays of which they had built a new church.[109]

William of Tyre was less enthusiastic than the pilgrim visitors. The Hospitaller buildings were directly opposite the south door of the Holy Sepulchre and he saw them as an overt challenge to the patriarch with whom the Hospitallers had a running dispute over the reception of the excommunicate and the payment of tithes. Matters deteriorated to such an extent that the Hospitallers deliberately rang their bells during times of interdict and when the patriarch preached from the Calvary chapel to the east of the south door, but what was most intolerable to William was the size of the main hall, which he said was higher and more costly than the church of the Holy Sepulchre itself.[110] Indeed, the whole complex was larger than that of the Holy Sepulchre, including the patriarch's palace and the canons' convent, since it encompassed, among many other buildings, not only the wards for the sick, but two churches, a series of conventual buildings, including a dormitory for the Knights, stables and at least two dozen cisterns.[111]

The location of gold- and silversmiths on the Street of Palms running between the Holy Sepulchre and the Hospital underlines the economic importance of pilgrimage to the city. For those who could afford it, the acquisition of reliquaries to hold their precious acquisitions was high on their list of priorities, providing employment for a considerable community of craftsmen from an early date. One of the most striking examples is the True Cross reliquary given to a noble pilgrim called Berthold by Patriarch Warmund in the mid-1120s, which he took back to the monastery of the Holy Sepulchre recently founded at Denkendorf, near Stuttgart. This silver-gilt double-armed

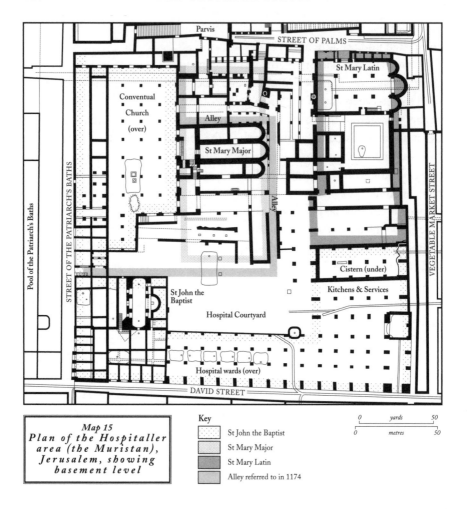

Map 15
*Plan of the Hospitaller
area (the Muristan),
Jerusalem, showing
basement level*

Key

St John the Baptist
St Mary Major
St Mary Latin
Alley referred to in 1174

cross, set with semi-precious stones, contained splinters of the True Cross set
in slits.[112] This represented the top end of the market, but many less expensive
reliquaries were produced as well as other mementoes such as badges. It is no
coincidence that the sale of palm fronds took place in the same area.[113]

Theoderic was equally impressed by the Templar headquarters at the
southern end of the Haram al-Sharif. The area was entered by the Beautiful
Gate on the western side, close to the Temple of the Lord. The Templars had
taken over the al-Aqsa mosque after Baldwin II had moved to the other side
of the city and had repaired the damage done by his predecessor. By the 1160s,
they had built a new cloister to the west of the al-Aqsa, enclosed by vaulted
buildings which included what Theoderic calls a new palace, and they were in
the process of erecting a church that Theoderic says was 'of magnificent size
and workmanship', although it was unfinished at the time of his visit. They

had also developed the area to the east with houses, halls and water supplies, perhaps in a manner not dissimilar to the compound of the Temple of the Lord. Below the south-east corner was a large vaulted area, the exact size of which is now difficult to determine, but which was used for stabling. Both John of Würzburg and Theoderic were shown these stables, although their very different figures for the numbers of horses and camels that could be accommodated are clearly only guesses. Five hundred might be a reasonable estimate, judging by the present size. The whole quarter was well fortified, strengthened by the order's construction of a barbican to the south which protected the two gates on that side.[114]

Building on this scale seems to have persuaded the Templars to establish their own workshop, probably located in the south-east corner above the stables. The sculptural fragments that survive indicate that the order had recruited craftsmen of high skill, possibly from among the Italians who had worked on the Holy Sepulchre, where there was now less demand for their labour. The results fully justified Theoderic's praise: the decoration of the buildings must have been characterised by foliate sculpture of great originality, at the centre of which were acanthus leaves carved in a manner suggestive of wet drapery. This does not seem to have been primarily a commercial atelier. Indeed, there seems to have been quite enough work to keep it fully occupied but, when the opportunity arose, it may also have produced pieces for other clients as well.[115]

Grand as they had become, the very existence of the orders of the Hospital and the Temple derived from the need to provide for those who required help and protection. The heaving mass of humanity that descended upon the holy shrines every year included many who could not support themselves or who saw the opportunities available to beggars. Jerusalem attracted the poor and destitute as much as the powerful and wealthy, a situation that placed great strain upon the city's services. The Hospitallers not only looked after the sick but also gave proper burials to many of the poor, whom they took to Akeldama (the Field of Blood), situated to the south of Mount Sion. Here they had built a chapel and a charnel pit to which the bodies were carried in procession from the Hospital in the city. They had received the land from William of Messines, the patriarch, in 1143, but it had particular resonance for the pilgrims as it had been used for the burial of strangers since the first century. According to Matthew 27, the area had been purchased by the priests with the thirty pieces of silver that Judas had flung down in the Temple.[116]

Even if care for the sick and needy was not their primary function, all the great institutions were drawn into its provision. Typical therefore was a grant of the tithes of the *casal* of al-Dafis in 1128–9 by the former patriarch,

Evremar of Chocques, archbishop of Caesarea, to the canons of the Holy Sepulchre, in order to provide 'food and refreshment for the poor'.[117] In 1173, the current patriarch, Amalric of Nesle, wrote to Louis VII of France to appeal for help for the multitudes who were drawn to Jerusalem. 'Much is needed to sustain their miserable, impoverished lives and it is evident that helpers are few, while the Eastern Church cannot provide for all their needs as it is oppressed by many tribulations and attacks by the pagans. Hence we make all their benefactors participants and associates of all our prayers and our generosity and particularly of those who are or in future will be in the holy city of Jerusalem.'[118]

For some, however, poverty was voluntary, for the tradition of eremitical life had begun in Syria, Palestine and Egypt in the third century and had been kept alive there ever since. In June 1099, the crusaders had met a hermit on the Mount of Olives, who advised them to storm Jerusalem the following day, as the Lord would give them the city.[119] In the event this proved to be a particularly maladroit prophecy, but this did not deter his many successors during the twelfth century. Although many sought out wild and remote caves, they were also a familiar sight on the walls and in the streets of Jerusalem and its immediate vicinity.[120] In the late 1160s, Theoderic described 'a great number of dwellings of servants of God, that is hermits, who all belong to the Abbot of the Blessed Mary', grouped around the tomb of Jehoshaphat in the middle of the Kidron valley.[121]

Gerard of Nazareth, bishop of Latakia, wrote a treatise about these men, *De conversatione servorum Dei*. Among those well known in Jerusalem were three men, Ralph, Alberic and Bartholomew, who devoted themselves to the care of lepers, probably those belonging to the Order of St Lazarus, whose house was just outside the north-west corner of the city. Alberic ate their leftover food, kissed them after mass, washed their feet, made their beds and carried them on his shoulders, while Bartholomew laboured to carry water to them from the ponds (presumably the Pool of the Hospital).[122] These lepers received special mention in Amalric of Nesle's letter to Louis VII: 'We commend to you the bearer of this letter, a brother sent by the poor to your excellency in their need. When you have heard him, as you think fit and with the inspiration of God, may you help them in their need, as they no longer look like humans nor have any of their pleasures.'

All, rich or poor, had to be sustained by some means. If the amount of living space was restricted by the grandiose schemes of the great institutions of the kingdom, it was further reduced by the need to feed the citizens and the many crusader and pilgrim visitors. Large open areas adjacent to the northern and western walls contained orchards and gardens, while near David's Gate there were grain and pig markets and to the south a sizeable cattle market with its associated tanneries and butcheries.[123] Most of the produce sold in Jerusalem's markets came from the rural hinterland which, on three sides of the city, was intensively farmed, largely by Christians, both Latin and Syrian. The area extending from al-Bira in the north to Bethlehem in the south seems to have been particularly geared to the Jerusalem market. Under Baldwin III, the countryside and the roads were safer than they had been in the past. The Templars had built castles and forts along the main pilgrim routes from the ports and eastwards towards the Jordan, while the capture of Ascalon in 1153 had finally ended Egyptian raiding from the south, all of which made a crisis on the scale of 1120 much less likely.[124]

Greater security combined with Frankish organisational skill and the rapid acquisition of new techniques had effected a considerable agricultural revival, so that farmers produced not only the Mediterranean staples of wheat, barley, olives and grapes with which they were already familiar, but crops new to them, including dates, sugar cane, figs, bananas and citrus fruit.[125] They established new villages, developed farms based around fortified manor houses and adopted the technology of irrigation and sugar production. They built and adapted appropriate road systems, enabling them both to supply cities like Jerusalem, often on a daily basis, and to reach the ports for the export market. Frankish rural settlement in the kingdom of Jerusalem was much more extensive than has previously been thought, although it is more difficult to gauge its extent in Antioch and Tripoli. Probably about half the Frankish population lived in cities and towns, a high proportion in comparison to anywhere else in the West, even in central Italy, the most urbanised region of medieval Europe, but by no means enough to characterise the settlers and their descendants as primarily urban dwellers.

Among the settlements in the vicinity of Jerusalem was al-Bira (called by the Franks Magna Mahumeria), about 10 miles to the north of the city, the largest of the villages established by Godfrey of Bouillon's original grant of 1100. This was a typical Frankish village strung out along a main street, next to which individual plots had been allocated. At the north end stood the church and to the south a tower and enclosure which, with overall dimensions of 61 by 46 metres, was large enough to provide refuge for the inhabitants in times of emergency. By the time of Baldwin's death the population was between 500 and 600, among whom were builders, carpenters, metalworkers and agricultural labourers.[126] West of al-Bira, on the coast road, was Qubeiba (Parva Mahumeria), which was also part of the holdings of the Holy Sepulchre, but here there was greater specialisation among its smaller population. The village had ten installations for processing olives, and the

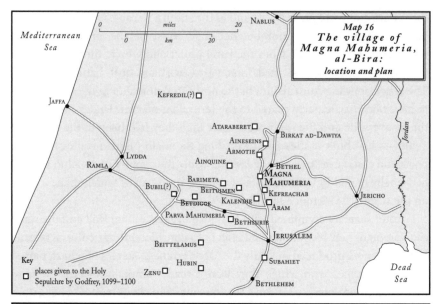

Map 16
*The village of
Magna Mahumeria,
al-Bira:*
location and plan

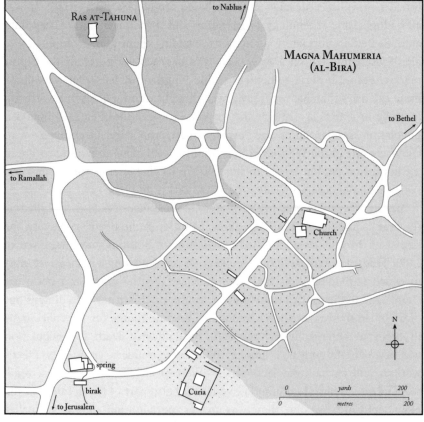

RAS AT-TAHUNA

MAGNA MAHUMERIA
(AL-BIRA)

to Nablus

to Bethel

to Ramallah

Church

N

spring

birak

Curia

to Jerusalem

yards   200

metres   200

inhabitants were primarily occupied with supplying oil to the canons for liturgical use.[127] The first mention of the village in the records is in 1159, so it is
not likely to have been part of Godfrey's original grant, but its existence
presumably reflects the expansion of Jerusalem itself over the previous half-
century. Specialist production became more common in the course of the
twelfth century, as capital projects like mills, for both flour and sugar production, were seen to be profitable. Sugar was an attractive export, and in the
course of the twelfth century many sugar refineries were established, most
commonly along the northern coastal plain and in the Jordan valley.[128]

As in the contemporary West, ecclesiastical institutions played a key role in
agrarian development in the twelfth century, especially when additional
capital was needed. While the canons of the Holy Sepulchre had made full use
of Godfrey's original grant to the north of the city, the Hospitallers had an
equally impressive network to the west, centred upon their castle of Belmont
(Suba), just over 6 miles from Jerusalem. Belmont is situated on a conical hill
about 762 metres high, giving it extensive views of the surrounding area and
placing it in a good position to defend both Hospitaller estates and travellers
along the Ramla to Jerusalem road. Originally it had probably been a courtyard house belonging to a secular lord, but the Hospitallers held it from at
least 1157, and they developed it into a concentric castle, occupied by about
ten knights and around 330 support staff. Although it had a double line of
walls and an oblique entrance, there were no towers, and it does not compare
with great castles of the military orders like Belvoir or Safad. Its primary
purpose was to act as a centre for the Hospitallers' estates in the area, which
produced wheat, barley and legumes, and kept livestock, including cattle,
sheep and goats. Like the canons of the Holy Sepulchre, the Hospitallers
revived agriculture in their own territories, rebuilding terraces and clearing
springs, so that they were able to irrigate large quantities of vegetables, most
of which must have been sold in the Jerusalem markets.[129] Just along the
Ramla to Jerusalem road lay another Hospitaller building, that of Aqua Bella
(see plate 10), a large fortified courtyard that may have been used as an infirmary or even an isolation hospital, and Abu Ghosh (Emmaus), where the
fortified church built over a spring became a pilgrimage centre as it was
believed to be the place where Christ had appeared to two of the disciples after
the Resurrection. To the east of the church, a ninth-century caravanserai was
converted into a hospice for pilgrims.[130]

However, not all agrarian lands were in institutional hands; in the areas
close to Jerusalem some Frankish lords lived in fortified manor houses in the
midst of their rural estates, at least for part of the year. They were not great
barons, but knights or burgesses with more modest holdings. One such estate

was at Khirbat al-Lawza, where a collection of vaulted buildings around a courtyard show Frankish construction. There is an aqueduct from a spring to a reservoir and two networks of irrigation channels. The eastern side of the wadi in which it is situated is terraced and must have been used for vines and olives. Although clearly a rural residence, it is only about 2½ miles from Jerusalem and does not appear to have been fortified in any serious manner.[131]

Although the Franks had colonised the rural areas quite extensively, there remained a substantial Muslim population, primarily inhabiting the villages to the north of Nablus rather than in the vicinity of Jerusalem.[132] The lords, whether institutions or individuals, drew their rents and produce through the *rais*, who in turn might be responsible to the lord's officials, such as the dragoman. These offices, although adapted by the Franks for their own purposes, were evidently in existence well before the Frankish conquest.[133] Unlike their Frankish counterparts, many of the Arab and Syrian peasants can be classified as 'villeins' in that they were tied to the land and subject both to a *chevage*, or head tax, and to payments for seigneurial monopolies such as the use of mills, ovens or baths. Although in the 1180s these peasants were seen as contemptibly passive by the Spanish Muslim traveller Ibn Jubayr, the system survived with relatively little disruption because there was little opportunity or indeed point in fleeing to Muslim-controlled areas, where other, perhaps even more oppressive elites, such as the Turks or Kurds, dominated.[134]

Although the Frankish occupation was a comparatively short interlude in the long history of outside occupation of these lands, by the 1160s in some areas, especially in Jerusalem and the surrounding region, their impact upon both the built and the natural environment was quite profound. Urban II's declaration that these were 'our lands' was taken very seriously indeed.

CHAPTER 10

King Amalric

THEODORA was seventeen years old when Baldwin died. She had borne him no children, even though they had been married for over four years.[1] Baldwin's hereditary successor was therefore his brother, Amalric, and, indeed, the chronicle of Ernoul, an Old French version of the events of the 1170s and 1180s emanating from the Ibelin family circle, says that Baldwin had named his brother as his heir.[2] Even so, he did not command general acceptance. The succession, says William of Tyre, 'was the occasion of much discord among the barons of the realm, who were variously affected by the change of monarchs. In fact, it came near to causing a serious quarrel involving the danger of a schism.' Amalric, though, had the strong support of 'the clergy and the people, as well as a few of the great men of the kingdom', and the opposition was obliged to give way. He was therefore crowned and anointed by the patriarch in the church of the Holy Sepulchre on 18 February 1163, eight days after his brother's death, and apparently on the same day as the funeral.[3] Amalric himself makes no mention of these problems. On 8 April, he wrote to Louis VII of France announcing his brother's death and confirming his own succession. 'We now rule his kingdom as of hereditary right and are firmly established on the throne of our kingdom. There was no impediment and all our subjects showed their goodwill.'[4]

However, the king's letter was disingenuous, for there had been a further complication which had needed to be resolved during this eight-day period. Amalric had married Agnes of Courtenay, the elder daughter of Joscelin II of Edessa. Agnes's early years had been traumatic, for she had lost her first husband, Reynald of Marash, in the defeat at Inab in 1149, and in the following year her father had been captured and taken to Aleppo and had not been seen since.[5] By then the remnants of the county of Edessa had disinte-grated, and after her mother, Beatrice, had sold what remained to the

Byzantines, the family had emigrated to the lordship of Saone in the principality of Antioch, where Beatrice still held dower lands from her first marriage
to William of Saone.[6] Agnes has married Amalric, then count of Jaffa and
Ascalon, apparently in 1157.[7] She had no dowry, but she was the grand-
daughter of one of the crusaders of 1101 and therefore of appropriate rank to
be Amalric's wife. They had two children: Sibylla, apparently named after her
aunt, the countess of Flanders, and Baldwin, named after his uncle, King
Baldwin III, who stood as his godfather.[8]

All this seems completely normal and respectable, yet William says that
Amalric was 'forced to put away his wife' before Amalric of Nesle, the patriarch, would agree to the coronation, on the grounds that the couple were too
closely related, that is, 'within the fourth degree'. In this, the patriarch was
following the stand taken by his predecessor, Fulcher, a man known to adopt
a hard line on canonical matters whatever the political consequences. In fact,
the couple had a common great-great-grandfather, but such a relatively
distant kinship would not usually have been invoked unless it was demanded
by extraneous political circumstances. Moreover, it was agreed that, the
divorce notwithstanding, the couple's two children would retain full rights
of succession. As it happened, John, cardinal-priest of SS. Giovanni e Paulo,
the papal legate whose entry into the kingdom had previously caused so
much controversy, was still in Jerusalem, and he lent his authority to these
arrangements.[9]

This story is so unlikely that historians have been unwilling to accept it at
face value. William was still studying in the West at this time and there was
no contemporary chronicler in the Holy Land who could observe events at
first hand. Even William himself was puzzled by the claim of consanguinity
and later consulted Stephanie of Courtenay, abbess of the convent of St Mary
the Great in Jerusalem, who was the daughter of Joscelin I and consequently
Agnes's aunt, in order to clarify the exact relationship in his own mind. One
possible reason for dissent may have been baronial objections to an influx of
Edessan exiles associated with Agnes and her brother, Joscelin III, titular
count of Edessa since the death of their father in 1159. Joscelin was indeed
granted taxes and lands by Baldwin III in c.1158 and was arguably only the
most prominent of those left with status but no patrimony when the county
of Edessa collapsed. Baldwin's appointment of Joscelin as *bailli* of the fief of
Harim in the principality of Antioch seems to indicate the king's awareness of
discontent among the Jerusalem baronage.[10]

It may be, however, that Agnes's marital history presented further problems. William of Tyre says that after her divorce from Amalric, Agnes immediately married Hugh of Ibelin, the head of his family since the death of his

father, Barisan, in 1150.[11] The evidence of the late thirteenth-century *Lignages d'Outremer* suggests that Agnes was in fact already married to Hugh in 1157, and that therefore her marriage to Amalric was bigamous and perhaps even the result of an abduction.[12] Thus consanguinity was only a cover for the scandal that came to a head in 1163, rather as the crisis of Baldwin I's illness had led to the repudiation of Adelaide of Sicily, even though the bigamy had been known for some time before. Toleration of such behaviour would have created a situation in which the barons' own marriages could have been violated, with the consequent loss of any material and social advantages they might have gained from them. William of Tyre may well have known this, but was hardly likely to give it a public airing, although he hints at the problem when he says that Agnes was married to Amalric de facto and not de iure, as well as his more general comment that Amalric had a habit of seducing married women.[13]

A major objection to this explanation is that Amalric would not have been able to enter into a bigamous marriage in 1157 without incurring excommunication, even if Patriarch Fulcher was dead by the time the marriage actually took place.[14] Moreover, even if Agnes was already betrothed to Hugh, when she arrived in the kingdom he may not have been available to marry her, having been captured at Jacob's Ford in June 1157; the marriage to Amalric took place after Hugh's disappearance.[15] He was in fact released in late 1158 or early 1159, but sometimes such captivity could last for many years or, as can be seen in the case of Agnes's father, until death. In fact, there is no evidence of any objection to the marriage in 1157, except for that of Patriarch Fulcher. Indeed, it may be inferred that the influential *hautes dames* who were so important in the appointment of Amalric of Nesle as patriarch approved, given the choice of Sibylla as the name of the couple's first child.

In the end, even though there appears to have been no Edessan clique as such, baronial opposition does seem to have been aimed at Agnes and reflects the usual manoeuvring for position liable to take place with any change of regime. The barons were not proposing an alternative candidate to Amalric, but were concerned to prevent Agnes from becoming queen and thus gaining a position in which she could control patronage and power to their detriment. This is the more likely interpretation of Ernoul's enigmatic statement that the barons had told Amalric that Agnes 'ought not to be queen of so high a city as Jerusalem', rather than any oblique reference to her sexual morals.[16] The papal legate understood this climate of opinion and fell in with the wishes of the leading barons.[17]

The personality and physical characteristics of the new king are better known than those of his predecessors. This is because William of Tyre was a direct witness, for he finally returned to the kingdom in 1166, when he began a career in the Church and in politics that brought him into close and regular contact with the king and the royal circle. This is not surprising, for William was highly educated and now in the prime of life, having left the kingdom for France perhaps in the autumn of 1146 to embark on a course of study that lasted for the next twenty years. He had initially gone to the liberal arts school at Chartres, before moving on to the higher subjects of theology in Paris and then canon and civil law in Bologna.[18] As soon as he arrived back, he was given a prebend in the church of Acre by Bishop William, and two years later he was made archdeacon of Tyre by Archbishop Frederick. In 1174, he added the archdeaconry of Nazareth to this collection of benefices. These promotions were effectively arranged by the king with whom William had frequent conversations, often on an informal basis, since Amalric enjoyed serious discussions on a variety of topics, including matters of theology. William was sufficiently trusted to be sent on a mission to Manuel Comnenus in 1168 and, in 1170, he was appointed tutor to Baldwin, Amalric's son and heir. William says that it was Amalric who suggested that he write an account of the history of the kingdom since its foundation.[19]

As described by William, Amalric had a fair complexion with blond receding hair. He was taller than average and considerably overweight, so that he literally shook with laughter when something amused him. However, this cannot have been very often, since William says that he was taciturn and serious, in contrast to his brother's affability. Although William presents him as less well educated than Baldwin, it is evident that he had a very sharp mind and a powerful memory, and that he knew the value of obtaining the right information when he needed it. His piety was expressed by daily attendance at mass when circumstances allowed and, particularly meritorious in William's eyes, in ensuring that the Church received its tithes in full.

However, in keeping with his own self-imposed standards, William did not believe in sycophancy, so he could not ignore what he regarded as the king's faults. He was unrestrained in sexual matters and had affairs with married women. Moreover, he was what William calls 'a vehement assailant of the liberty of the churches', by which he meant that his exactions placed a heavy burden of debt upon them. This was part of his 'lust for money', which affected everyone, secular or ecclesiastical. Amalric justified his behaviour on the grounds that rulers needed money, especially if an unexpected contingency arose, which, of course, was a frequent occurrence in the crusader East. William seems to have accepted this, but he was less convinced by the king's claim that if a ruler were well provided for his subjects' property would be safe. The king, he said, exhausted patrimonies, often on trivial pretexts.[20]

William is primarily concerned with the effects of Amalric's policies upon the upper classes, but there are signs that the king was also interested in maximising commercial revenues, since it appears that the proliferation of lesser courts in ports controlled by the king – most notably the Court of the *Fonde* or Market and the Court of the Chain – occurred during Amalric's reign. These probably formalised systems already in operation, but it is highly likely that their creation led to a more systematic collection of tolls and customs than in the past, with consequent increases in returns.[21]

William's portrait conveys a picture of a forceful and intelligent ruler, unlikely to brook much opposition, wherever it originated. Yet Amalric had been obliged to renounce his wife, not only because of patriarchal intransigence, but because a majority of the leading barons – without whom there could be no effective government – had left him with no alternative. There had been serious opposition in the past. Daibert of Pisa had clearly intended to subordinate Godfrey of Bouillon to his own authority and, when he died, to prevent his brother Baldwin from seizing the Crown. Baldwin II twice faced challenges to his legitimacy, both at the time of his accession in 1118 and while he was in captivity in 1123–4. It seems probable that the issue of a document known as the *Etablissement de Baudouin de Borc*, which made explicit the king's right to confiscate the fiefs of rebellious vassals, was a reaction to these problems.[22] In 1134, Fulk only just avoided a major civil conflict when Hugh of Le Puiset revolted; even afterwards it is evident that his freedom of manoeuvre was considerably restricted by the need to conciliate Melisende and her supporters. Moreover, Amalric himself had had first-hand experience of the struggle for royal power in the conflict of 1152, from which he was fortunate to emerge relatively unscathed, despite choosing the wrong side.

During this period the leading baronial families had established a greater degree of dynastic continuity, a situation that contrasts with the volatility of the early years of the crusader states. Proof that these nobles were consolidating an increasingly privileged position can be seen in previous legislation, exemplified by *assises* prohibiting the arrest of nobles for debt and conceding the right of wreck to lords with coastal fiefs.[23] At the same time the kings do not seem to have exercised rights of feudal overlordship commonly seen in contemporary monarchies in France and England, since there are no examples of taking reliefs on the succession of new heirs and few instances of profiting from rights of wardship over minors.[24] Indeed, neither royal charters nor chronicles give any indication that the king entered the lordships of his great vassals except at times of war or rebellion, or if he wished to hold an assembly. When not otherwise on the move, the king was most frequently to be found in one of the four main administrative centres of his demesne at Jerusalem, Acre, Tyre or Nablus.[25]

This is the context of the *assise sur la ligece*, issued by Amalric, apparently near the beginning of the reign. This *assise* is drawn from the collection of law books known as the *Assises de Jerusalem*, which is a fourteenth-century compilation of works from different periods of the kingdom, none of which provides the exact wording of the *assise*.[26] However, it does seem that the leading jurists of the second half of the thirteenth century, John of Ibelin and Philip of Novara, believed that it had arisen from what they describe as a war between Amalric and Gerard Grenier, lord of Sidon and Beaufort, one of the king's tenants-in-chief, because of the latter's unjust seizure of a fief held by one of his vassals. The *assise* was issued following the making of peace, and it obliged rear-vassals (that is, vassals of the tenants-in-chief) to pay liege homage to the king, as well as doing the homage they owed to their own lords.[27] In theory this meant that, in the event of a conflict between the king and one of his tenants-in chief, the king took precedence.

The logical interpretation of this *assise* is that it is the action of a king attempting to limit the independence of his major fief-holders, perceived to have become too powerful, especially in the light of Amalric's conditional accession to the throne.[28] However, there is no evidence to show that any rear-vassal ever did use the *assise* to act against his lord in the High Court, in contrast to the royal court in Paris; indeed, in the thirteenth century, the legislation was actually invoked against the Crown since it enabled the king himself to be judged in the High Court by the peers acting together.[29] This is perhaps misleading, in that the *assise* appears to have been established not to provide a court of appeal for the rear-vassals, but as a vehicle for bringing action for treason against rebellious barons. In 1184, when Baldwin IV wished to begin a process for treason against Guy of Lusignan, count of Jaffa, he did so by convening a full session of the High Court at Acre.[30] It is, of course, possible that the *assise* was forced on the king by an assertive baronage, but it seems unlikely in the 1160s, when neither Amalric nor his barons could have foreseen the future application of such legislation.

This view is reinforced by an examination of the preceding circumstances. These have all the appearance of forceful rulers acting to control a recalcitrant vassal. Two eastern chroniclers who were much nearer to the events than the jurists of the 1260s – Michael the Syrian and Ibn al-Athir – knew that towards the end of the reign there had been a confrontation between Baldwin III and the lord of Sidon, although their notices are too brief to form a comprehensive picture of what was happening. According to Michael the Syrian, the Franks wished to seize 'a Frankish brigand, who was at Baghras' and who had fled from there and gone to find Nur al-Din. Supplied with Turkish forces, he had returned to the region of Antioch where he had continued to act in the same way.[31] 'This year,' says Ibn al-Athir, 'the Frankish ruler of Sidon sought out Nūr al-Dīn Mahmūd, ruler of Syria, to seek his protection. He gave him guarantees and also sent a force with him to protect him from the Franks. However a Frankish ambush overwhelmed them on their way and killed a number of the Muslims. The survivors fled.'[32] This ambush was evidently organised by the king: a charter of 16 March 1160 shows Baldwin III at the siege of Belhacem, close to Sidon, supported by his leading vassals.[33]

This was a serious confrontation. Gerard was the grandson of Eustace Grenier, royal constable under Baldwin II, and he had married Agnes, niece of William of Bures, prince of Galilee, and Eustace's successor as constable. As a leading baron of the kingdom, he had been present at the assembly near Acre before the attack on Damascus in 1148 and he had commanded the royal fleet that had attempted to blockade Ascalon during the siege of 1153.[34] If he really had allied with Nur al-Din his action was as treasonable as that of Hugh of Le Puiset in 1134, when he had called on Egyptian help. It may be that Gerard's truculence was the trigger for the *assise*, and that the accusation of failure to do justice was a pretext for its enactment. Moreover, if it is true that it was Gerard who had pointed out the consanguinity between Amalric and Agnes of Courtenay, the king would have had a very personal reason for enmity towards him.[35]

Amalric's strong personality was therefore bound to be the major determinant of policy in the kingdom of Jerusalem and, indeed, in the crusader states as whole. The centre of his ambitions was the conquest of Egypt. Between September 1163 and December 1169, he led five expeditions and, in 1167, even occupied Alexandria itself. Both the capture of Ascalon and the granting of anticipatory fiefs indicate that Baldwin had had similar aims, and the Egyptians had been sufficiently alarmed to agree to pay him an annual tribute.[36] Amalric, as William of Tyre says, worked without cease to expand the kingdom, and the wealthy country of Egypt must have been especially attractive to him because of what the archbishop saw as his extreme cupidity.[37] It was, though, more complicated than that. The upper echelons of the kingdom of Jerusalem formed a tight-knit little society in which the demand for land and patronage outstripped supply. Baldwin III's desire to capture Ascalon and his plans to invade Egypt may well have been partly driven by a need to find new lands. The dispossession of the Edessans added greatly to these problems, for the numbers may have been considerable; William of Tyre claims that Edessa was a productive land capable of supporting 500 knights, but the shrunken principality of Antioch offered little in the way of alternative outlets. Whatever Amalric's motives in attacking Egypt in the 1160s, he could not ignore the pressures upon his limited resources in the existing kingdom of Jerusalem. Moreover, the opportunity was obvious, for the Egyptian government was hardly functioning, as rival viziers, Dirgham, the chamberlain and former military commander, and Shawar, the governor of Upper Egypt, competed for control, unchecked by a caliph who wielded little real power.

As was to be expected, in 1163 the tribute was not paid and, in September, Amalric led a large army against Dirgham, the incumbent vizier, who, in desperation, opened the dykes on the Nile. In fact, Amalric came within 35 miles of Cairo and Dirgham agreed to pay an even larger tribute than before, providing guarantees in the form of hostages.[38] On his return, Amalric wrote to Louis VII, telling him that they had put the enemy to flight and that, had not the annual Nile floods impeded them, they would have taken Bilbais. It only needed the king's help for success to be assured.[39]

In fact, Amalric knew well that it would not be so easy, for Nur al-Din was equally well informed about the situation in Egypt. Although Dirgham had driven out Shawar, it was a short-lived success, since Shawar appealed to Nur al-Din for help. He, in turn, sent Asad al-Din Shirkuh, a Kurd from Takrit, who was one of his most able and determined generals. William of Tyre gives an unflattering physical picture of Shirkuh – short and fat and already quite elderly, and suffering from a cataract on one eye – but is full of praise for his military skills and endurance.[40] Neither ruler could afford to cede the field to the other, and the struggle became the defining feature of Amalric's reign. Even after the king's death in 1174, by which time Saladin had full control of Cairo, the Latins did not give up, unsuccessfully urging Philip, count of Flanders, who was on crusade in 1177–8, to lead a Franco-Byzantine expedition into the country.[41]

Shirkuh and Shawar were at first unsuccessful, but when Dirgham was killed in the fighting, Shawar was able to seize power, slaughtering all of Dirgham's relations and allies. However, it soon became evident that Shirkuh had every intention of conquering the country himself, for he showed no sign of leaving, but instead began an attack on the city of Bilbais. This was the occasion of Amalric's second expedition, for Shawar realised he needed help and, says William of Tyre, offered the king even greater rewards than those given by Dirgham. Amalric therefore set out again in July 1164. According to Ibn abi-Taiyi (a lost source extracted in the thirteenth-century anthology of the Damascene historian Abu Shama), Shawar covered Amalric's expenses, paying him a total of 27,000 dinars, made up of 1,000 dinars for each stage of his march into Egypt, and the costs of fodder for his horses and beasts of

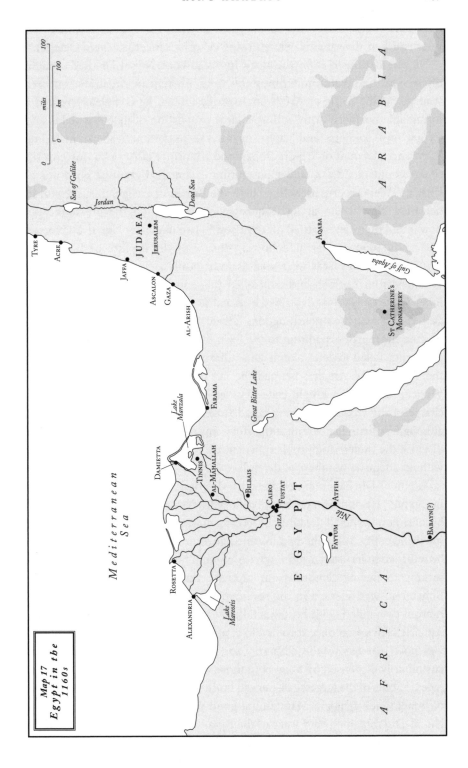

Map 17
Egypt in the
1160s

burden.[42] William's account is succinct. Amalric drove out Shirkuh and re-established Shawar as vizier, returning victorious to Jerusalem in October.[43]

He had no time to enjoy the glory. In his absence, Nur al-Din had brought disaster to the north, underlining the risks inherent in Amalric's southern strategy. In the battle of Artah on 10 August 1164, he completely routed a formidable northern army, killing a large proportion of its 600 knights and 12,000 foot soldiers, and capturing all the important leaders, including Raymond III, count of Tripoli, Bohemond III, prince of Antioch, Joscelin III, titular count of Edessa, and Constantine Coloman, Byzantine governor of Cilicia.[44] Western crusaders like Hugh the Brown of Lusignan, successful in defeating Nur al-Din at La Boquée in eastern Tripoli the previous year, now found themselves carted off to prison.[45] Two days later Nur al-Din forced the capitulation of Harim, following this with the capture of Banyas on 18 October. Both places were seen as strategically vital, for Harim was only 18 miles from Antioch and controlled the Iron Bridge across the Orontes River, while Banyas was described by Amalric of Nesle, patriarch of Jerusalem, as the gateway to the whole kingdom.[46] Even the arrival of Thierry of Flanders, now on his fourth expedition to the East, together with 'a considerable body of knights', failed to deter Nur al-Din.[47] Both Bertrand of Blancfort, master of the Temple, and Amalric blamed the fall of Banyas on traitors, named by William of Tyre as a knight called Walter of Quesnoy, who had been left in charge of the city, and a priest called Roger, who allegedly accepted bribes, although William is not sure if the story was true.[48] However, they could not disguise the underlying problem, which was that the kingdom had been left without adequate numbers of defenders.[49]

As Nur al-Din had intended, the crisis diverted Amalric from his campaigns in Egypt.[50] He and Thierry rapidly moved north and, in a process that had become familiar to all the kings of Jerusalem, set about restoring the affairs of the principality. When he had installed governors in all the important cities, he returned to Jerusalem, although throughout he seems to have been actively seeking to free Bohemond from captivity. Surprisingly, he succeeded, for Bohemond was released in the summer of 1165, on payment of part of the ransom demanded, with hostages taken for the rest. Bohemond (perhaps on Amalric's advice) at once travelled to Constantinople, where his sister, Maria, was now married to the emperor, and received the hospitality and gifts customarily dispensed by Manuel to those whom he regarded as his subordinates.[51] Some of the largesse dispensed must have gone towards the remainder of Bohemond's ransom. Maintaining good relations was evidently wise, for Nur al-Din remained very wary of the Byzantines. According to Ibn al-Athir, he refrained from attacking Antioch itself after the victory at Artah, partly because he believed that the citadel would be very difficult to take, but primarily because he did not want to provoke an appeal to Manuel for aid.[52] Both Ibn al-Athir and William of Tyre attribute the release of Bohemond to Nur al-Din's belief that he would be easier to cope with than the Byzantines.

Even had he wished to do so, Amalric could not ignore Egypt. While individual lords were, as William of Tyre puts it, 'anxious over their own affairs and eager to extend their lands', both the king and the masters of the military orders had a wider strategy to consider.[53] However, the sheer size of Egypt presented a huge challenge to their resources, for it was over 500 miles from the Nile Delta in the north to the First Cataract at Aswan in the south.[54] In 1163 and 1164, the master of the Temple, Bertrand of Blancfort, expressed his concerns in a series of letters to Louis VII. In the autumn of 1164, he returned from Egypt to find that his order had lost sixty knights at Artah and a larger number of sergeants and turcopoles.[55] 'Paneas [Banyas], the strongest city in the kingdom, had been handed over to the Turks by the ruse of traitors. Antioch is in a miserable, lamentable state and ready to be overthrown with a terrible, unspeakable slaughter of its inhabitants. There is no doubt that it will fall into the hands of the Greeks or the Turks, and very soon, unless divine pity and your super-excellent greatness come to its help with all speed.' The king's aid was vital because they simply did not have the resources to cope. 'Although our King Amalric is great and magnificent, thanks to God, he cannot organise a fourfold army to defend Antioch, Tripoli, Jerusalem and Babylon [Egypt], in which he remains with his sons and which is most to be feared. But Nur al-Din can attack all four at one and the same time if he so desires, so great is the number of his dogs.'[56]

Nevertheless, the conquest of Egypt was possible. Fatimid determination to defend Ascalon had been based on the assumption that, if it fell, Egypt would be open to Frankish invasion.[57] This was a realistic calculation as the Christian kingdoms of al-Maqurra and 'Alwa were located to the south, while Franco-Byzantine control of the sea meant that the ports of Alexandria, Rosetta and Damietta would be targets.[58] For his part, Saladin established himself as ruler of the country despite the obvious difficulties, overcoming a revolt against him in Cairo in August 1169, as well as surviving both Nur al-Din's antagonism and Frankish and Byzantine attacks.[59]

Amalric must have calculated that the potential rewards justified the risks, for the kingdom of Jerusalem would have been transformed into a major regional power, the southern territories would have been made safe, many more settlers from the expanding population of the West would have emigrated, and new resources would have been obtained, some of which might have been of value in defending the northern states. Alexandria, for

example, was a great port, with links to the West and Upper Egypt, but especially to the East via the Red Sea, a key spice route beyond the reach of the
kingdom of Jerusalem, while the local and regional trade which the Franks
had developed would have been further stimulated.[60] Moreover, as early as the
1120s, the Premonstratensians of St Samuel on Mountjoy found that most
of the sites around Jerusalem had already been acquired by other monasteries,
a situation that explains their interest in the south-west around Ascalon, a
region not fully encompassed until the 1150s.[61] Egypt was an obvious attraction for a crowded kingdom seeking new territorial outlets.

Louis VII, however, showed no sign of intending to lead a new expedition
in the near future, despite the blizzard of letters aimed at him.[62] Thus, their
condemnations of the Greeks in the letters to France notwithstanding, the
Latin leaders in the East continued to cultivate the Byzantines. Bohemond
must have taken an oath of fidelity to Manuel before he left Constantinople
since, in the words put into the emperor's mouth by John Kinnamos, 'the
city of Antioch was anciently tributary to the Romans and now is subject to
our majesty'.[63] When Bohemond returned to Syria he brought with him
Athanasius I Manasses, the latest in the line of titular Greek patriarchs of
Antioch appointed by the Comnenian emperors. Aimery of Limoges was
obliged to leave, taking up residence in his castle of al-Qusair, about 12 miles
south of Antioch, probably held by the patriarchs since 1134. He showed his
resentment by excommunicating the inhabitants of Antioch.[64] Soon after, in
the autumn of 1165, Amalric, unmarried since his enforced separation from
Agnes of Courtenay at the beginning of the reign, sent an embassy to
Constantinople led by Ernesius, archbishop of Caesarea, and Odo of Saint-
Amand, the royal butler, with the aim of negotiating a marriage alliance with
the imperial family.[65]

However, the Byzantines could not provide immediate help. The embassy
did not return for nearly two years, but in January 1167 news reached
Jerusalem that Shirkuh was marching through the desert towards Egypt at the
head of another army. William of Tyre says that Shirkuh had convinced the
Abbasid caliph at Baghdad that Egypt was a rich country, ruled by a decadent
dynasty that adhered to law and traditions quite contrary to Sunnite teaching.[66]
Nur al-Din was less enthusiastic but, says Ibn al-Athir, Shirkuh was 'extremely
eager to do this', and Nur al-Din agreed to furnish him with 2,000 cavalry and
the company of several emirs, as he feared that too weak a force would meet
with disaster. In early February, Shirkuh reached Atfih on the Nile, crossed
over to the west bank and encamped at Giza, opposite Old Cairo.[67] Meanwhile,
Amalric called a general council at Nablus at which a tax of a tenth on
movable property was agreed to finance the Christian response. Amalric set

out from Ascalon on 30 January, crossing what William calls the desolate wilderness between Gaza and al-Arish. The mobilisation had been extremely rapid and at al-Arish they had to wait for reinforcements before the army moved on to Bilbais. The king had hurried because he had hoped to catch Shirkuh before he crossed the Nile, but discovered he was too late. As William of Tyre realised, Shirkuh was 'a most vigilant leader'.[68]

Unlike the expedition of 1164, which he covered in a couple of lines, this campaign was of intense interest to William of Tyre. He was now resident in the kingdom and he had reliable informants who could give him first-hand information. Moreover, Amalric penetrated far deeper into the country than ever before, enabling William to set out the historical and religious context of famous places of central importance to the Classical and Christian past.[69] For some of this material he could, of course, call on his library, but his dramatic descriptions of the fighting and of the meeting of the Frankish envoys with the caliph himself are clearly based directly on information given by the participants immediately after they returned and written up very soon after. The most important of his sources was Hugh, lord of Caesarea since c.1154 and a member of one of the oldest families in the kingdom, since his grandfather was Eustace Grenier, who had served both Baldwin I and Baldwin II. He was the younger son of Walter of Caesarea, whose elder son, Eustace, appears to have contracted leprosy and entered the Order of St Lazarus. William describes Hugh as 'a young man of uncommon prudence and circumspection beyond that which is usually found at that age'.[70]

William says that Shawar could scarcely believe that Shirkuh was again threatening the country, but, once convinced, he was extremely anxious to secure Frankish support. He agreed to an annual tribute of 400,000 gold pieces (presumably dinars) of which half would be paid immediately, on condition that the Franks either destroy Shirkuh or drive him out. Hugh of Caesarea and the Templar Geoffrey Fulcher were sent to the caliph to confirm the treaty and, in a unique passage, William describes their entry into his palace in Cairo and their audience with him. No other westerners had been allowed into the place or into the presence of the caliph in the crusader era.[71] They were led by Shawar through a series of dark passages, the entrances of which were guarded by Ethiopians, until they came to a large, open court. Here they encountered an exotic world, quite unknown to them.

There, supported by columns of marble covered with designs in relief were promenades with fretted and gilded ceilings and pavements of various colored stones. Throughout the entire circuit royal magnificence prevailed. So elegant was both material and workmanship that involuntarily the eyes of all who saw it were

ravished by the rare beauty and never wearied of the sight. There were marble
fishpools filled with limpid waters; there were birds of many kinds, unknown to
our part of the world. These were larger than those familiar to us, their forms were
unusual, their colors strange, and their songs different. The food of each varied
according to its species and was suited to its own kind.[72]

From here they were conducted by the chief eunuch through elegant and
opulent buildings to the inner palace where the caliph resided, their sense of
having entered another world reinforced as they encountered animals from
Africa and Asia which William had not seen outside the pages of Solinus.[73]
Al-Adid, the caliph, still in his mid-teens, was seated on a golden throne,
concealed by curtains embroidered with pearls and gold. After Shawar had
prostrated himself three times the curtains opened and Shawar approached,
kissed the caliph's foot and then explained the agreement he had made and the
reasons for it. Al-Adid readily consented, but Hugh of Caesarea caused
consternation by asking not only that he confirm it by clasping hands but that
his hand should be uncovered, as would have been the case in the western
world. 'Finally, with extreme unwillingness, as if it detracted from his majesty,
yet with a slight smile which greatly aggrieved the Egyptians, he put his
uncovered hand into that of Hugh.'[74]

On the morning after the envoys' return, the Christians discovered that
Shirkuh had encamped on the opposite bank. Their reaction was to build a
wooden bridge, fortified with towers, that extended halfway across the river,
and a stalemate ensued that lasted for over a month. This was partly because
Amalric was waiting for reinforcements: Humphrey of Toron, the constable,
and Philip of Nablus joined the camp at this time, having been delayed by
their own affairs. Amalric now secretly moved his army 8 miles upstream,
where most of his men were ferried across to an island called al-Mahallah. A
force under Hugh of Ibelin was left to guard the wooden bridge and protect
the caliph in Cairo. The plan was hindered, however, by what William
describes as a whirlwind, which prevented the army from crossing the other
channel to the opposite bank, so losing the element of surprise and giving the
enemy time to react.

William of Tyre and Ibn al-Athir agree that Shirkuh now retreated upriver,
pursued by Amalric and his knights, the foot soldiers having been left behind
for greater speed. After three days the Franks caught up at 'a place called
Bābayn' and decided to give battle. William gives the date as 18 March. He
claims that Shirkuh had 12,000 Turks and 10,000 or 11,000 Arabs, whereas
Amalric had only 374 knights together with 'the worthless and effeminate
Egyptians' and some useless turcopoles. The situation must have looked

different from the other side, however, for there was a debate about whether to fight or attempt to escape back to Syria, 'because of their small numbers and their distance from their homes and homelands and the dangers of the route'. Urged on by a mamluk called Sharaf al-Din Buzghush, lord of Shaqif, and by Salah al-Din, Shirkuh's nephew, they chose to stand and fight. This, as Ibn al-Athir saw it, was fully justified by their rout of 'the armies of Egypt and the Franks of the Levant coast' with a force of only 2,000 cavalry.[75] William of Tyre is more equivocal, describing a rather incoherent battle broken up by the terrain into a series of smaller engagements, in which ultimately Amalric was obliged to regroup and retreat across the river to Lamonia, 10 miles away. When he reached Cairo he found that 100 knights were missing, whereas the enemy had lost 1,500. Among those not present was Hugh of Caesarea, taken prisoner by Saladin.[76]

Whatever the truth about the losses on both sides, the battle was evidently indecisive. Shirkuh did not wait for further contact, but rapidly took his army north to Alexandria, which at once submitted to him. Again he was followed by the Franks, who blockaded the city for a month by closing the branch of the Nile by which the inhabitants obtained food supplies from Upper Egypt. With famine imminent, Shirkuh managed to escape upriver, leaving Saladin in charge. Briefly Amalric pursued him, but was then persuaded by the Egyptians that the city itself could be taken. Alexandria was now fully besieged: ships were sent from Palestine, the Pisans brought their fleet, siege engines were constructed and the orchards around the city were cut down, much to the resentment of the inhabitants.[77] Inside the city there was increasing bitterness against the Turks, who were blamed for bringing these miseries on the population.

These circumstances forced Shirkuh to offer terms, which he discussed with Hugh of Caesarea and which were conveyed to the king by another captive, Arnulf of Turbessel. William of Tyre says that Alexandria was to be ceded to the king and the Turkish garrison allowed to depart, prisoners were to be exchanged, and Shirkuh and his forces were to leave Egypt. Ibn al-Athir has the Franks paying Shirkuh 50,000 dinars and promising to leave the country, but agrees with William of Tyre that the Franks were allowed to place a garrison in Alexandria to prevent Nur al-Din from sending in further forces. He says that the Franks were given an annual tribute of 100,000 dinars by the Egyptians. The Turks left Alexandria on 4 August and Shirkuh arrived back in Damascus on 5 September.[78] With the departure of Shirkuh, the Christians entered the city in triumph, where the king placed his banner on the Pharos, Alexandria's famous lighthouse. William of Tyre claims that they were welcomed, although the heavy exactions placed on the city by Shawar suggest that most of the tribute money was extracted from the local population, presumably as punishment for submitting to the Turks. In accordance with the agreement, the Franks then returned to the kingdom of Jerusalem, some by sea but mostly overland; Amalric reached Ascalon on 21 August.

Eight days later Amalric married Maria Comnena, daughter of Manuel's nephew, John, in the cathedral at Tyre in a ceremony conducted by Patriarch Amalric. She had arrived in the company of the envoys sent to Constantinople nearly two years before. Soon after, two south Italians from Manuel's court – Alexander, count of Gravina, and Michael Hydruntius from Otranto – also landed at Tyre, and immediately had a private conference with the king and selected notables.[79] The Byzantine envoys suggested that since Egypt was in such a feeble state it would soon fall under the control of another power unless the emperor and the king conquered it for themselves, a task which they said could easily be accomplished. William of Tyre evidently believed that the initiative had come from Amalric and, indeed, the marriage and the arrival of the ambassadors were obviously connected. Accordingly, a treaty was drawn up and William himself was chosen as one of the envoys to be sent to Manuel to ratify its terms, setting out from Tripoli soon after. Manuel himself was campaigning in Serbia and the royal representatives finally caught up with him near Ochrida, where both parties confirmed the treaty on oath. William and his companions then set out on the return journey on 1 October 1168. It is no coincidence that, during this period, Amalric is depicted on royal seals wearing a sash crossed over his chest, a style of dress that derives from the Byzantine *loros*, itself a symbol of imperial sovereignty.[80]

However, this new climate of cordiality is most vividly demonstrated by the extensive, high-quality mosaic programme that was now undertaken in the church of the Nativity at Bethlehem. Uniquely, this church had been inherited by the crusaders largely in the form in which it had been rebuilt in the sixth century at the time of Emperor Justinian. The first generation of settlers had added other buildings to the complex, including episcopal accommodation, a cloister and monastic structures for the Augustinian canons established there and, perhaps later, a hospital. The church itself had a narthex, a central nave flanked by double rows of columns, and three apses at the east end and on the transepts. Below the choir was the Cave of the Nativity, believed to be the place of Christ's birth, and beneath the north transept was the tomb of St Jerome. In c.1130, the body of Joseph of Arimathea was brought to a tomb on the west side of the choir.[81] For pilgrims, this site was therefore second only to that of the Holy Sepulchre and some showed their devotion by sponsoring paintings on the rows of columns in the nave, the earliest of which, an image of the Virgin and Child in the form known as Mary Glykophilousa, includes an inscription dating it to 1130.[82] At the foot of the column are two kneeling figures, evidently of western origin, assumed to be the donors.[83] There are forty-four columns in all, on twenty-seven of which are painted a variety of sacred figures, using a technique that involved fixing the pigment in oil or wax, and then applying it directly to the stone surface, following the outlines of the subject in sepia.[84] It seems likely that the earlier examples are a series of individual votive images, painted over the years between 1130 and 1167, when an attempt was made to integrate the column paintings with the redecoration of the church undertaken at that time.[85]

The mosaic programme must have been started soon after the marriage of Amalric and Maria; the use of an obviously Byzantine church already decorated with paintings heavily influenced by Byzantine models reflects the alliance that was sealed by this marriage. The work seems to have been overseen by Ephraim, apparently an Orthodox cleric-artist resident in Palestine, assisted by two others, Basil, a Syrian Melkite, and another mosaicist, whose name is not known. The inscription on the south side of the apse which records Ephraim's supervision of the decoration of this part of the church states that it had been done under the sponsorship of Manuel, ruler of the Greeks, and Amalric, who among other qualities is described as being 'the guardian of virtue', and during the episcopacy of Ralph, bishop of Bethlehem, teacher of the Church. As was appropriate at such a site, the mosaics in the sanctuary concentrate upon the Virgin and Child, while those in the two side apses illustrate the Life and Passion of Christ. On the south wall of the nave were set out seven ecumenical councils, beginning with Nicaea in 325 at the eastern end and continuing onto the north wall, which showed six provincial councils, the first of which was Carthage in 254. Inscriptions were in Greek and Latin, but in the conciliar series all but one were Greek. The aim was to show the ecumenical councils as the repositories of doctrine, while the provincial councils laid down the related disciplinary actions.[86]

This ambitious programme is a striking demonstration of the way Manuel viewed the world in the late 1160s, and it is significant that Amalric and his lay and ecclesiastical advisers were willing to accept this in return for the military and political support that could be obtained from a co-operative Byzantine emperor. The fact that Ralph was royal chancellor as well as bishop of Bethlehem must have had an influence on the choice of the church of the Nativity as the site for the mosaics, while Ralph himself must have seen the work as a means of elevating the status of his see following the resolution of a long dispute over the incorporation of the bishopric of Ascalon.[87] For Amalric, theological differences (such as the exclusion of the *filioque* clause in the Creed in the inscriptions) were of much less consequence than practical help. Thus Manuel was able to present himself as the successor of Constantine and Justinian, presiding over an ecumenical Church that encompassed not only Greeks and Latins, but also Armenians and Jacobites, whose reconciliation was part of a long-term programme projected through councils held under imperial auspices between 1157 and 1179. Both the human and divine natures of Christ, as seen in the apses, and the series of councils along the nave walls were integral to Manuel's ecumenical programme. He himself was portrayed in the sanctuary, probably next to the scene showing the Presentation of Christ. This would never have been accepted by the papacy, for, in a world in which theological and disciplinary matters were decided in councils called by the emperor, Roman claims to primacy were ignored. At the same time Manuel dispensed his patronage to other Orthodox sites in Palestine, including the church of the Holy Sepulchre and the Greek monasteries of the area, emphasising the continued presence of Orthodox clergy and monks in the kingdom of Jerusalem.[88] Not surprisingly in these circumstances, local Greek clergy were once again allowed access to the Holy Sepulchre. The contrast with the early years of the kingdom is stark, when the only matter upon which Daibert of Pisa and Arnulf of Chocques could agree was the expulsion of the Greeks.[89]

Therefore, when William of Tyre arrived back in the kingdom he was astonished to find that the king had already left on a new expedition to Egypt, having set out soon after 20 October.[90] William clearly thought that this was an extraordinary thing to have done. As he was absent at the time he could not be certain what had prompted the new campaign, apparently undertaken in contravention of the treaty made with Shawar in August 1167, not to mention in the face of the planned joint campaign with Manuel, for which the Byzantines could not possibly have been ready. There was, he says, a rumour that Shawar had been trying to obtain aid from Nur al-Din, and it was in order to prevent such an alliance that the hasty mobilisation was made. Indeed, Ibn al-Athir says that al-Kamil Shuja, Shawar's son, had offered allegiance and tribute to Nur al-Din soon after the Franks had left Egypt in August 1167. As a consequence, Nur al-Din had sent 'a large sum of money', although no military action had followed.[91]

William of Tyre clearly did not believe that this was the real reason for Amalric's invasion, however. 'There are those who claim that all these charges were false, that the Sultan Shawar was quite innocent and, far from deserving such treatment, had in good faith kept the treaty and all its stipulations. They assert that the war made against him was unjust and contrary to divine law; that it was merely a pretext invented to defend an outrageous enterprise.'[92] Ibn al-Athir places Shirkuh's intervention in Egypt in December, after Amalric had invaded, explaining that it was because the Franks had taken control of Cairo and had established 'a tyrannical rule over the Muslims'. He portrays Amalric as a reluctant aggressor, concerned in case Nur al-Din might be provoked, but eventually acceding to the pressure of what he calls 'the Frankish knights and policy makers'.[93]

Although it is difficult to pin down the exact circumstances, Amalric's fourth expedition to Egypt was therefore highly controversial within the kingdom. The upshot was serious disagreement, which profoundly affected the Frankish ability to achieve any permanent occupation. This expressed itself most dramatically in the attitude of the Templars, who refused to take part. They themselves have left no record of their reasons, but William of Tyre, who was not in Jerusalem at the time, speculates that they had either objected to the dissolution of the treaty with Shawar, which they saw as bad faith, or, less honourably, withdrew 'because the master of a rival house was apparently the originator and leader of the enterprise'.[94] The rival house was, of course, the Hospital, and had its master refused to participate Amalric could not have undertaken the expedition. In fact, the Hospitallers were instrumental. 'It is said,' William of Tyre reports, 'that Gerbert, surnamed Assallit, the master of the house of the Hospital at Jerusalem, was the prime mover, if not the originator, of this ill-fated campaign.' In an agreement with the king of 11 October 1168, the Hospitallers committed themselves to furnish 500 knights and 500 turcopoles, to be assembled at al-Arish before the marshal or the constable, a greater force than they had ever previously provided.[95]

This extravagant promise was matched by an extraordinary set of potential privileges, which suggests that Amalric was far from reluctant to undertake the enterprise. In return for their military help, the Hospitallers were offered the opportunity to create a vast lordship centred on Bilbais and extending as far as the coast, the return on which was estimated to be a rental of 100,000 old besants per annum.[96] There would then be another 50,000 besants from ten other places: Cairo, Tinnis, Damietta, the island of al-Mahallah, Alexandria, Qus, Aswan, al-Bahnasa, Atfih and Fayyum. In each of these places they would receive the best house or palace after the king, as well as a tenth of the caliph's treasure in Cairo and other cities. The Hospitallers could take their own proportion of the plunder before all others, after the king had had his half-share, and they would be entitled to all the spoils from any of their own military operations, unless the king were present in person. If the order could not muster as many men as had been agreed, its share would be proportionately lower, but if it could provide more men, then it would receive an even greater recompense.

In fact, Gilbert of Assailly stretched the resources of the Hospital to breaking point, borrowing large sums of money to hire additional knights the order could not provide itself. This evidently reflected the contrasting personalities of the two masters. William of Tyre offers a vivid portrait of Gilbert, whom he presents as a highly emotional and unstable man, given to extremes, whose actions eventually led to his resignation in a fit of depression. By contrast, Bertrand of Blancfort, says William, was 'a religious and God-fearing man', his policies perhaps tempered by his own bitter experience of nearly two years in a Muslim prison following the defeat of Baldwin III's army near Jacob's Ford in June 1157.[97] Although the Temple had participated in the earlier Egyptian campaigns, the Franks had failed to turn their invasions into permanent conquests, despite actually occupying Alexandria in 1167.

Moreover, the master was aware of the increasing responsibilities of the order. At some point before April 1168, possibly because of worries about attacks on the north while he was away in Egypt, Amalric had given Safad in northern Galilee to the Templars, a castle that overlooked all the places of pilgrimage in the northern part of the kingdom and that was only about 7 miles west of the Jordan.[98] Inevitably this brought additional expenses on a large scale.[99] At the same time Nur al-Din was able to inflict heavy losses on Antioch when the army of the kingdom of Jerusalem was absent, losses felt more acutely by the Templars, who had a greater stake in the principality than the Hospitallers, as can be seen by the fact that the Antiochene commander of the Templars ranked higher within his order than did his Hospitaller equivalent, reflecting the early date at which the Templars had become involved in Antioch's defence.[100] This belief in the vulnerability of the northern states was shared by the Muslims. The qadi Abu'l-Mahsin Yusuf, quoted by Abu Shama, describes the departure of the Christians from Egypt in 1167 as having been provoked by Nur al-Din, for the Franks feared for their possessions.[101]

Bertrand of Blancfort's reluctance may have been strengthened by an incident that had apparently occurred in 1166, although William of Tyre is vague about the date. William claims that, under siege by Shirkuh, a Templar garrison surrendered an unnamed cave fortress lying beyond the Jordan, despite the fact that Amalric had mounted a relief expedition. According to William, in his anger, Amalric hanged about twelve of the Templars responsible, which, if true, was an evident violation of the order's jurisdictional immunity.[102] This is a puzzling episode, since William provides no context, nor mentions any repercussions, but there may be a connection with the royal confirmation of a grant to the Temple of parts of the fief of Transjordan held by Philip of Nablus. This grant was made by Philip on the occasion of his entrance to the order on 17 January 1166 at Acre, and encompassed a considerable portion of the northern part of the fief, including the castle of Amman and half of the land Philip held in the Belqa, north of the Dead Sea.[103] If the cave fortress surrendered by the Templars had been situated in lands so recently entrusted to the care of the Temple, then the king's reaction is more comprehensible, the order's papal privileges notwithstanding.[104]

For the Templars, pragmatism may have been reinforced by principle, since the expedition involved the abandonment of the agreement with Shawar, made the previous year, to which the Templar, Geoffrey Fulcher, had made a major contribution. William of Tyre was always very aware of such issues and he thought that in the expedition of 1168 the Christians had broken their word, leading to the withdrawal of God's favour and therefore inevitable failure. Ibn Shaddad thus had some justification for his accusation that the Franks were 'breaking all the terms of the peace that had been agreed with the Egyptians and Asad al-Din, in their eagerness for the country'.[105]

In these circumstances, William makes no effort to present the campaign in a positive light.[106] After a siege of three days Bilbais was taken, the city plundered and the inhabitants massacred. Amalric then marched on to Cairo but, according to Ibn al-Athir, before he reached it, Shawar ordered Fustat or 'Old Cairo' to be set on fire and its contents plundered, starting a conflagration that lasted for fifty-four days and destroyed the city almost completely. 'All this was because of the fear that the Franks would seize it.'[107] Shawar had no real means of resistance, so he tried to gain time by offering a huge sum of money to Amalric, while simultaneously sending to Nur al-Din for help. William of Tyre says that he promised Amalric 2 million dinars, while Ibn al-Athir puts the figure at a million. Either way these are fantasy sums; as William puts it, 'the entire resources of the kingdom would scarcely have sufficed.'

William must be repeating a view of some of the participants when he says that Cairo could have been taken at this point, especially as the Christian fleet had now arrived, taken Tinnis and was attempting to block the Nile below the city. Shawar, however, after having paid a first instalment of 100,000 dinars, managed to persuade Amalric to retreat to a position a few miles away, ostensibly to give him time to collect the remainder. Meanwhile, he did all he could to strengthen the city's defences and to stiffen the morale of the population. Ibn al-Athir says that their determination to resist was increased when they heard the fate of the inhabitants of Bilbais. Nevertheless, William ascribes the failure to take the city to the king's avarice, in which he was encouraged by the seneschal, Miles of Plancy. If Cairo had been stormed, it would have been open to plunder, whereas all the tribute money would end up in the royal treasury.

Whatever his motives, Amalric's decision was fatal to the campaign. On 2 December, Shirkuh set out from Damascus with 8,000 cavalry, 2,000 of them selected from the standing army, paid for by Nur al-Din, who granted a sum of 200,000 dinars together with equipment.[108] News of his imminent arrival led Amalric to return to Bilbais, but he did not meet Shirkuh, who appears to have bypassed him and established himself on the other bank of the Nile. The king now decided that to challenge Shirkuh would be too dangerous and, on 2 January, the army set out for home. The fiasco of the campaign was compounded by the fact that Shirkuh was left unopposed in Egypt and, for the first time, was in a position to take over. 'He [Nur al-Din] dispatched messengers far and wide to spread the good news of that, for it was a reconquest of Egypt and a preservation of all Syrian and other lands.'[109]

Shawar did what he could to survive, but when the caliph bestowed a robe of honour upon Shirkuh he knew he was in great danger. Ibn al-Athir says that he plotted to invite Shirkuh and his emirs to a banquet and then arrest them, but that the plan was blocked by his son, al-Kamil. Thereafter, Shawar's end was not long in coming: he was murdered by Saladin and 'Izz al-Din Jurdik, one of the mamluk emirs, either by their own hands or through a manoeuvre that left Shirkuh no alternative but to have him put to death.[110] Shirkuh was appointed vizier in his place, and 'thus, strong through the power of the sword, Shirkuh became master of all Egypt'. In later reflections on these events, probably in 1182, William of Tyre attributes the ills of the kingdom to the outcome of the campaign of 1168–9. Cupidity had lost the political and commercial advantages that had previously prevailed, plunging the kingdom into 'a state of turbulence and anxiety'.[111]

However, Amalric had not mounted this expedition merely to engage in extortion. The agreement with the Hospital and the deployment of the fleet confirm his intention to gain control of Egypt and it is not surprising to find that in the summer of 1169 he began preparations for a fifth expedition. Aware that the forces of the kingdom alone had not proved sufficient in the past, he once more sought help in the West, sending letters to the emperor, the kings of France, England and Sicily, and the counts of Flanders, Troyes and Chartres. He was undeterred when the first embassy was forced back by storms, appointing new envoys for a second attempt, led by Frederick, archbishop of Tyre, and John, bishop of Banyas. William of Tyre is dismissive of this embassy. Bishop John died in Paris, while Frederick of Tyre was away two years but accomplished nothing.[112]

The kingdom was by means ignored in the West during Amalric's reign, but the Franks were unable to persuade either Louis VII or any other kings to come to their aid, while, among several high-profile visitors, only Thierry of

Flanders made any actual military contribution. There were, however, expeditions led by Stephen of Perche, chancellor of the kingdom of Sicily and archbishop-elect of Palermo, and William, count of Nevers, in the summer of 1168, as well as by three leading French lords, Stephen of Sancerre, brother of Theobald V, count of Blois, Stephen, count of Saône, and Hugh, duke of Burgundy, in 1171. Henry the Lion, duke of Saxony and Bavaria, more powerful than all three of them, also visited the holy places the following year. However, their help was quite limited: both Stephen of Perche and William of Nevers died in the East, while the arrivals of 1171 and 1172 saw themselves as pilgrims rather than warriors and stayed only a short time.[113] Even had they been inclined to fight, an expedition to Egypt was such a major undertaking that it is unlikely that any of them would have been willing to participate.

Only Stephen of Sancerre had seemed to offer more. The one concrete result of Frederick of Tyre's mission had been to persuade him to come to the East to marry Sibylla, Amalric's daughter, now aged about eleven. His lineage was impressive and, although a third son, he had a patrimony of his own. The plan, however, fell apart, perhaps because Stephen disliked what might have been seen as the kingdom's subservience to Constantinople, or perhaps because the detailed negotiations with Amalric suggested to him that the marriage was less desirable than he had been led to believe. William of Tyre was not disappointed to see him go, for he thought Stephen an immoral and worthless individual and claimed that he had made himself hated in the kingdom.[114]

William of Tyre was therefore realistic in seeing the main hope for a further attack on Egypt as lying with the Byzantines rather than with any western ruler. Moreover, his role as negotiator gave him a personal interest in the alliance. In the autumn Manuel did indeed send a formidable force, led by Andronicus Contostephanus, Alexander of Gravina and Theodore Maurozumes. Two of these men had had experience of the crusader states in the past: Andronicus had been a leader of Manuel's punitive expedition against Raymond of Antioch in 1144–5, while Alexander had been one of the Byzantine envoys in 1168. The emperor sent a powerful fleet, which included 150 galleys, sixty large ships capable of carrying and unloading horses, and between ten and twenty dromonds, carrying large quantities of supplies and equipment. The fleet arrived at Tyre before anchoring at Acre.[115]

Amalric had been making his own preparations during the summer. In August 1169, he confirmed the 1168 agreement with the Hospitallers, as well as bringing the Templars back into his army.[116] Bertrand of Blancfort had died on 2 January 1169, as Amalric returned from Egypt, opening the way for a new master more amenable to the king's policies. Philip of Nablus had joined the Temple in 1166 and had long been associated with Amalric, for they had both supported Melisende in her struggle with Baldwin III. In August 1169, Philip was elected master of the Temple, obviously as a result of royal influence. When Bertrand of Blancfort withdrew the Templars from the expedition of 1168 he disappeared from royal charters, but Philip's appearance as a signatory to the Hospitaller confirmation and to grants made to the Pisans of privileges in Cairo and other cities on 17 September shows that the Templars were once more involved.[117]

Common sense demanded that if the Christians were ever to regain control of Egypt, they needed to strike quickly before Shirkuh and Saladin had had time to establish themselves. Their position was precarious. William of Tyre says that the Egyptians hated the Turks, feelings that doubtless applied equally to Kurds and mamluks as well.[118] Amalric's plans were furthered by the sudden death of Shirkuh on 23 March 1169, apparently from the effects of overeating, and by Saladin's difficulties in the months which followed. Nur al-Din was angry at what he saw as Saladin's insubordination, particularly by the irresponsible way he spent money (a characteristic which he never lost), while Saladin himself was wary of the caliph, who he feared might have him killed. Resentment at the Turkish occupation came to a head in August when Egyptian discontent fused with the truculence of the black soldiers who served the caliph, creating a violent revolt in Cairo. After several days of fierce fighting, the revolt was quelled on 23 August and the remaining rebels were killed at Giza, but it showed what could happen if Saladin was obliged to face another external threat.[119]

The Franks and the Byzantines now attempted the difficult feat of a co-ordinated attack on Egypt: Amalric left Ascalon on 16 October, while the Byzantine fleet sailed from Acre a few days before. Although hindered by sea flooding on the coast road, Amalric reached Farama, which had been abandoned, and then, on 27 October, Damietta, where his army encamped nearby. Both William of Tyre and Niketas Choniates are critical of the delay that followed, allowing time for the Turks to send in reinforcements from further upriver, including men and supplies provided by Nur al-Din.[120] As the siege became increasingly drawn out, the Byzantines began to suffer from shortages of supplies, a problem not rectified by the Franks who, according to William, needed to conserve what little they had for themselves. The besiegers now began to lose heart: 'It was the general opinion that the expedition had been undertaken against the will of the Lord.' In the end they decided to make peace, for they foresaw only death, either by famine or the sword.[121]

There were repercussions for all parties. Amalric and his army successfully accomplished their return, reaching Ascalon on 21 December, but the kingdom of Jerusalem had not escaped unscathed. Nur al-Din had adopted his previous tactics when Egypt was under pressure, 'plundering and ruining' the undefended land, where he had reached 'areas not previously touched'.[122] Nor could Gilbert of Assailly avoid the consequences. He had burdened the Hospitallers with a debt of 100,000 pieces of gold which could not be repaid.[123] The disaster precipitated a personal crisis for Gilbert, who resigned the mastership, causing a schism within the order, and opening up arguments about both the extent of papal authority over the Hospital's affairs and the nature of the order's mission.[124] The Byzantine fleet was obliged to set out in December, well past the usual sailing season, and was hit by a storm from which few of their ships escaped.[125] To the Turks, however, the threat had been real enough. John Kinnamos says that envoys came from Egypt offering tribute in the hope of preventing another attack, but that Manuel rejected this 'as he intended to overrun their whole land again'.[126]

Inevitably there were recriminations. William of Tyre is reluctant to blame the Greeks, since he remained aware of his part in negotiating the original alliance, and says they fought bravely. However, his informants were less charitable, telling William that the disaster had been caused by Manuel, who had not spent enough money on supplies.[127] Michael the Syrian, who as a Jacobite was always ready to castigate the Byzantines, says that 'when the Greeks arrived in Egypt, driven by their inveterate malice, they wished to deceive the king, and to seize the country for themselves'. When Amalric was warned of this, he decided to take the customary Egyptian offer of gold and return to Jerusalem.[128]

The Greek sources are equally forthright. Both John Kinnamos and Niketas Choniates believed that the failure had been caused by procrastination on the part of the Latins, who had left the Greeks to do most of the fighting. Kinnamos saw this as treachery, which he claimed stemmed from Latin reluctance to share conquests equally, while Choniates ascribed the failure of supplies to the prolongation of the campaign. Manuel had provided the fleet with a supply of grain for three months, beginning in August.[129] Andronicus, he says, had been instructed to obey Amalric, but had finally lost patience with 'talking into the ear of the dead' and, ignoring 'the Latin drivel', had decided to conduct the campaign on his own. However, just as the Byzantines were about to take the city by storm, Amalric appeared and announced he had made a treaty with the Saracens, completely undermining the Greeks, whose only thought thereafter was to return home. It was this disorganised embarkation that had exposed the ships to the Mediterranean in December and caused the foundering of the Byzantine fleet.[130]

Within seven months the crusader states had suffered a new disaster, but this time the effects were felt in Antioch and Tripoli rather than Jerusalem.

The earthquake that struck on 29 June 1170 dealt a shattering blow to the inhabitants of Syria, Christian and Muslim alike.[131] In Antioch, the walls along the banks of the Orontes crumbled, several churches were destroyed and the sanctuary of the cathedral collapsed. Bohemond III was deeply affected, cutting his hair and dressing in sackcloth before leading a deputation to Aimery of Limoges, still in his castle of al-Qusair. Here he pressed the patriarch to return, but he would not be moved while Athanasius, the Greek patriarch, remained in the city. However, it happened that Athanasius was one of the victims of falling masonry in the cathedral of St Peter, where he was conducting a service. Although he was pulled out alive, he did not survive for long, enabling Aimery to be restored to the patriarchate.[132] In the county of Tripoli, the shield of castles granted to the military orders by Raymond II was torn apart. Crac des Chevaliers, Chastel Blanc and al-'Arimah needed major reconstruction; only the Templar castle of Tortosa escaped damage, while in Tripoli itself the cathedral of St Mary was brought down.

The Muslim cities were equally affected, and a temporary peace was made between Amalric and Nur al-Din while these regions recovered from the death and destruction brought by the earthquake. Even so, Ibn al-Athir says that each side feared the other while they set about repairing the damage.[133] In a letter written immediately after the events, in July or August, Amalric told Louis VII that an earthquake of unprecedented severity had struck the county of Tripoli and that its effects had been felt all the way north to Antioch. If help was not forthcoming, Tripoli, Arqa, Gibelet, Latakia, Marqab and Antioch would be occupied by the enemy.[134] At much the same time, Amalric, in his role as administrator of the county, granted the Hospitallers the castles of Arqa and Gibelacar, north-east of Tripoli, exempting them from the count's rights of overlordship, but leaving the order with the cost and responsibility of rebuilding.[135] It is unlikely that the order made much immediate progress, since it was still suffering from the effects of the huge debts incurred by Gilbert of Assailly in the Egyptian campaigns of 1168 and 1169.

Saladin's consolidation of his power in Cairo had, however, added another dimension to the Islamic *jihad*. Ibn Shaddad claims that, after the death of Shirkuh, Saladin became convinced that he was destined by God to conquer the coast (that is, the lands occupied by the Franks) and that he should therefore make appropriate changes to both his lifestyle and his policies. 'He renounced wine, gave up vain pastimes and donned the garments of seriousness and pious endeavour. He never retreated from that, but grew ever more serious until God gathered him to His mercy.'[136]

Although there is a suspicion that Ibn Shaddad is remoulding Saladin's earlier career to fit his presentation of later events, Saladin's own actions to some extent confirm this account. By the early 1170s, perhaps encouraged by the additional problems created for Amalric by the regency of the shattered county of Tripoli, he felt strong enough to attack the south of the kingdom of Jerusalem, both on the coast and in Jordan. In December 1170, he suddenly appeared at Darum (Dair al-Balah), about 9 miles south of Gaza, and the first Frankish settlement encountered by an army coming from Egypt. Darum was a square fortress of simple plan with four corner towers built by Amalric as a centre for the collection of taxes and tolls, and it was not equipped to withstand the kind of force brought against it by Saladin. By the time Amalric had gathered his forces, Saladin had already besieged it for two days and had broken into the compound. The king clearly believed that this was not simply a raid but the preliminary to an important battle, for he assembled an army of 250 knights and about 2,000 foot soldiers under the protection of the True Cross, as well as Templars from the garrison at Gaza. There may have been a more general summoning of the host, for sixty-five youths from the agrarian settlement of al-Bira, north of Jerusalem, were among those who came to Gaza.[137]

However, when they saw the Muslim army they were shocked by its size and could do little more than defend themselves. They were unable to prevent Saladin moving on to Gaza, where he again broke into the town, although the citadel held out under Miles of Plancy. During the fighting most of the youths from al-Bira were killed. The major battle, nevertheless, did not materialise and Saladin turned back to Egypt, leaving the Franks to contemplate the destruction he had left behind. Darum had particularly suffered, for it was left in a 'half-destroyed' state.[138] Amalric rebuilt it more strongly than before, but the change in the balance of power was evident. When, in late December, Saladin had some prefabricated boats transported across Sinai, and used them to attack and plunder Ailah, the Franks were powerless to stop him.[139] For the first time since the death of the vizier al-Afdal in 1121, there was a real threat from Egypt.

Both sides now acted to protect their positions. In the summer of 1171, Nur al-Din pressed Saladin to bring Egypt into Abbasid allegiance, a process that would involve the removal of the Shi'ite Fatimids. Saladin was aware of the dangers, but was greatly helped by the illness of al-Adid, who died on 13 September 1171. Two days before he had put on a show of military strength by parading the bulk of his army through Cairo. On 10 September, the Fatimid regime was brought to an end and the khutbah (Friday sermon and prayer) proclaimed in the name of al-Mustadi, the Abbasid caliph, apparently without provoking any general unrest.[140]

Amalric was equally active. Early in 1171, he held a general curia to discuss the state of the kingdom. He may well have announced the recoining of the *deniers* and *oboles* at this time and, like Baldwin, reasserted his authority through control of the currency (see plate 11).[141] However, the major reason for the assembly was to discuss future military policy. It was decided to ask for western help by means of embassies and letters to all the major rulers, and at the same time to send a mission to Emperor Manuel. To the shock and surprise of most of the barons, Amalric then proposed to visit Manuel himself, an action that suggests he placed little confidence in the prospect of effective western help in the foreseeable future, for no previous king of Jerusalem had visited Constantinople. He set out on 10 March, accompanied by leading nobles and royal officers, having sent Philip of Nablus ahead to prepare the ground. Philip had resigned his position as master of the Templars specifically for this purpose, and was replaced by Odo of Saint-Amand, a former royal marshal and butler who had served both Baldwin and Amalric since the mid-1150s and might be expected to continue to reflect royal interests within the order.[142]

Manuel was perhaps surprised by the visit, but he nevertheless arranged a lavish welcome, culminating in a personal greeting in a special audience room hung with precious curtains. When the curtains were drawn aside, the emperor was seen seated on a golden throne; Amalric was placed next to him but, like Baldwin III in 1158, on a slightly lower throne. Amalric and his delegation were shown every consideration, including being given access to the private imperial apartments, a special viewing of Constantinople's most precious relics, and musical and theatrical entertainments. The king was given a guided tour of Constantinople and was taken by ship to view the mouth of the Black Sea. At the same time intensive negotiations took place during which the Latins convinced Manuel that they should once more attempt 'the subjugation of Egypt'.[143]

The king finally returned from this fantasy world on 15 June, when he landed at Sidon. Despite the bitterness that had developed between the two armies at Damietta in 1169, he had gained a promise for a new joint attack on Egypt and, had he not died in 1174, there is no doubt that Amalric would have continued with this strategy. Manuel had his own agenda. Until the phenomenal expansion of Islam in the seventh century, Egypt had been an integral part of the Byzantine empire. As Kinnamos puts it, Manuel, 'who had already recovered many of the regions in the east for the Romans, longed very intensely to reclaim this one too'. Amalric was well aware of this. The price that the crusader states had to pay for Manuel's aid was subordination to the Byzantine concept of empire, and no amount of elaborate ceremonial in Constantinople could disguise this. Like his brother before him, Amalric had been obliged to agree to what Kinnamos calls 'his subjection' to the Romans.[144]

It seems very likely that one consequence was a much more overt Byzantine presence in the kingdom. The extensive fresco decoration of the east end of the Hospitaller church of Abu Ghosh, for example, dates from the early 1170s and was executed by Byzantine artists (although working under Hospitaller instruction), suggesting that other Byzantine figures, such as diplomats and military advisers, must also have been in Jerusalem, even though they have not left such material evidence of their existence.[145]

However, the treaty with the Byzantines did nothing to alleviate the immediate threats to the crusader states. Almost at once it was necessary to gather a force at the Springs of Saffuriya to meet an incursion by Nur al-Din in the region of Banyas, a threat exacerbated by Saladin's almost simultaneous attack on Montréal. According to Ibn al-Athir, in October 1171 Montréal was close to falling, but Saladin was advised that if Nur al-Din defeated Amalric at the same time, nothing would prevent him from forcing Saladin to submit to him, perhaps even depriving him of Egypt. This may not be the full truth, since Montréal was extremely difficult to capture, but whatever the reason, for a brief period, the distrust between Nur al-Din and Saladin prevented a concerted attack on the kingdom of Jerusalem.[146]

The next year Amalric was obliged to travel to Antioch, still suffering from the effects of the terrible earthquake, to block Malih, brother of Thoros II, who was trying to seize control of Cilicia after the latter's death. Not only had Malih expelled the Templars from their fortresses in Cilicia, but he had also obtained help from Nur al-Din. Malih excited the censure of both William of Tyre and Michael the Syrian. This remained unfinished business, because although the king obliged Malih to submit, he was forced to abandon the north when he heard that Kerak was under attack, only to find that the crisis had subsided by the time he reached Jerusalem.[147] Nur al-Din was adept at such diversionary tactics, creating a sense of insecurity that made long-term strategies difficult to implement.

Amalric, however, was not the type of personality who was content to take an entirely reactive role, and it may be that his extraordinary attempt to ally with the dissident Shi'ite sect of the Assassins in 1173 grew out of his frustration with the circumstances in which he found himself in the early 1170s. In William's version of events, Amalric agreed to remit an annual tribute of 2,000 gold pieces paid by the Assassins to the Templars, while for his part Rashid al-Din Sinan, the Assassin leader in Syria, had promised that he and his followers would convert to Christianity. Provisional agreement was reached, but while Abdullah, the envoy of the Assassins, was travelling back through the county of Tripoli, protected by a royal safe-conduct, he was attacked and killed by a group of Templars led by a knight called Walter of Mesnil.

The king was incensed by this violation and demanded that Odo of Saint-Amand, the Templar master, hand over the culprit, but the master exacerbated the situation by refusing to do so, replying that he had given the man a penance and that he 'was about to send him to the pope'. This was particularly galling for the king, whose evident influence in Odo's appointment must have led him to have expected greater co-operation from the master. Given his previous record, it is inconceivable that Amalric would let the matter rest there, and he went to Sidon himself, where Walter of Mesnil was being held, and had him seized and thrown into prison in Tyre. Amalric, says William, regarded this so seriously that he intended to take up the matter with other rulers, but he died before he was able to do so.[148]

Both William and the one other contemporary source that records the murder, the English secular canon Walter Map, present this as the loss of a striking opportunity to convert Muslims to the Christian path; indeed, Map alleged that the Templars were afraid that conversions of this kind would soon make their role redundant.[149] Such an initiative was indeed unique in the twelfth century, but it may have stemmed from the belief of Hasan II, the Assassin leader at Alamut, articulated by the abrogation of the law of the Prophet and by no means unlikely in a messianic sect, that the millennium had arrived. For his part Amalric need not have had any ideological motives; purely pragmatic considerations would suggest that an alliance with a sect feared in the Sunni world, whose centre of power was in the vulnerable area to the east of Valania, and which was a committed enemy of the Zengids, was a desirable goal. In the end the king was able to clear his name with Sinan, but there is no further sign of an alliance, perhaps because three months after Amalric's death in July 1174, Raymond III, count of Tripoli, whose father had been killed by the Assassins, was appointed regent.[150]

By coincidence, Nur al-Din and Amalric died within nine weeks of each other, on 15 May and 11 July 1174, respectively. As might be expected from the most pro-Zengid of the chroniclers, Ibn al-Athir presents Nur al-Din as the epitome of virtue. He paid for his personal affairs entirely from his own property, considering himself to be 'the custodian of the Muslims' for everything else, he maintained the Shariah even when it affected him directly, his bravery was 'of the highest order', he was the promoter of public works, including defensive walls, madrasas, hospitals, caravanserais and seminaries, and he was the creator of charitable trusts. 'In short, his good qualities were numerous and his virtues abundant, more than this book can contain.'[151] To William of Tyre, he had been 'a mighty persecutor of the Christian name and faith', but this did not preclude respect for his qualities as well, for he had been 'a just prince, valiant and wise, and, according to the traditions of his race, a religious man'.[152] Michael the Syrian says that Nur al-Din's death was 'joyous news', not only to the Christians, but also apparently to some of his emirs as well, as they had been subject to considerable constraints under his command. 'He did not permit the drinking of wine in the camp, nor tolerate music or dancing, and the camp was absolutely silent. He was assiduous in listening to reading from their Book; he considered himself like Muhammad, and was waiting for the Lord to speak to him as he had to Moses.'[153]

Naturally, Amalric had attempted to take advantage of the likely disruption in the Zengid empire caused by Nur al-Din's death by launching an attack on Banyas, but it did not succeed and he accepted a large sum of money to retreat.[154] It was during this withdrawal that he fell ill with dysentery. He managed to get back to Jerusalem, but the combined efforts of Greek, Syrian and Latin doctors could not save him. Although William of Tyre sums him up as a 'man of wisdom and discretion, fully competent to hold the reins of government in the kingdom', his comments on his character and actions are by no means always laudatory. Like William, however, Ibn al-Athir could see the enemy's strengths: 'He was one of the bravest of their kings, the most outstanding for policy, cunning and intrigue.'[155]

CHAPTER 11

The Disintegration of the Crusader States

According to Ibn al-Athir, Nur al-Din harboured a deep and justified mistrust of Saladin. By late 1171, it had become evident that Saladin was reluctant to commit himself to joint attacks on the Franks because he feared that if they were victorious there would be nothing to prevent Nur al-Din establishing his authority in Egypt. After Saladin's withdrawal from the siege of Montréal in October 1171, Nur al-Din 'resolved to enter Egypt and expel him'. When Saladin became aware of this he held a family conference during which his nephew, Taqi al-Din, expressed the view that any such move should be forcibly resisted. Najm al-Din Ayyub, Saladin's father, publicly rebuked him for his disloyalty, but in private assured his son that they would resist even if Nur al-Din wanted as much as 'a piece of sugar cane'. It was, nevertheless, better not to adopt an overtly hostile demeanour, which would only be regarded as provocative. 'It turned out as Ayyūb had expected. Nūr al-Dīn died without having made a move against him and Saladin ruled the land. This was an example of really good and excellent advice.' Even so, Nur al-Din would eventually have invaded Egypt. Ibn al-Athir says that he was in the midst of preparations when 'he received God's decree which cannot be averted'.[1]

Nur al-Din's successor was his son, al-Malik al-Salih Isma'il, aged only eleven. Inevitably he would be under the control of Nur al-Din's emirs, led by Shams al-Din Muhammad, leaving his father's lands vulnerable to attack. Saladin was obviously interested in Damascus, but was initially restrained, since he needed a pretext, but Saif al-Din, lord of Mosul, Nur al-Din's nephew, immediately seized the Jazira. In these circumstances Amalric's attack on Banyas had to be deflected, obliging Shams al-Din to buy him off, while simultaneously threatening to call in Saladin and Saif al-Din if he refused.[2]

In fact, Saladin soon had problems of his own. On 28 July 1174, a large Sicilian fleet suddenly appeared at Alexandria, and at once launched an attack. Saladin himself was 120 miles away, but although the Sicilians persisted for five days, they failed to take the port because of what William of Tyre saw as incompetent leadership, but which Ibn al-Athir called gallant Muslim resistance. This had been, albeit for a short time, a serious threat; both William of Tyre and Ibn al-Athir say that the Sicilians brought 200 ships, although the latter adds another thirty-six horse transports, six large ships carrying war materials and forty other vessels with provisions.[3] Moreover, they had been hoping to link up with dissident Fatimids who were plotting against Saladin. This had originally been intended as a combined land and sea attack, planned by Amalric and William II, king of Sicily, but Amalric's death was not known in Palermo before the fleet set out and therefore the Sicilians found themselves without the military support they had expected.[4] At the time this alliance must have seemed a considerable success for Amalric, for it was only the second Sicilian involvement with the crusader states since the insult to Queen Adelaide in 1117.

Relieved of this threat, Saladin was now in a position to respond to an invitation from Shams al-Din, who was fearful of the developing anarchy in Nur al-Din's lands, to take over Damascus. Keeping up the pretence that he was acting as the servant of al-Salih, Saladin entered the city on 28 October 1174. He at once set about establishing himself in Syria. Between December 1174 and March 1175, he acquired Hama, Homs and Baalbek, despite resistance from some of Nur al-Din's supporters, although Aleppo held out against him after a tearful appeal to the people by al-Salih.[5]

Less than nine months after the death of Amalric, the situation which the king had spent so much blood and resources to avoid had come about, for all of Egypt and most of Syria were now in the hands of one man, although Aleppo continued to resist. Some attempt had been made to create problems for Saladin. Raymond III, count of Tripoli, who had been a prisoner of Nur al-Din since the disaster at Artah in August 1164, had been ransomed for 80,000 dinars, probably early in 1174.[6] In January 1175, he led a force to relieve the defenders of the citadel at Homs, which Saladin had not been able to take. Although nothing was achieved, Saladin realised that Raymond had been drawn by the prospect of the release of hostages held to guarantee the payment of his ransom, and he used this as a lever to persuade him to desist from interfering again in the siege of the city. William of Tyre believes that Humphrey of Toron, the royal constable, had been the key figure in these negotiations, which he describes as done 'against our purpose'.[7] Indeed, the long-term consequences of the costs of this ransom had major repercussions for Raymond and were always a consideration for him in his future actions.

However, the major reason why the Franks had been unable to take advantage of Muslim disarray in the second half of 1174 was that Amalric's death had precipitated a crisis in Jerusalem every bit as serious as that in Damascus. Amalric's successor was Baldwin, his son by Agnes of Courtenay. As the previous king's only son, he evidently had the best hereditary claim, although he was only thirteen, barely older than al-Salih. Nevertheless, his succession, claims William of Tyre, accorded with the wishes of all, laymen and ecclesiastics, and he was crowned on 15 July. Indeed, in normal circumstances, the acceptance of a minor less than two years away from his majority would not be considered unusual in the twelfth century, but in this case it was complicated by the fact that he had serious health problems. William had been his tutor and was evidently very fond of him, and around 1170, when Baldwin was nine, he had noticed a numbness in his right arm and hand, which did not prove susceptible to treatment. By the time he had reached puberty, this was diagnosed as leprosy, of the kind that modern medicine recognises as the most serious, that is, lepromatous rather than tuberculoid, and which ultimately led to his premature death at the age of twenty-four.[8]

Acceptance of a possible leper in a kingdom in which there had been succession problems in the past seems puzzling, but the later actions of the principals involved suggest that they did not plan for this to be a permanent arrangement, as they well knew that Baldwin's condition would deteriorate quite rapidly. In 1174, there were no alternative candidates, but given time this could be rectified, most obviously by finding a sufficiently weighty figure as a husband for Sibylla, Baldwin's unmarried older sister, who had been brought up by her aunt Iveta in the convent at Bethany. It seems unlikely that contemporaries were unaware of the nature of his disease, although admittedly it was not always easy to recognise in its early stages.[9] Leprosy, however, was sufficiently common for the formation of a charitable order, that of St Lazarus, in the 1130s, which was run by lepers and which provided an honourable retreat for members of the nobility with the disease. Many families were therefore familiar with its characteristics.[10] Indeed, Amalric's search for medical help in Fatimid Egypt must have been connected to his realisation that his son was ill; his use of a famous doctor and astrologer, Abu Sulayman Dawud, originally from Jerusalem but now settled in Egypt, to treat Baldwin, shows his concern.[11] The members of the High Court therefore knew that Baldwin might have leprosy, but still went ahead with the coronation.[12]

In these circumstances, Miles of Plancy took over the running of the government. He had come to the East in the 1160s and had been seneschal since 1169. More recently he had become lord of Transjordan through marriage to Stephanie of Milly, daughter of Philip of Nablus, a highly favourable match granted by Amalric. He had been a close adviser of Amalric, especially on his Egyptian campaigns; indeed, he was a member of the Montlhéry family and therefore kin of Baldwin II and his descendants. As seneschal, he controlled finance and castles and was the chief judicial officer after the king.[13] However, he did not impress William of Tyre, who describes him as being 'of degenerate morals, one who neither feared God nor reverenced man. Milon de Plancy was a man without shame, a brawler and a slanderer, ever active in stirring up trouble.'[14] During the 1170s, William became increasingly involved in the politics of the kingdom, so he is not an unbiased observer; nevertheless, there seems to be some truth in his observation that Miles provoked resentment among the baronage by blocking access to the king and excluding them from the processes of government. The most important of these barons was Humphrey of Toron, the constable, without whom Miles could not summon the host, so there was no prospect of fulfilling the obligations to the Sicilians, even had this been a practical proposition at this time. This conflict came to a head quite quickly, for Miles was stabbed to death in the streets of Acre, probably in October 1174, by unknown plotters.[15]

Although William of Tyre is vague about the exact sequence of events, it seems that soon afterwards Raymond of Tripoli appeared before the High Court in Jerusalem in order to obtain a judgment 'about the petitions which he had previously presented'. After two days of discussion it was agreed to popular acclaim that 'there should be surrendered to him, after the king, the administration and rule of the whole realm', an office the Franks described as bailli.[16] Soon afterwards he was granted the hand of Eschiva II, widow of Walter, lord of Galilee, giving him a fief owing 100 knights and making him the leading baron in the kingdom of Jerusalem, since the county of Tripoli also owed 100 knights.[17]

Raymond's first attempt to obtain control of the kingdom appears to have been in August, when Miles of Plancy was still alive. Although the matter had been postponed as only a few of the barons were present, on that occasion Raymond had justified himself on the grounds that he was the king's nearest blood relative, that he was the richest and most powerful of the king's subjects, and that he had granted Amalric full powers in his county while he was in prison, making him his heir should he be unfortunate enough never to obtain his release.[18] Raymond was the son of Raymond II and Hodierna, Baldwin II's third daughter, and was thus one generation closer to the royal family than Bohemond III of Antioch, grandson of Alice, Baldwin's second daughter. William of Tyre says that he had widespread support, naming Humphrey of

Toron, Baldwin of Ramla, Balian, his brother, and Reynald of Sidon among the barons, as well as all the bishops.

William of Tyre has a very favourable view of Raymond of Tripoli, at least partly because of what he saw as his high moral character: dynamic in action, disinclined to extremes of behaviour, modest in eating and drinking, generous to strangers. Although Eschiva had no children by him, William presents him as a faithful and loving husband, who treated her children as if they were his own. The archbishop sums him up as 'a diligent man and esteemed by all', whom he contrasts with others around the king who sought only their own advantage.[19] However, from 1174 onwards, William's judgements on individuals – inevitably in the circumstances – are more politicised than in any other part of his chronicle. With Raymond in power, William's own fortunes began to rise; in December 1174, he succeeded Ralph of Bethlehem as chancellor and, in June 1175, Frederick of Tyre as archbishop.[20]

In fact, Raymond was far from disinterested.[21] His actions were usually driven by his own personal ambitions and needs and, even when they were not – as on the eve of the battle of Hattin in July 1187 – his enemies believed them to have been, given his previous record. This was at once evident. Raymond had never forgiven Manuel for reneging on the marriage negotiations with his sister, Melisende, in 1160–1, an affront he had followed up by a series of attacks on Byzantine lands.[22] He therefore dropped the Byzantine alliance of 1171 and attempted to obtain the help of the German emperor, Frederick Barbarossa, Manuel's western rival.[23] The first priority was a husband for Sibylla, and it was agreed that she should marry William Longsword, son of William V, marquis of Montferrat, one of Frederick Barbarossa's main supporters in Lombardy. This was achieved in November 1176, a month after William Longsword had arrived in the kingdom, and he received the lordship of Jaffa and Ascalon.[24]

This was a marriage at the level of that of Fulk of Anjou in 1129, for William was a cousin of both Louis VII of France and Frederick Barbarossa. William of Tyre says that there was some opposition to him when he actually arrived, although he claims the original decision had been unanimous. The potential was considerable. If Frederick Barbarossa had succeeded in his ambition to conquer the city-states of Lombardy, he might have been able to extend his rule into the kingdom of Sicily. Both areas contained maritime resources essential to the crusader states. In fact, Raymond's policy foundered within a year: in May 1176, Frederick Barbarossa was defeated by the forces of the Lombard League at the battle of Legnano, north-west of Milan, forcing him to come to terms after eighteen years of struggle and leaving the crusader states low on his list of priorities. Then, in June 1177, William Longsword died of an illness contracted two months before, a not unusual occurrence among those not acclimatised to the Levant. He was buried in the vestibule of the Hospitaller church in Jerusalem, where William of Tyre conducted the service, for the patriarch was unwell. Sibylla, probably no more than seventeen years of age, was left a widow, and pregnant with William Longsword's child. This was a double blow, for Longsword's death destroyed the idea that he might at some point take over from the ailing Baldwin IV, while Sibylla's pregnancy meant that a new husband would know that his own children would probably not inherit, undermining her prospects of a second marriage.

It looks as if Raymond's role as *bailli* ended in July 1176, when Baldwin turned fifteen and thus, according to John of Ibelin, attained his majority.[25] Baldwin now reverted to his father's Byzantine alliance, despite the fact that the Byzantines too had suffered a very serious military defeat when, in September, they were overcome by the Seljuk sultan of Rum, Kilij Arslan II, at the battle of Myriocephalon, north of Lake Egirdir in western Asia Minor. William of Tyre portrays this as a very great disaster, which had a huge impact upon Manuel's health and demeanour, but it did not prevent the emperor from implementing plans for a joint invasion of Egypt.[26] Perhaps he saw in this a means of restoring imperial prestige and reputation. In the winter of 1176–7, Baldwin sent Reynald of Châtillon to Constantinople to negotiate the terms of a new agreement, and in September 1177, high-level imperial ambassadors arrived in Jerusalem, including once again the Sicilian Alexander of Gravina. They brought with them a substantial fleet of seventy galleys plus support ships.[27]

Reynald and Joscelin of Courtenay had been released from prison in the summer of 1176 as a result of negotiations between Bohemond III and Gumushtekin, atabeg of Aleppo, who was apprehensive following Saladin's victory over a Zengid coalition led by Saif al-Din of Mosul in April. 'Imad al-Din, who entered Saladin's service in 1175 and provides first-hand information about his career thereafter, says that their release was the consequence of Aleppan anger at Saladin's behaviour. Even so, Gumushtekin demanded a heavy price: 50,000 dinars for Joscelin and 120,000 for Reynald.[28] This in itself is enough to explain Reynald's changed attitude towards Byzantium, for Manuel was the only person capable of paying such a sum. It does not seem likely that it could have been raised by his friends alone, as William of Tyre says, although Agnes of Courtenay was probably able to provide some of Joscelin's ransom.[29] Indeed, Agnes of Courtenay was now the key figure. Her position as mother of Baldwin and Sibylla gave her the kind of status and influence she had lost after the forced separation from Amalric in 1163. In c.1171, she had married Reynald of Sidon, one of the most important barons of the kingdom. Clearly, in these circumstances, husband and wife could function to mutual benefit.[30]

Neither Joscelin of Courtenay nor Reynald of Châtillon had lands of their own, despite their status, so they both returned to the kingdom of Jerusalem, further complicating the politics of the court of the leper king. Joscelin was appointed seneschal, the chief administrative office of the kingdom, as well as marrying Agnes of Milly, daughter of Henry the Buffalo, brother of Philip of Nablus. The marriage brought a dowry that included Castellum Novum (Miʻiliya) and Montfort, situated in the hills to the north-east of Acre. By the autumn of 1179, he had become prosperous enough to augment these holdings with a series of purchases in the region, creating a lordship that, although scattered, was of considerable value. During this same period, in 1178, Bohemond III granted him a fief in the principality of Antioch, which included an abbey and several *casalia*. These were to be relinquished if Joscelin ever regained his Edessan lands.[31]

Reynald was married to Stephanie of Milly, Agnes's cousin, widow of Humphrey III of Toron and, very recently, Miles of Plancy.[32] As the only surviving heir of Philip of Nablus, she brought to Reynald the southern part of the great fief of Transjordan, received by her father in 1161. Reynald therefore became lord of Kerak and Montréal, and thus overlooked the routes between Cairo and Damascus, crucial links in Saladin's empire.[33] The rise of Joscelin and Reynald provides a striking index of the new importance of the Courtenays and their allies. Both immediately outranked Humphrey II of Toron, the constable, previously a dominant figure under Baldwin III and Amalric, appearing above him on witness lists of charters from 1176 onwards, a position even Miles of Plancy had been unable to achieve.[34]

At the beginning of August 1177, Philip of Alsace, count of Flanders, landed at Acre with a considerable army. He was no ordinary crusader. From the beginning the counts of Flanders had committed themselves heavily to the cause, something they were able to do because they had more resources than any other French baron and perhaps even than the monarchy. Philip's father, Thierry, had been to the Holy Land four times and his mother, Sibylla, had entered the convent at Bethany. Philip was closely related to the royal house of Jerusalem, for King Fulk was his grandfather, and Baldwin IV his cousin.[35] William of Tyre says that his appearance had been 'expected for a long time', so it is probable that the Byzantines anticipated that his army would be a major element in any new assault on Egypt. They would have been encouraged in that belief by the Latin leaders in Jerusalem, for King Baldwin had become very ill, and Philip of Flanders was an obvious replacement, even if only temporarily. Accordingly, the count was offered what William of Tyre calls 'the rule and general administration of the entire kingdom'.[36]

In fact, both were disappointed, for Philip said that he had come 'to subject himself to divine service', not to take power, and that he wished to be free to return to Flanders when needed. He would accept any other procurator whom the king might appoint. Moreover, after what William of Tyre presents as a series of excuses and devious ploys, he refused to take part in an invasion of Egypt. He did, nevertheless, agree to fight in the north in conjunction with Raymond of Tripoli and Bohemond of Antioch, a campaign the king reinforced with 100 knights and 2,000 foot. In September, Philip and Raymond attacked Hama and then, in December, joined up with Bohemond to besiege Harim. Both the count of Tripoli and the prince of Antioch had a personal interest in its recapture. Its loss in 1164 had not only resulted in the imprisonment of both of them, but it had also left in enemy hands a strategically important fortress only 18 miles from Antioch. William of Tyre, heavily committed to the alliance with the Byzantines, was sufficiently irritated by what he saw as a diversion to comment that some said that both rulers had dissuaded Philip from the Egyptian venture so that they could enlarge their own lands.[37]

This formidable force established a tight blockade, but William of Tyre believed that the target was too close to Antioch to maintain proper discipline, blaming Philip and his entourage for continually returning to the city to indulge in drinking and the pleasures of the flesh. Morale was not helped by Philip's frequent references to his desire to return home. Although, as William claims, they were close to taking the castle, in the end Raymond allowed himself to be bought off and Philip returned to Jerusalem in time to celebrate Easter on 9 April. Ibn al-Athir says that the siege had brought the Franks 'to the end of their efforts and they had become as though exhausted'. Some confirmation of William's version of events can be found in the timing of the abandonment of the siege, for it enabled Philip to undertake the spring sailing, taking ship from Latakia for Constantinople soon after Easter.[38]

The behaviour of the count of Flanders needs more explanation than that offered by William of Tyre. If they had invaded Egypt, Philip may have feared that he would have been blamed for any defeat (on past record quite a likely outcome); if they had succeeded, on the other hand, it would have been to somebody else's advantage, either that of Baldwin IV or of the Byzantines.[39] Baldwin was evidently experiencing a long-term physical deterioration, but the state of his health was inconsistent and there were periods when he recovered sufficiently to lead military expeditions, even though after 1179 he had to be carried on a litter. Two years before, for example, he had led a foray into the Hauran in a now familiar attempt to undermine the Damascene economic base, and in August of that same year he and Raymond had fought a pitched battle near Baalbek with Shams al-Dula, Saladin's brother, now governor of Damascus.[40] Such considerations may have been reinforced by Philip's lack of ambition in the East, to which he had come, as he said, out of piety. Moreover, the decision to take part in the northern campaign was based on a 'sound appreciation' of the military advice given by Raymond and Bohemond.[41] Philip's attitudes demonstrate the fundamental problem faced by the crusader states in their relations with western powers: if the crusaders were powerful enough to deploy large resources, they usually had their own agenda, which was unlikely to be changed by the Franks of the East, while if they were minor lords, they could never make a decisive difference in any campaign against the Muslims.

William of Tyre was clearly biased against Philip of Flanders, for he was unwilling to give due recognition to the dilemmas that faced the count. Even so, the archbishop's assessment of the overall situation may well have been correct. Saladin evidently expected to be attacked in Egypt and, indeed, left Syria in the late summer of 1176 after defeating Saif al-Din and making peace with Aleppo and the Is'mailis.[42] When, however, in the autumn of 1177, he realised that the major part of Frankish forces had gone north to Harim, he seized the opportunity to invade the southern part of the kingdom. Neither Ibn al-Athir nor Ibn Shaddad explains his reasons, but to William of Tyre it was obvious that he hoped either to damage the kingdom or to force the abandonment of the siege of Harim. It may have been because of this perceived weakness that, in Ibn al-Athir's words, the Muslims 'became over eager and relaxed, moving about the country secure and confident'. Saladin therefore left his heavy baggage at al-Arish and, accompanied by his more lightly armed troops, made a sudden appearance in front of Ascalon. Baldwin had assembled all the forces he could find, but was obliged to retreat into Ascalon on the night of 24 November, leaving the Muslim forces to raid the entire area as far as Jerusalem. William of Tyre paints a bleak picture of an abandoned Ramla and of the citizens of Jerusalem huddled in the Tower of David for protection.[43]

William's account heightens the dramatic effect of the Christian victory that followed the next day. Baldwin's army was heavily outnumbered, even though William's figures of 375 knights opposed to 26,000 light cavalry, 1,000 of whom were Saladin's personal mamluks, cannot be taken seriously. The Christian army included Odo of Saint-Amand, master of the Temple, with eighty brethren, some of whom had come from the garrison at Gaza, and the leading barons, Baldwin of Ramla and his brother, Balian, Reynald of Sidon and Joscelin of Courtenay, the royal seneschal. It was commanded by Reynald of Châtillon, who had been made 'procurator of the kingdom and the army' following the refusal of Philip of Flanders to take responsibility for the kingdom in the autumn of 1177.[44] They took with them the True Cross under the care of Albert, bishop of Bethlehem.

The armies met on 25 November, below a hill known as Mont Gisard (Tell al-Safiya) between Ramla and Ibelin. William of Tyre says that initially the engagement was indecisive, but that soon the Christians broke Saladin's lines, chasing his army into a nearby marsh. Saladin later explained to Ibn Shaddad what had happened: his army had been charged by the Franks while it was carrying out a manoeuvre that involved the right flank moving to the left and the left into the centre.[45] According to Ibn al-Athir, the Franks caught them as they were trying to cross a river, and one of them almost reached Saladin before himself being killed. Saladin later turned this incident to his own advantage, claiming that he had been spared by God 'for a purpose that He had in mind'.[46]

Ibn Shaddad calls this 'a terrible reverse', for many men and animals and much equipment were lost in the aftermath. The following eleven days were exceptionally wet and cold and few of the fugitives succeeded in returning to Cairo. Some suffered so much that they gave themselves up rather than spend any more time in the open. However, it had been a very bloody battle for both sides: 1,100 Christians had been killed and 750 were treated for wounds in the Hospital in Jerusalem.[47] Indeed, with so many wounded, the Hospitallers would have been hard-pressed to cope, first treating survivors in their field hospital, which was a large tent they took with them whenever a major confrontation was expected, and then carrying them back to Jerusalem as soon as possible using relays of camels, horses, mules and donkeys.[48] William of Tyre attributes the victory to divine help, but cannot resist adding that had the counts of Flanders and Tripoli been present, they would have claimed it for themselves.[49]

The Franks knew, of course, that Saladin's rise meant that there would be further such battles in the future and that they would not be confined to the south. Saladin had established his brother, Turanshah (Shams al-Daula), in Damascus, and had shown his determination to capture Aleppo. The comprehensive agreement between the masters of the Temple and the Hospital, made in February 1179, which was intended to settle a series of disputes between the orders, reflects Frankish awareness of the need for solidarity, for it was sealed by King Baldwin, Prince Bohemond and Count Raymond, as well as leading barons, all of whom were present in person.[50] It may be therefore that the victory at Mont Gisard together with the perception that Saladin would have to be fended off in the east encouraged the Franks to start building a new castle at Jacob's Ford (Bait al-Ahzan) on the Jordan, between Lake Huleh and the Sea of Galilee, in October 1178.[51] The Franks had already broken the truce made after Mont Gisard by attacking Hama in August, but this was much more serious. The Templars, established on the heights of Safad by early 1168 at the latest, appear to have been the driving force, perhaps intending to create a semi-autonomous district around the two castles not dissimilar to their enclaves in the county of Tripoli. Further south, but in an equally exposed frontier position, the possession of Amman and the parts of the Belqa which the order had received in 1166 might have served as a precedent.[52]

Jacob's Ford had in the past been left unfortified, but the Frankish inability to recover Banyas, north of Lake Huleh, previously regarded as of great strategic importance to the kingdom, together with Saladin's control of Damascus, persuaded the Franks that a castle there was a priority, both as an obstacle to invaders of Galilee and as a base for raiding the Hauran. William of Tyre says that it took six months to build, but it was still not finished by the following spring, for this was intended to be a formidable construction. Modern excavations and contemporary descriptions show an extensive enceinte with a tower on the western side and a very large cistern at the northern end, all built with heavy blocks, mortared with lime, but this was only the first stage. By the spring of 1179 only the inner wall had been erected, but ultimately it would have been a concentric castle built with a double line of walls (see plate 12).[53]

Most of the work was done while Saladin was engaged in the siege of Baalbek, but he was well aware of the potential military threat. Moreover, he appears to have regarded the new castle as an intrusion into Muslim territory, as well as occupying the site of an important shrine, circumstances that reinforced his determination to prevent its construction.[54] At first he tried to persuade the Franks to dismantle it, offering 60,000 dinars, which he gradually increased to 100,000, but with no success. He therefore spent the money instead on soldiers, who were used to raid the surrounding area and, in late May 1179, in an attempt to test the strength of its defences, in a sortie against the castle itself. Inevitably, such tactics led to confrontations with the Franks in one of which – a raid by the Franks into the region of Banyas in April – the constable, Humphrey of Toron, was fatally wounded.[55] The human and material costs of this border warfare were therefore often very high. Ibn al-Athir acknowledges this: 'How can you be made to realize just what this Humphrey was! His bravery and skill in battle were proverbial. He was a tribulation that God inflicted on the Muslims and God gave relief from his wickedness.'[56] Humphrey was a well-known figure, but the destruction of villages and the burning of crops led to many more anonymous deaths every year. This was especially true of 1179, a year of severe drought and famine in the region.

Sometimes these skirmishes developed an impetus of their own. On 10 June, the Christians suffered a serious defeat at Marj Ayun, an area that lay between the Leontes River and the Upper Jordan, to the north-west of Banyas. The king had assembled an army at Tiberias and marched north in attempt to stop Saladin from devastating the lands to the east of Sidon. On first contact, the invaders were put to flight, but Saladin rallied his forces and attacked what had now become a series of dispersed groups. Reynald of Sidon, coming from the west, was deterred from proceeding by some of the survivors and turned back. Some took refuge in the castle of Beaufort, but even so Christian losses were considerable and included the capture of Baldwin of Ramla, Hugh of Tiberias and Odo of Saint-Amand, master of the Temple. At this time William of Tyre was away in Rome, attending the Third Lateran Council, so he could only gather his material later from participants. These blamed Odo of Saint-Amand, although the archbishop needed little encouragement to condemn a man whom he believed to be insufferably arrogant and deeply tainted by the sin of pride. Odo, he says, died in prison within a year, 'lamented by no one'.[57]

Saladin began a massive assault on Chastellet, the new castle at Jacob's Ford, on 24 August. It took him five days to break down the defences, although he breached the outer wall on the first day. When it was all over the castle was a smouldering ruin and the cistern was crammed with the bodies of the dead. The Templar commander had killed himself by immolation in one of the many fires burning across the site. Most of the 700 prisoners were either executed or killed while being taken to Damascus. Disease spread in Saladin's army, killing, among others, more than ten of his emirs. The garrison had received no help from outside since the army, assembling at Tiberias, had taken a considerable time to muster, a situation perhaps created both by the losses at Marj Ayun and by the need to incorporate the forces of important crusaders who had arrived only in July, including Henry of Troyes, count of Champagne, Peter of Courtenay, brother of King Louis VII, and Philip, bishop-elect of Beauvais.[58] They heard the news of the castle's fall while they were still at Tiberias. Saladin followed this up with another series of raids, ravaging the lands around Tiberias, Tyre and Beirut, with the specific intention of spreading terror.[59]

Baldwin IV had shown remarkable resilience and courage in the circumstances, but his health was visibly deteriorating. William of Tyre says that each day there were more and more signs of his leprosy. Yet the problem of the kingship had not been resolved, despite the fact that he had now been on the throne for nearly seven years. The king knew that he needed to find another husband for Sibylla and, in October 1178, he had deputed Joscius, bishop of Acre, who was part of the kingdom's delegation to the Third Lateran Council, to approach Hugh III, duke of Burgundy. Hugh was already known in Jerusalem, for he had visited the Holy Land in the summer of 1171 at the same time as his uncle, Stephen, count of Saône, and, William says, the decision to make the offer was unanimous.[60]

However, although it was believed that the duke had sworn an oath to marry Sibylla, he had still not appeared by the spring of 1180. William of Tyre says that he does not know why, but it was probably because of the succession crisis in France caused by the paralysis of King Louis VII, who eventually died in September, a circumstance that made it difficult for the duke to leave his lands.[61] Baldwin must have been aware that such a situation could drag on for months, and in Holy Week he suddenly married Sibylla to Guy of Lusignan, a Poitevin who was a relative newcomer to the kingdom. As husband of Sibylla, Guy now became count of Jaffa and Ascalon.[62] He was the younger brother of Aimery of Lusignan, who had recently replaced the late Humphrey of Toron as constable. The brothers came from a crusading family, participants in eastern campaigns since the crusade of 1101. Their grandfather, Hugh VII, had been on the Second Crusade, and their father, Hugh VIII, had died in one of Nur al-Din's prisons.[63] Aimery had been in the kingdom since at least 1173 and probably earlier and, as constable, was evidently an influential figure. Nevertheless, the marriage was quite unexpected and, in some quarters, by no means welcome.

William of Tyre was not present during these events – he did not land at Saint Simeon en route from Italy and Constantinople until May – but his whole narrative makes clear his disapproval of Guy of Lusignan. When Guy became *bailli* in 1183, he condemned him as a man who possessed neither the strength of character nor the judgement required for such a role.[64] He may have been influenced by Guy's reputation as a rebel and troublemaker. The English chroniclers Roger of Howden and William of Newburgh record that he had been exiled from England and Poitou by King Henry II because of his behaviour, which, according to Howden, included the killing of Patrick, earl of Salisbury, while he was returning from a pilgrimage to Compostela. Guy had therefore taken the Cross and sailed to the East.[65] Nevertheless, whatever his reasons for his dislike of Sibylla's new husband, William of Tyre's explanation of Baldwin's apparently precipitate action appears quite plausible, which is that Raymond of Tripoli and Bohemond of Antioch had arrived in the kingdom ostensibly for the celebration of Easter on 20 April but, in the king's eyes, they had actually come with the aim of deposing him and seizing power for themselves. If such a plan existed,

Sibylla's marriage blocked it and, after completing their devotions, they retreated to Tiberias.[66]

The problems caused by Baldwin's leprosy were now fully exposed. Raymond of Tripoli, whose support the kingdom could ill-afford to lose, did not return for two years. Moreover, Baldwin of Ramla, the oldest surviving brother of the very ambitious Ibelin family, became alienated since, according to Ernoul, who was more or less the family's house chronicler, he had hoped to marry Sibylla himself and believed that he had obtained her agreement. Indeed, Baldwin seems to have been the husband intended for Sibylla by Raymond and Bohemond. Ernoul is not a sober writer in the manner of William of Tyre and, in keeping with the genre in which he wrote, he chose to weave an elaborate and romantic story around this rejection; nevertheless, the fact remains that Baldwin's exclusion created another disgruntled baron in the kingdom.[67]

Baldwin's hasty decision to marry Guy to Sibylla inadvertently established a focal point for a 'court party', clustered around the king's maternal kin, which excluded his relatives descended from Queen Melisende's sisters, Raymond of Tripoli and Bohemond of Antioch, as well as the powerful and ambitious Ibelin family.[68] Moreover, the dowager queen, Maria Comnena, mother of Isabella, Sibylla's half-sister, and, since 1177, wife of Balian of Ibelin, Baldwin's younger brother, had seen her place usurped by Agnes of Courtenay.[69] Her position was further undermined in the autumn when Reynald of Châtillon secured the betrothal of Isabella, then aged eight, to Humphrey IV of Toron.[70] This tied the second sister into the ruling group since Humphrey was the son of Stephanie, now Reynald's wife, and Humphrey III of Toron, who had died in c.1173. Soon after, Baldwin IV secured the exchange of Humphrey's hereditary lands of Toron, Chastel Neuf and Banyas for a large money fief, a move that gave the king greater control over the defences to the north-east of the kingdom, but which may also have been intended to create a buffer against Raymond of Tripoli, preventing direct access to his Galilean lands.[71]

In the autumn the Church became involved, for Amalric of Nesle, patriarch of Jerusalem, died in October. He was replaced by Eraclius, archbishop of Caesarea since 1175. He had originated in Gévaudan in Provence, and had studied at Bologna before emigrating to the East, where, in 1169, he became archdeacon of Jerusalem. Although William of Tyre records his appointment without comment, Ernoul claims that the archbishop of Tyre had been a candidate for the patriarchate but that through the process of dual postulation, which left the king to choose between two candidates, Agnes of Courtenay had ensured that Eraclius became patriarch, even though William was the preferred choice of the clergy. In Ernoul's presentation, corruption was manifest, for he alleges that Eraclius was the lover of the queen mother, as well as keeping a mistress called Pasque of Rivieri, wife of a mercer from Nablus, by whom he had a daughter. This matter was so well known that Pasque was referred to as the 'patriarchess'.[72] It has been shown that Ernoul had 'defamatory intent', but that in itself suggests that he regarded Eraclius as belonging to a group hostile to the Ibelins.[73] At a time when they should have been concentrating on thwarting Saladin, the leaders of the Latin states allowed themselves to become preoccupied with the politics of faction.[74]

In retrospect, the year 1180 can be seen as a major turning point. Thereafter there were no more victories like Mont Gisard, while the castle at Jacob's Ford was never rebuilt. Although Saladin made a truce soon after, it was, William of Tyre notes, the first ever in which the Latins were in no position to set conditions. Indeed, William thinks that Saladin's main reason for making the truce had nothing to do with the Christians, but was because the Damascus region had suffered five successive years of drought.[75] With the notable exception of the attacks made by Reynald of Châtillon from his base at Kerak between 1180 and 1187, Latin military activity was now almost entirely reactive; the rebuilding of castles like Belvoir, Kerak, Montréal, Safad and Crac des Chevaliers in concentric form, already being undertaken during the 1170s, reflects this attitude, for improved Muslim siege techniques had led to significant losses even while Amalric was pursuing his expansive plans (see plate 13).[76]

The events of the summer illustrate the point. The truce did not cover the county of Tripoli, and Saladin took the opportunity to invade the coastal plain, burning the harvest and depopulating the area. He was not opposed, for neither the Hospitallers nor the Templars ventured out of their castles, while Count Raymond retreated to the city of Arqa, near the coast. Communication between the parts of the elaborately constructed defensive system of the county broke down completely. This way the strongholds at least remained intact, but the economic base upon which they depended was devastated. Saladin was even able to deploy galleys off the coast of Beirut and, in June, he seized the island of Ruad, off Tortosa. He eventually retreated, having done immense damage, and made a truce with Raymond of Tripoli.[77]

In recent years the feasibility of the Egyptian plans had depended upon the alliance with Byzantium, but on 24 September, Emperor Manuel died, leaving Alexius II, aged only eleven, as his successor, under the regency of his mother, Maria of Antioch, Bohemond III's sister. William of Tyre had made his return journey from the Third Lateran Council through Constantinople because he had been empowered to renew the alliance and, indeed, soon afterwards Baldwin sent Joscelin of Courtenay, his seneschal, and Baldwin of Ramla to finalise the arrangements. Manuel's death occurred while Joscelin was still in Constantinople and, although this did not in itself change the policy, the accession of a minor meant that the government was vulnerable. When Andronicus Comnenus seized power in April 1182, exploiting anti-Latin feeling in the capital to overthrow the existing regime, the Franks in the East knew they could expect no more help from the Greeks.[78]

Relations in Antioch were no more harmonious. Bohemond III took advantage of Manuel's death to leave his wife, Theodora, the emperor's great-niece, in order to marry a Frankish noblewoman called Sibylla, an act for which he was excommunicated by Aimery of Limoges, the patriarch.[79] The schism in the north was potentially very dangerous; William of Tyre describes Bohemond's behaviour as 'madness'. Bohemond besieged Aimery and the clergy in a fortress of the Church, presumably al-Qusair, which led to the imposition of an interdict. The king sent a delegation to mediate, led by Patriarch Eraclius and Reynald of Châtillon, and joined by Raymond of Tripoli en route on the basis that his friendship with Bohemond would make the envoys more acceptable. After a meeting at Latakia they departed in the belief that they had reached a settlement, for Bohemond agreed to restore the possessions of the Church and accepted that if he did not take back Theodora he would remain excommunicate. But once they had gone he ignored the agreement, creating further conflict by driving out some of the nobles who opposed him and obliging them to take refuge in Cilicia.[80]

The Franks were fortunate that the truce with Saladin held during this time, since William of Tyre conveys a strong sense that Baldwin had difficulty keeping them together. According to William, one reason for such a high-level delegation to Bohemond was the fear that news of such behaviour would alienate the pope and western rulers. Even so, when Raymond of Tripoli tried to visit Tiberias in the spring of 1182, the king was worried that he would attempt another coup, and prevented him from entering the kingdom. William of Tyre blames this on the malicious advice of Agnes of Courtenay and her brother, Joscelin, supported by what he calls a few of their followers. In this instance, William makes no attempt to conceal his opinions, denying that Raymond had any such intention and calling Agnes of Courtenay 'a woman completely odious to God'. In the end, the king reluctantly relented, persuaded by other leading barons that the exposure of such divisions could only make the land more vulnerable. In fact, the king's health was deteriorating by the day, and he was less and less able to cope.[81]

However, when fighting broke out again in the summer of 1182, in what must have been a singular effort of will, Baldwin forced himself to lead out the army to counter a series of attacks by Saladin against different parts of the kingdom. The advantages of possessing both Cairo and Damascus now became very evident. While Baldwin faced Saladin near Kerak in Transjordan, Turkish forces from Damascus, Bostrum, Baalbek and Homs captured 500 villagers from Dabburiya near Mount Tabor and then seized the cave fortress of Habis Jaldak (Sawad), set in the cliffs south of the Yarmuk River, about 20 miles east of Tiberias, in a region where previously there had been a division of authority between the Franks and the Muslims. William of Tyre blames Syrian disaffection for the fall of the fortress, which may be indicative of the effects these attacks were having upon the local population.[82] Although there was no battle at Kerak, Saladin intensified the pressure on Galilee, which forced Baldwin to keep an army in the field and provoked a series of quite serious confrontations. In an exceptionally hot summer, the fighting was even more painful than usual, with many deaths from heatstroke on both sides.

At the same time Saladin had been attempting to revive Egyptian sea power, largely moribund since the fall of Ascalon in 1153. He already held a large pilgrim ship which had been forced south towards Damietta by the prevailing winds. In August, he was sufficiently confident to send ships to blockade Beirut. A simultaneous attack by his brother, al-Adil, in the south-west of the kingdom was intended to divert the Franks, while Saladin himself moved in from the Beqa valley to besiege Beirut on its landward side. Baldwin and the barons, encamped at Saffuriya, chose to defend the place they regarded as being in the greatest danger, and turned the army towards the relief of Beirut, while at the same time a fleet of thirty-three ships was sent out from Acre and Tyre.[83] These moves were enough to persuade Saladin to retreat, but he does seem to have been serious in his intention to take Beirut, since he seldom undertook sieges unless he thought he could succeed.[84]

These attacks were intended to inflict economic damage on the crusader states as well as to undermine morale. They may well, too, have been undertaken for their propaganda value, underlining Saladin's commitment to the *jihad* against the Christians in the eyes of both the caliph and the Muslim world as a whole. Saladin may have thought it necessary to send out such a message, since in the autumn of 1182 he switched his attention to the northeast, setting off without even making a truce with the Franks in a campaign to extend and consolidate his power into the Zengid heartlands. He crossed the Euphrates into the Jazira and in the following months seized Edessa, Harran and Sinjar, although Mosul proved too strong for him to take. Although Raymond of Tripoli and King Baldwin took advantage of his absence to conduct destructive campaigns to the east and south of Damascus, and even regained control of Habis Jaldak, they could not do enough damage to divert Saladin from his campaign in the Jazira.[85]

The Franks were well aware of this. A measure of their anxiety can be seen in the calling of a general council in February 1183, where it was agreed to make a *census* or survey of the whole kingdom, as a preliminary to the levy of an extraordinary tax 'for the common benefit of the kingdom'. Consent was obtained from the upper classes, and assent from 'the people', although it is not clear in what form.[86] The tax was universal, encompassing all social classes, from the prelates and high barons to the peasantry. Four men were chosen from each city to collect the money, taking account of ability to pay. Owners of urban property would pay 1 besant on every 100 besants' worth of property or on money owed to them and 2 besants on every 100 of revenue. Those with an income below this level paid a hearth tax of a besant (or a proportion of a besant). All churches and monasteries, nobles and their vassals, and others holding rents were to pay 2 besants for every 100 of rental income. All those who held *casalia* were liable for the equivalent of 1 besant per hearth, which they could recover from the peasantry, having taken into account differentials in income among the rural population. The money was to be deposited in two boxes, in Jerusalem and Haifa, for which there were to be three separate keyholders, and was to be used exclusively for 'the defence of the land'.

Such a levy had never previously been taken in the crusader states and, indeed, the decree states explicitly that the tax was once only, and could not be used as a precedent. However, there were examples in the West: Henry II and Louis VII had levied general taxes for the defence of the Holy Land in 1166 and, given the frequent contact between Jerusalem and these two monarchies, these seem the most likely models. Certainly the Franks could have learned about the methods used to collect Louis VII's tax from Stephen of Sancerre when he visited the Holy Land in 1170, since he brought some of the proceeds with him.[87]

It may have been at about this time that Patriarch Eraclius sent a general encyclical to all the ecclesiastical and secular leaders in the West and to 'all the sons of the Church'. The letter is undated, but it must have been written before the battle of Hattin in 1187. Whatever the precise details, the patriarch's attempt to persuade individuals to provide material help is in keeping with the mood that prompted the special levy of 1183. Eraclius describes a land surrounded by enemies, which the Christians would be forced to abandon unless they received help. He was therefore sending a delegation of canons from the Holy Sepulchre, whose aim was to gather whatever support they could through offers of remission of sins and of confraternity with the Holy

Sepulchre community. If their present situation prevented them from coming in person, 'may you give these utterly reliable men the means of support from the wealth God bestowed on you'. In return, such donors would receive the same remission of sins as those who actually made the journey to the East. Moreover, anybody who sent a horse, mule or any other mount, weapons and armour, or ecclesiastical ornaments, books or vestments would receive remission of a third of the penance imposed on them. He was supported in this by Aimery of Limoges, patriarch of Antioch, and seventeen archbishops and bishops in the kingdom of Jerusalem, who each offered forty days of absolution.[88]

At the same time the patriarch was offering inducements to join the confraternity of the canons in return for an annual donation. This brought not only a quarter remission of penance, but also an additional range of privileges, including burial in areas under interdict, individual masses for the dying, and annual offerings on the anniversary of the death of those in the confraternity. The patriarch was anxious to garner as much support as possible: even if vows already taken could not be fulfilled because of illness, infirmity 'or some other serious reason', they could be absolved in exchange for the money that had been saved for the journey.[89] In principle, such offers were not unprecedented: the canons of the Holy Sepulchre had been constructing a fraternal network since the 1130s, while in 1155 Patriarch Fulcher had offered possible commutation of vows in return for financial support. But Eraclius was making more sweeping promises in keeping with what the Franks in the East perceived to be a highly perilous situation.[90]

The Christians were right to be alarmed for, on 11 June 1183, Saladin had achieved his last great goal in Muslim Syria when Aleppo surrendered to him. Its ruler, 'Imad al-Din Zengi, agreed to exchange it for Sinjar and some lesser cities and towns. Members of Saladin's entourage were contemptuous. The qadi, al-Fadil, said: 'We gave him for Aleppo such-and-such places. This is an exchange in truth! We took dinars from him and gave him dirhams. We gave up villages and acquired major cities.'[91] William of Tyre no doubt reflects the general perception when he says that in practice the Christians were now surrounded, leaving them almost besieged.[92]

Rumours were now rife among the Latins, for nobody knew what Saladin would do next. However, the signs were ominous. When Baldwin granted Bohemond 300 knights for the defence of Antioch, Saladin made a truce with him before departing for Damascus, which suggested that he was preparing a major attack on the kingdom of Jerusalem. In the kingdom itself, there was now an urgent need to appoint a new *bailli* as Baldwin had become extremely ill. In contrast to previous occasions, February's assembly had been convened and conducted by the leaders of the kingdom and not the king, and in October Guy of Lusignan was placed in charge. He was, however, obliged to swear an oath that he would not attempt to gain the crown in Baldwin's lifetime, a condition that suggests that the king did not entirely trust him, and may reflect the division of opinion over his appointment recorded by William of Tyre. His experiences with Raymond of Tripoli and Bohemond of Antioch may have made the king wary, but William of Tyre had also picked up rumours that Guy had been attempting to buy support among the baronage and Baldwin must have been warned about this.[93]

Fears of Saladin's next move were entirely justified, for on 29 September he crossed the Jordan south of the Sea of Galilee and invaded the plain of Baisan. Ibn Shaddad says that he planned a pitched battle, an assertion supported by other Muslim sources.[94] The Christians were not unprepared, for the new tax had enabled them to raise a formidable and well-equipped force: William of Tyre says that they had 1,300 cavalry and more than 15,000 foot.[95] They encamped at the Springs of Saffuriya where there were adequate supplies of fresh water, although Muslim raiding parties made it difficult to keep so many men properly supplied with food. William says that this was the greatest army assembled in living memory, which means that it was larger than those taken to Egypt by Amalric. With the notable exception of Bohemond of Antioch, all the major leaders were present, including Raymond of Tripoli, the Ibelin brothers, Reynald of Sidon, Walter of Caesarea and Joscelin of Courtenay. They were reinforced by Henry, duke of Louvain, and Ralph of Mauleon from Aquitaine, a man with a formidable military reputation; both men were at that time on expeditions to the Holy Land. In addition, there were seamen from the ships of the Italian maritime cities who had not yet embarked on the autumn passage.

In the course of the next nine days, there was bitter fighting and many men were lost on both sides, but the battle clearly expected by both William of Tyre and the Muslim chroniclers did not take place, since Guy of Lusignan either chose not to engage the enemy, or was prevented from doing so by influential elements within the army. The Christians did not remain static, leaving Saffuriya to challenge Saladin at the Springs of Tubania, about 16 miles to the south-east. However, when Saladin suddenly moved away towards Baisan, the fighting broke down into a series of smaller engagements. Turkish detachments did considerable damage to Le Petit Gerin and Forbelet, and caused panic in Nazareth, where most of the remaining inhabitants were noncombatants. One group even climbed Mount Tabor, but was unable to break into the cloister of the Greek monastery of St Elias, which was fortified with walls and a tower. Eventually, on the ninth day, Saladin gave up and retreated towards

Damascus. Even then the Christians were uneasy, returning to Saffuriya until they were certain he was not coming back.[96]

When it was all over there were immediate repercussions on the Christian side. According to William of Tyre, the king thought that Guy of Lusignan had 'lacked both vigour and sense' and, having taken 'sounder advice', dismissed him as *bailli* and took back power directly to himself, even though Guy had held the position for less than a month.[97] This suggests that, although Saladin had been obliged to retreat, Baldwin thought that Guy had lost a rare opportunity to inflict a defeat that would have undermined his power and weakened his prestige in the Muslim world, making it much more difficult for him to mount the same kind of challenge again. These were no ordinary border skirmishes: the Christians had taken the True Cross with them and for over a week two very large armies, both assembled with great expense and effort, had been separated by no more than 6 miles.[98] William of Tyre was, of course, an archbishop and so did not accompany the army, but he received his information from those who had been present, and he came to the conclusion that Saladin had been reckless and had left himself open to potential disaster.[99] In the light of his attitude to Guy of Lusignan in the aftermath, the king must have thought the same.

William records something of the debate that followed. Some argued that Saladin had been so entrenched that it would have been impossible to attack him, but others thought that this was merely an excuse to avoid battle, since if they had succeeded Guy would have taken all the credit. In short, whatever Guy himself had wanted to do (and this cannot be known for certain), any move towards battle had been sabotaged by his enemies in the army, motivated not by tactical considerations, but by personal rivalry and hatred.[100] These same people then persuaded the king that the failure to attack Saladin lay entirely with the *bailli*. William, who makes no secret of his low opinion of Guy of Lusignan, nevertheless chooses to sit on the fence rather than seize the opportunity to blame him for what was thought by other contemporaries to have been a dismal failure.

In the short term, Guy's enemies certainly succeeded, for the king now decided to make Sibylla's five-year-old son, Baldwin, co-ruler, and on 20 November 1183, he was crowned in the church of the Holy Sepulchre.[101] William of Tyre claims that the advice the king received was unanimous, naming Bohemond III, Raymond of Tripoli, Reynald of Sidon, Baldwin of Ramla and his brother, Balian. William says that Agnes of Courtenay actually suggested this and was especially keen to see him crowned, which shows that she was more interested in retaining power through her influence over the Crown than she was in defending Guy of Lusignan, since the coronation blocked any ambition Guy had to become king himself. It now appears that efforts were made to isolate Guy completely. In contrast to all the other barons present, he was not asked to do homage to the boy-king, while at the same time Baldwin IV had decided that his marriage to Sibylla must be ended, demanding from the patriarch that a day be set for the annulment. Both William of Tyre and Ernoul emphasise Baldwin's animosity towards Guy, which was reinforced by Guy's refusal to accede to the king's request to exchange Jerusalem for Tyre. William characterises this as gross ingratitude on Guy's part, although Tyre was, of course, more commercially valuable than Jerusalem. In these circumstances it looks as if Baldwin and many of the leading barons intended to drive Guy out of the kingdom.[102]

Guy of Lusignan may have been saved by Saladin. News had reached Jerusalem that, little more than a month after his campaign in Galilee, Saladin had launched another attack, this time in Transjordan. Saladin had brought a large force to besiege Kerak in Moab, situated about 12 miles to the east of the southern end of the Dead Sea, and had called on his brother, al-Adil, to bring more men from Egypt. Reynald of Châtillon had become lord of Kerak and Montréal following his marriage to Stephanie of Milly in 1177, and was not present at the coronation of Baldwin V because he had hurried to Kerak on hearing the news of Saladin's approach.[103] There is no doubt that the king realised that this was a major threat and, as soon as he was able, he organised a relief army, which set out under the protection of the True Cross.

Kerak was a powerful castle against which Saladin had failed before. It had been strengthened by previous lords from the time of Pagan the Butler in 1142 and by the 1180s its excellent natural defences had been heavily augmented by a series of building campaigns. It was built in a large wedge shape extending south along a ridge created by the meeting of two wadis. At the wider end of the wedge on the north side was a town and the whole complex was protected by a deep fosse which had been dug right across the ridge. Between the castle and the town there was another, similar ditch, while the southern end of the castle contained a cistern that served as a moat in the event of attack from the neighbouring high ground. The sides of the ridge, reinforced with masonry, sloped steeply down to the wadis, making access impossible from the east or the west (see plate 14).[104]

Kerak was not a random choice, for it occupied a position overlooking the main route between Cairo and Damascus and therefore was of vital strategic importance. However, Saladin had not mounted the attack for this reason alone, for he held a grudge against Reynald of Châtillon, a grudge that he pursued right up to the time of Reynald's capture in July 1187 after the battle of Hattin, when he personally executed him. It was Reynald, Saladin claimed, who had first broken the truce in 1182, when he attacked a caravan from Egypt that had halted near the castle of Montréal, believing that its safety was guaranteed by the terms of the truce.[105] Saladin was right to identify Reynald as a dangerous enemy. He had shown great energy since his release in 1176, and it is now generally recognised that he was committed to the war against Islam in a way that had not been evident during his time as prince of Antioch. Despite his sixteen years in prison, he had emerged with sufficient physical strength to begin campaigning at once.[106]

More seriously, in February 1183, Reynald had outraged Saladin by carrying his attack into the Red Sea. He had built a number of ships, constructed in pieces so that they could be carried overland, and launched these on the gulf of Aqaba. They were divided into two squadrons, one of which besieged Aqaba, a fortress described by al-Fadil as 'at the head of the sea', while the other ranged along the coast of the Hidjaz. Much damage was done to Aydhab, on the western side of the Red Sea, where merchants were captured and goods seized. 'Imad al-Din claims that Medina was in danger, while al-Fadil, inflating his rhetoric for the benefit of the caliph at Baghdad, said the inhabitants of Mecca were terrified, believing that the Last Judgment had come. Saladin must certainly have feared the potential damage to vital Red Sea trading links should the Franks manage to penetrate the region on a regular basis. In Cairo, al-Adil ordered his fleet commander, the formidable Husam al-Din Lu'lu, to eliminate them, and after he had captured and killed those at Aqaba, he pursued the others along the coast, forcing them to abandon their ships before finally trapping them in a ravine. The survivors were taken back to Cairo on Saladin's orders, since, according to 'Imad al-Din, the sultan was determined that no one should remain alive who had any knowledge that might be useful to any future Frankish attempt to invade the area.[107]

Saladin had therefore assembled a powerful army to besiege Kerak, later reinforced by al-Adil with troops brought from Egypt. Ibn al-Athir says that he had seven trebuchets 'which continued to hurl stones night and day'. Reynald chose to defend the town, a decision that William of Tyre criticises as showing a lack of foresight, since the Muslims seized the town and all its contents, which were then used to help sustain them during the siege. The castle quickly became crowded with noncombatants, including both the inhabitants of the town and Syrians from the surrounding area. Added to these were guests and entertainers who had come for the wedding of Humphrey of Toron and Isabella, betrothed in 1180.[108] In these circumstances Baldwin could hardly afford to spend more time dealing with Guy of Lusignan. He assembled a relief army and, taking the True Cross, set out for

Kerak. However, when they reached the Dead Sea he was unable to continue and handed over command to Raymond of Tripoli. By this time Saladin had learned of the approaching army and, on 3 or 4 December, after a siege of a month, decided to retreat.[109]

Guy of Lusignan had accompanied the relief army to Kerak, but as soon as he could he set out for Ascalon, sending a message for Sibylla to join him. 'For he feared,' says William of Tyre, 'that if Baldwin should have her in his power he would not permit her to return to her husband.' Summoned by the king, he declined to appear, claiming illness, and when Baldwin actually went to Ascalon he was refused entry. However, Baldwin gained access to Jaffa without difficulty and installed his own governor, evidently the first step in depriving Guy of his lordship on the basis that he was a recalcitrant vassal. He then went directly to Acre, where he called a general council, apparently planned before Saladin's siege of Kerak, since the main business was consideration of a plan to send a new mission to the West. In fact, the council became the scene of a dramatic quarrel, since Eraclius and the masters of the Hospital and Temple, who had been designated the chief envoys, tried to intercede for Guy before any discussion of the mission could take place and, when they were not given priority, withdrew in anger.[110]

Guy, however, seems to have been determined to defy the king and, at some time after early October 1184, launched an attack on some Bedouin encamped near the royal fief of Darum on the southern borders of the kingdom. As the Bedouin had paid for royal protection, they had believed themselves to be safe. Guy's attack, not very different from his behaviour as an unruly vassal of Henry II in Poitou, looks as if it was intended as retaliation for the confiscation of Jaffa. Baldwin's response was to hand over government to Raymond of Tripoli, a decision that William of Tyre says was supported by the whole populace and what he calls 'the greatest part of the barons'.[111] To the archbishop, it was evident that the only hope of survival was to place Raymond in charge.[112]

William certainly considered ending the work at this point, perhaps because he had decided that he no longer wished to record what he saw as the ruin of his country, but he says that he was persuaded to continue, and he therefore embarked on the first chapter of a new book. Even so, he was very depressed. After his failure to become patriarch, William's fortunes had begun to decline, at least in part because his former patron, Raymond of Tripoli, no longer had any influence in the kingdom, making the archbishop 'a marked man' in the eyes of the *camarilla* surrounding Agnes of Courtenay. His role as chancellor had been increasingly marginalised and, in the spring or summer of 1184, he appears to have left the post, possibly because he had been excommunicated by the patriarch.[113] Ernoul claims that this took place on Maundy Thursday, which in 1184 fell on 29 March, and that afterwards he was poisoned by a corrupt doctor.[114] Neither the year of William's death nor the exact circumstances in which it happened are known for certain, but it has been shown that he died on 29 September, very probably in 1186.[115] What is clear is that without the archbishop's narrative it is much more difficult to follow the course of events in the crusader states, especially as Ernoul is an unreliable guide, while the complicated manuscript tradition of the Old French continuations of William of Tyre adds further to the confusion.[116]

Ernoul is particularly anxious to tell the story of the internal struggles in the kingdom, a story that, in combination with the appeals made by the patriarch, gives the impression that the West had abandoned the crusader states. In fact, crusaders and pilgrims continued to visit, among them the famous William Marshal. William had attended the deathbed of King Henry, Henry II's eldest son, in June 1183, and, as the king writhed in contrition for his frivolous life, he had promised that he would fulfil Henry's crusading vow and that he would carry his cloak, marked with the Cross, to Jerusalem. William probably reached the Holy Land during the spring of 1184, and stayed about two years, for he was back in France in 1186. Almost nothing is known of his activities there, which are accorded only a few lines by his biographer, but it seems likely that a man of his temperament would have been involved in fighting the infidel at some stage. Certainly the experience had a profound effect upon him, for he promised to enter the Order of the Temple at the time of his death and, in 1219, was indeed buried in the Temple church in London.[117]

Nor does Ernoul choose to mention the departure of the high-level mission to the West. The embassy set out in the summer of 1184, led by Patriarch Eraclius and the masters of the military orders, Roger des Moulins of the Hospital and Arnau of Torroja of the Temple. Evidently the quarrel at the council had been patched up, perhaps because the king took no further action against Guy of Lusignan. Both masters were experienced men, elected to stabilise their orders after recent problems. Roger des Moulins had been master since 1177 and had served in the East since at least 1175. Arnau of Torroja had been master of Spain and Provence, where he had administered the province with considerable success for twenty-five years, and he had probably been chosen as master in the East in 1180 for the financial and diplomatic skills which he had displayed during this period.[118]

The embassy landed at Brindisi and in September it met Pope Lucius III and Emperor Frederick Barbarossa at Verona, where they were attempting to resolve their differences following the Peace of Constance of June 1183. While the envoys were there they received a letter from King Baldwin informing them that, in July and August, Saladin had again launched an unsuccessful attack on Kerak, and had penetrated central Galilee, where Nablus, Sebaste and various properties of the military orders had suffered losses and destruction. These campaigns included an unsuccessful attack upon the major Hospitaller castle of Belvoir.[119] According to Ralph of Diceto, canon at St Paul's in London, and a well-informed contemporary with contacts both in Henry's court and in France and Italy, it was agreed that a new offer of remission of sins should be made to those who would go to the aid of the Holy Land, although in fact the pope, who had been driven out of Rome, was in no position to take immediate action.[120] He did, however, write to Henry II, asking him to offer help when the embassy reached England.[121]

Arnau of Torroja died at Verona at the end of September, which was a serious loss given his diplomatic background, but the others pressed on to Paris and, in early January 1185, met Philip II. Philip was never a very keen crusader, even though he took part in the recapture of Acre in 1191, and the envoys had to be content with a council held in Paris in which it was agreed that the French clergy should, through preaching and sermons, rouse the population to set out for Jerusalem. They could not persuade him to undertake any direct responsibilities towards the Holy Land, however, even though they offered him the keys of Jerusalem and the Holy Sepulchre.[122] Probably they were not too surprised at this, since their greatest hope lay in England. Fulk of Anjou was grandfather to both Henry II and Baldwin IV, and Henry could be expected to take a direct interest in the state of the East. Ever since 1172, when he had been absolved of the murder of Thomas Becket, Henry had been accumulating large sums of money in Jerusalem, apparently intended for use when he eventually travelled to the East. In his will of 1182, he had bequeathed 5,000 marks of silver each to the Templars and Hospitallers for the service of the Holy Land, plus another 5,000 marks for general defence to be held by the two masters.[123] On 29 January 1185, in an emotional meeting at Reading, Eraclius preached before him, presenting the king with the banner of the kingdom and the keys to the Tower of David and the Holy Sepulchre.

Despite the belief of the royal clerk, Gerald of Wales, who was present at court at this time, that the king was not interested in helping the Holy Land, Henry took the matter very seriously, summoning all his vassals and the leading clergy as well as King William of Scotland to a council at the house of the Hospitallers in Clerkenwell. The meeting lasted for a week, between 10 and 17 March, but the patriarch now undid much of what he had achieved at Reading by criticising the king, and some of the emotion generated was dissipated. Indeed, by this time the patriarch must have decided that there was little chance of Henry actually making a personal appearance in the Holy Land and, according to Gerald of Wales, had an almighty row with the king at Dover while they were waiting to cross the Channel, in the course of which Eraclius repeated his prophesy that in a very short time Henry would meet with many misfortunes. In fact, Henry was well aware that even his departure on crusade, let alone acceptance of any responsibility for the government of the kingdom of Jerusalem, would be certain to cause upheaval in the Angevin lands, for his sons could not be trusted. Nor was this to be wondered at, said the patriarch tartly, 'since they have come from the devil, and to the devil they will go'.[124]

Although Henry would not leave his lands, in April he did travel to Vaudreuil in Normandy to meet Philip II and the two kings agreed that they would levy a special tax, assessed according to income, for three years for the aid of the Holy Land.[125] But the envoys had wanted much more than this. Gerald of Wales claims that Eraclius lamented that everybody was willing to offer money, but nobody would actually come to Jerusalem. Certainly his offer of the keys suggests real desperation; indeed, Baldwin may have intended to abdicate in favour of Henry II and at least temporarily hand over government until Baldwin V came of age.[126] This was the single most important mission to the West in the twelfth century and the patriarch had left no one in any doubt about the extent of the crisis facing the crusader states.[127]

CHAPTER 12

The Battle of Hattin and its Consequences

W HEN Patriarch Eraclius returned to Jerusalem in July 1185, he cannot have been surprised to learn of the death of Baldwin IV. The exact date is not known, but the king had been dead for at least three months by the time he arrived.[1] According to Roger of Howden, the patriarch had hoped that he would be able to bring back the king of England, or one of his sons, or 'some other man of great authority', but he had achieved none of these things, and he had left Vaudreuil 'grieving and confounded'.[2]

In Jerusalem, Eraclius found a new regime in power. Baldwin had not been reconciled to Guy of Lusignan, despite the patriarch's efforts the previous spring, and the king, again very ill, had appointed Raymond of Tripoli as temporary governor, probably in early 1185.[3] However, it had soon become evident that this time the king would not recover, so more long-term arrangements had to be made. According to Ernoul, Baldwin had called the barons together and they had sworn an oath to accept Raymond until the king's nephew came of age. The presence of Bohemond III in Acre in April suggests that the assembly took place at this time and, indeed, that Baldwin wanted the adherence of Tripoli and Antioch as well as that of the barons of Jerusalem.[4] If he died prematurely they would either choose Raymond as king, since he was the nearest male relative, or, if they wanted an outsider from the West, 'they should act in accordance with the count's advice and wishes'. Raymond had agreed on conditions, the nature of which reflect the fragility of relations between the leaders. If Baldwin V died he wanted it to be clear that it was not his responsibility, so care of the boy was handed over to the seneschal, Joscelin of Courtenay. Raymond was to be *bailli* for ten years, although if the child died before then, the position would pass to the closest heir until the great rulers of the West – the pope, the emperor, and the kings of England and France – should judge between the two sisters, Sibylla and Isabella, since 'the barons were not in agreement that the elder sister should have the throne'. All the fortresses and castles were to be held under the guard of the Temple and the Hospital. Raymond, ever short of money because of the burden of his ransom, also wanted recompense for his expenses and this he received in the form of the grant of the city of Beirut.[5]

Baldwin V had been crowned co-ruler in November 1183; his uncle, aware that he had only a short time to live, now arranged a ceremonial crown-wearing for the boy. Ernoul says that he was carried on the shoulders of Balian of Ibelin to the Temple of the Lord, that is, the Dome of the Rock, in a ceremony that apparently imitated the offering of Christ in the Temple as described in chapter two of the Gospel of Luke. Baldwin V wore the crown from the church of the Holy Sepulchre, and when he arrived at the Temple of the Lord he offered the crown and then bought it back. 'For it used to be the custom that when a mother had her first male child she would offer him at the Temple and buy him back with a lamb or with two pigeons or two turtledoves.' After the king had received the crown, he and the barons and 'all those who wished to eat' sat down together in the Temple of Solomon, where the food was served by the burgesses of Jerusalem.[6]

In these circumstances it is not difficult to see the kingdom as lurching towards an inevitable crisis. Eraclius had brought money but no major western leader, while the kingdom itself was under the governorship of a man barely tolerated by some of the most powerful in the land. The king was only seven or eight years old and therefore would not reach his majority for another seven to eight years.[7] Some thought they could see the writing on the wall: at some point during this period, an English Templar called Robert of St Albans apostasised, promising Saladin he would deliver Jerusalem to him. Furnished with troops, he caused considerable damage in Galilee before he was beaten off.[8] To make matters worse, the following summer was especially hot and dry. Ernoul says that no rain fell for a year after Baldwin IV's death and he tells the story of how a charitable burgess of Jerusalem called Germain, accustomed to providing drinking water for the poor, was obliged to resort to prayer when all the cisterns dried up. He was rewarded by God, who revealed the location of an old well near the Spring of Siloam to the south of the city, which Germain then refurbished.[9]

In fact, this picture is misleading. Although the chronology is unclear, Raymond was able to negotiate a four-year truce with Saladin, probably in the spring of 1185, as Saladin wished once more to turn his attention to Mosul, which still eluded his grasp. Saladin besieged Mosul during the summer, although the extreme heat seems to have taken the impetus out of the attack. He returned in November, but again failed to take it and, on 26 December, retreated to Harran.[10] By this time Saladin was seriously ill, although attempts were made by his entourage to hide the fact. According to Ibn Shaddad, 'He arrived at Harran very sick and extremely weak. His life was despaired of and a rumour went round that he had died.'[11] At the same time feuding between the Turcomans and the Kurds over which he had no control was disrupting the Jazira and the Diyar Bakr and causing huge casualties.[12] For his part, 'Izz al-Din, atabeg of Mosul, had received no help from elsewhere in the Islamic world and had decided that his best hope was to seek peace. The result was an agreement, negotiated by Ibn Shaddad, who was not yet in Saladin's service, at the beginning of March 1186, by which time Saladin was convalescing. 'Izz al-Din agreed to accept Saladin's overlordship and to provide military aid. Even so, Saladin did not arrive in Aleppo until 6 April.[13]

In view of what happened just over a year later at Hattin, it is important to assess the situation in the spring of 1186. It is possible to see Saladin's position in a very positive light, with the peace agreement with Mosul as the final piece in a 'grand coalition', added to which was the possession of Egyptian resources not available to Nur al-Din.[14] This, though, is too favourable a picture. He had not actually made any inroads into Frankish territory, while his attacks on Kerak had ended in failure, leaving Reynald of Châtillon as a continuing threat. Indeed, part of the reason for making peace with Mosul may have been the fear that the Franks would take the initiative and attack Damascus. Saladin's expenditure on his armies was disproportionate and unsustainable unless he continued to expand his empire; even then, his grip on the lands he did occupy was not always certain. He was very close to death in 1186. Had that happened, 'the Franks could confidently have looked forward to a period of discord' and the Muslim capture of Jerusalem would have remained a dream.[15] However, like Nur al-Din in 1157, Saladin survived and, according to 'Imad al-Din, the effects of his recovery were salutary, reawakening in him his proper objective, which was the *jihad* against the Franks.

At the same time, despite the political instability that a minority inevitably caused, the Latins continued to maintain and develop their infrastructure in the manner that had characterised them throughout the twelfth century. A case in point is the rebuilding and embellishment of the church of the Annunciation in Nazareth, the third most holy site in the kingdom. This project had begun after the earthquake of 1170, although the connection between the disaster and the rebuilding seems to have been exaggerated. The site was particularly associated with Lethard II, whose longevity as archbishop of Nazareth between 1158 and 1190 provided a continuity that enabled him to oversee the erection of a very large church, replacing the relatively small building which Tancred had endowed. There had probably been a church here since the time of Constantine; indeed, the Christians believed that the Apostles had changed the home of the Virgin Mary into a church. However, in contrast to the sites at the Holy Sepulchre and at Bethlehem, in practice Lethard was unencumbered by the legacy of the past and was free to build an entirely new church.[16]

Although the church was destroyed by the Mamluk sultan Baybars in 1263, it is possible to reconstruct the overall plan. It was nearly 173 metres long, with a nave of three aisles and six bays, ending in a choir with three apses. There were two portals, on the west and the north, the second of which gave access to the conventual buildings of the Augustinian canons. Within the church on the north side was the aedicule or shrine grotto where the Virgin received the Annunciation from the Angel Gabriel.[17] This was where Christ spent his childhood and where Joseph was buried. According to John Phocas, who saw it in 1185, above the entrance 'is painted the winged angel coming down beside her who is to be a Mother, yet has no husband'.[18]

However, the characteristic of the building was an elaborate series of figural sculptures quite unlike the fresco and mosaic traditions seen in the other two great churches. Only a small proportion of the work is known, but there was a major programme on the west front centred upon the Incarnate Lord, who was surrounded by angels, saints and prophets, together with an important inscription on the door arch.[19] Inside, the Latins had built a two-storey chapel around the shrine grotto on which they had planned to place a number of capitals. Five of these capitals were discovered in 1908, seemingly having been hidden at the time of the defeat at Hattin in July 1187.[20] One of the capitals was rectangular and the other four polygonal and, although made from relatively soft local limestone, all were in good condition, apparently because they had never been put into position (see plate 15).

The large rectangular capital was one of several perhaps intended for the lower storey of the chapel, although another possible location was the nave arcade. It shows the Virgin leading an apostle through the perils of Hell where they are assailed by grotesque demons, an appropriate theme within the wider context of the twelfth-century cult of the Virgin, whose popularity as an intercessor had continued to grow over the previous decades. The other four capitals were destined for the exterior of the unfinished baldacchino or architectural canopy above, and they depict the stories of the missions of the apostles Thomas, Peter, James the Greater and Matthew in the East. All these capitals are of very high quality and bear obvious affinities to contemporary French Romanesque sculpture, especially in Berry and the Rhône valley. Nevertheless, they are the work of local sculptors, some of whom had perhaps worked in Jerusalem or at the Hospitaller castle of Belvoir, and are not directly derived from any specific French prototypes.[21] None of this would have been possible if the finance, skills and materials had not been available locally, nor likely if the archbishop and his advisers had perceived themselves to be part of a society on the brink of disaster. While William of Tyre offers a persuasive analysis of contemporary conditions in crusader states, projects like this suggest that not everybody shared his gloomy view of the future.[22]

Not surprisingly, Raymond of Tripoli did not last the ten years he had set out in his conditions when he became *bailli*. In the late summer of 1186, the young king, Baldwin V, died, still less than nine years old, provoking a new governmental crisis in Jerusalem barely a year after the last one.[23] In the twelfth century, when there was more than one candidate for a throne, the issue was usually settled by speed rather than by legal argument and, in this case, those around Sibylla acted faster. Her mother, Agnes, had died, probably earlier in the year, but Joscelin, her uncle, delivered Baldwin's body to the Templars to be taken to Jerusalem for burial. According to Ernoul, he advised Raymond to go to Tiberias and he foolishly followed this advice. Joscelin then took advantage of the time gained to seize both Acre and Beirut, while telling Sibylla and her supporters to secure Jerusalem. Once the boy had been buried, she could then have herself crowned.[24]

Ernoul sees Joscelin's actions as a great betrayal, but it must be assumed that Raymond planned to become king and had taken a conscious decision to stay away from the funeral to give himself time to muster his own supporters. This he did by calling a *curia* at Nablus, to which, as *bailli*, he summoned all the barons. Ernoul says that they all came except for Joscelin of Courtenay and Reynald of Châtillon. However, as Ernoul's own narrative shows, they were not the sole men of influence present in Jerusalem. Apart from these two, the masters of the military orders, the patriarch and William V, marquis of Montferrat, all attended the boy's funeral. The presence of William of Montferrat shows that this was not a simple polarisation of two distinct parties, divided by deep-rooted enmities, as it has sometimes been presented. William had decided to commit himself to the kingdom of Jerusalem soon after Baldwin V's coronation and had ceded his lands in Lombardy to Conrad, his oldest surviving son. On arrival in the East – welcomed, according to Ernoul, by Raymond of Tripoli and all the barons, as might be expected of a veteran of the Second Crusade – he was granted the castle of St Elias in Judaea, which was part of the royal demesne.[25] It was quite natural and legitimate for him to oversee his grandson's welfare in these circumstances, and it must therefore have seemed to him entirely appropriate to attend Baldwin's funeral and to support the succession of the boy's mother. Once the funeral was over, Sibylla summoned all the barons at Nablus to attend her coronation, but they refused, instead sending two Cistercian abbots to forbid the patriarch and masters of the military orders from doing this on the grounds that it was contrary to the oath they had all sworn to Baldwin IV. But Sibylla's supporters had control of the key cities as well as the support of Eraclius and, far from obeying, now closed Jerusalem to outsiders.

Raymond's position was further weakened by a long-standing quarrel with the new master of the Temple, Gerard of Ridefort, who had succeeded Arnau of Torroja in 1185. Like many others, Gerard had come to the East to improve himself, at first serving both the Crown and the count of Tripoli for pay, but eventually becoming marshal of the kingdom, a position in the military establishment second only to that of the constable. In 1180, Raymond had promised him marriage to the daughter of William Dorel, lord of the small coastal town of Botron between Gibelet and Nephin, but the count had reneged on his promise when a Pisan merchant called Plivain had offered him a substantial sum for the heiress. Raymond was probably influenced by the burden of the large debts still outstanding for his ransom, but Gerard, a man very conscious of his social position as a member of the knightly class, was deeply insulted. He never forgave Raymond and, in accordance with the values of the class to which he was so proud to belong, thereafter sought the opportunity to take revenge. At some time before 1183, after an illness, he had entered the Order of the Temple, where he rose to be seneschal, before becoming master two years later.[26] The situation prevailing in Jerusalem in the autumn of 1185 gave him a power which he had never held before and he determined to take full advantage of it.

Reynald of Châtillon and Gerard of Ridefort now took Sibylla to the Holy Sepulchre to be crowned by the patriarch, where she was acclaimed by all those present, but they needed the keys to the Treasury where the crowns were kept, keys held by the masters of the Temple and the Hospital. Ernoul was well aware of the drama of this story, describing how Roger des Moulins, who was against the enterprise from the beginning, would not co-operate, at first hiding and then, when found, flinging the key into the middle of the room in anger after being harassed by Eraclius, Gerard and Reynald.

There is no eyewitness account of the coronation, since Ernoul was presumably with the barons at Nablus and claims to have obtained his information from a spy who had gained access to Jerusalem through a postern gate, while western chroniclers like Roger of Howden derived their versions from conversations with Guy's supporters at the siege of Acre in 1190 and 1191.[27] Ernoul has Eraclius place one crown on the altar and the other on Sibylla's head. The patriarch then asked her to give the other crown to the man who could govern the kingdom and she at once chose Guy, placing the crown on his head as he knelt before her. Gerard of Ridefort helped her to do this, saying that this was worth the marriage of Botron. Eraclius, Ernoul says, did this for love of her mother, a reference to the story that Agnes of Courtenay had been his mistress. As far as Ernoul was concerned, they had all broken their oaths, but it seems probable that after his experiences in 1185 Eraclius saw no point in consulting western rulers.[28]

In contrast to Ernoul, two later crusaders – Guy of Bazoches, who came to the East in July 1190, and Roger of Howden, who arrived in June 1191 – both say that Sibylla had been pressed to divorce Guy because her marriage represented a disparagement of her rank, but that she had refused to accept any one as ruler other than her husband. In Roger of Howden's version, she actually agreed to a divorce, only to choose Guy once she had been crowned, although it is by no means clear how this was actually implemented.[29] These stories seem to indicate that there was considerable tension among the supporters of Sibylla in Jerusalem at this time, some of whom perhaps had an eye to reconciling those barons who could accept Sibylla's hereditary rights, but could not stomach Guy of Lusignan.[30] The anonymous author of a work called *Libellus de expugnatione Terrae Sanctae per Saladinum*, who was in the Holy Land at this time, describes a fraught atmosphere in which some shouted that the coronation was the will of God, while others believed that, because of it, the Sepulchre of the Lord and the city of Jerusalem would be destroyed. 'There arose dissension in the land which was so great, that scarcely two people would agree with each other.'[31]

The exact sequence of events is not therefore known, but it does not change the fact that Raymond and the barons were left to react to events rather than taking the initiative themselves. Their response was to find a candidate of their own and then take Jerusalem by force. Among the barons at Nablus was Humphrey IV of Toron, husband of Isabella, Sibylla's half-sister, and therefore an obvious counter, for Isabella had been born while Amalric was king and her mother, Maria Comnena, had been legitimately married to him at the time. But Humphrey could not face the consequences of such a move, which would have meant civil war. During the night he fled to Jerusalem and the next day submitted to Sibylla, effectively undermining baronial resistance.[32] The barons therefore saw no alternative but to swear homage to the new rulers; only Baldwin of Ramla, his resentment at Guy's marriage to Sibylla in 1180 still strong, refused to agree, although he may have done homage in the end in order to protect his son's inheritance. He then rode north to Antioch, where he was received by Bohemond III, apparently delighted to see him. According to Ernoul, anxious to fashion his story to apportion blame for the eventual outcome, Baldwin had told the barons at Nablus that Guy was a madman and a fool and would lose the land.[33]

Raymond of Tripoli, however, represented a bigger problem. Gerard of Ridefort advised Guy to assemble the host and besiege Tiberias, advice that probably stemmed from his hatred of the count, but that also represented a legitimate means of dealing with a recalcitrant vassal. Ernoul says that Raymond was pleased when he heard this news, presumably because he believed it would give him the opportunity to overcome Guy by force. He then 'sent to Saladin who was lord of Damascus telling him that King Guy was gathering his troops to make war on him, and Saladin replied that if he should need help he would come to his aid'. Saladin had troops stationed at Banyas, about 40 miles away.[34]

The Muslim sources provide corroboration for Raymond's move, for they show that Saladin knew of these dissensions, which were evidently to his advantage. According to 'Imad al-Din, Guy had demanded that Raymond give an account of his rule, but he neither obeyed nor responded. Ibn al-Athir says that Raymond had been asked specifically to account for money collected and he had replied that everything had been spent on Baldwin V's government. Saladin had responded to Raymond's overtures by releasing some of the knights of his whom he had been holding, and promising the help he needed to make himself 'an independent ruler for all the Franks'.[35] After this, Raymond's enthusiasm for the Muslims only increased. 'At this point,' says 'Imad al-Din, 'if he had not feared the people of his own religion, he would have embraced Islam.'[36] Whatever the truth of this, if the revolts of Hugh of Le Puiset in 1134 and of Gerard of Sidon in 1160 were treasonable, then so too was Raymond's alliance with Saladin in 1186.[37]

Guy now seems to have been convinced by Balian of Ibelin that to attack the count in these circumstances, with winter coming on, would be reckless. Tiberias appears to have been defended by both Christian and Muslim forces (part of the agreement with Saladin), and Balian assured the king that Saladin would meet any attack with such force that 'if you go there not a man will escape'. Instead, Balian volunteered to act as mediator, but Raymond would not relent unless Beirut was restored to him, creating a stand-off that lasted over the winter of 1186-7.[38] Certainly the divisions were stark. On the one hand, there was Raymond of Tripoli, whose record suggested he could not be trusted and who harboured ambitions for the throne, and on the other, Guy of Lusignan, who found it difficult to create a broad base of loyalty, not the least because many thought that he was not competent to rule.

Guy may also have been influenced by an awareness of his weak position. He knew that he was resented by a significant proportion of the baronage and that, as Balian of Ibelin pointed out, he could not afford to lose both Raymond of Tripoli and Baldwin of Ramla. Moreover, even his own partisans could not be relied upon. In the midst of this crisis Reynald of Châtillon had heard of a rich caravan travelling from Cairo to Damascus and he at once left for Kerak. Assembling as many men as he could, he seized the caravan, taking prisoners and booty back to Kerak. As this was a violation of the four-year truce made by Raymond of Tripoli, Saladin demanded that Guy order the return of the people and the spoils. Reynald, nevertheless, replied that 'he would not do so, for he was lord of his land, just as Guy was lord of his, and he had no truces with the Saracens'.[39] In short, he believed that he was entitled to extract what he could from caravans passing through his territories. At this point, the kingdom of Jerusalem was showing signs of having lost its cohesion, on the brink of breaking up into a collection of semi-autonomous fiefdoms, none of which, on its own, was capable of resisting Saladin's coalition.

In fact, both 'Imad al-Din and Ibn al-Athir claim that Reynald had broken an agreement with Saladin to allow free passage of caravans. 'The prince of Kerak Arnaud was the most perfidious and the most wicked of the Franks,' says 'Imad al-Din, 'the most avaricious, the most eager to cause harm and to do evil, to break firm promises and serious oaths, to violate his word and to perjure himself.' Despite Saladin's demands, Reynald refused to return men, horses or goods. 'Imad al-Din says that 'the sultan swore then that he would have his life'.[40]

Nobody therefore would have been surprised to learn that, shortly before Easter 1187 (29 March), Saladin was gathering his forces for a full-scale invasion. 'This year,' says Ibn al-Athir, 'Saladin wrote to all his lands, summoning men to the Jihad. He wrote to Mosul, the Mesopotamian regions, Irbil and other places in the east and to Egypt and all of Syria, calling upon them to engage in the Jihad and ordering them to make all possible preparations.' Saladin himself set out for Bosra with the intention of preventing Reynald from attacking pilgrims coming from Mecca, or blocking the forces he had called up from Egypt. He then besieged Kerak directly, destroying the crops there and at Montréal, effectively confining Reynald to his castle.[41]

It was now imperative that the quarrel between Raymond of Tripoli and Guy of Lusignan be settled, so the king agreed to send a delegation to Tiberias to make peace. Ernoul's account of what followed is convincing because it must have been drawn from a close personal knowledge of events, as Balian of Ibelin was a key player and Ernoul seems to have accompanied him throughout.[42] The masters of the military orders, Joscius, archbishop of Tyre, and Balian set out as a group, while a fifth member, Reynald of Sidon, travelled by another route. They spent the night at Nablus, where Balian stayed behind to deal with personal business, promising to catch up with them the next night. However, at the same time, Saladin ordered his son, al-Afdal, to

send a force into the territory around Acre to lay waste to the region.[43] Ernoul
says that this was retaliation for the activities of Reynald of Châtillon, but this
seems to be a contrivance to shift the blame onto Reynald, for it is not
confirmed by the Muslim sources. The Muslim force was commanded by
Muzaffar al-Din, lord of Harran and Edessa, and to reach the area he needed
to travel through Raymond of Tripoli's Galilean lands. Raymond had no
option but to allow this under the terms of his agreement with Saladin, but he
set conditions that the Muslims should do no damage to any towns or villages,
while warning the Franks not to venture out as they would be killed. The force
was to cross the Jordan at sunrise and return at sunset.

Among those who received warning from the count were the members of
the party coming to negotiate peace with him, who by this time had reached
the Templar castle of La Fève (al-Fula), and to Gerard of Ridefort it must have
seemed bizarre that such an enemy force should be allowed into the kingdom,
intent on destroying valuable Christian resources at a time when the threat
from Saladin was so imminent. La Fève was an important Templar base in the
centre of the kingdom, garrisoned by between fifty and sixty knights, and
stocked with supplies.[44] From here Gerard sent out for reinforcements to
another Templar castle, at Caco (Khirbat Qara) about 4 miles away. Ernoul
says that eighty Templar knights, the ten Hospitallers who had formed the
escort for Roger des Moulins and another forty secular knights from the royal
garrison at Nazareth now gathered to confront Muzaffar al-Din's force.

It seems most unlikely that the Christians knew the size of the Muslim force
beforehand, but when they sighted it they must have realised at once that they
were heavily outnumbered, for it may have contained as many as 7,000 men.
Ernoul says that an argument broke out, during which Roger des Moulins and
a leading Templar called James of Mailly tried to dissuade Gerard of Ridefort
from making an attack, but Gerard derided Mailly as a coward.[45] The author
of the *Libellus*, however, says nothing about a dramatic clash of opinions,
instead recording inspiring speeches given by both Gerard and Roger des
Moulins when they heard about the Turkish incursion.[46] If, of course, at this
point the size of the Muslim force was not known, then the *Libellus* is not
incompatible with Ernoul's account.

They met at the Spring of the Cresson, north-east of Nazareth, on or near
the road between Saffuriya and Tiberias, just over 2 miles west of Kafr Sabt,
on 1 May 1187, and the Christians were overwhelmed.[47] Only Gerard and
three knights escaped, while the remainder were killed or captured, as well as
the people of Nazareth who, apparently at Gerard of Ridefort's instigation, had
come out expecting to find spoils after a Christian victory. In a letter to Pope
Urban III, Gerard himself said they had had 110 knights against 6,000 and

that Roger des Moulins, Robert Frenellus, the Templar marshal, and James of Mailly, together with fifty Templar knights and ten sergeants, had died.[48] It was, says Ibn al-Athir, a battle to turn black hair to grey. Raymond of Tripoli had to endure the sight of the heads of men he knew fixed to Muslim lances as the returning Muslims rode back through his lands.[49]

Balian of Ibelin arrived at La Fève to find it deserted and was told the news by a Templar knight. Had he not stopped for mass with the bishop of Sebaste, says Ernoul, he too would have been involved in the battle. Balian and Joscius of Tyre reached Tiberias on 2 May, as did Reynald of Sidon, where they found a very shaken Raymond of Tripoli. Gerard of Ridefort had initially set out with them, but was unable to continue because of the pain of his wounds. Shock must have hastened the reconciliation between the count and the king that was then agreed. They met at the Hospitaller castle of St Job outside Jerusalem, where both dismounted and Raymond fell on his knees before the king, who lifted him up and embraced him.

It was only just in time, for the crisis was upon them. Saladin now had an army of at least 30,000 trained troops, which was considerably augmented by an unknown number of volunteers. Taqi al-Din, Saladin's nephew, who had been sent to watch the northern frontier, had made a truce with Bohemond of Antioch, and had joined the main Muslim army at 'Ashtara, on the Damascus road, about 28 miles to the east of Tiberias. By 27 June, the army had taken up a position near the crossing of the Jordan at as-Senebra, just to the south of the Sea of Galilee. The excitable 'Imad al-Din described the army as similar to an ocean, enveloping the area to such an extent that the land disappeared under the spread of the tents.[50] In response, King Guy now mustered the host, while Raymond left to collect his own men from Tiberias. Help was requested from Bohemond III, who sent Raymond, his eldest son, with fifty knights. The army then gathered at the Springs of Saffuriya, as it had done in the past, and Eraclius took out the True Cross, which he entrusted to the prior of the Holy Sepulchre, 'for he had an excuse and could not go'.[51] Gerard of Ridefort advised the king to announce that all those who would join them would be well paid, as he would release the money deposited with the Temple by Henry II. This money enabled Guy to assemble a formidable army of his own, although he could not match Saladin. He had about 1,200 knights at his disposal, plus mounted sergeants, turcopoles and foot soldiers. The *Libellus* describes the turcopoles as 'innumerable' and puts the number of foot soldiers at over 18,000, although Ernoul's final figure for the whole army is more than 40,000.[52]

Messages then reached them that Tiberias was under siege and Countess Eschiva was in great distress. Guy of Lusignan had schemed to become king and now the responsibility lay on his shoulders. According to a letter from the Genoese consuls to Pope Urban III, written in late September, which is based on information from a Genoese merchant in Acre, Guy had originally intended 'to fortify his cites and localities rather than make an immediate attack on the invader'.[53] He twice took counsel from his leading vassals and the military orders and on both occasions the advice was conflicting. Raymond of Tripoli wanted him to send to Antioch for more help, including from Baldwin of Ramla, during which time he argued that Saladin's army, worn down by the heat, would lose momentum. Raymond's view seems to have been that either Saladin would be forced to retreat, giving the Christians the opportunity to fall on his rearguard, or he would push into the kingdom, exposing himself to counterattack. The place to camp would be in front of Acre, where they would be well supplied with food and water, and into which they could retreat should things go wrong. In contrast, Gerard of Ridefort and Reynald of Châtillon, as might be expected from their previous records, wanted to take the initiative and drive Saladin out of the kingdom. Raymond's advice, they said, was duplicitous, for Saladin would take advantage of the king's passivity and Guy would lose his kingdom.[54]

On the evening of Thursday 2 July, the king held a third council, and this time appears to have accepted Raymond's view that he did not have the strength to confront Saladin and that he should therefore stay where he was. According to Ernoul, however, after nightfall, Gerard of Ridefort convinced Guy that Raymond was a traitor whose main motive was to put the king to shame, and that they should tackle Saladin at once. It is not known how long the Christians had been at Saffuriya, but Saladin had begun to move his army on the previous Friday, 26 June, so they may have been there for up to five days. Indeed, during this time Saladin had advanced to Kafr Sabt, on the plateau overlooking the Roman road and hardly more than 10 miles away, in an attempt to draw out the Franks but, although he had waited for two days, he had been unsuccessful.[55] It was therefore to the surprise of the other leaders that, in the early hours of the morning of 3 July, Guy ordered his forces to leave the springs in order to march east along the Roman road that led along the valley to the south of Mount Turan.[56]

As presented by Ernoul, the aim was to relieve Tiberias. When they heard that the countess had sent for help, the knights were supposed to have said: 'Let us go and rescue the ladies and maidens of Tiberias.' Such a chivalric gesture may well have appealed to the audiences of the Old French continuations of William of Tyre, but it seems hardly credible as the basis for a serious military decision, especially given the previous enmity between Guy and Raymond. Moreover, Raymond was opposed to the idea, for he knew that, although the town had fallen, the countess was quite well defended in the moated citadel and, should she need to abandon it, she could take to the boats on the lake. On the other hand, both 'Imad al-Din and Ibn al-Athir claim that Saladin had attacked Tiberias as a means of persuading the Franks to leave Saffuriya. 'For he did not doubt,' says 'Imad al-Din, 'that the Franks, as soon as they knew of his arrival, would be eager to help the town and he [Saladin] would thus be able to engage them in battle and destroy them.'[57]

In fact, both sides were influenced by pragmatic military reasons, largely derived from the dire experiences of the campaign of September and October 1183.[58] On that occasion, Saladin had indeed been obliged to retreat, but the human and material costs to both sides had been heavy. Many men had been killed and the Christian army had suffered an acute shortage of supplies. Raymond's advice that they should fall back on Acre suggests that he believed that Saffuriya was a far from ideal place to make a stand because, as in 1183, communications with the coast could be cut off. Mere defence based on the springs would not have been enough to see off a coalition on this scale; indeed, Saladin's credibility as a leader of the *jihad* rested upon the success of this campaign.[59] Guy, however, drew a different lesson from the events of 1183, for he had lost his position as *bailli* as a result and had effectively been forced into a kind of internal exile by Baldwin IV. It would not have been difficult to persuade him that Raymond of Tripoli was motivated by malice. William of Tyre, who had a very unfavourable view of Guy, nevertheless said that some thought that he had been undermined by those who did not want him to receive credit for any victory.[60] Moreover, Reynald of Châtillon's policy of unrelenting aggression towards Saladin had had some success. Despite great efforts, Saladin had not been able to take Kerak, while Reynald had proved a constant threat to the caravans travelling between Cairo and Damascus. Ibn al-Athir, aware of these disputes, saw the arguments as a direct confrontation between Reynald and Raymond. 'That is enough making us frightened of the Muslims!' he has Reynald say to Raymond, 'There is no doubt that you are on their side and favour them, otherwise you would not have spoken so.'[61]

Gerard of Ridefort had his own reasons, for he was driven not only by a hatred of Raymond of Tripoli, but also by what Ernoul calls his desire 'to avenge the shame and loss that they [the Saracens] had inflicted on him and on Christendom', meaning of course the defeat at the Spring of the Cresson, the site of which was very close to Kafr Sabt, where Saladin had positioned his army. The master's whole outlook was profoundly affected by an acute noble class-consciousness, which demanded that he follow a code of knightly behaviour quite distinct from those whom he dismissed contemptuously as Italian usurers. Such a code required that affronts, real or imagined, be avenged.[62] However, there was another dimension to the master's actions, for he had released the money so carefully accumulated by Henry II over the previous fifteen years, including the large sums deposited with the military orders as a result of Henry's will in 1182. Until 1187, none of this had been spent; Henry had enjoyed the credit for such generosity while keeping a tight hold on the money itself. Moreover, the 5,000 marks bequeathed 'for the defence of the land of Jerusalem' in 1182 carried the caveat that it could not be used without Henry's permission. Failure to obtain this meant that Henry would have to be compensated by the military orders. Thus, nothing less than a spectacular success would have been sufficient to assuage Henry's anger, and that could not have been achieved by the defensive tactics recommended by the count of Tripoli and his barons.[63]

On Friday 3 July, the march across Galilee proved as arduous as Raymond of Tripoli had predicted. Raymond himself led the column, as was apparently customary for the lord of the region through which the army was passing. They had set out, according to the *Libellus*, lacking necessities, but in the course of the morning they passed springs near the village of Turan on the south side of the mountain. However, these were no alternative to Saffuriya; discharge measurements show that the springs at Saffuriya are capable of producing as much as 600 times more water.[64] Progress was slow and soon men and horses began to suffer from thirst and exhaustion in the heat. Ernoul says that around midday they came to a stop when Raymond wrongly advised that they should make camp, but the author of the *Libellus*, who seems to have been in Raymond's part of the army, ascribes the decision to the king, claiming that it was contrary to the count's wishes. The halt was at Maskana, just over halfway to Tiberias from Saffuriya. There may have been some water here, although in summer it would have been quite inadequate for an army of this size.[65] Maskana was evidently the wrong place to stop, but there may have been no alternative, for at the rear of the army the Templars had come under heavy attack from Saladin's forces on Kafr Sabt, who must have been bearing down on them from above.[66]

Once the Christians had committed themselves, Saladin sent Taqi al-Din and Muzzafar al-Din, commanding the right and left wings respectively, to surround them, cutting off access to Turan and to the much larger springs at the village of Hattin, just over 3 miles away to the north-east.[67] If the Franks had planned to push on in the hope of reaching these springs, as one of the Old French continuations of William of Tyre suggests, these moves effectively prevented them.[68] The Muslim forces were now oppressively close; on the night of 3 July, the main army seems to have been at Lubiya, not much more than a mile away.[69] The next morning the Christians attempted to continue their march towards Tiberias, but at various points during the day the Muslims lit brushwood and other combustible materials they had gathered overnight, adding to the immense suffering of the army. At the same time Saladin refrained from launching a major attack until the sun was fully up.

Direct confrontation followed. As constable, Aimery of Lusignan organised the army into units. Raymond of Tripoli, his four stepsons and Raymond of Antioch were stationed in the van, while Balian of Ibelin and Joscelin of Courtenay protected the rear. The *Libellus* shows that considerable effort was made to co-ordinate the knights and the infantry, with the former acting as a shield for the foot soldiers, who would then be able to fire their arrows at on the enemy.[70] The exact sequence of events thereafter is not known for certain and has caused considerable controversy among historians, so any reconstruction remains problematic. Saladin, apparently warned by deserters from Raymond's ranks, moved quickly to prevent the Franks from settling into an effective battle formation, causing the infantry to retreat rapidly to the north up the hill known as the Horns of Hattin. Neither orders from the king, nor pleas from the bishop of Acre, custodian of the True Cross, could persuade them to come back.

Either on his own initiative or on the orders of the king, Raymond of Tripoli now charged the enemy, apparently hoping to gain the springs at the village of Hattin, since he was aiming at Taqi al-Din on the Muslim right wing. However, as they approached, the Muslim forces parted, not, it seems, for tactical reasons, but because they knew they could not withstand its ferocity. The *Libellus* says that in the confined space the knights trampled down some of their own men and Ernoul thought that only about ten or twelve survived. These included Raymond himself, his stepsons, Raymond of Antioch, Reynald of Sidon, Balian of Ibelin and Joscelin of Courtenay. Once through the Muslim ranks, they did not turn back, but made their way first to Safad, about 10 miles to the north, and eventually to Tyre.[71]

At the same time the military orders at the rear were having great difficulty holding out against the encircling Turks, since they had no infantry support, and the remains of the army now retreated up the Horns of Hattin.[72] Although probably forced on them, this was the best move, since they might have been able to regroup on the higher ground, as well as defending themselves inside what appears to have been the remains of Iron and Bronze Age fortifications.[73] Here, too, they had the rallying point of the True Cross, around which they tried to erect a barrier of tents. The knights were then able to make at least two charges against the Muslim centre, but when these failed resistance at last began to falter. Most appallingly for the Christians, Taqi al-Din seized the True Cross itself. The exhausted Christians were now overwhelmed and, around the middle of the afternoon, the Muslims captured the major leaders, including King Guy, Gerard of Ridefort, Reynald of Châtillon, William of Montferrat, Aimery of Lusignan, Humphrey of Toron and Hugh of Gibelet. Ironically, among the other captives was Plivain of Botron, whose acquisition of the port was, according to Ernoul, the original cause of Gerard of Ridefort's hatred of the count of Tripoli.[74]

It was almost impossible for those who wrote about the battle to remain uninfluenced by its result, so that a sense of inevitability pervades almost all descriptions then and since. At the time, however, it did not look like that to participants on either side. The decision to camp at Maskana on the Friday may have been unavoidable, given the condition of the army, but both Ernoul and the *Libellus* thought that they had a chance of fighting their way through to the Sea of Galilee had they not stopped. Ernoul goes as far as to say that some thought that 'if the Christians had pressed on to meet the Saracens, Saladin would have been defeated'. The author of the *Libellus* thought this was a crucial decision, claiming that when Raymond of Tripoli had heard the king's command, he exclaimed that the land was destroyed.[75] Again, this is hindsight. According to information obtained by Genoese merchants in Acre at the time, the turning point came with the desertion of six of the king's knights on the Saturday morning, when they informed the sultan of the condition of the Christian army. 'This renewed Saladin's resolve as he had been anxious and in doubt about the outcome of an all-out battle.'[76]

Most telling, however, is the account given by Ibn al-Athir, who says that, even after the flight of the count, 'they understood that they would only be saved from death by facing it boldly, so they carried out successive charges, which almost drove the Muslims from their positions despite their numbers, had it not been for God's grace'. Ibn al-Athir derived this information from a conversation he had with al-Afdal, Saladin's son, who twice believed that victory had been achieved when the Frankish charges were beaten back, only to be reprimanded by his father, who told him that they would not be defeated until the fall of the tent erected by Guy on the hillside. When this happened, 'the sultan dismounted, prostrated himself in thanks to God Almighty and wept for joy'.[77] Even the triumphalist 'Imad al-Din acknowledged the extent of the resistance. After they had learned of Raymond's flight, the Franks were at first downcast, but then their courage revived: 'far from conceding, they held firm to their positions, and even once more took the offensive, charging us and penetrating our ranks.'[78]

This scenario is confirmed by an anonymous account known as the *Persecutio Saalardini*, which is perhaps based on a letter sent by one of the participants. This tells how Guy held another conference early on Saturday

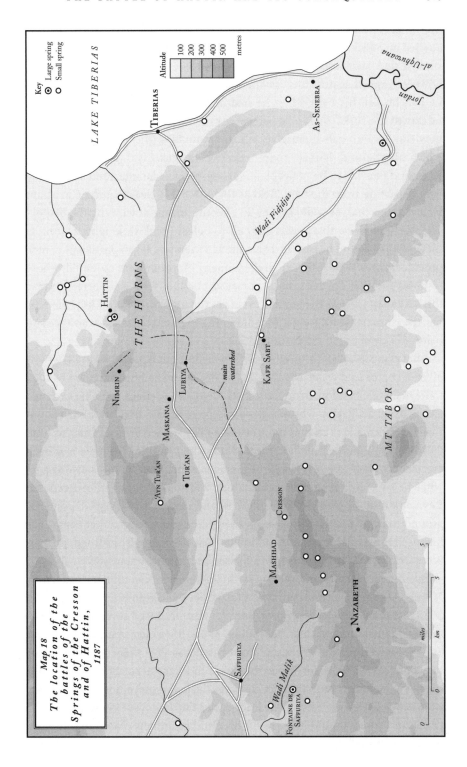

Map 18
The location of the
battles of the
Springs of the Cresson
and of Hattin,
1187

morning. Here a knight called John, 'who had often fought in Turkish armies', advised an attack on the enemy's centre, where Saladin's banner could be seen, since if they succeeded there the battle could be won. Raymond of Tripoli, however, argued against this, 'saying that [John] was not to be believed, since he had broken his oath when he had abjured us and when he had sworn fidelity to the Turks', that is, he had twice proved to be untrustworthy. Instead, they should entrench themselves on the mountain (meaning Hattin), from which they could launch more effective attacks. The author considers Raymond's advice to be malevolent, largely because he interprets the count's later departure from the battlefield as flight, but it is clear that the Christians believed that charges could still be an effective means of winning the battle.[79] The Muslims knew that it was difficult to defeat Frankish knights as long as they retained sound horses, and Saladin had therefore taken particular care to provide himself with sufficient archers, many of whom were mounted, whose task was to bring down as many horses as possible.[80] He was correct to take this seriously. Despite the terrible events of the night of Friday 3 July, the next day the Christians still fought for something like six hours under a fierce sun before succumbing to exhaustion.

After the battle the captured leaders were brought before Saladin. Guy was given a cup of iced water which, after he had quenched his thirst, he handed to Reynald of Châtillon. Ernoul presents Reynald as defiant, refusing to drink, although 'Imad al-Din, who was probably present, says that he did drink, but that Saladin made it clear it did not oblige him to accord the *aman* to him. Saladin then mounted his horse and did not return until his tents had been erected. He then called Reynald to his tent, struck him with his sword and, while he lay on the ground, beheaded him.[81] Ernoul says that 'he ordered that Reynald's head be brought to Damascus, and there it was dragged along the ground to show the Saracens whom the prince had wronged that vengeance had been exacted'.[82] Ibn Shaddad thought that this was fully justified, for 'this accursed Reynald was a monstrous infidel and terrible oppressor'.[83]

Saladin was equally unforgiving to the members of the military orders. By Monday morning, he had retrieved them from their captors, who were given 50 dinars each to hand them over, an offer that produced several hundred of them. He then ordered their beheading, a task for which many scholars and Sufis volunteered, although when it came to it not all of them could face it, or they botched the blow, for which they were mocked. According to the senior surviving member of the Temple, Terricus, the grand preceptor, 230 Templars were beheaded at this time.[84] The leaders and the other captives were taken to prison in Damascus and 'the fire of this band of infidels ceased to burn and was extinguished'.[85]

'About two years later,' writes Ibn al-Athir, 'I passed by the site of the battle and saw the ground covered with their bones, visible from afar, some of them heaped up and others scattered about and this was apart from those that torrents had swept away or wild beasts in those thickets and hollows had taken.'[86] The battle was a huge defeat for the Christians, but they had survived disasters before. Hattin was different, however, in that Guy had committed all the manpower he could muster, so that the land now lay open to Saladin. Indeed, this situation suggests strongly that Guy had not originally intended to confront the Muslims in a full-scale battle and had only changed his mind on the evening of 2 July, by which time he could not redeploy his forces. Saladin went at once to Tiberias, where Eschiva assumed that Raymond and her sons had been killed or captured, and therefore surrendered in return for a safe-conduct to Tripoli.[87] According to the *Libellus*, Saladin then moved to Saffuriya, symbolically taking up the position that had been occupied by the army of Jerusalem. Here he divided out booty among his emirs, whose support he now needed to effect the conquest of the crusader states.[88]

Although he did not expect any immediate challenge, he needed to take advantage of the situation as soon as possible, for his coalition would only hold together for a few more months. In the kingdom of Jerusalem, the three most important cities were Acre and Tyre, the commercial leaders and key ports, and Jerusalem itself, the capture of which was essential if Saladin were to justify his claim to be the leader of the *jihad*. Initially he sent Taqi al-Din to seize Acre and he quickly agreed a surrender with Joscelin of Courtenay, only to meet resistance from the local population, who rioted, setting fire to a number of places in the city. Saladin's arrival on 8 July and his promise of safe-conduct calmed the situation and the citizens were given forty days to leave.[89] Ibn al-Athir says that the Muslims took over on 9 July, in time to celebrate Friday prayers in the former mosque, the first occasion this had been done on the Syrian littoral since the Frankish conquest. There were large stocks of goods in the warehouses, as demand had been depressed in the West and they had not been exported. These included gold, jewels, textiles and weapons, as well as the sugar manufactured in the vicinity. Again these were distributed among the sultan's followers, largely by al-Afdal, who had been given charge of the city.[90]

A series of rapid capitulations followed. When Terricus wrote to the Templars in the West in late July or early August, he told them that only Jerusalem, Ascalon, Tyre and Beirut still remained in Christian hands.[91] Terricus was either exaggerating or not fully informed, for the great inland castles of Beaufort, Safad, Belvoir, Kerak and Montréal were still in Christian hands, but nevertheless between 10 July and 6 August, when Beirut fell, the major coastal cities of Jaffa, Arsuf, Caesarea, Haifa, Sidon and Gibelet all surrendered.[92] This did not involve any great loss of life, but large numbers of Christians were enslaved. Ibn al-Athir describes a scene in Aleppo, which he thought was typical, when a Muslim and his slave went to a house in the city. 'Then he [the owner of the house] brought out another Frankish woman. When the first one caught sight of this other, they both cried out and embraced one another, screaming and weeping. They fell to the ground and sat talking. It transpired that they were two sisters. They had a number of family members but knew nothing about any one of them.'[93]

Tyre, however, proved to be much more difficult. Its position on a peninsula presented special problems for besiegers and it was the only city that had a considerable complement of defenders, since those who had escaped from the battle or had been expelled from other cities had made their way there. The witness list of a privilege granted to the Genoese in mid-July shows who was present: the archbishops of Tyre, Nazareth and Caesarea, Raymond of Tripoli, Joscelin of Courtenay, Reynald of Sidon, Balian of Ibelin and Walter of Caesarea, as well as the acting heads of the military orders, Terricus of the Temple and Borellus of the Hospital.[94] Even so, Ibn al-Athir thought that Saladin overestimated its strength, especially as Raymond of Tripoli appears to have left soon after the agreement with the Genoese, presumably to attend to the defences of Tripoli.[95] At any rate, Saladin decided to concentrate on easier targets.

The delay was crucial. Reynald of Sidon had, in fact, already promised to surrender the city, but was prevented by the arrival of Conrad of Monferrat, son of the marquis, William, captured at Hattin. Conrad had sailed in a Genoese ship from Constantinople, ignorant of events in Palestine. On 13 July, his ship reached Acre and, as was the custom, waited outside the harbour for a bell and the dispatch of a small boat. Nothing happened and, when in turn the Genoese sent their own boat, they quickly discovered that the garrison in the Tower of the Flies, on the outer end of the eastern wall of the harbour, was Muslim. Conrad sailed on to Tyre, where he found Saladin's banners already flying over the city. Welcomed by the citizens, he threw down the banners and at once began to organise a defence. Ernoul says that Reynald of Sidon did not dare contradict him and left for Tripoli. Soon afterwards they were reinforced by three Pisan ships, so that when Saladin returned he found the city defiant. An attempt to offer Conrad his father's freedom in exchange for the city failed; Ernoul dramatically claims that to emphasise the point Conrad even shot a crossbow bolt at the marquis.[96]

Ascalon also resisted, its inhabitants encouraged by the strength of its fortifications on which the Franks had spent considerable sums. This time Saladin

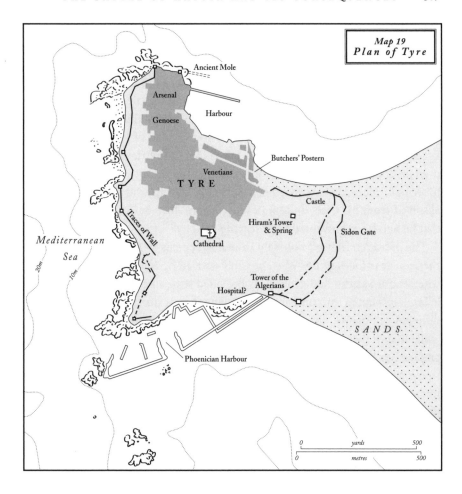

Map 19
Plan of Tyre

Ancient Mole
Arsenal
Harbour
Genoese
Butchers' Postern
Venetians
TYRE
Castle
Hiram's Tower & Spring
Sidon Gate
Cathedral
Mediterranean Sea
Traces of Wall
20m
10m
Tower of the Algerians
Hospital?
SANDS
Phoenician Harbour

0   yards   500
0   metres   500

brought the king as a bargaining counter, but the defenders were not persuaded to capitulate, and Saladin began a regular siege. Finally, after two weeks, on 4 September, believing that no help was at hand, they gave in on conditions, most importantly their safe passage to Jerusalem. Gerard of Rideforts presence was significant, because the Templars had held key fortresses in the south since the middle of the century, most importantly Gaza and Latrun (Toron des Chevaliers). As their vow of obedience demanded, the Templars acceded to the master's command to submit. In return, Saladin agreed to free ten nominated persons, including Guy himself, Aimery, his brother, the marshal, and Gerard of Ridefort, although the king's release would be delayed until the following July.[97] Saladin then allowed Sybilla to join Guy in Nablus as 'he did not want her in Jerusalem once he was besieging it'.[98] This was a particularly important gain for Saladin since he needed to make the passage of troops and provisions from Egypt as easy as possible and could not afford to leave Ascalon and its surrounding complex of fortresses in Frankish hands.[99]

Meanwhile, in Jerusalem itself the inhabitants were braced for the inevitable attack. The city was hugely crowded. Many had fled there from other places now held by the Muslims, so it may have contained double its usual population.[100] The chief men of authority were Balian of Ibelin and Patriarch Eraclius. Balian had been allowed to travel there to retrieve his wife and children on condition that he spent only one night in the city before taking them to Tripoli. He had, however, been persuaded by Eraclius that he could be absolved from his oath, and had excused himself to Saladin on the grounds that he had been prevented from leaving the city.[101]

The patriarch himself now sent dramatic appeals to Pope Urban III and to the secular princes of the West, possibly carried by Maria Comnena, Balian's wife, whom Saladin had generously provided with an escort to the coast. The letters are similar in content, but the language is adapted to appeal to the different recipients. The letter to Urban is replete with biblical references, while that to the princes bewails the misfortunes that have afflicted them and emphasises the magnitude of a military defeat that had cost 25,000 lives in a single day. Both stress the devastating loss of the True Cross and the enemy's intention to wipe the Christian name from the face of the earth. Eraclius tells the pope that he is not confident that they can defend the Holy Land for another six months and he lists twenty-eight places in the kingdom that have already been lost. Only Jerusalem and Tyre survive, he says. The letter to the princes names thirty-two places that have been lost, as well as a further thirty castles and casalia. In words reminiscent of Urban II's Clermont speech, he paints a picture of Muslims using the churches as stables and copulating with Christian women before the altars. Saladin is now so close to Jerusalem that they expect to be under siege at any moment. Defence can only be mounted with men and money from the West, and Eraclius offers a plenary indulgence and the promise of eternal life to any who will come to their aid.[102]

Saladin knew, of course, that above all he had to capture Jerusalem, and on 20 September he encamped his forces along the western and north-western walls, opposite the Jaffa and Damascus Gates respectively.[103] After an initial attempt at negotiation by Saladin, who offered the same terms that had been accepted at Ascalon, was rejected, fierce fighting began almost at once. The author of the Libellus was one of those trapped in the city and he describes how showers of arrows poured over the walls, filling the hospitals with the wounded and overwhelming the doctors. He himself suffered an arrow in the bridge of his nose and, although the wooden shaft was removed, the metal remained in his face for the rest of his life.[104] However, despite the intensity of the attack, the besiegers were unable to break in or force a surrender and, after five days, Saladin moved round to the eastern side on the Mount of Olives. From here his petraries and mangonels bombarded the city, and his miners began to burrow beneath the wall. Nobody could be found inside the city to defend the resulting gaps; the *Libellus* says that even an offer of 5,000 besants by the patriarch was insufficient to produce volunteers.[105] Penitential processions had no effect, for God, believed Ernoul, would not listen to their prayers. 'For the stench of adultery, of disgusting extravagance and of sin against nature would not let their prayers rise to God. God was so very angered at that people that He cleansed the city of them.'[106]

In reality the defenders knew that they could not survive and now tried to negotiate on the basis of Saladin's previous offer. Two attempts by Balian of Ibelin were rebuffed, partly because Saladin knew he had the upper hand and partly because the sultan must himself have been under pressure from religious leaders anxious to requite 'evil with evil' by avenging the massacre of 1099. In the end Balian used what leverage he had. They would, he told Saladin, kill their women and children, destroy the Dome of the Rock and the al-Aqsa mosque, and slaughter the 5,000 Muslim prisoners they held. 'Then we shall come forth, all of us, against you and fight you like desperate men fighting for their lives. Not one of us will be killed at that time until he kills many more of you. We shall die nobly or win victory gloriously.'[107]

Saladin's response was to offer to ransom the inhabitants: ten dinars for each man, five for a woman and two for a child. Anyone who did not pay would be enslaved, although Balian bought out 18,000 of the poor for the lump sum of 30,000 dinars. Even so, Ibn al-Athir says this still left another 16,000 who were taken as slaves.[108] Most of the men would have ended up as forced labourers, but about half of those who had not been ransomed were women and children, who were divided up among their captors. Many of the more attractive women were obliged to become concubines, or were otherwise sexually abused, whatever their previous status in Frankish society.[109] In these circumstances the Hospitallers released their portion of Henry II's deposits, for Saladin would have the money in any case if the city fell.[110] Thus, on 2 October 1187, the keys of Jerusalem were handed over to Saladin, and the gates sealed to prevent any departures without payment of a ransom.

Nevertheless, says 'Imad al-Din, this did not enrich the public treasury, because 'the tax was not guarded as it ought to have been'. A combination of negligence, disorder and corruption meant that many escaped without making the full payment. Muslim officials were bribed so that people were let down over the walls on ropes, concealed in baggage or disguised as Muslim soldiers. Important leaders obtained immunities: Muzaffar al-Din, for example, claimed 1,000 prisoners on the pretext that they were Armenians who came from the lands he held around around Edessa. Saladin, often castigated for his financial naïvety by 'Imad al-Din, granted him and others such requests.[111] Muzaffar al-Din was not the only one to take advantage. Ibn al-Athir says that Saladin knew that Eraclius was a rich man and that he was taking out a huge sum from the churches, but refused to break his oath and only charged him the standard ten dinars.[112] 'Imad al-Din thought that the patriarch was worth 200,000.[113] At the other end of the scale, Saladin seems to have been willing to let those who were completely destitute leave without paying, setting up a checkpoint at the postern gate near the house of St Lazarus. However, when one of the Muslims pierced a gourd carried by one of the 'poor', thinking it contained wine, money spilled forth and the concession was immediately abandoned.[114] On the Christian side, Ernoul says that the Templars and Hospitallers, freed from the threat of plunder, did not give as much as they might have. 'Had they thought that violence would be done them, they would have given more than they did.'[115] The losses that 'Imad al-Din regretted were compounded by Saladin's own generosity. Between the capture of the city on the 2nd and Saladin's departure on the 30th, he distributed to his emirs and the *ulema* (Islamic scholars) sums amounting to 220,000 dinars and kept nothing for himself.[116]

The refugees who escaped enslavement were accompanied for part of their journey by armed escorts provided by Saladin.[117] Their numbers were too great to travel in one body and they were divided into three groups, led by the Templars, the Hospitallers and, finally, by Balian of Ibelin and Patriarch Eraclius. The Muslim writers lose interest in them once they had entered Christian territory, but some went to Tyre while others tried to make their way to Tripoli. Ernoul, however, says that they were plundered of what little they had by Reynald, lord of Nephin, and that those who escaped were treated in the same way by the count of Tripoli's men after the count had refused them entry to the city. Some reached Antioch, and others eventually managed to settle in Tripoli. It is not clear if Ernoul is referring to Raymond of Tripoli in this passage, since at some point in the autumn Raymond had become ill (from pleurisy, according to Ibn Shaddad) and died, leaving his lands to Bohemond, second son of Bohemond III of Antioch.[118] Others went south and joined the exiles from Ascalon and Gaza. These managed to reach Alexandria, where they were allowed to stay by the local governor until they could take ship for the West in the next spring sailing. The visiting Italian merchants were reluctant to take them, but were forced to do so by the governor, who refused to return their steering oars, deposited with him during the winter to ensure that they paid the required taxes, until they had agreed.[119]

In these circumstances, with survival the evident priority, it is unlikely that anybody gave much thought to the preservation of the kingdom's archives. Seventy years later the Cypriot jurist Philip of Novara claimed that 'the *assises*, good *usages* and good customs' had all been deposited in a chest in the Holy Sepulchre, locked with nine separate keys. 'All was lost when Saladin took Jerusalem. Never again was there an *assise* or *usage*, or agreed custom written down.'[120] If this was true, then the disappearance of the so-called *Letres dou Sepulcre* removed nearly ninety years of legislation that had underpinned the administration of the kingdom. However, the *Letres* probably never existed in the first place: they were a convenient fiction invented for contemporary political reasons.[121] Of course, many documents belonging to both public and private bodies must genuinely have been lost, including the royal archives, which had certainly been in existence in 1180 when, as chancellor, William of Tyre recorded the deposit of a royal charter there.[122] However, it seems improbable that such a valuable (and presumably portable) chest as that referred to by Philip would not have been removed or hidden in anticipation of the attack on the city, just as the Nazareth capitals appear to have been.

The Muslim sources convey a powerful sense that momentous events had taken place. The surrender on Friday 27 Rajab (2 October) was on the eve of the Prophetic Ascension recorded in the Koran, according to Ibn Shaddad. In stark contrast to Ernoul's diatribe about the stench of Christian sin, Ibn Shaddad said that the timing of events meant that God had enabled Jerusalem to be returned to the Muslims on the anniversary of the Prophet's Night Journey, a sign of his acceptance of 'this professed obedience'. The wider Muslim world was well aware of what had happened, for when news that Saladin was moving his army to besiege Jerusalem spread, it attracted 'a vast crowd of men of religion, Sufis and mystics' to witness the conquest, and the *ulema* from Egypt and Syria all travelled there. Ibn Shaddad says no one of any importance was absent.[123]

Saladin then set about the purification of the city, restoring buildings to their states prior to the Christian conquest. The gilded cross on top of the Dome of the Rock was pulled down and, according to the Templar Terricus in a letter to Henry II of England early in 1188, it was 'publicly beaten for two days as it was carried around the city'. The marble pavement placed over the rock itself to prevent pilgrim souvenir hunters from breaking off bits was removed. Christian carvings around the shrine were broken up. A carved wooden pulpit, made on the orders of Nur al-Din for the time when Jerusalem would be reconquered, was brought from Aleppo. Additional buildings, especially those erected by the Templars on the western side of the al-Aqsa, were cleared away. Inside the al-Aqsa the *mihrab* was uncovered and the building refurnished with carpets and prayer mats. Madrasas were established in former Christian buildings, including those once occupied by the Hospitallers. Saladin's family performed various acts of piety; among these was the sprinkling of rose-water in and around the Dome of the Rock by Taqi al-Din.[124] The Christian presence was not entirely erased, however, for Terricus says that the Syrians were allowed custody of the Holy Sepulchre for a year, while ten Hospitaller brothers were permitted to continue to tend the sick in their house for the same period.[125]

The taking of Jerusalem was a huge coup, which Saladin hoped would finally establish his reputation throughout the Muslim East as the great leader of the *jihad*. Indeed, when Saladin left Jerusalem on 30 October, his men spread out across the plain, apparently gripped by a state of euphoria. 'One of their desires,' says 'Imad al-Din, 'was to plunge the blood of the infidels into the ocean.'[126] In fact, an-Nasir, the Abbasid caliph, was far from enthusiastic about the increase in Saladin's power and made his discontent known in a letter to the sultan in December 1187.[127] Moreover, practical problems remained: Tyre was under the control of Conrad of Montferrat, who had no intention of capitulating, while key inland castles were still resisting despite sieges begun soon after Hattin. At Tyre, Conrad had taken the opportunity to strengthen the defences, deepening the ditch and ensuring that the sea wall was continuous. Extensive underwater rocks made it difficult for hostile ships to come close to the walls.[128] 'The city,' says Ibn al-Athir, 'became like an island in the midst of the sea, impossible to reach or approach.'[129] On the landward side siege operations could only be conducted against the relatively short eastern face, and attackers could be harassed by crossfire from small boats on the inlets to the north and south.

Saladin arrived on 12 November, and, on the 25th, began an assault. Conrad responded by asking for help from Tripoli, but the ships sent were caught in a storm and did not reach him.[130] Saladin also tried to use sea power, bringing in ten galleys from Acre, a move that almost succeeded. However, early one morning five of his galleys blockading the entrance to the harbour were caught by surprise and quickly overwhelmed. Their crews were killed or dived into the sea, leaving insufficient ships to continue, and Saladin was obliged to order them to sail to Beirut. According to Terricus, looking for some good news amidst the gloom, the fleet commander and his subordinates were captured and Saladin had his remaining galleys drawn up on land and burnt.[131] This encouraged the defenders to make a sortie, during which the

Muslims wrongly thought they had captured Conrad. As 'Imad al-Din comments, the Muslims had become used to easy victories; they now became increasingly disgruntled and Saladin found it difficult to persuade them to continue. Finally, on 1 January, as the bad weather closed in, he decided to lift the siege and retreat to Acre.[132] 'He gave leave to all the armies to return to their homelands, to rest during the winter and return in the spring. The armies of the East, Mosul and others departed, as did those of Syria and those of Egypt. His special guard remained resident in Acre.'[133]

Ibn al-Athir is blunt in his assessment of where the blame lay. Saladin was responsible for the failure, for he had given the Frankish knights safe-conducts which enabled them to assemble at Tyre, as well as time to send for help from overseas, which greatly strengthened their morale. He admits, however, that to an extent Saladin's hand had been forced by some of his emirs, who feared that as his money ran low, the sultan would start to borrow from them; as a consequence, their efforts had been less than wholehearted.[134] Tyre, neverthe-less, was the most difficult of the coastal cities to take. Apart from Ascalon, it had been the last major port to fall to the Franks, who had been unable to capture it until 1124, a quarter of a century after the fall of Jerusalem. Even then, it had taken nearly five months to bring about its surrender, despite the presence of a powerful Venetian fleet.[135] Conrad had arrived at Tyre by chance, but he was the right man in the right place.

While Tyre held out on the coast, isolated pockets of resistance remained inland. As might be expected, these were the strongest Frankish castles, mainly controlled by the military orders, where most of their surviving personnel had found refuge. Although Chastel Neuf had surrendered while he was besieging Tyre, in early 1188 Saladin had not taken Kerak and Montréal in Transjordan, nor the Galilean castles of the Hospital at Belvoir and the Temple at Safad, all of which had been expensively rebuilt in the 1170s.[136] He had left forces around these enclaves in order to keep the garrisons pinned inside the walls since, as there was no prospect of relief, it was only a matter of time before they ran out of supplies and surrendered, but such patient waiting was hardly a practical way of managing his main army, which required more action and the returns that went with it.

At Belvoir, which overlooked the route along the Jordan valley, part of his objective was to maintain a free passage, and Saladin was much distressed when one stormy night in January his men were surprised by a Hospitaller sortie. Many of the besiegers were killed or captured and their supplies seized, enabling the Hospitallers to hold out for another year, as Belvoir did not fall until 5 January 1189. This was a notable, if small-scale, success for the garrison. Terricus says that the besiegers had been supporting themselves with arms and provisions from the Templar supply depot at La Fève, which the Muslims had taken in July 1187, and that most of these had been regained in the Hospitaller raid.[137] Saladin now decided that he could not succeed here until he had gathered what Ibn Shaddad calls 'a concentration of forces' and therefore raised the siege.[138]

If there were to be no more rapid capitulations in the kingdom of Jerusalem, it was now time for Saladin to turn his attention to the two northern crusader states.[139] In the spring he had moved from Acre to Damascus, and he set out from there in mid-May 1188. Qadas, south of the lake of Homs, was used as an assembly point, and here he met 'Imad al-Din Zengi, lord of Sinjar, and forces from Mosul and the Jazira.[140] The ensuing campaign is well documented, for the three most important contemporary Muslim chroniclers – Ibn al-Athir, 'Imad al-Din and Ibn Shaddad – were all eyewitnesses.[141] Saladin's immediate target was Tripoli, although neither Ibn al-Athir nor Ibn Shaddad says so, perhaps because it turned out to be his second failure to take a major coastal city in the space of a few months. Tripoli appears to have been saved by the arrival of a formidable Sicilian fleet which may have consisted of as many as sixty galleys. It had been sent by King William II, who apparently intended to crusade himself in partnership with his brother-in-law, Henry II of England. This was only the second serious intervention in Outremer by the kings of Sicily since the repudiation of Queen Adelaide in 1117, an action for which the successors of Baldwin I had paid dearly.[142] Ernoul claims that William was trying to assuage his guilt; he had planned an attack on Constantinople and for the previous two years he had been recruiting crusaders and pilgrims who might otherwise have given their services to the crusader states.[143]

Neither William nor Henry lived long enough to put the plan of a joint crusade into action – if, indeed, it had ever amounted to more than a pious hope – since both died in the course of 1189. But there is no doubt that William was serious in his attempt to bring aid to the stricken crusader states, for the fleet was commanded by Margaritus of Brindisi, the most famous and capable admiral of the day, and must have been very costly to equip, since it carried an army of 200 knights and their support staff. Ernoul says that William sent another 300 knights the following August. The fleet had originally sailed for Tyre, but news of Saladin's approach diverted it north. 'Imad al-Din asserted that the fleet was of no consequence, staying largely inactive for several months, but Ernoul believed it's presence had convinced Saladin that he could not take the city at that time.[144] According to 'Imad al-Din, Saladin was persuaded by the argument that a siege of Tripoli would take too long, for it was well fortified with numerous defenders.[145]

However, little else stood in Saladin's way. On 3 July, at Tortosa, he found that the inhabitants had retreated into two towers that formed part of the fortification of the Templar compound in the north-west corner of the city, and his troops were able to plunder the town at will. The defenders of one of the towers soon capitulated and Saladin threw the smashed masonry into the sea, but he was unable to dislodge the Templars from the other tower, where they were commanded by Gerard of Rideford, previously released by Saladin. The sultan took his frustration out on the town, demolishing its walls and burning many of the important buildings, including the cathedral.[146] Nevertheless, in response to a reminder from Queen Sibylla, who was living in Tripoli, Saladin did bring the other captive Christian leaders to Tortosa, where he freed Guy of Lusignan and William of Montferrat on condition that they did not bear arms against him and that Guy went overseas. In an anecdote typically designed to appeal to the audience for his work, Ernoul describes how Guy then crossed to the island of Ruad, just off the coast at Tortosa, in the company of Saladin's representatives, to demonstrate how he had indeed kept his promise to cross the sea. In October the following year, after fierce fighting outside Acre, Saladin accused Guy of breaking his oath, but if the story of the trip to Ruad is true he cannot have had much confidence that Guy was about to disappear from the scene.[147]

As in the kingdom of Jerusalem, he did not waste time on the great Tripolitan castles of the military orders; a day's survey of Crac des Chevaliers, for example, showed him that it presented too many problems. One castle, however, was unavoidable, for it blocked the coast road into the principality of Antioch, preventing access to Jabala and Latakia, which Saladin believed were ready to submit. This was Marqab, recently taken over by the Hospitallers from the Mazoir family. The Mazoirs had created a formidable castle, built largely of black basalt and set on a triangular plateau high above the sea on its western side and overlooking a narrow defile to the east. Ibn al-Athir describes it as impregnable. 'Nobody,' he says, 'can have any hope of conquering it because of its height and strength.'[148]

The Mazoirs were one of the most important families in the principality and had held the castle and the small associated town of Valania since 1140. However, after the damage caused by the earthquake of 1170, they had found it increasingly difficult to maintain and, in February 1187, had sold it to the Hospitallers.[149] The brothers already had a considerable presence in the territory and at once set about reconstructing the castle, although they could not have done very much by the time Saladin's army appeared in mid-July 1188. Even so, Saladin had no intention of launching an attack; indeed, he was more concerned to pass it in safety than to capture it. The soldiers needed to

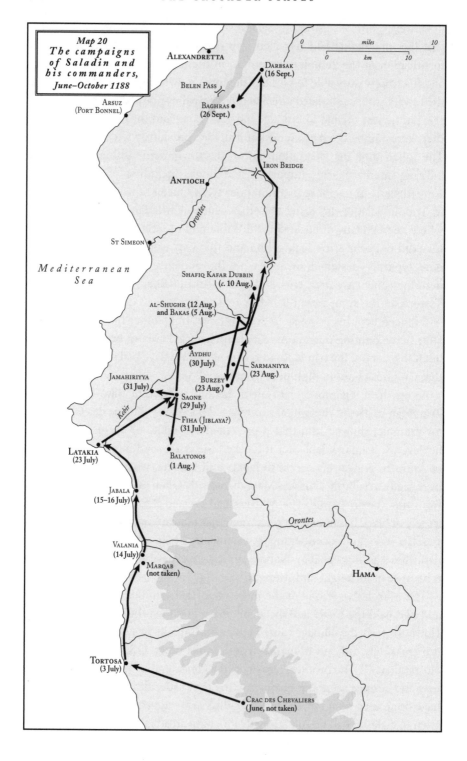

Map 20
The campaigns
of Saladin and
his commanders,
June–October 1188

ALEXANDRETTA

DARBSAK
(16 Sept.)

BELEN PASS

BAGHRAS
(26 Sept.)

ARSUZ
(PORT BONNEL)

IRON BRIDGE

ANTIOCH

Orontes

ST SIMEON

Mediterranean
Sea

SHAFIQ KAFAR DUBBIN
(c. 10 Aug.)

AL-SHUGHR (12 Aug.)
and BAKAS (5 Aug.)

AYDHU
(30 July)

SARMANIYYA
(23 Aug.)

JAMAHIRIYYA
(31 July)

BURZEY
(23 Aug.)

SAONE
(29 July)

Kabir

FIHA (JIBLAYA?)
(31 July)

LATAKIA
(23 July)

BALATONOS
(1 Aug.)

JABALA
(15–16 July)

Orontes

VALANIA
(14 July)

MARQAB
(not taken)

HAMA

TORTOSA
(3 July)

CRAC DES CHEVALIERS
(June, not taken)

miles   10

km   10

construct palisades to defend themselves from the rain of arrows both from
the castle above and from the Sicilian ships along the shore, for Margaritus
had been tracking the army ever since it left Tripoli. Saladin was obliged to
establish a special rearguard of archers to counter the fierce fire.[150]

Once through the defile, Saladin was able to acquire Valania, Jabala and
Latakia with relative ease. Valania, seat of the bishopric, had been abandoned
by Bishop Anterius and his flock, who had taken refuge in Marqab. Ernoul
says that Saladin chose not to leave a garrison there because of its proximity
to Marqab, but instead destroyed the town.[151] Anterius and his successors
were obliged to use the castle as their seat, where they lived thereafter in an
uneasy relationship with the Hospitallers.[152] Saladin's confidence that he
could take Jabala was based on a visit from Mansur ibn Nabil, qadi of Jabala,
who had, according to Ibn al-Athir, been inspired by 'zeal for the faith' and
had offered to deliver Jabala, Latakia and other towns in the region. This was
not an empty promise. When Saladin arrived on 15 July, the qadi raised his
banners on the walls and handed over the town, for the Frankish inhabitants
had retreated into the citadel.

The fall of Jabala offers some insight into the methods used by the princes
of Antioch to rule their possessions, for the Franks were evidently a minority
in a part of the principality in which the indigenous population was largely
Muslim. The qadi had 'enjoyed much respect and high status, wielding
authority over all the Muslims in Jabala and its districts in whatever concerned
Bohemond'. In these circumstances there was little that Bohemond could do
to oppose Saladin, unless he was willing to confront him in open battle, hardly
an attractive prospect after the debacle at Hattin. Bohemond had taken
Muslim hostages from Jabala, but when the qadi persuaded the Franks in the
citadel to surrender, he was provided with a bargaining counter, which soon
led to an exchange of hostages.[153]

At Latakia the pattern was very similar. The Franks abandoned the town,
but held out in two forts on the higher ground. The Muslim accounts describe
fierce fighting, but once more Mansur ibn Nabil was able to negotiate,
warning the Franks of their fate if they held out. On 23 July, they too capitulated, much to the frustration of Margaritus, who had brought his fleet up to
help in its defence. After the town had fallen, he came ashore to meet Saladin
in the hope that he could persuade him to resettle the Franks as his subjects,
but could achieve nothing. The Muslim chroniclers were impressed with
Latakia. Ibn al-Athir says that it 'was constructed with the most beautiful
buildings, very decorated and with plentiful marble of various sorts', while
'Imad al-Din describes it as the most beautiful of the coastal towns with an
incomparable port. It had been 'a paradise inhabited by the damned'. 'Imad

al-Din's regret at the plunder of the marble and the destruction of the churches is palpable.[154]

Saladin now began a systematic conquest of the principality of Antioch. In less than a month between 29 July, when he took the castle of Saone, and 23 August, when he forced the capitulation of Burzey, he gained control of the entire southern part of the state. Both castles were heavily fortified, yet fell by assault. Saone's formidable perimeter walls overlooking deep ravines, huge keep and rock-cut channel were undone by a weak point on the northern side, where the central ditch between the upper and lower enceintes had not been finished. After bombarding it with trebuchets, the Muslims broke into the lower enclosure and then crossed the unfinished ditch separating it from the main castle, forcing the garrison to retreat into the keep. Almost all of them were wounded, having been showered with arrows.[155] Ibn Shaddad was an observer. 'I was watching our men seize the cooking pots, in which food had just been prepared, and eat while battling against the castle. The defenders of the bailey joined those in the castle and took whatever property they could carry. The rest was plundered. Our soldiers surrounded the castle walls and the enemy, when they stared destruction in the face, sought relief by asking for terms. Hearing this, the sultan offered them terms and graciously allowed them their lives and their property, except that ten dinars should be taken from each man, five from each woman and two from every child.'[156] As 'Imad al-Din saw it, the taking of Saone 'assured the security of Latakia and strengthened the hope that they would soon possess Antioch, as it was the key and most important of its dependencies: the gate was open and the road completely laid out'.[157]

Burzey had been captured by the Byzantines during the campaign of 974–5, when they had taken Saone. The Franks had hung on to it because it was inaccessible, high above the Orontes on the eastern slopes of the Nusairi mountains. It was unlikely to receive any help once Saladin had decided to focus on it because it was so isolated, but it nevertheless presented a formidable obstacle. Ibn al-Athir says that the only feasible approach was from the west. When he failed to break it down with his trebuchets, Saladin used his superior numbers to mount a series of assaults from this side, forcing the Franks to retreat to the citadel at the same moment that a smaller group took advantage of the situation to climb in on the undefended eastern side. The castle fell after three days, on 23 August, but the lord of Burzey was saved from imprisonment by his wife, sister of Sibylla, wife of Bohemond III. The couple were released by Saladin because, according Ibn al-Athir, she was in correspondence with the sultan and 'used to inform him of many significant matters'. In keeping with his policy in this region, Saladin handed out both Saone and

Burzey to the emir Nasir al-Din Mankubars, whose lordship of Apamea, situated on the other side of a lake and marsh from Burzey, had long been menaced by the garrison there.[158]

Saladin now moved his forces north to the Iron Bridge on the Orontes, only about 9 miles north-east of Antioch, which was the place from which the crusaders had begun their approach to the city in 1097. Antioch was so close that 'Imad al-Din says they had an ardent desire to move on the city, but that it was unanimously accepted that its approaches were protected by the Templar castles of Darbsak and Baghras and that when these were destroyed 'the fall of Antioch would be next'.[159] Both castles were situated to the south-east of the Amanus mountains. Darbsak was 25 miles to the north of Antioch, while Baghras was closer, about 16 miles away, facing the Belen Pass which led to the port of Alexandretta. The defenders of Darbsak sent for help from Bohemond III, but nothing was forthcoming and, on 16 September, they surrendered on terms that allowed them to leave for Antioch, although they could take nothing with them and were obliged to pay an indemnity of 5,000 dinars.

This capitulation may have influenced the garrison at Baghras, evidently a far more formidable target judging by Saladin's hesitation before deciding to besiege it. When he did finally launch an assault, he took the precaution of placing a screening force between the castle and Antioch, as well as ravaging the surrounding lands upon which Baghras depended. An ineffective attack with trebuchets undermined Muslim confidence, for the castle was set too high for the machines to have any impact, but just as the besiegers were becoming weary and the work seemed never-ending, according to 'Imad al-Din, on 26 September, the commander suddenly emerged from the gate and asked for an *aman* for the defenders in exchange for the castle and everything in it. In view of the isolation of Baghras, his decision is not surprising.[160] The contents alone were a great prize: 'Imad al-Din says that, among many other things, there were 12,000 sacks of corn.[161]

The two castles were given to the emir 'Alam al-Din, lord of 'Azaz, but Baghras was not garrisoned. Instead, the emir, whom 'Imad al-Din describes as poor, took advantage of the shortages in Antioch created by the current fighting and sold off the stocks to the Christians at very high prices, before dismantling the fortress.[162] 'Imad al-Din disapproved, believing this behaviour to be to the detriment of true believers, but he must have been influenced in his judgement by his knowledge that the abandoned remains were later occupied by Leo of Armenia, a ruler who emerged unscathed from the effects of Saladin's triumphs, for Cilicia was never attacked.[163]

Antioch, however, was now virtually encircled. Earlier in the year, Aimery of Limoges, patriarch since 1140 and witness to more triumphs and disasters in the crusader states than any other contemporary leader, had written a great lament to Henry II, to whom he pleaded for help. 'Should you delay,' he said, 'the Lord's Sepulchre together with the noble city of Antioch and its adjacent land will be forever disgracefully subject to foreign nations.'[164] It seemed as if Aimery's prediction was about to come true. In November, Armengarde of Aspe, the new master of the Hospital, wrote to Leopold V, duke of Austria, describing the inroads made by Saladin over the previous months. 'This summer the unspeakable Saladin totally destroyed the city of Tortosa except for the Templar citadel, burnt down the city of Valania before moving on to the region of Antioch, where he claimed the famous cities of Jabala and Latakia, the strongholds of Saone, Gorda, Cavea and Rochefort [Burzey] and the lands as far as Antioch. Beyond Antioch he besieged and captured Darbsak and Gaston [Baghras].'[165]

However, the expected blow was never struck. Bohemond – described by Ibn al-Athir as 'the greatest of the Franks and their most extensive ruler' – asked Saladin for a truce, offering to release the large numbers of Muslim prisoners he held. He used as his negotiator his brother-in-law, which presumably enabled him to make use of continuing contacts with the Muslim camp through Sibylla's sister.[166] 'Saladin,' says Ibn al-Athir, 'consulted the regional rulers and others who were with him and the majority advised that he should accept this, to allow the troops to go home, rest and renew what they needed. He therefore agreed and made a truce for eight months, beginning 1 Tishrīn [1 October 1188] and ending 31 Ayyār [31 May].'[167] Ibn Shaddad says that the truce was for seven months and adds the significant rider that if help did not come, the city of Antioch would be handed over at the end of this period.[168] For Armengarde of Aspe this was 'a pitiful agreement', that a city 'acquired with the blood of valiant Christians' would be surrendered 'without even a stone being thrown'.

After the dispersal of his armies, Saladin went first to Aleppo and then to Damascus. He was clearly impatient to continue his campaigns and the obvious solution was to turn his attention to those pockets of resistance in the kingdom of Jerusalem which he had not had time for in the spring. He was encouraged by news of the fall of the Transjordanian castles, including Kerak, Montréal and Li Vaux Moise, and was not deterred by the exceptionally poor weather conditions, forcing the capitulation of Safad on 6 December and Belvoir on 5 January.[169] The qadi al-Fadil thought the fall of Belvoir was particularly important. It was an observation post above a junction of routes, now made safe by the removal of the Franks. The area round about was already being repopulated and the countryside was once more prosperous and calm. Only Tyre remained, which he said was not a fortress protecting its inhabitants, but a prison that enclosed them.[170]

After the conquest of these castles, said Ibn al-Athir, 'the Muslims acquired everything from as far as Ayla to the furthest districts of Beirut with only the interruption of Tyre and also all the dependencies of Antioch, apart from al-Qusayr'. Satisfying as this was, it still irked him that Saladin had freed their defenders, most of whom made their way to Tyre. 'Every valiant, devilish champion of the Franks gathered there. Their offensive power became great and their zeal burned brightly. They sent a succession of envoys to Andalusia, Sicily and other islands of the Mediterranean, seeking aid and reinforcements, while support was coming to them little by little. All this was due to Saladin's being remiss in releasing all whom he besieged, so that he ended up biting his thumb in regret and chagrin when that was of no use.'[171]

CHAPTER 13

The Third Crusade

Aₜₜₑₙ Saladin had taken Latakia on 22 July 1188, Margaritus of Brindisi, commander of the Sicilian fleet which lay off the coast, requested a safe-conduct. 'Imad al-Din must have been present when he came ashore.

Having obtained it, he arrived, presented himself in a humble and suppliant attitude and, after a moment of reflection and meditation, expressed himself as follows. 'You are a great sultan, a generous king, your justice is known to all, your merit is spread afar, your power is redoubtable, manifest is your goodness. If you pardon the fearful people who live along these shores, if you render this country to them, they will become for you a servant people submissive to your laws both near and far. But, if you refuse, legions will rise up from beyond the sea, as numerous as the waves. The kings of the Christians will march against you from every country. But, since you can easily do this, let the people of this country free and grant them your pardon.' The sultan replied: 'It is God who has ordered the submission of the land to us: it is our obligation to obey him and to devote ourselves to the holy war; it is He who has made us master of this country. When all the nations of the world unite against us, we will invoke the power of God and we will combat them, without caring about the number of our enemies.'[1]

These enemies were already gathering. Although Pope Urban III had died on 20 October 1187, soon after receiving the news of Hattin, nine days later his successor, Gregory VIII, issued the encyclical *Audita tremendi*, in which he blamed all Christians for what had happened, not simply those directly involved in the battle or those who lived in the crusader states. 'Faced by such great distress concerning that land, moreover, we ought to consider not only the sins of its inhabitants but also our own and those of the whole Christian people, and we ought also to fear lest what is left of that land will be lost and the power of the infidels rage in other regions, since we hear from all parts of the world about quarrels between kings and princes, cities against cities, and about scandals.' For those who set out in the right frame of mind there would be a full indulgence. Whether they lived or died, they should know that, through the mercy of God and the authority of the apostles Peter and Paul, 'they will have relaxation of the reparation imposed for all their sins, of which they have made proper confession'.[2]

Margaritus was quite correct. None of the great rulers of the West could ignore the events in the Holy Land, whatever their personal feelings about crusading. In October, the defenders of Tyre had sent an embassy to the West led by Joscius, the archbishop, and this had inspired William II to equip his fleet and to begin his own preparations. Supplied with horses and money by William, Joscius had then travelled on to Rome and then Ferrara, where he met Gregory VIII.[3] The pope, however, died on 20 December and it was left to his successor, Clement III, to activate his plans. Most importantly he sent Henry, cardinal-bishop of Albano, to the German emperor, Frederick Barbarossa, a veteran of the Second Crusade and the obvious leader of a new rescue mission. On 27 March, at Mainz, Frederick took the Cross, followed by many of the leading princes and ecclesiastics of the empire.[4]

Joscius, meanwhile, had continued his journey north and, in January, found Henry II and Philip II of France in conference at their traditional meeting place on the borders of Normandy between Gisors and Trie. Roger of Howden credits his inspired preaching with convincing the two kings and Philip of Alsace, count of Flanders, that they should undertake the expedition and, on 21 January, they too took the Cross. Many others rushed to join them, Roger says, because of the miraculous appearance of a cross in the sky.[5] They did so in the knowledge that Richard, count of Poitou and duke of Aquitaine, eldest surviving son of Henry II, had already committed himself. If William of Newburgh is correct, this was apparently an impulsive act, for Richard took the Cross in November 1187 at Tours, within twelve hours of receiving the news, and was later rebuked by his father for not seeking his permission first.[6]

Given their past record, it is reasonable to assume that neither Henry nor Philip were enthusiastic crusaders, although Philip of Flanders had made a controversial appearance in the East in 1177–8.[7] However, Henry in particular had little choice. Joscius was not the only envoy he received from the East, for the northern states had sent Anterius, bishop of Valania, and the bishop of Jabala, who perhaps carried the appeal of Aimery of Limoges in which he had told Henry that he should be 'mindful of your renown and fame so that the God who raised you onto your throne may in turn be raised by you'.[8] Later in the year Henry wrote to both patriarchs promising assistance 'more quickly than you could believe'. He assured them that he and his son had set aside all worldly pleasures and that they would very soon be present in person.[9]

In fact, Saladin was in no immediate danger, for the organisation, financing and transportation of large-scale armies took many months, while the two principal figures were quite elderly men, who had suddenly been called upon to undertake the rescue of the Holy Land after long careers in which both had spent most of their time fighting to hold together and expand their huge domains in the West. Indeed, Henry was still struggling in the summer of 1189 when he was taken ill and died on 6 July.[10] It does seem though that, whatever the obstacles, Frederick Barbarossa was determined that his reign should culminate in the recapture of Jerusalem. Even though he was in his mid-sixties and lacked the administrative machinery of his contemporaries in France and England, his was the first of the western armies to set out. On 11 May 1189, he left Ratisbon (Regensburg), aiming to take the land route through the Balkans and Asia Minor. No crusaders had done this since the Second Crusade, as the sea route was now safer and quicker. Frederick himself must have had misgivings; in his youth he had been a member of Conrad III's disastrous expedition of 1148. However, the sheer size of his army seems to have determined the choice, for he and his son Frederick, duke of Swabia, were accompanied by an archbishop, eight bishops, an abbot, a duke, two margraves and twenty-six counts.[11] It is thought that the total number of men was between 12,000 and 15,000, of whom around 3,000 were knights.[12]

Extensive negotiations had been conducted in advance to ensure a smooth passage, especially with Isaac II Angelus, the Byzantine emperor, and Kilij Arslan II, the Seljuq sultan of Rum, whose representatives had reached an agreement with Frederick at the Diet of Nuremberg in late December 1188. Isaac had gained power in June 1185, when the unstable and violent regime of Andronicus II had collapsed and the emperor had been killed, but the Byzantines were no longer in a position to play a major role in Levantine politics in the way they had in the days of John and Manuel Comnenus, and inevitably Isaac was nervous, fearing that the crusade could be turned against him.[13] Not surprisingly, therefore, he had been in contact with Saladin as well. In the summer of 1189, Ibn Shaddad says that they had agreed to establish a mosque in Constantinople and that a preacher had delivered the *khutbah* for the Abbasid caliph. Soon afterwards Isaac wrote to tell Saladin that the Germans had crossed into Byzantine territory, but that they had been so weakened by his troops that 'they will be no benefit to their kindred and no harm to your Excellency'. It is evident, however, who was the stronger party, for Isaac chided Saladin for his failure to recognise 'any of the good intentions and efforts of our Majesty'.[14]

Isaac had certainly been hindering Barbarossa's army. Nicetas Choniates, who was governor of the *theme* of Philippopolis at the time, blames the Byzantine envoys for provoking the Germans and Isaac for ordering attacks on the army. He says these actions caused him 'a host of troubles' and evidently would have preferred to have eased the passage of the crusaders through the lands that he administered.[15] In a long letter to his son Henry, written in November 1189, Frederick complained that they had run into trouble as soon as they had reached Byzantine territory. As they travelled through Bulgaria they were harassed by archers and refused the market facilities promised at the Diet of Nuremberg. After six weeks they reached Philippopolis, which was deserted, and there they learned that Isaac had imprisoned Barbarossa's envoys. 'This,' commented Ernoul, 'is not something to be surprised at, for the Greeks have always hated the Church of Rome and Latin Christians.'[16] A series of attacks on Byzantine towns obliged Isaac to return the ambassadors 'with great pomp', but a prolonged exchange of messages served only to delay the army until the onset of winter, leaving Frederick no alternative but to wait until spring. Anticipating trouble, he ordered Henry to make secret arrangements with Genoa, Venice, Ancona and Pisa, so that the following March they could launch a combined attack on Constantinople, without which he could not see how they were going to be able to cross into Asia Minor.[17] On 22 November, the German army established itself in winter quarters at Adrianople, which was deserted just like Philippopolis.[18]

Isaac was exaggerating when he told Saladin that 'they have been so weakened that they will hardly reach your lands', but he had nonetheles made a considerable impact. Although not many men had been killed, the Germans had lost large numbers of horses, the shortage of which remained a problem for the rest of the crusade, while delays crossing Bulgaria had postponed the confrontation with Saladin until the summer of 1190, three years after the battle of Hattin. Eventually, on 14 February, after a winter during which, at times, the discipline of the German army showed signs of breaking down, a new agreement was made with Isaac and, in late March, the army was able to cross at Gallipoli, well away from Constantinople itself.[19]

The march across Asia Minor was, as Frederick knew, even more difficult, firstly because of Greek harassment and then, from late April, because of attacks by the Seljuqs under Qutb al-Din Malikshah, the son of Kilij Arslan. By the time they reached Iconium on 17 May, the Germans were in a poor condition, suffering from severe shortages and growing manpower losses, yet they still managed to take the city, forcing Kilij Arslan to make peace and arrange markets. Moreover, this victory brought a large quantity of plunder, the value of which may have been as high as 100,000 marks.[20] On 30 May, they re-entered Christian territory at Laranda (Karaman) on the borders of Cilicia.[21]

Despite previous setbacks, therefore, at this point the army remained formidable, as well as quite well endowed with financial resources, but on 10 June 1190, the whole enterprise was undermined by the death of the emperor. In the heat of midsummer he decided that he would swim the River Saleph, apparently despite receiving advice to the contrary. According to the anonymous cleric responsible for the chronicle of 'Ansbert', Frederick drowned in a whirlpool, although the effort may have precipitated a heart attack first.[22] Nicetas Choniates, who had initially described him as 'the evil beyond our borders', clearly believed that Frederick's death was a great blow to the Christian cause. 'His burning passion for Christ,' he said, 'was greater than that of any other Christian monarch of his time.'[23] It is perhaps indicative of the toll taken by the journey that, although Frederick of Swabia was able to take command, the German crusade began to disintegrate. The emperor's body was taken to Tarsus. From here, some sailed to Tripoli, while others went to Saint Simeon and from there to Antioch. A third group carried on overland to Antioch. Frederick of Swabia reached Antioch on 21 June, only for there to be an outbreak of disease which struck 'both nobles and the poor, old as well as young'.[24]

Saladin had dismissed Margaritus by telling him that it made no difference how many enemies were sent against him as his mission was blessed by God. In fact, the news of Frederick Barbarossa's crusade had caused him deep anxiety. Ernoul says that he dismantled the walls of Latakia, Jabala, Gibelet and Beirut so that the emperor would not be able to garrison them, which, if true, suggests that Saladin was not confident he could prevent the Germans from marching south.[25] This accords with the information given by Ibn al-Athir. Some of Saladin's advisers wanted him to oppose Frederick before he could link up with the Franks, but he decided instead to send contingents from Aleppo, Jabala, Latakia and Shaizar to keep a watch on the frontier rather than committing himself entirely to the north.[26]

Ibn Shaddad was sent to call up the lords of Sinjar, the Jazira, Mosul and Irbil, and, on 23 October 1189, set out to inform an-Nasir, the caliph at Baghdad, and ask for his help. They had heard, says Ibn Shaddad, that the emperor led a great host of 200,000 or perhaps even 260,000 men.[27] Saladin had little faith in Kilij Arslan, whom he believed had made a secret agreement with the emperor, and it was therefore a huge relief when he heard that Frederick had drowned.[28] Even so, a letter from Gregory IV, the Armenian Catholicos, was hardly reassuring: according to him, the crusaders still had

42,000 men, who remained determined. 'Their cause is a great one and they are serious in their enterprise and of prodigious discipline ...'[29] However, observation of those who travelled overland to Antioch led to a second letter from which it is clear that the Germans were not in a good state. They had been attacked by the small garrison left at Baghras and had lost many of their possessions, apparently because they had incautiously believed that the castle was still in the hands of the Templars.[30] 'They are very numerous, but they are weak, short of horses and equipment. Most of them have their baggage on donkeys and weak horses.' Gregory had heard that both Leo of Armenia and Bohemond of Antioch were planning to take advantage of them.[31]

Saladin's reluctance to commit large forces to intercept Frederick Barbarossa was primarily caused by the problems he faced in the kingdom of Jerusalem. In his survey of Saladin's conquests, Ibn al-Athir had overlooked one important fortress, that of Beaufort (Shaqif Arnun), situated high above the Litani River, about 17 miles to the north-east of Tyre.[32] This was the seat of Reynald of Sidon, who had escaped from Hattin in the breakout led by Raymond of Tripoli. Reynald was a fluent Arabic-speaker and familiar with Islamic history and religious belief; consequently, he seems to have captured the interest of the Muslim chroniclers. When Saladin camped outside his castle on 5 May 1189, his forces had been besieging Beaufort for a year and it had nearly run out of provisions. With the fall of the other castles Reynald knew he was totally isolated and realised that his only hope was to play for time, since he must have imagined that sooner or later substantial numbers would arrive from the West.

Apparently, one day he suddenly appeared at the entrance to Saladin's tent. He was honourably received and offered to become 'the sultan's mamluke', since once he had surrendered he would no longer be able to live among the Franks and would need a fief in Damascus to support himself and his family. Both Saladin and Ibn Shaddad seem to have taken pleasure in his company, and he was given three months to retrieve his family and retainers from Tyre, but in fact he used the period to reinforce the defences and bring in provisions. It now became obvious to the Muslims that, as Ibn Shaddad put it, his whole purpose was procrastination. On 13 August, Reynald was finally forced to agree that the time limit had expired, but he was apparently unable to persuade the garrison to capitulate, although Saladin soon realised that this was a ploy that had been arranged beforehand. He was taken to Banyas and put under guard, where 'neither words nor torture' succeeded in forcing him to give in and he was sent on to Damascus, where he was thrown into prison.[33]

Ibn Shaddad says Saladin was furious at the delay. He had good reason to be because, on 22 August, he heard the extraordinary news that Guy of Lusignan was leading a force towards Acre. According to Ernoul, Guy's brother, Geoffrey, together with Andrew, brother of Erard, count of Brienne, had sailed to Tyre without waiting for the main crusader armies. He was told that Guy had gone to Antioch with his other brother, Aimery, and Gerard of Ridefort, master of the Temple. Together they assembled a force of some 600 knights and returned to Tyre, only to find that Conrad of Montferrat would not allow them entry. At this point Guy had few options: there was nothing for him at home in Poitou, his military reputation (never great) had been destroyed, his kingdom was almost entirely in the hands of Saladin, and the only city holding out, Tyre, was controlled by a man who clearly believed that Guy had forfeited the right to rule and that he should take his place. Geoffrey told him that crusaders from the West would soon arrive. 'It is,' he said, 'much better that they should find that you have besieged a city than that you have been idle.'[34] Guy, reinforced by absolution from his oath to Saladin, and urged on by his brothers and Gerard of Ridefort, therefore decided to move on Acre, even though his force was totally inadequate.[35]

They made their way along the coast, shadowed by Pisan ships to which they could retreat if necessary. The presence of Ubaldo, archbishop of Pisa, the papal legate, who had arrived on 6 April, added a layer of official backing to the venture.[36] Ibn al-Athir presents Saladin as keen to attack them en route, but deterred by his emirs, who argued it would be easier to eliminate them when they reached Acre.[37] Consequently, on 28 August, Guy was able to establish himself on a low hill called Tell al-Fukhkhar, about 36 metres high, and about half a mile to the east of the city. This was quite a good position since Acre was situated on a plain and gave good views in all directions, while enabling Guy to press the city quite closely. Any further away and they would not have had sufficient men to make any real impact. The Pisans established a beachhead, while also attempting to blockade the harbour. Saladin, with far more men at his disposal, spread out along the surrounding hills, placing himself on Tell Kaisan, about 5 miles south-east of Acre, and then extending right to Tell al-'Ayadiya and left to the Na'aman River.[38]

Guy's attempted siege of Acre had profound effects upon the military situation. In the view of the Norman poet Ambroise, who arrived with Richard I's forces in June 1191, 'this was the beginning of the deliverance of Christendom'.[39] Ibn al-Athir says that Saladin had planned to attack Tyre in 1189 since he was worried about its constant reinforcement, but he did not want to leave Beaufort uncaptured in his rear.[40] Moreover, although the truce with Antioch had expired in May, Saladin was in no position to take advantage during the

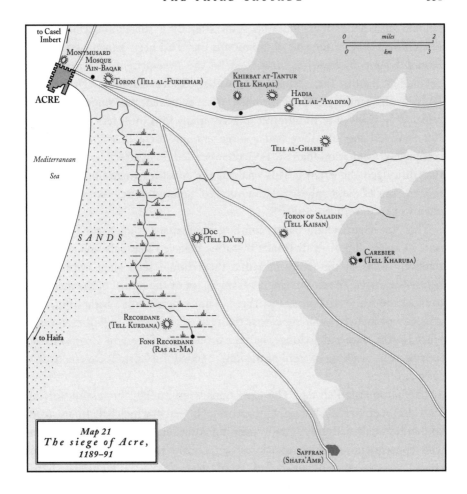

Map 21
*The siege of Acre,
1189–91*

summer of 1189, saving Antioch from what, the previous autumn, had looked like its inevitable fall. The threat that Guy's forces presented was not as negligible as has sometimes been suggested. According to the author of the first book of the *Itinerarium*, who seems to have acquired his information from participants quite soon after the events, Guy had just under 9,000 men when he set out from Tyre, of whom 700 were knights.[41] Once outside Acre, they were augmented both by men coming from Tyre and by new crusaders arriving from the West, so that by the end of August Ibn Shaddad estimated their strength at 2,000 mounted men and 30,000 foot, sufficient to cover about half of the city.[42]

There are no unbiased observers and nobody counted these men, but the list of new arrivals is impressive. These included James, lord of Avesnes-sur-Helpe, a prominent vassal of both the counts of Flanders and of Hainaut, who landed on 1 September, followed soon after by a substantial Danish and Frisian fleet. Before the end of the month they had been joined by Philip of Dreux, bishop of Beauvais, described by the *Itinerarium* as 'a man more devoted to battles than books', his brother, Robert, count of Dreux, and Ludwig III, landgrave of Thuringia, who achieved the singular feat of persuading Conrad of Montferrat to accompany him to Acre.[43] By this time Ibn Shaddad thought they had a large enough force to encompass Acre completely, a situation that, on 14 September, led to an attack by Taqi al-Din that dislodged the Franks. This enabled the Muslims to resupply the city; indeed, on 17 September, Saladin himself entered Acre and viewed the enemy's camp from the walls.[44]

This may have been the trigger for the general attack made by the Christians on 4 October. Ibn al-Athir thinks that they believed that Saladin's army was relatively weak at this point and that they should seize their opportunity before the arrival of reinforcements from Egypt or the return of the men sent to blockade Antioch, Tripoli and Tyre.[45] They emerged on a wide front, 'like a plague of locusts, creeping across the face of the earth', says Ibn al-Athir. Since Hattin, they had no longer had the protection of the True Cross; instead four persons, walking in front of the king, carried the Gospels covered with a satin cloth.

The battle lasted all day. The Christians were initially successful, forcing Taqi al-Din on the Muslim right into a strategic retreat which Saladin misread, so that he weakened the centre by sending additional troops to support him. The consequent Frankish attack caused considerable panic; the Muslim chroniclers describe how many fled – some, they claimed, as far as Damascus. Ibn al-Athir thought that this would have turned into a rout had the Christians thrown down Saladin's tents, as the rest of the army would have seen this as a signal of defeat. However, the Muslim left was untouched and, fearing isolation, the Christians in the centre began to stream back down the hill, only to be attacked by Saladin and both wings of his army, losing many men before they regained their trenches near Acre.[46] This was an appallingly bloody battle. Among the high-profile victims were Gerard of Ridefort and Andrew of Brienne, both killed trying to protect the rearguard during the attempted retreat to the camp.[47] Ibn Shaddad was told by one of those in charge of disposing of the bodies that he had counted 4,100 Christian dead thrown into the river from the left wing alone, excluding those killed on other parts of the battlefield.[48]

Saladin did not try to follow up this victory, but instead ordered withdrawal to al-Karruba, just over 7 miles to the south-east, 'fearing the smells of the corpses and the unhealthy effects of the battlefield on the troops'. 'Imad al-Din saw this as a serious mistake, prompted by the advice of self-interested emirs, for it gave the Christians time to excavate deeper trenches and to build up ramparts and palisades. These ditches, he said, extended right around Acre from one side to the other. 'Their camp was transformed into a powerful and formidable town, rich in defensive works and inaccessible even to a bird on the wing.' This view is confirmed by Ibn al-Athir: what they achieved, he says, was beyond expectation.[49]

Not surprisingly there was little appetite for fighting on either side after this; apart from sorties against the Christian trenches from Acre itself, there was little contact, since once the winter set in both sides were separated by a sea of mud.[50] Ibn Shaddad says that the Muslim soldiers, who had been fifty days under arms, were exhausted, and their horses were upset and fretful. Saladin himself was ill and tired.[51] Conditions in the Christian camp were worse. Saladin had ordered the bodies from the battle to be thrown into the river that the Franks used as drinking water, and the spread of disease was almost inevitable. 'The earth', says Ibn al-Athir, 'became unwholesome from the stink of the corpses and the corruption of the air and the atmosphere.'[52]

The pattern established in the autumn of 1189 was repeated over the next eighteen months: long periods of attritional warfare punctuated by short and often vicious bouts of more intensive conflict. These circumstances completely changed the nature of the fighting. In the past year Saladin had been mobile and successful. He had suffered few losses and had extended his control as far north as the Amanus mountains. Christian resistance had, in general, been slight and mostly in isolated pockets, so they too had sustained relatively few casualties. In contrast, in 1189, both sides became entrenched in static positions, the fighting was uncompromising and the death toll consequently much higher. In such conditions it was hard to keep armies well fed and healthy, and to maintain morale. Nor was it easy to break this cycle. The city was so closely invested that it was extremely difficult for Saladin to supply it or even to keep in regular contact with the defenders, while the besiegers found themselves fighting on two fronts, making it impossible for them to give their entire attention to the attacks on the city. Although both sides were losing many men, neither could prevent the other from receiving reinforcements, as new crusaders came by sea and Saladin called on contingents from throughout the Islamic world to join the *jihad*.

Spring brought a renewal of hostilities. Both sides were so close they had quite good information about each other, doubtless acquired both by spies and by open observation. In late March or early April, the Christians tried to take advantage of Saladin's absence by attacking the Muslim left under al-Adil, hoping they could damage his forces by trapping them next to the boggy ground along the Na'aman River, where they would be unable to receive help from the rest of the army. The Muslims were forced to fight desperately and were nearly overcome, but managed to hold out until nightfall, obliging the Christians to retreat to their earthworks. According to Ambroise, there was an equally fierce battle at sea as Conrad of Montferrat had led fifty vessels, mostly Genoese and Pisan, against the Turkish fleet outside Acre, presumably timed to coincide with the land battle.[53] Saladin had not anticipated any action and reacted by once more tightening his grip on the besiegers by moving back to Tell Kaisan, where he had been based the previous autumn, and by using fresh arrivals at the end of April to re-establish the long front along the hills over-looking the plain of Acre.[54] Soon after, on 22 April, Saladin was relieved of another distraction when the defenders of Beaufort finally decided to give up, realising 'that there was no-one to save them from what God had in store'. Reynald was released and went to Tyre, while the Muslims gained the money and supplies left by the garrison.[55]

As a result there was no further Christian attack until late July when, on the 25th, another assault was launched on al-Adil and the Egyptian troops, presumably based on intelligence that Saladin had sent some of his forces north to counter the expected arrival of the Germans. Again it failed: Ibn al-Athir says that the Franks were cut down on all sides and that after this they became less aggressive.[56] 'Imad al-Din composed thirty or forty bulletins describing the victory so that they could be sent out across the Islamic world. In the evening he and Ibn Shaddad rode out to inspect the bodies, lying muti-lated and naked, including a woman killed in combat.[57] There was no hiding the extent of this defeat, but the compiler of the *Itinerarium* blames it on the lesser members of the army, intent on plunder, who ignored the advice of the leaders, although he adds that the nobility did nothing to help them when they were being slaughtered by the Turks.[58] No source, Christian or Muslim, puts the number of Christian dead at fewer than 5,000.[59] The Muslims did not follow up their victory, for the next day they heard of the death of Frederick Barbarossa and were, says Ibn al-Athir, 'too preoccupied by this good news'. Their triumph was short-lived, for, on 27 July, the Franks had their own celebration when Henry, count of Champagne, landed with large forces and considerable funds, 'so that their spirits rose again and became confident'.[60]

Engagements like this, however, were exceptional. Most of the time the Christians concentrated upon the siege, deploying their increasing expertise in the use and construction of machines. On 27 April, having managed to fill in part of the fosse, the Franks brought up three massive siege towers, all taller than the walls. After an eight-day struggle, the defenders set them on fire with the help of a specialist artificer from Damascus, but the besiegers had come

close to success. Ibn al-Athir thought that, before the conflagration, the city
had been on the point of falling, and the *Itinerarium* even claims that the
defenders had offered to surrender, only to be turned down by the overconfident Christians.[61] In August, they used some of the funds brought by Henry
of Champagne to build new trebuchets, one of which the defenders destroyed,
although they were unable to reach the other two, which were screened by a
low mound.[62]

For his part, Saladin responded with strenuous efforts to keep the city
supplied, something that would not have been possible in the past, but was
practical now that he controlled so many of the ports along the littoral.
Although losses were often high, he achieved some successes: on 15 June,
most of an Egyptian fleet reached the harbour, having survived a battle with
the Christian ships trying to conduct a blockade, never easy for vessels
dependent on wind conditions; and again in late August, a Muslim buss from
Beirut managed to evade the enemy ships by pretending to be Christian.[63]
Although a single ship, Ibn Shaddad says that it was loaded with 400 *ghiraras*
of wheat, as well as cheese, corn, onions and sheep, and that relief was vital
since the garrison was by this time in serious need.[64] Nevertheless, the
margins for survival remained narrow. By the middle of September, they
were once more facing a crisis, saved this time by the arrival of three busses
from Egypt.[65] The Christian reaction to that was to attempt to set fire to the
Tower of the Flies, but this failed when one ship caught fire and another
capsized.[66]

Early in October, Frederick of Swabia and the remaining German forces
finally arrived from Tyre, having travelled down the coast to Tripoli and taken
ships from there. 'Imad al-Din says that, between Latakia and Jabala, they had
lost sixty to seventy horses from their cavalry force, which was already
severely weakened. Had Frederick Barbarossa survived with most of his army
intact, this might have proved the decisive moment in the crusade, for the
French and English kings did not appear until April and June the next year.
As it was, 'Imad al-Din did not think Frederick of Swabia was more dangerous
than any ordinary count.[67] Frederick, though, believed he could break the
stalemate and, against advice, attacked Saladin's advance guard on Tell
al-'Ayadiya, only to be beaten back.

Much more threatening to the Muslims was the construction of a huge
wheeled battering ram, metal-tipped and propelled by a large number of
soldiers protected by iron sheets. The initiative for this seems to have come
from Thierry of Montfaucon, archbishop of Besançon. On 15 October, the
ram was the centrepiece of a general attack, but it was again repelled. The ram
was set on fire and, still ablaze, pulled into the city, while large numbers of

men who had taken up position in the fosse in expectation of a breach in the walls were mown down by crossbowmen above.[68] Two days later the Christians sent another ship to try to destroy the Tower of the Flies, but again it was fired by the defenders.[69]

These new failures had a serious effect on Christian morale. 'They [the Germans],' says Ibn Shaddad, 'were overwhelmed with grievous disappointment and a general dejection fell upon them.' On 16 September, a large party of English crusaders had arrived at Tyre, including Baldwin of Ford, archbishop of Canterbury, Hubert Walter, bishop of Salisbury, and Ranulf Glanville, the former justiciar of England.[70] On 21 October, the archbishop moved to the camp at Acre and was shocked by what he found. Baldwin's chaplain sent a very depressing letter to the convent at Canterbury. 'The army is given over to shameful activity. It is with sorrow and sighs that I tell you that it indulges in idleness and vice rather than in virtue. The Lord is not in the camp: there is none that doeth good. The princes envy one another and jockey for position. The lesser men are in want and find no support. In the camp there is no chastity, sobriety, faith, love or charity, and, as God is my witness, I should not have believed it had I not seen it.'[71] According to the *Itinerarium*, Baldwin thought that 'the army had lost all discipline, concentrating on taverns, prostitutes and games of dice'.[72] While some allowance needs to be made for ecclesiastical moralising, there seems to have been much truth in what he was saying. 'Imad al-Din, for example, has a long, undated passage describing the arrival of a ship carrying 300 prostitutes, probably in the previous autumn.[73]

This dip in morale was not, however, surprising. The siege had begun well over a year ago, in late August 1189, and the army had been reinforced by a stream of crusaders ever since, while Guy's small encampment on Tell al-Fukhkhar had developed into a great semicircle of trenches around the city. Yet no progress had been made. A high death rate in the fighting had been exacerbated by disease and famine. 'In their terrible distress,' writes the author of the *Itinerarium*, 'their limbs swelled up and their whole body was swollen with liquid as if they had dropsy. The violence of the disease was such that some people's teeth fell out, torn away completely at the roots.'[74] When Baldwin's chaplain wrote to the convent, Ranulf Glanville was already dead, as were Queen Sibylla and her two young daughters. By this time Patriarch Eraclius was ill and Baldwin had become the effective spiritual head of the crusaders. On 11 November, although an elderly man, he was fit enough to absolve the army before accompanying it in an attack against Saladin's forces in the hills, but by the 19th he too was dead.[75] On 20 January the following year, Frederick of Swabia died, followed soon after by Theobald, count of Blois.[76]

The attack for which Baldwin gave absolution began on Monday, 12 November, when the Christians attempted to overcome Saladin's forces on Tell al-'Ayadiya in an action partly motivated by the situation prevailing in the trenches. Ibn Shaddad says that there had been many desertions among the Franks, who 'came to give themselves into our hands because of their intense hunger', and, apparently as a consequence, that 'the rest made up their minds to move against us'. But the Muslims proved elusive and retreated south to Tell Kaisan. Three days of manoeuvres followed, as the Franks moved down the Na'aman River, intending, it seems, to march to Haifa, where they had heard there was food. On the 15th they were hit by a determined Muslim attack at Recordane, forcing them to retreat, and on Thursday, Frederick of Swabia, who had been keeping his forces in reserve, retaliated. Despite 'Imad al-Din's claim that the Christians had been humiliated, neither side achieved an unambiguous victory, but the fighting had been fierce and the losses heavy, and Imad was probably correct when he asserted that this deterred the Franks from emerging again.[77] As the Franks had taken four days of supplies but had gained nothing, this foray failed to alleviate the famine in the camp.

The Muslims were aware of what was happening. Ibn Shaddad knew that conditions in the Christian camp were deteriorating. 'After winter had come with its incessant rainfall and change of airs, the plain became very unhealthy and, as a result, there was great mortality amongst the enemy. In addition to that there were the severe shortages and the fact that the sea was closed to them, from which supplies had been reaching them from every quarter. Daily, from 100 to 200 were dying, according to reports, and some said more than that.'[78] According to Ambroise's informants, the famine had been exacerbated by Conrad of Montferrat for his own political ends, for when supplies did arrive at Tyre, he had prevented them from reaching the army, causing acute distress among the poorer people. Many existed on carob beans, normally used for animal feed, for little else was available.[79]

Rivalries among the leaders reduced the effectiveness of the army still further, as Baldwin's chaplain had also noted. New contingents of crusaders provided welcome reinforcements, but inevitably their arrival meant that Guy of Lusignan's control of the army had begun to slip away. James of Avesnes, Ludwig of Thuringia, Henry of Champagne and Frederick of Swabia had at various times all seen themselves as commanders, while the struggle between Guy and Conrad of Montferrat for the kingship remained unresolved.[80] An apparent reconciliation between them at Easter 1190 did not last; indeed, the author of the *Itinerarium* alleges that Conrad was only pretending to be friendly, for he was still plotting to seize the kingdom.[81] In the autumn of 1190, Sibylla's death presented Conrad with the opportunity to argue that Guy no longer had any legitimacy, and he now set his sights on marrying Isabella, Sibylla's half-sister, despite the fact that she had been married to Humphrey of Toron since 1183 and the widespread belief that he himself already had two living wives.[82]

The sources closest to events – the Old French continuations, Ambroise and the *Itinerarium* – are all hostile to Conrad, so it is difficult to obtain a balanced view of events. Conrad's defence of Tyre was much admired by many in the West: the troubadours, for example, contrasted this activity with the long wait for the arrival of the kings.[83] Nevertheless, the story that the chroniclers tell carries conviction: that Conrad bribed the princes in the army to agree to the marriage, that Maria Comnena, supported by Reynald of Sidon, Pagan of Haifa and Balian of Ibelin, her husband, browbeat her daughter into leaving Humphrey, and that Ubaldo of Pisa, the papal legate, and Philip of Dreux, bishop of Beauvais, accepted and promoted the match.[84] Only Baldwin of Canterbury stood out against it and his death on 19 November removed the last obstacle.

Conrad therefore married Isabella on 24 November.[85] Both Ambroise and the author of the *Itinerarium* take satisfaction from a Muslim attack upon some of the marriage guests, who, less than sober, were ambushed by the Turks. One of them, Guy of Senlis, butler of France, who had challenged Humphrey to single combat during the wrangles that led up to the marriage, was captured and never heard of again. Ambroise says that twenty of the wedding guests were captured or killed and that 'they were well-paid for the marriage'.[86] There is no mistaking the bitterness these events caused. For Maria Comnena and her supporters, it was revenge for Guy and Sibylla's coup of 1186, but the *Itinerarium* describes Maria as 'steeped in Greek filth from the cradle' and as having a husband, Balian of Ibelin, 'whose morals matched her own'.[87] Nor was this a dispute exclusive to the ruling classes, for it impinged on the whole army. Conrad had gathered support by offering food supplies, a promise manifestly not kept during the winter famine that followed.

By the spring of 1191, the need for fresh men and resources from the monarchies of England and France had become acute. Hubert Walter, writing to Richard FitzNeal, bishop of London, at about the beginning of the year, thought that the army was actually diminishing in size, as men abandoned the siege, 'burdened beyond measure by sickness in body, or by labour and expense'. As his later record as archbishop of Canterbury and justiciar and chancellor of England shows, Hubert was a man of keen intellect and sober judgement. He estimated at this time that, unless the two kings arrived by Easter, the money would run out and 'the hope of worldly consolation will die away'.[88] Meanwhile, Saladin had taken advantage of the winter to bring in fresh forces by sea, although this was not an unmitigated success, for the replacements were far fewer than the original garrison, a situation that Ibn al-Athir ascribes to the negligence of Saladin's subordinates.[89]

Certainly the delays had seemed interminable: Richard, duke of Aquitaine, had taken the Cross in November 1187 and Kings Henry and Philip in the following January. However, Richard had not lost his determination to go on crusade and his father's death relieved him of the worry that he was about to be disinherited. On 3 September 1189, he was crowned king of England at Westminster Abbey, leaving him master of his own policies with no need to take any farther cognisance of his reluctant father. Richard was fully aware that he would stand little chance against the type of coalitions that Saladin was capable of putting together unless he could mobilise sufficient resources. According to Roger of Howden, there were about 100,000 marks in the English treasury.[90] Further large sums were then extracted from Henry's leading administrators, all of whom had enriched themselves while in office. Ranulf Glanville had been Henry's chief justiciar since 1180 and more recently sheriff of Yorkshire and Westmorland, but despite a fine of 15,000 pounds of silver he could still afford to fulfil a crusade vow taken in 1185.[91] Richard also effected a major redistribution of the offices of sheriff, all of whom had to make proffers for their positions, except for the counties he granted to John, his brother.[92] Even William Longchamp, whom Richard appointed to run the country in his absence, suffered confiscations, as well as paying £3,000 sterling for the office of chancellor.[93]

Although a policy of fines and confiscations combined with the sale of public offices and demands for payment for the renewal of royal grants was quite usual for a new ruler, Richard nevertheless raised sums far beyond the norm. Henry II had already started to collect a tax known as the 'Saladin tithe', which aimed to take a tenth of revenues and movables. This was established in January 1188, when Henry and Philip of France had agreed to go on crusade, and was deeply resented in both countries, partly because of its scale and partly because of the fear of precedent: Philip, in fact, was forced to give it up.[94]

Delay had its advantages. Roger of Howden believed that immense sums had been raised from those who now wished to be released from their vows; the proceeds were granted to Richard by Pope Clement III.[95] More serious for long-term government was the alienation of considerable parts of the royal demesne, which raised money in the short term but which Glanville knew would be damaging in the future. The financial pressure caused by the crusade can be seen in the distinct spike in the Exchequer returns in 1190, which show record receipts of £31,000 in contrast to £21,000 in 1188 (Henry II's last complete year) and a steep fall in the years 1191–3, when the average was £11,000.[96] The unique place of the Holy Land within the Latin Christian world of the twelfth century is shown very dramatically in these figures, for the events of one hot July day in Galilee in 1187 had, in the years that followed, profound repercussions in every part of the Anglo-Norman lands.

The translation of the money collected into practical means for crusading meant the acquisition of both horses and ships. Thus, for example, the king instituted a levy of two palfreys and two sumpter horses on every city and one each from every royal manor, apparently for use by himself and his immediate followers.[97] In contrast to Frederick Barbarossa, both Richard and Philip planned to travel by sea. Richard's fleet was assembled from all over his extensive territories: the Anglo-Norman lands carried the greatest burden of taxation, but the ports of the Atlantic coast were essential for the shipping. The aim was to sail first to Lisbon and then to Marseille, where the ships would be met by Richard, although in the event this junction never took place because the fleet did not arrive in time. At Lisbon there were 106 ships, but numbers were increasing all the time: when the fleet left Sicily in the spring of 1191, it had reached a total of 219 vessels of various sorts.[98]

While Richard's administrators concentrated on the logistics of this huge operation, many thousands of other participants made their own preparations. One such person was Robert IV, lord of Sablé, holder of one of the principal lordships in northern Anjou, situated along the valley of the Sarthe extending north-eastwards to La Suze. Robert was an important figure on the crusade because he was a direct vassal of Richard I and, in early March 1190, was one of the five men appointed as justiciars of the royal fleet. Like many other crusaders, he may not have intended to return, for he was a widower when he set out and joined the Templars when he reached the East. In the second half of 1191, evidently through the king's influence, he became master of the order in succession to Gerard of Ridefort. Indeed, Robert did not return, dying in September 1193. As his charters show, he had made extensive preparations, founding a new monastery, granting exemptions to other local religious houses, ratifying previous donations and repairing past wrongs.[99] These actions were given powerful visual endorsement when, in June 1190, just before he departed with the fleet, Robert recognised that he held the fief of Codoingel from the abbey of Evron. He took the abbot onto the roof of the castle keep and from this vantage point showed the estate laid out before them. Then, witnessed by his mother and his son, he brought wine and fell on his knees before him. The abbot was unable to persuade him to rise until he had served him the wine, in return for which he was granted the favour of the house.[100] In accordance with his crusade vow, Robert, like thousands of others, was able to set out with his affairs settled and his sins remitted.

The rank-and-file did not mark their departures in charters, but they nevertheless responded in considerable numbers. In a preaching tour of Wales in March and April 1188, Archbishop Baldwin recruited around 3,000 men, most of whom were archers, vital members of an army in which their skills would be needed in sieges, for fighting on the march and in major battles. The men of Gwent, says Gerald of Wales, were more skilled with the bow and arrow than those from other parts of Wales. Even though their bows were fairly rough, at short range they had great penetrative force. 'You could not shoot far with them; but they are powerful enough to inflict serious wounds in a close fight.' Even so, enthusiasm was not universal. Gerald describes how some resisted or were dissuaded by their wives and consequently received their just deserts from a vengeful deity.[101]

Much less is known about the preparations made by the French king, Philip II. Although Philip had begun a process of bureaucratisation and financial development that, by the time of his death in 1223, had transformed Capetian France into a major power, he had made only limited progress by the late 1180s.[102] The contract made by Hugh III, duke of Burgundy, with the Genoese on Philip's behalf, in February 1190, was for the transport of 650 knights, 1,300 squires and 1,300 horses: a relatively modest army.[103] However, this does not take account of the forces brought by the king's leading vassals, Hugh of Burgundy himself, Philip of Alsace, count of Flanders, and Hugh, count of St-Pol, as well as those such as the Blois-Champagne contingent, which had travelled in advance of the royal army. 'There did not remain in France,' says Ambroise, 'any great men who did not come to the army at Acre at that time, sooner or later.'[104]

Richard I and Philip II set out from Vézelay in Burgundy on 4 July 1190 in accordance with their previous agreement, but Philip did not arrive in the Holy Land until 20 April 1191, and Richard was even later, only appearing on 8 June.[105] This is despite the fact that Roger of Howden believed – admittedly unrealistically – that the sailing time from the southern French ports was about fifteen days.[106] Part of the problem was logistical, for nobody had had any experience of transporting soldiers, horses, supplies and equipment on this scale by sea; Richard even thought it necessary to carry especially hard stones from Messina for use in his siege engines.[107] Even allowing for such problems, to take nearly a year for a journey of little more than two to three weeks at a time of acute crisis in the siege of Acre seems excessive, and demands some explanation.

At Vézelay, the kings had agreed to meet again at Messina, presumably with the intention of undertaking an autumn passage. Richard arrived on 23 September, a few days after Philip, having waited fruitlessly at Marseille for the fleet.[108] Richard had a direct interest in the kingdom as Joanna, his sister, had been married to William II since 1177 and, as his widow, she was entitled to the return of her dower. However, Tancred of Lecce, who had seized the throne after William had died without direct heirs, proved unco-operative, an attitude exacerbated both by Richard's belligerence and the mutual hostility between the crusaders and the local population, as well as by the evident mistrust between the two kings, which Tancred was able to exploit. Eventually, on 4 October, Richard forced Tancred into a settlement by seizing Messina, and Tancred paid 20,000 ounces of gold in lieu of the dower and a further 20,000 ounces claimed under William II's will, as well as contributing four busses and fifteen galleys to the crusade.[109]

While extra financing for the expedition was evidently welcome, these affairs served to detain Richard late enough in the season to make the passage of a fleet of this size too risky.[110] While the besiegers outside Acre suffered in the appalling conditions of the winter of 1190–1, the two kings thus postponed their departure until the spring. During this time they settled their differences over Richard's proposed marriage to Alice, Philip's sister, which had been constantly delayed since 1169 and was now abandoned. Instead, Richard arranged to marry Berengaria of Navarre and she was brought to Sicily at the end of March 1191 by Eleanor of Aquitaine.[111] Nevertheless, it was costly to remain in Messina. Ambroise says that both Richard and Philip had to subsidise their followers, who 'moaned and complained and grumbled at the expense they incurred'.[112]

Richard finally sailed on 10 April 1191, fortified both by an elaborate ceremony of repentance for his sins undertaken before the English prelates at Messina and by the prophecy of the famous Cistercian abbot Joachim of Fiore that Saladin would be driven out of the Holy Land.[113] 'Never,' says Ambroise admiringly, 'has the sun risen over such a rich fleet.'[114] Richard took a cautious route via Crete and Rhodes, keeping the coasts in sight, for ships carrying horses needed regular stops to take on water, while galleys could be easily swamped in bad weather.[115] Nevertheless, on 12 April, storms broke up the fleet, driving some of his ships well ahead of the main body. Among these were three ships wrecked on the coast of Cyprus, probably on 24 April, causing the drowning of Roger Malcael, Richard's vice-chancellor and seal-bearer.[116] Survivors were taken prisoner by Isaac Comnenus, the independent ruler of the island. Other vessels, including the dromond carrying Joanna and Berengaria, were forced into Limassol.

Isaac had been Byzantine governor of Cyprus and, according to Ambroise, had formed his own alliance with Saladin. Ambroise, with an eye on his potential audience, describes Isaac as 'more treacherous than Judas or Ganelon', and claims that the alliance had been sealed by drinking each other's blood.[117] These apparently chance circumstances caused Richard to launch an attack upon Isaac and, in under a month, between 6 May and 1 June, after meeting comparatively weak resistance, he was able to seize control of the island and to capture Isaac. It was a very useful acquisition, as it was only three days' sailing from the Palestinian mainland and produced a wide array of foodstuffs, vital for a long campaign.[118] Moreover, Isaac was isolated and the island had been there for the taking, as neither Constantinople, from which he had been estranged since 1183, nor Saladin could come to his aid. It was therefore quite possible that the operation was planned in advance; even so, it delayed the king's arrival at Acre even further.[119] Indeed, delegations from the mainland, led by Guy of Lusignan and Philip of Dreux, bishop of Beauvais, on 11 and 20 May respectively, did nothing to deflect him from his evident intention of consolidating his hold on the island.[120]

On 5 June, Richard set out for the Holy Land, landing at Acre three days later. He had spent the previous night before Tyre and then, according to Ambroise, God had sent them a north wind, which blew them south past Scandelion and Casal Imbert. Ambroise is evidently drawing on his own experiences when he describes the king's arrival: 'Then he saw Acre, clearly exposed, with the flower of the world encamped around it. He saw the slopes and the mountains, the valleys and the plains, covered with Turks and tents and men who had it in their hearts to harm Christianity, all there in very great numbers. He saw the tents of Saladin and those of his brother Saphadin, so near to our Christian army that the pagans pressed upon them.'[121]

It is significant that Richard could sail so freely down the coast for, despite some notable successes, the Muslim ships had found it difficult to maintain supplies for Acre in the face of the Christian fleets. Even when they did manage to reach the besieged, they often found they could not sail out again, and when Acre did fall, one of the conditions imposed was that the Muslims should not destroy the ships in the harbour. Richard's galleys actually met a large dromond coming from Beirut, loaded with soldiers, camels, weapons and provisions, and after a fierce battle forced the captain to scuttle it. In true epic style, Ambroise puts words into Saladin's mouth: 'When Saladin heard tell of it he pulled his beard three times, out of sorrow. Then he spoke as a man overcome: "God! Now I have lost Acre, and my people of whom I was sure. You have brought too much misfortune upon me."'[122] Of course, Ambroise did not know what Saladin had actually said, but Ibn Shaddad does interpret the sinking of this ship as one of the signs that the city would fall.[123]

By this time Philip II was already fully engaged in the siege, having arrived on 20 April. His voyage from Messina to Acre had taken twenty-two days, covering 1,325 miles at an average speed of 2.3 knots, considerably quicker than Richard's much larger fleet which went from Messina to Limassol in thirty days, averaging 1.36 knots over a distance of 1,075 miles.[124] Despite 'Imad al-Din's low opinion of his forces, Philip made an immediate impact.[125] Rigord, the Saint-Denis chronicler, says that the whole army welcomed him as 'an angel of the Lord, with hymns, songs of praise and great effusions of tears', an understandable reaction given the suffering of the previous months.[126] Importantly, his provision of subsidies and the appearance of fresh troops made a huge difference to the morale of an army that had been in a very poor state. Even Ambroise, who never has a good word to say for the French, admits that he 'had conducted himself well'.[127]

However, the Muslim sources do not record a major attack until 30 May, which might suggest that it had taken this long to revive the strength and spirits of the besiegers, but the delay may also have been connected to news of the imminent arrival of Richard I. Certainly, the view expressed by Rigord and the *Estoire d'Eracles* that Philip could have taken the city but instead chose to wait for Richard stretches credibility, given the rivalry between the two kings that had emerged while they were in Sicily.[128] As the equally biased author of the second book of the *Itinerarium* sees it, Philip 'was eaten up with envy over King Richard's noble character and success'.[129] On 4 June, furious assaults with trebuchets were supported by tenacious efforts to fill the fosse which, says Ibn Shaddad, 'went so far that they were throwing in all their dead horses and, finally, they were even throwing in their own dead'.[130] There is no doubt that, although the besiegers had endured a terrible winter, the garrison too was worn down; Ibn al-Athir, always more inclined to be critical of Saladin than the two chroniclers in the sultan's employ, thinks that it had not been properly resupplied during the winter.[131] Saladin nevertheless took this new assault very seriously, bringing up forces to Tell al-'Ayadiya in an effort to divert the attackers, apparently with some success as the initial intensity seems to have slackened. Even so, Ibn Shaddad says that this situation lasted until the arrival of King Richard on 8 June.

On the night after Richard's landing, the Muslims could see large fires in the Christian encampment, indicating sizeable reinforcements. 'Their princes', says Ibn Shaddad, 'had been threatening us with his arrival and deserters had been telling us that they were putting off the great push against the city that they wanted to make until his arrival.'[132] Philip II, who in retrospect can be seen to have been planning to return to France as soon as it became possible, wanted to begin a large-scale attack at once. If ever Saladin reflected upon the advice of some of his emirs at the time of Acre's capture that he should destroy the city, it must have been now, for, with the sea covered by Christian ships and the city tightly encircled by trenches, he could do little to help his men within the walls.[133] The only barrier to an immediate assault was Richard's state of health, for almost as soon as he landed, he began to suffer from an unidentified illness, called *arnaldia* or *leonardie* by the chroniclers, which may have been a recurrence of a previous condition.[134] Understandably, he was therefore reluctant to launch an attack, citing the fact that a large part of his fleet, together with the catapults it was carrying, was still detained at Tyre by adverse winds.[135]

Ibn Shaddad says that the Muslims were heartened when they heard of Richard's illness, but in practice it made little difference to the siege since the Franks were now so numerous that they were able to operate in shifts, leaving the defenders without relief and close to exhaustion. By this time their trebuchets had taken the equivalent of a man's height from the tops of the walls.[136] The most serious assault came on 1 July, when an attack led by the French succeeded in breaking down some of the walls.[137] The next day the defenders sent a message to Saladin telling him that unless something were done they would be obliged to surrender. Then, on 4 July, to the sultan's consternation, a group of emirs from inside Acre appeared before him to ask for mercy, having fled the city. Particularly shocking was the desertion of 'Abd al-Qadir al-Halabi, leader of an elite regiment, who, according to 'Imad al-Din, only made amends for his blameworthy act by returning to the city the following night.[138]

Both sides now realised that the end was near and sporadic talks had been under way since late June, but Christian demands for the release of all prisoners and the restoration of all the coastal cities were too great and on 11 July negotiations broke down. 'Our scope for finding ways of dealing with them became limited,' says Ibn Shaddad. On 12 July, a swimmer arrived with a message from the garrison telling Saladin that they were no longer able to continue and soon after 'Imad al-Din reports that they saw Christian flags flying over the town, although they did not know exactly what had happened. In a passage that rings true, Ibn Shaddad describes how he tried to console a distraught Saladin by reminding him of his past achievements. Even then, however, Saladin had not completely given up, beseeching God to induce the Franks to come out to challenge him in a battle that might turn everything around. 'The enemy, however', says Ibn Shaddad, 'did nothing of the sort.'[139]

The terms of the surrender negotiated by al-Mastub, the commander of the garrison, were that the city was to be given up, including all engines, equipment and ships, and payment of 200,000 dinars was to be made. The Muslims were to hand over 1,500 prisoners from the common people and another 100 selected by the Franks, and the True Cross was to be returned. As Conrad of Montferrat had acted as intermediary, he was to receive 10,000 dinars together with another 4,000 dinars for his men. In return the garrison would be permitted to leave with their dependants and personal goods.[140] The kings now divided the spoils between them, causing much resentment among those who had suffered for nearly two years in the siege; the fulfilment of promises that they would receive a share was so delayed that, says Roger of Howden, 'many, forced by poverty, withdrew from them'.[141]

One prominent crusader – Leopold V, duke of Austria – was especially offended. He had arrived from Vienna in the spring of 1191 before the two kings, and at once became *de facto* leader of the German contingent, for Frederick of Swabia was already dead. He therefore believed himself to be entitled to a share of the spoils. According to Richard of Devizes, writing with knowledge of King Richard's later imprisonment in Austria, 'he appeared to claim for himself a part of the triumph. If not at the order at least with the consent of the offended king, the duke's banner was cast into the dirt and trampled upon as an insult to him by his mockers.' The duke did not stay to be humiliated further. 'Later, as quickly as he could, full of wrath, he sailed back to his own land.'[142]

Richard now seems to have tried to persuade Philip to commit himself to another three years in the East, with the aim of achieving a complete conquest. But Philip believed he had done his duty, and on 31 July he sailed to Tyre and from there to France, much to the righteous indignation of the Anglo-Norman chroniclers.[143] Like Richard, he had been ill and, not unreasonably, feared that he might die in Palestine, as so many others had done during the siege. Rank was no protection from disease, as had been shown by the death of Philip of Flanders on 1 June.[144] Moreover, he had concrete political reasons for his renewed presence in France for, with the death of Philip of Flanders, he claimed that Péronne now belonged to the royal demesne.[145] His departure was an evident worry to Richard I, since the French king would certainly threaten his continental lands, despite past promises and Richard's status as a crusader. On the other hand, the situation had its attractions for a man of Richard's personality, leaving him undisputed leader of the crusade. Hugh, duke of Burgundy, left in command of the French, was in no better position to compete with him than Leopold of Austria had been.

Richard's first important act after Philip's departure has been the subject of great controversy ever since, for, on the afternoon of 20 August, he brought 2,700 prisoners held since the fall of Acre to the plain between Tell al-'Ayadiya and Tell Kaisan, and had them all killed. When the Franks retreated 'Imad al-Din was among those who went out to see what had happened. Passing among the naked bodies strewn across the ground, he saw them as martyrs who 'had been stripped in order to be clothed in a robe of the silk of paradise that Allah had generously offered them'.[146] Richard was apparently convinced that Saladin was procrastinating in fulfilling the terms of the agreement made at the fall of the city with the aim of delaying any attempt at reconquest or attempt on Jerusalem and, knowing that he could not take them with him on the forthcoming march, the king had decided to kill them.[147] The Muslim reaction to what was regarded as the king's 'perfidy' was to return the Frankish prisoners due for release to Damascus and to put the True Cross into the treasury. It was never recovered or seen by the crusaders again.

The recapture of Acre was a great triumph for the crusaders, but no substantial damage had been inflicted on Saladin's army and most of his conquests were untouched. Most importantly, he still held Jerusalem and the holy places, which remained the central goal of the crusade and the chief justification for its immense costs in lives and money. Richard therefore had important strategic decisions to make and, despite his flamboyant image, he chose not to take a direct route to Jerusalem, but instead decided to follow the more cautious option which was to lead the army south along the coast, taking advantage of his control of the sea to protect his right flank and using the more mobile elements as a screen on the landward side.[148]

Starting out on 22 August, in a striking demonstration of the skills of fighting on the march, for the next sixteen days the Christians pushed south along the coastal road, most of the time protected at the front by Richard and his household and at the rear by the military orders. Even so, it was hard going. Showers of arrows fell into the main body of the army, killing and wounding both men and horses, while at night the heat and the insects allowed little rest. Captured men and women were taken to Saladin, who had them executed, often having them tortured and mutilated first, 'as he was still in an extreme rage at what had been done to the prisoners at Acre'.[149] For Ambroise, the pain of the human and environmental hazards almost seems to merge. The Turks, he says, were like 'an annoying venomous fly'. In an age when horse armour was a rarity, the damage to and loss of horses were very high, driving the Templars in the rearguard close to despair. The reluctance of many to join the host is hardly surprising, preferring as they did the wine and women of Acre to the hardships and dangers of the march.[150]

On 5 September, talks between Richard and al-Adil had broken up in anger, when Richard had demanded that the Muslims restore the lands they had taken and that they return to what he called their 'own countries'. Sooner or later matters had to come to a head, and they did so on the morning of Saturday the 7th, after the Christian army emerged from a wooded area known as the forest of Arsuf, to the north of the town, and encamped on the plain near the Rochetaille River.[151] Richard had anticipated battle, as he was aware that Saladin had been gathering as large an army as possible, having called in forces from across his empire. Indeed, Saladin had been reconnoitring potential sites almost since the march began. Ibn Shaddad says that he had 'every intention of bringing the enemy to a pitched battle that day'.[152]

The Christian army set out for Arsuf at dawn, organised into twelve squadrons, with the Templars in the van and the Hospitallers in the rearguard.[153] There appear to have been about 1,200 knights and approximately 20,000 foot, a force not dissimilar in size to that at Guy of Lusignan's disposal at Hattin. The Muslims attacked incessantly during the morning and thought that they had the enemy 'in their power', only to be surprised by a mass cavalry charge once the infantry had reached the open ground of the Arsuf plantations. Ibn Shaddad was in the centre when he saw three separate groups charging at the right, left and centre simultaneously and, by his own account, ran first to the left and then to the right in a desperate attempt to save himself. In the end he managed to get back to Saladin and his personal guard, although he had very few men with him. All around men were fleeing in what Ibn Shaddad describes as 'a complete rout'. However, when the attackers pulled up, fearing an ambush, the Muslims had a chance to counterattack, only to be charged again. A third attack by the Christian cavalry enabled them to reach a series of hillocks, where they again halted.[154]

This broadly accorded with what Richard had intended, although the constant fighting during the morning, when many horses were lost, seems to have provoked the Hospitallers into a premature charge, forcing the king's hand. He reacted at once by following up with the Anglo-Norman and Templar forces, and it must have been the sight of these galloping towards him that had put Ibn Shaddad into a panic.[155] This was a Christian victory in the sense that Muslim losses had been very heavy, including several prominent emirs. However, the Muslim army may have been as much as twice the size of that of the Christians, so the damage inflicted was not as great as this figure suggests. It is noticeable that the Muslims were still able to attack the Christian army on 9 September as it made its way to Jaffa, whereas a comparable Christian counter after Hattin would have been inconceivable.[156] Christian losses had been much less, although there was great lamentation at the death of James of Avesnes, unhorsed during the battle and, together with his kinsmen, surrounded by a large group of Turkish soldiers.[157]

The significance of this battle has been much debated. For some it was no more than 'a temporary tactical success', while others think that it provided a second chance to march on Jerusalem, for Saladin's forces were in disarray and crusader morale was high.[158] It is evident, though, that the Muslims who were there did not see it as a routine engagement. Ibn Shaddad says that Saladin could not be consoled, while the troops were 'either wounded in body or wounded in the heart', and Ibn al-Athir's opinion is that, had the Franks continued their pursuit, 'the Muslims would have been destroyed'.[159] The nature of the battle confirms this view. Modern studies show that the lance was the weapon most likely to kill, since its impact and its accuracy were both much greater than those of arrows. Since in this engagement the most evident feature is the series of Christian charges, it is probable that the Muslims suffered far more fatalities than at any other point on the march.[160] Ambroise is equally forthright about the intensity of the battle. Echoing the fears of Fulcher of Chartres over ninety years before, he says: 'In the whole army there was no man who was so confident that he did not wish in his heart that he had finished his pilgrimage.'[161]

Yet, when the Christians reached Jaffa on 10 September, they remained there until 31 October, while Richard refortified and resupplied it and other smaller nearby fortresses, convinced that the coast had to be secured first if it was ever to be viable to hold Jerusalem again. To this end, Jaffa, as it had done ever since the First Crusade, remained a vital means of maintaining the essential links with the West. Saladin's view cannot have been very different, for he spent most of the rest of September dismantling the defences of Ascalon, although he had initially hoped to garrison it. The latter idea appears to have horrified some of his councillors, clearly scarred by recent experiences. 'Imad al-Din says that 'they had been frightened by the events at Acre and its defence over three years which finally ended to the disadvantage of the Muslims'. 'Imad al-Din much regretted what he saw as cowardly advice, but Ibn Shaddad says they argued that otherwise 'the Franks might gain control of it intact, destroy the garrison and use it to take Jerusalem . . . and cut our communications with Egypt'.[162] Much of the demolition was accomplished before the Franks even found out about it.[163]

On the face of it Richard remained confident. In a letter of 1 October, probably meant for general consumption, he said that he hoped to take Jerusalem by mid-January, but in another letter of the same date, sent to Garnier of Rochefort, abbot of Clairvaux, he wrote that, while he believed that the Lord's inheritance would be fully restored, nevertheless money was running out and

'we can in no way remain in Syria beyond next Easter', a perspective somewhat different from that adopted less than three months before, when he had
tried to persuade Philip II to commit himself for the next three years.[164] A
measure of Richard's uncertainty can be seen in his willingness to negotiate,
since, as his letter indicates, it was in Saladin's interest to spin out talks as long
as possible. When, a year later, Richard proposed a truce, Saladin's emirs
advised him to accept on the grounds that, although the Franks could not be
trusted to keep their promises, nevertheless if they dispersed, there would be
no one left in Palestine capable of offering resistance.

At the same time Richard started to talk about mounting an invasion of
Egypt, a plan which, if serious, could not possibly have been implemented
without the Italian fleets. In his capacity as overlord, on 13 October, Richard
confirmed the privileges granted to the Pisans by King Guy, but he needed the
support of their rivals, the Genoese, as well.[165] Two days before, therefore, he
had written to the Genoese consuls, asking them to send forces for such a
venture. 'If indeed you bring your whole fleet of ships, you will receive your
share of the land which, by the help of God, we shall be able to win from the
Saracens in keeping with the agreement that we shall make between us.'[166] On
26 October, Guy confirmed the Genoese privileges at Richard's request.[167] It
is not at all clear whether Richard really intended to attack Egypt before
attempting to capture Jerusalem but, taken in the context of continuing negotiations with al-Adil, all this activity must at the least be seen as an attempt to
increase his bargaining power.

Even so, the Muslims were taken by surprise when, in late October 1191,
Richard made the extraordinary proposal that al-Adil should marry Joanna,
Richard's sister and widow of William II of Sicily. The seat of their power
would be in Jerusalem, and they would hold all the castles, but the local
Franks and the military orders would be satisfied by the restoration of their
lordships on the coast, while the priests and the monks would live in
Jerusalem under a guarantee of safe-conduct. Prisoners on both sides would
be released. According to Ibn Shaddad, who acted as the envoy between
Saladin and al-Adil, Saladin three times approved these terms, mainly because
he did not think that Richard was serious and that 'it was intended to mock
and deceive him'. However, judging by Joanna's furious reaction, it seems that
her brother really did mean it. Even Ibn Shaddad knew about the family row.
'It made her very displeased and angry . . . How could she possibly allow a
Muslim to have carnal knowledge of her!' As far as Richard was concerned, if
this was the problem, then he proposed that al-Adil become a Christian, a
suggestion that Ibn Shaddad thought was intended as a means of keeping the
door open for further negotiation.[168] 'Imad al-Din, who also took part in

discussions about the matter between al-Adil and several leading emirs, has a different view, for he was intrigued by the idea that 'the word war would be transformed into peace, thanks to a woman', and he presents Joanna as having been deterred by the Christian priests from giving her sex to a Muslim, claiming that she 'now abhorred what she had coveted'.[169]

By early 1192, it does seem as though Saladin's policy of delay was working, and to this end he aimed to undermine any peace talks. After one such session, in November 1191, he had told Ibn Shaddad, 'If death should happen to strike me down, these forces are hardly likely to assemble again and the Franks will grow strong. Our best course is to keep on with the Jihad until we expel them from the coast or die ourselves.'[170] Once again the winter weather prevented any large-scale campaigning, as the crusaders struggled to keep their equipment from rusting and rotting. The plan to move on Jerusalem in January was aborted on the advice of the leaders of the military orders and the local baronage, while much time and money were spent refortifying Ascalon after the damage done to it by Saladin's men during the previous September. 'When this news was known, revealed and it was realised that the army was to turn back (let it not be called retreat),' says Ambroise, 'then was the army, which had been so eager in its advance, so discouraged, that not since God created time was there ever seen an army so dejected and so depressed, so disturbed and so astounded, nor so overcome with great sadness.'

Ambroise, ever reluctant to criticise his hero, nevertheless sees this as a missed opportunity for, unknown to the Christians, the Turks were in a weak state, suffering from the winter snows, which had killed many of their horses and other animals. He thinks that had the crusaders attacked, the city would have been taken.[171] He is followed in this by Richard de Templo, but, unlike Ambroise, Richard does not think Jerusalem could have been held for long, for once their pilgrimage had been completed, most of the crusaders would have left for home.[172] Saladin was, indeed, more vulnerable, having allowed the dispersal of many of his troops during the winter season when, on 12 December, he had retreated to Jerusalem. However, he had also spent time reinforcing the city's defences with a deeper fosse and stronger walls, work done through the forced labour of nearly 2,000 Frankish prisoners.[173]

Meanwhile, Saladin knew that Richard was presiding over a fractious and disunited army. Some of the prostitutes whom the king had prevented from accompanying the march south had turned up in Jaffa, having sailed down the coast in whatever ships or boats were available.[174] When, in mid-November 1191, Conrad of Montferrat had proposed a separate peace, it is not surprising that Saladin had seized the opportunity to spread dissension within the Christian ranks.[175] In February 1192, Richard quarrelled with the duke of

Burgundy, who, in common with many other members of the army, returned to Acre. They had parted in acrimony when the duke had asked the king for more money to pay his troops, which Richard was unwilling to provide, presumably because he needed it for the rebuilding of Ascalon. Fighting between the maritime cities had also broken out, with the Pisans taking Guy of Lusignan's side and the Genoese supporting Conrad of Montferrat.[176] By his Easter deadline (which fell on 5 April in 1192), Richard was no nearer to recovering the holy places than he had been six months before. When news quickly followed of problems in England, Richard announced that he would have to leave.[177]

For all Richard's vigour and bravery and evident commitment to the holy war, there are signs that the crusade was beginning to disintegrate around him. He now had no real alternative but to accept the general will that Conrad of Montferrat become king, abandoning his previous support for Guy of Lusignan. As Ambroise says, Guy was now left without a kingdom, despite what the poet saw as his immense contribution to the Christian cause.[178] He was therefore compensated with the island of Cyprus, which Richard knew he could not hold indefinitely himself and which he had initially sold to the Templars.[179] As the Muslims rightly feared Conrad's martial qualities, this may not have been a bad outcome for the Franks in the East, but the arrangement fell apart when, on 28 April 1192, Conrad was killed in Tyre by two members of the Assassins, apparently in revenge for a past insult. This forced another change of policy, and Henry of Champagne was accepted as ruler, marrying the pregnant Isabella on 5 May, only a week after her last husband had been murdered.[180]

The king was now torn between continuing the crusade just when campaigning had become feasible again, or returning to the West to sort out the deteriorating political situation in his own lands. In the end he chose the former, setting about the task with his customary energy. On 22 May, he captured Darum, south of Gaza, and the next month, on 23 June, seized a rich Muslim caravan at the Round Cistern, south of Bait Jibrin, bringing extra resources at a time when, as his letter to the abbot of Clairvaux shows, even the huge sums he had collected for the crusade were running out.[181]

The key event, however, was Richard's decision to make another attempt to reach Jerusalem, and by 11 June he had led the army to Bait Nuba, only about 12 miles from the city, but once there stopped again, waiting for Henry of Champagne to gather further troops from Acre. Again, the leaders discussed the feasibility of an attack, an idea that was strongly supported by the French, but opposed by the Syrian barons and the military orders. In the event both Christians and Muslims were profoundly influenced by the mistakes of the past. Richard was particularly worried about the availability of water in high summer, and ultimately he judged there was no practical way that such a large army could be supplied, a decision that must have been taken in the context of what the local leaders had told him about Hattin.[182] Saladin, on the other hand, was faced with similar divisions within his own camp, for although he wanted to defend Jerusalem, his leading mamluks and emirs feared that, according to Ibn Shaddad, 'they will suffer what happened to those in Acre and then all the lands of Islam will be lost'. They believed they should meet the Franks in pitched battle, an idea unacceptable to Saladin since it risked the loss of Jerusalem.[183]

On 3 July, as if in answer to their Friday prayers, messengers brought Saladin the news that the Christians were withdrawing from their second attempt to march on the holy city. The crusaders were now completely demoralised. 'When, whatever efforts they might put into it,' says Ambroise, '[they realised] all could come to nothing; they would not worship at the Holy Sepulchre which was four leagues away, their hearts were filled with sorrow and they turned back so disheartened and miserable that you never saw a chosen people so depressed and dismayed.'[184] Richard de Templo, writing for a clerical audience, presents it as the just judgment of God, who 'directs times and seasons for the human emotions with inscrutable dispensation'.[185]

There was now talk of an attack on Egypt – a policy much favoured in the thirteenth century as well as previously by King Amalric – but it was never likely that those who had suffered so much to recapture Jerusalem would have been willing to set off in the opposite direction. It is not clear if Saladin thought that Egypt was really threatened, but at the least he did not want his communications with Cairo disrupted, which was a danger after the capture of Darum. This explains his sudden attack on Jaffa on 28 July, which would have succeeded had not Richard launched a daring rescue from the sea.[186]

This was the last great engagement of the Third Crusade. For all its drama, the relief of Jaffa did not change the fundamental situation: ultimately Richard could not destroy Saladin's army, and he could not risk a direct attack on Jerusalem until he had done so. He had left Vézelay in July 1190, over two years before, and now his advisers were pressing him to return to attend to his affairs in the West. He himself was again ill and, according to Ambroise, could see his forces draining away. 'So he would rather seek a truce than leave the land in danger, for everyone else was leaving, openly making for their boats.' On 2 September, he reluctantly agreed to a three-year truce. The Christians would retain the lands between Tyre and Jaffa, but would be obliged to dismantle Ascalon, a condition that particularly upset the king after he had spent so much money restoring it. Antioch and Tripoli were to be included in the peace.[187] The crusaders would be permitted to make pilgrimages to Jerusalem in groups, although in a last vindictive spasm Richard prevented the French from taking part. Those who visited the city did so in a state of some apprehension, believing that Saladin might use the opportunity to take revenge for the massacre outside Acre in August 1191.[188] Those who remained were no more confident. In April 1193, Geoffrey of Donjon, the Hospitaller master, told William of Villaret, the order's preceptor in the West: 'We know for certain that since the loss of the land the inheritance of Christ cannot easily be regained. The land held by the Christians during the truces remains virtually uninhabited.'[189]

The great survivor was Bohemond III. He had made no contribution to the crusade, having appeared only once at the siege of Acre in the summer of 1191, apparently to consult Kings Philip and Richard.[190] Yet Saladin's preoccupation with the crusade had saved Antioch from what, in October 1188, had looked like its inevitable capitulation the following year. In the autumn, after Richard's departure, Bohemond emerged to meet Saladin at Beirut where, says Ibn al-Athir, he 'did obeisance', in return for which 'Saladin bestowed a robe of honour upon him'.[191]

For Saladin, like Richard, the truce represented a scaling down of his ambitions after the triumphs of 1187 and 1188, but he was no more confident than Richard that he could hold his army together. Ibn al-Athir says that some of the emirs argued that if the Franks were not given the opportunity to leave on the autumn sailing, they would be present in Palestine for another year, and the Muslim forces could not sustain that.[192] 'The sultan', says Ibn Shaddad, 'saw that this was for the best because of the weakness, scant resources and longing for home that had overwhelmed our men, and also because of their lack of zeal at Jaffa that he witnessed on the day when he ordered them to attack and they would not. He feared that he might need them and find them gone. He decided to rest them for a while so that they might recover and forget this present state they had come to, and so that he might make the land productive again, supply Jerusalem with all the weapons that he could and have an opportunity to strengthen its defences.' Ibn Shaddad knew that this was not what Saladin had wanted, since he had told him only the previous November that making peace would give the Franks the opportunity to grow strong, but he discerned God's hand in the making of the peace, for Saladin died unexpectedly, on 4 March 1193, less than five months after Richard's departure. 'Had that happened in the course of hostilities, Islam would have been in peril. The peace was nothing but a providential blessing for him.'[193]

Richard I sailed from Acre on 9 October 1192, fully intending to return. As Ambroise presents it: 'In the morning, in the light of day, he turned his face towards Syria and said, that his men could hear and others could listen, "Ah! Syria! I commend you to God. May the Lord God, by His command, grant me the time, if it is His will, that I may come to your help! For I still expect to save you." Then did his ship begin to travel at speed.'[194]

Conclusion

The land of Jerusalem is situated in the centre of the world. It is for the most part mountainous, but the land is extremely fertile. To the east lies Arabia, to the south Egypt, to the west is the Great Sea, and to the north Syria. From ancient times it has been the common homeland of the nations, since they have flocked there from every part to worship at the holy places, as can be read in the Acts of the Apostles about the gift of the Holy Spirit [to] 'the Parthians, the Medes and the Elamites', and others.[1]

THE establishment and maintenance of the crusader states in the littoral of Syria and Palestine and, more briefly, inland beyond the Euphrates was one of the most extraordinary achievements of the high middle ages. Until the battle of Hattin in July 1187, the fall of these states was not inevitable, despite the loss of Edessa in 1144 and the evident internal conflicts and external dangers. The very capable leaders of the first generation of settlers overcame the huge problems that faced them and struggled hard to put down roots in an often hostile environment, and their successors built on their efforts, leaving a lasting mark upon both the urban and rural landscapes.

Their pragmatic approach to the challenge of providing for defence, administration and economic development produced political entities which resist the stereotyping of modern historical constructs and predetermined models.[2] Lacking existing traditions, they produced founding myths of their own, endowing the first crusaders with legendary qualities and solidifying their institutions by imaginative use of the distant past. At their core was the belief – as true for the Latin West as it was for the crusader East – that the holy places belonged to the Christians, even though they had been seized by the Muslims, most particularly by the Arabs, the Kurds and the Turks. Their determination to right this wrong not only took the form of military conquest, but also entailed the rebuilding and embellishment of the holy shrines, actions that, although heavily influenced by both Byzantium and the Latin West, ultimately produced their own independent and vibrant culture.

There could therefore be no compromise with this ideological drive, which had initially been fatally misunderstood by al-Afdal, the Egyptian vizier, when, after driving the Turks out of Jerusalem in 1098, he offered the crusaders access to the holy places in small parties of 200 or 300 under the supervision of his own officials.[3] There is some irony in the fact that, by September 1191, the wheel of fortune had turned full circle, when only designated groups of Christian pilgrims were allowed to make hasty and fearful obeisance at the shrines in and around Jerusalem to which Saladin had granted them entry.[4] Richard I knew he had left unfinished business, but the Nazareth capitals, with their confident theme of the mission of the Apostles, remained buried until 1908, symbolising both the sophisticated achievements of the crusader states in the twelfth century and the dramatic destruction of the society that had created them.

Chronology

18–28 November 1095	Council of Clermont
March 1098	Baldwin of Boulogne takes over rule of Edessa
3 June 1098	Fall of Antioch to the crusaders
17 June 1099	Crusader ships occupy Jaffa
15 July 1099	Crusaders capture Jerusalem
22 July 1099	Election of Godfrey of Bouillon as ruler of Jerusalem
1 August 1099	Election of Arnulf of Chocques as patriarch of Jerusalem
12 August 1099	Crusaders defeat the Egyptians at Ascalon
25 December 1099	Daibert, archbishop of Pisa, crowned patriarch of Jerusalem
18 July 1100	Death of Godfrey of Bouillon
Mid-August 1100	Capture of Bohemond by the Danishmend Turk, Malik Ghazi
20 August 1100	Capture of Haifa by the Latins
2 October 1100	Baldwin of Boulogne departs from Edessa, which he cedes to Baldwin of Bourcq
25 December 1100	Coronation of Baldwin of Boulogne as king of Jerusalem
c.28 March 1101	Tancred becomes regent of Antioch
29 April 1101	Capture of Arsuf by the Latins
17 May 1101	Capture of Caesarea by the Latins
August–September 1101	Defeat of crusading forces in Asia Minor by the Seljuk sultan, Kilij Arslan

7 September 1101	Baldwin defeats the Egyptians at the battle of Ramla
14 April 1102	Raymond of Toulouse defeats forces from Damascus and Homs near Tortosa
17–27 May 1102	Baldwin meets the Egyptians, finally defeating them near Jaffa
May 1103	Release of Bohemond
7–8 May 1104	Defeat of combined Christian forces at the battle of Harran, and capture of Baldwin of Bourcq and Joscelin of Courtenay
26 May 1104	Capture of Acre by the Latins
Autumn 1104	Bohemond and Daibert sail for the West
28 February 1105	Death of Raymond of Toulouse, who is succeeded by William-Jordan, count of Cerdagne, his cousin
27 August 1105	Baldwin defeats the Egyptians at the third battle of Ramla
Mid-August 1108	Release of Baldwin of Bourcq
September 1108	Treaty of Devol between Bohemond and Alexius I
June 1109	Royal assembly near Tripoli
Late June 1109	Murder of William-Jordan
26 June 1109	Fall of Tripoli to the Latins
13 May 1110	Fall of Beirut to the Latins
5 December 1110	Fall of Sidon to the Latins
March 1111	Death of Bohemond
Before 3 February 1112	Death of Bertrand of Toulouse and succession of his son, Pons
12 December 1112	Death of Tancred, leaving regency of Antioch to Roger of Salerno
15 February 1113	Grant of *Pie postulatio voluntatis* to the Hospitallers by Pope Paschal II
August 1113	Marriage of Baldwin I to Adelaide of Sicily
2 October 1113	Murder of Mawdud of Mosul
1114	Arnulf of Chocques, patriarch of Jerusalem, imposes the Augustinian Rule on the canons of the Holy Sepulchre
29 November 1114	Major earthquake in Syria
14 September 1115	Victory of Roger of Antioch over Bursuq, lord of Hamadhan

Autumn 1115	Establishment of the castle of Montreal (Shawbak)
25 April 1117	Departure of Adelaide of Sicily from the kingdom of Jerusalem after the annulment of her marriage to Baldwin I
22 March 1118	Latin forces under Baldwin I take Farama in the Nile Delta
2 April 1118	Death of Baldwin I
14 April 1118	Consecration of Baldwin of Bourcq as king of Jerusalem
15 August 1118	Death of Alexius Comnenus, Byzantine emperor
25 December 1119	Coronation of Baldwin II and Morphia
28 June 1119	Defeat and death of Roger of Antioch at Balat, the 'Field of Blood', by Il-Ghazi, ruler of Mardin
August–September 1119	Joscelin of Courtenay becomes count of Edessa
c.1119	Beginnings of the Templars
16 January 1120	Council of Nablus
5 December 1121	Death of al-Afdal, Egyptian vizier
1122–4	Venetian Crusade
13 September 1122	Capture of Joscelin of Courtenay by Nur al-Daulak Balak
8 November 1122	Death of Il-Ghazi
18 April 1123	Capture of Baldwin II by Balak
1123	*Pactum Warmundi*
8 August 1123	Escape of Joscelin of Courtenay from captivity
February–July 1124	Siege and capture of Tyre by the Latins
6 May 1124	Death of Balak
24 August 1124	Release of Baldwin II
October 1124–January 1125	Failed siege of Aleppo by Baldwin II
2 May 1125	*Privilegium Balduini*
Autumn 1126	Arrival of Bohemond II in Antioch
1127	Death of Fulcher of Chartres
Autumn 1127	Embassy from the kingdom of Jerusalem to Fulk of Anjou
September 1127	'Imad al-Din Zengi appointed governor of Mosul

11 February 1128	Death of Tughtigin of Damascus
31 May 1128	Fulk of Anjou takes the Cross
June 1128	Zengi granted Aleppo
13 January 1129	Council of Troyes
2 June 1129	Marriage of Fulk of Anjou and Melisende of Jerusalem
Early November 1129	Assassins hand over Banyas to the Latins
Mid-November –6 December 1129	Failed attack on Damascus by Baldwin II and Fulk of Anjou
1130	Revolt of Alice of Antioch
February 1130	Death of Bohemond II
21 August 1131	Death of Baldwin II
1 October 1131	Death of Joscelin of Courtenay, who is succeeded by his son, Joscelin II
Autumn 1131	Revolt of Pons of Tripoli
December 1132	Latins lose Banyas
Late 1134	Revolt of Hugh of Le Puiset and Romanus of Le Puy
c.1135	Commissioning of the Melisende Psalter
Autumn 1135	Death of Bernard of Valence, first Latin patriarch of Antioch
Late 1135/early 1136	Revolt of Alice of Antioch
Spring 1136	Raymond of Poitiers marries Constance of Antioch
25 March 1137	Death of Pons of Tripoli
Summer 1137	Campaign of John Comnenus, Byzantine emperor, in Cilicia and Antioch
August 1137	Defeat of Fulk at Montferrand by Zengi and loss of the town
Before 1138	Marriage of Raymond II of Tripoli to Hodierna of Jerusalem
5 February 1138	Establishment of the convent of Bethany
April–May 1138	Failed attempt to take Shaizar by the Byzantines and the Latins
June 1138	Zengi takes Homs
Summer 1139	Pilgrimage of Thierry of Flanders
Spring 1140	Aimery of Limoges chosen as patriarch of Antioch
12 June 1140	Latins regain Banyas
December 1140	Council of Antioch

1142	Building of the castle of Kerak by Pagan the Butler
1142	Raymond II of Tripoli cedes Le Crat (Hisn al-Akrad) to the Hospitallers
Autumn 1142	John Comnenus campaigns in Antioch and Edessa
8 April 1143	Death of John Comnenus
10 November 1143	Death of King Fulk
25 December 1143	Coronation of Melisende and Baldwin III
23–24 December 1144	Capture of Edessa by Zengi
1 December 1145	Bull *Quantum praedecessores*
14 September 1146	Death of Zengi
November/December 1146	Joscelin II and Baldwin of Marash retake Edessa
December 1146	Nur al-Din, Zengi's second son, regains Edessa
May 1147	Unsuccessful invasion of the Hauran by Baldwin III
Early April 1148	Arrival of Conrad III of Germany at Acre
24 June 1148	Assembly of the leaders of the Second Crusade at Palmarea
24–28 July 1148	Unsuccessful attack on Damascus by the forces of the Second Crusade
29 June 1149	Defeat and death of Raymond of Poitiers by Nur al-Din at the battle of Inab
15 July 1149	Consecration of the church of the Holy Sepulchre
May 1150	Capture of Joscelin II of Edessa
August 1150	Evacuation of the Latins from the county of Edessa
31 March 1152	Baldwin III's crowning with a laurel in Jerusalem, resulting in the partition of the kingdom
April 1152	Baldwin III seizes power and Melisende retires to Nablus
April/May 1152	Baldwin III holds a High Court at Tripoli. Murder of Raymond II of Tripoli by Assassins
Spring 1153	Reynald of Châtillon marries Constance of Antioch

22 August 1153	Latins capture Ascalon
25 April 1154	Nur al-Din takes over Damascus
1155	Reynald of Châtillon attacks Byzantine Cyprus
19 June 1157	Defeat of Baldwin III at Jacob's Ford by Nur al-Din
Autumn 1157	Third expedition of Thierry of Flanders
September 1158	Marriage of Baldwin III and Theodora, niece of Manuel Comnenus
December 1158	Submission of Reynald of Châtillon to Manuel Comnenus at Mamistra
12 April 1159	Ceremonial entry of Manuel Comnenus into Antioch
Early 1161	Campaign of Baldwin III to al-Arish
11 September 1161	Death of Queen Melisende
November 1161	Capture of Reynald of Châtillon by Majd al-Din of Aleppo
10 February 1163	Death of Baldwin III
18 February 1163	Coronation of King Amalric
1163	Bohemond III gains power in Antioch
c.1163	Issue of the *assise sur la ligece* by King Amalric
September 1163	First campaign of King Amalric to Egypt
August–October 1164	Amalric's second Egyptian campaign
10 August 1164	Battle of Artah
12 August 1164	Capture of Harim by Nur al-Din
18 October 1164	Capture of Banyas by Nur al-Din
1165	Athanasius Manasses installed as Orthodox patriarch of Antioch
January–August 1167	Amalric's third Egyptian campaign
1167	Beginning of Franco-Byzantine redecoration of the church of the Nativity at Bethlehem
August 1167	Frankish occupation of Alexandria
29 August 1167	Marriage of Amalric and Maria Comnena
October 1168–January 1169	Amalric's fourth Egyptian campaign
23 March 1169	Death of Shirkuh
October–December 1169	Amalric's fifth Egyptian campaign
29 June 1170	Major earthquake in Syria
From 1170	Hospitaller rebuilding of Crac des Chevaliers

Spring 1171	Amalric's visit to Constantinople
10 September 1171	Saladin proclaims Egyptian allegiance to the Abbasid caliphate
1173	Murder of the Assassin envoy by the Templars
Early 1174	Raymond III of Tripoli released from Muslim captivity
15 May 1174	Death of Nur al-Din
11 July 1174	Death of Amalric
15 July 1174	Coronation of Baldwin IV
28 July–2 August 1174	Unsuccessful Sicilian attack on Alexandria
October 1174	Murder of Miles of Plancy, seneschal of Jerusalem. Raymond of Tripoli chosen as *bailli* of Jerusalem
28 October 1174	Saladin enters Damascus
Summer 1176	Release of Reynald of Châtillon and Joscelin of Courtenay from Muslim captivity
17 September 1176	Battle of Myriocephalon
November 1176	Marriage of Sibylla of Jerusalem and William Longsword
August 1177–April 1178	Crusade of Philip of Alsace, count of Flanders
25 November 1177	Battle of Mont Gisard
10 June 1179	Victory of Saladin over Latin forces at Marj Ayun
24–29 August 1179	Destruction of the castle at Jacob's Ford by Saladin
April 1180	Marriage of Sibylla of Jerusalem and Guy of Lusignan
May 1180	Truce between Saladin and Baldwin IV
24 September 1180	Death of Manuel Comnenus
February 1183	Council agrees levy of an extraordinary general tax in the kingdom of Jerusalem
February 1183	Reynald of Châtillon's ships attack Aqaba and Aydhab on the Red Sea
11 June 1183	Saladin gains control of Aleppo
29 September–8 October 1183	Stand-off between the armies of Saladin and Guy of Lusignan in Galilee
20 November 1183	Guy of Lusignan removed as *bailli*
November 1183	Baldwin V crowned co-ruler

July 1184–July 1185	Embassy of the patriarch and the masters of the military orders to the West
Early April 1185	Raymond of Tripoli reappointed *bailli*
Spring 1185	Raymond of Tripoli makes four-year truce with Saladin
15 April 1185	Probable date of the death of Baldwin IV
Late summer 1186	Death of Baldwin V and coronation of Sibylla and Guy
Early 1187	Attack by Reynald of Châtillon on a Muslim caravan, breaking the truce
February 1187	Hospitallers purchase the castle of Marqab
1 May 1187	Battle of the Springs of the Cresson
4 July 1187	Battle of Hattin
10 July 1187	Capture of Acre by Saladin
14 July 1187	Arrival of Conrad of Montferrat at Tyre
2 October 1187	Fall of the city of Jerusalem to Saladin
29 October 1187	Issue of *Audita tremendi*
November–December 1187	Unsuccessful siege of Tyre by Saladin
Summer 1188	Arrival of Sicilian fleet under Margaritus of Brindisi off Syrian coast
October 1188	Saladin agrees to eight-month truce with Bohemond III of Antioch
28 August 1189	Beginning of the siege of Acre by Guy of Lusignan
4 October 1189	Defeat of Christian forces outside Acre by Saladin
22 April 1190	Surrender of Beaufort to Saladin
7 October 1190	Arrival of Frederick of Swabia at Acre
Before 21 October 1190	Death of Queen Sibylla and her daughters
24 November 1190	Marriage of Conrad of Montferrat and Isabella of Jerusalem
May 1191	Richard I seizes Cyprus from Isaac Comnenus
12 July 1191	Fall of Acre to the combined crusader forces
20 August 1191	Massacre of the Muslim prisoners by Richard
7 September 1191	Battle of Arsuf
21 October 1191	Richard proposes that al-Adil marry his sister, Joanna
After 6 January 1192	Richard abandons march on Jerusalem

28 April 1192	Murder of Conrad of Montferrat by the Assassins
c.2 May 1192	Henry of Champagne elected king of Jerusalem
5 May 1192	Marriage of Henry of Champagne and Isabella of Jerusalem
After 5 May 1192	Guy of Lusignan takes over government of Cyprus
3 July 1192	Richard abandons march on Jerusalem a second time
1 August 1192	Richard retakes Jaffa from Saladin
2 September 1192	Treaty of Jaffa
9 October 1192	Richard leaves the Holy Land
4 March 1193	Death of Saladin

Abbreviations

AA	Albert of Aachen, *Historia Ierosolimitana*, ed. and tr. S.B. Edgington, Oxford, 2007
Cart.	*Cartulaire général de l'Ordre des Hospitaliers de Saint-Jean de Jérusalem, 1100–1310*, 4 vols, ed. J. Delaville Le Roulx, Paris, 1894–1905
Cont. WT	*La Continuation de Guillaume de Tyr (1184–1197)*, ed. M. R. Morgan, Documents relatifs à l'histoire des croisades publiés par l'Académie des Inscriptions et Belles-Lettres, Paris, 1982
Eracles	*L'Estoire d'Eracles empereur et la conqueste de la Terre d'Outremer*, in RHCr, Occidentaux, vols 1 and 2, Paris, 1859
Ernoul-Bernard	*Chronique d'Ernoul et de Bernard le Trésorier*, ed. L. de Mas Latrie, Société de l'Histoire de France, Paris, 1871
FC	*Fulcheri Carnotensis Historia Hierosolymitana*, ed. H. Hagenmeyer, Heidelberg, 1913
JP	*Jerusalem Pilgrimage, 1099–1185*, ed. J. Wilkinson, Hakluyt Society, series II, 167, London, 1988
MGHSS	Monumenta Germaniae Historica, Scriptores
ODCC	*The Oxford Dictionary of the Christian Church*, ed. F.L. Cross; 3rd edn, ed. E.A. Livingstone, Oxford, 1997
PL	*Patrologiae cursus completus: Series Latina*, ed. J.P. Migne
RHCr	*Recueil des historiens des croisades*
RHG	*Recueil des historiens des Gaules et de la France*
ROL	*Revue de l'Orient Latin*
RRH	*Regesta Regni Hierosolymitani*, ed. R. Röhricht, 2 vols, Innsbruck, 1893–1904
RS	Rolls Series

ULKJ   *Die Urkunden der Lateinischen Könige von Jerusalem*, 4 vols, ed. H.E. Mayer, Altfranzösische Texte erstellt von Jean Richard, Monumenta Germaniae Historica, Hanover, 2010

WC   *Galterii Cancellarii Bella Antiochena*, ed. H. Hagenmeyer, Innsbruck, 1896

WT   Guillaume de Tyr, *Chronique*, ed. R.B.C. Huygens, 2 vols, Corpus Christianorum, Continuatio Mediaevalis, 63 and 63A, Turnhout, 1986

Notes

Introduction

1. Baha' al-Din Ibn Shaddad, *The Rare and Excellent History of Saladin*, tr. D.S. Richards, Crusade Texts in Translation, 7, Aldershot, 2001, pp. 185–6.

1 The Expedition to Jerusalem

1. *Die Kreuzzugsbriefe aus Jahren 1088–1100*, ed. H. Hagenmeyer, Innsbruck, 1901, no. II, pp. 136–7. Tr. L. and J. Riley-Smith, *The Crusades: Idea and Reality 1095–1274*, Documents of Medieval History, 4, London, 1981, p. 38. Accounts of the treatment of Christian pilgrims are inadequate and contradictory, but the belief in the persecution of the eastern Church seems to have been a fixed element of papal rhetoric since the time of Gregory VII.
2. M. Bull, 'The Roots of Lay Enthusiasm for the First Crusade', *History*, 78 (1993), 360–1.
3. FC, 1.6, pp. 153–63, 1.10, pp. 183–5. Fulcher of Chartres (1059–1127) was probably a canon in the cathedral chapter. He set out on the crusade in the army of Stephen of Blois, but in October 1097 became chaplain to Baldwin of Boulogne, accompanying him on his expedition to Edessa. He seems to have written his chronicle in three phases, from 1100–1 to 1105, from 1109 onwards, and then a revision after 1124. See V. Epp, *Fulcher von Chartres: Studien zur Geschichtsschreibung des ersten Kreuzzuges*, Düsseldorf, 1990, pp. 24–35.
4. See J. France, *Victory in the East: A military history of the First Crusade*, Cambridge, 1994, pp. 2–3, 122–42.
5. FC, 1.6, p. 161.
6. See J.H. Pryor, 'A View From a Masthead: the First Crusade From the Sea', *Crusades*, 7 (2008), 148.
7. Ibn al-Qalanisi, *The Damascus Chronicle of the Crusades*, tr. H.A.R. Gibb, London, 1932, p. 41.
8. France, *Victory in the East*, p. 95. On 'arms-bearers', see M. Bull, *Knightly Piety and the Lay Response to the First Crusade: The Limousin and Gascony, c.970–c.1130*, Oxford, 1993, p. 16. This term is intended to cover a wide range of warriors from great territorial princes to ordinary mounted soldiers. It avoids the connotations of the word 'knight'.
9. France, *Victory in the East*, p. 102.
10. See T. Asbridge, *The First Crusade: A New History*, London, 2004, for a detailed and balanced account of the expedition.
11. Hagenmeyer, *Kreuzzugsbriefe*, no. IV, p. 139. *Letters from the East: Crusaders, Pilgrims and Settlers in the 12th–13th Centuries*, tr. M. Barber and K. Bate, Crusade Texts in Translation, 18, Farnham, 2010, no. 1, p. 16.
12. France, *Victory in the East*, p. 116.
13. AA, 2.18, pp. 88–91.
14. AA, 2.16, pp. 84–7.
15. *Le 'Liber' de Raymond d'Aguilers*, ed. J.H. and L.L. Hill, Documents relatifs à l'histoire des croisades publiés par l'Académie des Inscriptions et Belles-Lettres, Paris, 1969, p. 41. Raymond d'Aguilers, *Historia Francorum Qui Ceperunt Iherusalem*, tr. J.H. and L.L. Hill, Philadelphia, 1968, pp. 23–4. See J.H. and L. Hill, *Raymond IV, Count of Toulouse*, New York, 1962, p. 51.

16. Anna Comnena, *The Alexiad of the Princess Anna Comnena*, tr. E.A.S. Dawes, London, 1928, 10.5, p. 250, 11.4, p. 258.
17. See P. Magdalino, 'The Pen of the Aunt: Echoes of the Mid-Twelfth Century in the Alexiad', in *Anna Komnene and her Times*, ed. T. Gouma-Peterson, New York, 2000, pp. 15-43.
18. See B.Z. Kedar, 'The Jerusalem Massacre of July 1099 in the Western Historiography of the Crusades', *Crusades*, 3 (2004), 15-75. He concludes that the killings that took place between 15 and 17 July were on a considerably greater scale than massacres in other towns taken by storm, but that near-contemporaries who were not present and post-medieval writers have been more strongly influenced by 'basic values and attitudes' than by the eyewitnesses.
19. France, *Victory in the East*, pp. 2-3. The distance from Paris or Cologne via Constantinople.
20. An atabeg was in origin a guardian of a young Seljuk prince, but often became a ruler in his own right, as was the case with Kerbogha. He had brought together his own coalition of Muslim forces. See Asbridge, *First Crusade*, pp. 202-4. For the fleets, see Pryor, 'A View from a Masthead', 143-7.
21. See N. Jaspert, 'Ein Polymythos: Die Kreuzzüge', in *Mythen in der Geschichte*, ed. H. Altrichter, K. Herbers and H. Neuhaus, Freiburg im Breisgau, 2004, pp. 205-8.
22. S. Runciman, *A History of the Crusades*, vol. 1, Cambridge, 1951, pp. 104-5.
23. Imperial representatives had travelled as far as southern England for this purpose: see C.J. Tyerman, *England and the Crusades 1095-1588*, Chicago, 1988, p. 14.
24. Anna Comnena does not mention any request by Alexius, since if he had initiated the expedition he could have been blamed for the problems that the Latins caused the empire: see Magdalino, 'Pen of the Aunt', pp. 25-6.
25. E.O. Blake and C. Morris, 'A Hermit Goes to War: Peter and the Origins of the First Crusade', in *Studies in Church History*, 22 (1985), pp. 79-108. See also A. Jotischky, 'The Christians of Jerusalem, the Holy Sepulchre and the Origins of the First Crusade', *Crusades*, 7 (2008), 35-57. For Symeon II, see J. Pahlitzsch, *Graeci und Suriani im Palästina der Kreuzfahrerzeit*, Berliner Historische Studien, 33, Berlin, 2001, pp. 46-60.
26. AA, 1.2-5, pp. 1-9.
27. Michael the Syrian, *Chronique de Michel le Syrien, Patriarche Jacobite d'Antioche*, ed. and tr. J.-B. Chabot, vol. 3, Paris, 1905, 15.7, p. 182.
28. Hagenmeyer, *Kreuzzugsbriefe*, no. XVI, p. 164.
29. See P.E. Chevedden, '"A Crusade from the First": The Norman Conquest of Islamic Sicily, 1060-1091', *Al-Masāq*, 22 (2010), 191-225.
30. See I.S. Robinson, 'Gregory VII and the Soldiers of Christ', *History*, 58 (1973), 169-92.
31. Gregory VII, *The Correspondence of Gregory VII*, ed. and tr. E. Emerton, New York, 1959, pp. 60-1.
32. See F.H. Russell, *The Just War in the Middle Ages*, Cambridge, 1975, 16-39, and C. Erdmann, *The Origin of the Idea of the Crusade*, tr. M.W. Baldwin and W. Goffart, Princeton, NJ, 1977 (originally 1935), pp. 229-68.
33. See A.C. Krey, 'Urban's Crusade – Success or Failure', *American Historical Review*, 53 (1948), 235-50; J.A. Brundage, 'Adhemar of Le Puy: The Bishop and his Critics', *Speculum*, 34 (1959), 201-12.
34. AA, 1, 2-5, pp. 4-7, 6.39, pp. 452-3; Hagenmeyer, *Kreuzzugsbriefe*, no. VI, pp. 141-2; no. IX, pp. 146-9. France, *Victory in the East*, p. 210, thinks that Adhémar actually sailed to Cyprus to meet the patriarch and helped compose Symeon's letter of January 1098.
35. See Bull, *Knightly Piety*, pp. 115-54, and J. Riley-Smith, *The First Crusaders, 1095-1131*, Cambridge, 1997, pp. 23-39.
36. Bull, 'Roots', 369.
37. Ralph of Caen, *Radulphi Cadomensis Tancredus*, ed. E. D'Angelo, Corpus Christianorum Continuatio Mediaevalis, 231, Turnhout, 2011, pp. 6-7. Tr. B.S. Bachrach and D.S. Bachrach, Crusade Texts in Translation, 12, Aldershot, 2005, p. 22. This passage is convincing because the expiatory pilgrimage to Jerusalem was a marked feature of Norman aristocratic life throughout the twelfth century: see, for example, Orderic Vitalis, *Ecclesiastical History*, vol. 2, ed. and tr. M. Chibnall, Oxford, 1969, pp. 10-11, 14-15, 68-9. Orderic was a monk at St Evroul, south of La Ferté in Normandy, who, among many other subjects, wrote about the Normans and their participation in the crusades during the first four decades of the twelfth century.
38. For example, as described by the anonymous Norman participant and chronicler, *Gesta Francorum*, ed. and tr. R. Hill, London, 1982, p. 40.
39. Hagenmeyer, *Kreuzzugsbriefe*, no. VI, p. 142. Tr. Barber and Bate, *Letters from the East*, no. 2, p. 18.
40. J. Richard, 'Départs de pèlerins et de croisés bourguignons au XIe s.: à propos d'une charte de Cluny', *Annales de Bourgogne*, 60 (1988), 140-2.

41. On the attraction of the religious sites in the Holy Land, see N. Jaspert, 'Das Heilige Grab, das Wahre Kreuz, Jerusalem und das Heilige Land. Wirkung, Wandel und Vermittler hochmittelalterlicher Attraktoren', in *Konflikt und Bewältigung. Die Zerstörung der Grabeskirche zu Jerusalem im Jahre 1009*, ed. T. Pratsch, Berlin, 2011, pp. 69–74. See Riley-Smith, *First Crusaders*, pp. 15–22, for a review of modern explanations of the motives of the crusaders, and J. Richard, *The Crusades, c.1071-c.1291*, tr. J. Birrell, Cambridge, 1999 (originally 1996), p. 7, for the issues raised by the idea of a 'land crisis' in the late eleventh century.

42. J. Riley-Smith, *The First Crusade and the Idea of Crusading*, London, 1986, pp. 43–6.

43. G. Duby, *La société aux XIe et XIIe siècles dans la région maconnaise*, Paris, 1971, p. 239.

44. G. Constable, 'The Financing of the Crusades in the Twelfth Century', in *Outremer: Studies in the Crusading Kingdom of Jerusalem Presented to Joshua Prawer*, ed. B.Z. Kedar, H.E. Mayer and R.C. Smail, Jerusalem, 1982, pp. 64–88. See, too, the value of wills as a means of understanding motivation, Jaspert, 'Das Heilige Grab, das Wahre Kreuz, Jerusalem und das Heilige Land', pp. 74–83.

45. FC, 1.32, pp. 318–22. For example, Robert of Normandy, who is presented by Orderic Vitalis as motivated by a desire to escape the problems of governing Normandy, but at the same time driven by a powerful need to visit the holy places and to expiate his sins; see W.M. Aird, *Robert Curthose, Duke of Normandy (c.1050-1134)*, Woodbridge, 2008, pp. 158–9.

46. AA, 6.36, pp. 448–9; FC, 2.6, p. 388.

47. Robert the Monk, *Historia Iherosolimitana*, in RHCr, Occid., vol. 3, Paris, 1866, 1.1, p. 728. Tr. C. Sweetenham, *History of the First Crusade*, Crusade Texts in Translation, 11, Aldershot, 2005, p. 80.

48. Bull, *Knightly Piety*, p. 169.

49. Raymond of Aguilers, p. 141. Tr. Hill and Hill, p. 119: *Histoire Anonyme de la Première Croisade*, ed. L. Bréhier, Paris, 1924, p. 14.

50. Raymond of Aguilers, p. 88. Moreover, Raymond had not made extensive alienations and sales before his departure; Hill and Hill, *Raymond IV*, p. 37. William of Malmesbury, *Gesta Regum Anglorum: The History of the English Kings*, vol. 1, ed. and tr. R.A.B. Mynors, completed by R.M. Thomson and M. Winterbottom, Oxford, 1998, pp. 696–7, says that he had resolved never to return to Provence, but he was writing in the knowledge of Raymond's endeavours in Asia Minor and Syria between 1100 and 1105. William (c.1095-c.1143) had entered the Benedictine house of Malmesbury as an oblate. His view of Raymond of Toulouse probably dates from the mid-1120s.

51. Raymond of Aguilers, pp. 152–5. Tr. Hill and Hill, pp. 129–32.

52. Raymond of Aguilers, p. 46. See Hill and Hill, *Raymond IV*, pp. 62–3.

53. WT, 11.2, p. 497.

54. Richard, *Crusades*, p. 77.

55. H.E. Mayer, 'Études sur l'histoire de Baudouin Ier roi de Jérusalem', in *Mélanges sur l'histoire du royaume latin de Jérusalem*, Paris, 1984, pp. 15–16, 21–31, 43–7.

56. AA, 6.37, pp. 450–1. This observation is supported by modern research. Jonathan Riley-Smith identified twenty-eight individuals who stayed with Godfrey, of whom twelve came from the duke's household. These included important lords like his relative Warner, count of Grez in Brabant: 'The motives of the earliest crusaders and the settlement of Latin Palestine, 1095–1100', *English Historical Review*, 98 (1983), 724–30.

57. WT, 10.1, p. 453.

58. Mayer, 'Études', pp. 13–15, 32–50.

59. Ralph of Caen, pp. 7–8. See E. Jamison, *The Norman Administration of Apulia and Capua*, ed. D. Clementi and T. Közler, Darmstadt, 1987 (originally 1913), p. 226; R.B. Yewdale, *Bohemond I, Prince of Antioch*, Princeton, NJ, 1924, pp. 26–33.

60. Richard of Poitiers, *Chronica*, MGHSS, vol. 26, Hanover, 1882, p. 79. See Yewdale, *Bohemond I*, pp. 10–24.

61. See G. Beech, 'A Norman-Italian Adventurer in the East: Richard of Salerno, 1097–1112', in *Anglo-Norman Studies*, 15, *Proceedings of the XV Battle Conference and of the XI Colloquio Medievale of the Officina di Studi Medievali*, ed. M. Chibnall, Woodbridge, 1992, pp. 25–9.

62. Ekkehard of Aura, *Hierosolymitani*, in RHCr, Occid., vol. 5, Paris, 1895, cap. VIII, p. 17.

63. For example, one of the villages in Godfrey's grant was al-Bira, called Magna Mahumeria by the Franks, a name that suggests a previous Muslim population; see Chapter 9, pp. 227–8.

64. See M. Nader, *Burgesses and Burgess Law in the Latin Kingdoms of Jerusalem and Cyprus (1099-1325)*, Aldershot, 2006, pp. 2–3.

65. FC, 1.29, p. 304.

66. France, *Victory in the East*, pp. 122–42; Riley-Smith, *First Crusade and the Idea of Crusading*, pp. 63–5.
67. *Le Cartulaire du Chapitre du Saint-Sépulcre de Jérusalem*, ed. G. Bresc-Bautier, Documents relatifs à l'histoire des croisades publiés par l'Académie des Inscriptions et Belles-Lettres, Paris, 1984, no. 26, pp. 86–8, which is the 1114 confirmation of King Baldwin. The greater part of this cartulary was compiled c.1165 and can be considered an organic whole. Further acts, which extend as far as 1244, are of a more fragmentary nature. See the editor's analysis, pp. 8–20. See D. Pringle, 'Magna Mahumeria (al-Bīra): The Archaeology of a Frankish New Town in Palestine', in *Crusade and Settlement*, ed. P.W. Edbury, Cardiff, 1985, pp. 147–8.
68. FC, 1.14, pp. 203–15.
69. See France, *Victory in the East*, pp. 319–23.
70. Raymond of Aguilers, p. 143. Tr. Hill and Hill, p. 121.
71. Raymond of Aguilers, p. 152.
72. William of Malmesbury, pp. 702–3; Henry, archdeacon of Huntingdon, *Historia Anglorum: The History of the English People*, ed. and tr. D. Greenway, Oxford Medieval Texts, Oxford, 1996, 7.18, pp. 442–3. These chroniclers were evidently making a moral point, asserting that his later, blighted life was the consequence of his refusal, which had incurred God's displeasure. See C.W. David, *Robert Curthose, Duke of Normandy*, Cambridge, Mass., 1920, p. 114, who calls this story 'a later invention', and Aird, *Robert Curthose*, pp. 185–6, who is less sceptical and thinks that he may have been seriously considered as a candidate. Unlike Raymond, Robert had no historian in his retinue; had there been such a writer, the respective parties might have been presented rather differently.
73. R. Hiestand, 'Some Reflections on the Impact of the Papacy on the Crusader States and the Military Orders in the Twelfth and Thirteenth Centuries', in *The Crusades and the Military Orders: Expanding the Frontiers of Medieval Latin Christianity*, ed. Z. Hunyadi and J. Laszovsky, Budapest, 2001, pp. 10–11.
74. See A.V. Murray, *The Crusader Kingdom of Jerusalem: A Dynastic History, 1099–1125*, Oxford, 2000, pp. 63–77, for a full discussion of the issues raised by Godfrey's titles and the literature on the subject. Jonathan Riley-Smith has pointed out that the title *advocatus* is used only once in contemporary sources and that this is in a letter composed when Godfrey was not present, even though he is presented as a party to it: 'The Title of Godfrey of Bouillon', *Bulletin of the Institute of Historical Research*, 52 (1979), 83–6.
75. Raymond of Aguilers, p. 58. Indeed, it appears that later in the twelfth century it was said in Zengid circles that the Egyptians had actually invited the Franks to invade Syria so that they could serve as a buffer against the Seljuks; Ibn al-Athir, *The Chronicle of Ibn al-Athīr for the Crusading Period from al-Kāmil fi'l-ta'rīkh*, Part 1, tr. D.S. Richards, Crusade Texts in Translation, 13, Aldershot, 2006, p. 14. Ibn al-Athir (1160–1233) was born into a family notable for its administrative and scholarly achievements. The family was centred on Mosul and especially associated with the Zengids, although Ibn al-Athir does not seem to have held any official position under the dynasty.
76. Raymond of Aguilers, pp. 109–10; WT, 7.19, pp. 367–8. See Gibb, in *A History of the Crusades* vol. 1, *The First Hundred Years*, ed. M. W. Baldwin, Madison, 1969, vol. 1, p. 95.
77. FC, 1.31, pp. 311–12.
78. *Gesta Francorum*, p. 95. See Aird, *Robert Curthose*, pp. 187–8.
79. Hagenmeyer, *Kreuzuggsbriefe*, no. XVIII, p. 170; AA, 6.49, pp. 466–7.
80. *Gesta Francorum*, pp. 96–7.
81. Ibn al-Qalanisi, p. 54.
82. See C. Hillenbrand, *The Crusades: Islamic Perspectives*, Edinburgh, 1999, pp. 19–20.
83. See Chapter 3, pp. 52, 60–1, Chapter 4, p. 65.
84. Raymond of Aguilers, pp. 153–4; *Gesta Francorum*, p. 93.
85. B. Hamilton, *The Latin Church in the Crusader States: The Secular Church*, London, 1980, pp. 13–14.
86. See J. Richard, 'Quelques textes sur les premiers temps de l'église latine de Jérusalem', in *Recueil Clovis Brunel*, vol. 2, Paris, 1955, pp. 420–3, on the question of Arnulf's authority.
87. Ralph of Caen, pp. 81–2.
88. See J.G. Rowe, 'Paschal II and the Relation between the Spiritual and the Temporal Powers in the Kingdom of Jerusalem', *Speculum*, 32 (1957), 472.
89. Riley-Smith, *Crusades*, p. 54.
90. See H.E. Mayer, 'The Origins of the Lordships of Ramla and Lydda in the Latin Kingdom of Jerusalem', *Speculum*, 60 (1985), 537–41.

91. Raymond of Aguilers, p. 154. A bull of Paschal II in 1117 named two women with whom he was alleged to have had sexual relations, one a Christian, the wife of a certain Girard, the other a Muslim, by whom he had a son; *Cartulaire du Saint-Sépulcre*, no. 91, p. 208.

92. Guibert de Nogent, *Dei Gesta per Francos*, ed. R.B.C. Huygens, Corpus Christianorum, Continuatio Mediaevalis, 127A, Turnhout, 1996, 7.15, p. 291. *Gesta Dei per Francos*, tr. R. Levine, Woodbridge, 1997, pp. 135-6.

93. Ralph of Caen, p. 93. Tr. Bachrach and Bachrach, p. 127. The bishop came from a poor see in Calabria where he was a suffragan of the archbishopric of Cosenza, and he may have joined the expedition with the Italian Normans in the hope of improving his status and wealth. See A.V. Murray, 'Norman Settlement in the Latin Kingdom of Jerusalem, 1099-1131', *Archivio Normanno-Svevo*, 1 for 2008 (2009), 68-9.

94. Hamilton, *Latin Church*, p. 12. Symeon died at about this time, but the crusaders would not have known this. He may have left Cyprus for Constantinople before his death; after him a succession of Greek patriarchs in exile was elected.

95. Raymond of Aguilers, p. 154. The bishop of Martirano was still with the Christians in early August, when he was sent by Godfrey from Ramla to Jerusalem to report on the position of the Egyptian army to the counts waiting there. Raymond of Aguilers, p. 156. According to the *Gesta Francorum*, p. 94, he was taken by the Saracens while on the return journey from Jerusalem.

96. Ralph of Caen, pp. 107-8, 111-16. Tr. Bachrach and Bachrach, pp. 144-5, 148-54. See Raymond of Aguilers, p. 154, who says that Arnulf despoiled other clerics by taking away their benefices.

97. AA, 8.1-48, pp. 586-637; FC, 2.16, pp. 428-33. See J.L. Cate, 'The Crusade of 1101', in *A History of the Crusades*, vol. 1, *The First Hundred Years*, ed. M.W. Baldwin, pp. 343-67.

98. FC, 2.6, pp. 388-9. Tr. F.R. Ryan, *A History of the Expedition to Jerusalem, 1095-1127*, ed. H. Fink, Knoxville, Tenn., 1969, pp. 149-50.

99. France, *Victory in the East*, pp. 117-18.

100. C. J. Tyerman, *God's War: A New History of the Crusades*, London, 2006, pp. 33-5.

101. Stephen's motives for leaving the crusade, ranging from illness to cowardice, are not agreed among contemporaries but the end result was the same. See J.A. Brundage, 'An Errant Crusader: Stephen of Blois', *Traditio*, 16 (1960), 388-90.

102. J. France, 'Byzantium in Western Chronicles before the First Crusade', in *Knighthoods of Christ: Essays on the History of the Crusades and the Knights Templar Presented to Malcolm Barber*, ed. N. Housley, Aldershot, 2007, pp. 3-16.

103. *Gesta Francorum*, p. 72; AA, 5.3, pp. 340-3. Albert's version seems to have been written in the knowledge that Alexius had turned back, accusing him of failing to provide promised aid and informing him that, as a consequence, they considered their oaths to him invalid. However, the *Gesta* says the legation was sent immediately after the defeat of Kerbogha on 28 June, at which time the crusaders could not have known about the meeting at Philomelium, and that its purpose was to ask Alexius 'to come to take over the city and fulfil the obligations which he had undertaken towards them'.

104. Hagenmeyer, *Kreuzzugsbriefe*, no. XVI, pp. 164-5. Tr. Barber and Bate, *Letters from the East*, no. 8, p. 33.

105. France, 'Byzantium in Western Chronicles', p. 5.

106. See Pahlitzsch, *Graeci und Suriani*, pp. 73-7.

107. Anna Comnena, *Alexiad*, 11.6, pp. 282-3.

108. Hagenmeyer, *Kreuzzugsbriefe*, no. XX, p. 176. Tr. A.C. Krey, *The First Crusade: The Accounts of Eyewitnesses and Participants*, Princeton, NJ, 1921, pp. 264-5.

2 Syria and Palestine

1. *Gesta Francorum*, p. 27.

2. Ralph of Caen, p. 57. Tr. Bachrach and Bachrach, p. 85.

3. Ibn Butlan, in *Palestine under the Moslems: A Description of Syria and the Holy Land from A.D. 650 to 1500*, tr. G. Le Strange, introd. W. Khalidy, Khayats Oriental Reprints, 14, Beirut, 1965 (originally 1890), p. 370.

4. Ibn Butlan, p. 370. See R. Rogers, *Latin Siege Warfare in the Twelfth Century*, Oxford, 1992, pp. 26-8, and Asbridge, *First Crusade*, pp. 160-2.

5. Ralph of Caen, p. 47.

6. Raymond of Aguilers, p. 48. Tr. Hill and Hill, p. 31.

7. FC, 1.33, pp. 326–30. See G. Downey, *A History of Antioch in Syria from Seleucus to the Arab Conquest*, Princeton, NJ, 1961, pp. 17–18, and J.M. Wagstaff, *The Evolution of Middle Eastern Landscapes: An Outline to A.D. 1840*, London, 1985, p. 12.
8. Michael the Syrian, 19.9, pp. 348–9.
9. Ralph of Caen, p. 54. Tr. Bachrach and Bachrach, p. 81.
10. Hagenmeyer, *Kreuzzugsbriefe*, no. X, p. 150. Tr. Barber and Bate, *Letters from the East*, no. 5, p. 23.
11. AA, 5.13, pp. 354–5.
12. Ralph of Caen, p. 100. Tr. Bachrach and Bachrach, p. 136; Ibn al-Qalanisi, p. 295. See P.D. Mitchell, *Medicine in the Crusades: Warfare, Wounds and the Medieval Surgeon*, Cambridge, 2004, pp. 1–4.
13. Mukaddasi, *Description of Syria, including Palestine*, tr. G. Le Strange, Palestine Pilgrims' Text Society, 3, London, 1896, p. 85.
14. J. Richard, *Le Comté de Tripoli sous la dynastie toulousaine (1102–1187)*, Paris, 1945, pp. 1–2.
15. WT, 13.3, pp. 588–9. Tr. Babcock and Krey, *A History of Deeds Done beyond the Sea*, Records of Civilization, Sources and Studies, 35, New York, 1943, vol. 2, p. 5.
16. Richard, *Comté*, p. 3.
17. Ralph of Caen, pp. 100–1.
18. *Peregrinationes Tres: Saewulf, John of Würzburg, Theodericus*, ed. R.B.C. Huygens, Corpus Christianorum. Continuatio Mediaevalis, 139, Turnhout, 1994, p. 146; JP, p. 277. Huygens, pp. 27–9, dates Theoderic's pilgrimage to 1169.
19. B. Z. Kedar, 'The *Tractatus de locis et statu sancte terre ierosolimitane*', in *The Crusades and their Sources: Essays Presented to Bernard Hamilton*, ed. J. France and W.G. Zajac, Aldershot, 1998, p. 128. See M. Lombard, 'Une carte du bois dans la Méditerranée musulmane (VIIe–XIe siècles)', *Annales ESC*, 14 (1959), 236–40.
20. Ibn Butlan, p. 370.
21. FC, 1.14, p. 209. Tr. Ryan, p. 90. See Wagstaff, *Evolution of Middle Eastern Landscapes*, p. 16, and M. Amouroux-Mourad, *Le Comté d'Édesse, 1098–1150*, Bibliothèque Archéologique et Historique de l'Institut Français d'Archéologie du Proche-Orient, 128, Paris, 1988, pp. 19–20.
22. Matthew of Edessa, *Armenia and the Crusades, Tenth to the Twelfth Centuries: The Chronicle of Matthew of Edessa*, tr. A.E. Dostourian, Lanham, 1993, 2.130–1, p. 175.
23. Daniel the Abbot, 'The Life and Journey of Daniel, Abbot of the Russian Land', in JP, p. 161.
24. FC, 2.5, pp. 376–7. Tr. Ryan, p. 145. If Fulcher is following Roman practice, then a stade was 125 paces, equivalent to a little under an eighth of an English mile. The figures, however, are taken from Josephus, *The Jewish War*, 4.482.
25. Daniel, in JP, p. 141.
26. FC, 2.5, pp. 380–4.
27. FC, 2.56, pp. 594–5. It is possible that Baldwin built a fort here: see D. Pringle, *Secular Buildings in the Crusader Kingdom of Jerusalem: An Archaeological Gazetteer*, Cambridge, 1997, P5, p. 113.
28. Downey, *History of Antioch*, p. 20; Wagstaff, *Evolution of Middle Eastern Landscapes*, p. 13.
29. John Phocas, 'A General Description of the Settlements and Places Belonging to Syria and Phoenicia on the Way from Antioch to Jerusalem, and the Holy Places of Palestine', in JP, p. 328.
30. Mukaddasi, pp. 39–41.
31. WT, 8.4, p. 388. *A History of Deeds Done beyond the Sea*, tr. E.A. Babcock and A.C. Krey, vol. 1, Records of Civilization, Sources and Studies, 35, New York, 1943, p. 346. See A.J. Boas, *Jerusalem in the Time of the Crusades: Society, Landscape and Art in the Holy City under Frankish Rule*, London, 2001, pp. 171–7, for the problems in supplying Jerusalem with water.
32. Mukaddasi, p. 85.
33. Raymond of Aguilers, p. 54.
34. M.-L. Bulst-Thiele, *Sacrae Domus Templi Hierosolymitani Magistri*, Göttingen, 1974, Anhang 1, no. 2, pp. 360–1. Tr. M. Barber and K. Bate, *The Templars*, Manchester Medieval Sources, Manchester, 2002, p. 100.
35. FC, 1.15, p. 224, 2.34, p. 505, 2.51, pp. 574–5, 2.52, pp. 578–9, 2.54, p. 590, 2.61, p. 605. Cf. the accounts of Walter the Chancellor and Matthew of Edessa of the great earthquake in Antioch in 1114: WC, 1.1, pp. 63–5, and Matthew of Edessa, 3.67, pp. 216–17. See also Ibn al-Qalanisi, pp. 326, 338, on the earthquakes of 1156 and 1157, which particularly affected Aleppo and Hama.

36. WT, 20.18, pp. 934–6. See H.E. Mayer, 'Das syrische Erdbeben von 1170: Ein unedierter Brief König Amalrichs von Jerusalem', *Deutches Archiv für Erforschung des Mittelalters*, 45 (1989), 474–7.
37. WC, Prologus, pp. 61–2. Tr. T.S. Asbridge and S.B. Edgington, *The Antiochene Wars*, Crusade Texts in Translation, 4, Aldershot, 1999, p. 78. Cf. FC, 2.52, p. 578, 2.60, pp. 602–3 (locusts, worms and mice), 3.62, pp. 822–3 (rats).
38. Ambroise, *The History of the Holy War*, ed. and tr. M. Ailes and M. Barber, 2 vols, Woodbridge, 2003, vol. 1, p. 95, vol. 2, p. 113.
39. WT, 19.16, pp. 885–6. Tr. Babcock and Krey, vol. 2, p. 317.
40. Raymond of Aguilers, p. 54.
41. See R. Dussaud, *Topographie historique de la Syrie antique et médiévale*, Haut-Commissariat de la République Française en Syrie et Liban, Service des Antiquités et des Beaux-Arts, Bibliothèque Archéologique et Historique, Paris, 1927, map XIV.
42. Much of it had survived because of falling population in the past, especially between the fifth and seventh centuries.
43. Ralph of Caen, p. 120. Tr. Bachrach and Bachrach, p. 159. See Dussaud, *Topographie*, pp. 413–15.
44. FC, 3.10, pp. 644–5. Even today, Jerash retains much of its splendour. It must have been awe-inspiring in the twelfth century, when so much more of it survived.
45. See Dussaud, *Topographie*, pp. 37–8, for Sidon, pp. 64–73, for Byblos. Sidon still had rich remains in the 1920s, including Greek sarcophagi and several layers of buildings. The description of the building of 'Atlit (or Pilgrims' Castle) is by Oliver of Paderborn, master of the cathedral school at Cologne: *Historia Damiatina*, ed. O. Hoogeweg, *Die Schriften des Kölner Domscholasters*, in *Bibliothek des Litterarischen Vereins in Stuttgart*, 202, Tübingen, 1894, pp. 169–72.
46. WT, 17.12, p. 776. Tr. Babcock and Krey, vol. 2, p. 202.
47. WT, 13.1, pp. 584–7. Tr. Babcock and Krey, vol. 2, pp. 1–4.
48. Mukaddasi, p. 4.
49. Downey, *History of Antioch*, pp. 5–13.
50. *Gesta Francorum*, p. 27.
51. Downey, *History of Antioch*, p. 272.
52. WT, 4.9, pp. 244–5. Tr. Babcock and Krey, vol. 1, p. 200.
53. WT, 8.1–2, pp. 381–4. Tr. Babcock and Krey, vol. 1, pp. 339–41. David actually captured a pre-existing settlement and Hadrian's rebuilding only partially coincided with that of the earlier city.
54. S. Schein, *Gateway to the Heavenly City: Crusader Jerusalem and the Catholic West (1099–1187)*, Aldershot, 2005, pp. 1, 18–20.
55. ODCC, pp. 868–9.
56. Baldric of Dol, *Historia Jerosolimitani*, in RHCr, Occid., vol. 4, p. 12. Tr. L. and J. Riley-Smith, *Crusades: Idea and Reality*, p. 49.
57. WC, 1.1, p. 63. Tr. Asbridge and Edgington, p. 81.
58. *Peregrinationes Tres*, p.137. See A. Grabois, 'Le pèlerin occidental en Terre Sainte à l'époque des croisades et ses réalités: La relation de pèlerinage de Jean de Wurtzbourg', in *Études de civilisation médiévale (IXe–XIIe siècles): Mélanges offerts à Edmond-René Labande*, Poitiers, 1974, pp. 367–76.
59. Hamilton, *Latin Church*, pp. 159–60. See, however, the inadequacies of conventional nomenclature, as well as the confusion this caused the Latins: A. Jotischky, 'Ethnographic Attitudes in the Crusader States: The Franks and the Indigenous Orthodox People', in *East and West in the Crusader States: Context - Contacts - Confrontations*, III, Acta of the Congress Held at Hernen Castle in September 2000, ed. K. Ciggaar and H. Teule, Leuven, 2003, pp. 3–4.
60. See Pahlitzsch, *Graeci und Suriani*, pp. 181–213.
61. Michael the Syrian, 15.7, p. 183.
62. Hagenmeyer, *Kreuzzugsbriefe*, no. XVI, p. 164.
63. WT, 4.23, p. 265. Tr. Babcock and Krey, vol. 1, p. 221.
64. WT, 5.11, p. 286. Tr. Babcock and Krey, vol. 1, p. 241. See C. MacEvitt, *The Crusades and the Christian World of the East: Rough Tolerance*, Philadelphia, PA, 2008, pp. 101–34, 169.
65. Hamilton, *Latin Church*, p. 188.
66. A.S. Atiya, *A History of Eastern Christianity*, London, 1968, pp. 305–33; Hamilton, *Latin Church*, pp. 200–1.
67. Kedar, 'Tractatus', p. 124.

68. *ODCC*, pp. 1104–5. There were many variants.
69. Hamilton, *Latin Church*, pp. 190–1.
70. See A. Palmer, 'The History of the Syrian Orthodox in Jerusalem', *Oriens Christianus*, 75 (1991), 16–37, and D. Pringle, *The Churches of the Crusader Kingdom of Jerusalem: A Corpus*, vol. 3, Cambridge, 2007, pp. 327–35.
71. WT, 22.9(8), pp. 1018–19. Tr. Babcock and Krey, vol. 2, pp. 458–9.
72. See R.W. Crawford, 'William of Tyre and the Maronites', *Speculum*, 30 (1955), 222–8.
73. Atiya, *Eastern Christianity*, pp. 16–97.
74. *ODCC*, pp. 1138–9; Hamilton, *Latin Church*, pp. 209–10; Atiya, *Eastern Christianity*, pp. 239–66. Atiya thinks that in the early middle ages the Nestorians formed the single largest Christian Church.
75. See Pringle, *Churches of the Crusader Kingdom*, vol. 2, Cambridge, 1998, no. 145, pp. 33–40.
76. Daniel, in JP, p. 150; John Phocas, in JP, p. 326; PL, vol. 162, p. 730.
77. PL, vol. 162, p. 730.
78. See J. Pahlitzsch, 'Georgians and Greeks in Jerusalem (1099–1310)', in *East and West in the Crusader States: Context – Contacts – Confrontations*, vol. 3, *Acta of the Congress Held at Hernen Castle in September 2000*, ed. K. Ciggaar and H. Teule, Louvain, 2003, pp. 35–9.
79. J. Prawer, *The History of the Jews in the Latin Kingdom of Jerusalem*, Oxford, 1988, pp. 153–9.
80. France, *Victory in the East*, p. 355.
81. See A. Grabois, 'The First Crusade and the Jews', in *The Crusades: Other Experiences, Alternate Perspectives*, ed. K.I. Semaan, Binghampton, New York, 2003, p. 22.
82. R. Ellenblum, *Frankish Rural Settlement in the Latin Kingdom of Jerusalem*, Cambridge, 1998, p. 260.
83. *The Itinerary of Benjamin of Tudela: Travels in the Middle Ages*, introd. M.A. Signer, M.N. Adler and A. Asher, Malibu, CA, 1983, p. 82.
84. B.Z. Kedar, 'The Frankish Period', in *The Samaritans*, ed. A.D. Crown, Tübingen, 1989, pp. 82–7.
85. Ibn Shaddad, p. 18.
86. Ibn al-Athir, part 2, p. 331.
87. See F.E. Peters, 'The Quest of the Historical Muhammad', *International Journal of Middle East Studies*, 23 (1991), 291–315.
88. AA, 3.59, pp. 230–1. Cf. WT, 4.24, pp. 267–8. Tr. Babcock and Krey, vol. 1, pp. 223–4. For William, 'a deep and inveterate enmity had existed between the Orientals and the Egyptians, arising out of differences in their religious beliefs and their opposite dogmas'.
89. WT, 19.21, pp. 890–2. Tr. Babcock and Krey, vol. 2, pp. 323–5.
90. Some explanation of this seems to have been given by the Egyptian envoys who negotiated with the Latins during the First Crusade, since Raymond of Aguilers heard a story that the Turks had promised to revere Ali, 'the brother-in-law (*de genere*) of Muhammed', if the Fatimid vizier would ally with them against the Franks. Raymond of Aguilers, p. 110. Tr. Hill and Hill, p. 89.
91. AA, 8.19, pp. 612–13.
92. *Gesta Francorum*, p. 21. Cf. WT, 1.7, pp. 114–17. Tr. Babcock and Krey, vol. 1, pp. 71–4.
93. B.Z. Kedar, 'A Western Survey of Saladin's Forces at the Siege of Acre', in *Montjoie: Studies in Crusade History in Honour of Hans Eberhard Mayer*, ed. B.Z. Kedar, J. Riley-Smith and R. Hiestand, Aldershot, 1997, pp. 116–17, 122. This appears as an addition to the survey known as the *Tractatus*: see p. 374, n. 19.
94. See B. Lewis, 'The Isma'ilites and the Assassins', in *A History of the Crusades*, vol. 1, *The First Hundred Years*, ed. M.W. Baldwin (Madison, 1969), pp. 99–132. The Assassins had previously made an unsuccessful attempt to establish themselves at Banyas, but did not survive there beyond 1130. See Ibn al-Qalanisi, pp. 186–95.
95. WT, 20.29, p. 953.
96. Ellenblum, *Frankish Rural Settlement*, pp. 36–7, 222–76.
97. *Peregrinationes Tres*, p. 187. Tr. JP, pp. 310–11.
98. WT, 1.7, pp. 114–17. Tr. Babcock and Krey, vol. 1, pp. 71–4.
99. Michael the Syrian, 21.5, pp. 400–2.
100. See J. Schenk, 'Nomadic Violence in the First Latin Kingdom of Jerusalem and the Military Orders', *Reading Medieval Studies*, 36 (2010), 39–47.
101. WT, 18.11, p. 825; Ibn al-Qalanisi, pp. 327–8.
102. See Epp, *Fulcher von Chartres*, pp. 38–44. These attitudes can be seen particularly in Fulcher's revised version of his chronicle, made after 1124.
103. FC, 3.37, pp. 748–9. Tr. Ryan, pp. 271–2. Isaiah 65:25.

3 The First Settlers

1. AA, 7. 17–21, pp. 508–17. For Warner, see Murray, *Crusader Kingdom*, pp. 234–5, n. 133.

2. WT, 9.23, p. 449. Tr., vol. 1, p. 413; Ekkehard of Aura, cap. XX, pp. 26–7; caps XXIII–XXIV, pp. 29–30, for his visit in 1101. William of Malmesbury, pp. 658–9 says that he had an attack of 'his old fever' immediately after the battle of Ascalon, a piece of information that he may have derived from an oral source. It is clear that in both Outremer and the West many suffered from low-level fevers at his period, and that these could quite suddenly become serious. On the inevitable rumours that he had been poisoned, especially after his visit to the emir of Caesarea, see Edgington in AA, pp. 512–13, n. 24.

3. AA, 3.4, pp. 142–5, for the bear attack. Ibn al-Qalanisi, p. 51, says that he was killed by an arrow while attacking Acre, perhaps wanting to claim that it was the Muslims who had ended the life of such a famous Christian hero.

4. AA, 6.34–5, pp. 446–9.

5. Baldric of Dol, p. 110. Baldric used material from the *Gesta Francorum*, but this information seems to have come from eyewitnesses.

6. AA, 6.51, pp. 470–1.

7. Ralph of Caen, p. 117. Tr. Bachrach and Bachrach, p. 154; William of Malmesbury, pp. 698–9.

8. According to Albert of Aachen, 6.51, pp. 472–3, a few days later Raymond acted in the same way at Arsuf, when frustrated in his desire to obtain it for himself. J.H. and L.L. Hill, *Raymond IV*, p. 137, point out that the events of 13–17 August have been largely reconstructed from chroniclers who were not there and that all of them show anti-Raymond bias. However, the two leaders certainly quarrelled over the city, a circumstance that according to Ibn al-Qalanisi, p. 49, not only prevented them from taking Ascalon, but also lost them the tribute that had been promised. Whatever the truth of the matter, the incident was sufficiently well known to be used a century later by Geoffrey of Villehardouin to demonstrate the dangers of rivalry within the Christian ranks: see J.M. Powell, 'Myth, Legend, Propaganda, History: The First Crusade, 1140–ca.1300', in *Autour de la Première Croisade*, ed. M. Balard, Paris, 1996, p. 134.

9. WT, 9.19, pp. 446–7. Tr. Babcock and Krey, vol. 1, pp. 408–10.

10. FC, 1.33, pp. 330–3.

11. AA, 7.1–6, pp. 486–95.

12. AA, 7.9–15, pp. 498–507. For Gerard, see Murray, *Crusader Kingdom*, no. 47, p. 199.

13. AA, 7.16–17, pp. 506–11.

14. AA, 7.2–3, pp. 486–91, 9, pp. 498–9.

15. AA, 7.16, pp. 506–7.

16. See J. Richard, 'La noblesse de Terre Sainte (1097–1187)', *Arquivos do centro cultural português*, 26 (1989), 323–5.

17. Murray, *Crusader Kingdom*, pp. 79–81.

18. See D. Pringle, *The Churches of the Crusader Kingdom of Jerusalem: A Corpus*, vol. 1, Cambridge, 1993, pp. 223–4.

19. See H.E. Mayer, 'Die Herrschaftsbildung in Hebron', *Zeitschrift des Deutschen Palästina-Vereins*, 101 (1985), 66, and Murray, *Crusader Kingdom*, no. 110, p. 225.

20. For Geldemar, see Murray, *Crusader Kingdom*, no. 44, p. 198.

21. AA, 7.15, pp. 506–7, 12, pp. 502–3, 22, pp. 516–17, 37, pp. 540–1.

22. WT, 9.19, p. 446. Such an edict makes sense in the context within which Godfrey was obliged to operate, although it may be that William attributed it to him more because of his perception of Godfrey's founding role than because he actually had solid documentary evidence.

23. See Chapter 1, p. 17.

24. See A.V. Murray, 'Sex, death and the problem of single women in the armies of the First Crusade', in *Shipping, Trade and Crusade in the Medieval Mediterranean: Studies in honour of John Pryor*, ed. R. Gertwagen and E. Jeffreys, Farnham, 2012 (forthcoming).

25. See Boas, *Jerusalem in the Time of the Crusades*, pp. 7, 97–101.

26. D. Pringle, 'Magna Mahumeria (al-Bīra): The Archaeology of a Frankish New Town in Palestine', in *Crusade and Settlement*, ed. P.W. Edbury, Cardiff, 1985, pp. 147–68.

27. FC, 3.33, pp. 731–2.

28. AA, 7.16–17, pp. 506–11.

29. Ralph of Caen, p. 117. Tr. Bachrach and Bachrach, p. 155.

30. Letter of Daibert, Godfrey and Raymond of Toulouse to the pope (September, 1099), Hagenmeyer, *Kreuzzugsbriefe*, no. XVIII, p. 170.

31. WT, 8.9, p. 99.

32. *Peregrinationes Tres*, pp. 63–4.
33. Hagenmeyer, *Kreuzzugsbriefe*, no. XVIII, p. 170.
34. Guibert de Nogent, 7.38, p. 338. Tr. Levine, *Gesta Dei per Francos*, Woodbridge, 1997, p. 159.
35. Ibn al-Qalanisi, introd. Gibb, pp. 21–38.
36. J.H. Pryor, *Geography, Technology and War: Studies in the Maritime History of the Mediterranean, 649–1571*, Cambridge, 1988, pp. 114–15.
37. Pryor, *Geography, Technology and War*, p. 116.
38. AA, 7.6, pp. 494–5.
39. G. Fedalto, *La Chiesa Latina in Oriente*, vol. 1, Verona, 1973, pp. 91–3, Hamilton, *Latin Church*, pp. 14–15, and M. Matzke, *Daibert von Pisa. Zwischen Pisa, Papst und erstem Kreuzzug*, Sigmaringen, 1998, p. 137, believe that he was, or had been, the papal legate, contrary to the view of Krey, 'Urban's Crusade – Success or Failure', 240–2. Krey's view that the Pisan fleet set sail before Urban could have had news of Adhémar's death is unconvincing. The fleet could have set out in spring 1099 and still have had time to occupy various islands in the eastern Mediterranean before arriving at Latakia in September 1099: H. Hagenmeyer, *Chronologie de la Première Croisade, 1094–1100*, Paris, 1902, no. 428, pp. 269–70. See Murray, *Crusader Kingdom*, p. 82, for a summary of the arguments.
40. See Murray, *Crusader Kingdom*, pp. 81–93.
41. Ralph of Caen, p. 118. Tr. Bachrach and Bachrach, p. 156. See Chapter 1, p. 22. Arnulf does not seem to have been consecrated bishop at this time.
42. See Hamilton, *Latin Church*, pp. 14–16. Albert of Aachen, 6.39, pp. 452–55, says that they appointed Arnulf 'as chancellor of the holy church of Jerusalem, procurator of the holy relics, and keeper of the alms of the faithful'. He may well have held the second and third of these positions, but there was no patriarchal chancellor until the mid-1130s: see H.E. Mayer, *Die Kanzlei der lateinischen Könige von Jerusalem*, vol. 1, Hanover, 1996, p. 47.
43. WT, 9.15, p. 440. Tr. Babcock and Krey, vol. 1, p. 403. No contemporary chronicler was present to record this investiture but, if a passing reference to it by Fulcher of Chartres in 1124, 3.34, p. 741, is any indication, it appears to have been well known, for Fulcher evidently did not think it required further explanation.
44. WT, 10.4, p. 456. As Daibert put it in a letter to Bohemond: 'With the assent of the clergy, leaders, and the people alike, you brought about my election.' See also Yewdale, *Bohemond I*, p. 91.
45. AA, 6.54–9, pp. 474–85. See also Pahlitzsch, *Graeci und Suriani*, pp. 84–5, who argues that this shows that not all the crusaders had turned against Byzantium. However, it made little practical difference as the two dukes were on their way home in any case, leaving Raymond as the only important crusade leader willing to defend Byzantine claims.
46. Ralph of Caen, p. 118. Tr. Bachrach and Bachrach, p. 156. See Hamilton, *Latin Church*, pp. 16, 22–5.
47. AA, 7.8, pp. 496–9; FC, 1.33, p. 334.
48. WT, 9.15–16, pp. 440–2. Tr. Babcock and Krey, vol. 1, pp. 402–4; 10.4, p. 456. Tr. Babcock and Krey, vol. 1, p. 419, for Daibert's version.
49. WT, 9.17–18, pp. 442–4. Tr. Babcock and Krey, vol. 1, pp. 405–8. See J. Prawer, 'The Patriarch's Lordship in Jerusalem', in *Crusader Institutions*, Oxford, 1980, pp. 296–303, showing the area concerned, and Pahlitzsch, *Graeci und Suriani*, pp. 42–6.
50. AA, 7.27, pp. 522–3. See Murray, *Crusader Kingdom*, pp. 87–9, and P.W. Edbury and J.G. Rowe, *William of Tyre: Historian of the Latin East*, Cambridge, 1988, pp. 49–50.
51. Murray, *Crusader Kingdom*, p. 86.
52. This in itself is evidence that the letter reproduced in William's chronicle is not the original.
53. *Work on Geography*, in JP, p. 210.
54. Murray, *Crusader Kingdom*, pp. 89–90.
55. Hiestand, 'Some Reflections', p. 10.
56. J. Riley-Smith, *The Crusades: A History*, 2nd edn, London, 2005, pp. 62–5.
57. Hagenmeyer, *Kreuzzugsbriefe*, no. XXI, pp. 176–7. The choice of the German people was presumably meant to appeal to their pride in Godfrey's election.
58. FC, 1.33, pp. 333–4. Tr. 132; WT, 10.4, p. 457. Tr. Babcock and Krey, vol. 1, p. 421.
59. Murray, *Crusader Kingdom*, p. 83.
60. AA, 7.6–7, pp. 494–7; WT, 9.15, p. 440.
61. *Monachi Anonymi Littorensis Historia de Translatio Sanctorum Magni Nicolai*, in RHCr, Occid., vol. 5, Paris, 1895, pp. 272, 275; ULKJ, vol. 1, no. 9, pp. 105–7; Hagenmeyer, *Chronologie*, no. 472, pp. 299–300, no. 478, pp. 302–3. The right to goods from ships wrecked on the coast would

normally have belonged to the ruler, so this was a useful concession for the Venetians. D.E. Queller and I.B. Katele, 'Venice and the Conquest of the Latin Kingdom of Jerusalem', *Studi Venetiani*, 12 (1986), 24–5, argue that these concessions, although they seem generous, reflect the size of the Venetian expedition, which seems to have involved between 8,100 and 9,000 men.

62. Pryor, *Geography, Technology and War*, pp. 1–3.
63. *Translatio*, p. 275; Hagenmeyer, *Chronologie*, no. 484, pp. 306–7, no. 487, pp. 308–9. Hagenmeyer fixes the date of the message of Tancred and Daibert to the Venetians, in which they inform them they are now intending to attack Haifa, as 23 July, which makes it quite possible that the change of target was determined by the news of Godfrey's death.
64. AA, 7.23–6, pp. 516–23; *Translatio*, pp. 275–8. The Venetians did not take part in the actual storming of the city and therefore appear to have gained little from the enterprise, despite the terms of their agreement with the Franks: Queller and Katele, 'Venice and the Conquest of the Latin Kingdom', 25–6.
65. AA, 7.30, pp. 528–9.
66. WT, 10.4, p. 457. Tr. Babcock and Krey, vol. 1, pp. 420–1.
67. WT, 10.3, p. 455. Tr. Babcock and Krey, vol. 1, p. 418.
68. See Murray, *Crusader Kingdom*, pp. 89–90. The phrase is *absque herede masculo*, translated as 'without male issue' by Babcock and Krey, vol. 1, p. 419, which makes a crucial difference. William, 9.16, p. 441, paraphrases this as *absque legitimo . . . herede*, translated by Babcock and Krey, vol. 1, p. 404, as 'legitimate heir'.
69. AA, 7.27, pp. 522–3, and n. 30 for a discussion about the authenticity of the letter.
70. A.V. Murray, 'Daimbert of Pisa, the *Domus Godefridi* and the Accession of Baldwin I', in *From Clermont to Jerusalem: The Crusades and Crusader Societies, 1095-1500*, ed. A.V. Murray, Turnhout, 1998, pp. 81–99.
71. AA, 7.27, pp. 522–3, 47, pp. 554–5.
72. Hagenmeyer, *Chronologie*, nos 497–9, pp. 318–21.
73. FC, 2.1, pp. 352–3. Tr. Ryan, p. 137.
74. Albert of Aachen says 400 knights and 1,000 foot, but Fulcher was actually with what he calls Baldwin's 'little army'.
75. Matthew of Edessa, 2.134, p. 177.
76. Hagenmeyer, *Chronologie*, no. 504, pp. 325–6.
77. WT, 10.5, p. 458.
78. AA, 7.31, pp. 530–1.
79. Caffaro, *Liber de liberatione civitatum Orientis*, in *Annali Genovesi di Caffaro e de' suoi continuari*, ed. L.T. Belgrano, vol. 1, Rome, 1890, pp. 112–13. Caffaro was the son of Rustico of Caschifellone. He took part in this expedition and provides first-hand knowledge of events. See R. Face, 'Secular History in Twelfth-Century Italy: Caffaro of Genoa', *Journal of Medieval History*, 6 (1980), 169–84.
80. FC, 2.2–3, pp. 357–65.
81. FC, 2.3, p. 366.
82. AA, 7.35–6, pp. 538–41.
83. FC, 2.3, pp. 367–9.
84. WT, 10.8, p. 462. Tr. Babcock and Krey, vol. 1, p. 426.
85. FC, 2.4–5, pp. 370–84; AA, 7.38–40, pp. 542–7. Hagenmeyer, *Chronologie*, nos 516–20, pp. 336–41.
86. AA, 7.38, pp. 542–3.
87. *Peregrinationes Tres*, pp. 71–2. Saewulf says that the rest of the town, however, was ruined.
88. Daniel, in JP, p. 143.
89. FC, 2.6, pp. 384–7. Tr. Ryan, pp. 148–9. Murray, *Crusader Kingdom*, p. 96, suggests that the messianic fervour of the previous year had much diminished.
90. See J.F.A. Mason, 'Saint Anselm's Relations with Laymen: Selected Letters', in *Spicilegium Beccense, I, Congrès international du IXe centenaire de l'arrivée d'Anselme au Bec*, Paris, 1959, pp. 556–9.
91. WT, 10.9, p. 463.
92. AA, 7.44, pp. 550–1. See Hamilton, *Latin Church*, p. 55. The coronation was later confirmed by Paschal II.

4 The Origins of the Latin States

1. AA, 7.44–5, pp. 550–5.
2. Ralph of Caen, p. 119. Tr. Bachrach and Bachrach, p. 158.

NOTES to pp. 66-9

3. WT, 10.9, pp. 463–4. Tr. Babcock and Krey, vol. 1, p. 428.

4. FC, 2.6, pp. 387–90.

5. See K. Elm, 'Kanoniker und Ritter vom Heiligen Grab: Ein Beitrag zur Entstehung und Frühgeschichte der palästinensischen Ritterorden', in *Die geistlichen Ritterorden Europas*, ed. J. Fleckenstein and M. Hellmann, Sigmaringen, 1980, pp. 156–9. WT, 22.17(16), p. 1032, disapproved of canons appearing on the battlefield, but it seems they were still doing so in the 1180s.

6. A.V. Murray, 'The Origins of the Frankish Nobility in the Kingdom of Jerusalem, 1100–1118', *Mediterranean Historical Review*, 4 (1989), 282–3.

7. AA, 9.11, pp. 648–51. See J. Pryor, 'The Voyages of Saewulf', in *Peregrinationes Tres*, p. 36.

8. P.A. Adair, 'Flemish Comital Family and the Crusades', in *The Crusades: Other Experiences, Alternate Perspectives*, ed. K.I. Semaan, Binghampton, New York, 2003, pp. 101–12.

9. Riley-Smith, *Crusades*, pp. 90–4. For a contrary view, see S. Tibble, *Monarchy and Lordships in the Latin Kingdom of Jerusalem, 1099–1291*, Oxford, 1989, pp. 5–65. There are difficulties over contemporary terminology, especially the use of the word 'vassal', which was not common in the twelfth-century Latin East. However, men did swear oaths of fidelity and they did supply essential military forces raised from the lands or monetary incomes they received as grants. This does not presuppose an existing 'system' – indeed, it could not, given the initial nature of the settlement – but it does reflect the necessary arrangements of practical men. For a concise summary of the arguments, see J. Rubin, 'The Debate on Twelfth-Century Frankish Feudalism: Additional Evidence from William of Tyre's *Chronicon*', *Crusades*, 8 (2009), 53–62.

10. See D.M. Metcalf, 'East Meets West, and Money Changes Hands', in *East and West in the Crusader States: Context – Contacts – Confrontations*, III. *Acta of the Congress Held at Hernen Castle in September 2000*, ed. K. Ciggaar and H. Teule, Louvain, 2003, p. 231.

11. WT, 10.13(14), p. 468. Tr. Babcock and Krey, vol. 1, p. 433.

12. Caffaro, *Liber*, in *Annali Genovesi*, vol. 1, pp. 111–12. See F. Cardini, 'Profilo di un crociato Guglielmo Embriaco', *Archivio Storico Italiano*, 136 (1978), 405–36, and S. Epstein, *Genoa and the Genoese, 958–1528*, Chapel Hill, NC, 1996, pp. 27–31.

13. WT, 10.15, p. 470.

14. FC, 2.25, pp. 462–3. Tr. Ryan, p.176.

15. Epstein, *Genoa and the Genoese*, pp. 10–28.

16. See D. Jacoby, 'The Economic Function of the Crusader States of the Levant: A New Approach', in *Europe's Economic Relations with the Islamic World, 13th–18th Centuries*, ed. S. Cavaciocchi, Florence, 2007, p. 179.

17. *Codice diplomatico della Repubblica di Genova*, ed. C. Imperiale di Sant'Angelo, vol. 1, Rome, 1936, p. 20; RRH, no. 43, p. 8. See Epstein, *Genoa and the Genoese*, pp. 31–2.

18. There is controversy over this. Hans Mayer and Marie-Luise Favreau believe that the charter of privileges was forged and that therefore the inscription never existed: 'Das Diplom Balduins I. für Genua und Genuas Goldene Inschrift in der Grabeskirche', *Quellen und Forschungen aus italienischen Archiven und Bibiliotheken*, 55–6 (1976), 22–95, and ULKJ, vol. 1, no. 29, pp. 137–44. However, Benjamin Kedar has argued that, although the charter may have been tampered with later in the twelfth century, it contains the core of the privileges granted and that this was publicly acknowledged in the inscription: 'Genoa's golden inscriptions in the Church of the Holy Sepulchre: a case for the defence', in *I Comuni Italiani nel Regno Crociato di Gerusalemme*, ed. G. Airaldi and B.Z. Kedar, Genoa, 1986, pp. 317–35, and 'Again: Genoa's Golden Inscription and King Baldwin I's Privilege of 1104', in *Chemins d'Outre-Mer: Études d'histoire sur la Méditerranée médiévale offertes à Michel Balard*, ed. D. Coulon, C. Otten-Froux, P. Pagès and D. Valérian, vol. 1, Paris, 2004, pp. 495–502. It was prestigious for the Genoese to be involved in the creation of the new kingdom and therefore tempting for them to magnify their role, but it is clear that their help in the capture of the coastal cities was indispensable, so Kedar's view seems the more credible.

19. C. Marshall, 'The crusading motivation of the Italian city republics in the Latin East, 1096–1104', in *The Experience of Crusading*, vol. 1, *Western Approaches*, ed. M. Bull and N. Housley, Cambridge, 2003, pp. 60–79.

20. AA, 9.30, pp. 674–5.

21. AA, 7.55–6, pp. 562–5.

22. FC, 2.9, p. 403. David Hay, 'Gender Bias and Religious Intolerance in Accounts of the "Massacres" of the First Crusade', in *Tolerance and Intolerance: Social Conflict in the Age of the Crusades*, ed. M. Gervers and J.M. Powell, Syracuse, NY, 2001, pp. 3–10, 135–9, argues that, in fact, even during the First Crusade, the massacres described by the chroniclers were exaggerated, partly for ideological reasons, and that some modern historians have taken these accounts too literally.

23. See Y. Friedman, *Encounter between Enemies: Captivity and Ransom in the Latin Kingdom of Jerusalem*, Leiden, 2002, pp. 30–1.
24. See J. Prawer, 'The Settlement of the Latins in Jerusalem', *Speculum*, 27 (1952), 490–503.
25. AA, 10.49, pp. 762–3.
26. FC, 2.10–14, pp. 404–24.
27. Guibert of Nogent, 7.24, p. 316. Guibert depended greatly on written sources, but he does include anecdotes from participants, which is presumably the case here. When Arpin returned to France, he became a monk at Cluny and Guibert probably heard the story on the monastic grapevine. See Orderic Vitalis, vol. 5, pp. 350–3.
28. FC, 2.15, pp. 424–8, 2.18–21, pp. 435–55; AA, 9.2–12, pp. 638–53.
29. The crusaders were already familiar with the *tourkopouloi*, troops of Turkish origin used in the Byzantine army. See J. Richard, 'Les turcoples au service des royaumes de Jérusalem et de Chypre: Musulmans convertis ou chrétiens orientaux?', in *Mélanges Dominique Sourdel/Revue des études islamiques*, 54 (1986), 259–70, and R.C. Smail, *Crusading Warfare, 1097–1193*, Cambridge, 1956, pp. 111–12. The reference is not, however, precise, and the mounted warriors may also have included westerners equipped as horse archers.
30. FC, 2.31–2, pp. 489–501.
31. Raymond of Aguilers, p. 131. Raymond is the only chronicler to associate Arnulf with this discovery, but, given his antipathy towards him, it seems unlikely he would have credited it to him if it had not been achieved through his efforts. Riley-Smith, *First Crusade and the Idea of Crusading*, p. 98, suggests that he might have found it in the 'garden area' of the Holy Sepulchre compound.
32. AA, 6.38, pp. 450–3, 6.44, pp. 460–1.
33. FC, 2.21, pp. 453–4. Tr. Ryan, p. 173. See also 2.11, pp. 409–10 (1101), 2.32, p. 495 (1105).
34. FC, 2.31–2, pp. 493–5. See A.V. Murray, '"Mighty against the Enemies of Christ": The Relic of the True Cross in the Armies of the Kingdom of Jerusalem', in *The Crusades and their Sources: Essays Presented to Bernard Hamilton*, ed. J. France and W.G. Zajac, Aldershot, 1998, pp. 217–38, and Jaspert, 'Das Heilige Grab, das Wahre Kreuz, Jerusalem und das Heilige Land', pp. 69–70, 87–9.
35. FC, 2.26, pp. 466–7. Tr. Ryan, p. 177.
36. WT, 10.24(25)–25(26), pp. 483–5. Tr. Babcock and Krey, vol. 1, pp. 452–3. See Murray, *Crusader Kingdom*, no. 36, p. 195.
37. WT, 11.4, p. 500. See H. Hagenmeyer, 'Chronologie de l'histoire du royaume de Jérusalem: Règne de Baldouin I (1101–1118)', *ROL*, 12 (1909–11), no. 747, pp. 312–13, for the date.
38. Hagenmeyer, 'Chronologie de l'histoire du royaume', *ROL*, 9 (1902), no. 539, p. 404.
39. AA, 7.46–51, pp. 554–61. Albert wrongly implies that Maurice had been appointed in response to a royal appeal lodged against Daibert at the papal curia: 7.46–7, pp. 554–7.
40. AA, 7.58–63, pp. 568–75.
41. AA, 9.14–17, pp. 654–9.
42. AA, 10.58, pp. 772–3.
43. FC, 2.37, pp. 512–14. Tr. Ryan, pp. 190–1.
44. *Cartulaire du Saint-Sépulcre*, no. 90, pp. 204–6; WT, 11.4, p. 500, says that Evremar set out before news of Daibert's death had arrived (*antequam de obitu eius*), which could not be the case if Hagenmeyer's argument that he died in June 1105 is correct. For a discussion of this matter, see Edgington, pp. 772–3, n. 68.
45. WT, 10.25(26), pp. 484–5, 11.4, p. 501. William therefore did not accept that Evremar had been patriarch in the first place.
46. WT, 11.4, p. 501. Tr. Babcock and Krey, vol. 1, p. 468. See Fedalto, *La Chiesa Latina*, vol. 2, p. 60, and Hamilton, *Latin Church*, pp. 57–8.
47. AA, 10.59, pp. 772–3.
48. 17 October 1097. Hagenmeyer, *Chronologie de la Première Croisade*, no. 199, p. 103.
49. W.B. Stevenson, *The Crusaders in the East*, Cambridge, 1907, pp. 22–3 and n. 2; Amouroux-Mourad, *Le Comté d'Édesse*, pp. 58–61; Asbridge, *First Crusade*, pp. 140–2.
50. AA, 4.9, pp. 260–3.
51. Matthew of Edessa, 2.113, p. 166; WT, 4.2, p. 235.
52. AA, 3.17, pp. 164–5. Pakrad's existence must have been known to the leaders of the army, even if it was Baldwin who had taken him on.
53. FC, 1.14, p. 210. Matthew of Edessa, 2.113, p. 166, 2.117, p. 168, says that he had 100 horsemen at Turbessel, but this was reduced to sixty for the journey to Edessa.
54. See Chapter 1, p. 16.
55. AA, 3.17, pp. 164–5. WT, 4.1, p. 233, places all the blame on Baldwin in keeping with his view that Tancred was one of the heroes of the First Crusade.

56. FC, 1.14, pp. 206–15. Tr. Ryan, p. 91. See Hagenmeyer, *Chronologie*, pp. 213–14, n.36.

57. See A.A. Beaumont, 'Albert of Aachen and the County of Edessa', in *The Crusades and Other Historical Essays Presented to Dana C. Munro*, ed. L.J. Paetow, New York, 1928, pp. 105–7.

58. AA, 3.17–25, pp. 164–81; Matthew of Edessa, 2.118, pp. 169–70; WT, 4.6, pp. 239–40. See Beaumont, 'Albert of Aachen', pp. 107–13.

59. WT, 4.2, pp. 234–5. See Amouroux-Mourad, *Le Comté d'Édesse*, pp. 40–2.

60. AA, 3.18, pp. 166–7.

61. AA, 5.22, pp. 364–5. Balduk had taken part in Kerbogha's battle with the crusaders at Antioch on 28 June which in itself was sufficient reason for Baldwin to regard him as an enemy: AA, 4.8, pp. 260–1, 4.51, pp. 328–9.

62. AA, 5.5, pp. 344–5, 5.13, pp. 354–5.

63. FC, 1.33, p. 324. Tr. Ryan, p. 129.

64. WT, 5.14, pp. 289–90. William has been followed in this view by most historians, but Asbridge, *First Crusade*, p. 205, thinks that Bohemond could have brought about the fall of Antioch much sooner had it suited him and that therefore the timing was not so crucial. William bases his three weeks on Fulcher of Chartres, 1.19, p. 242, who makes no comment on its significance but who is the most reliable witness since he was in the city at the time. Albert of Aachen, 4.12, pp. 266–7, says the siege lasted only three days, while Matthew of Edessa, 2.119, p. 170, has forty days, although this seems to represent the total time Kerbogha spent in the region, rather than the siege alone.

65. AA, 3.19–20, pp. 168–9.

66. Guibert de Nogent, 7.39, pp. 338–9. Tr. Levine, p. 159.

67. AA, 3.32, pp. 188–9; WT, 10.1, p. 453. Baldwin had been promised a large payment as well, but Albert says he only received a small proportion.

68. WT, 4.2, pp. 234–5.

69. See Amouroux-Mourad, *Le Comté d'Édesse*, pp. 97–100, who suggests that there was less trouble from the Syrians because they had never been the dominant group in the past. See also C. MacEvitt, 'Christian Authority in the Latin East: Edessa in Crusader History', in *The Medieval Crusade*, ed. S.J. Ridyard, Woodbridge, 2004, pp. 71–83, who argues that historians have been unduly influenced by Matthew of Edessa, and that relations between Latins and Armenians were more complex than they have sometimes been presented.

70. AA, 5.16, pp. 356–61.

71. Ralph of Caen, p. 118. Tr. Bachrach and Bachrach, pp. 156–7. Matthew of Edessa, 2.134, pp. 176–7; AA, 7.28, pp. 532–5. Hagenmeyer, *Chronologie*, pp. 313–16, giving c.15 August.

72. Anna Comnena, *Alexiad*, 11.7, p. 288.

73. Hagenmeyer, *Kreuzzugsbriefe*, no. XIII, pp. 155–6; no. XIV, p. 156; RRH, no. 12, p. 2.

74. *Codice diplomatico della Repubblica di Genova*, vol. 1, p. 16; RRH, no. 35, p. 5. There is clearly a difference between *ruga* and *fundus*, but there remains some ambiguity about their meaning.

75. FC, 1.35, pp. 347–9; AA, 7.29, pp. 526–7.

76. Ralph of Caen, p. 123. Matthew of Edessa, 3.14, pp. 191–2, says that Kogh Vasil contributed 10,000 pieces himself. Various stories circulated about the circumstances of his release, perhaps promoted by Bohemond himself. See, for example, AA, 9.36, pp. 684–7, and Orderic Vitalis, vol. 5, pp. 358–78.

77. FC, 2.23, p. 460.

78. FC, 2.27, p. 473 (*atrociorem*).

79. WT, 10.29(30), p. 491 (*periculosum*). Tr. Babcock and Krey, vol. 1, p. 459.

80. WT, 10.23(24), pp. 482–3. See R.L. Nicholson, *Joscelyn I, Prince of Edessa*, Urbana, IL, 1954, pp. 1–5, and Amouroux-Mourad, *Le comté d'Édesse*, pp. 63–4.

81. Ibn al-Qalanisi, p. 60; WT, 10.28(29), pp. 488–9.

82. Ralph of Caen, pp. 124–6, presents Tancred as the only leader who was properly prepared. AA, 9.38–41, pp. 688–95, has broadly the same story, but with much less emphasis on Tancred. See Beaumont, 'Albert of Aachen', pp. 124–7.

83. Matthew of Edessa, 3.18–19, pp. 192–4.

84. Ibn al-Qalanisi, p. 61.

85. AA, 9.42–4, pp. 694–701.

86. Ibn al-Qalanisi, p. 69.

87. Ralph of Caen, pp. 128–9. Tr. Bachrach and Bachrach, p. 170. See T. Asbridge, 'The significance and causes of the battle of the Field of Blood', *Journal of Medieval History*, 23 (1997), fig. 2, p. 305, for maps showing the losses experienced by Antioch at this time.

88. See Yewdale, *Bohemond I*, pp. 106–34. Anna Comnena allocates much space to this, including giving the details of the treaty, as it enhanced her father's reputation to have overcome the great

Bohemond: see *Alexiad*, 13.1–12, pp. 323–58. See R.J. Lilie, *Byzantium and the Crusader States, 1096–1204*, tr. J.C. Morris and J.E. Ridings, Oxford, 1993, pp. 75–82, who sees the treaty more as a negotiated settlement than as a defeat for Bohemond.

89. Ralph of Caen, p. 17. Tr. Bachrach and Bachrach, pp. 35–6.
90. See Beech, 'A Norman-Italian Adventurer', pp. 35–6. According to Matthew of Edessa, 3.40, pp. 201–2, he 'caused the ruin of many persons'.
91. AA, 9.47, pp. 702–4, 10.20–4, pp. 734–41; Ralph of Caen, pp. 129–31; Ibn al-Qalanisi, pp. 69–70, 72–4.
92. RRH, no. 53, p. 11.
93. See D.M. Metcalf, *Coinage of the Crusades and the Latin East in the Ashmolean Museum Oxford*, 2nd edn., London, 1995, pp. 22–30. On one issue it was thought he was wearing a turban, but this now seems unlikely: p. 27.
94. AA, 9.47, pp. 702–3. See also Friedman, *Encounter between Enemies*, pp. 31–2.
95. FC, 2.28, p. 479. Tr. Ryan, pp. 180–1.
96. Matthew of Edessa, 3.39, p. 201, claims that 2,000 Christians were killed in the battle. See Nicholson, *Joscelyn I*, pp. 12–22.
97. AA, 8.43, pp. 632–3. Ralph of Caen, p. 122, says that Raymond 'abjured or swore whatever he was ordered to'. For the date, see Hagenmeyer, 'Chronologie de l'histoire du royaume', *ROL*, 10 (1903–4), no. 627, pp. 396–8. See also Chapter 4, p. 81.
98. See Fedalto, *La Chiesa Latina*, vol. 2, p. 33, and Hamilton, *Latin Church*, pp. 10–11, 23.
99. J. Richard, 'Note sur l'archidiocèse d'Apamée et les conquêtes de Raymond de Saint-Gilles en Syrie du Nord', *Syria*, 25 (1946–8), 103–6; Hamilton, *Latin Church*, pp. 10–11, 23. Peter was, it appears, initially consecrated by John IV, the Greek patriarch: *Gesta Francorum*, p. 75.
100. See T. Asbridge, 'The Principality of Antioch and the Jabal as-Summāq', in *The First Crusade: Origins and Impact*, ed. J. Phillips, Manchester, 1997, pp. 142–52.
101. Anna Comnena says her father trusted Raymond and often discussed important matters with him: *Alexiad*, 10.11, p. 267. See Richard, *Comté*, pp. 27–30. The Byzantines had not held Tripoli since the seventh century, but retained a strong interest in the north around Tortosa and Maraclea.
102. See France, *Victory in the East*, pp. 311–23; Richard, 'Note sur l'archdiocèse d'Apamée', 103–5. See also Chapter 1, p. 18.
103. Richard, *Comté*, p. 12.
104. Raymond of Aguilers, bk 13, pp. 124–5. Tr. Hill and Hill, pp. 83–4.
105. AA, 8.43, pp. 632–4; FC, 2.17, pp. 434–5. Tortosa had been taken in 1099, but had been lost again.
106. *Gesta Francorum*, pp. 83–4; Raymond of Aguilers, bk 11, p. 108; AA, 5.31, pp. 376–7. See Hill and Hill, *Raymond IV*, p. 143, for the territories taken by Raymond in this region in 1098 and 1099.
107. Ibn al-Athir, vol. 1, pp. 105–6.
108. Ibn al-Athir, vol. 1, pp. 59–60. Translated as 'men', but it cannot have been his total force: see Richard, *Comté*, pp. 52–3. Janah al-Daula was nominally dependent on Aleppo, but in practice was an independent ruler: Richard, *Comté*, p. 13.
109. Ibn al-Qalanisi, p. 55.
110. H. Kennedy, *Crusader Castles*, Cambridge, 1994, p. 63.
111. WT, 10.26(27), p. 486.
112. Ibn al-Qalanisi, p. 65; Ibn al-Athir, part 1, p. 104.
113. AA, 9.27, pp. 670–1; Caffaro, *Liber*, in *Annali Genovesi*, vol. 1, p. 121. There is some controversy whether this occurred in this year, as WT, 11.9, pp. 509–10, places its capture in 1109, but 1104 seems more probable: see Edgington, pp. 670–1, n. 55. The Genoese received a third of the town.
114. Fedalto, *La Chiesa Latina*, vol. 2, p. 231; Hamilton, *Latin Church*, p. 25. He took up the position in 1109 after the capture of the city.
115. J. Richard, 'Le Chartrier de Sainte-Marie-Latine et l'établissement de Raymond de Saint-Gilles à Mont-Pèlerin', in *Mélanges de l'histoire du Moyen Age dédiés à la mémoire de Louis Halphen*, Paris, 1951, pp. 605–12; Richard, *Comté*, p. 59.
116. *Cartulaire du Saint-Sépulcre*, no. 79, pp. 185–7. This is a confirmation, probably of 1143. See D. Pringle, 'The Church of the Holy Sepulchre in the Castle of Tripoli (Mont-Pèlerin)', in *Egypt and Syria in the Fatimid, Ayyubid and Mamluk Eras*, ed. U. Vermeulen and K. D'Hulster, Orientalia Lovaniensia Analecta, 169, Louvain, 2007, pp. 167–82. The present remains of the church do not appear to incorporate any Muslim building, so it was probably newly built rather than a conversion from the mosque. An octagon to the east may have been a family burial crypt.

117. A confirmation by Pons of Tripoli in 1116 shows that the monks had successfully established themselves: Richard, 'Le Chartrier', pp. 610–12.
118. RRH, no. 38, p. 6 (16 January 1103), for St Victor.
119. See R. Hiestand, 'Saint-Ruf d'Avignon, Raymond de Saint-Gilles et l'église latine du comté de Tripoli', *Annales du Midi*, 98 (1986), 327–36.
120. Ralph of Caen, p. 122. For Byzantine relations with Raymond and his successors, see Richard, *Comté*, pp. 27–30.
121. AA, 9.51, pp. 710–11. See J. Richard, 'Questions de topographie tripolitaine', *Journal asiatique*, 236 (1948), 53–9, who shows that, despite being forced to scale down their ambitions, the counts of Tripoli did not really abandon them until 1186.
122. *The Register of Pope Gregory VII, 1073–1085: An English Translation*, tr. H.E.J. Cowdrey, Oxford, 2002, 1.46, pp. 50–1.
123. See Hill and Hill, *Raymond IV*, pp. 3–21.
124. WT, 11.2, pp. 496–7. Tr. Babcock and Krey, vol. 1, p. 463.
125. Richard, *Comté*, pp. 3, 15, 24–5.
126. Ibn al-Qalanisi, pp. 83–7; Ibn al-Athir, part 1, pp. 132–3.
127. J. Richard, 'Les Saint-Gilles et le comté de Tripoli', in *Islam et chrétiens du Midi (XIIe–XIVe s.): Cahiers de Fanjeaux*, 18 (1983), pp. 65–75.
128. See A.V. Murray, 'A Note on the Origin of Eustace Grenier', *Bulletin of the Society for the Study of the Crusades and the Latin East*, 6 (1986), 28–30.
129. AA, 11.10–12, pp. 780–3; WT, 11.9, pp. 507–8; FC, 2.41, p. 531, is typically brief, but nevertheless makes it clear that Baldwin had made peace between the parties. See also Richard, *Comté*, pp. 5–6, and Nicholson, *Joscelyn I*, pp. 22–4.
130. See the discussion by Edgington, in AA, pp. 786–7, n. 22.
131. See Murray, 'Norman Settlement in the Latin Kingdom of Jerusalem', 73–4.
132. *English Historical Documents*, vol. 2, *1042–1189*, ed. D.C. Douglas and G.W. Greenway, 2nd edn, Oxford, 1981, no. 50, pp. 481–3. See D.C. Douglas, *William the Conqueror: The Norman Impact on England*, London, 1964, pp. 306–9.
133. FC, 2.41, p. 533; AA, 9.13, pp. 782–7, who also has a story about 500 soldiers hiding inside the city, ready to attack the Christians, but who were thwarted when they were betrayed. FC, ed. Hagenmeyer, p. 534, n. 14, for the date.
134. Ibn al-Qalanisi, p. 89, giving the date as 12 July.
135. RRH, no. 55, pp. 11–12.
136. Ibn al-Qalanisi, p. 91.
137. Pryor, *Geography, Technology and War*, pp. 113–24. In the past the Fatimids had relied on the control of the ports of North Africa and the Syro-Palestinian coast to provide watering facilities for what had once been a strong navy. See J. Richard, 'Les bases maritimes des Fatimides, leur corsairs et l'occupation franque en Syrie', in *Egypt and Syria in the Fatimid, Ayyubid and Mamluk Eras*, II, Orientali Lovaniensia Analecta, 83, ed. V. Vermeulen and D. De Smet, Louvain, 1998, pp. 115–16.
138. See M. Lombard, 'Une carte du bois dans la Méditerranée musulmane (VIIe–XIe siècles)', *Annales ESC*, 14 (1959), 240–5, 253.
139. See M. Lombard, 'Arsenaux et bois de marine dans la Méditerranée musulmane (VIIe–XIe siècles)', in *Le navire et l'économie maritime du Moyen Âge au XVIIIe s., principalement en Méditerranée*, Actes II Colloque international d'histoire maritime, 1957, Paris, 1958, pp. 61–5.
140. WT, 11.10, p. 509. Tr. Babcock and Krey, vol. 1, p. 477.
141. FC, 2.42, pp. 534–5, 2.44, pp. 543–8; AA, 11.15–17, pp. 786–91, 11.26, pp. 798–801, 11.30–4, pp. 802–9; Ibn al-Qalanisi, pp. 99–101, 106–8.
142. WT, 11.14, p. 519.
143. Arguably his kingdom encompassed Tripoli as well, a situation that led to the later struggle with Pons of Tripoli; see Chapter 7, pp. 152–3.
144. WT, 11.12, p. 514. See J. Prawer, 'The Origin of the Court of Burgesses', in *Crusader Institutions*, Oxford, 1980, pp. 263–95, and Nader, *Burgesses*, pp. 29–30. The first reference to an actual *curia* is in 1149: *Cartulaire du Saint-Sépulcre*, no. 110, p. 231.
145. See Nader, *Burgesses*, pp. 71–99.
146. John VIII died at some point before 1116/17, when a new patriarch, Sabas, bishop of Caesarea, was appointed, but he too was resident in Jerusalem for only a short time. See Pahlitzsch, *Graeci und Suriani*, pp. 101–38, and Hamilton, *Latin Church*, pp. 179–80.
147. See E.H. Byrne, 'The Genoese Colonies in Syria', in *The Crusades and Other Historical Essays Presented to Dana C. Munro*, ed. L.J. Paetow, New York, 1928, pp. 145–59.

148. See W. Müller-Wiener, *Castles of the Crusaders*, London, 1966, pp. 64-5, plates 85-7; Kennedy, *Crusader Castles*, pp. 64-7.
149. A. V. Murray, 'Ethnic Identity in the Crusader States: The Frankish Race and the Settlement of Outremer', in *Concepts of National Identity in the Middle Ages*, ed. S. Forde, L. Johnson and A.V. Murray, Leeds, 1995, pp. 59-73; 'How Norman Was the Principality of Antioch? Prolegomena to a Study of the Origins of the Nobility of a Crusader State', in *Family Trees and the Roots of Politics: The Prosopography of Britain and France from the Tenth to the Twelfth Century*, ed. K.S.B. Keats-Rowan, Woodbridge, 1997, pp. 349-59.
150. See Jaspert, 'Ein Polymythos', pp. 211-12, and N. Morton, 'The defence of the Holy Land and the memory of the Maccabees', *Journal of Medieval History*, 30 (2010), 6-7, 10-11. Even so, Ralph of Caen, p. 38. Tr. Bachrach and Bachrach, p. 61, did claim Baldwin's descent from Charlemagne, thus making him born 'to take his seat on David's throne': see Riley-Smith, *First Crusade and the Idea of Crusading*, p. 112.
151. See Mayer, *Die Kanzlei*, vol. 1, pp. 30-4. Charters are a good indicator of the difficulties faced in establishing a new political entity where there are no models or archives, leaving the drafters with little more than their own intuition and their memories of their lands of origin. Not surprisingly the early charters of the kingdom exhibit many inconsistencies: see ULKJ, vol. 1, pp. 42-51.
152. AA, 11.10, pp. 780-1.

5 The Military, Institutional and Ecclesiastical Framework

1. Ibn al-Qalanisi, pp. 83-7.
2. See R. Ellenblum, *Crusader Castles and Modern Histories*, Cambridge, 2007, pp. 203-6.
3. *Chronique d'Ernoul et de Bernard le Trésorier*, ed. L. de Mas Latrie, Société de l'Histoire de France, Paris, 1871, pp. 315-16. This is a history of the kingdom in Old French, part of which was probably written in the early 1190s by Ernoul, a squire of Balian II, lord of Ibelin. It contains information not found in William of Tyre. This section, however, is unlikely to have been written by Ernoul. See Chapter 11, pp. 275, 286.
4. Ibn al-Qalanisi, pp. 145-6.
5. AA, 11.16-19, pp. 788-93; Matthew of Edessa, 3.45, pp. 203-4. See Beaumont, 'Albert of Aachen', pp. 133-4, who does not think that either chronicler is credible on the stories of the Franco-Turkish alliances.
6. FC, 2.43, pp. 537-43.
7. Ibn al-Qalanisi, pp. 101-4.
8. See Hillenbrand, *The Crusades: Islamic Perspectives*, pp. 89-109, on the *jihad*. She does not, however, think that the campaigns of the first two decades of the twelfth century can be given the title of *jihad*, p. 108. In contrast, see Richard, *Crusades*, p. 134, who accepts René Grousset's term, 'counter-crusades', as appropriate for this period.
9. Ibn al-Qalanisi, pp. 103-4; FC, 2.43, pp. 542-3; AA, 11.20-4, pp. 792-9.
10. Matthew of Edessa, 3.47, p. 205.
11. Ibn al-Qalanisi, pp. 110-12.
12. Ibn al-Qalanisi, pp. 112-13.
13. Ibn al-Athir, part 1, p. 155.
14. See H.S. Fink, 'The Foundation of the Latin States, 1099-1118', in *A History of the Crusades*, vol. 1, *The First Hundred Years*, ed. M.W. Baldwin, Madison, 1969, 1, pp. 400-1.
15. Ibn al-Qalanisi, p.119.
16. Ibn al-Athir, part 1, p. 159; FC, 2.46, pp. 560-1.
17. Ibn al-Qalanisi, p. 126.
18. Ibn al-Qalanisi, p. 130; Ibn al-Athir, part 1, pp. 157-9.
19. Ibn al-Qalanisi, pp. 142-3.
20. WT, 11.19, p. 523.
21. FC, 2.49, pp. 565-72.
22. Ibn al-Qalanisi, pp.141-2.
23. Ibn al-Athir, part 1, p. 163.
24. FC, 2.51, p. 578. Tr. Ryan, p. 209. FC, 2.53, p. 582.
25. Matthew of Edessa, 3.63, p. 214.
26. Ibn al-Athir, part 1, pp. 163, 166-7.
27. Ibn al-Qalanisi, p. 127.

28. See Beech, 'A Norman-Italian Adventurer', pp. 38–9. He had held this lordship since at least 1108. A potential struggle over the control of Antioch between Roger and Bohemond II never took place because of the former's death in 1119.

29. Roger's sister, Maria, married Joscelin of Courtenay before 1119, but the date is not known: see Nicholson, *Joscelyn I*, p. 62.

30. WT, 11.22, pp. 527–9. See Nicholson, *Joscelyn I*, pp. 25–47, and Amouroux-Mourad, *Le comté d'Édesse*, pp. 69–70. WT says that King Baldwin recognised Joscelin's military value, perhaps because of his wars in Edessa. In addition, he may have taken part in the battle of Ramla in May 1102, along with Arpin of Bourges and others from the army of Stephen of Blois: see Orderic Vitalis, vol. 5, bk 10, pp. 324–5, for this group. See Chapter 4, p. 70.

31. Ibn al-Athir, part 1, p. 172; WC, 1.2, pp. 66–7.

32. WC, 1.4, pp. 69–71. Tr. Asbridge and Edgington, pp. 96–7.

33. WC, 1.6–7, pp. 73–7. Tr. Asbridge and Edgington, pp. 106–7; FC, 2.54, pp. 586–90; Ibn al-Athir, part 1, pp. 172–3; Matthew of Edessa, 3.70, pp. 218–19. Ibn al-Qalanisi, who must have been well informed about the battle, chooses not to mention it.

34. FC, 2.55, pp. 592–3. Tr. Ryan, p. 215.

35. WT, 11.26, p. 535.

36. See D. Pringle, 'Churches and settlement in crusader Palestine', in *The Experience of Crusading*, vol. 2, *Defining the Crusader Kingdom*, ed. P. Edbury and J. Phillips, Cambridge, 2003, pp. 171–2; Pringle, *Churches*, vol. 2, no. 229, pp. 307–11, no. 230, pp. 311–14.

37. See Kennedy, *Crusader Castles*, pp. 24–6; Pringle, *Secular Buildings*, no. 157, pp. 75–6.

38. AA, 12.21, pp. 856–7. For the wider context, see H.E. Mayer, *Die Kreuzfahrerherrschaft Montréal (Sôbak): Jordanien im 12. Jahrhundert*, Wiesbaden, 1990.

39. See Mayer, *Die Kanzlei*, vol. 1, pp. 59–60. T. Asbridge, *The Creation of the Principality of Antioch, 1098–1130*, Woodbridge, 2000, p. 5, surmises that Walter the Chancellor held the office in the principality from c.1114 to c.1122, but he appears in no actual charters. There was a chancellor called Jacob in Edessa in 1126: RRH, no. 113a, p. 8.

40. See Mayer, *Die Kanzlei*, vol. 1, pp. 11–54.

41. Epp, *Fulcher von Chartres*, p. 27; Richard, 'Quelques textes', p. 421.

42. See H.E. Mayer, 'Die Hofkapelle der Könige von Jerusalem', *Deutsches Archiv*, 44 (1988), 489–509.

43. See J. Strayer, 'The Laicization of French and English Society in the Thirteenth Century', in *Change in Medieval Society: Europe North of the Alps, 1050–1500*, ed. S. Thrupp, New York, 1964 (originally 1940), p. 113.

44. WT, 18.4–5, pp. 814–17. See R. Hiestand, 'Die Anfänge der Johanniter', in *Die geistlichen Ritterorden Europas*, ed. J. Fleckenstein and M. Hellmann, Vorträge und Forschungen 26, Sigmaringen, 1980, pp. 33–47, and A. Luttrell, 'The Earliest Hospitallers', in *Montjoie: Studies in Crusade History in Honour of Hans Eberhard Mayer*, ed. B.Z. Kedar, J. Riley-Smith and R. Hiestand, Aldershot, 1997, pp. 37–42.

45. The obscurity of his origins made him an ideal vessel for later Hospitaller myths, giving him a semi-legendary status: see Hiestand, 'Anfänge der Johanniter', pp. 42–3.

46. *Cartulaire général de l'Ordre des Hospitaliers de Saint-Jean de Jérusalem, 1100–1310*, vol. 1, ed. J. Delaville Le Roulx, Paris, 1894, no. 1, pp. 21–2; ULKJ, vol. 1, no. 3, pp. 98–9; AA, 7.70, pp. 584–5.

47. *Cart.*, vol. 1, no. 20, pp. 21–2, no. 25, pp. 25–6, no. 28, pp. 27–8, no. 29, pp. 28–9; ULKJ, vol. 1, no. 42, pp. 165–8, no. 51, pp. 176–7, no. 52, pp. 177–9.

48. See Hiestand, 'Anfänge der Johanniter', pp. 47–8, and Luttrell, 'Earliest Hospitallers', pp. 39–40. The process by which the change of allegiance from St Mary Latin to the Holy Sepulchre took place is by no means clear.

49. *Cart.*, vol. 1, no. 30, p. 29. The importance of this privilege can be exaggerated. Hiestand, 'Anfänge der Johanniter', pp. 50–3, makes clear that it neither established the hospital as a separate order, nor exempted it from episcopal jurisdiction. In other words, it was a privilege of a kind received by many other ecclesiastical institutions.

50. AA, 7.62, pp. 572–5. See Chapter 4, pp. 73–4.

51. See Luttrell, 'Earliest Hospitallers', pp. 46–52.

52. Daniel, in JP, p. 120.

53. *Gesta Francorum*, pp. 92, 98. See Jaspert , 'Das Heilige Grab, das Wahre Kreuz, Jerusalem und das Heilige Land', pp. 73–4, for the context.

54. Daniel, in JP, pp. 127–8.

55. See Pringle, *Churches*, vol. 3, pp. 6–15; J. Folda, *The Art of the Crusaders in the Holy Land, 1098–1187*, Cambridge, 1995, pp. 48, 177.

56. AA, 6.41, pp. 454–5.

57. *Cartulaire du Saint-Sépulcre*, no. 19, pp. 72–4.
58. *Cartulaire du Saint-Sépulcre*, no. 20, pp. 74–7.
59. See C.H. Lawrence, *Medieval Monasticism: Forms of Religious Life in Western Europe in the Middle Ages*, 2nd edn, London, 1989, pp. 163–9, who describes the Rule of St Augustine as 'the identity card of the regular canonical life'. WT, 11.15, p. 519. For Raymond's foundation, see Chapter 4, p. 89.
60. *Cartulaire du Saint-Sépulcre*, no. 3, pp. 36–7. The canons had been in conflict with the patriarch in the past, most notably with Daibert, FC, 2.5, p. 384. Epp, *Fulcher von Chartres*, pp. 31–2, thinks that Fulcher might have become a canon of the Holy Sepulchre at this time, perhaps replacing some of those who could not accept the reform. Papal intervention of this kind emphasised the need for institutions like the Holy Sepulchre to have direct access to the papacy. In 1144, Celestine II granted them a church in Rome where they could stay 'when you come to the curia on behalf of the affairs of your church': *Cartulaire du Saint-Sépulcre*, no. 13, pp. 58–9.
61. This chapel was one of the earliest of the crusader constructions on this site. It enclosed the area that was thought to have been where St Helena found the True Cross. See Pringle, *Churches*, vol. 3, pp. 9, 45.
62. See Folda, *Art of the Crusaders*, pp. 57–60, 204, 500, and Pringle, *Churches*, vol. 3, pp. 17–18, 45–6, 58–63. Pringle argues that the canons' cloister was laid out sufficiently far to the east to allow for the future extension of the church, suggesting that at least some planning had been done while Arnulf was patriarch. He thinks, too, that the cloister was not completed until the reconstruction of the church was begun. However, a definitive chronology is not possible.
63. See Pringle, *Churches*, vol. 3, p. 125.
64. FC, 1.30, p. 308; WT, 9.9, p. 431.
65. See Pringle, *Churches*, vol. 3, pp. 398–401.
66. FC, 1.26, pp. 289–90. See H.E. Mayer, *Bistümer, Klöster und Stifte im Königreich Jerusalem*, Stuttgart, 1977, pp. 222–4.
67. *Peregrinationes Tres*, p. 70; Daniel in JP, pp. 36–7. See Pringle, *Churches*, vol. 3, pp. 262–4.
68. Daniel, in JP, p. 135. See Pringle, *Churches*, vol. 3, pp. 72–3.
69. *Cart.*, vol. 1, no. 25, pp. 25–6, no. 28, pp. 27–8. See B. Hamilton, 'Ideals of Holiness: Crusaders, Contemplatives and Mendicants', *International History Review*, 17 (1995), 695–6.
70. See Pringle, *Churches*, vol. 3, pp. 287–9.
71. WT, 9.9, p. 431. See Pringle, *Churches*, vol. 3, pp. 287–9.
72. *Peregrinationes Tres*, p. 69; RRH, Add., no. 36c, p. 3. Baldwin seems to have been forgiven his fraudulent claim to have been marked with a cross in order to raise money for his journey: see Murray, *Crusader Kingdom*, pp. 184–5.
73. WT, 9.13, pp. 437–8. Tr. Babcock and Krey, p. 399. For example, Tancred's grant of 1101 to the monastery of Mount Tabor: ULKJ, vol. 1, no. 20, pp. 124–5.
74. *Peregrinationes Tres*, pp. 73–4. Tr. JP, p. 111. Daniel, in JP, pp. 163–4. Bishop Bernard is first documented in 1109, but it looks as if he held the see from at least 1106, the time of Daniel's visit. On him, see Hamilton, *Latin Church*, p. 60. For the church, see Pringle, *Churches*, vol. 2, pp. 116–19.
75. *Peregrinationes Tres*, p. 74; Daniel, in JP, p. 161. See Pringle, *Churches*, vol. 2, pp. 63–5.
76. See Hamilton, 'Ideals of Holiness', 698.
77. AA, 12.9–11, pp. 838–41. There is a grant to the abbot and monks there in June 1115: RRH, no. 77, pp. 17–18.
78. See J. Riley-Smith, 'Government in Latin Syria and the Commercial Privileges of Foreign Merchants', in *Relations between East and West in the Middle Ages*, ed. D. Baker, Edinburgh, 1973, pp. 109–32.
79. See Jacoby, 'Economic Function of the Crusader States', p. 188.
80. In the mid-thirteenth century the exchequer was called by the Byzantine name, the *Secrète*, but the term does not seem to have been used in the time of Baldwin I.
81. Ibn al-Qalanisi, pp. 130–1.
82. AA, 12.2–4, pp. 826–9.
83. AA, 12.8, pp. 834–5. See Rogers, *Latin Siege Warfare*, pp. 79–82.
84. *Cartulaire du Saint-Sépulcre*, no. 25, pp. 85–6. See Hamilton, *Latin Church*, pp. 61–2.
85. WT, 11.21, pp. 525–7. Tr. Babcock and Krey, vol. 1, p. 496. The key phrase is *quibuscumque conditionibus parentes*.
86. Murray, *Crusader Kingdom*, p. 116.
87. See Mayer, 'Études', pp. 68–72, for discussion of the evidence.
88. Murray, *Crusader Kingdom*, p. 116. Roger was, of course, crowned king of Sicily in 1130 by the anti-pope, Anacletus II, thus establishing a dynasty of Norman kings, but this could not have been anticipated at this time.

89. AA, 12.13, pp. 842–5; FC, 2.51, pp. 575–7. Edgington, in AA, pp. 842–3, n. 25, suggests that Albert's description is modelled on Plutarch's portrayal of Cleopatra.
90. WT, 11.21, p. 526. Tr. Babcock and Krey, vol. 1, p. 497.
91. See Murray, 'Norman Settlement in the Latin Kingdom of Jerusalem', 78–9.
92. AA, 12.14, pp. 844–7.
93. See Pringle, *Churches*, vol. 3, no. 305, p. 142, for the background to this site. A likely date for the repudiation was c.1103, for William of Tyre claims that the illegality of Baldwin's action was one of the grounds for Daibert's complaint about the king's behaviour when he appealed to the pope in 1104: see Chapter 4, p. 78.
94. WT, 11.1, pp. 495–6. Tr. Babcock and Krey, vol. 1, p. 461.
95. See Mayer, 'Études', pp. 57–8.
96. Guibert of Nogent, 7.48, p. 349. Tr. Levine, p. 164.
97. AA, 12.23, pp. 860–1.
98. FC, 2.59, pp. 600–1. Tr. Ryan, pp. 217–18.
99. WT, 11.29, p. 542. Tr. Babcock and Krey, vol. 1, pp. 513–14.
100. AA, 12.24, pp. 861–3. Albert also claims consanguinity. See Hamilton, *Latin Church*, pp. 61–4, and Mayer, 'Études', p. 65.
101. Mayer, 'Études', pp. 67–8.
102. FC, 2.60, p. 602.
103. *Cartulaire du Saint-Sépulcre*, no. 91, pp. 206–8.
104. WT, 11.29, pp. 542–3. In fact, a fleet was sent to Egypt by William II in 1174, but the archbishop may have written this beforehand and then failed to revise it later, since he does describe the 1174 campaign. See Babcock and Krey, trs. vol. 1, p. 514, n. 99. The Sicilians also attacked and plundered Tinnis in July 1154: Ibn al-Qalanisi, pp. 321–2.
105. FC, 2.62, pp. 605–6. Pringle, *Secular Buildings*, no. 106, p. 51.
106. AA, 11.35–7, pp. 808–11; Ibn al-Qalanisi, pp. 108–10.
107. WT, 11.20, p. 525, 11.24, pp. 531–2.
108. As early as 1102–3, Baldwin had referred to himself as king of Babylon and Asia, *Cartulaire du Saint-Sépulcre*, no. 19, p. 73, while in his grant of privileges to the Genoese in 1104 he promised them a third of Cairo if he conquered it with their help: *Codice Diplomatico*, vol. 1, p. 20. See J. Richard, *The Latin Kingdom of Jerusalem*, tr. J. Barlow, vol. 1, Amsterdam, 1978 (originally 1953), pp. 19–41, and Chapter 4, p. 68.
109. AA, 12.25, pp. 862–3; Ibn al-Athir, part 1, p. 196. See also J. Clédat, 'Le raid du roi Baudouin Ier en Egypt', *Bulletin de l'Institut Français d'Archéologie Orientale*, 26 (1925), 71–81.
110. For comparison, see the force of 200 knights that Baldwin took mainly to reconnoitre the Red Sea in 1116. See Chapter 2, p. 32.
111. AA, 12.26–8, pp. 864–9. See Mitchell, *Medicine in the Crusades*, pp. 24–5.
112. FC, 2.64, p. 610.
113. AA, 9.22–3, pp. 664–8. See Edgington, in AA, p. 666, n. 51 and p. 860, n. 52, and Mitchell, *Medicine in the Crusades*, p. 160.
114. See E. Hallam, 'Royal Burial and the Cult of Kingship in France and England, 1060–1330', *Journal of Medieval History*, 8 (1982), 359–80.
115. AA, 12.29, pp. 870–3. Although now destroyed, there is a reproduction of the layout in the chapel of Mount Calvary as seen in the seventeenth century in E. Hallam, *Chronicles of the Crusades*, New York, 1989, p. 107, taken from British Library MS Add. 33566, f. 90, and an illustration of the tomb and its epitaph in Folda, *Art of the Crusaders*, pp. 74–5, taken from Horn, MS. Vat. Lat. 9233.
116. *Peregrinationes Tres: Theodericus*, p. 167.
117. See K. Elm, 'La liturgie de l'Eglise latine de Jérusalem au temps des croisades': in *Les Croisades: L'Orient et l'Occident d'Urbain II à Saint Louis, 1096–1270*, ed. M. Rey-Delqué, Milan, 1997, p. 244.
118. AA, 12.28, pp. 868–9.
119. WT, 12.2, pp. 547–8; FC, 3.1, p. 616.
120. AA, 12.30, pp. 872–3.
121. See Mayer, 'Études', pp. 73–91, and Murray, *Crusader Kingdom*, pp. 115–23, for detailed discussion of the succession issue.
122. FC, 3.1, p. 616. Fulcher uses the phrase *communiter electus*. AA, 12.30, pp. 872–3.
123. WT, 12.3, pp. 548–50. Tr. Babcock and Krey, vol. 1, pp. 519–20. See Nicholson, *Joscelyn I*, pp. 52–3.
124. See A.V. Murray, 'Dynastic Continuity or Dynastic Change? The Accession of Baldwin II and the Nobility of the Kingdom of Jerusalem', *Medieval Prosopography*, 13 (1992), 1–27. The fact that

William of Tyre took so much trouble to explain these events suggests that, even in the 1170s, in some quarters in the West, this was still regarded as a live issue. See B. Hamilton, *The Leper King and his Heirs: Baldwin IV and the Crusader Kingdom of Jerusalem*, Cambridge, 2000, p. 120.

125. This problem has long been identified. Krey, in WT, vol. 1, p. 521, n. 11, thought the embassy left after the choice of Baldwin, whereas La Monte, *Feudal Monarchy*, p. 8, thought that it was before.

126. See Mayer, 'Études', pp. 76-7, and Murray, *Crusader Kingdom*, pp. 120-3.

127. Riley-Smith, *Crusades*, p. 95.

128. H. Tanner, 'In his Brothers' Shadow: The Crusading Career and Reputation of Count Eustace III of Boulogne', in *The Crusades: Other Experiences, Alternate Perspectives*, ed. K.I. Semaan, Binghampton, New York, 2003, pp. 83-99. Eustace was uneasy at leaving his lands in the hands of his illegitimate sons, and he felt he owed loyalty to Henry I of England, his brother-in-law, in his conflict with Louis VI of France.

129. Murray, *Crusader Kingdom*, pp. 122-3.

130. FC, 3.7, p. 635. AA, 12.30, pp. 872-3, says that he was crowned (*coronatus*) at this time, but Fulcher must have been present, so is a more reliable witness. William of Tyre follows Fulcher, 12.12, p. 562. In one of the Albert manuscripts, the word is *honoratus*, which might be rendered 'invested'.

131. Matthew of Edessa, 3.75, p. 221.

132. See H.E. Mayer, 'Das Pontifikale von Tyrus und die Krönung der lateinischen Könige von Jerusalem. Zugleich ein Beitrag zur Forschung über Herrschaftszeichen und Staatssymbolik', *Dumbarton Oaks Papers*, 21 (1967), 152-4. For the chronology, see R. Hiestand, 'Chronologisches zur Geschichte des Königreiches Jerusalem um 1130', *Deutsches Archiv*, 26 (1970), 226-9.

133. See B. Hamilton, 'Women in the Crusader States: The Queens of Jerusalem (1100-1190)', in *Medieval Women: Dedicated and Presented to Professor Rosalind M.T. Hill on the Occasion of her Seventieth Birthday*, ed. D. Baker, Studies in Church History, Subsidia, 1, Oxford, 1978, p. 148. Mayer points out that Morphia was the first queen to be crowned in the crusader kingdom. It may be that Fulcher's reference to Baldwin's consecration in 1118 should be understood to mean that he was crowned at the same time, in which case there is no need to seek an explanation for the delay. However, William of Tyre did not read Fulcher's account in this way and Fulcher himself uses different words to describe the two ceremonies.

6 Antioch and Jerusalem

1. Ibn al-Qalanisi, p. 45.

2. See C. Hillenbrand, 'The Career of Najm al-Dīn Il-Ghāzī', *Der Islam*, 58 (1981), 254-5.

3. See Hillenbrand, 'Najm al-Dīn Il-Ghāzī', 259-67, 271-5.

4. Matthew of Edessa, 3.78, p. 223.

5. WC, 2.14, p. 109. Tr. Asbridge and Edgington, p. 162.

6. Asbridge, 'Field of Blood', 310-13, and map.

7. See Hillenbrand, 'Najm al-Dīn Il-Ghāzī', 267-9.

8. *Extraits de la chronique d'Alep par Kemal ed-Din*, in RHCr, Orientaux, vol. 3, Paris, 1884, p. 616. Kamal al-Din was born in Aleppo in 1191 or 1192 and died in Cairo in 1262.

9. Ibn al-Qalanisi, pp. 157-8.

10. Ibn al-Qalanisi, p. 159.

11. Kemal ed-Din, p. 616.

12. WC, 2.1, p. 79.

13. WC, 2.1, p. 79, 2.5, p. 89; FC, 3.4, pp. 624-6.

14. WC, 2.1, p. 80. Tr. Asbridge and Edgington, p. 112.

15. Kemal ed-Din, p. 617.

16. WC, 2.2, p. 81. See Asbridge, 'Field of Blood', 313.

17. WC, 2.3, pp. 83-4.

18. WC, 2.4, p. 85.

19. WC, 2.5, pp. 87-9. Tr. Asbridge and Edgington, p. 127.

20. WC, 2.6, p. 90. Tr. Asbridge and Edgington, p. 130.

21. WC, 2.5, pp. 88-9; Matthew of Edessa, 3.79, pp. 223-4.

22. FC, 3.3, p. 621.

23. WC, 2.6, p. 91.

24. See Asbridge, 'Field of Blood', 307-8. Walter also records, 2.4, p. 86, the deaths of Jordan of Jordan and Odo of Forestmoutiers, not previously mentioned, but who must have been well-known figures in the principality.

25. WC, 2.14, pp. 107–9; *An Arab-Syrian Gentleman in the Period of the Crusades: Memoirs of Usāmah Ibn-Munqidh*, tr. P.K. Hitti, Princeton, NJ, 1929, pp. 149–50. Usamah came from Shaizar and observed the Franks for most to the twelfth century. He says that Robert was executed by Tughtigin, which angered Il-Ghazi, who had wanted the ransom money to pay his Turcomans.
26. See Asbridge and Edgington, WC, introduction, pp. 1–2.
27. WC, 2.1 and Prologus, pp. 78–80. Tr. Asbridge and Edgington, p. 113.
28. FC, 3.3, pp. 620–1.
29. WC, 2.8, p. 95. Tr. Asbridge and Edgington, p. 138.
30. Matthew of Edessa, 3.79, p. 223. Under the year 1117–18, Matthew of Edessa, 3.74, pp. 220–1, complains bitterly about the treatment of the Armenians by Baldwin, when he was count of Edessa, and by Galeran of Le Puiset, lord of Bira.
31. Matthew of Edessa, 3.79, p. 224; WC, 2.8, p. 95. Tr. Asbridge and Edgington, p. 138.
32. Michael the Syrian, 15.12, p. 204.
33. WC, 2.8, p. 94, 2.10, p. 99, 2.11, pp. 101–2. Asbridge, 'Field of Blood', 314, thinks he may have abandoned the first two when he turned to al-Atharib and Zardana.
34. WC, 2.9–12, pp. 96–105.
35. Asbridge, *Creation of the Principality*, p. 143, suggests that some in Antioch had doubts about the acceptance of Bohemond and were concerned to create safeguards against any changes.
36. FC, 3.7, p. 635.
37. Kemal ed-Din, p. 620; WC, 2.11, pp. 100–2.
38. Matthew of Edessa, 3.79, p. 224. Michael the Syrian, however, 15.12, p. 205, says that the Turks suffered 'a great defeat'.
39. FC, 3.5, pp. 630–1.
40. WC, 2.12, p. 105.
41. Asbridge, 'Field of Blood', 304–5, for comparative maps. However, Roger had been drawing tribute from the inhabitants of the territories of Aleppo and Shaizar and this would have been lost, undermining the ability of the rulers of Antioch to hire soldiers; see Asbridge, *Creation of the Principality*, p. 69.
42. See Chapter 4, pp. 81–2.
43. See Chapter 2, p. 26.
44. Ibn al-Qalanisi, p. 161. See also Hillenbrand, 'Najm al-Dīn Il-Ghāzī', 276–8.
45. Ibn al-Qalanisi, pp. 149–50, 161; WC, 2.7, pp. 91–4, 2.8, p. 95, 2.15, pp. 110–12. See Asbridge, 'Field of Blood', 315.
46. Ibn al-Qalanisi, pp. 160–1.
47. See Asbridge, 'Field of Blood', 315–16.
48. Ibn al-Athir, part 1, pp. 214–15. FC, 3.11, pp. 647–8, says that they never remained in any one area for long.
49. Hillenbrand, 'Najm al-Dīn Il-Ghāzī', 271–5.
50. FC, 3.5, p. 631.
51. The date is not known, but Nicholson, *Joscelyn I*, p. 56, thinks late August or early September 1119.
52. FC, 3.7, pp. 633–5.
53. WT, 12.12, p. 526.
54. See Amouroux-Mourad, *Le Comté d'Édesse*, pp. 121–5.
55. See Amouroux-Mourad, *Le Comté d'Édesse*, pp. 114–19. The first reference to a chancellor is in 1126, and to a constable in 1134; see below, n. 56.
56. C. Kohler, 'Chartes de l'abbaye de Notre-Dame de la Vallée de Josaphat en Terre Sainte (1108–1291): Analyses et extraits', *ROL*, 7 (1899), no. 11, pp. 121–2 (1126); *Cart.*, vol. 1, no. 104, pp. 89–90, is a confirmation of 1134 by Joscelin II of a grant to the Hospital made by his father.
57. Matthew of Edessa, 3.81, p. 225.
58. See MacEvitt, 'Christian Authority in the Latin East', pp. 74–7.
59. FC, 3.6–7, pp. 632–3, 635. There is no definite evidence of coronation *laudes* in the kingdom, but they were probably sung on this occasion, given the references to *laudes* at other key moments in Baldwin's reign. Baldwin's accession had not been without controversy and he would surely have been keen to promote a liturgical ruler cult: see Mayer, 'Das Pontifikale von Tyrus', 187–90.
60. WT, 12.13, pp. 563–4.
61. For the articles, see B.Z. Kedar, 'On the Origins of the Earliest Laws of Frankish Jerusalem: The Canons of the Council of Nablus', *Speculum*, 74 (1999), 331–4. The phrase used is *quasi vim legis*. The use of *quasi* suggests a slight ambiguity about the legal status of these decrees. See also ULKJ, vol. 1, no. 84, pp. 222–4.
62. Hamilton, *Latin Church*, p. 53.

63. See La Monte, *Feudal Monarchy*, p. 123, n. 2; Tibble, *Monarchy and Lordships*, pp. 23–4, 41, 43, 93, 157; P. Edbury, *John of Ibelin and the Kingdom of Jerusalem*, Woodbridge, 1997, pp. 4–5; Mayer, 'Origins of the Lordships of Ramla and Lydda', 543–6.

64. H.E. Mayer, 'The Concordat of Nablus', *Journal of Ecclesiastical History*, 33 (1982), 531–43.

65. See Mayer, 'Concordat of Nablus', 539–41, who suggests a possible deal between Baldwin and Arnulf.

66. See Hamilton, *Latin Church*, pp. 144–50 (tithes) and p. 38 (parish churches).

67. See G. Constable, *Monastic Tithes from their Origins to the Twelfth Century*, Cambridge, 1964, pp. 225, 229, and J. Richard, 'Le paiement des dîmes dans les états des croisés', *Bibliothèque de l'École des Chartes*, 150 (1992), 73–4. At this time only a limited number of individual houses had been allowed to keep the tithes but, as Constable shows, p. 238, from 1138 under Innocent II, the papacy made frequent use of such privileges, a policy that caused considerable friction between monastic institutions and the secular clergy in the crusader states.

68. Jean Richard, 'Le statut de la femme dans l'Orient latin', *Recueils de la Société de Jean Bodin*, 12 (1962), 383, suggests that in the early days of the settlement the Franks may have taken Muslim concubines, but that there is no evidence for this practice after this time. This raises some interesting questions. If the canons derive from actual cases, then this might be an indication that the prohibitions were effective. However, as they are the only evidence for this, they might not reflect a real situation and could be seen as a kind of propitiation of a God who would have been angry at any sexual transgressions. Perhaps some of the canons should not be taken too literally.

69. See Kedar, 'Laws of Frankish Jerusalem', 324–5.

70. See Elm, 'Kanoniker und Ritter', pp. 156–9.

71. H. Buchthal, *Miniature Painting in the Latin Kingdom of Jerusalem*, Oxford, 1957, pp. 35–8.

72. *Cartulaire du Saint-Sépulcre*, no. 27, pp. 88–9; FC, 3.8, pp. 636–7; WT, 12.15, p. 565. The problem may have been exacerbated by the alienation of the kingdom of Sicily, which in the past seems to have exported food supplies to Palestine and Syria. See J. Richard, 'Agricultural Conditions in the Crusader States', in *A History of the Crusades*, vol. 5, *The Impact of the Crusades on the Near East*, ed. N.P. Zacour and H.W. Hazard, Madison, 1985, p. 265.

73. Cf. Kedar, 'Laws of Frankish Jerusalem', 331.

74. *Historia Compostellana*, ed. E. Falque Rey, Corpus Christianorum, Continuatio Mediaevalis, 70, Turnhout, 1988, 2.28, pp. 270–2. Tr. Barber and Bate, *Letters from the East*, no. 13, pp. 42–4.

75. See R.A. Fletcher, *Saint James's Catapult: The Life and Times of Diego Gelmírez of Santiago de Compostela*, Oxford, 1984, especially chaps 6 and 8. Although his architects did not have the originality of those who worked for Suger of Saint-Denis, Diego's programme was comparable in scale and achieved more concrete results, including major reconstruction of the cathedral, as well as the associated complex of chapter buildings, cloister, palace and public facilities for pilgrims: pp. 174–9.

76. *Historia Compostellana*, 2.3, p. 225, 2.10, p. 240.

77. *Historia Compostellana*, 2.71, p. 370, 2.78, p. 379.

78. *Historia Compostellana*, 3.26, p. 463. The Holy Sepulchre already held four churches in Galicia and ultimately found that its expansion across the Latin West necessitated the establishment of a provincial organisation rather than reliance on sporadic visits by individual canons. See N. Jaspert, ' "Pro nobis, qui pro vobis oramus, orate": Die Kathedralkapitel von Compostela und Jerusalem in der ersten Hälfte des 12. Jahrhunderts', in *Santiago, Roma, Jerusalén: Actas del III Congreso Internacional de Estudios Jacobeos*, ed. P.C. von Saucken, Santiago de Compostela, 1999, pp. 195–200.

79. Richard, 'Quelques textes', pp. 426–30.

80. Jaspert, ' "Pro nobis, qui pro vobis oramus, orate" ', pp. 200–12. The *Historia Compostellana* was produced to further the interests of the see, and the inclusion of the two letters from the patriarchs of Jerusalem needs to be seen in this context: p. 206.

81. See M. Barber, *The New Knighthood: A History of the Order of the Temple*, Cambridge, 1994, pp. 3–10, and Schenk, 'Nomadic Violence', 39–55.

82. Ernoul-Bernard, pp. 7–9. See A. Luttrell, 'The Earliest Templars', in *Autour de la Première Croisade: Actes du Colloque de la Society for the Study of the Crusades and the Latin East* (Clermont-Ferrand, 22–25 juin 1995), ed. M. Balard, Paris, 1996, pp. 193–202. For a review of the various theories concerning their origins, see P.V. Claverie, 'Les débuts de l'Ordre du Temple en Orient', *Le Moyen Age*, 111 (2005), 545–57.

83. *Cartulaire du Saint-Sépulcre*, no. 63, pp. 157–8; no. 135, p. 262. This payment was exchanged for three villages in the early 1160s, but it is not clear when it was first instituted. J. Riley-Smith, *Templars and Hospitallers as Professed Religious in the Holy Land*, Notre Dame, IN, 2009, p. 11, suggests that this was a levy, perhaps imposed on other religious houses as well.

84. WT, 12.7, pp. 553–5. William says that the Templars were granted a Rule and a habit at the council of Troyes, which he says took place in the ninth year after their foundation. As the council took place in January 1129, this is not consistent with his statement that the original group was established in 1118.

85. FC, 1.26, p. 291, and n. 30.

86. See Chapter 4, p. 71.

87. Mayer, 'Concordat of Nablus', 541–2; Kedar, 'Laws of Frankish Jerusalem', 327.

88. Kedar, 'Laws of Frankish Jerusalem', 327–9.

89. Daniel, in JP, pp. 126–7.

90. See Hamilton, 'Ideals of Holiness', 699.

91. Sancti Bernardi Opera, vol. 8, Epistolae, ed. J. Leclercq and H.M. Rochais, Rome, 1977, no. 253, p. 150.

92. See B. Hamilton, 'The Cistercians in the Crusader States', in One Yet Two: Monastic Tradition East and West, ed. M.B. Pennington, Kalamazoo, 1976, pp. 405–8, and D. Pringle, 'Cistercian Houses in the Kingdom of Jerusalem', in The Second Crusade and the Cistercians, ed. M. Gervers, New York, 1992, pp. 183–90.

93. See H.E. Mayer, 'Sankt Samuel auf dem Freudenberge und sein Besitz nach einem unbekannten Diplom König Balduins V', Quellen und Forschungen aus italienischen Archiven und Bibliotheken, 44 (1964), 36–41, 48–67.

94. See Lawrence, Medieval Monasticism, pp. 169–72.

95. See Hamilton, Latin Church, pp. 101–2, who suggests such evangelisation was not in the interests of the local baronage, who did not wish to provoke problems with the Muslim population.

96. See K. Elm, 'Nec minori celebritate a catholicis cultoribus observatur et colitur. Zwei Berichte über die 1119/20 erfolgte Auffindung und Erhebung der Gebeine der Patriarchen Abraham, Isaak und Jakob', Zeitschrift für Religions- und Geistesgeschichte, 49 (1997), 325–9, and Mayer, 'Die Herrschaftsbildung in Hebron', 65–75. Reynald of Châtillon became lord of Hebron in 1177: see Chapter 11, p. 268.

97. See Hamilton, Latin Church, p. 77.

98. See Elm, 'Nec minori celebritate', 318–44, and Pringle, Churches, vol. 1, pp. 223–9.

99. WT, 20.3, p. 914. Tr. Babcock and Krey, vol. 2, p. 346.

100. FC, 3.9, pp. 638–42.

101. H.E. Mayer, 'Jérusalem et Antioche sous le règne de Baudouin II', Comptes-rendus des séances de l'Académie des Inscriptions et Belles-Lettres, année 1980 (1981), 718–19.

102. Mayer, 'Jérusalem et Antioche', 721–2. See Epp, Fulcher von Chartres, pp. 27–8, who thinks that by this time Fulcher had become a canon of the Holy Sepulchre and that the intensity of his language suggests that he might have been among those responsible for guarding the relic.

103. Ibn al-Qalanisi, p. 162.

104. See Mayer, Die Kanzlei, vol. 1, pp. 66–7.

105. FC, 3.34, p. 739.

106. WT, 12.14, p. 564.

107. FC, 3.12, pp. 651–2; Ibn al-Qalanisi, p. 166.

108. Matthew of Edessa, para. 87, pp. 228–9.

109. FC, 3.16, pp. 658–9; Ibn al-Qalanisi, p. 167. See Nicholson, Joscelyn I, pp. 62–72.

110. FC, 3.23–6, pp. 676–93, 3.38, pp. 749–51; Matthew of Edessa, para. 96, pp. 232–3. Fulcher has an uncharacteristically long and detailed account of the adventures of Joscelin after his escape, although he admits it was difficult to find out the truth. The story obviously appealed to him, but it does have some romantic elements.

111. Ibn al-Qalanisi, p. 166.

112. WC, 2.16, pp. 114–15. Tr. Asbridge and Edgington, p. 171.

113. FC, 3.31, pp. 721–7.

114. See Chapter 5, pp. 112, 116.

115. See J. Riley-Smith, 'The Venetian Crusade of 1122–1124', in I Comuni Italiani nel Regno Crociato di Gerusalemme, ed. G. Airaldi and B.Z. Kedar, Genoa, 1986, pp. 340–2. There is no extant letter from the East, although it is most likely to have been sent at around the same time as that to Diego Gelmírez. Venetian sources say that nuncios were sent first to Rome and then to Venice: Cerbani Cerbani, Clerici Veneti, Translatio Mirifici Martyris Isidori a Chio Insula in Civitatem Venetam (Jun. 1125), in RHCr, Occid., vol. 5, pp. 322–3, and Historia Ducum Veneticorum, in MGHSS, vol. 14, p. 73. Reference to letters and envoys sent by Baldwin is made in the treaty between the Venetians and the leaders of the kingdom in 1123: WT, 12.25, p. 578.

116. *Decrees of the Ecumenical Councils*, vol. 1. *Nicaea to Lateran V*, ed. N. P. Tanner, London, 1990, pp. 191-2.
117. See Queller and Katele, 'Venice and the Conquest of the Latin Kingdom', 16-28, for Venetian activity in the East in the first decade of the twelfth century.
118. WT, 12.22, p. 573.
119. FC, 3.14-15, pp. 655-8.
120. See Riley-Smith, 'Venetian Crusade', p. 343.
121. FC, 3.17-20, pp. 661-72; WT, 12.22-3, pp. 573-5. A continuous sea blockade was difficult to achieve so the obvious solution was to eliminate any enemy fleet before the siege actually began. See Rogers, *Latin Siege Warfare*, p. 68.
122. WT, 12.24, p. 576.
123. FC, 3.27, p. 694.
124. *Historia Ducum Veneticorum*, p. 74.
125. FC, 3.16, pp. 659-61, 3.22, pp. 674-5.
126. See Chapter 4, p. 91.
127. Pagan had become increasingly powerful, taking a more active political role and leaving more of the work of drafting charters to his staff, notably the notary Hemelin, who, in c.1124, became vice-chancellor and, in 1130, succeeded Pagan as chancellor: see Mayer, *Die Kanzlei*, vol. 1, pp. 67-8.
128. Sidon fell in 1110 with the help of Norwegian and Venetian fleets, but an unsuccessful attack was made on it in 1107-8, in conjunction with the Italians, including the Venetians: AA, 10.46, pp. 760-1. See Chapter 4, p. 93.
129. M. Pozza, 'Venezia e il Regno di Gerusalemme dagli Svevi agli Angioini', in *I Comuni Italiani nel Regno Crociato di Gerusalemme*, ed. G. Airaldi and B.Z. Kedar, Genoa, 1986, Appendix, no. 1, pp. 373-9; WT, 12.25, pp. 577-8. FC, 3.36, pp. 745-6, makes it clear that the Venetians had properties both around the harbour and in the city itself. According to the *Historia Ducum Veneticorum*, p. 74, the Venetians had first been offered two-thirds of the city, but had said they were content with a third.
130. FC does not mention any such controversy.
131. WT, 13.13, p. 601. For Scandelion, see Chapter 5, p. 116.
132. FC, 3.11, pp. 646-7. See Fedalto, *La Chiesa Latina*, vol. 2, p. 234, and Hamilton, *Latin Church*, p. 66. This would have been a preliminary to the appointment of suffragan bishops for the other coastal dioceses. In fact, Odo died before the city was taken and Warmund does not seem to have appointed anybody else until c.1127, when William, prior of the Holy Sepulchre, was chosen.
133. WT, 13.7, pp. 594-5.
134. See M. Balard, 'Communes italiennes, pouvoir et habitants des états francs de Syrie-Palestine au XIIe siècle', in *Crusaders and Muslims in Twelfth-Century Syria*, ed. M. Shatzmiller, Leiden, 1993, pp. 53-4. Balard points out that the Italians were chiefly interested in certain key ports, which meant Acre, Tyre, Tripoli, Latakia and Saint Simeon (for Antioch).
135. Ibn al-Qalanisi, pp. 163-4, 170-1.
136. FC, 3.28, pp. 695-6, 3.34, p. 735, gives 7 June; Ibn al-Qalanisi, p. 172, gives 8 June. See Rogers, *Latin Siege Warfare*, pp. 82-3.
137. WT, 13.7, p. 594, 13.9, pp. 595-7. There had been a temporary estrangement between Baldwin and Pons in 1122, when the king had been ready to use force to compel his submission, but this had been settled by mediation; FC, 3.11, pp. 647-8.
138. WT, 13.6, pp. 593-4, 13.10, pp. 597-8.
139. WT, 13.9, pp. 595-7
140. Ibn al-Qalanisi, pp. 171-2.
141. FC, 3.34, pp. 736-7.
142. FC, 3.56, pp. 803-5.
143. FC, 3.38-40, pp. 749-57; WT, 13.15, pp. 603-4.
144. Pozza, 'Venezia e il Regno di Gerusalemme', no. 2, pp. 179-85; ULKJ, vol. 1, no. 93, pp. 241-7. See D. Jacoby, 'The Venetian Privileges in the Latin Kingdom of Jerusalem: Twelfth- and Thirteenth-Century Interpretations and Implementation', in *Montjoie: Studies in Crusade History in Honour of Hans Eberhard Mayer*, ed. B.Z. Kedar, J. Riley-Smith and R. Hiestand, Aldershot, 1997, pp. 155-75. Jacoby points out that, far from creating a quasi-independent enclave as has sometimes been argued, the Venetians were obliged to undertake some 'tough bargaining' and evidently believed the *Pactum Warmundi* was 'more advantageous than the charter of 1125'.
145. FC, 3.42, pp. 761-5; Kemal ed-Din, p. 644. See Chapter 5, pp. 102-3.
146. Ibn al-Qalanisi, p. 173; FC, 3.42, pp. 763-4.

147. FC, 3.42, p. 765; WT, 13.16, pp. 604–6; Ibn al-Qalanisi, pp. 169–70 (wrongly placing this in 1123–4); Matthew of Edessa, para. 102, pp. 234–6. See also Nicholson, *Joscelyn I*, pp. 75–6.
148. FC, 3.44, pp. 769–71.
149. See Asbridge, *Creation of the Principality*, pp. 81–9.
150. WT, 13.16, p. 605.
151. FC, 3.42, p. 763.
152. A. Murray, 'Baldwin II and his Nobles: Baronial Factionalism and Dissent in the Kingdom of Jerusalem, 1118–34', *Nottingham Medieval Studies*, 38 (1994), 69–75.
153. Galbertus Notarius Brugensis, *De Multro, Traditione, et Occisione Gloriosi Karoli Comitis Flandriarum*, ed. J. Rider, Corpus Christianorum, Continuatio Mediaevalis, 131, Turnhout, 1994, pp. 14–15; Tr. Galbert of Bruges, *The Murder of Charles the Good*, tr. and ed. J.B. Ross, Toronto, 1967 (originally 1959), pp. 92–3.
154. Galbertus, p. 31. See Galbert, tr. Ross, p. 113, n. 8, for possible dates. Charles was probably in his thirties at this time.
155. FC, 3.50, pp. 784–93; WT, 13.18, pp. 608–10.
156. Ibn al-Qalanisi, p. 174. It was presumably also meant to deter Tughtigin from mustering an attack from this region now that the Christians held Tyre.
157. Murray, 'Baldwin II and his Nobles', 75–81, offers some speculations as to the identity of those involved, but there is no solid evidence.
158. FC, 3.61, pp. 819–22; WT, 13.21, pp. 613–14. See Asbridge, *Creation of the Principality*, pp. 146–7.
159. See R. Hiestand, 'Chronologisches zur Geschichte des Königreiches Jerusalem um 1130', *Deutches Archiv*, 26 (1970), 223. Morphia died on 1 October, but the precise year is not known, other than that it must have been 1126–8. If she died in 1126, this in itself might have been a significant reason for seeking a husband for Melisende.
160. WT, 13.26, p. 620.
161. WT, 13.24, p. 618, 14.2, p. 633. See Murray, 'Baldwin II and his Nobles', 76.
162. Pozza, 'Venezia e il Regno di Gerusalemme', no. 2, p. 382. His companions are listed in the Latin Rule of the Temple, given to the order at the council of Troyes in 1129; *Regula pauperum commilitonum Christi Templique Salomonici*, ed. S. Cerrini, Corpus Christianorum, Continuatio Mediaevalis, Prologue (forthcoming).
163. WT, 14.1, pp. 631–3.
164. *Recueil d'annales angevines et vendômoises*, ed. L. Halphen, Paris, 1903, pp. 8, 120; Orderic Vitalis, vol. 6, pp. 308–11, who dates the pilgrimage to 1120. WT, 14.2, p. 633, records the funding of the 100 knights, but places his pilgrimage after the death of his wife, Eremburge. This is highly unlikely as she did not die until late 1126: see the discussion by Hans Mayer, 'The Succession of Baldwin II in Jerusalem: English Impact on the East', *Dumbarton Oaks Papers*, 39 (1985), 145, n. 35.
165. Among the preparations would have been the need to obtain permission from King Louis VI as overlord. The Angevin chroniclers record that the offer was 'on the advice' of the king, but this does not mean that Louis chose Fulk; see Mayer, 'Succession', 140.
166. See J. Gillingham, *The Angevin Empire*, 2nd edn, London, 2001, pp. 8–12.
167. See Mayer, 'Succession', 146–7, for the chronology.
168. *Cartulaire général de l'Ordre du Temple 1119?–1150: Recueil des chartes et des bulles relatives à l'Ordre du Temple*, ed. G.A.M. d'Albon, Paris, 1913, no. 8, pp. 5–6; no. 12, pp. 8–10. Ironically, William Clito had been killed in battle on 27 May 1128.
169. *Cartulaire général du Temple*, no. 12, pp. 8–10; RRH, no. 122, p. 30.
170. The phrase is *cum spe regni post regis obitum traderetur*, where *spes* carries a much stronger connotation than merely 'hope'. It has been argued by Hans Mayer that lengthy negotiations were needed before Fulk was convinced, and that Guy Brisbarre had travelled back to Jerusalem in the course of the year 1128–9 in order to obtain an assurance that Melisende was officially designated Baldwin's heir: 'Succession to Baldwin II', 143–5. This is chronologically possible but, given the comprehensive nature of the settlements in Anjou in the spring of 1128, seems unlikely. Guy Brisbarre may equally have been elsewhere in France, helping in the drive to persuade men to take the Cross.
171. WT, 13.24, pp. 618–19. It is not clear when Hugh and his companions returned, but other crusaders and pilgrims must have been arriving in separate groups throughout the summer.
172. See Barber, *New Knighthood*, pp. 11–19, and J. Phillips, 'Hugh of Payns and the 1129 Damascus Crusade', in *The Military Orders: Fighting for the Faith and Caring for the Sick*, ed. M. Barber, Aldershot, 1994, vol. 1, pp. 141–7. The patriarchs do not seem to have intended that the Templars

would develop in this way. Elm, 'Kanoniker und Ritter', pp. 163-7, suggests that they had originally seen them as their own *militia Sancti Sepulcri*, who would have formed a small cadre of
permanent knights in Jerusalem who could have acted as a focal point for the organisation of
visiting knights from the West.

173. *Gesta Ambaziensium dominorum*, in *Chroniques des comtes d'Anjou*, ed. L. Halphen and
R. Poupardin, Paris, 1913, p. 115. Hugh of Amboise died in Jerusalem on 24 July, presumably
in 1130. He was buried on the Mount of Olives, near the church. After the First Crusade he
had returned to Anjou at Easter 1100. One of his sons later joined Fulk in Jerusalem. On
the importance of these crusading exploits to the family, see N.L. Paul, 'Crusade, Memory
and Regional Politics in Twelfth-Century Amboise', *Journal of Medieval History*, 31 (2005),
127-41.

174. Ibn al-Qalanisi, pp. 179-95. See Lewis, 'The Ismāʿīlites and the Assassins', pp. 116-17.

175. Ibn al-Qalanisi, p. 196.

176. WT, 13.26, pp. 620-2; Ibn al-Qalanisi, pp. 195-200. Not surprisingly, given the large crusader
presence, news of the failure soon reached the West, where Henry of Huntingdon attributed it to
the debauchery of the settlers in Palestine: 7.40, pp. 484-5.

177. Michael the Syrian, 16.3, pp. 226-7.

178. Ibn al-Athir, part 1, p. 278, however, says that it was cold and wet – although, of course, he was
writing much later.

179. Ibn al-Qalanisi, p. 200.

7 The Second Generation

1. WT, 13.27-8, pp. 623-5.

2. WT, 14.2, pp. 633-4. See Mayer, 'Das Pontifikale von Tyrus', 154-5. The day chosen was one of
the great feasts of the Holy Sepulchre, for it was the date that commemorated the return of the
Cross to Jerusalem in 629 after the end of the Persian wars. Mayer argues that the appearance of
the two previous kings wearing crowns in the city of Jerusalem was sufficient precedent for the
shift from Bethlehem to the Holy Sepulchre.

3. WT, 13.28, p. 625, 12.4, pp. 550-1. See Chapter 6, p. 143.

4. Matthew of Edessa, 3.75, p. 221.

5. B.Z. Kedar, 'Gerard of Nazareth: A Neglected Twelfth-Century Writer in the Latin East.
A Contribution to the Intellectual and Monastic History of the Crusader States', *Dumbarton Oaks
Papers*, 37 (1983), 73.

6. Matthew of Edessa, 3.75, p. 222.

7. FC, 3.21, pp. 673-4, 3.24, p. 687. Tr. Ryan, p. 245. See Murray, 'Baldwin II and his Nobles', 74-5.

8. See Murray, 'Baldwin II and his Nobles', 73-4.

9. D. Gerish, 'Ancestors and Predecessors: Royal Continuity and Identity in the First Kingdom of
Jerusalem', in *Anglo-Norman Studies*, 20, *Proceedings of the Battle Conference in Dublin, 1997*,
Woodbridge, 1998, pp. 133-4, 141-2. See ULKJ, vol. 1, no. 83, pp. 220-2, no. 85, pp. 225-30,
no. 86, pp. 230-3.

10. See R. Hiestand, 'Chronologisches zur Geschichte des Königreiches Jerusalem im 12. Jahrhundert',
Deutsches Archiv, 35 (1979), 542-55, and Hamilton, *Latin Church*, pp. 67-8.

11. See Chapter 3, pp. 55-60, and Chapter 4, pp. 73-4.

12. WT, 13.25, pp. 619-20.

13. Ibn al-Qalanisi, p. 208.

14. WT, 13.21, pp. 613-14. See Asbridge, *Creation of the Principality*, pp. 89-90.

15. Ibn al-Qalanisi, pp. 177-8.

16. Ibn al-Athir, part 1, p. 273.

17. WT, 13.22, pp. 614-15; Ibn al-Athir, part 1, pp. 272-3.

18. WT, 13.27, p. 623. Michael the Syrian, 16.3, p. 227, says that Bohemond was killed because the
Turks did not recognise him, implying that he might otherwise have been ransomed.

19. WT, 13.27, pp. 623-5. See Nicholson, *Joscelyn I*, p. 88.

20. WT, 14.4, p. 636 (*regionis illius magnates*).

21. FC, 3.11, pp. 646-8.

22. Ibn al-Qalanisi, p. 215. See Richard, *Comté*, pp. 32-8, for a discussion of what he calls the 'limited
vassality' of the counts, which he sees as analogous to the position of the great fiefs of France at
the same period.

23. WT, 14.4-5, pp. 635-7. Rainald had been captured at the Field of Blood in 1119: see Chapter 6,
p. 124.

24. WT, 14.7, pp. 638–9; Ibn al-Qalanisi, pp. 222–3. Both agree that the Muslim forces were routed, but Ibn al-Qalanisi mentions further engagements in which the Aleppans were victorious.

25. WT, 14.1, p. 632. William had actually held Fulk prisoner for a time as a bargaining tool for lands he claimed from Fulk IV, but this does not seem to have deterred the king from seeking a husband for Constance at the Poitevin court.

26. WT, 14.9, pp. 640–1. See B. Hamilton, 'Ralph of Domfront, Patriarch of Antioch (1135–40)', *Nottingham Medieval Studies*, 28 (1984), 3. Constance was the great-granddaughter of Robert Guiscard, uncle of Roger II.

27. T. Asbridge, 'Alice of Antioch: a case study of female power in the twelfth century', in *The Experience of Crusading*, vol. 2, *Defining the Crusader Kingdom*, ed. P. Edbury and J. Phillips, Cambridge, 2003, pp. 29–47.

28. Asbridge, 'Alice of Antioch', p. 43. For the dating of the revolt and Fulk's return from Antioch in the late summer or autumn of 1134, see H.E. Mayer, 'Studies in the History of Queen Melisende of Jerusalem', *Dumbarton Oaks Papers*, 26 (1972), 104–5.

29. WT, 14.15, pp. 651–2. She must have remarried almost immediately, as she is designated as the wife of Hugh in a charter issued at Acre in 1123: RRH, no. 102a, p. 7. See J.L. La Monte, 'The Lords of Le Puiset on the Crusades', *Speculum*, 17 (1942), 100–18, and Murray, 'Dynastic Continuity or Dynastic Change?', 16–19. At the time of the marriage Baldwin was in prison, but there is no evidence he had any objection to the match when he returned to the kingdom in 1125. It does, however, appear that noble women had more freedom to marry without consent than was later the case: see S. Schein, 'Women in Medieval Colonial Society: The Latin Kingdom of Jerusalem in the Twelfth Century', in *Gendering the Crusades*, ed. S. Edgington and S. Lambert, Cardiff, 2001, p. 141.

30. WT, 15.21, pp. 703–4; ULKJ, vol. 1, no. 105, p. 263.

31. Murray, 'Baldwin II and his Nobles', 76–8.

32. Barisan had been third in the list of prominent seculars at the council of Nablus in 1120. See Chapter 6, p. 130.

33. WT, 14. 16–18, pp. 652–5.

34. WT, 14.15, p. 652. The phrase used by William is *cum domina regina familiaria nimis misceret colloquia*, which has a graceful ambiguity.

35. Mayer, 'Queen Melisende', 98–113, and Hamilton, 'Women in the Crusader States', pp. 148–51. From the beginning of the reign Fulk seems to have been anxious to emphasise his position. See the grant to the hospital for the poor at Nablus, dating from the mid-1130s, in which he stresses that Baldwin 'made me his heir in the kingdom of Jerusalem': R. Hiestand, 'Zwei unbekannte Diplome der lateinischen Könige von Jerusalem aus Lucca', *Quellen und Forschungen aus italienischen Archiven und Bibliotheken*, 50 (1970), 8–33, 54–5; ULKJ, vol. 1, no. 131, pp. 302–4.

36. Orderic Vitalis, vol. 6, bk 12, pp. 390–2. Orderic's comment that initially Fulk 'acted without the foresight and shrewdness he should have shown' is very similar to that of Ibn al-Qalanisi. See H.E. Mayer, 'Angevins versus Normans: The New Men of King Fulk of Jerusalem', *Proceedings of the American Philosophical Society*, 133 (1989), 1–25.

37. Murray, 'Baldwin II and his Nobles', 77–81.

38. See B. Kühnel, *Crusader Art of the Twelfth Century: A Geographical, an Historical or an Art Historical Notion?*, Berlin, 1994, pp. 34–41.

39. When Emma married Eustace Grenier, she had brought with her Jericho and its dependencies, worth 5,000 gold pieces annually in William of Tyre's time. This, says William, had belonged to the patriarchate of Jerusalem but had been conferred on her by Arnulf of Chocques: WT, 11.15, p. 519.

40. Richard, *Crusades*, pp. 139–40.

41. Asbridge, 'Alice of Antioch', 42–3. The political role of the sisters reflects the wider importance of women in the crusader states, where Jean Richard has characterised their status as 'more western than eastern'. Not only could they act as regents, but they could also govern lordships and receive homage and, in everyday affairs, could appear in public without a veil, in contrast to women in Palermo, another society of mixed cultural values. In the crusader states, the keeping of women in seclusion seems to have been exceptional. See Richard, 'Le statut de la femme', 388.

42. Mayer, 'Queen Melisende', 110.

43. See, for example, the confirmation to the canons of the Holy Sepulchre of 4 December 1138, made 'with the assent of Queen Melisende and her son Baldwin', *Cartulaire du Saint-Sépulcre*, no. 32, pp. 95–6; ULKJ, vol. 1, no. 141, p. 326. Cf. Baldwin II's confirmation to the canons in the last year of his life, made 'in the presence of the count of Anjou and my daughter Melisende, with their approval and consent', *Cartulaire du Saint-Sépulcre*, no. 31, pp. 94–5; ULKJ, vol. 1, no. 124, p. 288.

Even so, the queen did not have any role in Antioch, where her consent was not sought: see Mayer, 'Queen Melisende', 109–10.

44. WT, 14.18, pp. 655–6.

45. *Cartulaire du Saint-Sépulcre*, no. 74, pp. 173–4; ULKJ, vol. 1, no. 130, p. 302. His designation is *bajulus et tutor Antiocheni principatus*.

46. WT, 15.27, p. 711. William says that Amalric, whom he knew well, was aged seven when the king died, which is believed to have been in mid-November 1143.

47. WT, 14.20, p. 658. Tr. Babcock and Krey, vol. 2, p. 178.

48. Hodierna is shown as countess of Tripoli in a charter of 4 December 1138 at Acre: ULKJ, vol. 1, no. 141, p. 326.

49. WT, 17.19, pp. 786–7.

50. See Friedman, *Encounter between Enemies*, p. 183.

51. See Chapter 5, p. 114.

52. *Peregrinationes Tres*, p. 68.

53. See Pringle, *Churches*, vol. 3, pp. 142–3, 155; Folda, *Art of the Crusaders*, pp. 64–5, 133, 522, n. 71.

54. See H.E. Mayer, 'Fontevrault und Bethanien: Kirchliches Leben in Anjou und Jerusalem im 12. Jahrhundert', *Zeitschrift für Kirchengeschichte*, 102 (1991), 34–7, who argues that she was forced into monastic life and that Melisende's omission from the Obituary of the great house of Fontevrault in Maine, on which several other members of the family are enrolled, apparently at Iveta's request, reflects resentment of her elder sister. This may be significant because a house's obituary list recorded anniversary dates of those for whom they should pray. A claim based on the Byzantine concept of *porphyrogenitus* (that is, 'born in the purple') was twice used in the kingdom in the 1180s: see J. Riley-Smith, *The Feudal Nobility and the Kingdom of Jerusalem, 1174–1277*, London, 1973, pp. 104, 108.

55. John 11: 1–45; Luke 10: 38–42; Mark 11: 1–11.

56. *Cartulaire du Saint-Sépulcre*, no. 34, pp. 98–100; ULKJ, vol. 1, no. 138, pp. 315–21. Mayer, 'Fontevrault und Bethanien', 15, stresses the importance of this document, as ninety-one people participated, and it has a witness list longer than any other issued by a king of Jerusalem. Thecua, however, was in a more exposed position than Bethany. In 1139, it was abandoned by its inhabitants, who, when they realised they were about to be attacked, hid in caves. A force sent to drive off the attackers was badly beaten. See WT, 15.6, pp. 681–4, and Chapter 7, p. 163.

57. According to an anonymous pilgrim account, as early as the first decade of the twelfth century, the place was 'much frequented by the faithful, and by the Jews as well': tr. JP, p. 188. The east church, originally that of St Lazarus, had been rededicated to Mary and Martha in the early twelfth century: Pringle, *Churches*, vol. 1, p. 124.

58. See Pringle, *Churches*, vol. 1, nos 59–60, pp. 122–37, and plans.

59. WT, 15.26, pp. 709–10; *L'Estoire d'Eracles empereur et la conqueste de la Terre d'Outremer*, in RHCr, Occid., vol. 1 (i), p. 700. The *Eracles* is a French translation of William of Tyre, composed as an epic chronicle for a western, knightly audience. It was written sometime between 1204 and 1234 by a cleric who was in the Holy Land after c.1180 and was therefore in a position to add extra details from his own observation. He could easily have visited Bethany. See J.H. Pryor, 'The *Eracles* and William of Tyre: An Interim Report', in *The Horns of Hattin*, ed. B.Z. Kedar, London, 1992, pp. 270–93, and B. Hamilton, 'The Old French Translation of William of Tyre as an Historical Source', in *The Experience of Crusading*, vol. 2, ed. P.W. Edbury and J. Phillips, Cambridge, 2003, pp. 93–112.

60. Mayer, 'Fontevrault und Bethanien', 14–16, 25–6.

61. In addition, Bethany had a dependency in the city of Jerusalem and local priories near Nablus and in Tripoli: see Mayer, 'Fontevrault und Bethanien', 18. See also, however, Pringle, *Churches*, vol. 1, p. 124, who does not believe that this was a double house. However, Pringle's plan and Mayer's belief in a double house are not necessarily incompatible.

62. *Cartulaire du Saint-Sépulcre*, no. 38, p. 108; ULKJ, vol. 1, no. 210, p. 393, mentions Matilda as abbess (1144); RRH, no. 327, p. 84, shows that Iveta had succeeded by 1157. See Mayer, 'Fontevrault und Bethanien', 19, 30–8. Mayer believes she may have been Fulk's daughter, Matilda of Anjou. She had become a nun at Fontevrault in 1128, at the time when Fulk was finalising his arrangements before his departure for the East; Mayer argues that William of Tyre, who had left the kingdom in 1145, was mistaken in his belief that the abbess had died in office, as in 1149 Matilda became abbess of Fontevrault. Matilda, however, was a common name, and it would be surprising if William was unaware that she was Fulk's daughter, despite his absence from the kingdom.

63. Robert of Torigni, 'Chronicle', in *Chronicles of the Reigns of Stephen, Henry II and Richard I*, vol. 4, ed. R. Howlett, RS 82, London, 1889, p. 205. Robert was abbot of Mont-Saint-Michel between 1154 and his death in 1186 and, as such, was well placed to gather information from pilgrims. See Hamilton, 'Ideals of Holiness', 698–9.

64. See Folda, *Art of the Crusaders*, p. 154.

65. See Mayer, *Die Kanzlei*, vol. 1, pp. 173–4, and H.E. Mayer, 'Guillaume de Tyr à l'école', *Mémoires de l'Académie des Sciences, Arts et Belles-Lettres de Dijon*, 127 (1988), 257–65, where he shows that William retained his admiration for John throughout his life.

66. Buchthal, *Miniature Painting*, pp. 21–2.

67. Folda, *Art of the Crusaders*, pp. 100–5, and colour plates 5–7.

68. See J. Backhouse, 'The Case of Queen Melisende's Psalter: An Historical Investigation', in *Tributes to Jonathan J.G. Alexander: The Making and Meaning of Illuminated Medieval and Renaissance Manuscripts, Art and Architecture*, ed. S. L'Engle and G. Guest, London, 2006, p. 458; Folda, *Art of the Crusaders*, pp. 162–3, who suggests that the Armenian element may be the result of Melisende's patronage, given her mother's background.

69. Folda, *Art of the Crusaders*, p. 155, thinks that the library had been abandoned by the Greeks in 1099.

70. It did not, however, disappear, for the chapter of the Holy Sepulchre was initially re-established in Tyre (which Saladin had not taken) and then in Acre, when the city was recaptured in 1191: see Buchthal, *Miniature Painting*, pp. xxx.

71. Folda, *Art of the Crusaders*, pp. 282–3, 337–47, colour plate 16, for the Gospel of St John.

72. For the most thorough analyses, see Buchthal, *Miniature Painting*, pp. 1–14, and Folda, *Art of the Crusaders*, pp. 137–62, colour plates 8–13.

73. WT, 14.22, pp. 659–60.

74. WT, 14.8, pp. 639–40.

75. *Eracles*, 14.8, p. 617.

76. WT, 14.22, p. 659. Tr. Babcock and Krey, vol. 2, p. 80.

77. WT, 14.22, pp. 659–61. See Pringle, *Churches*, vol. 1, p. 95.

78. *Cart.*, vol. 1, no. 116, pp. 97–8; ULKJ, vol. 1, no. 135, pp. 310–14. See A. Forey, 'The Militarisation of the Hospital of St John', *Studia Monastica*, 26 (1984), 82.

79. See A. Kloner and M. Cohen, 'Die Kreuzfahrerburg Beth Guvrin', in *Burgen und Städte der Kreuzzugszeit*, Studien zur internationalen Architektur- und Kunstgeschichte, 65, Petersberg, 2008, pp. 285–92.

80. See A.J. Boas and A.M. Maeir, 'The Frankish Castle of Blanche Garde and the Medieval and Modern Village of Tell es-Safi in the Light of Recent Discoveries', *Crusades*, 8 (2009), 19–22.

81. WT, 15.24–5, pp. 706–9. Barisan is called Balian the Elder in William's narrative, apparently because of changes in fashion in pronunciation. He may also have received the castle of Mirabel on the road between Jerusalem and Caesarea at this time, although this is not certain, see Edbury, *John of Ibelin*, pp. 4–5.

82. *Cart.*, vol. 1, no. 399, pp. 272–3 (1168), no. 509, p. 350 (1177–87). See J. Riley-Smith, *The Knights of St John in Jerusalem and Cyprus, c.1050–1310*, London, 1967, pp. 435–7.

83. See Smail, *Crusading Warfare*, pp. 204–9, for a discussion of the functions of these castles.

84. WT, 15.6, pp. 681–4. The attempts to defend the kingdom in the king's absence were among the earliest recorded military engagements of the Templars, in this case under Robert of Craon, who had succeeded Hugh of Payns as master.

85. See Chapter 5, pp. 104–5.

86. WT, 15.21, pp. 703–4. See Smail, *Crusading Warfare*, pp. 218–21; Kennedy, *Crusader Castles*, pp. 45–51; Pringle, *Secular Buildings*, no. 124, pp. 59–60, for discussion and literature.

87. WT, 22.29(28), p. 1056.

88. See M.-L. Favreau-Lilie, 'Landesausbau und Burg während der Kreuzfahrerzeit: *Safad* in Obergalilaea', *Zeitschrift des Deutschen Palastina-Vereins*, 96 (1980), 67–71.

89. WT, 14.17, 19, pp. 654, 656–7. William says that at this time Fulk and Rainier were engaged in the siege of Jaffa in the conflict with Hugh of Le Puiset, but Ibn al-Qalanisi places the siege of Banyas in December 1132, when the king must still have been preoccupied in the north. Not surprisingly, William's dating of the events of the 1130s lacks precision.

90. Ibn al-Qalanisi, pp. 215–18.

91. WT, 14.22, p. 660.

92. Mukaddasi, p. 24.

93. For a summary of its history and layout, see A. Grabois, 'La cité de Baniyas et le château de Subeibeh pendant les croisades', *Cahiers de civilisation médiévale*, 13 (1970), 43–55.

94. WT, 15.7–11, pp. 684–91; Ibn al-Qalanisi, pp. 245, 247–8, 253–61.
95. WT, 13.19, pp. 610–11.
96. WT, 14.29, pp. 669–70; Ibn al-Qalanisi, pp. 242–3. These events were soon known in the West, since Orderic Vitalis, vol. 6, pp. 494–503, recounts stories about them in his thirteenth and last book. His information had come from returning pilgrims.
97. Ibn al-Qalanisi, p. 252.
98. *Cart.*, vol. 1, no. 144, pp. 116–18. The charter is dated 1142, indiction 7, but 1142 is indiction 5, so it may belong to 1144. However, the mistake is more likely to be in the indiction than the year, of which everybody would have been aware, while the cession of rights held five years before would only make sense if Raymond were talking about 1137 and not 1139, when he had already lost Montferrand and Raphaniya.
99. Ibn al-Qalanisi, p. 127. Shortly before his death, Tancred had urged Pons to marry his widow, Cecilia, so the settlement of these fiefs may have been part of such an arrangement. Pons was still a boy in 1112 and the marriage did not take place until 1115. See Chapter 5, p. 103.
100. See J. Richard, '*Cum omni raisagio montanee* . . . À propos de la cession du Crac aux Hospitaliers', in *Itinéraires d'Orient; Hommages à Claude Cahen (Res Orientales, VI)*, Paris, 1994, pp. 187–93.
101. Although the counts had had a constable since at least 1110–11, in the person of the long-serving Roger, last mentioned in 1127, RRH, no. 58, p. 13, no. 118, p. 29, there is little evidence of other leading officials. However, in addition to the three named in the charter, Raymond II had a seneschal and a chamberlain: RRH, no. 191, p. 47, dated December 1139. See Richard, *Comté*, pp. 71–8, on the operation of the High Court in the county, and pp. 81–3, on the court of the burgesses.
102. *Cart.*, vol. 1, no. 160, p. 130; ULKJ, vol. 1, no. 170, p. 349.
103. See Luttrell, 'The Earliest Hospitallers', pp. 53–4, and Richard, *Comté*, p. 62.
104. See Riley-Smith, *Knights of St John*, pp. 55–6, and Forey, 'Militarisation of the Hospital', 81–3.
105. WT, 14.23, pp. 661–2.
106. See J. Richard, 'Vassaux, tributaires ou alliés? Les chefferies montagnardes et les Ismaîliens dans l'orbite des Etats des croisés', in *Die Kreuzfahrerstaaten als multikulturelle Gesellschaft*, Schriften des historischen Kollegs, Kolloquien, 37, ed. H.E. Mayer, Munich, 1997, pp. 141–52.
107. Richard, 'À propos de la cession du Crac', 192.
108. WT, 14.12, p. 658. See Chapter 7, p. 153.
109. WT, 14.10, p. 641. Tr. Babcock and Krey, vol. 2, p. 60.
110. Hamilton, 'Ralph of Domfront', 4–6.
111. WT, 14.20–1, pp. 657–9. Tr. Babcock and Krey, pp. 77–80.
112. Edbury and Rowe, *William of Tyre*, p. 46, suggest that he may have had access to a narrative for the period, but there is nothing extant, and that personal witness was equally likely to have been his main source.
113. Asbridge, 'Alice of Antioch', 44–5.
114. John Kinnamos, *Deeds of John and Manuel Comnenus*, tr. C.M. Brand, Columbia Records of Civilization, 95, New York, 1976, p. 22. Most historians see this proposal as emanating from Alice, but there is no evidence for this. Kinnamos places the events after Bohemond's death and refers to the Antiochene leaders as the proponents. Asbridge, 'Alice of Antioch', 46, questions the traditional chronology.
115. WT, 14.24, p. 663. Tr. Babcock and Krey, vol. 2, p. 83. WT, 14.30, p. 670; Kinnamos, pp. 22–4; *Continuation of Gregory the Priest*, in *Armenia and the Crusades*, tr. Dostourian, p. 241. Gregory came from Kesoun and appears to be continuing the chronicle of Matthew of Edessa. See G. Beech, 'A Little-Known Armenian Historian of the Crusading Period: Gregory the Priest (1136–62)', in *Truth as Gift: Studies in Medieval Cistercian History in Honor of John R. Sommerfeldt*, ed. M.L. Dutton, D.M. La Corte and P. Lockey, Cistercian Studies Series, 204, Kalmazoo, 2004, pp. 119–21. Gregory says that Leon and his family were removed to Constantinople, where Leon died.
116. WT, 14. 24, pp. 662–3. Tr. Babcock and Krey, p. 84. Pope Innocent II was sufficiently alarmed to issue a bull forbidding any Latins serving in the imperial army or living in Byzantine territories from taking part in any attack on Antioch: *Cartulaire du Saint-Sépulcre*, no. 10, pp. 51–2.
117. WT, 14.30, pp. 670–1. William says he swore *ligiam* and *fidelitatem*. Kinnamos, p. 24.
118. Kinnamos, p. 25; *O City of Byzantium: Annals of Niketas Choniates*, tr. H.J. Magoulias, Detroit, 1984, p. 18; Ibn al-Qalanisi, p. 248. Shaizar was the home city of Usamah ibn Munqidh, but he has only anecdotes about the siege: *Memoirs of Usâmah Ibn-Munqidh*, pp. 122, 143–4.
119. Ibn al-Qalanisi, pp. 249–51, for the attack on Aleppo.
120. WT, 15.1–3, pp. 674–8. See B. Hamilton, 'William of Tyre and the Byzantine Empire', in *Porphyrogenita: Essays on the History and Literature of Byzantium and the Latin East in Honour*

of Julian Chrysostomides, ed. C. Dendrinos, J. Harris, E. Harvalia-Crook and J. Herrin, Aldershot, 2003, p. 223.

121. WT, 15,4–5, pp. 678–81.
122. Kinnamos, p. 25.
123. Kinnamos, pp. 26–7.
124. WT, 15.19, pp. 700–1.
125. WT, 15.20, pp. 701–2. Tr. Babcock and Krey, pp. 124–5. The phrase *per ignaviam Grecorum* suggests cowardice as well as idleness.
126. WT, 14.30, p. 670. Tr. Babcock and Krey, p. 92.
127. Niketas Choniates, p. 22. See J. Harris, *Byzantium and the Crusades*, London, 2003, pp. 82–9, for the differing perceptions of the Greeks and Latins of the proper order in Syria and Palestine.
128. Kinnamos, pp. 27–31; WT, 15.23, pp. 705–6.
129. Hamilton, 'Ralph of Domfront', 20–1.
130. Ibn al-Qalanisi, pp. 245–6.
131. WT, 15.12–17, pp. 691–9, sets out the history of these events in Rome and Antioch.
132. A previous legate, Peter, archbishop of Lyon, had died at Acre in May 1139: WT, 15.11, pp. 688–9.
133. See R. Hiestand, 'Ein neuer Bericht über das Konzil von Antiochia 1140', *Annuarium Historiae Conciliorum*, 20 (1988), 314–50. Hiestand suggests that the witness could be Baldwin, chancellor of the patriarch of Jerusalem (later archbishop of Caesarea).
134. Innocent's attitude to this dispute was, as Hamilton shows, to some extent determined by the state of his relations with Roger II of Sicily: 'Ralph of Domfront', 11–15.
135. WT, 15.27, pp. 710–11. See Mitchell, *Medicine in the Crusades*, p. 164.
136. Stevenson, *Crusaders in the East*, p. 135, does not mince his words: 'Fulk neither understood the true interests of Jerusalem nor realised the gravity of the situation in the north.'
137. WT, 14.6, p. 638. Tr. Babcock and Krey, vol. 2, p. 56.

8 The Zengid Threat

1. WT, 18.27, p. 850.
2. Edbury and Rowe, *William of Tyre*, pp. 80–1.
3. Mayer, 'Queen Melisende', p. 98.
4. Edbury and Rowe, *William of Tyre*, pp. 82–3.
5. *Sancti Bernardi Opera*, vol. 8, *Epistolae*, no. 354, pp. 297–8. *The Letters of St Bernard of Clairvaux*, tr. B.S. James, introd. B.M. Kienzle, Stroud, 1998, no. 273, p. 346.
6. *Sancti Bernardi Opera*, vol. 8, *Epistolae*, no. 289, pp. 205–6. *Letters of St Bernard*, no. 274, pp. 347–8. These letters are not dated, but the first must have been written soon after Fulk's death. The second may be as late as 1153, as suggested in the translation of the *Letters*, p. 546, but could be earlier.
7. See Chapter 8, p. 197. Ibn al-Qalanisi, pp. 287–8, says his mother and does not mention a sister.
8. WT, 16.28, p. 756.
9. See K. Ciggaar, 'The Abbey of Prémontré – Royal Contacts, Royal News: The Context of the So-Called *Continuatio Praemonstratensis*', in *East and West in the Crusader States: Context – Contacts – Confrontations*, III, *Acts of the Congress Held at Hernen Castle in September 2000*, ed. K. Ciggaar and H. Teule, Louvain, 2003, pp. 21–33.
10. Modern historians are similarly divided. Edbury and Rowe carefully express themselves in the passive voice. 'Melisende can be seen as an ambitious, scheming woman who clung to power, and whose behaviour endangered the stability of the kingdom. In this she can be thought of as a true sister of Alice of Antioch, whose reckless ambition William had condemned.' Edbury and Rowe, *William of Tyre*, p. 82. This might be compared with Bernard Hamilton's view. 'Melisende has often been criticised for not resigning power gracefully to her son at this time [1151–2]: it is difficult to see what justification she would have felt for doing so; she obviously had the support of the Church and most of the southern lords; she was not a regent clinging tenaciously to power after the heir had reached his majority, but the acknowledged co-ruler of the kingdom; she had governed well, but her son was inexperienced and had shown little capacity for government hitherto.' Hamilton, 'Women in the Crusader States', p. 153.
11. See Chapter 6, p. 140.
12. See H.E. Mayer, 'Manasses of Hierges in East and West', *Revue belge de philologie et d'histoire*, 66 (1988), 757–60. See La Monte, *Feudal Monarchy*, pp. 118–20, on the role of the constable.

13. WT, 17.13, pp. 777–8. Tr. Babcock and Krey, vol. 2, p. 204. Although William remembers seeing Manasses, he was not in the kingdom after 1145, but several of the main protagonists were alive in the late 1160s and after from whom he could have formed this view.

14. For the situation of the family at this time, see Edbury, *John of Ibelin*, pp. 5–6.

15. See M. Barber, 'The career of Philip of Nablus in the kingdom of Jerusalem', in *The Experience of Crusading*, vol. 2, *Defining the Crusader Kingdom*, ed. P. Edbury and J. Phillips, Cambridge, 2003, pp. 61–5.

16. See Mayer, 'Queen Melisende', pp. 118–20.

17. See Mayer, 'Queen Melisende', pp. 115–16.

18. WT, 16.17, p. 738. See Mayer, *Die Kanzlei*, vol. 1, pp. 83–101.

19. RRH, no. 172, p. 43, no. 173, p. 43. See Mayer, *Bistümer, Klöster und Stifte*, p. 224.

20. See R. Hiestand, 'Gaudfridus abbas Templi Domini: an underestimated figure in the early history of the kingdom of Jerusalem', in *The Experience of Crusading*, vol. 2, ed. P.W. Edbury and J. Phillips, Cambridge, 2003, pp. 48–59. As an intellectual, Hiestand compares Geoffrey to Aimery of Limoges.

21. See W.R. Taylor, 'A New Syriac Fragment Dealing with Incidents in the Second Crusade', *The Annual of the American Schools of Oriental Research*, 11 (1929–30), 120–30, and A. Palmer, 'The History of the Syrian Orthodox in Jerusalem, Part Two: Queen Melisende and the Jacobite Estates', *Oriens Christianus*, 76 (1992), 76–85.

22. See B.Z. Kedar, 'Palmarée, abbaye clunisienne du XIIe siècle, en Galilee', *Revue bénédictine*, 93 (1983), 261–4.

23. WT, 16.17, pp. 738–9, who says that Ralph was strongly supported by both the king and his mother. See Mayer, 'Queen Melisende', pp. 126–7, and *Die Kanzlei*, vol. 1, pp. 101–12.

24. WT, 16.4, p. 718. Tr. Babcock and Krey, vol. 2, pp. 140–1. William makes Joscelin permanently resident in Turbessel, but Ibn al-Qalanisi, p. 266, and Ibn al-Athir, p. 372, think that his absence was temporary. His son, Joscelin III, was royal seneschal in the 1170s and '80s and was associated with a group in government of which William of Tyre strongly disapproved; see Chapter 11, pp. 268, 285. This may well have influenced the way he portrayed his father.

25. Ibn al-Athir, part 1, p. 372.

26. Gregory the Priest, p. 243. On the city itself, see Amouroux-Mourad, *Le Comté d'Édesse*, pp. 40–2.

27. Michael the Syrian, 17.2, p. 262. Hugh was in his mid-sixties, a Fleming who had been archbishop since at least 1122. Later attempts to present him as a martyr did not succeed: see R. Hiestand, 'L'archevêque Hugues d'Edesse et son destin posthume', in *Dei gesta per Francos: Etudes sur les croisades dédiées à Jean Richard*, ed. M. Balard, B.Z. Kedar and J. Riley-Smith, Aldershot, 2001, pp. 171–7.

28. Ibn al-Qalanisi, pp. 267–8; Michael the Syrian, 17.2, pp. 260–4. For dating, see Stevenson, *Crusaders in the East*, p. 151, n. 1.

29. Michael the Syrian, 17.2, pp. 262–3.

30. Nersēs Šnorhali, *Lament on Edessa*, tr. T.M. van Lint, in *East and West in the Crusader States: Context – Contacts – Confrontations*, II, *Acta of the Congress Held at Hernen Castle in May 1997*, ed. K. Ciggaar and H. Teule, Louvain, 1999, p. 53. However, as Nerses is primarily concerned to present Zengi as the unwitting instrument of God, intent on punishing Christian sin, ultimately this made no difference. See T.M. van Lint, 'Seeking Meaning in Catastrophe: Nersēs Šnorhali's *Lament on Edessa*', in *East and West in the Crusader States: Context – Contacts – Confrontations*, II, *Acta of the Congress Held at Hernen Castle in May 1997*, ed. K. Ciggaar and H. Teule, Louvain, 1999, p. 42.

31. Mayer ascribes this to Melisende's determination to marginalise her son by depriving him of the opportunity to gain a military reputation, which, of course, was denied to her: 'Queen Melisende', pp. 117–18.

32. See Chapter 3, p. 62.

33. Ibn al-Qalanisi, p. 269.

34. Ibn al-Qalanisi, pp. 267–8.

35. Ibn al-Athir, part 1, p. 373.

36. Kinnamos, pp. 35–6. See Lilie, *Byzantium and the Crusader States*, pp. 144–5.

37. Loyalty to the Franks could never be certain. William of Tyre, 4.2, p. 235, says that the inhabitants of the city itself were Christian, but that the surrounding region contained a mixed population. Matthew of Edessa's disillusion with the Franks can be seen as early as 1105–6: 3.30, pp. 197–8, 3.40, pp. 201–2.

38. Ibn al-Qalanisi, p. 266.

39. See C. Hillenbrand, '"Abominable acts": the career of Zengi', in *The Second Crusade: Scope and Consequences*, ed. J. Phillips and M. Hoch, Manchester, 2001, pp. 111–32, and N. Elisséeff, *Nūr ad-Dīn: Un grand prince musulman de Syrie au temps des croisades (511–569 H./1118–1174)*, vol. 2, Damascus, 1967, pp. 293–388.

40. Ibn al-Qalanisi, p. 260.

41. Ibn al-Qalanisi, pp. 271–2, who says that the man was one of Zengi's attendants and that the matter was personal. According to him, the murderer was Frankish in origin which, given the number of Frankish women held as prisoners, is quite possible. There must have been many men of mixed background in the service of Muslim rulers in the East at this period. For the possible Damascene connection, see Hillenbrand, '"Abominable Acts"', p. 130, n. 63.

42. Ibn al-Qalanisi, p. 272.

43. See G. Beech, 'The Crusader Lordship of Marash in Armenian Cilicia, 1104–1149', *Viator*, 27 (1996), 45–50. Baldwin may have been a younger brother of Raymond of Poitiers, and Beech speculates that this support for Joscelin may have been the cause of a quarrel between them.

44. WT, 16.14–16, pp. 734–8; Ibn al-Qalanisi, pp. 274–5. Michael the Syrian, 16.5, p. 271, says that Baldwin's body was never found. See Elisséeff, *Nūr ad-Dīn*, vol. 2, pp. 396–401. Nur al-Din's rapid response was a consequence of his excellent system of communication, inherited from his father. He reacted as soon as he heard that Joscelin had left Turbessel.

45. Michael the Syrian, 16.5, pp. 271–2.

46. See Elisséeff, *Nūr ad-Dīn*, vol. 1, pp. 261–75. WT, 22.21(20), pp. 1038–9, has a description of the cisterns.

47. Ibn al-Qalanisi, p. 275, who dates the marriage contract 30 March 1147.

48. WT, 16.9, p. 726. The phrase used is *plebs indiscreta*. Mayer, 'Queen Melisende', pp. 122–4, thinks that the king was having second thoughts.

49. Ibn al-Qalanisi, p. 277.

50. Mayer, 'Queen Melisende', p. 124.

51. WT, 16.8–13, pp. 723–34. See Smail, *Crusading Warfare*, pp. 158–9, who uses it as an example of the ability of the Franks to fight in a marching column, a method used with varying degrees of success by other crusading leaders in the twelfth century, most notably by Louis VII of France and Richard I of England.

52. Ibn al-Qalanisi, p. 278.

53. Otto of Freising, *Chronica sive Historia de duabus civitatibus*, ed. A. Hofmeister, MGHSS, vol. 45, Hanover, 1912, 7.33, pp. 363–5. Tr. C.C. Mierow, *The Two Cities: A Chronicle of Universal History to the Years 1146 A.D.*, New York, 1928, p. 443. See J. Phillips, 'Armenia, Edessa and the Second Crusade', in *Knighthoods of Christ: Essays on the History of the Crusades and the Knights Templar Presented to Malcolm Barber*, ed. N. Housley, Aldershot, 2007, pp. 39–50.

54. 'Der Text der Kreuzzugsbulle Eugens III', ed. P. Rassow, *Neues Archiv*, 45 (1924), 302–5. Tr. L. and J. Riley-Smith, *Crusades*, pp. 57–9. See J. Riley-Smith, *What Were the Crusades?*, 3rd edn, Basingstoke, 2002, pp. 59–64, on the significance of the pope's offer.

55. WT, 16.18, pp. 739–41. Tr. Babcock and Krey, pp. 163–4.

56. Otto of Freising, *Gesta Friderici I. Imperatoris auctoribus Ottone et Ragetvino praeposito Frisingensibus*, ed. R. Wilmans, MGHSS, vol. 20, Hanover, 1925, 1.39, pp. 372–3. There is good evidence that, unlike Louis VII, Conrad had already been on a pilgrimage/crusade to the Holy Land in 1125, twelve years before he became king: see R. Hiestand, '"Kaiser" Konrad III., der zweite Kreuzzug und ein verlorenes Diplom für den Berg Thabor', *Deutsches Archiv*, 35 (1979), 124–5.

57. See J. Phillips, *The Second Crusade: Extending the Frontiers of Christendom*, New Haven and London, 2007, pp. 61–79, and M. Bull, 'The Capetian Monarchy and the Early Crusade Movement: Hugh of Vermandois and Louis VII', *Nottingham Medieval Studies*, 40 (1996), 43–6. Bull, p. 45, stresses that Louis was committing the full prestige of the dynasty to the crusade and not simply using it as a means of undertaking a penitential pilgrimage.

58. See G. Constable, 'The Second Crusade as Seen by Contemporaries', *Traditio*, 9 (1953), 213–79.

59. *Diplomatum Regum et Imperatorum Germaniae*, ed. F. Hausmann, vol. 9, MGH, Diplomata, Vienna, Cologne, Graz, 1969, no. 195, pp. 354–5; Otto of Freising, *Gesta Friderici I.*, 1.44, p. 375, 1.58, p. 385.

60. WT, 16.28, pp. 755–6.

61. Odo of Deuil, *De profectione Ludovici VII in Orientem*, ed. and tr. V.G. Berry, New York, 1948, bk 4, pp. 68–70, bk 6, pp. 111–41.

62. Ibn al-Qalanisi, pp. 280–2.

63. Ibn al-Qalanisi, p. 282.
64. *Diplomatum Regum*, no. 195, p. 355. According to John of Salisbury, at this time in papal service at Rome, 'they [the Germans] would wait for no-one whatsoever until Edessa, which they came to liberate, had been captured': *Historia Pontificalis*, ed. and tr. M. Chibnall, Oxford, 1956, chap. 24, p. 54.
65. See Hiestand, '"Kaiser" Konrad', 85–7.
66. Otto of Freising, *Gesta Friderici I.*, 1.34, p. 370. Otto says that Louis desired to fulfil a vow to go to Jerusalem made by his late brother, Philip (died 1131). Odo of Deuil, bk 1, pp. 6–7, implies that Edessa was the king's original goal. On the situation in Edessa, see Amouroux-Mourand, *Le Comté d'Édesse*, pp. 86–7.
67. Phillips, *Second Crusade*, p. 208.
68. WT, 16.27, pp. 754–5. Tr. Babcock and Krey, p. 180.
69. John of Salisbury, 23, p. 53. See Phillips, *Second Crusade*, pp. 210–12.
70. WT, 17.1, pp. 760–1.
71. Otto of Freising, *Gesta Friderici I.*, 1.58, p. 385. See Mayer, 'Queen Melisende', p. 127.
72. See Barber, *New Knighthood*, pp. 66–8.
73. See Hiestand, '"Kaiser" Konrad', 93–7, 113–26.
74. WT, 16.28, p. 756.
75. See J. Richard, 'Le siège de Damas dans l'histoire et dans la légende', in *Cross Cultural Convergences in the Crusader Period*, ed. M. Goodich, S. Menache and S. Schein, New York, 1995, p. 228; M. Hoch, 'The Choice of Damascus as the Objective of the Second Crusade: A Re-evaluation', in *Autour de la Première Croisade: Actes du Colloque de la Society for the Study of the Crusades and the Latin East (Clermont-Ferrand, 22–25 juin 1995)*, ed. M. Balard, Paris, 1996, pp. 359–69; and G. Loud, 'Some Reflections on the Failure of the Second Crusade', *Crusades*, 4 (2005), 9–14.
76. WT, 17.2–6, pp. 761–8.
77. Ibn al-Qalanisi, pp. 282–7.
78. Krey argues that the army was not large and that there were 'too many officers and not enough troops': tr. Babcock and Krey, pp. 194–5, n. 13. This is based on William's statement, 16.22, p. 747, that only about a tenth of Conrad's army escaped the defeat at Dorylaeum. Krey, p. 172, n. 43, thinks that this proportion of losses 'is probably fairly accurate'.
79. *Diplomatum Regum*, no. 197, pp. 356–7.
80. Ibn al-Qalanisi, p. 196. See Chapter 6, p. 147.
81. Ibn al-Athir, part 2, pp. 21–2.
82. Stevenson, *Crusaders in the East*, pp. 161–2. Richard, *Crusades*, p. 167. See Phillips, *Second Crusade*, pp. 224–6.
83. Among modern historians, see, for example, Mayer, 'Queen Melisende', p. 128, who suggests possible reasons for the queen's interest in promoting failure.
84. Richard, 'Le siège de Damas', p. 229, n. 11, suggests that William has confused this with the attribution of Shaizar to Thierry in 1157. See Chapter 9, pp. 211–12.
85. WT, 17.7, pp. 768–9. If it had been generally known that the money was worthless, it seems unlikely that those who had received it would have remained anonymous.
86. Michael the Syrian, 17.6, p. 276.
87. *Annales Herbipolensis*, ed. G.H. Pertz, MGHSS, vol. 16, Hanover, 1859, p. 7. John of Salisbury reports this story, 25, p. 57, but says that King Louis 'always endeavoured to exonerate the brothers of the Temple'.
88. *Diplomatum Regum*, no. 197, pp. 357.
89. See Chapter 10, pp. 238, 241–2.
90. See Taylor, 'A New Syriac Fragment', 123–4.
91. See Pringle, 'Churches and Settlement', p. 169.
92. *Peregrinationes Tres*, p. 124.
93. WT, 16.22, p. 747, 16.25, p. 752, 17.5, p. 766, 17.8, pp. 769–70. Cf. Otto of Freising, *Gesta Friderici I.*, 1.60, pp. 386–7.
94. Edbury and Rowe, *William of Tyre*, pp. 160–1.
95. WT, 16.13, p. 734. Tr. Babcock and Krey, vol. 2, p. 157.
96. See M. Hoch, 'The price of failure: The Second Crusade as a turning-point in the history of the Latin East?', in *The Second Crusade*, ed. Phillips and Hoch, pp. 183–5, 193.
97. WT, 17.6, pp. 767–8. Tr. Babcock and Krey, pp. 192–3.
98. WT, 16.25, pp. 751–2. Tr. Babcock and Krey, p. 177.

99. WT, 17.9, pp. 770-2; Ibn al-Qalanisi, pp. 290-2. William dates the battle to 27 June while Ibn al-Qalanisi gives the 29th. Kinnamos, p. 97, says that Raymond would have preferred to camp on a nearby hill. Under pressure from his exhausted forces and against his better judgement, he had settled for a place he knew to be vulnerable.

100. Ibn al-Qalanisi, p. 292; Ibn al-Athir, vol. 2, p. 31.

101. RHG, vol. 15, pp. 540-1.

102. WT, 17.10, pp. 772-3.

103. The suits of armour were valuable, as they often had to be ordered individually or in small batches from specialist western manufacturers.

104. WT, 17.11, pp. 774-5.

105. Michael the Syrian, 17.6, pp. 277-8, 17.9, pp. 283-8, 17.11, pp. 294-6. See C. Cahen, *La Syrie du Nord à l'époque des croisades*, Paris, 1940, pp. 341-3. Part of the problem was Joscelin's lack of money, exacerbated by the loss of Edessa.

106. WT, 17.15, pp. 780-1.

107. Ibn al-Qalanisi, pp. 300-1.

108. WT, 17.15-17, pp. 780-4. The dating of these events is problematical, since their position in William of Tyre's account suggests they occurred in 1152, as does his reference to Humphrey of Toron as constable, a position he did not attain until that year. However, the refusal of the supporters of Queen Melisende to take part, the fact that this was a response to Joscelin's capture in May 1150 and the references to these campaigns in Ibn al-Qalanisi all suggest that 1150 is more likely. See Mayer, 'Queen Melisende', pp. 148-9.

109. See Hamilton, 'Women in the Crusader States', pp. 152-3, who makes it clear she was in fact co-ruler.

110. Mayer, 'Queen Melisende', pp. 118, 136-7, 148-9.

111. The word used by William is *laureatus*. Hamilton, 'Women in the Crusader States', p. 153, presumes that the patriarch would not allow him access to the crown jewels. See Mayer, 'Das Pontifikale von Tyrus', 167-8, who stresses that the form was less important than the manifest demonstration to the people.

112. William of Tyre refers to him as constable during Baldwin's campaigns in the north in 1149 and 1150, although he does not appear with this title in a charter until 1153.

113. ULKJ, no. 226, p. 415. See Mayer, *Die Kanzlei*, vol. 1, pp. 113-16. Between 1146 and 1152, while Ralph was archbishop-elect of Tyre, the kingdom had been without a chancellor, for it was not customary to hold both this post and an episcopal see simultaneously. This had led to the creation of rival scriptoria, hardly conducive to stable government. However, Ralph did ultimately gain ecclesiastical preferment without relinquishing his position as chancellor when he was chosen as bishop of Bethlehem in 1156, achieved, according to William of Tyre, 16.17, p. 739, through the favour of Pope Hadrian IV, 'since he was his fellow-countryman'.

114. WT, 17.13-14, pp. 777-80.

115. Mayer, 'Queen Melisende', pp. 175-8; Barber, 'Philip of Nablus', pp. 66-8. When Ascalon fell in 1153, Baldwin ensured that both in the city and in the *contado* the new fiefs were held by his own followers before he granted it to Amalric the following year. Even then Baldwin was reluctant to allow his brother too much freedom of action, for Amalric was obliged to accept Ralph of Bethlehem, the royal chancellor, as chancellor in his double county as well. See Mayer, *Die Kanzlei*, vol. 1, pp. 116-29.

116. Ibn al-Qalanisi, pp. 287-8; Kinnamos, p. 143; WT, 18.25, p. 849. William calls him 'a certain (*quendam*) Bertrand', which suggests that he knew very little about him and was probably unaware of the circumstances of his capture in 1148.

117. Ibn al-Athir, part 2, pp. 22-3.

118. J. Riley-Smith, 'The Templars and the castle of Tortosa in Syria: an unknown document concerning the acquisition of the fortress', *English Historical Review*, 74 (1969), 278-88, which includes the text of the 1157 confirmation. See Mayer, 'Queen Melisende', pp. 159-60, for a discussion of the chronology.

119. See Barber, *New Knighthood*, pp. 79-83.

120. See Richard, 'Les Saint-Gilles et le comté de Tripoli', 72-5.

121. See Mayer, 'Queen Melisende', p. 158.

122. WT, 17.19, pp. 786-7. Ralph of Merle had been one of the proposed husbands for Constance in the discussions that had preceded these murders.

123. See N. Elisséeff, 'The Reaction of the Syrian Muslims after the Foundation of the First Latin Kingdom of Jerusalem', in *Crusaders and Muslims*, pp. 166-72, and Elisséeff, *Nūr ad-Dīn*, vol. 3, pp. 750-79.

9 The Frankish Imprint

1. Matthew Paris, *Chronica Majora*, vol. 4, RS 57, London, 1877, pp. 143–4. Tr. Barber and Bate, *Letters from the East*, no. 66, p. 140.
2. Ibn Shaddad, p. 216.
3. WT, 17.12, pp. 775–6; Ibn al-Qalanisi, p. 297. William's phrase is *quasi regni limes*.
4. Ibn al-Qalanisi, p. 312.
5. Ibn al-Qalanisi, p. 314.
6. See P.M. Holt, *The Age of the Crusades: The Near East from the Eleventh Century to 1517*, London, 1986, pp. 46–7.
7. WT, 17.25, pp. 794–5; Ibn al-Qalanisi, p. 316.
8. For alternative versions, see H. Nicholson, 'Before William of Tyre: European Reports on the Military Orders' Deeds in the East, 1150–1185', in *The Military Orders*, vol. 2, *Welfare and Warfare*, ed. H. Nicholson, Aldershot, 1998, pp. 112–14. Palestinian nobles who had failed to support the Templars may well have been anxious to protect their own reputations by presenting William of Tyre with this version of events. William disliked the Templars, mainly because he believed that their exemptions undermined diocesan authority, so the story of Templar greed fitted his preconceptions.
9. WT, 17.27, pp. 797–9.
10. WT, 17.30, p. 805.
11. For the dating, see Stevenson, *Crusaders in the East*, p. 171, n. 3. See Pringle, *Churches*, vol. 1, pp. 61–9, for a plan of the town and the positions of the churches in the period up to 1191.
12. See Fedalto, *La Chiesa Latina*, vol. 2, p. 51, and Hamilton, *Latin Church*, p. 59.
13. WT, 17.30, p. 804. The phrase used is *matris consilio*.
14. Usamah, pp. 42–54; WT, 18.9, pp. 822–3.
15. See Barber, *New Knighthood*, pp. 75–6.
16. ULKJ, vol. 1, no. 249, pp. 457–9. See H.E. Mayer, 'Ein Deperditum König Balduins III. von Jerusalem als Zeugnis seiner Pläne zur Eroberung Ägyptens', *Deutches Archiv für Erforschung des Mittelalters*, 36 (1980), 549–66.
17. '*Le Livre des Assises* by John of Jaffa', in Edbury, *John of Ibelin*, XI, pp. 114, 193.
18. See Mayer, 'Ein Deperditum', 563–4, and J. Prawer, *Histoire du royaume latin de Jérusalem*, vol. 1, tr. G. Nahon, Paris, 1969, p. 423. ULKJ, vol. 1, no. 242, pp. 446–9, for the agreement with Pisa.
19. WT, 17.21–30, pp. 789–805.
20. Edbury and Rowe, *William of Tyre*, pp. 161–3.
21. See Chapter 6, p. 121.
22. WT, 17.20, pp. 787–9. Tr. Babcock and Krey, p. 216.
23. Ibn al-Qalanisi, p. 289.
24. Ibn al-Qalanisi, pp. 289–318, for the pressure exerted by Nur al-Din.
25. Ibn al-Qalanisi, p. 320.
26. See J. Drory, 'Hanbalis of the Nablus Region in the Eleventh and Twelfth Centuries', in *The Medieval Levant: Studies in Memory of Eliyahu Ashtor (1914–1984)*, ed. B.Z. Kedar and A.L. Udovitch, Haifa, 1988, pp. 93–9. They migrated in two groups, totalling 119 persons. Members of the family later fought in Saladin's armies.
27. WT, 17.26, p. 796.
28. Ibn al-Qalanisi, pp. 348, 353.
29. WT, 17.26, pp. 795–6 (*viri militi quasi gregario nubere dignaretur*).
30. PL, vol. 155, pp. 1263–4. Tr. Barber and Bate, *Letters from the East*, no. 19, p. 50.
31. Michael the Syrian, 17.10, p. 290.
32. WT, 18.1, p. 809.
33. WT, 17.10, p. 773. See Chapter 8, pp. 193–4.
34. WT, 15.18, pp. 699–700. This cluster of men from the Limousin may reflect Raymond's attempt to counter the predominantly Norman nature of the principality.
35. See B. Hamilton, 'Aimery of Limoges, Patriarch of Antioch: Ecumenist, Scholar and Patron of Hermits', in *The Joy of Learning and the Love of God: Studies in Honor of Jean Leclercq*, ed. E.R. Elder, Cistercian Studies, 160, Kalamazoo, 1995, pp. 270–1.
36. R. Hiestand, 'Un centre intellectual en Syrie du Nord? Notes sur la personnalité d'Aimery d'Antioche, Albert de Tarse et *Rorgo Fretellus*', *Le Moyen Age*, 5th series, 8 (1994), 8–16.
37. See Kedar, 'Gerard of Nazareth', 74.
38. See Chapter 4, pp. 92–3.

39. See L. Cochrane, *Adelard of Bath: The First English Scientist*, London, 1994, pp. 32–40. It is hard to pin down the chronology of Adelard's travels, but his reference to the earthquake of 1114, which he experienced in Mamistra, suggests he was in Syria at about this time.

40. Hugh Eteriano, *Contra Patarenos*, ed., tr. and introd. J. Hamilton, S. Hamilton and B. Hamilton, Leiden, 2004, pp. 129–30. See K. Ciggaar, 'Manuscripts as Intermediaries: The Crusader States and Literary Cross-Fertilization', in *East and West in the Crusader States: Context - Contacts - Confrontations. Acta of the Congress Held at Hernen Castle in May 1993*, ed. K. Ciggaar, A. Davids and H. Teule, Louvain, 1996, pp. 133–7.

41. Hiestand, 'Un centre intellectuel', 19–36, and P.C. Boeren, *Rorgo Fretellus de Nazareth et sa description de la Terre Sainte: Histoire et édition du texte*, Amsterdam, 1980.

42. See Hamilton, 'Aimery of Limoges', 278.

43. Kinnamos, 3.14, pp. 97–8. Nor was Constance, who, 'because she was aged, regarded him with displeasure'.

44. PL, vol. 155, pp. 1263–4. Tr. Barber and Bate, *Letters from the East*, no. 19, pp. 49–50.

45. WT, 18.23, p. 845.

46. WT, 18.1, p. 809; Kinnamos, 4.18, pp. 138–9.

47. See R.W. Edwards, 'Baǧras and Armenian Cilicia: A Reassessment', *Revue des études arméniennes*, 17 (1983), 415–35, and *The Fortifications of Armenian Cilicia*, Washington, DC, 1987, pp. 31–3, 102, 253, who found few signs of Armenian construction, and Claverie, 'Les débuts de l'Ordre du Temple en Orient', 558–9.

48. WT, 18.10, pp. 823–5. Tr. Babcock and Krey, pp. 253–4. Kinnamos, 4.17, pp. 136–7.

49. WT, 18.11, p. 825. Tr. Babcock and Krey, p. 255.

50. WT, 17.24, pp. 793–4.

51. Ibn al-Qalanisi, p. 327.

52. WT, 18.11, pp. 825–6.

53. WT, 18.12–14, pp. 826–32; Ibn al-Qalanisi, pp. 333–7.

54. RHG, vol. 15, no. 34, pp. 681–2. Letter of the pope to Samson, archbishop of Reims, and his suffragans (13 November 1157).

55. Ibn al-Qalanisi, p. 337.

56. WT, 18.15, pp. 832–3.

57. Ibn al-Qalanisi, pp. 338–40. Earthquakes had been felt since the previous September: pp. 326, 328–9.

58. WT, 18.17, p. 835; Ibn al-Qalanisi, pp. 341–2.

59. WT, 18.18, pp. 836–7; Ibn al-Qalanisi, p. 342, makes brief mention of this campaign, but attributes the Frankish retreat to the appearance of a host of Muslim fighters gathered to save the city. However, it seems unlikely that such an ad hoc force would have intimidated an army as strong as that of the Franks.

60. WT, 18.19, pp. 838–40, does not name the fortress, but says that it had formerly been under Reynald's control, implying that it had only been lost a short time before. Ibn al-Qalanisi, p. 344, identifies it as Harim.

61. WT, 18.14, p. 831. Tr. Babcock and Krey, pp. 261–2.

62. WT, 18.16, p. 834. Mayer, 'Ein Deperditum', 560, dates the embassy to before 4 October 1157.

63. Gregory the Priest, p. 272. This implies that Baldwin accepted the emperor's view of the Byzantine position in the north.

64. WT, 18.22, pp. 842–4.

65. See Hamilton, *Latin Church*, pp. 75–6.

66. This must have been an especially bitter occasion for Gerard of Nazareth, whose anti-Greek views were deeply entrenched. Andrew Jotischky speculates that, at this time, he might even have been replaced as bishop of Latakia by a Greek: see 'The Frankish Encounter with the Greek Orthodox in the Crusader States: The Case of Gerard of Nazareth and Mary Magdalene' in *Tolerance and Intolerance: Social Conflict in the Age of the Crusades*, ed. M. Gervers and J.M. Powell, Syracuse, NY, 2001, pp. 100–14, 168–72.

67. Gregory the Priest, p. 273.

68. Ibn al-Qalanisi, p. 355. Nevertheless, ransoms were paid. Among those released was Hugh of Ibelin, captured in 1157; WT, 18.24, p. 847. Early in 1160, he made a grant to the canons of the Holy Sepulchre in thanks for their help with his ransom, while John Gotman, captured at the same time, had been obliged to sell four *casals* to the Holy Sepulchre to raise the money for his release: *Cartulaire du Saint-Sépulcre*, no. 53, pp. 140–2, no. 88, pp. 201–3.

69. These events are covered by WT, 18, 23–5, pp. 844–9, and Kinnamos, 4.17–21, pp. 136–45. Both narratives tell essentially the same story with minor variations of detail, but with considerable

differences in emphasis. As might be expected, Kinnamos is especially concerned to show the extent of the imperial triumph. Paul Magdalino argues that Manuel intended to carry through the campaign against Nur al-Din, but was prevented by news of a conspiracy in Constantinople: *The Empire of Manuel I Komnenos, 1143–80*, Cambridge, 1993, p. 71.

70. See Harris, *Byzantium and the Crusades*, pp. 15–32, for the historical context of this imperial image-making.

71. See H. Möhring, *Saladin: The Sultan and his Times, 1138–1193*, tr. D.S. Bachrach, Baltimore, MD, 2008, pp. 20–2.

72. WT, 18.27–8, pp. 850–1, 18.30, pp. 854–5. For the dating of Reynald's capture, see B. Hamilton, 'The Elephant of Christ: Reynald of Châtillon', *Studies in Church History*, 15 (1978), pp. 98–9, n. 13.

73. Kinnamos, pp. 158–9. In contrast, one of the Byzantine envoys, Konstantinos Manasses, described Melisende as very beautiful, 'whom I thought worthy of the emperor': see W.J. Aerts, 'A Byzantine Traveller to One of the Crusader States' in *East and West in the Crusader States: Context – Contacts – Confrontations*, Vol. 3, *Acta of the Congress Held at Hernen Castle in September 2000*, ed. K. Ciggaar and H. Teule, Louvain, 2003, pp. 184–5.

74. In fact, although William of Tyre says that the same envoys were found in Antioch, it seems that the Byzantines were actually conducting parallel negotiations, which would explain the delaying tactics: Aerts, 'Byzantine Traveller', p. 170.

75. WT, 18.31, pp. 856–7, 18.33, pp. 858–9. William does not identify which Byzantine lands were attacked.

76. Michael the Syrian, 18.10, p. 324. Bohemond III first appears in charters in 1163: RRH, no. 387, pp. 101–2, no. 388, p. 102.

77. See Hamilton, 'Women in the Crusader States', pp. 154–5.

78. WT, 18.19, p. 838.

79. See, for example, Baldwin III's 1159 grant of the *casal* of Casracos to the abbey of St Mary of Jehoshaphat at Melisende's request: *Chartes de Terre Sainte provenant de l'abbaye de Notre-Dame de Josaphat*, ed. F. Delaborde, Paris, 1880, nos 33 and 34, pp. 80–2; ULKJ, vol. 1, no. 248, pp. 455–7.

80. WT, 18.20, pp. 840–1; *Eracles*, vol. 1 (ii), p. 854, says that *ces hautes dames*, Melisende and Sibylla, went to great trouble to ensure that this appointment was made.

81. WT, 18.29, pp. 852–4. The chief supporter of Alexander was Peter, archbishop of Tyre, William's predecessor but one. See also Mayer, 'Guillaume de Tyr à l'école', 260–1.

82. *Papsturkunden für Kirchen im Heiligen Lande*, ed. R. Hiestand, Vorarbeiten zum Oriens Pontificus, 3, Göttingen, 1985, no. 83, pp. 225–6. Tr. Barber and Bate, *Letters from the East*, no. 20, pp. 50–1.

83. RRH, no. 356, p. 93.

84. WT, 18.27, pp. 850–1, 18.32, p. 858.

85. *Tabulae Ordinis Theutonici*, ed. E. Strelhke, Berlin, 1869, no. 3, pp. 3–5; ULKJ, vol. 1, no. 263, pp. 479–86. See Barber, 'Philip of Nablus' 68–71. Philip had held his fief directly from the queen.

86. Bulst-Thiele, *Sacrae Domus Templi Hierosolymitani Magistri*, p. 80; Hamilton, 'Women in the Crusader States' p. 158, n. 80.

87. '*Le livre des assises* by John of Jaffa', XIII, pp. 118, 196. However, this figure may be misleading, in that key fortresses in exposed positions would need to be adequately garrisoned at all times, even when the king summoned the host. The lord of Transjordan must therefore have had additional military resources.

88. Mayer, 'Queen Melisende', pp. 179–80.

89. WT, 18.34, pp. 859–60. William says *cum dissinteria*.

90. See D.M. Metcalf, 'Describe the Currency of the Latin Kingdom of Jerusalem', in *Montjoie: Studies in Crusade History in Honour of Hans Eberhard Mayer*, ed. B.Z. Kedar, J. Riley-Smith and R. Hiestand, Aldershot, 1997, pp. 192–3. He dates the recoining to the 1140s, but the period of Baldwin's sole rule in the 1150s seems more likely.

91. See P.W. Edbury, 'The Baronial Coinage of the Latin Kingdom of Jerusalem' in *Coinage in the Latin East*, ed. P.W. Edbury and D.M. Metcalf, Oxford, 1980, p. 66. As Edbury points out, it was not usual to legislate against a hypothetical situation, so it is likely that there was some baronial coinage in circulation. Thereafter, there is little evidence of such coinage in the kingdom before 1187, except for some issues of Reynald of Sidon in the mid-1180s.

92. See B. Hamilton, 'Rebuilding Zion: The Holy Places of Jerusalem in the Twelfth Century', in *Studies in Church History*, 14 (1977), pp. 105–16, and 'The Impact of Crusader Jerusalem on Western Christendom', *Catholic Historical Review*, 80 (1994), 695–713.

93. However, see Chapter 2, pp. 44-5, for Jewish residents, and B.Z. Kedar, 'A Twelfth-Century Description of the Jerusalem Hospital', in *The Military Orders*, vol. 2, *Welfare and Warfare*, ed. H. Nicholson, Aldershot, 1998, pp. 6-7, for admissions by the Hospitallers of both Jews and Muslims to their facilities.

94. See J.C. Russell, *Medieval Regions and their Cities*, Newton Abbot, 1972, pp. 200-7. For a contrary view, see D. Pringle, 'Crusader Jerusalem', *Bulletin of the Anglo-Israel Archaeological Society*, 10 (1990-1), 106, who suggests 20,000-30,000.

95. See Nader, *Burgesses*, pp. 74-6.

96. Pringle, 'Crusader Jerusalem', 108.

97. *Peregrinationes Tres*, p. 156. See Folda, *Art of the Crusaders*, pp. 228-9, 542.

98. *Abbot Suger on the Abbey Church of St.-Denis and its Art Treasures*, ed. and tr. E. Panofsky, 2nd edn, G. Panofsky-Soergel, Princeton, NJ, 1979, pp. 111-21.

99. WT, 8.3, p. 386.

100. See Folda, *Art of the Crusaders*, pp. 177-229, and Pringle, *Churches*, vol. 3, pp. 21-3, 38-58.

101. *Peregrinationes Tres*, p. 151. Tr. JP, pp. 281-2.

102. WT, 18.3, p. 812.

103. See A. Borg, 'Observations on the Historiated Lintel of the Holy Sepulchre, Jerusalem', *Journal of the Warburg and Courtauld Institutes*, 32 (1969), 25-40, and M. Lindner, 'Topography and Iconography in Twelfth-Century Jerusalem', in *The Horns of Hattin*, ed. B.Z. Kedar, London, 1992, pp. 81-98. Lindner, p. 96, also points out the 'common stewardship of the Augustinian canons' of the sites illustrated.

104. See Folda, *Art of the Crusaders*, pp. 225-7, and Pringle, *Churches*, vol. 3, pp. 29, 54-5.

105. *Peregrinationes Tres*, p. 146. See A.J. Boas, *Jerusalem in the Time of the Crusades: Society, Landscape and Art in the Holy City under Frankish Rule*, London, 2001, pp. 73-82, 167; Pringle, *Churches*, vol. 3, no. 329, p. 217; and R. Ellenblum, 'Frankish Castles, Muslim Castles, and the Medieval Citadel of Jerusalem', in *In Laudem Hierosolymitani: Studies in Crusades and Medieval Culture in Honour of Benjamin Z. Kedar*, ed. I. Shagrir, R. Ellenblum and J. Riley-Smith, Aldershot, 2007, pp. 93-109.

106. Kedar, 'A Twelfth-Century Description of the Jerusalem Hospital', pp. 8, 19, 24.

107. *Peregrinationes Tres*, pp. 131, 157-8.

108. See C. Schick, 'The Muristan, or the Site of the Hospital of St. John of Jerusalem', *Palestine Exploration Fund: Quarterly Statement* (1902), 50.

109. See D. Pringle, 'The Layout of the Jerusalem Hospital in the Twelfth Century: Further Thoughts and Suggestions', in *The Military Orders*, vol. 4, *On Land and Sea*, ed. J. Upton-Ward, Aldershot, 2008, pp. 91-110.

110. WT, 18.3, pp. 812-14. In the spring of 1155, Patriarch Fulcher and several bishops travelled to Italy to present their case against the order to the pope but, according to William of Tyre, 18.6-8, pp. 817-21, they were unsuccessful because of Hospitaller bribery.

111. See Schick, 'Muristan', 42-56, including plan. In addition, the two abbey churches of St Mary Major and St Mary Latin stood on the site, housing communities of Benedictine nuns and monks respectively. See Pringle, *Churches*, vol. 3, no. 334, pp. 236-53, no. 335, pp. 253-61.

112. See Folda, *Art of the Crusaders*, pp. 97-100, and colour plates 3 and 4.

113. Ernoul-Bernard, p. 193. See Boas, *Jerusalem in the Time of the Crusades*, pp. 197-8.

114. *Peregrinationes Tres*, pp. 134, 164-5. See Pringle, *Churches*, vol. 3, nos 368-9, pp. 417-34, and A.J. Boas, *Archaeology of the Military Orders: A Survey of the Urban Centres, Rural Settlement and Castles of the Military Orders in the Latin East (c.1120-1291)*, London, 2006, pp. 19-28. Boas thinks that there were two cloisters east and west of the al-Aqsa, but that the new church was laid out on the eastern side. This does not tally with Theoderic's description, which places both the palace and the church on the western side. It is not clear if it was ever finished, but whatever its condition it was entirely dismantled after Saladin took over Jerusalem in 1187.

115. See Folda, *Art of the Crusaders*, pp. 441-56, 595, who believes that it was created specifically for the Templar building campaign in the mid-twelfth century, and Z. Jacoby, 'The Workshop of the Temple Area in Jerusalem in the Twelfth Century: Its Origin, Evolution and Impact', *Zeitschrift für Kunstgeschichte*, 45 (1982), 325-94, who thinks it catered for a wider range of commissions.

116. See Pringle, *Churches*, vol. 3, no. 332, pp. 222-8, and J. Riley-Smith, 'The Death and Burial of Latin Christian Pilgrims to Jerusalem and Acre, 1099-1291', *Crusades*, 7 (2008), 171-4.

117. *Cartulaire du Saint-Sépulcre*, no. 58, pp. 149-50.

118. RHG, vol. 16, no. 492, p. 168. Tr. Barber and Bate, *Letters from the East*, no. 37, p. 71.

119. Raymond of Aguilers, p. 139.

120. Kedar, 'Gerard of Nazareth', 72; *Cart.*, vol. 1, no. 858, p. 531.
121. *Peregrinationes Tres*, p. 145; JP, p. 276.
122. Kedar, 'Gerard of Nazareth', p. 72.
123. Ernoul-Bernard, pp. 189–210, which contains a description of the city probably written after the Christian recovery in 1229. See Boas, *Jerusalem in the Time of the Crusades*, pp. 142, 165–7.
124. See D. Pringle, 'Templar Castles on the Road to the Jordan', in *The Military Orders: Fighting for the Faith and Caring for the Sick*, ed. M. Barber, Aldershot, 1994, pp. 148–66, and 'Templar Castles between Jaffa and Jerusalem', in *The Military Orders*. vol. 2, *Welfare and Warfare*, ed. H. Nicholson, Aldershot, 1998, pp. 89–109.
125. The standard products listed on the Templar estates dependent on the Holy Sepulchre in the early 1160s are wine, oil, wheat, rye, barley, oats, beans, chickpeas, lentils, sesame, rice and millet: *Cartulaire du Saint-Sépulcre*, no. 64, p. 159. See Fulcher of Chartres's comments, 2.5, pp. 378–9, on the taste of dates, which he had never encountered before. For a concise overview, see Richard, 'Agricultural Conditions in the Crusader States', pp. 251–66.
126. See J. Prawer, 'Colonization Activities in the Latin Kingdom', in *Crusader Institutions*, Oxford, 1980, pp. 126–35; Pringle, 'Magna Mahumeria', 147–68; Ellenblum, *Frankish Rural Settlement*, pp. 82–4; A.J. Boas, *Crusader Archaeology: The Material Culture of the Latin East*, London, 1999, pp. 63–5; Nader, *Burgesses*, p. 188.
127. See Ellenblum, *Frankish Rural Settlement*, pp. 86–94.
128. See Ellenblum, *Frankish Rural Settlement*, pp. 205–8, for flour mills, and A. Peled, 'The Local Sugar Industry in the Latin Kingdom', in *Knights of the Holy Land: The Crusader Kingdom of Jerusalem*, ed. S. Rozenberg, Jerusalem, 1999, pp. 251–7. AA, 5.38, pp. 388–9, refers to sugar processing, and WT, 13.3, p. 589, says that it was exported all over the world. See Jacoby, 'Economic Function of the Crusader States', pp. 163–4, 170–2.
129. See R.P. Harper and D. Pringle, *Belmont Castle: The Excavation of a Crusader Stronghold in the Kingdom of Jerusalem*, British Academy Monographs in Archaeology, 10, Oxford, 2000.
130. See D. Pringle, 'Aqua Bella: The Interpretation of a Crusader Courtyard Building', in *The Horns of Hattin*, ed. B.Z. Kedar, London, 1992, pp. 147–67, and Pringle, *Churches*, vol. 1, no. 1, pp. 7–17.
131. See Ellenblum, *Frankish Rural Settlement*, pp. 181–5.
132. See Ellenblum, *Frankish Rural Settlement*, pp. 213–87, for the spatial distribution.
133. See J. Riley-Smith, 'Some Lesser Officials in Latin Syria', *English Historical Review*, 87 (1972), 1–26.
134. See H.E. Mayer, 'Latins, Muslims and Greeks in the Latin Kingdom of Jerusalem', *History*, 63 (1978), 179–87; P.L. Sidelko, 'Muslim Taxation under Crusader Rule', in *Tolerance and Intolerance: Social Conflict in the Age of the Crusades*, ed. M. Gervers and J.M. Powell, Syracuse, NY, 2001, pp. 65–74, 156–60; D.E.P. Jackson, 'Some Considerations Relating to the History of the Muslims in the Crusader States', in *East and West in the Crusader States. Context – Contacts – Confrontations. Acta of the Congress Held at Hernen Castle in May 1993*, ed. K. Ciggaar, A. Davids and H. Teule, Louvain, 1996, pp. 21–9.

10 King Amalric

1. William of Tyre, 18.22, pp. 843–4, says the marriage was happy and that Baldwin gave up his previous frivolous conduct. See J. B. Post, 'Age at Menopause and Menarche: Some Medieval Authorities', *Population Studies*, 25 (1971), 83–7, where it is suggested that the age of menarche was equivalent to that of the mid-twentieth-century, i.e. 12 to 14 years. Theodora later had two children by Andronicus Comnenus, cousin of the Byzantine emperor, Manuel. See Hamilton, 'Women in the Crusader States', pp. 161–2, for her later life. She died before 1182.
2. Ernoul-Bernard, p. 16. It should be emphasised, however, that the whole text does not necessarily emanate from Ernoul. There are few references to the Ibelins after 1187. See J. Gillingham, 'Roger of Howden on Crusade', in *Richard Coeur de Lion: Kingship, Chivalry and War in the Twelfth Century*, London and Rio Grande, 1994, p. 147, n. 33.
3. WT, 19.1, p. 864.
4. RHG, vol. 16, no. 121, p. 36. Tr. Barber and Bate, *Letters from the East*, no. 22, pp. 52–3. He uses the phrase *sine omni impedimento*. The date of 1164 given in RHG is most unlikely given the nature of the news.
5. See Chapter 8, pp. 193–5.
6. See Hamilton, *Leper King*, p. 24.

7. Robert of Torigni, p. 194, for the year. However, while Robert had access to good information, the rubrics in his chronicle were inserted by members of his staff and are not always reliable, so it would be unwise to build an argument based on the dating. Agnes, in fact, does not appear on any charters in the kingdom until the mid-1160s: *Cart.*, vol. 1, no. 328, p. 232 (1164–8), vol. 1, no. 371, pp. 254–5 (1167).

8. WT, 18.29, p. 854.

9. WT, 19.4, pp. 868–70. Tr. Babcock and Krey, pp. 300–1. The words used by William make it clear that compulsion was involved: *uxorem suam . . . coactus est abiuare*. According to *Eracles*, 23.3, p. 5, Amalric sent an embassy to Rome, apparently to ensure papal confirmation. See H.E. Mayer, 'The Beginnings of King Amalric of Jerusalem', in *The Horns of Hattin*, ed. B. Z. Kedar, London, 1992, pp. 132–4.

10. B. Hamilton, 'The Titular Nobility of the Latin East: the Case of Agnes of Courtenay', in *Crusade and Settlement*, ed. P.W. Edbury, Cardiff, 1985, pp. 197–203. See also J. Richard, *Le royaume latin de Jérusalem*, Paris, 1953, p. 77.

11. See Chapter 8, p. 176.

12. Mayer, 'Beginnings of King Amalric', pp. 125–6.

13. WT, 19.4, p. 869, 19.2, p. 866.

14. Hamilton, *Leper King*, p. 25. Fulcher did not die until 20 November 1157, which leaves only a brief period in which Amalric and Agnes could have married if the event really did take place in 1157. In any case, it seems unlikely that Aimery of Limoges, the senior cleric in Jerusalem at this time, would have been any more accommodating than Fulcher. Neither man bears much resemblance to Arnulf of Chocques.

15. Edbury, *John of Ibelin*, pp. 6–8. Hugh of Ibelin is described as recently released in late 1158 or early 1159; WT, 18.24, p. 847.

16. Ernoul-Bernard, p. 17. *Car telle n'est que roine doine iestre, de si haute cité comme de Jherusalem.* See Hamilton, 'Women in the Crusader States', p. 160.

17. Hiestand, 'Some Reflections on the Impact of the Papacy', p. 11, says that the legate acted against the wishes of the barons, but provides no evidence for this assertion.

18. See Mayer, *Die Kanzlei*, vol. 1, pp. 174–7.

19. WT, 19.12, pp. 881–2, 20.1, p. 913, 20.4, pp. 915–17, 21.1, p. 961. See Mayer, *Die Kanzlei*, vol. 1, pp. 177–84. In 1962, Robert Huygens discovered the lost 'autobiographical' chapter from William's chronicle, from which his career up to 1165 can be put together. See R.B.C. Huygens, 'Guillaume de Tyr étudiant: Un chapitre (XIX.12) de son "Histoire" retrouvé', *Latomus*, 21 (1962), 811–28. Edbury and Rowe, *William of Tyre*, pp. 13–17, 23–5, make it clear that William was not writing directly at the royal command, nor producing an official history either of Amalric's reign or of the kingdom as a whole.

20. WT, 19.2–3, pp. 846–8.

21. See Riley-Smith, *Feudal Nobility*, pp. 62–98, and Nader, *Burgesses*, pp. 158–61, for the context of these courts. The Court of the *Fonde* collected market taxes as well as hearing intercommunal commercial cases. The Court of the Chain derived its name from the chain across the harbour entrance used to close the port in times of danger. It functioned as a maritime court and was responsible for the operation of the port, including customs.

22. See Richard, *Crusades*, p. 92.

23. J. Prawer, 'The Nobility and the Feudal Regime in the Latin Kingdom of Jerusalem', in *Lordship and Community in Medieval Europe: Selected Readings*, ed. F.L. Cheyette, New York, 1968, pp. 162–3, 167–8. However, none of the twelfth-century *assises* can be dated with certainty.

24. See Riley-Smith, *Feudal Nobility*, p. 38.

25. See ULKJ, vol. 1, pp. 59–64.

26. Philip of Novara, *Le Livre de forme de plait*, ed. and tr. P. Edbury, Nicosia, 2009, cap. 47, pp. 118–20, 259–61. 'We only know the *assises* by hearsay and usage.'

27. John of Ibelin, *Livre de Jean d'Ibelin*, RHCr, Lois, vol. 1, cap. 140, pp. 214–15, cap. 199, pp. 319–20; Philip of Novara, cap. 49, pp. 123–7, 261–3. Nader, *Burgesses*, p. 130, points out that this was already the existing practice for burgesses, as can be seen in the charter for Magna Mahumeria of c.1155: *Cartulaire du Saint-Sépulcre*, no. 117, p. 240.

28. See J. Richard, 'Pairie d'Orient latin: les quatre baronies des royaumes de Jérusalem et de Chypre', *Revue historique de droit français et étranger*, series 4, 28 (1950), 76–7; Riley-Smith, *Crusades*, pp. 99–100. See also Richard, *Crusades*, pp. 92–3, Riley-Smith, *Feudal Nobility*, pp. 34–6, and Hamilton, *Leper King*, p. 60.

29. Prawer, 'Nobility and the Feudal Regime', pp. 168–74.

30. WT, 23.1, pp. 1062–4. See Richard, 'Prairie d'Orient latin', 77. See also G. Loud, 'The *Assise sur la Ligece* and Ralph of Tiberias', in *Crusade and Settlement*, ed. P.W. Edbury, Cardiff, 1985, p. 205. The issue of the *assise* might be seen, at least in part, as an attempt to prevent a repeat of the kind of confrontation which the kingdom had just experienced.

31. Michael the Syrian, 18.8, p. 318. Michael's account is not entirely trustworthy. He says that this man was captured and burnt to death but, in fact, Gerard did not die until c.1171. However, at this time Reynald of Châtillon was the ruler of Antioch and, given his own propensities, it would not have been surprising to find him giving refuge to Gerard of Sidon.

32. Ibn al-Athir, part 2, pp. 130–1.

33. ULKJ, vol. 1, no. 254, pp. 462–4. See Richard, 'Prairie d'Orient latin', 76. It seems probable that Gerard had escaped the ambush and had taken refuge in Belhacem.

34. WT, 14.19, p. 656, 17.1, p. 761, 17.21, p. 790, 17.23, p. 792, 17.25, p. 795. See J.L. La Monte, 'The Lords of Sidon in the Twelfth and Thirteenth Centuries', *Byzantion*, 17 (1944–5), 188–90.

35. WT, 19.4, p. 870. For the interpretation of William, see R. Hiestand, 'Die Herren von Sidon und die Thronfolgekrise des Jahres 1163 im Königreich Jerusalem', in *Montjoie: Studies in Crusade History in Honour of Hans Eberhard Mayer*, ed. B.Z. Kedar, J. Riley-Smith and R. Hiestand, Aldershot, 1997, pp. 77–90.

36. WT, 19.5, p. 870.

37. WT, 19.2, pp. 865–6.

38. WT, 19.5, pp. 870–2.

39. RHG, vol. 16, no. 194, p. 60.

40. WT, 19.5, p. 871.

41. WT, 21.13(14)–18(19), pp. 979–87.

42. Abu Shama, *Le livre des deux jardins*, in RHCr, Orient., vol. 4, Paris, 1898, p. 125.

43. WT, 19.11, pp. 877–8.

44. WT, 19.9, pp. 874–5; Ibn al-Athir, part 2, pp. 146–8; RHG, vol. 16, no. 195, pp. 60–1, which is a letter of Geoffrey Fulcher, preceptor of the Temple, written in September, giving the figures for the army.

45. WT, 19.8, pp. 873–4.

46. See Dussaud, *Topographie*, pp. 171–2, for the position of Harim, and *Cart.*, vol. 1, no. 404, p. 280, for the patriarch's description.

47. WT, 18.12, pp. 826–7; Ibn al-Athir, part 2, pp. 148–50.

48. RHG, vol. 16, no. 244, pp. 79–80, no. 243, p. 79; WT, 19.10, p. 877. The claim that Banyas was betrayed was known in the West, since it was retold by the Augustinian William of Newburgh, *Historia Rerum Anglicarum*, in *Chronicles and Memorials of the Reigns of Stephen, Henry II and Richard I*, vol. 1, ed. R. Howlett, RS 82, London, 1884, 2.23, p. 156. He obtained his information from a participant in Amalric's campaigns of 1164 and 1167.

49. WT, 19.10, p. 876.

50. Ibn al-Athir, part 2, p. 147.

51. WT, 19.11, pp. 877–8.

52. Ibn al-Athir, part 2, p. 148.

53. WT, 16.29, p. 757. Tr. Babcock and Krey, vol. 2, p. 182.

54. Elisséeff, *Nūr ad-Dīn*, vol. 2, p. 563, argues that, in fact, Nur al-Din's successes obliged the Franks to turn to Egypt, since they had no hope of further conquests in Syria.

55. RHG, vol. 16, no. 197, pp. 62–3.

56. RHG, vol. 16, no. 244, pp. 79–80. Tr. Barber and Bate, *Letters from the East*, no. 31, p. 61. See also RHG, no. 123, p. 38, no. 125, p. 39, no. 245, pp. 80–1.

57. See WT, 17.22, p. 792.

58. See Holt, *Age of the Crusades*, p. 130.

59. See M.C. Lyons and D.E.P. Jackson, *Saladin: The Politics of the Holy War*, Cambridge, 1982, pp. 26, 34–9.

60. WT, 19.27, pp. 902–3. See Jacoby, 'Economic Function of the Crusader States', pp. 165–7.

61. See Mayer, 'Sankt Samuel', 59–60, 63–5.

62. See J. Phillips, *Defenders of the Holy Land: Relations between the Latin East and the West, 1119–1187*, Oxford, 1996, pp. 141–9.

63. Kinnamos, 5.13, p. 179.

64. Michael the Syrian, vol. 3, 18.11, p. 326. See Hamilton, 'Aimery of Limoges', 275–6, and 'Three Patriarchs of Antioch, 1165–70', in *Dei gesta per Francos: Etudes sur les croisades dédiées à Jean Richard*, ed. M. Balard, B.Z. Kedar and J. Riley-Smith, Aldershot, 2001, pp. 199–201.

65. WT, 20.1, p. 913. See Magdalino, *Empire of Manuel I Komnenos*, pp. 72–4.

66. WT, 19.13, pp. 882-3.
67. Ibn al-Athir, part 2, p. 163.
68. WT, 19.14, p. 883, 19.16, p. 885.
69. William devotes nineteen chapters of Book 19 to the subject; 19.13-32, pp. 882-909.
70. WT, 19.18, p. 887, 19.19, p. 889, 19.20, p. 889, 19.30, p. 906, for references to his information from participants, and 19.17, pp. 886-7, for his character sketch of Hugh of Caesarea. The last charter reference to Hugh is in 1168; ULKJ, vol. 2, no. 327, p. 568. For Hugh's family, see J.L. La Monte, 'The Lords of Caesarea in the Period of the Crusades', *Speculum*, 22 (1947), 145-61.
71. WT, 19.23, pp. 895-6.
72. WT, 19.18, p. 887. Tr. Babcock and Krey, vol. 2, p. 319.
73. In the third century, Solinus collected together elements of Pliny's *Natural History*.
74. WT, 19.19, p. 889. Tr. Babcock and Krey, vol. 2, p. 321.
75. Ibn al-Athir, part 2, pp. 163-4. Mamluks were originally slaves who came from Central Asia. They were trained for military service and often obtained positions of importance in Islamic armies.
76. Among those who were wounded was the chancellor, Ralph, bishop of Bethlehem, who also lost all his baggage: WT, 19.25, p. 899. It is not clear if Ralph actually took part in the fighting, but it does show that the king thought it necessary to bring his chancellor with him, perhaps because, if he had been successful, Amalric would have issued charters to those who would have been established in the new conquests.
77. On 18 May 1168, Amalric made grants to the commune of Pisa in Acre in return for services rendered in the siege of Alexandria: ULKJ, vol. 2, no. 327, pp. 564-8. It is not clear if the ships to which William refers were in fact Pisan, or whether they were in addition to the fleet from the kingdom of Jerusalem. See Rogers, *Latin Siege Warfare*, pp. 83-4.
78. Ibn al-Athir, part 2, pp. 164-5. See Lyons and Jackson, *Saladin*, pp. 16-19.
79. WT, 20.4, pp. 915-17. William says they arrived during the same summer, but he places his account after the marriage. Moreover, the king did not return from Egypt until 21 August.
80. See Mayer, 'Das Pontifikale von Tyrus', 174-6, 234.
81. See Pringle, *Churches*, vol. 1, no. 61, pp. 137-56.
82. See G. Kühnel, *Wall Painting in the Latin Kingdom of Jerusalem*, Berlin, 1988, pp. 15-22, who characterises this type of iconography as a 'maternal genre scene'.
83. See Folda, *Art of the Crusaders*, pp. 91-7, and colour plates 1 and 2.
84. See Kühnel, *Wall Painting*, p. 6.
85. See Folda, *Art of the Crusaders*, pp. 163-5, 364-71. In contrast, Gustave Kühnel believes that, with the exception of the painting of 1130, there was an overall plan from the 1150s onwards: *Wall Painting*, pp. 1-147
86. See L.-A. Hunt, 'Art and Colonialism: The Mosaics of the Church of the Nativity in Bethlehem (1169) and the Problem of "Crusader" Art', *Dumbarton Oaks Papers*, 45 (1991), 69-85. The Orthodox community maintained an active artistic and intellectual life in the kingdom in the twelfth century: see Pahlitzsch, *Graeci und Suriani*, pp. 201, 206-9.
87. See Mayer, *Die Kanzlei*, vol. 1, pp. 137-9.
88. See A. Jotischky, 'Manuel Comnenus and the Reunion of the Churches: The Evidence of the Conciliar Mosaics in the Church of the Nativity at Bethlehem', *Levant*, 26 (1994), 207-23, and MacEvitt, *Crusades and the Christian World of the East*, pp. 112-18.
89. See Mayer, 'Latins, Muslims and Greeks', 188-92. Mayer believes that this had been achieved by 1164. This did not mean, however, that Manuel could appoint Greek Orthodox prelates from Constantinople.
90. WT, 20.6, p. 918. ULKJ, vol. 2, no. 337, p. 584, shows the king at Ascalon, the usual departure point for Egypt at that date.
91. Ibn al-Athir, part 2, p. 165.
92. WT, 20.5, p. 917. Tr. Babcock and Krey, vol. 2, p. 350. The key phrase is *aliquam haberet excusationem*.
93. Ibn al-Athir, part 2, pp. 171-2
94. WT, 20.5, p. 918. Tr. Babcock and Krey, vol. 2, pp. 350-1.
95. *Cart.*, vol. 1, no. 402, pp. 275-6; ULKJ, vol. 2, no. 336, pp. 578-82. See Riley-Smith, *Knights of St John*, pp. 71-3, 324. William of Tyre's assertion that Gilbert of Assailly was the driving force behind this campaign is confirmed by this charter, which seems to have been prepared by the Hospitallers themselves, as was the agreement with the order made the following summer. See Mayer, 'Die Hofkapelle', 506.

96. 'Old besants' seems to mean dinars of Alexandria rather than the Frankish imitations from Acre, which were between one-third and two-fifths lighter. See G. Schlumberger, *Numismatique de l'Orient latin*, Paris, 1878, pp. 130–43, *Additions et rectifications*, p. 10, and the discussion in Metcalf, *Coinage of the Crusades*, pp. 43–6.

97. WT, 18.14, p. 831, 20.5, pp. 917–18; RHG, vol. 15, pp. 681–2. See also Chapter 9, pp. 210–11.

98. ULKJ, vol. 2, no. 325, pp. 562–3.

99. Favreau-Lilie, 'Landesausbau und Burg', 84–5, suggests that some of the cost was offset by taxes in kind from the dependent villages as well as contributions from local farmers, now much better protected from raids and plundering than in the past, perhaps enabling them to expand the cultivated area.

100. See J. Burgtorf, 'The Military Orders in the Crusader Principality of Antioch', in *East and West in the Medieval Eastern Mediterranean*, vol. 1, *Antioch from the Byzantine Reconquest until the End of the Crusader Principality*, ed. K. Ciggaar and D.M. Metcalf, Orientalia Lovaniensia Analecta, 147, Louvain, 2006, pp. 226, 233.

101. Abu Shama, vol. 4, p. 110.

102. WT, 19.11, p. 879. William first places this at around the same time as the death of King William I of Sicily, which occurred in May 1166, but then concludes the book by saying that the year was the third of the reign, which would mean that it was before 18 February 1166.

103. J. Delaville Le Roulx, 'Chartes de Terre Sainte', *ROL*, 11 (1905–8), no. 2, pp. 183–4; ULKJ, vol. 2, no. 314, pp. 548–50.

104. For possible identification, see P. Deschamps, *Les Châteaux des Croisés en Terre Sainte*, vol. 2, *La défense du royaume de Jérusalem*, Paris, 1939, p. 116.

105. Ibn Shaddad, p. 43.

106. WT, 20.6–9, pp. 918–23.

107. Ibn al-Athir, part 2, p. 172. His worries may have been compounded by the knowledge that Fustat was largely inhabited by Christians and Jews.

108. Ibn al-Athir, part 2, pp. 173–4.

109. Ibn al-Athir, part 2, p. 174.

110. Ibn al-Athir, part 2, pp. 174–5; Ibn Shaddad, p. 44. See Lyons and Jackson, *Saladin*, pp. 24–7.

111. WT, 20.10, p. 924.

112. WT, 20.12, p. 926. His view may have been coloured by an apparent quarrel he had with the archbishop, which led him to travel to Rome in 1169 in an attempt to settle the matter: 20.17, p. 934. See Phillips, *Defenders of the Holy Land*, pp. 168–207, for the mission.

113. WT, 20.3, pp. 914–15, 20.25, p. 947. See E. Joranson, 'The Pilgrimage of Henry the Lion', in *Medieval and Historiographical Essays in Honor of James Westfall Thompson*, Chicago, 1938, pp. 146–225.

114. WT, 20.25, p. 947. See Phillips, *Defenders of the Holy Land*, pp. 177–9, 204–7, and Hamilton, *Leper King*, pp. 30–1.

115. WT, 20.13, pp. 926–7. Niketas Choniates, pp. 91–2, says that Andronicus met Amalric in Jerusalem before the expedition began. Kinnamos, 6.9, p. 208, has the fleet go straight to Egypt, but this is not likely.

116. *Cart.*, vol. 1, no. 409, p. 283; ULKJ, vol. 2, no. 341, pp. 591–5.

117. See Barber, 'Philip of Nablus', pp. 73–4.

118. WT, 20.11, p. 925.

119. Ibn al-Athir, part 2, pp. 176–80. See Lyons and Jackson, *Saladin*, pp. 27–36.

120. Ibn al-Athir, part 2, p. 183; Ibn Shaddad, p. 46.

121. WT, 20.16, pp. 931–3. Tr. Babcock and Krey, vol. 2, p. 368. See Rogers, *Latin Siege Warfare*, pp. 84–6.

122. Ibn al-Athir, part 2, p. 183.

123. WT, 20.5, pp. 917–18. See H. Nicholson, *The Knights Hospitaller*, Woodbridge, 2001, pp. 21–2.

124. See Riley-Smith, *Knights of St. John*, pp. 60–3. The date of his resignation is not known, but it was probably early in 1170. Such a resignation was unprecedented in the Hospital, although the Templar master, Everard des Barres, resigned to join the Cistercians in 1152. Gilbert was, in fact, persuaded by the patriarch to rescind his decision, but the imposition of conditions by the chapter precipitated a second resignation.

125. Niketas Choniates, p. 96; WT, 20.17, p. 933.

126. Kinnamos, 6.9, p. 209. Niketas Choniates, p. 96, confirms this, but says nothing about plans for any further attack.

127. WT, 20.17, p. 934. See also Möhring, *Saladin*, p. 35.

128. Michael the Syrian, 19.6, p. 336.

129. This has the ring of truth, since the end of October was effectively the close of the sailing season, except in very unusual circumstances. As Amalric did not even arrive at Damietta until 27 October, only a very quick victory would have sufficed.
130. Kinnamos, 6.9, pp. 208–9; Niketas Choniates, pp. 91–6.
131. See Mayer, 'Das syrische Erdbeben', 474–84.
132. Michael the Syrian, 19.7, p. 339. See Hamilton, 'Aimery of Limoges', 276.
133. WT, 20.18, p. 935; Ibn al-Athir, part 2, pp. 185–6.
134. Mayer, 'Das syrische Erdbeben', 484, for the text. The rather abrupt ending suggests that this is not the complete letter.
135. Cart., vol. 1, no. 411, pp. 284–6; ULKJ, vol. 2, no. 346, pp. 601–5. See Riley-Smith, Knights of St John, pp. 66–7. Mayer, 'Das syrische Erdbeben', 478, points out that this brought the Hospitallers considerably closer to Tripoli itself, and would not have met with much support from Raymond had he been in a position to intervene. In the end the Hospitallers did not take over these castles, despite holding other properties in the region, perhaps because Raymond III did not confirm the grant after his release from prison in 1174. See J. Richard, 'Le comté de Tripoli dans les chartes du Fonds des Porcellet', Bibliothèque de l'École des Chartes, 130 (1972), 344–7.
136. Ibn Shaddad, p. 45.
137. It is not clear if they were volunteers, or part of a wider call-up.
138. WT, 20.19–21, pp. 936–40. See Lyons and Jackson, Saladin, pp. 42–3.
139. Ibn al-Athir, part 2, p. 194.
140. Ibn al-Athir, pp. 196–8. See Lyons and Jackson, Saladin, pp. 44–6. Al-Adid's heirs seem to have been held in a form of house arrest, prevented from having contact with women, so that the dynasty slowly died out.
141. See Metcalf, 'Describe the Currency', p. 193. He suggests a date of c.1169. See Chapter 9, p. 218, for Baldwin's recoining.
142. For Odo's career, see Bulst-Thiele, Sacrae Domus Templi Hierosolymitani Magistri, pp. 87–105.
143. WT, 20.22–4, pp. 940–6. See S. Runciman, 'The Visit of King Amalric I to Constantinople in 1171', in Outremer: Studies in the History of the Crusading Kingdom of Jerusalem Presented to Joshua Prawer, ed. B.Z. Kedar, H.E. Mayer and R.C. Smail, Jerusalem, 1982, pp. 153–8. Runciman believes that William was part of Amalric's entourage. However, William does not say so, and Edbury and Rowe, William of Tyre, p. 55, think he reconstructed the account from eyewitnesses, as he does on other occasions.
144. Kinnamos, 6.9, pp. 208–9. The reference to Amalric is very brief, as Kinnamos was much more interested in Manuel's general arrest of the Venetians in the empire, which had occurred in March, shortly before Amalric's arrival. William of Tyre was apparently unaware of the arrest of the Venetians, but devotes three chapters to Amalric's visit. Kinnamos, 5.13, p. 179, says that Amalric took an oath to Manuel at the time of his marriage to Maria Comnena, 'as his brother Baldwin had done', but it is difficult to know what this means in western feudal terms. See Lilie, Byzantium and the Crusader States, pp. 204–9, J.L. La Monte, 'To What Extent Was the Byzantine Empire the Suzerain of the Latin Crusading States?', Byzantion, 7 (1932), 253–64, and Hamilton, 'William of Tyre and the Byzantine Empire', pp. 226–7.
145. See Kühnel, Wall Painting, pp. 149–80, and Folda, Art of the Crusaders, pp. 382–90. The reason for the failure to decorate the whole church has been the subject of much speculation. It might, however, be connected to the decline of Byzantine influence in the kingdom during the next reign, especially as a result of the anti-Byzantine policies of Raymond III of Tripoli, bailli between late 1174 and July 1176: see Chapter 11, pp. 265–7.
146. Ibn al-Athir, part 2, pp. 198–200. William of Tyre, 20.25, p. 946, does not link the two attacks, but in this instance Ibn al-Athir appears to have greater inside knowledge. See also Lyons and Jackson, Saladin, pp. 47–8. Möhring, Saladin, pp. 45–6, even speculates that there might have been a secret agreement between Saladin and Amalric offering mutual protection against Nur al-Din should circumstances demand it.
147. WT, 20.26, pp. 948–50; Michael the Syrian, 19.3, p. 331, 19.6, p. 337.
148. WT, 20.29–30, pp. 953–6. The French translation expresses this more forcefully. Amalric sent letters to all Christian princes, not only telling them about the great damage that the order had done to the faith, but also encouraging them to act against the Templars in their own lands; Eracles, vol. 1 (ii), p. 999.
149. Walter Map, De nugis curialium, ed. and tr. M.R. James, rev. edn. C.N.L. Brooke and R.A.B. Mynors, Oxford, 1983, pp. 66–7. Nicholson argues that Walter Map could have learned of these events from William of Tyre at the Third Lateran Council of 1179 and that he is not therefore an independent source. See Nicholson, 'Before William of Tyre', p. 112.

150. See Barber, *New Knighthood*, pp. 100-5, for this incident.
151. Ibn al-Athir, part 2, pp. 222-3.
152. WT, 20.31, p. 956. Tr. Babcock and Krey, vol. 2, p. 394.
153. Michael the Syrian, 19.11, p. 353.
154. Ibn al-Athir, part 2, pp. 225-6. See also the historian of Aleppo, Kamal al-Din, *L'histoire d'Alep*, tr. E. Blochet, *ROL*, 3 (1895), 518-19, who describes the setting-up of colleges and caravanserais and the gathering together of wise men and experts in law in the city by Nur al-Din.
155. WT, 20.32, pp. 956-7. Tr. Babcock and Krey, vol. 2, p. 396; Ibn al-Athir, part 2, p. 234. Michael the Syrian, 20.1, p. 356, saw his death as a tragedy, for, after Nur al-Din's death, the Christians had hoped that Amalric would be their saviour.

11 The Disintegration of the Crusader States

1. Ibn al-Athir, part 2, pp. 198-200, 221.
2. Ibn al-Athir, part 2, pp. 223-6.
3. WT, 21.3, p. 963; Ibn al-Athir, part 2, pp. 229-30.
4. See Hamilton, *Leper King*, pp. 75-6, 86-8, and Phillips, *Defenders of the Holy Land*, pp. 222-4.
5. WT, 21.6, pp. 967-8; Ibn al-Athir, part 2, pp. 231-5. See Lyons and Jackson, *Saladin*, pp. 77-95.
6. Neither the exact date nor the reason for Raymond's release is known, which is unfortunate given the huge consequences of his presence in the crusader states in the 1170s and 1180s. William of Tyre, 20.28, p. 952, says that Amalric paid part of the ransom, which is likely, as he must have found the government of Tripoli an extra burden, but Nur al-Din's motives are not clear. Ibn al-Athir, part 2, p. 234, says he was released by the emir Gumushtekin, Sa'd al-Din, formerly Nur al-Din's deputy in Mosul, early in 1175. As Gumushtekin was holding al-Salih in Aleppo at the time and was desperate to fend off Saladin, such a move would have been in his interests. However, William of Tyre is quite clear that the release occurred while Amalric was still alive, a statement confirmed by Raymond's appearance as a witness on a royal charter for the Hospitallers on 18 April 1174: ULKJ, vol. 2, no. 362, p. 629. See M.W. Baldwin, *Raymond III of Tripolis and the Fall of Jerusalem (1140-1187)*, New York, 1936, pp. 11, 14-15, for this issue.
7. WT, 21.8, pp. 972-4; Ibn al-Athir, part 2, p. 234, says that Raymond's siege of Homs began on 1 February. According to William of Tyre, the whole campaign lasted from January to May.
8. WT, 21.1-2, pp. 961-2. On the nature of the disease, see P.D. Mitchell, 'An Evaluation of the Leprosy of King Baldwin IV in the Context of the Medieval World', in Hamilton, *Leper King*, pp. 245-58. Saladin's information, however, was that the Franks did not immediately agree on Amalric's successor. See Lyons and Jackson, *Saladin*, p. 75.
9. See S. Lay, 'A leper in purple: the coronation of Baldwin IV of Jerusalem', *Journal of Medieval History*, 23 (1997), 317-34, who argues that it was not obvious that he had leprosy until around the age of fifteen when skin lesions began to appear.
10. See M. Barber, 'The Order of St Lazarus and the Crusades', *Catholic Historical Review*, 80 (1994), 439-56.
11. See E. Kohlberg and B.Z. Kedar, 'A Melkite Physician in Frankish Jerusalem and Ayyubid Damascus: Muwaffaq al-Dīn Ya'qūb b. Siqlāb', in *Asian and African Studies*, 22 (1988), 114.
12. Hamilton, *Leper King*, p. 38.
13. Any claims that might have been made by Agnes of Courtenay as the king's mother (perhaps based on the precedent of Queen Melisende) were negated by the fact that she was not the dowager queen. Her exclusion in 1163 suggests baronial anticipation that such a situation might arise. Similarly, Maria Comnena, Amalric's widow, who was dowager queen, was not the king's mother. In these circumstances, it is possible that Amalric might have designated Miles of Plancy as head of the government during the minority. See H.E. Mayer, 'Die Legitimität Balduins IV. von Jerusalem und das Testament der Agnes von Courtenay', *Historisches Jahrbuch*, 108 (1988), 66-7.
14. WT, 20.9, p. 921. Tr. Babcock and Krey, vol. 2, pp. 354-5.
15. WT, 21. 3-4, pp. 963-5. See B. Hamilton, 'Miles of Plancy and the Fief of Beirut', in *The Horns of Hattin*, ed. B.Z. Kedar, London, 1992, pp. 136-46, and *Leper King*, pp. 91-3.
16. WT, 21.5, p. 966. William says that he received *procuratio et potestas*. A parallel may be drawn with Amalric, described in 1170 as *procurans* of the county of Tripoli: *Cart.*, vol. 1, no. 411, p. 284; ULKJ, vol. 2, no. 346, p. 604. Cf. Fulk's position in Antioch in 1135; see Chapter 7, p. 156. The term *regens* in the sense of regent does not seem to have been used until the fourteenth century. William does not date these events, but places them after the assassination of Miles of Plancy.

17. In John of Ibelin's list of the mid-1260s, Galilee and Tripoli are presented as two of the four great baronies of the kingdom: *Le livre des assises*, X, pp. 113–14, 193. However, this can only give an approximate picture of the situation in the 1160s.
18. WT, 21.3, pp. 963–4.
19. WT, 21.5, pp. 965–7; 22.10(9), p. 1019.
20. William says that Ralph died during the summer and his last signed charter is 18 April 1174: ULKJ, vol. 2, no. 362, p. 629. On 3 July, the king was using Peter, the vice-chancellor: ULKJ, vol. 2, no. 364, p. 635. William first appears on 13 December: ULKJ, vol. 2, no. 381, p. 657. However, he does not seem to have exercised the office immediately, partly because he was probably on a mission to Constantinople between late 1175 and early 1176, and partly because of the hostility of Agnes of Courtenay. See Mayer, *Die Kanzlei*, vol. 1, pp. 166, 210–37, and Edbury and Rowe, *William of Tyre*, pp. 18–19.
21. For a more jaundiced Muslim view, see Lyons and Jackson, *Saladin*, p. 197.
22. See Chapter 9, p. 215.
23. See B. Hamilton, 'Manuel I Comnenus and Baldwin IV of Jerusalem', in *Kathegetria: Essays Presented to Joan Hussey for her 80th Birthday*, ed. J. Chrysostomides, Camberley, 1988, pp. 355–7.
24. WT, 21.12(13), pp. 977–8.
25. See Hamilton, 'Manuel I Comnenus and Baldwin IV', p. 357.
26. WT, 21.11(12), pp. 976–7. See M. Angold, *The Byzantine Empire, 1025–1204: A Political History*, London, 1984, pp. 192–4.
27. WT, 21.15–16, pp. 981–3. See Hamilton, 'Manuel I Comnenus and Baldwin IV of Jerusalem', pp. 359–60.
28. WT, 21.10(11), p. 976; 'Imad al-Din, in Abu Shama, vol. 4, p. 183; Michael the Syrian, vol. 3, 20.3, pp. 365–6. Saladin made peace with Aleppo on 29 July, so presumably the two men were released well before this date: Ibn al-Athir, part 2, pp. 243–4.
29. See R.L. Nicholson, *Joscelyn III and the Fall of the Crusader States, 1134–1199*, Leiden, 1973, pp. 37–9, 63–4.
30. See Hamilton, 'Titular Nobility', pp. 200–1, and Mayer, 'Die Legitimität', 68–9.
31. See Nicholson, *Joscelyn III*, pp. 73–7. Bohemond's motives are not known, but he may have been attempting to revive traditional Antiochene claims of lordship over the rulers of Edessa.
32. WT, 21.4, p. 964. Humphrey III died c.1173, predeceasing his father.
33. Reynald was 'lord of Hebron and Montréal' by November 1177; RRH, no. 551, p. 146. The northern part of the fief had been granted to the Templars in 1166; see Chapter 10, pp. 250–1.
34. ULKJ, vol. 2, no. 390, p. 670; RRH, no. 539, pp. 143–4, no. 572, p. 152. See Mayer, 'Die Herrschaftsbildung in Hebron', 75–6, 80.
35. See the genealogy in Hamilton, *Leper King*, p. xx. Philip had been one of the targets of the delegation led by Frederick, archbishop of Tyre, in 1169: see Chapter 10, p. 252. Philip developed his financial resources very effectively: see D. Nicholas, *Medieval Flanders*, London, 1992, pp. 79–81.
36. WT, 21.13(14), p. 979: *obtulit ei potestatem et liberam et generalem administrationem super regnum universum.*
37. WT, 21.17(18), p. 985. Ibn al-Athir, part 2, pp. 254–5, thought that Philip had left for the north because he believed Saladin was no longer a danger after his defeat at Mont Gisard on 25 November, but William says clearly that he left at the beginning of October.
38. WT, 21.18(19), pp. 986–7, 21.24(25), pp. 994–6; Ibn al-Athir, part 2, pp. 255–6.
39. Hamilton, *Leper King*, p. 124.
40. WT, 21.9(10)–10(11), pp. 974–6; Ibn al-Athir, part 2, pp. 249–50.
41. See J. Dunbabin, 'William of Tyre and Philip of Alsace, Count of Flanders', *Mededelingen var de Koninklijke Academie voor Wetenschappen, Letteren en Schone Kunsten van België: Klasse der Letteren*, 48 (1986), 110–17, and M.R. Tessera, 'Philip Count of Flanders and Hildegard of Bingen: Crusading against the Saracens or Crusading against Deadly Sin?', in *Gendering the Crusades*, ed. S.B. Edgington and S. Lambert, Cardiff, 2001, pp. 77–93.
42. Ibn al-Athir, part 2, p. 249.
43. WT, 21.19(20)–20(21), pp. 987–9.
44. WT, 13(14), p. 980. See Hamilton, 'Elephant of Christ', p. 100.
45. Ibn Shaddad, p. 54.
46. Ibn al-Athir, part 2, pp. 253–4.
47. See R. Röhricht, *Beitrage zur Geschichte der Kreuzzüge*, vol. 2, Berlin, 1878, n. 45, pp. 127–8. Tr. Barber and Bate, *Letters from the East*, no. 38, pp. 72–3. See Mitchell, *Medicine in the Crusades*, pp. 108–23, for weapon injuries sustained in battles like this. Many recovered if they escaped infection.

48. B.Z. Kedar, 'A Twelfth-Century Description of the Jerusalem Hospital', pp. 7, 21.

49. WT, 21.19(20)–23(24), pp. 987–94.

50. *Cart.*, vol. 1, no. 558, pp. 378–9; ULKJ, vol. 2, no. 407, pp. 693–7.

51. See M. Barber, 'Frontier Warfare in the Latin Kingdom of Jerusalem: The Campaign of Jacob's Ford, 1178–9', in *The Crusades and their Sources: Essays Presented to Bernard Hamilton*, ed. J. France and W.G. Zajac, Aldershot, 1998, pp. 2–22.

52. See Chapter 10, p. 250.

53. Excavation shows very clearly that a great deal of work remained to be done: see R. Ellenblum, 'Frontier Activities: The Transformation of a Muslim Sacred Site into the Frankish Castle of Vadum Jacob', *Crusades*, 2 (2003), 91–3, and *Crusader Castles and Modern Histories*, pp. 261–74

54. See Ellenblum, 'Frontier Activities', 83–92. Ellenblum believes that the construction of Hunin (Chastel Neuf) at about the same time was much less provocative, since it was seen as being within Christian territory.

55. WT, 21.26(27), p. 999.

56. Ibn al-Athir, part 2, p. 262.

57. WT, 21.28(29), pp. 1001–2; Ibn al-Athir, part 2, p. 264. The death of William's brother, Ralph, in this engagement must have coloured his view of the master, p. 1002n., and Mayer, *Die Kanzlei*, vol. 1, p. 172. See G.A.M. d'Albon, 'La mort d'Odon de Saint-Amand, Grand maître du Temple', *Revue de l'Orient latin*, 12 (1909–11), 279–82.

58. WT, 21.29(30), pp. 1003–4.

59. 'Imad al-Din, in Abu Shama, vol. 4, pp. 205–6.

60. See Chapter 10, p. 253.

61. Philip II was crowned on 1 November 1179, aged fourteen, but Louis did not die until 19 September 1180, a situation that produced a prolonged period of uncertainty as the powerful barons of France manoeuvred for position. See J.W. Baldwin, *The Government of Philip Augustus: Foundations of French Royal Power in the Middle Ages*, Berkeley, 1986, pp. 3–17.

62. Ernoul-Bernard, p. 60; ULKJ, vol. 2, no. 423, p. 720 (March 1181). Sibylla had become countess of Jaffa when she married William of Montferrat in 1176.

63. See S. Painter, 'The Lords of Lusignan in the Eleventh and Twelfth Centuries', *Speculum*, 32 (1957), 27–47, and Chapter 10, p. 240.

64. WT, 22.26(25), p. 1050.

65. Roger of Howden, *Chronica*, vol. 1, ed. W. Stubbs, RS 51, London, 1869, pp. 273–4; William of Newburgh, vol. 1, 3.16, p. 255. Roger was a royal clerk between 1174 and 1189–90, and took part in the Third Crusade in 1190–1. Thereafter he remained mainly in his parish at Howden in Yorkshire. He wrote the *Chronica* in the decade between 1192 and 1202.

66. WT, 22.1, p. 1007. As close kin, Raymond and Bohemond could legitimately expect some role in the choice of a husband for Sibylla.

67. Ernoul-Bernard, pp. 56–60. See Baldwin, *Raymond III*, pp. 35–40, and Hamilton, *Leper King*, pp. 151–8, for interpretations of these complicated events.

68. See Hamilton, *Leper King*, p. 158.

69. WT, 21.17(18), p. 986, for Maria's remarriage.

70. WT, 22.5, p. 1012.

71. See Hamilton, *Leper King*, pp. 160–2. Agnes of Courtenay topped off this triumph when she obtained the lordship or usufruct of Toron from Baldwin IV in c.1183, although the king retained Chastel Neuf. See Mayer, 'Die Legitimität', 69–71. However, it should be noted that the lordship was much reduced by this time; most importantly, Banyas had been lost in 1164. See Chapter 10, p. 240.

72. WT, 21.9(10), p. 974; 22.4, pp. 1011–12. Ernoul was a squire or page of Balian of Ibelin at this time and was probably in his teens when these events took place. There is no definitive text, but this story is found in two versions, one of which provides much more detail than the other; Ernoul-Bernard, pp. 82–7 (the longer version) and *La Continuation de Guillaume de Tyr (1184–1197)*, ed. M.R. Morgan, Documents relatifs à l'histoire des croisades publiés par l'Académie des Inscriptions et Belles-Lettres, Paris, 1982, c. 38, pp. 50–1. See Hamilton, *Leper King*, pp. 7–11, for a concise discussion of these texts.

73. See B.Z. Kedar, 'The Patriarch Eraclius', in *Outremer: Studies in the History of the Crusading Kingdom of Jerusalem Presented to Joshua Prawer*, ed. B.Z. Kedar, H.E. Mayer and R.C. Smail, Jerusalem, 1982, pp. 177–89; P.W. Edbury and J.G. Rowe, 'William of Tyre and the Patriarchal Election of 1180', *English Historical Review*, 93 (1978), 1–25; Edbury and Rowe, *William of Tyre*, pp. 20–2; Hamilton, *Leper King*, pp. 96–7, 162–3.

74. Since the publication of M.W. Baldwin's *Raymond III of Tripolis* in 1936, the idea of the development of two factions consisting of a 'court party' and one of 'native barons' has become well established: see especially pp. 44–5. However, this interpretation was effectively picked apart by Peter Edbury, 'Propaganda and Faction in the Kingdom of Jerusalem: The Background to Hattin', in *Crusaders and Muslims in Twelfth-Century Syria*, ed. M. Shatzmiller, Leiden, 1993, pp. 173–89. There were certainly deep-seated rivalries and resentments in Jerusalem in the 1180s, but they do not accord with Baldwin's presentation.
75. WT, 22.1, pp. 1007–8.
76. See R. Ellenblum, 'Frankish and Muslim Siege Warfare and the Construction of Frankish Concentric Castles', in *Dei gesta per Francos: Etudes sur les croisades dédiées à Jean Richard*, ed. M. Balard, B.Z. Kedar and J. Riley-Smith, Aldershot, 2001, pp. 187–98, and *Crusader Castles and Modern Histories*, pp. 62–72, 231–57.
77. WT, 22.2, p. 1008.
78. WT, 22.5, p. 1012, 22.11(10)–14(13), pp. 1020–5. See Hamilton, 'Manuel I Comnenus and Baldwin IV', pp. 371–5.
79. Bohemond's first wife was Orgollosa of Harim, whom he had married sometime before 1170: RRH, no. 478, p. 125. She is last mentioned in February 1175: RRH, no. 523, p. 139. It must therefore be assumed that Bohemond was a widower when he married Theodora, an event that is conventionally dated to c.1177. Bohemond's eventual heir, Bohemond IV (prince of Antioch from 1201), was his second son by Orgollosa. On the circumstances of the marriage to Theodora, see Hamilton, 'Manuel I Comnenus and Baldwin IV', pp. 365–6.
80. WT, 22.5–7, pp. 1012–16; Michael the Syrian, 21.2, pp. 388–9, who calls Sibylla a prostitute. See Hamilton, 'Aimery of Limoges', 277–8.
81. WT, 22.10(9), pp. 1019–20.
82. WT, 22, 15(14)–16 (15), pp. 1026–30; Ibn al-Athir, part 2, pp. 281–2.
83. WT, 22.19(18), p. 1034. This was not a permanent fleet, but one put together to meet this crisis. William of Tyre was surprised that it had been done in only a week.
84. WT, 22.18(17)–19 (18), pp. 1032–6; Ibn al-Athir, part 2, pp. 283–4. See Lyons and Jackson, *Saladin*, pp. 165–72
85. WT, 22.20(19)–24(23), pp. 1037–43; Ibn al-Athir, part 2, pp. 284–8; Ibn Shaddad, pp. 57–8. See Lyons and Jackson, *Saladin*, pp. 173–85.
86. WT, 22.24(23), pp. 1043–6. William quotes directly from the decree, in which the words used are *de communi omnium principum tam ecclesiaticorum quam secularium et de assensu universe plebes regni Ierosolimorum.*
87. See B.Z. Kedar, 'The General Tax of 1183 in the Crusading Kingdom of Jerusalem: Innovation or Adaptation?', *English Historical Review*, 89 (1974), 339–45.
88. A clerical gathering of this size further suggests that the letter was written soon after the general council of 1183.
89. N. Jaspert, 'Zwei unbekannte Hilfsersuchen des Patriarchen Eraclius vor dem Fall Jerusalems (1187)', *Deutches Archiv für Erforschung des Mittelalters*, 60 (2004), no. 1, pp. 508–11. Tr. Barber and Bate, *Letters from the East*, no. 39, pp. 73–5.
90. Jaspert, 'Zwei unbekannte Hilfsersuchen', 494–5.
91. Quoted by Ibn al-Athir, part 2, p. 294. See Lyons and Jackson, *Saladin*, pp. 195–200.
92. WT, 22.25(24), pp. 1046–7; Ibn al-Athir, part 2, pp. 293–5; Ibn Shaddad, pp. 59–60
93. WT, 22.26(25), pp. 1048–50.
94. Ibn Shaddad, p. 61; Abu Shama, vol. 4, pp. 244–8, quoting 'Imad al-Din and al-Fadil.
95. WT, 22.28(27), p. 1053. 'Imad al-Din says the Franks had 1,500 knights, the same number of turcopoles, and 15,000 foot soldiers: Abu Shama, vol. 4, p. 245.
96. WT, 22.27(26)–28(27), pp. 1050–5. See Lyons and Jackson, *Saladin*, pp. 205–8.
97. WT, 22.30(29), p. 1057.
98. In the fighting in Galilee in 1182, Baldwin had about 700 knights at his disposal: WT, 22.17(16), p. 1031.
99. WT, 22.28(27), p. 1054. They had crossed the Jordan *inconsiderate nimis.*
100. See R.C. Smail, 'The Predicaments of Guy of Lusignan, 1183–87', in *Outremer: Studies in the History of the Crusading Kingdom of Jerusalem Presented to Joshua Prawer*, ed. B.Z. Kedar, H.E. Mayer and R.C. Smail, Jerusalem, 1982, pp. 164–72.
101. WT, 22.30(29), pp. 1057–9. William says that Raymond of Tripoli would be the ideal person to replace Guy as *bailli*, but Hamilton argues that this did not occur until late 1184 or, more probably, early 1185: *Leper King*, pp. 194–5, 205. See Chapter 11, p. 289.
102. WT, 23.1, p. 1062; *Cont. WT*, c. 1, p. 17.

103. See Chapter 11, p. 268.

104. See Chapter 7, p. 163.

105. Ibn Shaddad, p. 74. William of Tyre, 22.15(14), p. 1026, however, saw this as a pretext for holding the pilgrim ship which had been blown towards Damietta in the spring of that year, and mentions only that Reynald had seized 'certain Arabs'.

106. See C. Hillenbrand, 'The Imprisonment of Reynald of Châtillon', in *Texts, Documents and Artifacts: Islamic Studies in Honour of D.S. Richards*, ed. C.F. Robinson, Leiden, 2003, pp. 79–101, and Hamilton, 'Elephant of Christ', pp. 97–108.

107. Abu Shama, vol. 4, quoting 'Imad al-Din, pp. 230–2, and al-Fadil, pp. 232–5; Ibn al-Athir, part 2, pp. 289–90.

108. Ernoul-Bernard, p. 103, says that Saladin desisted from bombarding the tower in which the marriage celebrations were taking place, following an appeal by Stephanie of Milly, who had held him in her arms when he was a child hostage. This must be a romantic fiction, since Saladin was at least eight when Stephanie was born. It does indicate, however, how quickly the image of 'the chivalrous Saracen' developed around Saladin.

109. WT, 22.29(28), pp. 1055–7, 31(30), pp. 1059–60; Ibn al-Athir, part 2, pp. 297–8; Ibn Shaddad, p. 62.

110. WT, 23.1, pp. 1062–4. Tr. Babcock and Krey, vol. 2, p. 507. Lying behind this quarrel may have been Baldwin's desire to dissolve Guy and Sibylla's marriage, which Eraclius could not do under canon law.

111. William's phrase is *principum ex parte plurima*, which suggests there was opposition.

112. The chronology of events is not, however, very clear. William's narrative places them soon after the council at Acre in the spring of 1184, but Bernard Hamilton argues that the attack on the Bedouin occurred after 6 October and that Raymond was probably not appointed *bailli* before early 1185: *Leper King*, pp. 203–5.

113. See Mayer, *Die Kanzlei*, vol. 1, pp. 242–52.

114. *Cont. WT*, c. 39, pp. 51–2. The whole story may be fiction (see Kedar, 'Patriarch Eraclius', pp. 178–80), but both Edbury and Rowe, *William of Tyre*, pp. 20–1, and Hamilton, *Leper King*, pp. 199–201, think there may be some truth in the excommunication, but not the poisoning, although they differ in their dating.

115. See H.E. Mayer, 'Zum Tode Wilhelms von Tyrus', *Archiv für Diplomatik*, 5–6 (1959–60), 182–201; R. Hiestand, 'Zum Leben und zur Laufbahn Wilhelms von Tyrus', *Deutsches Archiv*, 34 (1978), 351.

116. See P.W. Edbury, 'The Lyon *Eracles* and the Old French Continuations of William of Tyre', in *Montjoie: Studies in Crusade History in Honour of Hans Eberhard Mayer*, ed. B.Z. Kedar, J. Riley-Smith and R. Hiestand, Aldershot, 1997, pp. 139–53.

117. *History of William Marshal*, ed. A.J. Holden, tr. S. Gregory, introd. D. Crouch, Anglo-Norman Text Society, vol. 1, London, 2002, ll. 7275–95, pp. 370–1. For the circumstances and dating, see D. Crouch, *William Marshal: Court, Career and Chivalry in the Angevin Empire*, London, 1990, pp. 49–53.

118. See Riley-Smith, *Knights of St John*, pp. 64–5, and N. Jaspert, 'The Election of Arnau de Torroja as Ninth Master of the Knights Templar (1180): An Enigmatic Decision Reconsidered', in *Actas do V Encontro sobre Ordens Militares*, ed. I.C.F. Fernandes, Colecção Ordens Militares, 2, Palmela, 2009, pp. 371–97. In the kingdom of Jerusalem, Bernard, bishop of Lydda, was chosen to deputise for the patriarch, which was another direct snub to William of Tyre: see Mayer, *Die Kanzlei*, vol. 1, pp. 249–50.

119. Ibn al-Athir, part 2, pp. 300–1, says that Saladin tried to bring Baldwin's relief army to battle, but without success.

120. Ralph of Diceto, *Ymagines Historiarum*, vol. 2, ed. W. Stubbs, RS 68, London, 1876, pp. 27–8, 30. Ralph incorporates Baldwin's letter to the envoys into his narrative.

121. Roger of Howden, *Gesta Henrici Secundi*, vol. 1, ed. W. Stubbs, RS 49, London, 1867, pp. 332–3. Roger seems to have written this between 1169 and 1192 almost contemporaneously and was therefore able to use it as a basis for his *Chronica*.

122. Rigord, *Histoire de Philippe Auguste*, ed. and tr. E. Carpentier, G. Pon and Y. Chauvin, Sources d'histoire médiévale publiées par l'Institut de Recherche et d'Histoire des Textes, 33, Paris, 2006, 1.30–1, pp. 178–83. Rigord (died c.1209) was a monk at Saint-Denis, whose chroniclers provided powerful historiographical support for the Capetian house. He would have had direct knowledge of this meeting but, unlike some of the Anglo-Norman chroniclers, he was not present on the Third Crusade in 1191.

123. See H.E. Mayer, 'Henry II of England and the Holy Land', *English Historical Review*, 97 (1982), 721–34. However, C.J. Tyerman, *England and the Crusades, 1095-1588*, Chicago, 1988, pp. 54–6,

doubts that, in practice, there had been any substantial accumulation of funds, behaviour that would, he thinks, 'on the face of it, have been highly eccentric'. For the will, see *Recueil des actes de Henri II, roi d'Angleterre et duc de Normandie*, vol. 2, ed. L. Delisle and E. Berger, Chartes et diplômes relatifs à l'histoire de France, Paris, 1920, no. 612, pp. 219–21.

124. Ralph of Diceto, vol. 2, pp. 32–4; Roger of Howden, *Gesta*, vol. 2, pp. 335–6; Gerald of Wales, *De Principis Instructione Liber*, ed. G.F. Warner, in *Giraldi Cambrensis Opera*, ed. J.S. Brewer, J.F. Dimock and G.F. Warner, vol. 8, RS 21, London, 1891, pp. 202–12. According to Gerald, p. 212, the prophecy was fulfilled, for the first thirty years of the reign had brought him 'worldly glory', but the last five nothing but misfortunes. The patriarch's comment is recorded by Gerald.

125. See F.A. Cazel, 'The Tax of 1185 in Aid of the Holy Land', *Speculum*, 30 (1955), 385–92.

126. See W.L. Warren, *Henry II*, London, 1973, pp. 604–6. He assumes that Henry was offered the throne of Jerusalem.

127. See, among several accounts, Phillips, *Defenders of the Holy Land*, pp. 251–63, and Kedar, 'Eraclius', pp. 191–5.

12 The Battle of Hattin and its Consequences

1. Roger of Howden, *Chronica*, vol. 2, pp. 304, 307, says he had returned before the Feast of St Peter's Chains (1 August). Roger des Moulins is not recorded as being in the kingdom until 1 February 1186, RRH, no. 647, p. 171, so it is not certain that they travelled back together. He was with Henry II at Dover on 10 April 1185, so he presumably went on to Vaudreuil: RRH, Add., no. 641a, p. 42. For Baldwin's death, see Hiestand, 'Chronologisches zur Geschichte des Königreiches Jerusalem', 545–53, who argues for 15 April 1185, and Hamilton, *Leper King*, p. 210, who leaves the matter open.

2. Roger of Howden, *Chronica*, vol. 2, p. 304, says *dolens et confusus*.

3. See Hamilton, *Leper King*, p. 205.

4. See Hiestand, 'Chronologisches zur Geschichte des Königreiches Jerusalem', 551–3.

5. *Cont. WT*, cc. 3–4, pp. 13–14. Tr. P.W. Edbury, *The Conquest of Jerusalem and the Third Crusade: Sources in Translation*, Aldershot, 1996, pp. 14–15; Ernoul-Bernard, pp. 115–17.

6. *Cont. WT*, c. 5, p. 21. Tr. Edbury, *Conquest*, p. 15; Ernoul-Bernard, pp. 117–18; *Eracles*, vol. 2, 23.5, pp. 7–9. See Mayer, 'Das Pontifikale', 158–60.

7. On his age, see Hamilton, *Leper King*, p. 139, n. 47. He was born sometime in the winter of 1177–8.

8. Roger of Howden, *Gesta*, vol. 2, p. 307. This is dated to 1185 by Roger, who presumably obtained his information from his English contacts. It is not mentioned in the Old French sources.

9. *Cont. WT*, cc. 7–9, pp. 22–4; Ernoul-Bernard, pp. 121–4. See Boas, *Jerusalem in the Time of the Crusades*, pp. 173–4, 177, on Germain's previous work, including the improvement of an additional cistern for the city.

10. *Cont. WT*, c. 9, pp. 23–4; Ernoul-Bernard, p. 124; Kamal-ad-Din, *L'histoire d'Alep*, tr. E. Blochet, *ROL*, 4 (1896), 173–5, who describes the problems Saladin faced at this time. See Baldwin, *Raymond III*, p. 70, n. 2, on the truce. Presumably Saladin would have wanted to secure his western flank before setting out for Mosul, which makes the spring of 1185 the most likely date.

11. Ibn Shaddad, p. 68.

12. Ibn al-Athir, part 2, p. 310; Ibn Shaddad, p. 69.

13. See Lyons and Jackson, *Saladin*, pp. 221–39.

14. H.A.R. Gibb, 'The Rise of Saladin, 1169–1189', in *A History of the Crusades*, vol. 1, ed. M.W. Baldwin, Madison, 1969, p. 580, and Möhring, *Saladin*, p. 57.

15. See Ibn al-Athir, part 2, pp. 313–15, for the signs of such divisions while Saladin was ill. The conflicts after his death in 1193 strongly suggest that a similar situation would have arisen in 1186. See Lyons and Jackson, *Saladin*, pp. 239–44, who, in contrast to Gibb and Möhring, describe this time as 'the nadir of Saladin's career'.

16. See Folda, *Art of the Crusaders*, p. 440.

17. See Pringle, *Churches*, vol. 2, pp. 116–20, 123–34, and Folda, *Art of the Crusaders*, pp. 415–18.

18. John Phocas, in JP, p. 320.

19. See Folda, *Art of the Crusaders*, pp. 430–2.

20. Nazareth is only 11 miles from Hattin and the capitals may have been buried as a precaution even before the battle, given the proximity of the two armies. It had fallen before the end of the month.

21. See J. Folda, *The Nazareth Capitals and the Crusader Shrine of the Annunciation*, Philadelphia, PA, 1986, and M. Barasch, *Crusader Figural Sculpture in the Holy Land*, New Brunswick, NJ, 1971, pp. 69-176. Folda, p. 49, thinks that eight apostles were originally planned, all of whom were associated with Galilee.

22. Folda, *Art of the Crusaders*, p. 415, draws attention to the rebuilding of neighbouring churches either before or at the same time as that of Nazareth, most importantly St Anne's at Saffuriya, the cathedral of St John at Sebaste and the church of the Resurrection at Nablus.

23. The reason for his death is not known, but Raymond's care in ensuring that he did not have custody of the child might imply doubts about his health. On the dates of Baldwin's birth and death, see Hiestand, 'Chronologisches zur Geschichte des Königreiches Jerusalem', 553-5.

24. *Cont. WT*, c. 17, pp. 30-1; Ernoul-Bernard, pp. 129-30. Joscelin had his own plans. After the coronation he attempted to expand his holdings in the north of the kingdom by adding Toron to his territories around Acre. As Mayer says, 'Die Legitimität', 87-9, in the end his complicated manoeuvres were negated by Saladin's victory at Hattin.

25. *Cont. WT*, c. 10, pp. 24-5, c. 17, pp. 30-1; Ernoul-Bernard, pp. 125-6, 130-1. WT, 17.1, p. 760, records his presence on the Second Crusade.

26. *Cont. WT*, c. 33, pp. 45-6; Ernoul-Bernard, p. 114. The story derives from the Old French continuations of William of Tyre with some variations in the details. See M. Barber, 'The Reputation of Gerard of Ridefort', in *The Military Orders*, vol. 4, *On Land and by Sea*, ed. J. Upton-Ward, Aldershot, 2008, pp. 111-19.

27. For a reconstruction, see Kedar, 'Eraclius', pp. 195-8. See also H. Nicholson, '"La roine preude femme et bonne dame": Queen Sibyl of Jerusalem (1186-1190) in History and Legend, 1186-1300', *Haskins Society Journal*, 15 (2004), 115-18, 124, for the extent to which the sources were influenced by gender stereotyping.

28. *Cont. WT*, c. 18, pp. 32-3; Ernoul-Bernard, pp. 131-4. As Mayer, 'Das Pontifikale von Tyrus', 161, points out, there were many irregularities with the procedures that followed, not the least of which was the closing of the gates of the city, which prevented public access to the acclamation normally associated with coronations.

29. The key section from Guy of Bazoches is quoted by Kedar, 'Eraclius', p. 197, n. 70; Roger of Howden, *Chronica*, vol. 2, pp. 315-16. The relevant passages are translated by Edbury, *Conquest*, pp. 154-5.

30. See Baldwin, *Raymond III*, p. 77, n. 21, on the evidence of possible opposition.

31. *Libellus de expugnatione Terrae Sanctae per Saladinum*, ed. J. Stevenson, RS 66, London, 1875, p. 209. It is generally thought that the author may have been English and that he probably wrote up his experiences in the early thirteenth century. However, John Pryor places it within a corpus of material that was altered in various ways in order to encourage participation in a new expedition to the Holy Land, or at least as a means of soliciting contributions. See J.H. Pryor, 'Two *excitationes* for the Third Crusade: The Letters of Brother Thierry of the Temple', *Mediterranean Historical Review*, 26 (2011), 15.

32. Hamilton, 'Elephant of Christ', p. 106, suggests that Reynald of Châtillon may have persuaded his stepson that this was the best course of action.

33. *Cont. WT*, c. 18-21, pp. 33-6. Ernoul-Bernard, pp. 138-9, says that he did homage, but this passage is not in *Cont. WT*. Eracles, pp. 31-4.

34. *Cont. WT*, c. 23, p. 36. Tr. Edbury, *Conquest*, p. 29. Ernoul-Bernard, p. 141.

35. 'Imâd ad-Din al-Isfahânî, *Conquête de la Syrie et de Palestine par Saladin*, tr. H. Massé, Paris, 1972, pp. 19-20; Ibn al-Athir, part 2, p. 316.

36. 'Imad al-Din, in Abu Shama, vol. 4, p. 258. On the idea that Raymond was ready to convert to Islam, which he dismisses, see Baldwin, *Raymond III*, pp. 83-5, esp. n. 35.

37. See Hamilton, *Leper King*, p. 224. For the previous revolts, see Chapter 7, pp. 154-6, Chapter 10, pp. 236-7.

38. *Cont. WT*, c. 23, pp. 36-7. Tr. Edbury, *Conquest*, p. 30; Ernoul-Bernard, pp. 141-2. Given Ernoul's closeness to Balian, this is likely to be an accurate account of what happened.

39. *Cont. WT*, c. 22, p. 36. Tr. Edbury, *Conquest*, p. 29. Ernoul claims that Saladin's sister was among the prisoners, but this looks like an embellishment since the Muslim sources do not mention it.

40. 'Imad al-Din, in Abu Shama, vol. 4, pp. 258-9; Ibn al-Athir, pp. 316-17. Hamilton, *Leper King*, p. 225, thinks that neither man would have made such a truce, and suggests that it was a story later spread about by Saladin's advisers to justify the execution of Reynald in July 1187.

41. Ibn al-Athir, pp. 318-19; 'Abu Shama, vol. 4, pp. 260-1.

42. *Cont. WT*, cc. 25-8, pp. 37-43; Ernoul-Bernard, pp. 143-57, mentioning Ernoul by name, p. 149.

43. Ibn al-Athir, part 2, p. 319; 'Imad al-Din, in Abu Shama, vol. 4, p. 262. See Lyons and Jackson, *Saladin*, pp. 249-50.

44. See B.Z. Kedar and D. Pringle, 'La Fève: A Crusader Castle in the Jezreel Valley', *Israel Exploration Journal*, 35 (1985), 164–79.

45. As can be seen from the master's letter to the pope, James of Mailly was not in fact the Templar marshal as designated by Ernoul. He soon attained legendary status: see the *Itinerarium Peregrinorum et Gesta Regis Ricardi*, in *Chronicles and Memorials of the Reign of Richard I*, vol. 1, ed. W. Stubbs, RS 38, London, 1864, 1.2, pp. 6–7, the first book of which is a compilation about the Third Crusade, perhaps written in 1191–2, possibly by an English crusader. See *Das Itinerarium Peregrinorum: Eine zeitgenössische englische Chronik zum dritten Kreuzzug in ursprünglicher Gestalt*, ed. H.E. Mayer, Schriften der Monumenta Germaniae historica, 18, Stuttgart, 1962, pp. 52–161. The *Itinerarium* as a whole, including the first book, was put together by Richard de Templo, prior of the Augustinian house of the Holy Trinity, London, probably between 1217 and 1222. Although he made extensive use of other accounts, especially that of the Norman poet Ambroise, nevertheless he was himself a crusader and added valuable material and opinions of his own. For a concise summary of the nature of the *Itinerarium*, see Helen Nicholson, *Chronicle of the Third Crusade: A Translation of the Itinerarium Peregrinorum et Gesta Regis Ricardi*, Crusade Texts in Translation, 3, Aldershot, 1997, pp. 6–14.

46. *Libellus*, pp. 211–12. See P.W. Edbury, 'Gerard of Ridefort and the Battle of Le Cresson (1 May 1187): The Developing Narrative Tradition', in *On the Margins of Crusading: The Military Orders, the Papacy and the Christian World*, Crusades Subsidia 4 ed. H. Nicholson, Farnham, 2011, pp. 45–60, on the differences between the Old French continuations of William of Tyre, where he shows that in some versions the master's actions are treated in a more neutral fashion than in the Lyon manuscript.

47. See D. Pringle, 'The Spring of the Cresson in Crusading History', in *Dei gesta per Francos: Etudes sur les croisades dédiées à Jean Richard*, ed. M. Balard, B.Z. Kedar and J. Riley–Smith, Aldershot, 2001, pp. 231–40.

48. *Papsturkunden für Kirchen im Heiligen Lande*, ed. Hiestand, no. 148, pp. 322–4. Tr. Edbury, *Conquest*, pp. 156–7. Ridefort's letter is not extant, but is mentioned in a letter of Urban III (3 September 1187).

49. Ibn al-Athir, part 2, pp. 319–20. See Lyons and Jackson, *Saladin*, pp. 249–50.

50. 'Imad al-Din, in Abu Shama, vol. 4, p. 263. See Lyons and Jackson, *Saladin*, pp. 252–6.

51. *Cont. WT*, c. 28, p. 42. Tr. Edbury, *Conquest*, p. 35.

52. *Libellus*, p. 218; *Cont. WT*, c. 31, p. 44. Given that he claimed 180,000 for Saladin's army, it seems probable that the *Libellus* is more reliable.

53. Roger of Howden, *Gesta*, vol. 2, p. 11. Tr. Barber and Bate, *Letters from the East*, no. 45, p. 82. Although this letter has been widely cited, some caution may be needed in its use as a source, since John Pryor believes it is 'an obvious forgery': 'Two *excitationes*', 16, n.167.

54. *Cont. WT*, cc. 30–2, pp. 43–5; Ernoul-Bernard, pp. 157–61; *Libellus*, pp. 221–2. The Genoese letter says that Raymond and Eschiva's sons persuaded the king to march on Tiberias, but a merchant based in Acre would naturally be less well informed about what happened at Saffuriya.

55. The witness is al-Muqaddasi, who, as a child, had lived near Nablus before his community had left for Damascus in 1156. He was a member of Saladin's army and the information comes from a letter he wrote in August 1187. It is quoted in Abu Shama, vol. 4, p. 286.

56. *Cont. WT*, c. 34, pp. 46–7; Ernoul-Bernard, pp. 161–2; *Libellus*, pp. 22–3.

57. 'Imad al–Din, in Abu Shama, vol. 4, p. 264; Ibn al-Athir, part 2, p. 321. 'Imad al-Din says that the fall of the town had provoked Raymond into action, perhaps because 'Imad wanted to emphasise the success of Saladin's manoeuvre: *Conquête de la Syrie*, p. 24.

58. See Chapter 11, pp. 281–2.

59. See, for example, the comments of Ibn Shaddad, p. 72; Ibn al-Athir, part 2, p. 320.

60. WT, 22.28(27), p. 1054.

61. Ibn al-Athir, part 2, p. 321.

62. See Barber, 'Reputation of Gerard of Ridefort', pp. 116–17.

63. See Mayer, 'Henry II', 728, 737. The implication is that the whole of Henry's deposits in the Holy Land needed his permission before they could be spent, although the 5,000 marks given for the general defence has the attached phrase *nisi eam in vita mea repetere voluero*. Thus, in addition, Henry could take back this money if he wished.

64. See B.Z. Kedar, 'The Battle of Hattin Revisited', in *The Horns of Hattin*, ed. B.Z. Kedar, London, 1992, pp. 196–7. Lyons and Jackson, *Saladin*, pp. 259–60, argue that Guy may have planned to return to the springs at Turan if he found that Saladin blocked the way east. These springs are not mentioned in western sources. J. Prawer, 'The Battle of Hattin', in *Crusader Institutions*, Oxford, 1980, pp. 492–3, thought they were inaccessible in any case.

65. Kedar, 'Battle of Hattin Revisited', pp. 200-1.
66. *Cont. WT*, c. 40, p. 52; *Libellus*, pp. 222-3. For a discussion, see Baldwin, *Raymond III*, pp. 115-19.
67. Lyons and Jackson, *Saladin*, p. 261. Al-Muqaddasi says that the Muslims now enveloped the Franks, to the extent that the centre was now behind them: Abu Shama, vol. 4, p. 287.
68. *Eracles*, p. 62. See Prawer, 'Battle of Hattin', pp. 493-6, and Kedar, 'Battle of Hattin Revisited', pp. 198-202.
69. 'Imad al-Din, in Abu Shama, vol. 4, p. 266.
70. *Libellus*, pp. 223-5; *Cont. WT*, c. 42, p. 53.
71. *Cont. WT*, c. 42, pp. 53-4; Ernoul-Bernard, pp. 169-70; *Libellus*, p. 226; 'Imad al-Din, in Abu Shama, vol. 4, pp. 269-70; Ibn al-Athir, p. 322. The presence of Balian of Ibelin, who had been in the rearguard, suggests that either the formation of the army had disintegrated or that Raymond had gathered together what the *Libellus* calls the *Pullani*.
72. Some confirmation for this is provided by the letter of the Genoese consuls, which says that there was no back-up for the Templars and that they were 'hemmed in and slaughtered'. As the informant was not actually at the battle, however, it is not absolutely clear that he is referring to the same incident: Roger of Howden, *Gesta*, p. 11.
73. See Kedar, 'Battle of Hattin Revisited', pp. 205-6.
74. *Cont. WT*, c. 42, pp. 54-5; *Libellus*, pp. 226-8; 'Imad al-Din, in Abu Shama, vol. 4, p. 274; Ibn al-Athir, p. 323.
75. *Cont. WT*, c. 40, p. 52. Tr. Edbury, *Conquest of Jerusalem*, p. 45. *Libellus*, pp. 222-3.
76. Roger of Howden, *Gesta*, vol. 2, pp. 11-12. Tr. Barber and Bate, *Letters from the East*, no. 45, p. 82.
77. Ibn al-Athir, part 2, pp. 322-3.
78. 'Imad al-Din, in Abu Shama, vol. 4, p. 270.
79. J. Richard, 'An Account of the Battle of Hattin Referring to the Frankish Mercenaries in Oriental Moslem States', *Speculum*, 27 (1952), 175-6. John appears to have been a Frankish mercenary serving for pay rather than from religious conviction. His position was far from unique.
80. 'Imad al-Din, in Abu Shama, vol. 4, pp. 271-2. See Lyons and Jackson, *Saladin*, p. 261.
81. *Cont. WT*, c. 43, pp. 55-6; 'Imad al-Din, *Conquête de la Syrie*, pp. 27-8; Ibn al-Athir, part 2, pp. 323-4. In certain circumstances non-Muslims in Islamic lands could claim the *aman*, that is the protection of the authorities. Ernoul says that the sultan's mamluks actually struck off his head.
82. Tr. Edbury, *Conquest*, p. 48.
83. Ibn Shaddad, p. 37.
84. Roger of Howden, *Chronica*, vol. 2, pp. 324-5. John Pryor has subjected the two letters that appear to have been written by Terricus from Tyre to close analysis and believes that they (and probably others) were among those later altered in order to serve as *excitationes* in the West. In that light he has redated this letter to early 1188, as well as suggesting that Terricus was not at Hattin as one version of the letter asserts. See 'Two *excitationes*', 1-28.
85. 'Imad al-Din, *Conquête de la Syrie*, pp. 30-2.
86. Ibn al-Athir, part 2, p. 324.
87. *Cont. WT*, c. 44, p. 56.
88. *Libellus*, p. 228.
89. *Cont. WT*, cc. 44-5, pp. 56-7; *Libellus*, pp. 234-5.
90. 'Imad al-Din, *Conquête de la Syrie*, p. 33; Ibn al-Athir, part 2, pp. 324-5.
91. Tr. Barber and Bate, *Letters from East*, no. 42, p. 78.
92. 'Imad al-Din, *Conquête de la Syrie*, pp. 34-44; Ibn al-Athir, par 2, pp. 326-8.
93. Ibn al-Athir, part 2, p. 326.
94. ULKJ, vol. 3, no. 769, pp. 1339-43.
95. Ibn al-Athir, part 2, p. 328.
96. *Cont. WT*, cc. 48-9, pp. 60-2; Ibn al-Athir, part 2, pp. 328-9. See D. Jacoby, 'Conrad, Marquis of Montferrat, and the Kingdom of Jerusalem (1187-1192)', in *Atti del Congresso internazionale 'Dai feudi monferrine e dal Piemonte ai nuovi mondi oltre gli Oceani'*, Alessandria 2-6 aprile, Alessandria, 1993, pp. 188-91. For the Genoese version of Conrad's arrival in the East, see M. Mack, 'A Genoese Perspective of the Third Crusade', *Crusades*, 10 (2011), 45.
97. *Cont. WT*, c. 49, pp. 62-3; 'Imad al-Din, in Abu Shama, vol. 4, p. 313.
98. This was apparently Ernoul's view: tr. Edbury, *Conquest*, p. 54. According to Ibn al-Athir, part 2, p. 333, Guy was held in the citadel at Nablus. The town itself had been taken soon after Hattin; *Libellus*, p. 233; 'Imad al-Din, *Conquête de la Syrie*, pp. 35-6.
99. Ibn al-Athir, part 2, pp. 329-30.

100. Ibn Shaddad, p. 77; Ibn al-Athir, part 2, p. 330.
101. *Cont. WT*, c. 45, p. 57, c. 49, p. 63; Ernoul-Bernard, pp. 186–7.
102. B.Z. Kedar, 'Ein Hilferuf aus Jerusalem vom September 1187', *Deutsches Archiv für Erforschung des Mittelalters*, 35 (1982), 112–22; Jaspert, 'Zwei unbekannte Hilfersuchen', no. 2, pp. 511–16.
103. *Cont. WT*, c. 50, pp. 63–4; Ibn al-Athir, part 2, p. 331.
104. *Libellus*, pp. 241–3.
105. *Libellus*, p. 245.
106. *Cont. WT*, c. 54, p. 67. Tr. Edbury, *Conquest*, p. 59.
107. Ibn al-Athir, part 2, p. 332.
108. Ibn al-Athir, part 2, p. 332. See also *Cont. WT*, c. 55, pp. 67–9; *Libellus*, pp. 246–8; 'Imad al-Din, in Abu Shama, vol. 4, p. 329; Michael the Syrian, 20.6, p. 404, for some variations in these figures, but all agree on the application of a set tariff.
109. See Friedman, *Encounter between Enemies*, pp. 163–72.
110. *Cont. WT*, c. 55, p. 68.
111. 'Imad al-Din, in Abu Shama, vol. 4, pp. 330–1. Ibn Shaddad, who wished to emphasise Saladin's virtues, comments on his generosity, both in the giving of alms and in making gifts and grants to individuals. Nevertheless, he implicitly accepts the dangers of this when he recounts how the sultan's officials hid sums of money in case they were needed in a crisis: pp. 19, 25–6.
112. Ibn al-Athir, part 2, pp. 333–4.
113. 'Imad al-Din, *Conquête de la Syrie*, p. 49.
114. *Cont. WT*, c. 57, p. 72.
115. *Cont. WT*, c. 57, pp. 70–1. Tr. Edbury, *Conquest*, p. 62.
116. Ibn Shaddad, p. 78.
117. *Cont. WT*, c. 59, p. 73.
118. On Raymond's death, see Ibn Shaddad, p. 74; Ernoul-Bernard, p. 178. See also Baldwin, *Raymond III*, pp. 137–8. Ralph of Diceto, vol. 2, p. 56, says that the count died fifteen days after the fall of Jerusalem, that is, on 17 October.
119. *Cont. WT*, cc. 59–61, pp. 73–5. The word used is *governaus*. See Pryor, *Geography, Technology and War*, pp. 31–2.
120. Philip of Novara, cap. 47, pp. 118–21, 259–61.
121. See P.W. Edbury, 'Law and Custom in the Latin East: *Les Letres dou Sepulcre*', in *Intercultural Contacts in the Medieval Mediterranean*, ed. B. Arbel, London, 1996, pp. 71–9.
122. WT, 22.5, p. 1012. See ULKJ, vol. 1, p. 11.
123. Ibn Shaddad, pp. 77–8; 'Imad al-Din, in Abu Shama, vol. 4, pp. 33–4.
124. 'Imad al-Din, *Conquête de la Syrie*, pp. 51–9; Ibn al-Athir, part 2, pp. 334–5; *Cont. WT*, c. 62, p. 75; *Libellus*, p. 250; Roger of Howden, *Chronica*, vol. 2, p. 346. Pryor (see note 84 above) dates this letter to post-July 1188.
125. Roger of Howden, *Chronica*, vol. 2, p. 346. By Syrians he meant indigenous Orthodox priests, who seem to have been allowed to continue to say the offices in the period between 1187 and 1192, when Saladin accepted two Latin priests and two deacons in each of the three great shrine churches of the Holy Sepulchre, Bethlehem and Nazareth as part of his agreement with Richard I: *Itinerarium*, 4.13, p. 438. See A. Jotischky, 'The Fate of the Orthodox Church in Jerusalem at the End of the 12th Century', in *Patterns of the Past, Prospects for the Future: The Christian Heritage in the Holy Land*, ed. T. Hummel, K. Hintlian and U. Carmesund, London, 1999, pp. 192–4.
126. 'Imad al-Din, *Conquête de la Syrie*, p. 63.
127. 'Imad al-Din, *Conquête de la Syrie*, pp. 85–92. See Lyons and Jackson, *Saladin*, pp. 280–1.
128. Wilbrand of Oldenburg. *Wilbrandi de Oldenborg Peregrinatio*, in *Peregrinatores Medii Aevi Quatuor*, ed. J.C.M. Laurent, 2nd edn, Leipzig, 1873, p. 164. Wilbrand was the son of Henry II, count of Oldenburg. He visited the Holy Land in 1211–12.
129. Ibn al-Athir, part 2, p. 335. See M. Mack, 'The Italian quarters of Frankish Tyre: mapping a medieval city', *Journal of Medieval History*, 33 (2007), 147–9.
130. *Cont. WT*, c. 63, p. 77, says ten galleys were sent by the count of Tripoli, presumably meaning Bohemond, since Raymond was dead by this date.
131. Roger of Howden, *Chronica*, vol. 2, p. 347. Tr. Barber and Bate, *Letters from the East*, no. 46, p. 84.
132. 'Imad al-Din, *Conquête de la Syrie*, pp. 63–80; *Cont. WT*, cc. 63–4, pp. 76–8.
133. Ibn al-Athir, part 2, p. 338; Ibn Shaddad, p. 79.
134. Ibn al-Athir, part 2, pp. 337–8.
135. See Chapter 6, pp. 141–2.

136. See Ellenblum, *Crusader Castles and Modern Histories*, pp. 213–57, and Chapter 11, p. 276.
137. Roger of Howden, *Chronica*, vol. 2, p. 346.
138. Ibn Shaddad, pp. 79–80; Ibn al-Athir, part 2, p. 344; 'Imad al-Din, *Conquête de la Syrie*, pp. 80–2.
139. See Lyons and Jackson, *Saladin*, pp. 286–91.
140. 'Imad al-Din, *Conquête de la Syrie*, pp. 116–20, describes the meeting with 'Imad al-Din Zengi in detail, significant because of the previously fraught relations: see Chapter 11, p. 280.
141. 'Imad al-Din was Saladin's secretary and was the oldest of the three, having served both Nur al-Din and Saladin. He presents what Donald Richards calls a 'genuine insider viewpoint'. See D.S. Richards, ''Imād al-Dīn al-Isfahāni: Administrator, Litterateur and Historian', in *Crusaders and Muslims in Twelfth-Century Syria*, ed. M. Shatzmiller, Leiden, 1993, pp. 133–46. Ibn Shaddad entered Saladin's service in May 1188. He says, p. 81, that all information previous to this was 'from eye-witnesses I trust'. Thereafter he was present at all the main events of Saladin's life until the sultan's death in March 1193, except for the period from October 1189 to April 1190, when he was away on a mission to gather support in the Islamic world to meet the threat of Frederick Barbarossa: p. 124.
142. See Chapter 5, p. 115: The only previous Sicilian action was an attack on Alexandria in July 1174: see Chapter 11, p. 263.
143. *Cont. WT*, c. 72, p. 82.
144. 'Imad al-Din, in Abu Shama, vol. 4, pp. 356–7; *Cont. WT*, c. 73, pp. 82–3, c. 75, pp. 85–6.
145. 'Imad al-Din, *Conquête de la Syrie*, pp. 122–3.
146. Ibn Shaddad, pp. 82–3; Ibn al-Athir, part 2, p. 345; 'Imad al-Din, in Abu Shama, vol. 4, pp. 353–4.
147. *Cont. WT*, c. 75, p. 86, c. 87, pp. 92–3.
148. Ibn al-Athir, part 2, p. 345; 'Imad al-Din, in Abu Shama, vol. 4, p. 357.
149. See J. Burgtorf, 'Die Herrschaft der Johanniter in Margat im Heiligen Land', in *Die Ritterorden als Träger der Herrschaft: Territorien, Grundbesitz und Kirche*, ed. R. Czaja and J. Sarnowsky, Ordines Militares, Colloquia Torunensia Historica 14, Toruń, 2007, pp. 27–39, and map 1. Rainald I Mazoir had originally been granted Marqab in 1118, but it was lost after the battle of the 'Field of Blood' the next year.
150. 'Imad al-Din calls Margaritus a bandit, 'one of the most ignoble rebels and the most deadly demons': *Conquête de la Syrie*, p. 125.
151. *Cont. WT*, c. 75, p. 87.
152. The bishop had in any case been in an invidious position since the sale of the fief of Marqab, since it meant that almost the entire diocese was dominated by the Hospitallers and Templars, who competed for control between themselves. Moreover, the fall of the coastal towns to the north cut off land communication with the patriarch of Antioch. See Hamilton, *Latin Church*, pp. 107, 212, and Burgtorf, 'Die Herrschaft der Johanniter in Margat', pp. 36–7.
153. Ibn al-Athir, part 2, pp. 345–6; Ibn Shaddad, p. 83; 'Imad al-Din, in Abu Shama, vol. 4, p. 358.
154. Ibn al-Athir, part 2, p. 346; 'Imad al-Din, in Abu Shama, vol, 4, p. 362. See also Chapter 2, p. 34.
155. Ibn al-Athir, part 2, pp. 347–8. See G. Saadé, 'Histoire du château de Saladin', *Studi Medievali*, 9 (1968), 980–1003. Saone had been held by the Byzantines from 975 to c.1108 and was really too large for the garrison of a secular Frankish lord. Robert of Zardana's sons, William (died 1132) and Garenton (died by 1175), seem to have mainly been responsible for the refortification of the north-west front.
156. Ibn Shaddad, pp. 84–5.
157. 'Imad al-Din, in Abu Shama, vol. 4, p. 367.
158. Ibn al-Athir, part 2, pp. 348, 351–2; Ibn Shaddad, p. 86; 'Imad al-Din, in Abu Shama, vol. 4, pp. 372–4. See Kennedy, *Crusader Castles*, pp. 79–84.
159. 'Imad al-Din, in Abu Shama, vol. 4, p. 376.
160. While the castle itself was in a formidable position, it had no intervisibility with other Frankish forts: see Edwards, 'Bağras and Armenian Cilicia: A Reassessment', 431–2.
161. Ibn al-Athir, part 2, pp. 352–3; Ibn Shaddad, p. 87; 'Imad al-Din, in Abu Shama, vol. 4, pp. 375–9; 'Imad al-Din, *Conquête de la Syrie*, pp. 142–4.
162. In fact, the destruction must have been limited, for there was a small garrison there which attacked a section of the German army travelling from Cilicia to Antioch in the summer of 1190; 'Imad al-Din, *Conquête de la Syrie*, p. 232. See Chapter 13, p. 329.
163. This led to a long and damaging war between the Armenians and the Templars after Saladin's death in 1193. The Templars did not regain control of the fortress until 1216. See Barber, *New Knighthood*, pp. 120–2.
164. Roger of Howden, *Chronica*, vol. 2, p. 341. Tr. Barber and Bate, *Letters from the East*, no. 47, p. 85.

165. 'Ansbert', *Historia de Expeditione Friderici Imperatoris*, ed. A. Chroust, MGHSS, n.s., vol. 5, Berlin, 1928, pp. 4–5. Tr. Barber and Bate, *Letters from the East*, no. 48, p. 86. For Armengarde of Aspe, see Riley-Smith, *Knights of St. John*, p. 107. He suggests that he may not have been master as such, but simply a temporary head until a new master was elected.

166. It is difficult to know what these contacts meant. Sibylla's sister might be seen as a spy, but she could equally have acted as a channel of communication between Bohemond and Saladin. Raymond of Tripoli, Bohemond's close friend, had had such links, and this might have been seen as prudent in the circumstances.

167. Ibn al-Athir, part 2, p. 353. 'Imad al-Din, *Conquête de la Syrie*, pp. 144–5, says that Saladin had no great wish for a truce, but that the 'foreign troops' did not want to fight any longer. As the Antiochenes would not have had time to bring in their harvest by May, he thought no great harm would arise from it.

168. Ibn Shaddad, p. 87.

169. Ibn Shaddad, pp. 88–90; Ibn al-Athir, part 2, pp. 354–7; 'Imad al-Din, in Abu Shama, vol. 4, pp. 381–8. See Lyons and Jackson, *Saladin*, pp. 291–4, and Favreau-Lilie, 'Landesausbau und Burg', 81–2.

170. Abu Shama, vol. 4, p. 388.

171. Ibn al-Athir, part 2, p. 356.

13 The Third Crusade

1. 'Imad al-Din, in Abu Shama, vol. 4, p. 363; Ibn al-Athir, part 2, p. 347. This exchange suggests that at this time Saladin perceived the *jihad* as meaning the total eclipse of the Frankish presence, a position he was forced to modify when combating the crusade that followed.

2. 'Ansbert', *Historia de Expeditione Friderici Imperatoris*, pp. 6–10. Tr. L. and J. Riley–Smith, *Crusades*, pp. 63–7. For the wider context, see Schein, *Gateway to the Heavenly City*, pp. 159–87.

3. *Cont. WT*, c. 72, p. 82, c. 74, pp. 83–4.

4. 'Ansbert', *Historia de Expeditione Friderici Imperatoris*, pp. 14–15. This is a composite text which includes important contemporary material written very close to the time of the events. See *The Crusade of Frederick Barbarossa: The History of the Expedition of the Emperor Frederick and Related Texts*, tr. G.A. Loud, Crusade Texts in Translation, 19, Farnham, 2010, pp. 1–7.

5. Roger of Howden, *Chronica*, vol. 2, pp. 334–5.

6. William of Newburgh, 3.23, p. 271. See J. Gillingham, *Richard I*, New Haven and London, 1999, pp. 87–8.

7. See Tyerman, *England and the Crusades*, pp. 39–54, for Henry II's past attitudes towards crusading, and Chapter 11, pp. 268–70, for the previous crusade of Philip of Flanders.

8. Roger of Howden, *Gesta*, vol. 2, p. 38, and Henry's encouraging reply, pp. 38–9. See Chapter 12, p. 322, for Aimery's letter.

9. Roger of Howden, *Chronica*, pp. 342–3. It is not clear if the two bishops had set out before or after the loss of their seats in July 1188, but in any case they must have known that the towns would be taken.

10. On the circumstances, see Warren, *Henry II*, pp. 607–26.

11. 'Ansbert', *Historia de Expeditione Friderici Imperatoris*, pp. 18–22, lists all the leading crusaders. See E.N. Johnson, 'The Crusades of Frederick Barbarossa and Henry VI', in HC, vol. 2, pp. 86–116, and R. Hiestand, '"precipua tocius christianismi columpna": Barbarossa und der Kreuzzug', in *Friedrich Barbarossa Handlungsspielräume und Wirkungsweisen des Staufischen Kaisers*, ed. A. Haverkamp, Vorträge und Forschungen, 40, Sigmaringen, 1992, pp. 51–108. The expedition can be followed in F. Opll, *Das Itinerar Kaiser Friedrich Barbarossas (1152–1190)*, Vienna, Cologne and Graz, 1978, pp. 97–109. Richard I needed as many as 219 ships for an army much smaller than that of the emperor: see Chapter 13, p. 340.

12. See A.V. Murray, 'Finance and Logistics of the Crusade of Frederick Barbarossa', in *In Laudem Hierosolymitani: Studies in Crusades and Medieval Culture in Honour of Benjamin Z. Kedar*, ed. I. Shagrir, R. Ellenblum and J. Riley–Smith, Aldershot, 2007, pp. 358–60.

13. See Harris, *Byzantium and the Crusades*, pp. 132–5, and Lilie, *Byzantium and the Crusader States*, pp. 230–7.

14. Ibn Shaddad, pp. 121–2. Ibn al-Athir, part 2, pp. 374–5, says that Isaac had promised he would not allow Frederick Barbarossa to cross his territory, but that in the event he was not strong enough to prevent him.

15. Niketas Choniates, pp. 221–2, 225. The *themes* were administrative units, organised on a military basis.

16. *Cont. WT*, c. 88, p. 93. Tr. Edbury, *Conquest*, p. 84.
17. 'Ansbert', *Historia de Expeditione Friderici Imperatoris*, pp. 40–3. See *Crusade of Frederick Barbarossa*, tr. Loud, pp. 16–17, for the context of these negotiations.
18. 'Ansbert', *Historia de Expeditione Friderici Imperatoris*, p. 53.
19. 'Ansbert', *Historia de Expeditione Friderici Imperatoris*, pp. 64–6, for the agreement, pp. 71–2, for the crossing.
20. See Murray, 'Finance and Logistics', pp. 366–7.
21. 'Ansbert', *Historia de Expeditione Friderici Imperatoris*, pp. 72–88; *Cont. WT*, cc. 89–91, pp. 93–6.
22. 'Ansbert', *Historia de Expeditione Friderici Imperatoris*, pp. 91–2.
23. Niketas Choniates, pp. 221, 229.
24. 'Ansbert', *Historia de Expeditione Friderici Imperatoris*, p. 92; *Cont. WT*, c. 97, p. 99.
25. *Cont. WT*, c. 96, p. 98.
26. Ibn al-Athir, part 2, p. 376. See also 'Imad al-Din, *Conquête de la Syrie*, p. 234, and Ibn Shaddad, p. 116.
27. Ibn Shaddad, p. 106.
28. Kilij Arslan had sent a letter of apology for his failure, excusing himself on the grounds that his sons now held the real power: Ibn al-Athir, part 2, p. 376.
29. Ibn Shaddad, pp. 114–16.
30. 'Imad al-Din, *Conquête de la Syrie*, pp. 232–3.
31. Ibn Shaddad, p. 117.
32. See Kennedy, *Crusader Castles*, pp. 41–5.
33. Ibn Shaddad, pp. 90–1, 95–6; Ibn al-Athir, part 2, pp. 360–1; 'Imad al-Din, in Abu Shama, vol. 4, pp. 397–400.
34. *Cont. WT*, c. 78–81, pp. 88–9. Tr. Edbury, *Conquest*, p. 80.
35. *Itinerarium*, 1.25, pp. 59–60. The release from the oath was justified on the usual ground that it was made under duress.
36. *Itinerarium*, 1.26, pp. 61–2. The Pisans had quarrelled with Conrad of Montferrat. See Jacoby, 'Conrad, Marquis of Montferrat', p. 200.
37. On this debate, see Lyons and Jackson, *Saladin*, p. 299, and H.A.R. Gibb, *The Life of Saladin from the Works of 'Imad al-Din and Baha' al-Din*, Oxford, 1973, pp. 59–61. Ibn al-Athir is not slow to criticise some of Saladin's decisions, so here he probably reflects the views expressed. 'Imad al-Din agrees; he thinks Saladin was proven to have had the better judgement: *Conquête de la Syrie*, p. 170.
38. Ibn Shaddad, p. 97. See Prawer, *Histoire du royaume latin*, vol. 2, pp. 43–4, and Pringle, *Churches*, vol. 4, pp. 16–17.
39. Ambroise, vol. 1, p. 45, tr. vol. 2, p. 71.
40. Ibn al-Athir, part 2, p. 360.
41. *Itinerarium*, 1.26, p. 61.
42. Ibn Shaddad, p. 97.
43. *Itinerarium*, 1.27–9, pp. 64–8. See also H. van Werveke, 'La contribution de la Flandre et du Hainaut à la Troisième Croisade', *Le Moyen Age*, 78 (1972), 58, 67–8, 85.
44. Ibn Shaddad, pp. 98–9; Ibn al-Athir, part 2, pp. 364–5.
45. Ibn al-Athir, part 2, p. 367.
46. Ibn Shaddad, pp. 101–4; Ibn al-Athir, pp. 366–8; 'Imad al-Din, *Conquête de la Syrie*, pp. 178–93; *Itinerarium*, 1.29–30, pp. 68–72. See Lyons and Jackson, *Saladin*, pp. 302–5.
47. *Itinerarium*, 1.29, pp. 70, 71. Ibn al-Athir, p. 368, says that the master of the Temple was captured and executed.
48. Ibn Shaddad, p. 104. *Itinerarium*, 1.30, p. 72, admits to 1,500 overall, but makes no attempt to conceal the scale of the defeat, while Ambroise, vol. 1, p. 49, says 5,000 lesser men.
49. 'Imad al-Din, in Abu Shama, vol. 4, p. 428; *Conquête de la Syrie*, p. 190; Ibn al-Athir, p. 369; *Itinerarium*, 1.31, p. 73.
50. 'Imad al-Din, *Conquête de la Syrie*, p. 201, says the rains were so heavy that the roads were a quagmire and it became impossible to attack the enemy.
51. Ibn Shaddad, pp. 105–6, 108.
52. Ibn al-Athir, part 2, pp. 368, 369; *Itinerarium*, 1.31, p. 74.
53. Ambroise, vol. 1, pp. 52–4.
54. 'Imad al-Din, in Abu Shama, vol. 4, pp. 440–1, 443, and *Conquête de la Syrie*, pp. 211–13; Ibn Shaddad, p. 107; Ibn al-Athir, part 2, p. 372.
55. Ibn Shaddad, p. 108; 'Imad al-Din, *Conquête de la Syrie*, p. 210.
56. Ibn al-Athir, part 2, p. 377.

57. 'Imad al-Din, *Conquête de la Syrie*, pp. 239–40. See H. Nicholson, 'Women on the Third Crusade', *Journal of Medieval History*, 23 (1997), 335–49, who points out that female warriors in the crusader armies are only mentioned in Muslim sources, evidently with the intention of emphasising the degenerate nature of Christian society. However, it does seem that a small number of women took part in the fighting, especially in the more desperate situations.

58. *Itinerarium*, 1.40, pp. 89–91.

59. See Ibn Shaddad's considered discussion of this, based on his own inspection and information from others, pp. 119–20.

60. Ibn al-Athir, part 2, p. 377. All the chroniclers thought that the count was important: 'Imad al-Din, *Conquête de la Syrie*, pp. 243–4; Ibn Shaddad, p. 120; *Itinerarium*, 1.42, p. 92, who provides a detailed list of other arrivals over the following months.

61. Ibn al-Athir, part 2, pp. 372–4; 'Imad al-Din, *Conquête de la Syrie*, pp. 215–20; *Itinerarium*,1.36, pp. 84–5.

62. Ibn Shaddad, pp. 122–3; Ibn al-Athir, part 2, pp. 377–8; 'Imad al-Din, *Conquête de la Syrie*, pp. 245–6.

63. 'Imad al-Din, *Conquête de la Syrie*, 224–6, 246–7; Ibn Shaddad, pp. 112–13.

64. Ibn Shaddad, pp. 123–4. The editor, Donald Richards, translates *ghiraras* as sacks, probably of about 440 lb (200 kg) each.

65. Ibn Shaddad, pp. 126–7; 'Imad al-Din, *Conquête de la Syrie*, pp. 248–9.

66. Ibn Shaddad, pp. 127–8; Ambroise, vol. 1, p. 61.

67. 'Imad al-Din, *Conquête de la Syrie*, pp. 250–1. See *Crusade of Frederick Barbarossa*, tr. Loud, pp. 27–8. Loud suggests that the disease that had afflicted the army even before the death of the emperor and that took such a high toll in Antioch was the major reason why the German army was so depleted.

68. Ibn Shaddad, pp. 130–1; 'Imad al-Din, *Conquête de la Syrie*, pp. 255–7; Ambroise, vol. 1, pp. 61–3.

69. Ibn Shaddad, p. 131.

70. *Epistolae Cantuarienses*, in *Chronicles and Memorials of the Reign of Richard I*, vol. 2, ed. W. Stubbs, RS 38, London, 1865, no. 345, p. 328; *Itinerarium*, 1.42, p. 93.

71. *Epistolae Cantuarienses*, no. 346, pp. 328–9. Tr. Edbury, *Conquest*, p. 171.

72. *Itinerarium*, 1.65, p. 123. Tr. Nicholson, *Chronicle of the Third Crusade*, p. 126.

73. 'Imad al-Din, *Conquête de la Syrie*, pp. 202–3. This is a typically overwritten passage, but it is still reasonable to assume a basis of truth beneath the linguistic exuberance.

74. *Itinerarium*, 1.70, p. 127. Tr. Nicholson, *Chronicle of the Third Crusade*, p. 129.

75. Ambroise, vol. 1, pp. 64–5; *Itinerarium*, 1.61–2, pp. 115–19, 1.65, pp. 123–4.

76. Ibn Shaddad, p. 143 (20 January); 'Imad al-Din, *Conquête de la Syrie*, p. 278 (10 January).

77. Ibn Shaddad, pp. 135–8; 'Imad al-Din, in Abu Shama, vol. 4, pp. 510–13; Ambroise, vol. 1, pp. 64–5. See Lyons and Jackson, *Saladin*, pp. 320–2, who judge that this was the fiercest fighting in the field since Hattin.

78. Ibn Shaddad, p. 143. 'Imad al-Din, *Conquête de la Syrie*, pp. 271, 278, 283, says that 1190–1 was an exceptionally hard winter and that spring was delayed. The Franks died in great numbers from diverse illnesses. See also Ibn al-Athir, part 2, p. 379.

79. Ambroise, vol. 1, pp. 66–71; *Itinerarium*, 1.66–81, pp. 124–37. Both authors have graphic accounts of the famine, told to them by survivors anxious to show what they had suffered.

80. *Itinerarium*, ll.43–4, pp. 94–5.

81. *Itinerarium*, 1.34, p. 79.

82. *Cont. WT*, cc. 104–6, pp. 105–7; Ambroise, vol. 1, pp. 66–7; *Itinerarium*, 1.63, pp. 119–23. See Hiestand, 'Zwei unbekannte Diplome', 31.

83. See Jacoby, 'Conrad, Marquis of Montferrat', pp. 192–3.

84. The adherence of the legate was obviously crucial and it may be that Conrad had promised the Pisans trade and property concessions, since they changed sides at this point, having previously supported Guy's initial attack on Acre. See Jacoby, 'Conrad, Marquis of Montferrat', p. 201.

85. *Eracles*, vol. 2, 25.11–12, pp. 151–4; Ernoul-Bernard, pp. 267–8. See S. Runciman, *A History of the Crusades*, vol. 3, Cambridge, 1954, pp. 30–2.

86. Ambroise, vol. 1, p. 67; *Itinerarium*, 1.63, pp. 121–3; Ibn Shaddad, pp. 139–40.

87. Tr. Nicholson, *Chronicle of the Third Crusade*, p. 123.

88. Ralph of Diceto, vol. 2, pp. 88–9. Tr. Edbury, pp. 171–2.

89. Ibn al-Athir, part 2, p. 380, echoing 'Imad al-Din's criticism.

90. Roger of Howden, *Chronica*, vol. 3, p. 8.

91. Richard of Devizes, *Chronicle*, ed. and tr. J.T. Appleby, London, 1963, pp. 5–7.

92. See K. Norgate, *Richard the Lion Heart*, London, 1924, p. 102.

93. See J.T. Appleby, *England without Richard, 1189-1199*, Ithaca, NY, 1965, pp. 15–16.
94. See S.K. Mitchell, *Taxation in Medieval England*, ed. S. Painter, New Haven, 1951, pp. 199–222. Cazel, 'Tax of 1185', 388, points out that the Saladin tithe was levied at a rate three or four times as heavy as the taxes of 1166 and 1185. Not surprisingly, there was widespread opposition.
95. Roger of Howden, *Chronica*, vol. 3, p. 17.
96. See N. Barratt, 'The English Revenue of Richard I', *English Historical Review*, 116 (2001), 636–41. The relatively low figure of £15,000 for 1189 reflects the drain on the country caused by the Saladin tithe, the receipts of which are not known; p. 640. Steep inflation from 1180 onwards further increased costs: see P. Harvey, 'The English Inflation of 1180–1220', *Past and Present*, 61 (1973), 3–30.
97. Roger of Howden, *Gesta*, vol. 2, p. 106. See Norgate, *Richard the Lion Heart*, p. 113.
98. Richard of Devizes, p. 28. See Appleby, *England without Richard*, p. 24. Henry II had considered the land route, but seems to have rejected it as impractical: see Tyerman, *England and the Crusades*, p. 60.
99. For the foundation of the monastery of Bois-Renou, near Sablé, see A. de Bertrand de Broussillon, *La Maison de Craon, 1050-1480: Étude historique accompagné du Cartulaire de Craon*, vol. 1, Paris, 1893, no. 173, p. 113. See Bulst-Thiele, *Sacrae Domus Militiae Templi Hierosolymitani Magistri*, pp. 123–34, for his career.
100. J. Boussard, *Le Comté d'Anjou sous Henri Plantagenêt et ses fils, 1151-1204*, Paris, 1938, Pièces justificatives, no. 7, pp. 179–81.
101. Gerald of Wales, *Itinerarium Kambriae*, ed. J.F. Dimock, in *Giraldi Cambrensis Opera*, ed. J.S. Brewer, J.F. Dimock and G.F. Warner, vol. 6, RS 21, London, 1868, 1.4, p. 54, 2.2, p. 113, 2.7, p. 126, 2.13, p. 147; Gerald of Wales, *The Journey through Wales and The Description of Wales*, tr. L. Thorpe, Harmondsworth, 1978, p. 113.
102. See Baldwin, *Government of Philip Augustus*, pp. 101–75, who sees the years between 1190 and 1203 as a period of 'extraordinary innovation in Capetian government', and J. Bradbury, *Philip Augustus: King of France 1180-1223*, Harlow, 1998, pp. 47–50, who attributes more progress to the years before the crusade than Baldwin. Neither would argue, however, that in 1190 Philip was able to draw on the resources available to Richard I.
103. *Recueil des actes de Philippe Auguste, roi de France*, vol. 1, ed. E. Berger and C. Brunel, Paris, 1916, no. 292, p. 354; Rigord, c. 76, pp. 274–5. See J. Richard, 'Philippe Auguste, la croisade et le royaume', in *La France de Philippe Auguste: Le temps des mutations*, ed. R.-H. Bautier, Paris, 1982, pp. 414–16, and Mack, 'Genoese Perspective', 48–52.
104. Ambroise, vol. 1, p. 73; tr. vol. 2, p. 94.
105. Roger of Howden, *Chronica*, vol. 3, p. 37.
106. Roger of Howden, *Chronica*, vol. 3, p. 51. See Norgate, *Richard the Lion Heart*, p. 120. In 1248, Louis IX of France sailed from Aigues–Mortes to Cyprus in twenty-four days, but this had been preceded by months of planning during which large quantities of supplies had been gathered in Cyprus. In 1190, there was no such base. See Pryor, *Geography, Technology and War*, p. 36.
107. Ambroise, vol. 1, p. 77. The stones were presumably used as ballast.
108. Roger of Howden, *Chronica*, vol. 3, pp. 54–5. Roger was present on the crusade between August 1190 and August 1191. See Gillingham, 'Roger of Howden on Crusade', pp. 141–53.
109. Roger of Howden, *Chronica*, vol. 3, pp. 58, 61–5. See Norgate, *Richard the Lion Heart*, pp. 132, 137.
110. The prevailing winds are westerly, but in winter easterlies are frequent, so they may well have found themselves sailing into the wind, a task for which twelfth-century ships were ill-equipped: see Pryor, *Geography, Technology and War*, pp. 3–4.
111. Roger of Howden, *Chronica*, vol. 2, pp. 99–100. The marriage to Berengaria was part of Richard's system for protecting his southern lands against his long-term enemy, Raymond V, count of Toulouse. Richard paid Philip 10,000 marks for this release: see Gillingham, *Richard I*, pp. 126–7, 140–2.
112. Ambroise, vol. 1, p. 17; tr., vol. 2, p. 46. Presumably at least some of the money extracted from Tancred was then spent on these subsidies.
113. Roger of Howden, *Chronica*, vol. 3, pp. 74–86.
114. Ambroise, vol. 1, p. 20; tr., vol. 2, p. 48.
115. See Pryor, *Geography, Technology and War*, pp. 70–7.
116. On the consequences of his death, see H.E. Mayer, 'Die Kanzlei Richards I. von England auf dem Dritten Kreuzzug', *Mitteilungen des Instituts für österreichische Geschichtsforschung*, 85 (1977), 22–35. The matrix of the great seal was recovered when his body was washed ashore. He was

replaced by one of the chamber clerks, Philip of Poitiers (later bishop of Durham), whose sometimes idiosyncratic formatting of charters did not entirely accord with usual chancery practice.

117. Ambroise, vol. 1, p. 23; tr. vol. 2, pp. 50–1. This was, of course, a convenient way of justifying an attack upon another Christian ruler.

118. Ambroise, vol. 1, pp. 22–8; *Itinerarium*, 2.28–33, pp. 180–94; Roger of Howden, vol. 3, pp. 105–10. The treatment of the queens is unclear. The *Itinerarium* says that they were safe in harbour and that Isaac tried unsuccessfully to persuade them to land, whereas Howden says that they were forced to remain outside at the mercy of the storms.

119. See J.A. Brundage, 'Richard the Lion-Heart and Byzantium', in *Studies in Medieval Culture*, 6–7, Kalamazoo, 1976, pp. 63–70.

120. Ambroise, vol. 1, pp. 28, 30–1.

121. Ambroise, vol. 1, p. 37; tr. vol. 2, p. 65.

122. Ambroise, vol. 1, p. 37; tr. vol. 2, p. 64.

123. Ibn Shaddad, p. 151. 'Imad ad-Din, *Conquête de la Syrie*, p. 299, equally emphasises the importance of what he calls a disaster. The chronology is not clear. Ambroise says that the incident occurred while Richard was en route to Acre, whereas Ibn Shaddad and Imad al-Din date it to 11 June, three days after Richard's arrival.

124. See Pryor, *Geography, Technology and War*, p. 74.

125. 'Imad al-Din, *Conquête de la Syrie*, pp. 289–90.

126. Rigord, c. 80, pp. 290–1.

127. Ambroise, vol. 1, p. 74; tr. vol. 2, p. 95.

128. Rigord, c. 80, pp. 290–1; *Eracles*, vol. 2, 25.15, p. 157. Ambroise, vol. 1, p. 34, presents Richard as hurrying to the mainland when he heard that the city might be taken without him. For contrasting views on Philip's contribution to the crusade, see Bradbury, *Philip Augustus*, pp. 85–101, and Gillingham, *Richard I*, pp. 165–6.

129. *Itinerarium*, 2.18, p. 166. Tr. Nicholson, *Chronicle of the Third Crusade*, p. 165.

130. Ibn Shaddad, pp. 148–50.

131. Ibn al-Athir, vol. 2, p. 380.

132. Ibn Shaddad, p. 150.

133. However, Möhring, *Saladin*, p. 70, argues that the destruction of Acre's defences was never a feasible option, unless Saladin had been prepared to take apart all the other coastal defences as well. Moreover, without the use of Acre's harbour, an attack on Tyre would not have been possible.

134. William of Newburgh, 4.4, p. 306, refers to this in 1189. Richard had already been ill while at Nicosia: Ambroise, vol. 1, p. 32. See T.G. Wagner and P.D. Mitchell, 'The Illnesses of King Richard and King Philippe on the Third Crusade: An understanding of *arnaldia* and *leonardie*', *Crusades*, 10 (2011), 23–44.

135. Ambroise, vol. 1, p. 74.

136. Ibn Shaddad, pp. 153, 155.

137. Ambroise, vol. 1, p. 75, 77–9; Ibn Shaddad, pp. 156–8.

138. 'Imad al-Din, *Conquête de la Syrie*, pp. 312–14. He was later captured and, after a year, ransomed by Saladin for 800 dinars.

139. Ibn Shaddad, pp. 160–2; 'Imad al-Din, *Conquête de la Syrie*, pp. 318–19.

140. Ibn Shaddad, p. 161; 'Imad al-Din, *Conquête de la Syrie*, p. 318; Roger of Howden, *Chronica*, vol. 3, pp. 120–1 (with some variations on the figures).

141. Roger of Howden, *Chronica*, vol. 3, p. 123.

142. Richard of Devizes, pp. 46–7; Rigord, c. 90, pp. 308–9. Richard was a monk of St Swithin's, Winchester. He acquired his information from those who had been present. On the sources for this incident, see Norgate, *Richard the Lion Heart*, pp. 330–1.

143. See Richard, 'Philippe Auguste, la croisade et le royaume', pp. 420–3, on Philip's contribution to the crusade.

144. Rigord, c. 88, pp. 304–5, says that Philip II was seriously ill. Ambroise, vol. 1, p. 90, claims that the deaths included the patriarch, six archbishops, twelve bishops, forty counts and 500 great landowners, some of whose names are recorded by Roger of Howden: *Gesta*, vol. 2, pp. 147–50. See Mitchell, *Medicine in the Crusades*, pp. 143–5, who estimates that between 25 and 40 per cent of the upper classes would have died in a campaign of the duration and intensity of the Third Crusade.

145. Roger of Howden, *Chronica*, vol. 3, p. 111, claims that from the time of the death of Philip of Flanders, Philip II was looking for an opportunity to return to France and gain control of the

county of Flanders. He may, too, have been short of funds by this time, although, if this were the case, none of the French chroniclers was prepared to admit it.

146. 'Imad al-Din, *Conquête de la Syrie*, pp. 330–1; Ibn Shaddad, pp. 164–5.

147. See Gillingham, *Richard I*, pp. 167–71. He sees most Christian contemporaries as viewing the event in favourable or at least neutral terms. However, there are signs of unease in both Ambroise and the *Itinerarium*: see M. Barber, 'The Albigensian Crusades: Wars Like Any Other?', in *Dei gesta per Francos: Etudes sur les croisades dédiées à Jean Richard*, ed. M. Balard, B.Z. Kedar and J. Riley-Smith, Aldershot, 2001, pp. 51–2. See also Lyons and Jackson, *Saladin*, p. 333, for consideration of the issues.

148. See Prawer, *Histoire du royaume latin*, vol. 2, p. 77, who argues that this was an opportunity lost, especially given the low state of morale in the Muslim forces.

149. Ibn Shaddad, pp. 168–70, 174. 'Imad al-Din says that 'all prisoners brought before Saladin were put to death': Abu Shama, vol. 5, p. 34.

150. Ambroise, vol. 1, pp. 91, 98; tr. vol. 2, pp. 110, 115. Richard's levy on horses in England during the preparations for the expedition is particularly pertinent in this context: see Chapter 13, p. 340. Horse armour was sufficiently unusual for Ibn Shaddad to make special mention of an important commander of the Franks whom, in November 1190, he saw 'mounted on a large horse, clothed in mail down to its hooves': p. 138.

151. Ambroise, vol. 1, p. 99.

152. Ibn Shaddad, pp. 173–4.

153. The *Itinerarium*, 4.17, p. 260, has six main sections, but the overall pattern is the same.

154. Ibn Shaddad, pp. 174–6.

155. Ambroise, vol. 1, pp. 101–4. The Hospitallers had twice asked the king to be allowed to charge and had twice been refused, but were finally provoked by the impetuosity of two men, including the marshal, who could not hold back. Ambroise believed that victory would have been total had this not happened.

156. Ibn Shaddad, pp. 176–7.

157. Ambroise, vol. 1, p. 107; *Itinerarium*, 4.20, pp. 275–6.

158. See Stevenson, *Crusaders in the East*, p. 276, n. 3, who calls the effects of the battle 'insignificant', despite the fact that it was 'hotly contested', and Smail, *Crusading Warfare*, pp. 164–5, who says that 'Any attempt to present it as a signal victory, or as "a crushing blow" is to misunderstand its place in the warfare of the period.' However, Prawer, *Histoire du royaume latin*, vol. 2, p. 83, is less dismissive, seeing it as a second opportunity lost. See also the discussion in Lyons and Jackson, *Saladin*, pp. 338–9, on the implications of the battle. They believe that if Richard had decided to turn inland without adequate preparation, then 'the tables could immediately be turned'.

159. Ibn Shaddad, pp. 175–6; Ibn al-Athir, vol. 2, p. 391.

160. See Mitchell, *Medicine in the Crusades*, p. 177.

161. Ambroise, vol. 1, p. 101; tr. vol. 2, p. 117. Richard de Templo has his own version of this, exclaiming, 'how different is the life of contemplation and meditation among the columns of the cloister from that dreadful exercise of war!' *Itinerarium*, 4.19, p. 270. Tr. Nicholson, *Chronicle of the Third Crusade*, p. 254.

162. Ibn Shaddad, pp. 177–80; 'Imad al-Din, *Conquête de la Syrie*, p. 346.

163. According to Ambroise, vol. 1, pp. 112–14, once the news reached him, Richard wished to stop the destruction of Ascalon as well, but was prevented from doing so by the French.

164. Roger of Howden, *Chronica*, vol. 3, pp. 130, 132. Tr. Edbury, *Conquest*, p. 181.

165. RRH, no. 706, pp. 189. This includes rights and liberties received from the Hospitallers and Templars, which, as Hans Mayer points out, seems highly unlikely: see 'Die Kanzlei Richards I.', 32. He speculates that perhaps the Pisans had submitted forged charters; however, both the masters are among the witnesses. Richard's actions show the readiness of western monarchs to issue their own charters in the East, whatever the rights of local institutions. As early as 1148, Conrad III had issued a diploma on behalf of the monastery of St Samuel at Mount Tabor, even though it in no way appertained to him: see Hiestand, '"Kaiser" Konrad', 98–113.

166. *Codice diplomatico della Repubblica di Genova*, vol. 3, pp. 19–21. Tr. Edbury, *Conquest*, pp. 181–2.

167. ULKJ, vol. 2, no. 485, pp. 825–8.

168. Ibn Shaddad, pp. 187–8.

169. 'Imad al-Din, *Conquête de la Syrie*, pp. 349–51. Ibn al-Athir, vol. 2, p. 392, blames the failure of the plan on 'the priests, bishops and monks', not on Joanna. Neither Ambroise nor Richard de Templo mentions this proposal, but it is inconceivable that Ibn Shaddad and 'Imad al-Din, both intimates of Saladin, would have invented the story. See Lyons and Jackson, *Saladin*, pp. 342–3.

It may be that Richard did not think it politic to make such a proposal widely known in the Christian army.

170. Ibn Shaddad, pp. 194–5.
171. Ambroise, vol. 1, pp. 125–31; tr. vol. 2, p. 137. Ambroise's view is shared by some modern historians: see M. Markowski, 'Richard Lionheart: bad king, bad crusader?', *Journal of Medieval History*, 23 (1997), 355–7, and Bradbury, *Philip Augustus*, pp. 98–9.
172. *Itinerarium*, 4.35, pp. 305–6, 5.1, p. 309.
173. 'Imad al-Din, *Conquête de la Syrie*, pp. 356–7, 371–3; Ibn al-Athir, vol. 2, pp. 393–4.
174. Ambroise, vol. 1, p. 127.
175. Ibn Shaddad, pp. 194–6; 'Imad al-Din, *Conquête de la Syrie*, pp. 353–4.
176. Ambroise, vol. 1, p. 132.
177. Ambroise, vol. 1, pp. 138–9.
178. Ambroise, vol. 1, p. 147.
179. *Cont. WT*, cc. 133–5, pp. 135–9. See P.W. Edbury, 'The Templars in Cyprus', in *The Military Orders: Fighting for the Faith and Caring for the Sick*, ed. M. Barber, Aldershot, 1994, pp. 189–91. There had been a revolt in Nicosia against the Templars earlier in April.
180. This was evidently a sensational event and was extensively reported by chroniclers on both sides. Ambroise, vol. 1, pp. 139–44; *Itinerarium*, 5.26–7, pp. 338–42; *Cont. WT*, p. 141; Ibn Shaddad, pp. 200–1; 'Imad al-Din, *Conquête de la Syrie*, pp. 376–8; Ibn al-Athir, vol. 2, pp. 396–7. Inevitably there were rumours that this was Richard's work, but Ibn al-Athir attributes it to Saladin, who had wanted Richard killed but, failing this, was prepared to pay the Assassins 10,000 dinars to kill Conrad. Neither idea seems likely.
181. Ambroise, vol. 1, pp. 148–51; Ibn Shaddad, pp. 203–9; 'Imad al-Din, *Conquête de la Syrie*, pp. 378–81.
182. Ambroise, vol. 1, pp. 157–73.
183. Ibn Shaddad, pp. 209–12.
184. Ambroise, vol. 1, p. 172; tr. vol. 2, p. 174.
185. *Itinerarium*, 6.7, p. 394. Tr. Nicholson, p. 345.
186. Ambroise, vol. 1, pp. 174–82; Ibn Shaddad, pp. 217–23; *Cont. WT*, cc. 139–40, pp. 143–6.
187. Ibn Shaddad, pp. 228–32; 'Imad al-Din, *Conquête de la Syrie*, pp. 388–91, who records that he wrote out the text of the agreement; Ambroise, vol. 1, pp. 189–90; tr. vol. 2, p. 186.
188. Ambroise, vol. 1, pp. 192–3, was among those who visited the city. He pitied the Franks and Syrians held there as slaves, many of whom must have been rebuilding the walls. Michael the Syrian, 20.6, p. 404, says that in October 1187, after the fall of Jerusalem, Saladin had assigned 5,000 of his prisoners to this task.
189. *Cart.*, vol. 1, no. 945, pp. 597–8. Tr. Barber and Bate, *Letters from the East*, no. 53, p. 93.
190. *Cont. WT*, cap. 152, p. 165.
191. Ibn al-Athir, part 2, p. 402.
192. Ibn al-Athir, part 2, pp. 401–2.
193. Ibn Shaddad, pp. 230, 232.
194. Ambroise, vol. 1, p. 198; tr. vol. 2, p. 193.

Conclusion

1. Kedar, '*Tractatus*', pp. 123–4. Tr. History Department, University of Leeds.
2. See the discussions in Jaspert, 'Ein Polymythos', 214–30, and Ellenblum, *Crusader Castles and Modern Histories*, pp. 43–61. For a concise summary, see A. Jotischky, *Crusading and the Crusader States*, Harlow, 2004, pp. 16–22.
3. WT, 7.19, pp. 367–8.
4. Ambroise, vol. 1, pp. 192–6.

Further Reading

Asbridge, T., *The Crusades. The War for the Holy Land*, London and New York: Simon & Schuster, 2010.

Edbury, P.W. and J.G. Rowe, *William of Tyre. Historian of the Latin East*, Cambridge: Cambridge University Press, 1988.

Eddé. A.-M., *Saladin*, tr. J.M. Todd, Harvard University Press, 2011.

Folda, J., *The Art of the Crusaders in the Holy Land, 1098–1187*, Cambridge: Cambridge University Press, 1995.

Harris, J., *Byzantium and the Crusades*, London: Hambledon, 2003.

Hillenbrand, C., *The Crusades. Islamic Perspectives*, Edinburgh: Edinburgh University Press, 1999.

Housley, N., *Fighting for the Cross. Crusading to the Holy Land*, New Haven and London: Yale University Press, 2008.

Jaspert, N., *The Crusades*, tr. P. G. Jestice, New York and London: Routledge, 2006.

Jotischky, A., *Crusading and the Crusader States*, Harlow: Longman, 2004.

Kennedy, H., *Crusader Castles*, Cambridge: Cambridge University Press, 1994.

Lyons, M.C. and D.E.P. Jackson, *Saladin. The politics of the Holy War*, Cambridge University Press, 1982.

Möhring, H., *Saladin. The Sultan and His Times, 1138–1193*, tr. D.S. Bachrach, Baltimore, MD: The Johns Hopkins University Press, 2008.

Murray, A.V., ed., *The Crusades. An Encyclopedia*, 4 vols, Santa Barbara and Oxford: ABC Clio, 2006.

Richard, J., *The Crusades c. 1071–c. 1291*, tr. J. Birrell, Cambridge: Cambridge University Press, 1999.

Riley-Smith, J., ed., *The Atlas of the Crusades*, London: Times Books, 1991.

Tyerman, C., *God's War. A New History of the Crusades*, London: Allen Lane, 2006.

Bibliography

Primary Sources

Abu Shama, *Le Livre des Deux Jardins*, in RHCr, Orient., vols 4 and 5, Paris, 1898.

Albert of Aachen, *Historia Ierosolimitana*, ed. and tr. S.B. Edgington, Oxford, 2007.

Ambroise, *The History of the Holy War*, ed. and tr. M. Ailes and M. Barber, 2 vols, Woodbridge, 2003.

Anna Comnena, *The Alexiad of the Princess Anna Comnena*, tr. E.A.S. Dawes, London, 1928.

Annales Herbipolensis, ed. G.H. Pertz, MGHSS, vol. 16, Hanover, 1859, pp. 1–12.

'Ansbert', *Historia de Expeditione Friderici Imperatoris*, ed. A. Chroust, MGH SS, n.s., vol. 5, Berlin, 1928.

Baha' al-Din Ibn Shaddad, *The Rare and Excellent History of Saladin*, tr. D.S. Richards, Crusade Texts in Translation, 7, Aldershot, 2001.

Baldric of Dol, *Historia Jerosolimitani*, in RHCr, Occid., vol. 4, Paris, 1879, pp. 1–111.

Barber, M., and K. Bate, trs, *The Templars*, Manchester Medieval Sources, Manchester, 2002.

—, *Letters from the East: Crusaders, Pilgrims and Settlers in the 12th–13th Centuries*, Crusade Texts in Translation, 18, Farnham, 2010.

Bernard of Clairvaux, *Sancti Bernardi Opera*, vol. 8, *Epistolae*, ed. J. Leclercq and H.M. Rochais, Rome, 1977.

—, *The Letters of St Bernard of Clairvaux*, trs. B.S. James, introd. B.M. Kienzle, Stroud, 1998.

Boeren, P.C., *Rorgo Fretellus de Nazareth et sa description de la Terre Sainte: Histoire et édition du texte*, Amsterdam, 1980.

Caffaro, *Liber de liberatione civitatum Orientis*, in *Annali Genovesi di Caffaro e de' suoi continuari*, ed. L.T. Belgrano, vol. 1, Rome, 1890.

Le Cartulaire du Chapitre du Saint-Sépulcre de Jérusalem, ed. G. Bresc-Bautier, Documents relatifs à l'histoire des croisades publiés par l'Académie des Inscriptions et Belles-Lettres, Paris, 1984.

Cartulaire général de l'Ordre des Hospitaliers de Saint-Jean de Jérusalem, 1100–1310, 4 vols, ed. J. Delaville Le Roulx, Paris, 1894–1905.

Cartulaire général de l'Ordre du Temple 1119?–1150: Recueil des chartes et des bulles relatives à l'ordre du Temple, ed. G.A.M. d'Albon, Paris, 1913.

Cerbani Cerbani, Clerici Veneti, *Translatio Mirifici Martyris Isidori a Chio Insula in Civitatem Venetam (Jun. 1125)*, in RHCr, Occid., vol. 5, Paris, 1895, pp. 321–34.

Chartes de Terre Sainte provenant de l'abbaye de Notre-Dame de Josaphat, ed. F. Delaborde, Paris, 1880.

Codice diplomatico della Repubblica di Genova, ed. C. Imperiale di Sant'Angelo, vols 1 and 3, Rome, 1936, 1942.

The Conquest of Jerusalem and the Third Crusade: Sources in Translation, tr. P.W. Edbury, Aldershot, 1996.

Continuation of Gregory the Priest: see Matthew of Edessa.

La Continuation de Guillaume de Tyr (1184–1197), ed. M. R. Morgan, Documents relatifs à l'histoire des croisades publiés par l'Académie des Inscriptions et Belles-Lettres, Paris, 1982.

The Crusade of Frederick Barbarossa: The History of the Expedition of the Emperor Frederick and Related Texts, tr. G.A. Loud, Crusade Texts in Translation, 19, Farnham, 2010.

Daniel the Abbot, 'The Life and Journey of Daniel, Abbot of the Russian Land', in JP, pp. 120–71.

Decrees of the Ecumenical Councils, vol. 1, *Nicaea to Lateran V*, ed. N.P. Tanner, London, 1990.

Delaville Le Roulx, J., 'Chartes de Terre Sainte', *ROL*, 11 (1905–8), 181–91.

Diplomatum Regum et Imperatorum Germaniae, ed. F. Hausmann, vol. 9, MGH, Diplomata, Vienna, Cologne, Graz, 1969.

Ekkehard of Aura, *Hierosolymita*, in RHCr, Occid., vol. 5, Paris, 1895, pp. 1–40.

English Historical Documents, vol. 2, 1042–1189, ed. D.C. Douglas and G.W. Greenway, 2nd edn, Oxford, 1981.

Epistolae Cantuarienses, in *Chronicles and Memorials of the Reign of Richard I*, vol. 2, ed. W. Stubbs, RS 38, London, 1865.

Eracles, *L'Estoire d'Eracles empereur et la conqueste de la Terre d'Outremer*, in RHCr, Occid., vols 1 and 2, Paris, 1859.

Ernoul, *Chronique d'Ernoul et de Bernard le Trésorier*, ed. L. de Mas Latrie, Société de l'Histoire de France, Paris, 1871.

Eugenius III, 'Der Text der Kreuzzugsbulle Eugens III', ed. P. Rassow, *Neues Archiv*, 45 (1924), 302–5.

Fulcher of Chartres, *A History of the Expedition to Jerusalem, 1095–1127*, tr. F. Ryan, ed. H. Fink, Knoxville, TN, 1969.

Fulcheri Carnotensis Historia Hierosolymitana, ed. H. Hagenmeyer, Heidelberg, 1913.

Gabrieli, F., *Arab Historians of the Crusades*, tr. E.J. Costello, Berkeley and Los Angeles, 1969.

Galbert of Bruges, *The Murder of Charles the Good*, tr. and ed. J.B. Ross, Toronto, 1967 (originally 1959).

Galbertus Notarius Brugensis, *De Multro, Traditione, et Occisione Gloriosi Karoli Comitis Flandriarum*, ed. J. Rider, Corpus Christianorum, Continuatio Mediaevalis, 131, Turnhout, 1994.

Gerald of Wales, *Itinerarium Kambriae*, ed. J.F. Dimock, in *Giraldi Cambrensis Opera*, ed. J.S. Brewer, J.F. Dimock and G.F. Warner, vol. 6, RS 21, London, 1868.

—, *De Principis Instructione Liber*, ed. G.F. Warner, in *Giraldi Cambrensis Opera*, ed. J.S. Brewer, J.F. Dimock and G.F. Warner, vol. 8, RS 21, London, 1891.

—, *The Journey through Wales and The Description of Wales*, tr. L. Thorpe, Harmondsworth, 1978.

Gesta Ambaziensium dominorum, in *Chroniques des Comtes d'Anjou*, ed. L. Halphen and R. Poupardin, Paris, 1913.

Gesta Francorum: Histoire Anonyme de la Première Croisade, ed. L. Bréhier, Paris, 1924.

Gesta Francorum et aliorum Hierosolimitanorum, ed. and tr. R. Hill, London, 1962.

Gregory VII, *The Correspondence of Gregory VII*, ed. and tr. E. Emerton, New York, 1959.

—, *The Register of Gregory VII, 1073–1085: An English Translation*, tr. H.E.J. Cowdrey, Oxford, 2002.

Gregory the Priest, *Continuation by Gregory the Priest*, in *Armenia and the Crusades; Tenth to the Twelfth Centuries: The Chronicle of Matthew of Edessa*, tr. A. Dostourian, Lanham, MD, 1993, pp. 241–79.

Guibert de Nogent, *Dei Gesta per Francos et cinq autres texts*, ed. R.B.C. Huygens, Corpus Christianorum, 127A, Turnhout, 1996.

Guibert of Nogent, *Gesta Dei per Francos*, tr. R. Levine, Woodbridge, 1997.

Hagenmeyer, H., ed., *Die Kreuzzugsbriefe aus den Jahren 1088–1100*, Innsbruck, 1901.

Henry, Archdeacon of Huntingdon, *Historia Anglorum: The History of the English People*, ed. and tr. D. Greenway, Oxford Medieval Texts, Oxford, 1996.

Historia Compostellana, ed. E. Falque Rey, Corpus Christianorum, Continuatio Mediaevalis, 70, Turnhout, 1988.

Historia Ducum Veneticorum, in MGH SS, vol. 14, Hanover, 1883, pp. 72–97.

History of William Marshal, ed. A.J. Holden, tr. S. Gregory, introd. D. Crouch, Anglo-Norman Text Society, 3 vols, London, 2002–6.

Hugh Eteriano, *Contra Patarenos*, ed., tr. and introd. J. Hamilton, S. Hamilton and B. Hamilton, Leiden, 2004.

Ibn al-Athir, *The Chronicle of Ibn al-Athīr for the Crusading Period from al-Kāmil fī' l-ta' rīkh*, parts 1 and 2, tr. D.S. Richards, Crusade Texts in Translation, 13, 15, Aldershot, 2006, 2007.

Ibn Butlan: see *Palestine under the Moslems*.

Ibn al-Qalanisi, *The Damascus Chronicle of the Crusades*, tr. H.A.R. Gibb, London, 1932.

'Imâd ad-Din al-Isfahânî, *Conquête de la Syrie et de Palestine par Saladin*, tr. H. Massé, Paris, 1972.

Itinerarium Peregrinorum et Gesta Regis Ricardi, in *Chronicles and Memorials of the Reign of Richard I*, vol. 1, ed. W. Stubbs, RS 38, London, 1864.

Das Itinerarium peregrinorum: Eine zeitgenössische englische Chronik zum dritten Kreuzzug in ursprünglicher Gestalt, ed. H.E. Mayer, Schriften der Monumenta Germaniae Historica, 18, Stuttgart, 1962.

—, *Chronicle of the Third Crusade: A Translation of the Itinerarium Peregrinorum et Gesta Regis Ricardi*, tr. H. Nicholson, Crusade Texts in Translation 3, Aldershot, 1997.

Jaspert, N., 'Zwei unbekannte Hilfsersuchen des Patriarchen Eraclius vor dem Fall Jerusalems (1187)', *Deutches Archiv für Erforschung des Mittelalters*, 60 (2004), 483–516.

Jerusalem Pilgrimage, 1099–1185, ed. J. Wilkinson, Hakluyt Society, series II, 167, London, 1988.

John of Ibelin, *Le Livre de Jean d'Ibelin*, in *Assises de Jérusalem*, vol. 1, *Assises de la Haute Cour*, ed. Comte Beugnot, RHCr, Lois, vol. 1, Paris, 1841, pp. 7–432.

John Kinnamos, *Deeds of John and Manuel Comnenus*, tr. C.M. Brand, Columbia Records of Civilization, 95, New York, 1976.

John Phocas, 'A General Description of the Settlements and Places Belonging to Syria and Phoenicia on the Way from Antioch to Jerusalem, and of the Holy Places of Palestine', in JP, pp. 315–36.

John of Salisbury, *Historia Pontificalis*, ed. and tr. M. Chibnall, Oxford, 1956.

John of Würzburg, 'Description of the Holy Land', in JP, pp. 244–73.

Kamal al-Din, *Extraits de la la Chronique d'Alep par Kemal ed-Din*, in RHCr, Orient., vol. 3, Paris, 1872, pp. 571–690.

—, *L'Histoire d'Alep*, tr. E. Blochet, ROL, 3 (1895), 509–654, 4 (1896), 145–225.

Kedar, B.Z., 'Ein Hilferuf aus Jerusalem vom September 1187', *Deutsches Archiv für Erforschung des Mittelalters*, 35 (1982), 112–22.

—, 'A Western Survey of Saladin's Forces at the Siege of Acre', in *Montjoie: Studies in Crusade History in Honour of Hans Eberhard Mayer*, ed. B. Z. Kedar, J. Riley-Smith and R. Hiestand, Aldershot, 1997, pp. 113–22.

—, 'The *Tractatus de locis et statu sancte terre ierosolimitane*', in *The Crusades and their Sources: Essays Presented to Bernard Hamilton*, ed. J. France and W. G. Zajac, Aldershot, 1998, pp. 111–33.

—, 'A Twelfth-Century Description of the Jerusalem Hospital', in *The Military Orders*, vol. 2, *Welfare and Warfare*, ed. H. Nicholson, Aldershot, 1998, pp. 3–26.

Krey, A.C., *The First Crusade: The Accounts of Eyewitnesses and Participants*, Princeton, NJ, 1921.

Libellus de expugnatione Terrae Sanctae per Saladinum, ed. J. Stevenson, RS 66, London, 1875, pp. 209–62.

'Le Livre des Assises' by John of Jaffa', in P.W. Edbury, *John of Ibelin and the Kingdom of Jerusalem*, Woodbridge, 1997, pp. 110–26, 191–200.

Le Livre du Roi, ed. M. Greilsammer, Documents relatifs à l'histoire des Croisades publiés par l'Académie des Inscriptions et Belles-Lettres, Paris, 1995.

Matthew of Edessa, *Armenia and the Crusades, Tenth to the Twelfth Centuries: The Chronicle of Matthew of Edessa*, tr. A. Dostourian, Lanham, MD, 1993.

Michael the Syrian, *Chronique de Michel le Syrien, Patriarche Jacobite d'Antioche (1166–1199)*, ed. and tr. J.-B. Chabot, vol. 3, Paris, 1905.

'Monk of Lido', *Monachi Anonymi Littorensis Historia de Translatio Sanctorum Magni Nicolai*, in RHCr, Occid., vol. 5, Paris, 1895, pp. 253–92.

Mukaddasi, *Description of Syria, including Palestine*, tr. G. Le Strange, Palestine Pilgrims' Text Society, 3, London, 1896.

Munro, D.C., 'Letters of the Crusaders Written from the Holy Land', in *Translations and Reprints from the Original Sources of European History*, ed. E.P. Cheyney, vol. 1 (4), Philadelphia, PA, 1902.

Nersēs Šnorhali, *Lament on Edessa*, tr. T.M. van Lint, in *East and West in the Crusader States: Context – Contacts – Confrontations*, II, *Acta of the Congress Held at Hernen Castle in May 1997*, ed. K. Ciggaar and H. Teule, Louvain, 1999, pp. 49–105.

Niketas Choniates, *O City of Byzantium: Annals of Niketas Choniates*, tr. H.J. Magoulias, Detroit, 1984.

Odo of Deuil, *De profectione Ludovici VII in Orientem*, ed. and tr. V.G. Berry, New York, 1948.

Oliver of Paderborn, *Historia Damiatina*, ed. O. Hoogeweg, *Die Schriften des Kölner Domscholasters*, in *Bibliothek des Litterarischen Vereins in Stuttgart*, 202, Tübingen, 1894.

Orderic Vitalis, *Ecclesiastical History*, vols 2, 5, 6, ed. and tr. M. Chibnall, Oxford, 1969–78.

Otto of Freising, *Chronica sive Historia de Duabus Civitatibus*, ed. A. Hofmeister, MGH SS, vol. 45, Hannover, 1912.

—, *The Two Cities: A Chronicle of Universal History to the Year 1146 A.D.*, tr. C.C. Mierow, New York, 1928.

Otto of Freising, *Gesta Friderici I. Imperatoris auctoribus Ottone et Ragewino praeposito Frisingensibus*, ed. R. Wilmans, MGHSS, vol. 20, Hanover, 1925.

Palestine under the Moslems: A Description of Syria and the Holy Land from A.D. 650 to 1500, tr. G. Le Strange, Khayats Oriental Reprints, 14, Beirut, 1965 (originally 1890).

Papsturkunden für Kirchen im Heiligen Lande, ed. R. Hiestand, Vorarbeiten zum Oriens Pontificus, vol. 3, Göttingen, 1985.

Papsturkunden für Templer und Johanniter, ed. R. Hiestand, Vorarbeiten zum Oriens Pontificus, vol. 2, Göttingen, 1984.

Peregrinationes Tres: Saewulf, John of Würzburg, Theodericus, ed. R.B.C. Huygens, Corpus Christianorum, Continuatio Mediaevalis, 139, Turnhout, 1996.

Philip of Novara, *Le Livre de Forme de Plait*, ed. and tr. P. Edbury, Nicosia, 2009.

Ralph of Caen, *Radulphi Cadomensis Tancredus*, ed. E. D'Angelo, Corpus Christianorum, Continuatio Mediaevalis, 231, Turnhout, 2011.

—, *Gesta Tancredi*, tr. B.S. Bachrach and D.S. Bachrach, Crusade Texts in Translation, 12, Aldershot, 2005.

Ralph of Diceto, *Ymagines Historiarum*, vol. 2, ed. W. Stubbs, RS 68, London, 1876.

Raymond d'Aguilers, *Historia Francorum Qui Ceperunt Iherusalem*, tr. J.H. and H.H. Hill, Philadelphia, PA, 1968.

Le 'Liber' de Raymond d'Aguilers, ed. J.H. and L.L. Hill, Documents relatifs à l'histoire des croisades publiés par l'Académie des Inscriptions et Belles-Lettres, Paris, 1969.

Recueil des actes de Henri II, roi d'Angleterre et duc de Normandie, vol. 2, ed. L. Delisle and E. Berger, Chartes et diplômes relatifs à l'histoire de France, Paris, 1920.

Recueil d'annales angevines et vendômoises, ed. L. Halphen, Paris, 1903.

Recueil des actes de Philippe Auguste, roi de France, vol. 1, ed. E. Berger and C. Brunel, Paris, 1916.

Regula Pauperum Commilitonum Christi Templique Salomonici, ed. S. Cerrini, Corpus Christianorum, Continuatio Mediaevalis (forthcoming).

Richard of Devizes, *Chronicle*, ed. and tr. J. Appleby, London, 1963.

Richard of Poitiers, *Chronica*, in MGH SS, vol. 26, Hanover, 1882.

Rigord, *Histoire de Philippe Auguste*, ed. and tr. E. Carpentier, G. Pon and Y. Chauvin, Sources d'histoire médiévale publiées par l'Institut de Recherche et d'Histoire des Textes, 33, Paris, 2006.

Riley-Smith, L. and J., trs, *The Crusades: Idea and Reality, 1095–1274*, Documents of Medieval History, 4, London, 1981.

Robert the Monk, *Historia Iherosolimitana*, in RHCr, Occid., vol. 3, Paris, 1866, pp. 717–882.

—, *History of the First Crusade*, tr. C. Sweetenham, Crusade Texts in Translation, 11, Aldershot, 2005.

Robert of Torigni, 'Chronicle', in *Chronicles of the Reigns of Stephen, Henry II and Richard I*, vol. 4, ed. R. Howlett, RS 82, London, 1889.

Roger of Howden, *Chronica*, vols 1–3, ed. W. Stubbs, RS 51, London, 1869.

Roger of Howden, *Gesta Henrici Secundi*, vol. 1, ed. W. Stubbs, RS 49, London, 1867 (published as Benedict of Peterborough).

Suger, *Abbot Suger on the Abbey Church of St.-Denis and its Art Treasures*, ed. and tr. E. Panofsky, 2nd edn, G. Panofsky-Soergel, Princeton, NJ, 1979.

Tabulae Ordinis Theutonici, ed. E. Strelhke, Berlin, 1869.

Theodoric, 'Book of the Holy Places', in JP, pp. 274–314.

Die Urkunden der Lateinischen Könige von Jerusalem, 4 vols, ed. H.E. Mayer, Altfranzösische Texte erstellt von Jean Richard, Monumenta Germaniae Historica, Hanover, 2010.

Usamah Ibn-Munqidh, *An Arab-Syrian Gentleman and Warrior in the Period of the Crusades: Memoirs of Usāmah Ibn-Munqidh*, tr. P.K. Hitti, Princeton, NJ, 1929.

Walter the Chancellor, *Galterii Cancellarii Bella Antiochena*, ed. H. Hagenmeyer, Innsbruck, 1896.

—, *The Antiochene Wars*, tr. T.S. Asbridge and S.B. Edgington, Crusade Texts in Translation, 4, Aldershot, 1999.

Walter Map, *De nugis curialium*, ed. and tr. M.R. James, rev. edn C.N.L. Brooke and R.A.B. Mynors, Oxford, 1983.

Wilbrand of Oldenburg, *Wilbrandi de Oldenborg Peregrinatio*, in *Peregrinatores Medii Aevi Quatuor*, ed. J.C.M. Laurent, 2nd edn, Leipzig, 1873, pp. 159–99.

William of Malmesbury, *Gesta Regum Anglorum: The History of the English Kings*, vol. 1, ed. and tr. R.A.B. Mynors, completed by R.M. Thomson and M. Winterbottom, Oxford, 1998.

William of Newburgh, *Historia Rerum Anglicarum*, in *Chronicles and Memorials of the Reigns of Stephen, Henry II and Richard I*, vol. 1, ed. R. Howlett, RS 82, London, 1884.

William of Tyre: Guillaume de Tyr, *Chronique*, ed. R.B.C. Huygens, 2 vols, Corpus Christianorum, Continuatio Mediaevalis, 63 and 63A, Turnhout, 1986.

—, *A History of Deeds Done beyond the Sea*, tr. E.A. Babcock and A.C. Krey, 2 vols, Records of Civilization, Sources and Studies, 35, New York, 1943.

Work on Geography, in JP, pp. 181–212.

Secondary Works

Adair, P.A., 'Flemish Comital Family and the Crusades', in *The Crusades: Other Experiences, Alternate Perspectives*, ed. K.I. Semaan, Binghampton, New York, 2003, pp. 101–12.

Aerts, W.J., 'A Byzantine Traveller to One of the Crusader States', in *East and West in the Crusader States: Context – Contacts – Confrontations, III. Acta of the Congress Held at Hernen Castle in September 2000*, ed. K. Ciggaar and H. Teule, Louvain, 2003, pp. 165–221.

Aird, W.M., *Robert Curthose, Duke of Normandy (c.1050–1134)*, Woodbridge, 2008.

Albon, G.A.M. d', 'La mort d'Odon de Saint-Amand, grand maître du Temple', *ROL*, 12 (1909–11), 279–82.

Amouroux-Mourad, M., *Le Comté d'Édesse, 1098–1150*, Bibliothèque Archéologique et Historique de l'Institut Français d'Archéologie du Proche-Orient, 128, Paris, 1988.

Angold, M., *The Byzantine Empire 1025–1204: A Political History*, London, 1984.

Appleby, J., *England without Richard, 1189–1199*, Ithaca, NY, 1965.

Asbridge, T., 'The Principality of Antioch and the Jabal as-Summāq', in *The First Crusade: Origins and Impact*, ed. J. Phillips, Manchester, 1997, pp. 142–52.

—, 'The significance and causes of the battle of the Field of Blood', *Journal of Medieval History*, 23 (1997), 301–16.

—, *The Creation of the Principality of Antioch, 1098–1130*, Woodbridge, 2000.

—, 'Alice of Antioch: A case study of female power in the twelfth century', in *The Experience of Crusading*, vol. 2, *Defining the Crusader Kingdom*, ed. P. Edbury and J. Phillips, Cambridge, 2003, pp. 29–47.

—, *The First Crusade: A New History*, London, 2004.

Atiya, A.S., *A History of Eastern Christianity*, London, 1968.

Backhouse, J., 'The Case of Queen Melisende's Psalter: An Historical Investigation', in *Tributes to Jonathan J.G. Alexander: The Making and Meaning of Illuminated Medieval and Renaissance Manuscripts, Art and Architecture*, ed. S. L'Engle and G. Guest, London, 2006, pp. 457–70.

Balard, M., 'Communes italiennes, pouvoir et habitants des états francs de Syrie-Palestine au XIIe siècle', in *Crusaders and Muslims in Twelfth-Century Syria*, ed. M. Shatzmiller, Leiden, 1993, pp. 43–64.

Baldwin, J.W., *The Government of Philip Augustus: Foundations of French Royal Power in the Middle Ages*, Berkeley, 1986.

Baldwin, M.W., *Raymond III of Tripolis and the Fall of Jerusalem (1140–1187)*, New York, 1936.

Barasch, M., *Crusader Figural Sculpture in the Holy Land*, New Brunswick, NJ, 1971.

Barber, M., *The New Knighthood: A History of the Order of the Temple*, Cambridge, 1994.

—, 'The Order of St Lazarus and the Crusades', *Catholic Historical Review*, 80 (1994), 439–56.

—, 'Frontier Warfare in the Latin Kingdom of Jerusalem: The Campaign of Jacob's Ford, 1178–9', in *The Crusades and their Sources: Essays Presented to Bernard Hamilton*, ed. J. France and W.G. Zajac, Aldershot, 1998, pp. 9–22.

—, 'The Albigensian Crusades: Wars Like Any Other?', in *Dei gesta per Francos: Etudes sur les croisades dédiées à Jean Richard*, ed. M. Balard, B.Z. Kedar and J. Riley-Smith, Aldershot, 2001, pp. 44–55.

—, 'The career of Philip of Nablus in the kingdom of Jerusalem', in *The Experience of Crusading*, vol. 2, *Defining the Crusader Kingdom*, ed. P. Edbury and J. Phillips, Cambridge, 2003, pp. 60–75.

—, 'The Reputation of Gerard of Ridefort', in *The Military Orders*, vol. 4, *On Land and by Sea*, ed. J. Upton-Ward, Aldershot, 2008, pp. 111–19.

Barratt, N., 'The English Revenue of Richard I', *English Historical Review*, 116 (2001), 635–56.

Beaumont, A.A., 'Albert of Aachen and the County of Edessa', in *The Crusades and Other Historical Essays Presented to Dana C. Munro*, ed. L.J. Paetow, New York, 1928, pp. 105–7.

Beech, G., 'A Norman-Italian Adventurer in the East: Richard of Salerno, 1097–1112', in *Anglo-Norman Studies*, 15, *Proceedings of the XV Battle Conference and of the XI Colloquio Medievale of the Officina di Studi Medievali*, ed. M. Chibnall, Woodbridge, 1992, pp. 25–40.

—, 'The Crusader Lordship of Marash in Armenian Cilicia, 1104–1149', *Viator*, 27 (1996), 35–52.

—, 'A Little-Known Armenian Historian of the Crusading Period: Gregory the Priest (1136–62)', in *Truth as Gift: Studies in Medieval Cistercian History in Honor of John R. Sommerfeldt*, ed. M.L. Dutton, D.M. La Corte and P. Lockey, Cistercian Studies Series, 204, Kalmazoo, 2004, pp. 119–43.

Bertrand de Broussillon, A., *La Maison de Craon, 1050–1480: Étude historique accompagné du Cartulaire de Craon*, vol. 1, Paris, 1893.

Blake, E.O., and C. Morris, 'A Hermit Goes to War: Peter and the Origins of the First Crusade', in *Studies in Church History*, 22 (1985), pp. 79–108.

Boas, A.J., *Crusader Archaeology: The Material Culture of the Latin East*, London, 1999.

—, *Jerusalem in the Time of the Crusades: Society, Landscape and Art in the Holy City under Frankish Rule*, London, 2001.

—, *Archaeology of the Military Orders: A Survey of the Urban Centres, Rural Settlement and Castles of the Military Orders in the Latin East (c.1120–1291)*, London, 2006.

—, and A.M. Maeir, 'The Frankish Castle of Blanche Garde and the Medieval and Modern Village of Tell es-Safi in the Light of Recent Discoveries', *Crusades*, 8 (2009), 1–22.

Borg, A., 'Observations on the Historiated Lintel of the Holy Sepulchre, Jerusalem', *Journal of the Warburg and Courtauld Institutes*, 32 (1969), 25–40.

Boussard, J., *Le Comté d'Anjou sous Henri Plantagenêt et ses fils, 1151–1204*, Paris, 1938.

Bradbury, J., *Philip Augustus. King of France 1180–1223*, Harlow, 1998.

Brundage, J.A., 'Adhemar of Le Puy: The Bishop and his Critics', *Speculum*, 34 (1959), 201–12.

—, 'An Errant Crusader: Stephen of Blois', *Traditio*, 16 (1960), 380–95.

—, 'Richard the Lion-Heart and Byzantium', in *Studies in Medieval Culture*, 6–7, Kalamazoo, 1976, pp. 63–70.

Buchthal, H., *Miniature Painting in the Latin Kingdom of Jerusalem*, Oxford, 1957.

Bull, M., 'The Roots of Lay Enthusiasm for the First Crusade', *History*, 78 (1993), 353–72.

—, *Knightly Piety and the Lay Response to the First Crusade: The Limousin and Gascony, c.970–c.1130*, Oxford, 1993.

—, 'The Capetian Monarchy and the Early Crusade Movement: Hugh of Vermandois and Louis VII', *Nottingham Medieval Studies*, 40 (1996), 25–46.

Bulst-Thiele, M.-L., *Sacrae Domus Templi Hierosolymitani Magistri*, Göttingen, 1974.

Burgtorf, J., 'The Military Orders in the Crusader Principality of Antioch', in *East and West in the Medieval Eastern Mediterranean*, vol. 1, *Antioch from the Byzantine Reconquest until the End of the Crusader Principality*, ed. K. Ciggaar and D.M. Metcalf, Orientalia Lovaniensia Analecta, 147, Louvain, 2006, pp. 217–46.

—, 'Die Herrschaft der Johanniter in Margat im Heiligen Land', in *Die Ritterorden als Träger der Herrschaft: Territorien, Grundbesitz und Kirche*, ed. R. Czaja and J. Sarnowsky, Ordines militares, Colloquia Torunensia Historica 14, Toruń, 2007, pp. 27–57.

Byrne, E.H., 'The Genoese Colonies in Syria', in *The Crusades and Other Historical Essays Presented to Dana C. Munro*, ed. L.J. Paetow, New York, 1928, pp. 139–82.

Cahen, C., *La Syrie du Nord à l'époque des croisades*, Paris, 1940.

Cardini, F., 'Profilo di un crociato Guglielmo Embriaco', *Archivio Storico Italiano*, 136 (1978), 405–36.

Cate, J.L., 'The Crusade of 1101', in *A History of the Crusades*, vol. 1, *The First Hundred Years*, ed. M.W. Baldwin, pp. 343–67.

Cazel, F.A., 'The Tax of 1185 in Aid of the Holy Land', *Speculum*, 30 (1955), 385–92.

Chevedden, P.E., '"A Crusade from the First": The Norman Conquest of Islamic Sicily, 1060–1091', *Al-Masāq*, 22 (2010), 191–225.

Ciggaar, K., 'Manuscripts as Intermediaries: The Crusader States and Literary Cross-Fertilization', in *East and West in the Crusader States: Context – Contacts – Confrontations. Acta of the Congress Held at Hernen Castle in May 1993*, ed. K. Ciggaar, A. Davids and H. Teule, Louvain, 1996, pp. 131–51.

—, 'The Abbey of Prémontré – Royal Contacts, Royal News: The Context of the So-Called *Continuatio Praemonstratensis*', in *East and West in the Crusader States: Context – Contacts – Confrontations*, III. *Acta of the Congress Held at Hernen Castle in September 2000*, ed. K. Ciggaar and H. Teule, Louvain, 2003, pp. 21–33.

Claverie, P.V., 'Les débuts de l'Ordre du Temple en Orient', *Le Moyen Age*, 111 (2005), 545–94.

Clédat, J.,'Le raid du roi Baudouin Ier en Egypt', *Bulletin de l'Insitut Français d'Archéologie Orientale*, 26 (1925), 71–81.

Cochrane, L., *Adelard of Bath: The First English Scientist*, London, 1994.

Constable, G., 'The Second Crusade as Seen by Contemporaries', *Traditio*, 9 (1953), 213–79.

—, *Monastic Tithes from their Origins to the Twelfth Century*, Cambridge, 1964.

—, 'The Financing of the Crusades in the Twelfth Century', in *Outremer: Studies in the Crusading Kingdom of Jerusalem Presented to Joshua Prawer*, ed. B.Z. Kedar, H.E. Mayer and R.C. Smail, Jerusalem, 1982, pp. 64–88.

Crawford, R.W., 'William of Tyre and the Maronites', *Speculum*, 30 (1955), 222–8.

Crouch, D., *William Marshal: Court, Career and Chivalry in the Angevin Empire*, London, 1990.

David, C.W., *Robert Curthose, Duke of Normandy*, Cambridge, MA, 1920.

Deschamps, P., *Les Châteaux des Croisés en Terre Sainte*, vol. 2, *La Défense du Royaume de Jérusalem*, Paris, 1939.

Douglas, D.C., *William the Conqueror: The Norman Impact on England*, London, 1964.

Downey, G., *A History of Antioch in Syria from Seleucus to the Arab Conquest*, Princeton, NJ, 1961.

Drory, J., 'Hanbalis of the Nablus Region in the Eleventh and Twelfth Centuries', in *The Medieval Levant: Studies in Memory of Eliyahu Ashtor (1914–1984)*, ed. B.Z. Kedar and A.L. Udovitch, Haifa, 1988, pp. 93–112.

Duby, G., *La société aux XIe et XIIe siècles dans la région maconnaise*, Paris, 1971.

Dunbabin, J., 'William of Tyre and Philip of Alsace, Count of Flanders', *Mededelingen var de Koninklijke Academie voor Wetenschappen, Letteren en Schone Kunsten van België: Klasse der Letteren*, 48 (1986), 110–17.

Dussaud, R., *Topographie historique de la Syrie antique et médiévale*, Haut-Commissariat de la République Française en Syrie et Liban, Service des Antiquités et des Beaux-Arts, Bibliothèque Archéologique et Historique, 4, Paris, 1927.

Edbury, P.W., 'The Baronial Coinage of the Latin Kingdom of Jerusalem', in *Coinage in the Latin East*, ed. P.W. Edbury and D.M. Metcalf, Oxford, 1980, pp. 59–72.

—, 'Propaganda and Faction in the Kingdom of Jerusalem: The Background to Hattin', in *Crusaders and Muslims in Twelfth-Century Syria*, ed. M. Shatzmiller, Leiden, 1993, pp. 173–89.

—, 'The Templars in Cyprus', in *The Military Orders: Fighting for the Faith and Caring for the Sick*, ed. M. Barber, Aldershot, 1994, pp. 189–95.

—, 'Law and Custom in the Latin East: *Les Letres dou Sepulcre*', in *Intercultural Contacts in the Medieval Mediterranean*, ed. B. Arbel, London, 1996, pp. 71–9.

—, 'The Lyon *Eracles* and the Old French Continuations of William of Tyre', in *Montjoie: Studies in Crusade History in Honour of Hans Eberhard Mayer*, ed. B.Z. Kedar, J. Riley-Smith and R. Hiestand, Aldershot, 1997, pp. 139–53.

—, *John of Ibelin and the Kingdom of Jerusalem*, Woodbridge, 1997.

—, 'Gerard of Ridefort and the Battle of Le Cresson (1 May 1187): The Developing Narrative Tradition', in *On the Margins of Crusading: The Military Orders, the Papacy and the Christian World*, ed. H. Nicholson, Crusades Subsidia 4, Farnham, 2011, pp. 45–60.

—, and J.G. Rowe, 'William of Tyre and the Patriarchal Election of 1180', *English Historical Review*, 93 (1978), 1–25.

—, and J.G. Rowe, *William of Tyre: Historian of the Latin East*, Cambridge, 1988.

Edwards, R.W., 'Bağras and Armenian Cilicia: A Reassessment', *Revue des études arméniennes*, 17 (1983), 415–35.

—, *The Fortifications of Armenian Cilicia*, Washington, DC, 1987.

Elisséeff, N., *Nūr ad-Dīn: Un grand prince musulman de Syrie au temps des croisades (511–569 H./1118–1174)*, 3 vols, Damascus, 1967.

—, 'The Reaction of the Syrian Muslims after the Foundation of the First Latin Kingdom of Jerusalem', in *Crusaders and Muslims in Twelfth-Century Syria*, ed. M. Shatzmiller, Leiden, 1993, pp. 162–72.

Ellenblum, R., *Frankish Rural Settlement in the Latin Kingdom of Jerusalem*, Cambridge, 1998.

—, 'Frankish and Muslim Siege Warfare and the Construction of Frankish Concentric Castles', in *Dei gesta per Francos: Etudes sur les Croisades dédiées à Jean Richard*, ed. M. Balard, B.Z. Kedar and J. Riley-Smith, Aldershot, 2001, pp. 187–98.

—, 'Frontier Activities: The Transformation of a Muslim Sacred Site into the Frankish Castle of Vadum Jacob', *Crusades*, 2 (2003), 83–97.

—, *Crusader Castles and Modern Histories*, Cambridge, 2007.

—, 'Frankish Castles, Muslim Castles and the Medieval Citadel of Jerusalem', in *In Laudem Hierosolymitani: Studies in Crusades and Medieval Culture in Honour of Benjamin Z. Kedar*, ed. I. Shagrir, R. Ellenblum and J. Riley-Smith, Aldershot, 2007, pp. 93–109.

Elm, K., 'Kanoniker und Ritter vom Heiligen Grab. Ein Beitrag zur Entstehung und Frühgeschichte der palästinensischen Ritterorden', in *Die geistlichen Ritterorden Europas*, ed. J. Fleckenstein and M. Hellmann, Sigmaringen, 1980, pp. 141–69.

—, 'La liturgie de l'Église latine de Jérusalem au temps des croisades', in *Les Croisades: L'Orient et l'Occident d'Urbain II à Saint Louis, 1096–1270*, ed. M. Rey-Delqué, Milan, 1997, pp. 243–5.

—, '*Neç minori celebritate a catholicis cultoribus observatur et colitur*. Zwei Berichte über die 1119/20 erfolgte Auffindung und Erhebung der Gebeine der Patriarchen Abraham, Isaak und Jakob', *Zeitschrift für Religions- und Geistesgeschichte*, 49 (1997), 318–44.

Epp, V., *Fulcher von Chartres: Studien zur Geschichtsschreibung des ersten Kreuzzuges*, Düsseldorf, 1990.

Epstein, S., *Genoa and the Genoese, 958–1528*, Chapel Hill, NC, 1996.

Erdmann, C., *The Origin of the Idea of the Crusade*, tr. M.W. Baldwin and W. Goffart, Princeton, NJ, 1977 (originally 1935).

Face, R., 'Secular History in Twelfth-Century Italy: Caffaro of Genoa', *Journal of Medieval History*, 6 (1980), 169–84.

Favreau-Lilie, M.-L., 'Landesausbau und Burg während der Kreuzfahrerzeit: *Safad* in Obergalilaea', *Zeitschrift des Deutschen Palastina-Vereins*, 96 (1980), 67–87.

Fedalto, G., *La Chiesa Latina in Oriente*, 2 vols, Verona, 1973, 1976.

Fink, H.S., 'The Foundation of the Latin States, 1099–1118', in *A History of the Crusades*, vol. 1, *The First Hundred Years*, ed. M.W. Baldwin, Madison, 1969, pp. 368–409.

Fletcher, R.A., *Saint James's Catapult: The Life and Times of Diego Gelmírez of Santiago de Compostela* (Oxford, 1984).

Folda, J., *The Nazareth Capitals and the Crusader Shrine of the Annunciation*, Philadelphia, PA, 1986.

—, *The Art of the Crusaders in the Holy Land, 1098–1187*, Cambridge, 1995.

Forey, A.J., 'The Militarisation of the Hospital of St John', *Studia Monastica*, 26 (1984), 75–89.

France, J., *Victory in the East: A military history of the First Crusade*, Cambridge, 1994.

—, 'Byzantium in Western Chronicles before the First Crusade', in *Knighthoods of Christ: Essays on the History of the Crusades and the Knights Templar Presented to Malcolm Barber*, ed. N. Housley, Aldershot, 2007, pp. 3–16.

Friedman, Y., *Encounter between Enemies: Captivity and Ransom in the Latin Kingdom of Jerusalem*, Leiden, 2002.

Gerish, D., 'Ancestors and Predecessors: Royal Continuity and Identity in the First Kingdom of Jerusalem', in *Anglo-Norman Studies*, 20, *Proceedings of the Battle Conference in Dublin, 1997*, Woodbridge, 1998, pp. 127–50.

Gibb, H.A.R., 'The Rise of Saladin, 1169–1189', in *A History of the Crusades*, vol. 1, *The First Hundred Years*, ed. M.W. Baldwin, Madison, 1969, pp. 563–89.

—, *The Life of Saladin from the Works of 'Imad al-Din and Baha' al-Din*, Oxford, 1973.

Gillingham, J., 'Roger of Howden on Crusade', in *Richard Coeur de Lion: Kingship, Chivalry and War in the Twelfth Century*, London and Rio Grande, 1994, pp. 141–53.

—, *Richard I*, New Haven and London, 1999.

—, *The Angevin Empire*, 2nd edn, London, 2001.

Grabois, A., 'La cité de Baniyas et le Château de Subeibeh pendant les Croisades', *Cahiers de civilisation médiévale*, 13 (1970), 43–62.

—, 'Le Pèlerin Occidental en Terre Sainte à l'Époque des Croisades et ses Réalités: La relation de Pèlerinage de Jean de Wurtzbourg', in *Études de civilisation médiévale (IXe–XIIe siècles): Mélanges offerts à Edmond-René Labande*, Poitiers, 1974, pp. 367–76.

—, 'The First Crusade and the Jews', in *The Crusades: Other Experiences, Alternate Perspectives*, ed. K.I. Semaan, Binghampton, NY, 2003, pp. 13–26.

Hagenmeyer, H., *Chronologie de la Première Croisade, 1094–1100*, Paris, 1898–1901.

—, 'Chronologie de l'histoire du royaume de Jérusalem: Règne de Baudouin I (1101–1118)', *ROL*, 9 (1902), 384–465; *ROL*, 10 (1903–4), 372–405; *ROL*, 11 (1905–8), 145–80, 453–85; *ROL*, 12 (1909–11), 68–103, 283–326.

Hallam, E., 'Royal Burial and the Cult of Kingship in France and England, 1060–1330', *Journal of Medieval History*, 8 (1982), 359–80.

—, *Chronicles of the Crusades*, New York, 1989.

Hamilton, B., 'The Cistercians in the Crusader States', in *One Yet Two: Monastic Tradition East and West*, ed. M.B. Pennington, Kalamazoo, 1976, pp. 405–22.

—, 'Rebuilding Zion: The Holy Places of Jerusalem in the Twelfth Century', in *Studies in Church History*, 14 (1977), pp. 105–16.

—, 'The Elephant of Christ: Reynald of Châtillon', in *Studies in Church History*, 15 (1978), pp. 97–108.

—, 'Women in the Crusader States: The Queens of Jerusalem (1100–1190)', in *Medieval Women: Dedicated and Presented to Professor Rosalind M.T. Hill on the Occasion of her Seventieth Birthday*, ed. D. Baker, *Studies in Church History*, Subsidia, 1, Oxford, 1978, pp. 143–74.

—, *The Latin Church in the Crusader States: The Secular Church*, London, 1980.

—, 'Ralph of Domfront, Patriarch of Antioch (1135–40)', *Nottingham Medieval Studies*, 28 (1984), 1–21.

—, 'The Titular Nobility of the Latin East: the Case of Agnes of Courtenay', in *Crusade and Settlement*, ed. P.W. Edbury, Cardiff, 1985, pp. 197–203.

—, 'Manuel I Comnenus and Baldwin IV of Jerusalem', in *Kathegetria: Essays Presented to Joan Hussey for her 80th Birthday*, ed. J. Chrysostomides, Camberley, 1988, pp. 353–75.

—, 'Miles of Plancy and the Fief of Beirut', in *The Horns of Hattin*, ed. B.Z. Kedar, London, 1992, pp. 136–46.

—, 'The Impact of Crusader Jerusalem on Western Christendom', *Catholic Historical Review*, 80 (1994), 695–713.

—, 'Aimery of Limoges, Patriarch of Antioch: Ecumenist, Scholar and Patron of Hermits', in *The Joy of Learning and the Love of God: Studies in Honor of Jean Leclercq*, ed. E.R. Elder, Cistercian Studies, 160, Kalamazoo, 1995, pp. 269–90.

—, 'Ideals of Holiness: Crusaders, Contemplatives and Mendicants', *International History Review*, 17 (1995), 693–712.

—, *The Leper King and his Heirs: Baldwin IV and the Crusader Kingdom of Jerusalem*, Cambridge, 2000.

—, 'Three Patriarchs of Antioch, 1165–70', in *Dei gesta per Francos: Etudes sur les croisades dédiées à Jean Richard*, ed. M. Balard, B.Z. Kedar and J. Riley-Smith, Aldershot, 2001, pp. 199–207.

—, 'The Old French Translation of William of Tyre as an Historical Source', in *The Experience of Crusading*, vol. 2, ed. P.W. Edbury and J. Phillips, Cambridge, 2003, pp. 93–112.

—, 'William of Tyre and the Byzantine Empire', in *Porphyrogenita: Essays on the History and Literature of Byzantium and the Latin East in Honour of Julian Chrysostomides*, ed. C. Dendrinos, J. Harris, E. Harvalia-Crook and J. Herrin, Aldershot, 2003, pp. 219–33.

Harper, R.P., and D. Pringle, *Belmont Castle: The Excavation of a Crusader Stronghold in the Kingdom of Jerusalem*, British Academy Monographs in Archaeology, 10, Oxford, 2000.

Harris, J., *Byzantium and the Crusades*, London, 2003.

Harvey, P., 'The English Inflation of 1180–1220', *Past and Present*, 61 (1973), 3–30.

Hay, D., 'Gender Bias and Religious Intolerance in Accounts of the "Massacres" of the First Crusade', in *Tolerance and Intolerance: Social Conflict in the Age of the Crusades*, ed. M. Gervers and J.M. Powell, Syracuse, NY, 2001, pp. 3–10, 135–9.

Hiestand, R., 'Chronologisches zur Geschichte des Königreiches Jerusalem um 1130', *Deutsches Archiv*, 26 (1970), 220–9.

—, 'Zwei unbekannte Diplome der lateinischen Könige von Jerusalem aus Lucca', *Quellen und Forschungen aus italienischen Archiven und Bibliotheken*, 50 (1970), 1–57.

—, 'Zum Leben und zur Laufbahn Wilhelms von Tyrus', *Deutsches Archiv*, 34 (1978), 345–80.

—, 'Chronologisches zur Geschichte des Königreiches Jerusalem im 12. Jahrhundert', *Deutsches Archiv*, 35 (1979), 542–55.

—, '"Kaiser" Konrad III., der zweite Kreuzzug und ein verlorenes Diplom für den Berg Thabor', *Deutsches Archiv*, 35 (1979), 82–126.

—, 'Die Anfänge der Johanniter', in *Die geistlichen Ritterorden Europas*, ed. J. Fleckenstein and M. Hellmann, Vorträge und Forschungen 26, Sigmaringen, 1980, pp. 31–80.

—, 'Saint-Ruf d'Avignon, Raymond de Saint-Gilles et l'église latine du comté de Tripoli', *Annales du Midi*, 98 (1986), 327–36.

—, 'Ein neuer Bericht über das Konzil von Antiochia 1140', *Annuarium Historiae Conciliorum*, 20 (1988), 314–50.

—, '"Precipua tocius christianismi columpna": Barbarossa und der Kreuzzug', in *Friedrich Barbarossa Handlungsspielräume und Wirkungsweisen des Staufischen Kaisers*, ed. A. Haverkamp, Vorträge und Forschungen, 40, Sigmaringen, 1992, pp. 51–108.

—, 'Un centre intellectual en Syrie du Nord? Notes sur la personnalité d'Aimery d'Antioche, Albert de Tarse et Rorgo Fretellus', *Le Moyen Age*, 5th series, 8 (1994), 7–35.

—, 'Die Herren von Sidon und die Thronfolgekrise des Jahres 1163 im Königreich Jerusalem', in *Montjoie: Studies in Crusade History in Honour of Hans Eberhard Mayer*, ed. B.Z. Kedar, J. Riley-Smith and R. Hiestand, Aldershot, 1997, pp. 77–90.

—, 'L'archevêque Hugues d'Edesse et son destin posthume', in *Dei gesta per Francos: Etudes sur les croisades dédiées à Jean Richard*, ed. M. Balard, B.Z. Kedar and J. Riley-Smith, Aldershot, 2001, pp. 171–7.

—, 'Some Reflections on the Impact of the Papacy on the Crusader States and the Military Orders in the Twelfth and Thirteenth Centuries', in *The Crusades and the Military Orders: Expanding the Frontiers of Medieval Latin Christianity*, ed. Z. Hunyadi and J. Laszlovszky, Budapest, 2001, pp. 3–20.

—, 'Gaudfridus abbas Templi Domini: an underestimated figure in the early history of the kingdom of Jerusalem', in *The Experience of Crusading*, vol. 2, *Defining the Crusader Kingdom*, ed. P.W. Edbury and J. Phillips, Cambridge, 2003, pp. 48–59.

Hill, J.H. and L.L. Hill, *Raymond IV, Count of Toulouse*, New York, 1962.

Hillenbrand, C., 'The Career of Najm al-Din Il-Ghazi', *Der Islam*, 58 (1981), 250–92.

—, *The Crusades: Islamic Perspectives*, Edinburgh, 1999.

—, '"Abominable acts": the career of Zengi', in *The Second Crusade: Scope and Consequences*, ed. J. Phillips and M. Hoch, Manchester, 2001, pp. 111–32.

—, 'The Imprisonment of Reynald of Châtillon', in *Texts, Documents and Artifacts: Islamic Studies in Honour of D.S. Richards*, ed. C.F. Robinson, Leiden, 2003, pp. 79–101.

Hoch, M., 'The Choice of Damascus as the Objective of the Second Crusade: A Re-evaluation', in *Autour de la Première Croisade: Actes du Colloque de la Society for the Study of the Crusades and the Latin East (Clermont-Ferrand, 22–25 juin 1995)*, ed. M. Balard, Paris, 1996, pp. 359–69.

—, 'The price of failure: the Second Crusade as a turning-point in the history of the Latin East?', in *The Second Crusade: Scope and Consequences*, ed. J. Phillips and M. Hoch, Manchester, 2001, pp. 180–200.

Holt, P.M., *The Age of the Crusades: The Near East from the Eleventh Century to 1517*, London, 1986.

Hunt, L.-A., 'Art and Colonialism: The Mosaics of the Church of the Nativity in Bethlehem (1169) and the Problem of "Crusader" Art', *Dumbarton Oaks Papers*, 45 (1991), 69–85.

Huygens, R.B.C., 'Guillaume de Tyr étudiant: Un chapitre (XIX.12) de son "Histoire" Retrouvé', *Latomus*, 21 (1962), 811–28.

Jackson, D.E.P., 'Some Considerations Relating to the History of the Muslims in the Crusader States', in *East and West in the Crusader States: Context – Contacts – Confrontations. Acta of the Congress Held at Hernen Castle in May 1993*, ed. K. Ciggaar, A. Davids and H. Teule, Louvain, 1996, pp. 21–9.

Jacoby, D., 'Conrad, Marquis of Montferrat, and the Kingdom of Jerusalem (1187–1192)', in *Atti del Congresso internazionale 'Dai feudi monferrine e dal Piemonte ai nuovi mondi oltre gli Oceani'*, Alessandria 2–6 aprile, Alexandria, 1993, pp. 187–238.

—, 'The Venetian Privileges in the Latin Kingdom of Jerusalem: Twelfth-and Thirteenth-Century Interpretations and Implementation', in *Montjoie: Studies in Crusade History in Honour of Hans Eberhard Mayer*, ed. B.Z. Kedar, J. Riley-Smith and R. Hiestand, Aldershot, 1997, pp. 155–75.

—, 'The Economic Function of the Crusader States of the Levant: A New Approach', in *Europe's Economic Relations with the Islamic World, 13th–18th Centuries*, ed. S. Cavaciocchi, Florence, 2007, pp. 159–91.

Jacoby, Z., 'The Workshop of the Temple Area in Jerusalem in the Twelfth Century: Its Origin, Evolution and Impact', *Zeitschrift für Kunstgeschichte*, 45 (1982), 325–94.

Jamison, E., *The Norman Administration of Apulia and Capua*, ed. D. Clementi and T. Közler, Darmstadt, 1987 (originally 1913).

Jaspert, N., '"Pro nobis, qui pro vobis oramus, orate": Die Kathedralkapitel von Compostela und Jerusalem in der ersten Hälfte des 12. Jahrhunderts', in *Santiago, Roma, Jerusalén: Actas del III Congreso Internacional de Estudios Jacobeos*, ed. P.C. von Saucken, Santiago de Compostela, 1999, pp. 187–212.

—, 'Ein Polymythos: Die Kreuzzüge', in *Mythen in der Geschichte*, ed. H. Altrichter, K. Herbers and H. Neuhaus, Freiburg im Breisgau, 2004, pp. 203–35.

—, 'The Election of Arnau de Torroja as Ninth Master of the Knights Templar (1180): An Enigmatic Decision Reconsidered', in *Actas do V Encontro sobre Ordens Militares*, ed. I. C. F. Fernandes. Colecção Ordens Militares, 2, Palmela, 2009, pp. 371–97.

—, 'Das Heilige Grab, das Wahre Kreuz, Jerusalem und das Heilige Land. Wirkung, Wandel und Vermittler hochmittelalterlicher Attraktoren', in *Konflikt und Bewältigung. Die Zerstörung der Grabeskirche zu Jerusalem im Jahre 1009*, ed. T. Pratsch, Berlin, 2011, pp. 67–95.

Johnson, E.N., 'The Crusades of Frederick Barbarossa and Henry VI', in *A History of the Crusades*, vol. 2, *The Later Crusades, 1189–1311*, ed. R.E. Wolff and H.W. Hazard, Madison, 1969, pp. 86–116.

Joranson, E., 'The Pilgrimage of Henry the Lion', in *Medieval and Historiographical Essays in Honor of James Westfall Thompson*, Chicago, 1938, pp. 146–225.

Jotischky, A., 'Manuel Comnenus and the Reunion of the Churches: The Evidence of the Conciliar Mosaics in the Church of the Nativity at Bethlehem', *Levant*, 26 (1994), 207–23.

—, 'The Fate of the Orthodox Church in Jerusalem at the End of the 12th Century', in *Patterns of the Past, Prospects for the Future: The Christian Heritage in the Holy Land*, ed. T. Hummel, K. Hintlian and U. Carmesund, London, 1999, pp. 179–94.

—, 'The Frankish Encounter with the Greek Orthodox in the Crusader States: The Case of Gerard of Nazareth and Mary Magdalene', in *Tolerance and Intolerance: Social Conflict in the Age of the Crusades*, ed. M. Gervers and J.M. Powell, Syracuse, NY, 2001, pp. 100–14, 168–72.

—, 'Ethnographic Attitudes in the Crusader States: The Franks and the Indigenous Orthodox People', in *East and West in the Crusader States: Context – Contacts – Confrontations*, III, *Acta of the Congress Held at Hernen Castle in September 2000*, ed. K. Ciggaar and H. Teule, Louvain, 2003, pp. 1–19.

—, *Crusading and the Crusader States*, Harlow, 2004.

—, 'The Christians of Jerusalem, the Holy Sepulchre and the Origins of the First Crusade', *Crusades*, 7 (2008), 35–57.

Kedar, B.Z., 'The General Tax of 1183 in the Crusading Kingdom of Jerusalem: Innovation or Adaptation?', *English Historical Review*, 89 (1974), 339–45.

—, 'The Patriarch Eraclius', in *Outremer: Studies in the History of the Crusading Kingdom of Jerusalem Presented to Joshua Prawer*, ed. B.Z. Kedar, H.E. Mayer and R.C. Smail, Jerusalem, 1982, pp. 177–204.

—, 'Gerard of Nazareth: A Neglected Twelfth-Century Writer in the Latin East. A Contribution to the Intellectual and Monastic History of the Crusader States', *Dumbarton Oaks Papers*, 37 (1983), 55–77.

—, 'Palmarée, abbaye clunisienne du XIIe siècle, en Galilee', *Revue bénédictine*, 93 (1983), 260–9.

—, 'Genoa's golden inscriptions in the Church of the Holy Sepulchre: a case for the defence', in *I Comuni Italiani nel Regno Crociato di Gerusalemme*, ed. G. Airaldi and B.Z. Kedar, Genoa, 1986, pp. 317–35.

—, 'The Frankish Period', in *The Samaritans*, ed. A.D. Crown, Tübingen, 1989, pp. 82–94.

—, 'The Battle of Hattin Revisited', in *The Horns of Hattin*, ed. B.Z. Kedar, London, 1992, pp. 190–207.

—, 'On the Origins of the Earliest Laws of Frankish Jerusalem: The Canons of the Council of Nablus', *Speculum*, 74 (1999), 310–35.

—, 'Again: Genoa's Golden Inscription and King Baldwin I's Privilege of 1104', in *Chemins d'Outre-Mer: Études d'histoire sur la Méditerranée médiévale offertes à Michel Balard*, ed. D. Coulon, C. Otten-Froux, P. Pagès and D. Valérian, vol. 1, Paris, 2004, pp. 495–502.

—, 'The Jerusalem Massacre of July 1099 in the Western Historiography of the Crusades', *Crusades*, 3 (2004), 15–75.

—, and D. Pringle, 'La Fève: A Crusader Castle in the Jezreel Valley', *Israel Exploration Journal*, 35 (1985), 164–79.

Kennedy, H., *Crusader Castles*, Cambridge, 1994.

Kloner, A., and M. Cohen, 'Die Kreuzfahrerburg Beth Guvrin', in *Burgen und Städte der Kreuzzugzeit*, Studien zur internationalen Architektur und Kunstgeschichte, 65, Petersberg, 2008, pp. 285–92.

Kohlberg, E., and B.Z. Kedar, 'A Melkite Physician in Frankish Jerusalem and Ayyubid Damascus: Muwaffaq al-Dīn Ya 'qūb b. Siqlāb', *Asian and African Studies*, 22 (1988), 113–26.

Krey, A.C., 'Urban's Crusade – Success or Failure', *American Historical Review*, 53 (1948), 235–50.

Kühnel, B., *Crusader Art of the Twelfth Century: A Geographical, an Historical or an Art Historical Notion?*, Berlin, 1994.

Kühnel, G., *Wall Painting in the Latin Kingdom of Jerusalem*, Berlin, 1988.

La Monte, J.L., 'To What Extent Was the Byzantine Empire the Suzerain of the Latin Crusading States?' *Byzantion*, 7 (1932), 253–64.

—, *Feudal Monarchy in the Latin Kingdom of Jerusalem, 1099–1291*, Cambridge, MA, 1936.

—, 'The Lords of Le Puiset on the Crusades', *Speculum*, 17 (1942), 100–18.

—, 'The Lords of Sidon in the Twelfth and Thirteenth Centuries', *Byzantion*, 17 (1944–5), 183–211.

—, 'The Lords of Caesarea in the Period of the Crusades', *Speculum*, 22 (1947), 145–61.

Lawrence, C.H., *Medieval Monasticism: Forms of Religious Life in Western Europe in the Middle Ages*, 2nd edn, London, 1989.

Lay, S., 'A leper in purple: the coronation of Baldwin IV of Jerusalem', *Journal of Medieval History*, 23 (1997), 317–34.

Lewis, B., 'The Ismā'īlites and the Assassins', in *A History of the Crusades*, vol. 1, *The First Hundred Years*, ed. M.W. Baldwin Madison, 1969, pp. 99–132.

Lilie, R.-J., *Byzantium and the Crusader States, 1096–1204*, tr. J.C. Morris and J.E. Ridings, Oxford, 1993.

Lindner, M., 'Topography and Iconography in Twelfth-Century Jerusalem', in *The Horns of Hattin*, ed. B.Z. Kedar, London, 1992, pp. 81–98.

Lombard, M., 'Arsenaux et bois de marine dans la Méditerranée musulmane (VIIe–XIe siècles)', in *Le navire et l'économie maritime du Moyen Âge au XVIIIe s., principalement en Méditerranée*, Actes II Colloque international d'histoire maritime, 1957, Paris, 1958, pp. 53–106.

—, 'Une carte du bois dans la Méditerranée musulmane (VIIe–XIe siècles)', *Annales ESC*, 14 (1959), 234–54.

Loud, G., 'The *Assise sur la Ligece* and Ralph of Tiberias', in *Crusade and Settlement*, ed. P.W. Edbury, Cardiff, 1985, pp. 204–12.

—, 'Some Reflections on the Failure of the Second Crusade', *Crusades*, 4 (2005), 1–14.

Luttrell, A., 'The Earliest Templars', in *Autour de la Première Croisade: Actes du Colloque de la Society for the Study of the Crusades and the Latin East* (Clermont-Ferrand, 22–25 juin 1995), ed. M. Balard, Paris, 1996, pp. 193–202.

—, 'The Earliest Hospitallers', in *Montjoie: Studies in Crusade History in Honour of Hans Eberhard Mayer*, ed. B.Z. Kedar, J. Riley-Smith and R. Hiestand, Aldershot, 1997, pp. 37–54.

Lyons, M.C., and D.E.P. Jackson, *Saladin: The Politics of the Holy War*, Cambridge, 1982.

MacEvitt, C., 'Christian Authority in the Latin East: Edessa in Crusader History', in *The Medieval Crusade*, ed. S.J. Ridyard, Woodbridge, 2004, pp. 71–83.

—, *The Crusades and the Christian World of the East: Rough Tolerance*, Philadelphia, PA, 2008.

Mack, M., 'The Italian quarters of Frankish Tyre: mapping a medieval city', *Journal of Medieval History*, 33 (2007), 147–65.

—, 'A Genoese Perspective of the Third Crusade', *Crusades*, 10 (2011), 45–62.

Magdalino, P., *The Empire of Manuel I Komnenos, 1143–80*, Cambridge, 1993.

—, 'The Pen of the Aunt: Echoes of the Mid-Twelfth Century in the Alexiad', in *Anna Komnene and her Times*, ed. T. Gouma-Peterson, New York, 2000, pp. 15–43.

Markowski, M., 'Richard Lionheart: bad king, bad crusader?', *Journal of Medieval History*, 23 (1997), 351–65.

Marshall, C., 'The crusading motivation of the Italian city republics in the Latin East, 1096–1104', in *The Experience of Crusading*, vol. 1, *Western Approaches*, ed. M. Bull and N. Housley, Cambridge, 2003, pp. 60–79.

Mason, J.F.A., 'Saint Anselm's Relations with Laymen: Selected Letters', in *Spicilegium Beccense, I, Congrès international du IXe centenaire de l'arrivée d'Anselme au Bec*, Paris, 1959, pp. 551–60.

Matzke, M., *Daibert von Pisa: Zwischen Pisa, Papst und erstem Kreuzzug*, Sigmaringen, 1998.

Mayer, H.E., 'Zum Tode Wilhelms von Tyrus', *Archiv für Diplomatik*, 5–6 (1959–60), 182–201.

—, 'Sankt Samuel auf dem Freudenberge und sein Besitz nach einem unbekannten Diplom König Balduins V', *Quellen und Forschungen aus italienischen Archiven und Bibliotheken*, 44 (1964), 35–71.

—, 'Das Pontifikale von Tyrus und die Krönung der lateinischen Könige von Jerusalem. Zugleich ein Beitrag zur Forschung über Herrschaftszeichen und Staatssymbolik', *Dumbarton Oaks Papers*, 21 (1967), 141–232.

—, 'Studies in the History of Queen Melisende of Jerusalem', *Dumbarton Oaks Papers*, 26 (1972), 95–182.

—, *Bistümer, Klöster und Stifte im Königreich Jerusalem*, Stuttgart, 1977.

—, 'Die Kanzlei Richards I. von England auf dem Dritten Kreuzzug', *Mitteilungen des Instituts für österreichische Geschichtsforschung*, 85 (1977), 22–35.

—, 'Latins, Muslims and Greeks in the Latin Kingdom of Jerusalem', *History*, 63 (1978), 175–92.

—, 'Ein Deperditum König Balduins III. von Jerusalem als Zeugnis seiner Pläne zur Eroberung Ägyptens', *Deutches Archiv für Erforschung des Mittelalters*, 36 (1980), 549–66.

—, 'Jérusalem et Antioche sous le règne de Baudouin II', *Comptes-rendus des séances de l'Académie des Inscriptions et Belles-Lettres, année 1980* (1981), 717–33.

—, 'The Concordat of Nablus', *Journal of Ecclesiastical History*, 33 (1982), 531–43.

—, 'Henry II of England and the Holy Land', *English Historical Review*, 97 (1982), 721–39.

—, 'Études sur l'histoire de Baudouin Ier roi de Jérusalem', in *Mélanges sur l'histoire du royaume latin de Jérusalem*, Paris, 1984, pp. 10–91.

—, 'Die Herrschaftsbildung in Hebron', *Zeitschrift des Deutschen Palästina-Vereins*, 101 (1985), 64–81.

—, 'The Origins of the Lordships of Ramla and Lydda in the Latin Kingdom of Jerusalem', *Speculum*, 60 (1985), 537–52.

—, 'The Succession of Baldwin II in Jerusalem: English Impact on the East', *Dumbarton Oaks Papers*, 39 (1985), 139–47.

—, 'Guillaume de Tyr à l'École', *Mémoires de l'Académie des Sciences, Arts et Belles-Lettres de Dijon*, 127 (1988), 257–65.

—, 'Die Hofkapelle der Könige von Jerusalem', *Deutsches Archiv*, 44 (1988), 489–509.

—, 'Die Legitimität Balduins IV. von Jerusalem und das Testament der Agnes von Courtenay', *Historisches Jahrbuch*, 108 (1988), 63–89.

—, 'Manasses of Hierges in East and West', *Revue belge de philologie et d'histoire*, 66 (1988), 757–66.

—, 'Angevins versus Normans: The New Men of King Fulk of Jerusalem', *Proceedings of the American Philosophical Society*, 133 (1989), 1–25.

—, 'Das syrische Erdbeben von 1170: Ein unedierter Brief König Amalrichs von Jerusalem', *Deutsches Archiv für Erforschung des Mittelalters*, 45 (1989), 474–84.

—, *Die Kreuzfahrerherrschaft Montréal (Šōbak). Jordanien im 12. Jahrhundert*, Wiesbaden, 1990.

—, 'Fontevrault und Bethanien: Kirchliches Leben in Anjou und Jerusalem im 12. Jahrhundert', *Zeitschrift für Kirchengeschichte*, 102 (1991), 14–44.

—, 'The Beginnings of King Amalric of Jerusalem', in *The Horns of Hattin*, ed. B.Z. Kedar, London, 1992, pp. 120–35.

—, *Die Kanzlei der lateinischen Könige von Jerusalem*, 2 vols, Hanover, 1996.

—, and M.-L. Favreau, 'Das Diplom Balduins I. für Genua und Genuas Goldene Inschrift in der Grabeskirche', *Quellen und Forschungen aus italienischen Archiven und Bibiliotheken*, 55–6 (1976), 22–95.

Metcalf, D.M., *Coinage of the Crusades and the Latin East in the Ashmolean Museum Oxford*, 2nd edn, London, 1995.

—, 'Describe the Currency of the Latin Kingdom of Jerusalem', in *Montjoie: Studies in Crusade History in Honour of Hans Eberhard Mayer*, ed. B.Z. Kedar, J. Riley-Smith and R. Hiestand, Aldershot, 1997, pp. 189–98.

—, 'East Meets West, and Money Changes Hands', in *East and West in the Crusader States: Context – Contacts – Confrontations*, III. *Acta of the Congress Held at Hernen Castle in September 2000*, ed. K. Ciggaar and H. Teule, Louvain, 2003, pp. 223–34.

Mitchell, P.D., 'An Evaluation of the Leprosy of King Baldwin IV in the Context of the Medieval World', in B. Hamilton, *The Leper King and his Heirs: Baldwin IV and the Crusader Kingdom of Jerusalem*, Cambridge, 2000, pp. 245–58.

—, *Medicine in the Crusades: Warfare, Wounds and the Medieval Surgeon*, Cambridge, 2004.

Mitchell, S.K., *Taxation in Medieval England*, ed. S. Painter, New Haven, 1951.

Möhring, H., *Saladin: The Sultan and his Times, 1138–1193*, tr. D.S. Bachrach, Baltimore, MD, 2008 (originally 2005).

Morton, N., 'The defence of the Holy Land and the memory of the Maccabees', *Journal of Medieval History*, 30 (2010), 1–19.

Müller-Wiener, W., *Castles of the Crusaders*, London, 1966.

Murray, A.V., 'A Note on the Origin of Eustace Grenier', *Bulletin of the Society for the Study of the Crusades and the Latin East*, 6 (1986), 28–30.

—, 'The Origins of the Frankish Nobility in the Kingdom of Jerusalem, 1100–1118', *Mediterranean Historical Review*, 4 (1989), 281–300.

—, 'Dynastic Continuity or Dynastic Change? The Accession of Baldwin II and the Nobility of the Kingdom of Jerusalem', *Medieval Prosopography*, 13 (1992), 1–27.

—, 'Baldwin II and his Nobles: Baronial Factionalism and Dissent in the Kingdom of Jerusalem, 1118–34', *Nottingham Medieval Studies*, 38 (1994), 60–81.

—, 'Ethnic Identity in the Crusader States: The Frankish Race and the Settlement of Outremer', in *Concepts of National Identity in the Middle Ages*, ed. S. Forde, L. Johnson and A.V. Murray, Leeds, 1995, pp. 59–73.

—, 'How Norman Was the Principality of Antioch? Prolegomena to a Study of the Origins of the Nobility of a Crusader State', in *Family Trees and the Roots of Politics: The Prosopography of Britain and France from the Tenth to the Twelfth Century*, ed. K.S.B. Keats-Rowan, Woodbridge, 1997, pp. 349–59.

—, 'Daimbert of Pisa, the *Domus Godefridi* and the Accession of Baldwin I', in *From Clermont to Jerusalem: The Crusades and Crusader Societies 1095–1500*, ed. A.V. Murray, Turnhout, 1998, pp. 81–99.

—, '"Mighty against the Enemies of Christ": The Relic of the True Cross in the Armies of the Kingdom of Jerusalem', in *The Crusades and their Sources: Essays Presented to Bernard Hamilton*, ed. J. France and W.G. Zajac, Aldershot, 1998, pp. 217–38.

—, *The Crusader Kingdom of Jerusalem: A Dynastic History, 1099–1125*, Oxford, 2000.

—, 'Finance and Logistics of the Crusade of Frederick Barbarossa', in *In Laudem Hierosolymitani: Studies in Crusades and Medieval Culture in Honour of Benjamin Z. Kedar*, ed. I. Shagrir, R. Ellenblum and J. Riley-Smith, Aldershot, 2007, pp. 375–68.

—, 'Norman Settlement in the Latin Kingdom of Jerusalem, 1099–1131', *Archivio Normanno-Svevo*, 1 for 2008 (2009), 61–85.

—, 'Sex, death and the problem of single women in the armies of the First Crusade', in *Shipping, Trade and Crusade in the Medieval Mediterranean. Studies in honour of John Pryor*, ed. R. Gertwagen and E. Jeffreys, Farnham, 2012 (forthcoming).

Nader, M., *Burgesses and Burgess Law in the Latin Kingdoms of Jerusalem and Cyprus (1099–1325)*, Aldershot, 2006.

Nicholas, D., *Medieval Flanders*, London, 1992.

Nicholson, H., 'Women on the Third Crusade', *Journal of Medieval History*, 23 (1997), 335–49.

—, 'Before William of Tyre: European Reports on the Military Orders' Deeds in the East, 1150–1185', in *The Military Orders*, vol. 2, *Welfare and Warfare*, ed. H. Nicholson, Aldershot, 1998, pp. 111–18.

—, *The Knights Hospitaller*, Woodbridge, 2001.

—, '"La roine preude femme et bonne dame": Queen Sibyl of Jerusalem (1186–1190) in History and Legend, 1186–1300', *Haskins Society Journal*, 15 (2004), 110–24.

Nicholson, R.L., *Joscelyn I, Prince of Edessa*, Urbana, IL, 1954.

—, *Joscelyn III and the Fall of the Crusader States, 1134–1199*, Leiden, 1973.

Norgate, K., *Richard the Lion Heart*, London, 1924.

Opll, F., *Das Itinerar Kaiser Friedrich Barbarossas (1152-1190)*, Vienna, Cologne and Graz, 1978.

The Oxford Dictionary of the Christian Church, ed. F.L. Cross, 3rd edn, ed. E.A. Livingstone, Oxford, 1997.

Pahlitzsch, J., *Graeci und Suriani im Palästina der Kreuzfahrerzeit*, Berliner Historische Studien, 33, Berlin, 2001.

—, 'Georgians and Greeks in Jerusalem (1099–1310)', in *East and West in the Crusader States: Context – Contacts – Confrontations*, III, *Acta of the Congress Held at Hernen Castle in September 2000*, ed. K. Ciggaar and H. Teule, Louvain, 2003, pp. 35–51.

Painter, S., 'The Lords of Lusignan in the Eleventh and Twelfth Centuries', *Speculum*, 32 (1957), 27–47.

Palmer, A., 'The History of the Syrian Orthodox in Jerusalem', *Oriens Christianus*, 75 (1991), 16–43.

—, 'The History of the Syrian Orthodox in Jerusalem, Part Two: Queen Melisende and the Jacobite Estates', *Oriens Christianus*, 76 (1992), 74–94.

Paul, N.L., 'Crusade, memory and regional politics in twelfth-century Amboise', *Journal of Medieval History*, 31 (2005), 127–41.

Peled, A., 'The Local Sugar Industry in the Latin Kingdom', in *Knights of the Holy Land: The Crusader Kingdom of Jerusalem*, ed. S. Rozenberg, Jerusalem, 1999, pp. 251–7.

Peters, F.E., 'The Quest of the Historical Muhammad', *International Journal of Middle East Studies*, 23 (1991), 291–315.

Phillips, J., 'Hugh of Payns and the 1129 Damascus Crusade', in *The Military Orders: Fighting for the Faith and Caring for the Sick*, ed. M. Barber, Aldershot, 1994, pp. 141–7.

—, *Defenders of the Holy Land: Relations between the Latin East and the West, 1119–1187*, Oxford, 1996.

—, 'Armenia, Edessa and the Second Crusade', in *Knighthoods of Christ: Essays on the History of the Crusades and the Knights Templar Presented to Malcolm Barber*, ed. N. Housley, Aldershot, 2007, pp. 39–50.

—, *The Second Crusade: Extending the Frontiers of Christendom*, New Haven and London, 2007.

Post, J.B., 'Age at Menopause and Menarche: Some Medieval Authorities', *Population Studies*, 25 (1971), 83–7.

Powell, J.M., 'Myth, Legend, Propaganda, History: The First Crusade, 1140–ca.1300', in *Autour de la Première Croisade*, ed. M. Balard, Paris, 1996, pp. 127–41.

Pozza, M., 'Venezia e il Regno di Gerusalemme dagli Svevi agli Angioini', in *I Comuni Italiani nel Regno Crociato di Gerusalemme*, ed. G. Airaldi and B.Z. Kedar, Genoa, 1986, pp. 351–99.

Prawer, J., 'The Settlement of the Latins in Jerusalem', *Speculum*, 27 (1952), 490–503.

—, 'The Nobility and the Feudal Regime in the Latin Kingdom of Jerusalem', in *Lordship and Community in Medieval Europe: Selected Readings*, ed. F.L. Cheyette, New York, 1968, pp. 156–79.

—, *Histoire du royaume latin de Jérusalem*, 2 vols, tr. G. Nahon, Paris, 1969.

—, 'The Battle of Hattin', in *Crusader Institutions*, Oxford, 1980, pp. 484–500.

—, 'Colonization Activities in the Latin Kingdom', in *Crusader Institutions*, Oxford, 1980, pp. 102–42.

—, 'The Origin of the Court of Burgesses', in *Crusader Institutions*, Oxford, 1980, pp. 263–95.

—, 'The Patriarch's Lordship in Jerusalem', in *Crusader Institutions*, Oxford, 1980, pp. 296–314.

—, *The History of the Jews in the Latin Kingdom of Jerusalem*, Oxford, 1988.

Pringle, D., 'Magna Mahumeria (al-Bīra): The Archaeology of a Frankish New Town in Palestine', in *Crusade and Settlement*, ed. P.W. Edbury, Cardiff, 1985, pp. 147–68.

—, 'Crusader Jerusalem', *Bulletin of the Anglo-Israel Archaeological Society*, 10 (1990–1), 105–13.

—, 'Aqua Bella: The Interpretation of a Crusader Courtyard Building', in *The Horns of Hattin*, ed. B.Z. Kedar, London, 1992, pp. 147–67.

—, 'Cistercian Houses in the Kingdom of Jerusalem', in *The Second Crusade and the Cistercians*, ed. M. Gervers, New York, 1992, pp. 183–98.

—, *The Churches of the Crusader Kingdom of Jerusalem: A Corpus*, 4 vols, Cambridge, 1993–2009.

—, 'Templar Castles on the Road to the Jordan', in *The Military Orders: Fighting for the Faith and Caring for the Sick*, ed. M. Barber, Aldershot, 1994, pp. 148–66.

—, *Secular Buildings in the Crusader Kingdom of Jerusalem: An Archaeological Gazetteer*, Cambridge, 1997.

—, 'Templar Castles between Jaffa and Jerusalem', in *The Military Orders*, vol. 2, *Welfare and Warfare*, ed. H. Nicholson, Aldershot, 1998, pp. 89–109.

—, 'The Spring of the Cresson in Crusading History', in *Dei gesta per Francos: Etudes sur les croisades dédiées à Jean Richard*, ed. M. Balard, B.Z. Kedar and J. Riley-Smith, Aldershot, 2001, pp. 231–40.

—, 'Churches and settlement in crusader Palestine', in *The Experience of Crusading*, vol. 2, *Defining the Crusader Kingdom*, ed. P. Edbury and J. Phillips, Cambridge, 2003, pp. 161–78.

—, 'The Church of the Holy Sepulchre in the Castle of Tripoli (Mont-Pèlerin)', in *Egypt and Syria in the Fatimid, Ayyubid and Mamluk Eras*, ed. U. Vermeulen and K. D'Hulster, Orientalia Lovaniensia Analecta, 169, Louvain, 2007, pp. 167–82.

—, 'The Layout of the Jerusalem Hospital in the Twelfth Century: Further Thoughts and Suggestions', in *The Military Orders*, vol. 4, *On Land and Sea*, ed. J. Upton-Ward, Aldershot, 2008, pp. 91–110.

Pryor, J.H., *Geography, Technology and War: Studies in the Maritime History of the Mediterranean, 649–1571*, Cambridge, 1988.

—, 'The *Eracles* and William of Tyre: An Interim Report', in *The Horns of Hattin*, ed. B.Z. Kedar, London, 1992, pp. 270–93.

—, 'The Voyages of Saewulf', in *Peregrinationes Tres: Saewulf, John of Würzburg, Theodericus*, ed. R.B.C. Huygens, Corpus Christianorum, Continuatio Mediaevalis, 139, Turnhout, 1996, pp. 35–57.

—, 'A View From a Masthead: the First Crusade From the Sea', *Crusades*, 7 (2008), 87–151.

—, 'Two *excitationes* for the Third Crusade: the letters of Brother Thierry of the Temple', *Mediterranean Historical Review*, 26 (2011), 1–28.

Queller, D.E., and I.B. Katele, 'Venice and the Conquest of the Latin Kingdom of Jerusalem', *Studi Venetiani*, 12 (1986), 15–43.

Richard, J., *Le Comté de Tripoli sous la dynastie toulousaine (1102–1187)*, Paris, 1945.

—, 'Note sur l'archidiocèse d'Apamée et les conquêtes de Raymond de Saint-Gilles en Syrie du Nord', *Syria*, 25 (1946-8), 102–8.

—, 'Questions de topographie tripolitaine', *Journal asiatique*, 236 (1948), 53–9.

—, 'Pairie d'Orient latin: les quatre baronies des royaumes de Jérusalem et de Chypre', *Revue historique de droit français et étranger*, series 4, 28 (1950), 67–88.

—, 'Le Chartrier de Sainte-Marie-Latine et l'établissement de Raymond de Saint-Gilles à Mont-Pèlerin', in *Mélanges de l'histoire du Moyen Age dédiés à la mémoire de Louis Halphen*, Paris, 1951, pp. 605–12.

—, 'An Account of the Battle of Hattin Referring to the Frankish Mercenaries in Oriental Moslem States', *Speculum*, 27 (1952), 168–77.

—, *Le royaume latin de Jérusalem*, Paris, 1953.

—, 'Quelques textes sur les premièrs temps de l'église latine de Jérusalem', in *Recueil Clovis Brunel*, vol. 2, Paris, 1955, pp. 420–30.

—, 'Le statut de la femme dans l'Orient latin', *Recueils de la Société de Jean Bodin*, 12 (1962), 377–88.

—, 'Le comté de Tripoli dans les chartes du Fonds des Porcellet', *Bibliothèque de l'École des Chartes*, 130 (1972), 339–82.

—, *The Latin Kingdom of Jerusalem*, tr. J. Barlow, vol. 1, Amsterdam, 1978 (originally 1953).

—, 'Philippe Auguste, la croisade et le royaume', in *La France de Philippe Auguste: Le temps des mutations*, ed. R.-H. Bautier, Paris, 1982, pp. 411–24.

—, 'Agricultural Conditions in the Crusader States', in *A History of the Crusades*, vol. 5, *The Impact of the Crusades on the Near East*, ed. N.P. Zacour and H.W. Hazard, Madison, 1985, pp. 251–66.

—, 'Les turcopoles au service des royaumes de Jérusalem et de Chypre: Musulmans convertis ou chrétiens orientaux?', in *Mélanges Dominique Sourdel/Revue des études islamiques*, 54 (1986), 259–70.

—, 'Départs de pèlerins et de croisés bouguignons au XIe s.: à propos d'une charte de Cluny', *Annales de Bourgogne*, 60 (1988), 139–43.

—, 'La noblesse de Terre Sainte (1097–1187)', *Arquivos do centro cultural português*, 26 (1989), 321–36.

—, 'Le paiement des dîmes dans les états des croisés', *Bibliothèque de l'École des Chartes*, 150 (1992), 71–83.

—, '*Cum omni raisagio montanee* ... À propos de la cession du Crac aux Hospitaliers', in *Itinéraires d'Orient: Hommages à Claude Cahen (Res Orientales, VI)*, Paris, 1994, pp. 187–93.

—, 'Le siège de Damas dans l'histoire et dans la légende', in *Cross Cultural Convergences in the Crusader Period*, ed. M. Goodich, S. Menache and S. Schein, New York, 1995, pp. 225–35.

—, 'Vassaux, tributaires ou alliés? Les chefferies montagnardes et les Ismaîliens dans l'orbite des etats des croisés', in *Die Kreuzfahrerstaaten als multikulturelle Gesellschaft*, Schriften des historischen Kollegs, Kolloquien, 37, ed. H.E. Mayer, Munich, 1997, pp. 141–52.

—, 'Les bases maritimes des Fatimides, leur corsairs et l'occupation franque en Syrie', in *Egypt and Syria in the Fatimid, Ayyubid and Mamluk Eras*, II, Orientali Lovaniensia Analecta, 83, ed. V. Vermeulen and D. De Smet, Louvain, 1998, pp. 115–29.

—, *The Crusades, c.1071–c.1291*, tr. J. Birrell, Cambridge, 1999 (originally 1996).

Richards, D.S., 'Imād al-Dīn al-Isfahāni: Administrator, Litterateur and Historian', in *Crusaders and Muslims in Twelfth-Century Syria*, ed. M. Shatzmiller, Leiden, 1993, pp. 133–46.

Riley-Smith. J., *The Knights of St John in Jerusalem and Cyprus, 1050–1310*, London, 1967.

—, 'The Templars and the castle of Tortosa in Syria: an unknown document concerning the acquisition of the fortress', *English Historical Review*, 74 (1969), 278–88.

—, 'Some lesser officials in Latin Syria', *English Historical Review*, 87 (1972), 1–26.

—, *The Feudal Nobility and the Kingdom of Jerusalem 1174–1277*, London, 1973.

—, 'Government in Latin Syria and the Commercial Privileges of Foreign Merchants', in *Relations between East and West in the Middle Ages*, ed. D. Baker, Edinburgh, 1973, pp. 109–32.

—, 'The Title of Godfrey of Bouillon', *Bulletin of the Institute of Historical Research*, 52 (1979), 83–6.

—, 'The motives of the earliest crusaders and the settlement of Latin Palestine, 1095–1100', *English Historical Review*, 98 (1983), 721–36.

—, *The First Crusade and the Idea of Crusading*, London, 1986.

—, 'The Venetian Crusade of 1122–1124', in *I Comuni Italiani nel Regno Crociato di Gerusalemme*, ed. G. Airaldi and B.Z. Kedar, Genoa, 1986, pp. 337–50.

—, *The First Crusaders, 1095–1131*, Cambridge, 1997.

—, *What Were the Crusades?*, 3rd edn, Basingstoke, 2002.

—, *The Crusades: A History*, 2nd edn, London, 2005.

—, 'The Death and Burial of Latin Christian Pilgrims to Jerusalem and Acre, 1099–1291', *Crusades*, 7 (2008), 165–79.

—, *Templars and Hospitallers as Professed Religious in the Holy Land*, Notre Dame, IN, 2009.

Robinson, I.S., 'Gregory VII and the Soldiers of Christ', *History*, 58 (1973), 169–92.

Röhricht, R., *Beitrage zur Geschichte der Kreuzzüge*, vol. 2, Berlin, 1878.

Rogers, R., *Latin Siege Warfare in the Twelfth Century*, Oxford, 1992.

Rowe, J.G., 'Paschal II and the Relation between the Spiritual and the Temporal Powers in the Kingdom of Jerusalem', *Speculum*, 32 (1957), 470–501.

Rubin, J., 'The Debate on Twelfth-Century Frankish Feudalism: Additional Evidence from William of Tyre's *Chronicon*', *Crusades*, 8 (2009), 53–62.

Runciman, S., *A History of the Crusades*, 3 vols, Cambridge, 1951–4.

—, 'The Visit of King Amalric I to Constantinople in 1171', in *Outremer: Studies in the History of the Crusading Kingdom of Jerusalem Presented to Joshua Prawer*, ed. B.Z. Kedar, H.E. Mayer and R.C. Smail, Jerusalem, 1982, pp. 153–8.

Russell, F.H., *The Just War in the Middle Ages*, Cambridge, 1975.

Russell, J.C., *Medieval Regions and their Cities*, Newton Abbot, 1972.

Saadé, G., 'Histoire du château de Saladin', *Studi Medievali*, 9 (1968), 980–1016.

Schein, S., 'Women in Medieval Colonial Society: The Latin Kingdom of Jerusalem in the Twelfth Century', in *Gendering the Crusades*, ed. S. Edgington and S. Lambert, Cardiff, 2001, pp. 140–53.

—, *Gateway to the Heavenly City: Crusader Jerusalem and the Catholic West (1099–1187)*, Aldershot, 2005.

Schenk, J., 'Nomadic Violence in the First Latin Kingdom of Jerusalem and the Military Orders', *Reading Medieval Studies*, 36 (2010), 39–55.

Schick, C., 'The Muristan, or the Site of the Hospital of St. John of Jerusalem', *Palestine Exploration Fund: Quarterly Statement* (1902), 42–56.

Schlumberger, G., *Numismatique de l'Orient latin*, Paris, 1878.

Sidelko, P.L., 'Muslim Taxation under Crusader Rule', in *Tolerance and Intolerance: Social Conflict in the Age of the Crusades*, ed. M. Gervers and J.M. Powell, Syracuse, NY, 2001, pp. 65–74, 156–60.

Smail, R.C., *Crusading Warfare, 1097–1193*, Cambridge, 1956.

—, 'The Predicaments of Guy of Lusignan, 1183–87', in *Outremer: Studies in the History of the Crusading Kingdom of Jerusalem Presented to Joshua Prawer*, ed. B.Z. Kedar, H.E. Mayer and R.C. Smail, Jerusalem, 1982, pp. 159–76.

Stevenson, W.B., *The Crusaders in the East*, Cambridge, 1907.

Strayer, J., 'The Laicization of French and English Society in the Thirteenth Century', in *Change in Medieval Society: Europe North of the Alps, 1050–1500*, ed. S. Thrupp, New York, 1964 (originally 1940), pp. 103–15.

Tanner, H., 'In his Brothers' Shadow: The Crusading Career and Reputation of Count Eustace III of Boulogne', in *The Crusades: Other Experiences, Alternate Perspectives*, ed. K.I. Semaan, Binghampton, NY, 2003, pp. 83–99.

Taylor, W.R., 'A New Syriac Fragment Dealing with Incidents in the Second Crusade', *The Annual of the American Schools of Oriental Research*, 11 (1929–30), 120–30.

Tessera, M.R., 'Philip Count of Flanders and Hildegard of Bingen: Crusading against the Saracens or Crusading against Deadly Sin?', in *Gendering the Crusades*, ed. S.B. Edgington and S. Lambert, Cardiff, 2001, pp. 77–93.

Tibble, S., *Monarchy and Lordships in the Latin Kingdom of Jerusalem, 1099–1291*, Oxford, 1989.

Tyerman, C.J., *England and the Crusades, 1095–1588*, Chicago, 1988.

—, *God's War: A New History of the Crusades*, London, 2006.

van Lint, T.M., 'Seeking Meaning in Catastrophe. Nersēs Šnorhali's *Lament on Edessa*', in *East and West in the Crusader States: Context – Contacts – Confrontations*, II, *Acta of the Congress Held at Hernen Castle in May 1997*, ed. K. Ciggaar and H. Teule, Louvain, 1999, pp. 29–47.

van Werveke, H., 'La contribution de la Flandre et du Hainaut à la Troisième Croisade', *Le Moyen Age*, 78 (1972), 55–90.

Wagner, T.G., and P.D. Mitchell, 'The Illnesses of King Richard and King Philippe on the Third Crusade: An understanding of *arnaldia* and *leonardie*', *Crusades*, 10 (2011), 23–44.

Wagstaff, J.M., *The Evolution of Middle Eastern Landscapes: An Outline to A.D. 1840*, London, 1985.

Warren, W.L., *Henry II*, London, 1973.

Yewdale, R.B., *Bohemond I, Prince of Antioch*, 1924.

Index